MASS MEDIA V

An Introduction to Modern Communication

Ray Eldon Hiebert
University of Maryland

Donald F. Ungurait
Florida State University

Thomas W. Bohn
Ithaca College

Longman
New York & London

Donation

Mass Media V

Longman Inc., 95 Church Street, White Plains, N.Y. 10601

Associated companies:
Longman Group Ltd., London
Longman Cheshire Pty., Melbourne
Longman Paul Pty., Auckland
Copp Clark Pitman, Toronto
Pitman Publishing Inc., New York

Executive editor: Gordon T. R. Anderson
Senior production editor: Ronni Strell
Text design: Mary Martylewski
Cover design: Paul Agule Design
Text art: J & R Services, Inc.
Production supervisor: Judith Stern

Library of Congress Cataloging-in-Publication Data

Hiebert, Ray Eldon.
  Mass media V.

  Includes index.
  1. Mass media. 2. Communication. I. Ungarait,
Donald F. II. Bohn, Thomas W. III. Title.
P90.H4792   1987   302.2'3   86-27401

ISBN 0-8013-0019-3

Compositor: TCSystems
Printer: R. R. Donnelley & Sons Company

87 88 89 90 91 92 9 8 7 6 5 4 3 2 1

Contents

Preface

You and I and the rest of humanity are living through a hyperrevolution. Radical changes in the way we live are being thrust on us and are being accepted and discarded at a rate that gives last year the look of ancient history. "That was *then*, this is *now!*" has always been the reality of cultures that are evolving. But *then* is growing ever closer to *now*. These changes, for better or worse, are in large part propelled by the engine of mass communication—what we call the mass media.

Books, newspapers, magazines, radio, television, motion pictures, and recordings are changing the world at a seemingly ever-accelerating rate.

The mass media have changed the American political process.

They have changed the way we learn and socialize the young.

They are an economic force with information power.

They open windows into every corner of the world and put the most private human endeavors under the media microscope.

They have changed how we think about ourselves and the others in our lives.

We, the people, do not always use the mass media to our best advantage. And there remains a lingering suspicion that it is the mass media that are doing the using.

If we are going to cope with, let alone control, the world we live in, an understanding of mass communication is essential.

The primary goal of *Mass Media V: An Introduction to Modern Communication* is to guide you along the path to becoming more learned mass communication scholars. We, the authors, believe that if you understand how the mass media work and what they do, you have taken an important step along the road to becoming a mass media professional as well as a critical consumer of mass communication products and services.

This volume of *Mass Media*, like its earlier editions, is a consumer-oriented text written for education's primary client—the student.

Mass Media V is essentially a toolbox, one that is well stocked with information, ideas, and analysis that can be used to fashion an understanding of mass communication. The master-craftsman faculty member and the apprentice student may not need all the tools herein. You may use one tool considerably more than another. A teacher's specialized knowledge, skills, and goals may emphasize some tools more than others. But with thoughtful comparison, *Mass Media V* contains most of what is needed to construct a basic understanding of the field.

This book was the first introductory text that had the process of mass communication as its core. The theories, models, systems, and elements of that process are central to what the mass media are and do. *Mass Media V* details every phase of the communication process from communicators to feedback.

The *Mass Media V* toolbox has been reorganized to emphasize its power tools. Part I—"What Are the Mass Media?"—and Part II—"What Do Mass Media Communicate?"—have been moved forward to enhance what the Introduction to Mass Communication (Media) survey courses emphasize.

The ordering of the chapters within Part I does not imply a preference for one medium over another; it symbolizes the order of the medium's development. Books came before newspapers, which developed before magazines, motion pictures, radio, television, and sound recording. The authors believe that all the uses, functions, and roles of the mass media are equally important. We try to avoid making judgments about the "morality" of the functions or establishing a hierarchy of values toward these roles. Much can be learned by taking a careful look at each mass medium separately, and that is what we will do in Part I. We will examine the historical development of each medium, the current scope of operation, the structure and organization, the new technological development, and basic characteristics and roles.

Part III—"How Does Mass Communication Work?"—places the mass media and their roles within a theoretical framework that is especially helpful to the neophyte who is preparing to enter one of mass communication's professions. The section begins with an examination of the source (Chapter 15, "Communicators") and how the content is structured (Chapter 16, "Codes: Symbols, Styles, and Formats") to move through the checkpoints of the process (Chapter 17, "Gatekeepers and Regulators") to the critical consumer (Chapter 18, "Audiences and Their Filters") and finally considers the ancillary issues (Chapter 19, "Feedback, Noise, and Amplification"). This analysis of the process is made available to expand understanding if covered rapidly in a classroom lecture.

As in many other fields of academic inquiry, the study of mass media is issue oriented. Part IV—"What Are the Key Mass Communication Issues?"—focuses on six critical areas. "International Systems" (Chapter 20) explores how nations other than the United States view their mass media and how those views influence our system and its coverage of the world view. "Economics" (Chapter 21) takes a hard detailed look at how the mass media interact with our capitalistic system and how economic realities influence mass media content. "Ethics" (Chapter 22) offers an overview of what the future leaders of our industry have to consider when making decisions or judgments about not only content issues, but also the leadership roles they must play and the examples they must set. "Effects: Mass Communication and the Individual" (Chapter 23) presents and analyzes the scientific research available on the impact of mass media on human behavior. "Impact: Mass Media and Society" (Chapter 24) examines the mass media's involvement with movements and issues. And "The Future of Mass Media" (Chapter 25) attempts to look forward to help you anticipate what is just ahead in our ever-changing field.

Some comments may be helpful to instructors as they use *Mass Media V* and integrate it with lectures and assignments. The book gives equal emphasis to all media and all media functions. It is more than an introduction to journalism or broadcasting. It is a *foundations* book; it reflects our concern that detailed information should be available on all media, intermedia relationships, and media functions. Because of the wealth of detail in *Mass Media V*, instructors can selectively emphasize particular media or functions and be assured that the basics outside their personal field of interest are covered in the text. All three authors teach the introductory mass communication course at their respective universities. Frankly, we all use the book differently and emphasize our specialized area of training and interest. We exercise our academic judgment, as every colleague must. We know there are time constraints in our lectures that limit discussion of certain topics. Nevertheless, we know the basics will be covered in detail in the text.

For students, we have this comment: *Mass Media V* is written for you and others like you. It is a beginning. It is an introduction to modern communication. We hope that it will serve as a guide in your personal journey to become a critical consumer and, perhaps, a media professional. It is a journey that all three authors began before you, and we now continue with you.

Ray Eldon Hiebert
Donald F. Ungurait
Thomas W. Bohn

1

The Process of Mass Communication and the Critical Consumer

Let there be no doubt. This is "the age of communication." Information is power, and cultural change seems to have shifted into "warp-drive." Central to our "age of communication" are the institutions known as the mass communication media. The mass media are the powerful, high-speed information systems that bring about change within societies, subcultures, families, and individuals, not only in the United States, but throughout the world.

Consider for a moment the importance of the mass media in our daily lives. For many Americans, the day begins with the voice of a local disc jockey on the clock radio. As we dress, a miniature television set brings us the Cable News Network (CNN) and keeps us "in tune with the world." At breakfast, we speedread the local newspaper or *USA Today*—the first national, capsule-comment newspaper. If we drive, the tape deck soothes our nerves; if we ride the subway or bus or if we walk, the Sony Walkman sets the pace. On campus, the text and the periodical fuel the educational machine. In the workplace, high-speed computers "process" our life styles as well as data. At home in the evening, MTV, HBO, CBN, BET, USA, ESPN, ABC, CBS, and NBC make up the alphabet soup we consume. Millions of us still curl up with a good book at bedtime. We see a movie or two on the weekend, or we watch that same movie on a VHS or Beta tape deck on a large-screen video beam projector, connected to a cable or a satellite dish in the backyard. Or we attend a concert to hear songs that the mass media have already taught us to sing. But more than likely, we stay at home and listen to that concert in the superior sound environment created by a compact-disc player. Mass communication consumption along with sleep and work and school are the activities that dominate Americans' lives. For many, they are equally time consuming. Media activities consume about one-third of the average day, and that is a conservative estimate.

Communication is the human cement that glues our society and all other cultures together. Communication links us emotionally and intellectually to other individuals, to groups, and to institutions. Communication is the cultural imperative that allows societies to exist and flourish.

Communication is a tool, a means, a process; it is neither good nor bad. Any morality in the act of communication depends on the people who generate the action.

Communication is often defined functionally as "the sharing of experiences" or "the transfer of meaning" or "the transmission of values." Communication is used to do all these things, but it is more than the sum of these actions. Communication is so diverse and so complex that one definition is difficult, if not impossible, to find. In fact, definitions of communication often limit our understanding of some human interactions. That is why this book evaluates communication as a process, as a complex series of cultural actions and reactions that is always moving toward changing goals. Communication in our accelerated existence is not a static entity fixed in time and space. It is the dynamic that underlies the development of humankind. Our institutions as well as our personal lives would crumble without the process of communication.

THE FOUR LEVELS OF COMMUNICATION

Because satisfactory definitions of communication are difficult to come by, describing the communication process may prove more fruitful. Daily routines involve myriad communication experiences. These activities tend to fall into four relatively discrete categories, or levels, of communication:

1. *Intrapersonal communication* describes one person talking to himself or herself. It is the thought process. All of us think things through before we speak or act.
2. *Interpersonal communication* may be dyadic (two persons) or triadic (three people), or it may involve a few individuals communicating with one another in close emotional or physical proximity. The closer the emotional or physical link, the more personal the communication. Talking on the telephone to someone you love may be a more intense experience than sending that person a letter, but both events are usually less involving than the first face-to-face encounter after a separation.
3. *Group communication* covers situations from participating in a busi-

ness meeting to going to a class to attending a rock concert. As the number of people increases, the level of involvement often changes. Some participants are more active than others; listeners drift in and out; and the total experience is often less immediate and intense than interpersonal communication. Group communication has been institutionalized in the world of work as *organizational communication;* the memo replaces the personal letter, and the conference call supersedes the trip to a meeting—work becomes a series of communication events.

4. *Mass communication* involves a communicator (almost always more than one person) using a mass medium to communicate with very large audiences. It has become the primary leisure industry in the United States.

The four levels of the process of communication can be visualized along a V-shaped continuum, with intrapersonal experiences at the closed end moving through interpersonal and group activities (which overlap in many cases) to mass communication at the open end of the model (Figure 1.1).

Four major changes occur as we move to the far right of the model into the process of mass communication.

1. The number of participants increases dramatically. Obviously, audiences for television, motion pictures, best-selling novels, and urban newspapers number in the millions. But what is just as important is that the sender evolves from one person into an organized group whose members take on specialized roles.
2. The message becomes less personal, less specialized, and more general. This step is necessary if the content is to be understood and accepted by the largest possible portion of the public.
3. The audience members become physically and emotionally sepa-

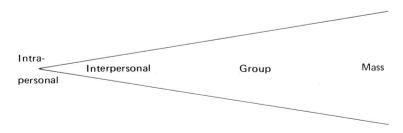

Figure 1.1. Gerhart D. Wiebe's V-shaped continuum of the communication process. (From Eugene L. Hartley and Ruth E. Hartley, *Fundamentals of Social Psychology,* New York: Knopf, 1959. Copyright © 1959 by Eugene L. Hartley and Ruth E. Hartley.)

rated in time and space from the members of other audiences and from the mass communicator. News magazines are read at different times and in different places by people who are usually different from other readers in that they do not care who wrote the articles. Emotional commitment to other participants is at a very low level.

4. A mass medium must always be involved for mass communication to occur. Mass communication incorporates not only complex technologies but never occurs without a complex organization—a newspaper or record company or publisher or radio station—acting as the channel of communication.

In spite of their differences, intrapersonal, interpersonal, group, and mass communication are basically similar. Variations on the same components contribute to the same basic structure. The most useful way to analyze the common parts of the process of communication is to examine models that visualize how communication works.

VISUALIZING THE COMMUNICATION PROCESS

At all levels of communication, three basic elements are evident in every model. Someone (A) sends something (m) to someone else (B). Students of communication use a variety of labels for these components, but essentially they are the same three things. Figure 1.2 illustrates that both the sender (A) and the receiver (B) must act on the message for communication to be successful. This model visualizes the idea that the more the receiver and the sender have in common, the more likely they will understand each other. The more likely it is that A and B share frames of reference, the more likely it is that the communication act will be successful.

One of the basic concerns of communication scholars has been to emphasize that the message sent may not be the message received. The model visualizes that in every communication experience, a wide range of

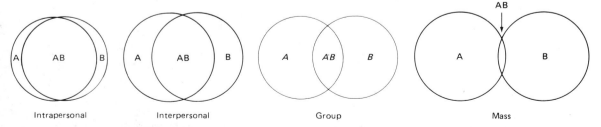

Intrapersonal	Interpersonal	Group	Mass

Figure 1.2. Visualizations of the relationship among the sender, the message, and the receiver. (From Wilbur Schramm, *Men, Message, and Media*, p. 43. Copyright © 1973 by Wilbur Schramm. Reprinted by permission of Harper & Row, Publishers, Inc.)

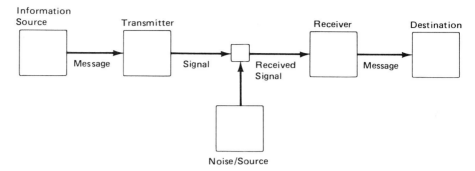

Figure 1.3. The Shannon-Weaver schematic diagram of a general communication system. (Copyright © 1948, American Telephone and Telegraph Company, reprinted by permission.)

factors come into play. The receiver has frames of reference that he or she uses to interpret the sender's message. The sender, in turn, tries to transmit messages that are easily understood and readily accepted by the receiver.

In intrapersonal communication, the circles almost always overlap, except when we cannot remember something. Depending on the closeness of a relationship or the amount of agreement on a subject, interpersonal communication can have considerable overlap and therefore a significant chance of success. The commonality of frames of reference in group communication varies tremendously, based on the purpose of the gathering or the cohesion of the organization. (In business parlance, organizational cohesion is known as teamwork.) By the time we reach mass communication, the two circles in the figure barely touch each other in some cases—for example, in avant-garde foreign films or recordings of Italian operas that are outside our experiences.

One of the earliest attempts to model the communication experience was the Shannon-Weaver "mathematical model of communication" (Figure 1.3). This model, developed for the American Telephone and Telegraph Company, identifies a number of elements based on the use of the telephone, which is often referred to as *telecommunication.* The transmitter, signal, received signal, and receiver are part of a system that can have noise, or disturbance, anywhere within it. The model emphasizes the movement of a message, using a systems approach to describe the communication process.

The Weaver-Ness model adds further dimensions: codes, which are the symbols used to carry the meaning; and feedback, which is the response of the receiver to the sender (Figure 1.4). This model emphasizes that communication is a circular, response-oriented activity that allows both source and destination to react, modify, and clarify the communiqué by using communication pathways, or channels.

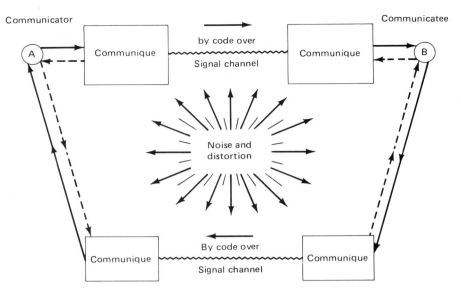

Figure 1.4. The Weaver-Ness model of speech communication. (From Andrew T. Weaver and Ordean G. Ness, *The Fundamentals and Forms of Speech.* Copyright © 1957 by the Odyssey Press, Inc. Reprinted by permission of the Bobbs-Merrill Co., Inc.)

In formal, structured organizations—the military, for example—the group becomes stratified; group members refer to the "chain of command" and "going through channels." The vertical nature of this kind of organization sets up layers through which a message must pass for approval or rejection or modification (Figure 1.5). Each level is a "gate" through which a message must pass, and each gate is "guarded" by the next level of authority, the gatekeeper. You can imagine what happens to messages in terms of content modification and time lapse as the private tells the corporal, who tells the sergeant, who tells the lieutenant, and so on up to the general, whose response moves down through the chain of command— ordering the colonel, who commands the major, who tells the captain, and on down to the troops. Messages are modified (expanded or contracted) or rejected. Each layer of the bureaucracy serves a gatekeeping function, which subordinates sometimes leapfrog by "going over someone's head." The more complex the organization, the more likely communication breakdown will occur. Memos and meetings become the primary pathways of communication, which depersonalizes interaction within the corporate setting.

Combining all the elements we have discussed, an intrapersonal, interpersonal, and group model emerges. It includes the components that appear in mass communication, albeit modified. Figure 1.6 illustrates nine identifiable elements:

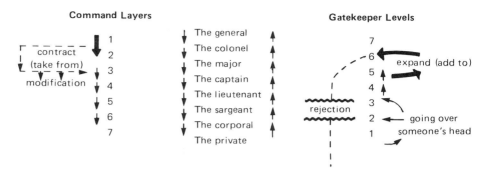

Figure 1.5. The chain-of-command model of organizational communication. Donald F. Ungurait designed this model for workshops in industry and government.

1. An individual acts as the *sender*
2. of a personal, specialized *message,*
3. using a *code* of commonly understood symbols
4. over a *channel* that is a pathway (airwave, paper and pencil, memos, or meetings)
5. through one or more members (bosses) acting as *gatekeepers* (if an organization is involved)
6. to another individual *receiver* or a small group,
7. passing through the receivers' *frames of reference,* which interpret the message
8. so that the receivers can react and respond in the form of verbal, nonverbal, or written *feedback* to the sender;
9. and, of course, *noise* and distortion can occur at any point in the

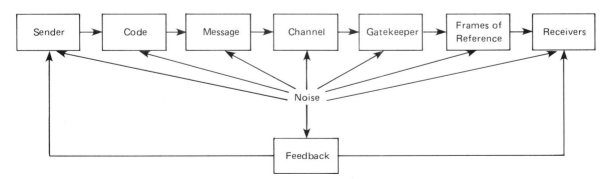

Figure 1.6. A summary model of intrapersonal, interpersonal, and group communication.

process and has to be eliminated by the sender, the receivers, or both.

The communication process, then, is modular; and individual components can be modified or can take on new variations that make them hybrids of the same aspects of intrapersonal-, interpersonal-, and group-communication models.

THE HUB MODEL OF MASS COMMUNICATION

When we make the leap to mass communication, the basic elements change significantly, and we add several new components. For our purpose, we need a model that visualizes mass communication as an interactive process. The HUB (**H**iebert, **U**ngurait, **B**ohn) model describes that process as a set of concentric elements always involved in a series of actions and reactions (Figure 1.7).

The HUB model pictures communication as a process similar to that of dropping a pebble into a pool. This action causes ripples that expand outward until they reach the sides of the pool, and then a few bounce back toward the center. The content of communication (an idea or an event) is like a pebble dropped into the pool of human affairs. Many factors affect that message as it ripples out to its audience and bounces back. These factors are the components of the total process.

The HUB model's rings also reflect the physical processes of sound conduction and electronic transmission. The goal, of course, is to present mass communication as clearly and completely as possible.

Let us now evaluate each element of the HUB model and examine the components that are not contained in other models or that are changed significantly once the process becomes mass communication.

Content

Each mass medium serves a variety of functions or, more correctly, is used by individuals, groups, and society to perform specified roles. In essence, these functions and uses are the content of mass communication. The content of mass communication is dissimilar to that of interpersonal or group communication messages in four basic areas. Mass communication messages are (1) less personal, (2) less specialized, (3) more rapid, and (4) more transient than other messages. Obviously, the number of people involved, the distance covered, and the time span are the overriding conditions that create these differences. There are at least six important tasks or categories of mass communication content.

News. The mass media provide timely and important facts that have consequences in our daily lives. They survey events in society and report them to the publics they serve.

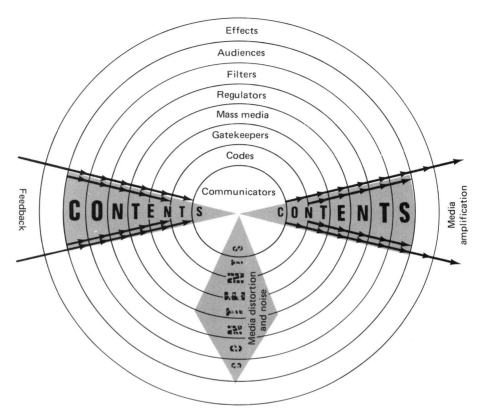

Figure 1.7. The HUB model of mass communication is visualized as pulsating, concentric circles, which emphasizes the relationship of all the elements of the mass communication process.

Commentary. The mass media provide us with an evaluation of events, placing them in perspective. In effect, the media take editorial positions and provide insights beyond the single event.

Public Relations. The mass media serve as instruments of propaganda and public persuasion. Governments, business corporations, political action groups, and individuals seek to establish or improve relationships through the mass media.

Advertising. The mass media are part of the marketing and distribution processes of our economic system. Advertising informs the members of the public about new products, convinces them of their value, and persuades them to buy.

Education. The mass media perform educational functions, such as socialization, general education, and classroom instruction. The media can serve to reinforce, modify, and replace the cultural heritage of the present society.

Entertainment. The mass media help people relax during their leisure time. The escapist use of the media is an overlay function. This means that media entertain as they inform, analyze, educate, persuade, and sell. Entertainment is the popular art of our time, but the mass media also contribute to the betterment of our cultural heritage through artistic achievement.

Communicators

In mass communication, it is extremely difficult, if not impossible, for an individual to be the sender. The mass communicator is a conglomerate or group of individuals, each of whom performs a specialized task. The communicator on "The Tonight Show Starring Johnny Carson" is not simply Johnny Carson, but an entire organization involving the network, local station, director, and technical staff, as well as the talent appearing on the show. *Time* magazine in the mid-twentieth century developed *group jour-*

Figure 1.8. No one individual serves as an independent communicator in the mass media. Cast and crew, literally dozens of specialists, await their call for the next shot in Jerry Reed's film *Whatever Comes Around*. Movies, like other media arts, depend on the members of a group working together to create. We call that group the *conglomerate communicator*.

nalism, in which the style and tone of the magazine required individual talents to blend into a successful format.

The communicators of *USA Today, People,* or *Mass Media V* are not only the writers or authors, but also reporters, copy editors, photographers, and many other specialists. Although individual personalities may dominate and become symbols for a television show (David Letterman), a film (George Lucas), a newspaper (Katherine Graham), or a magazine (Hugh Hefner), they are simply one part, albeit an important part, of the conglomerate communicator. An individual can be the dominant creative force, but a team of specialists is at work, and the sum of the team's talents form the conglomerate communicator.

Codes

In 1983, the *Pioneer 10* spacecraft left the solar system and raced toward the farther reaches of the universe. Before the spacecraft was launched in 1972, scientists had persuaded the National Aeronautics and Space Administration to place a plaque on board (Figure 1.9). The message was coded using

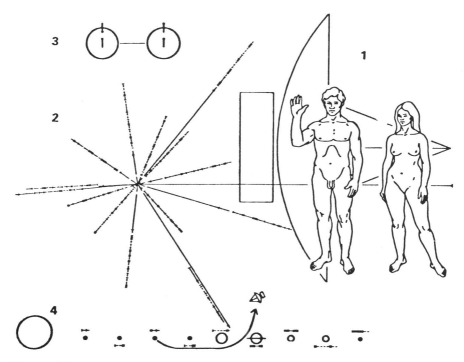

Figure 1.9. The design on the plaque on board *Pioneer 10,* depicting (1) the life forms who sent the message, with the male's hand raised in greeting; (2) the sun radiating radio waves; (3) the hydrogen molecule (hydrogen can be used as a universal clock); and (4) the solar system, with the path of *Pioneer 10* indicated.

a variety of symbols. The earthbound senders assumed that if the message was found by another intelligent life form, the code could be "broken." This code for interbeing communication is not unlike the codes of the mass media, whose messages are cast out and coded in what the sender hopes are understandable patterns.

Mass communication has modified and expanded the codes (languages and symbol systems) used in communication. For example, in the motion picture, new visual symbol systems often replace verbal language. Camera angles, freeze frames, and editing broaden, rather than limit, film's communicative capacities. The print media have utilized color printing, computer graphics, and a variety of typefaces to great effect in coding their messages.

Gatekeepers

Gatekeepers are individuals working in mass media organizations—for example, wire service editors, television network continuity personnel, or motion picture theater managers—who make decisions about what is communicated and how it is communicated. They are not usually originators of content; instead, they function as creative evaluators. In other words, gatekeepers can be positive forces, improving as well as eliminating content. They can delete, insert, emphasize, or deemphasize messages in mass media.

Mass Media

Mass communication never occurs without a mass medium, and that medium is more than a mechanical device to send messages. Mass media are social institutions created to perform the tasks that the society requires of them. The newspaper, book, magazine, motion picture, radio, television, and sound recording are mass communication media. They are complex industrial organizations.

The devices and products of the mass media—printing presses and books, newspapers, and magazines; transmitters and radio and television programs; cameras and motion pictures; and recording equipment and records and tapes—can be used for personal to narrowly organizational to completely mass communication ends. Books or movies are not the mass media; neither are computer terminals or tape decks. The mass media are the institutions and organizations that use mechanical devices to produce content for use by audiences.

When a mass medium becomes the channel in mass communication, it brings three characteristics to the process:

1. A *complex technology* becomes involved.
2. The *velocity* of the process increases in order to reach a huge audience.
3. The *amplitude* increases; because the potential to be heard is so powerful, it confers status on the sender.

Regulators

The regulators of the mass media—such as courts, government commissions, consumers, professional organizations, and public pressure groups—are external in the sense that they function outside the media institution. Regulation consists of laws, rules, restrictions, and informal pressures that control both the content and the structure of the media. Regulators of mass media have the ability to close down a theater, delete content, influence news coverage, and revoke television or radio licenses. Although these powers are not often used, regulators have considerable impact on decisions of the media because no one wants to incur the "wrath of regulators."

Filters

The filters are the frames of reference that audience members use to understand, accept, reject, or remember mass communication. These frames of reference are the rose-colored (depending on your preference) glasses we use to see the world. The extent and quality of the filters affect our ability to handle media content—to put mass communication to use rather than be manipulated by the mass media.

Audiences

Audiences are the component of mass communication that is most studied, both by academic scholars and professional research organizations. Mass communication receivers are aggregates that are more heterogeneous than homogeneous, relatively large, anonymous, and physically and emotionally separated from the mass communicator and most other members of the audience. The relationship between sender and receiver is impersonal at best. Audiences are fluid; they change from movie to movie, book to book, record to record.

Effects

The effects of mass communication can be placed into two overlapping categories: (1) the general impact that the mass media have on society; and (2) the specific effects that mass communication content has on specific individuals in the audience. Both issues are of ever-growing importance.

The effects of mass communication are real, but our ability to study them has not kept pace with other aspects of the process. Effects will be the central issue in the future of mass communication. This is the least understood and most debated aspect of the mass communication process.

Media Distortion and Noise

Mass communication has an increased possibility of media distortion and noise; and noise in the mass communication process can occur at any point, not simply in the medium. Because of its public nature, mass communication allows more interruption on a far broader level than does interpersonal communication. Noise can occur in a variety of forms: static on radio or television, a poorly printed newspaper, an out-of-focus motion picture. Noise is a breakdown somewhere in another element of the process.

Media Amplification

The mass media confer status. Appearance in the media gives credence to the importance of the individual, the message, and the event. That is why political events are staged for mass media. The mass media seldom, if ever, solve problems; rather, they identify what may need to be done or at least what some who gain access to the media think may need to be done.

Feedback

Feedback is the communicated response of audience members to a message sent by the system. In interpersonal communication, feedback is immediate. In mass communication, feedback is delayed and diffused. Television ratings are a form of feedback, but even with overnight ratings, TV program producers have no way of knowing if they lost the audience's attention halfway through the program.

In mass communication, feedback is often expressed quantitatively: a magazine's circulation figures or a film's box-office receipts. Feedback is institutionalized, representative, and indirect when evaluated in mass communication terms.

THE SIGNIFICANCE OF THE MASS MEDIA

In daily human activities, communicating is the most used conscious action. The mass media bring to the communication process an intensity and complexity that is overwhelming unless examined carefully. Entertainment media content usually comes under scrutiny in the popular press. Scholarly inquiry tends to focus on the audience and the effects of mass communication. The viewpoint of *Mass Media V* is that every part of the process is influenced by every other part. Therefore, this book seems to be both holistic (to provide an overview) and specific (to isolate each element in order to understand its specific contribution). All elements of the mass communication process are valid areas of scholarship.

Nevertheless, increased emphasis has been placed on the medium itself as an important element in the mass communication process. Indeed, the medium may be the key component in the process. Marshall McLuhan, in his book *Understanding Media: The Extension of Man*, coined the phrase "The medium is the message." What this means is that the carrier of communication—whether human voice or printed page, neon sign or electronic impulse—influences the message, the sender, the audience, and the effects of mass communication far more than was previously understood.

McLuhan later rephrased "The medium is the message" to "The medium is the massage." The use of the word *massage* rather than *message* emphasizes the carrier rather than the content. McLuhan stated that television itself, not television programs, massages us. Almost any program content is interchangeable, McLuhan argued, and content is relatively unimportant to the impact that this "electric window" will have on humankind.

Because the mass media affect the message's content, the message's sender, and the message's audience, we suggest that if we do not understand mass media, we cannot understand mass communication. The mass media speak new languages that we must learn.

The electronic media have homogenized America more in the past 30 years than was accomplished by other means in the previous 300 years. And the nations and peoples of the world are looking more alike all the time. When minuscule groups of terrorists want to emphasize their grievances, they grab us by our international electronic throats. All of us are held hostage on the starship earth because we participate mythically with all the other global villagers in their successes and their sorrows.

The United States is by far the largest producer and consumer of mass communication. Americans use four times as much newsprint as the Japanese, who are second in the world in newsprint consumption. Almost half of the world's telephones belong to Americans. The ratio of television sets per person in the United States is far above that of any other country. There are four times more radio sets in the United States than there are people to use them. America is a mass communication society.

American mass media have a great impact not only on our own society, but also on the rest of the world. In Africa, for example, one is more apt to hear American than African music on radio and television, in discos and night clubs, and on home phonographs. In Asia, American movies are shown more often than Asian movies. In Latin America, the *Reader's Digest* is more popular than any locally produced magazine. A United States Information Agency survey found that 15 to 30 percent of elite audiences in non-Communist countries read *Time*. More than 200 of the world's leading newspapers subscribe to the *New York Times* or the *Washington Post–Los Angeles Times* news services.

The world's masses are entertained and the "information elite" obtains much of what it feels it has to know from the mass media in the United States. Make no mistake; American mass communication industries remain in a leadership position and are a critical force in the world.

THE CRITICAL CONSUMER

In our discussion so far, a basic question remains: If the mass media play such an important role in our lives, are we their victims or their masters? That is, are we managed, manipulated, massaged, and brainwashed by the media, or do the media simply reflect us and our wishes, our purchases in the marketplace, our attention, and our dial twirling and page turning?

The best answer is probably a combination of both. We still do not know enough about the process to make final judgments. Although we speak of communication science, we have far to go to arrive at answers to some basic questions. One thing does seem clear: the more we know about a subject, the less we can be misled about it.

During the Korean War, when brainwashing in Communist prison camps became a great concern of Americans, a team of psychologists at the University of Illinois undertook an experiment. Two groups were tested to see how their opinions on a topic could be changed. One group was given advance information about the topic; the second group, which acted as the control, was not. The test results showed that the ideas of the group with the advance information were less likely to be changed than were those of the control group. The experimenters concluded that the more information a person has about a topic, the less likely that he or she can be brainwashed.

It seems certain that the mass media will play an ever-increasing role in our lives; therefore, the consumer of mass communication must continue to expand his or her knowledge of the process. Educated people must develop a critical attitude toward the mass media. They must be able to make judgments beyond their likes and dislikes. They must know when something is of high quality and when it is not. Universities offer courses on art appreciation, music appreciation, and literary appreciation in which students are taught to be critical of these forms. We need courses in mass communication that will teach us to become critically aware of the problems and processes of mass media.

Uncritical audiences are more likely to believe everything they see in print, hear on radio, or watch on television or at the movies. The power of print has intimidated human beings for hundreds of years, and the power of live-action pictures on television can be even more intimidating. Individuals who believe so completely in what they read in the newspaper or observe on television are apt to become disillusioned when they discover that what they read and see is not always 100 percent true. They may begin to be manipulated by those distant puppeteers behind the scenes—mass media newspeople and Madison Avenue advertisers.

Those who understand the process can achieve a truer perspective. The critical consumer can put what is artificial in mass communication into better balance with the reality of life. The study of mass media is important, then, because it helps the educated person understand one of the critical processes of modern life. Such understanding not only helps the participant in mass communication perform more effectively, but also enables the critical consumer to make more effective use of mass communication.

SUMMARY

Written and verbal communication are *the* processes that make us human beings, and mass communication is not an uncontrollable, mysterious force. Whether you wish to become a media professional or a critical consumer, you must learn to understand and, therefore, harness the power of mass communication to your needs. You must seek to manipulate the mass media rather than being manipulated by them. That is the essence of being a critical consumer.

Communication can be best understood as working on four levels: thinking about the first boy and girl you ever had a crush on (intrapersonal communication); talking on the telephone to your mother and father (interpersonal communication); listening to a lecture in class (group communication); and reading this book (mass communication). Remember that a mass medium must always be involved if the process is to be mass communication. A rock concert with thousands in attendance is not mass communication, but a music video of that concert broadcast on MTV is mass communication because a mass medium (broadcasting or cablecasting) is being used.

Visualizing (modeling) the various levels of communication clarifies the relationship among the elements of communication. The HUB model of mass communication identifies 12 components: (1) *content* as media uses and functions; (2) *communicators* as a conglomerate; (3) *codes* as symbol systems unique to each mass medium; (4) *gatekeepers* as checkpoints within the media to start, modify, or stop messages; (5) *mass media* as complex institutions of the host society; (6) *regulators* as external watchdogs that attempt to monitor and change media performance; (7) *filters* as the frames of reference that audiences use to understand or filter out messages; (8) *audiences* as individuals, often in very large aggregates, attending to a particular media event; (9) *effects* as the behavioral reaction of individuals and the impact of the mass media on a parent culture; (10) *noise* as any interruption of the communication process or any media distortion; (11) *media amplification* as the power of the media to focus on an issue, confer status on an individual, or give credence to a viewpoint; (12) *feedback* as the delayed, cumulative, and institutionalized response of the mass audience, usually reported numerically as attendance or monetary figures. If we could present the HUB model in motion, you could see that the concentric circles are not rigid but flex, or pulse, to the beat of a complex interaction of all the elements of the process of mass communication.

BIBLIOGRAPHY

Altheid, David L. *Media Power*. Beverly Hills, Calif.: Sage, 1985.

Conrad, Peter, *Television: The Medium and Its Manner*. Boston: Routledge and Kegan Paul, 1982.

Czitron, Daniel J. *Media and the American Mind: From Morse to McLuhan.* Chapel Hill: University of North Carolina Press, 1982.

Davis, Dennis K., and Stanley J. Baran. *Mass Communication and Everyday Life: A Perspective on Theory and Effects.* Belmont, Calif.: Wadsworth, 1985.

Fry, Don, ed. *Believing the News.* St. Petersburg, Fla.: Poynter Institute for Media Studies, 1985.

Goldman, Alan, ed. *Public Communication: Perception, Criticism, Performance.* Malamar, Fla.: Krieger, 1983.

Graber, Doris A. *Mass Media and American Politics.* 2nd ed. Washington D. C.: Congressional Quarterly, 1984.

Gurevitich, Michael, and Mark R. Levy, eds. *Mass Communication Yearbooks.* Beverly Hills, Calif.: Sage, 1985.

McLuhan, Marshall. *Understanding Media: The Extensions of Man.* New York: McGraw-Hill, 1964.

McLuhan, Marshall, and Quentin Fiore. *The Medium Is the Message: An Inventory of Effects.* New York: Bantam Books, 1967.

Martin, James. *Telematic Society: A Challenge for Tomorrow.* Englewood Cliffs, N.J.: Prentice-Hall, 1982.

Pember, Don. *Mass Media History.* Chicago: Science Research Associates, 1984.

Pool, Ithiel de Sola. *Technologies of Freedom.* Cambridge, Mass.: Harvard University Press, 1985.

Rogers, Everett M., and Francis Balle, eds. *The Media Revolution in America and Western Europe.* Norwood, N.J.: Albex, 1985.

Salvaggio, Jerry L., ed. *Telecommunications: Issues and Choices for Society.* New York: Longman, 1983.

PART I

What Are
the Mass Media?

2

Books

Of all the mass media, books may be the most specialized, and some people may not classify them as mass media at all. But many best-selling books have reached mass audiences, and like other media, books have developed from elite to mass to specialized forms. Of all the media, however, books are the most varied in content, but perhaps the least varied in form. More than 40,000 books are published each year, each with its own content, far more than the number of all newspapers, magazines, motion pictures, television and radio programs, and phonograph recordings combined. Except for a few best-sellers, most of those 40,000 titles reach relatively small audiences. And overall, the book industry has the lowest gross income of all the mass media.

In spite of their relatively weak economic position, books probably have the most long-term power and influence among the mass media. The book is still the medium used to communicate the most important thoughts of a society, the medium most used to present new ideas and to stimulate change, and the medium most used to educate—from preschool to post-doctoral programs. Libraries are often the central room in primary and secondary schools and, the central building on college and university campuses.

At the University of Maryland, as at other educational institutions in the United States, the campus is dominated by the library. Engraved in stone on the building are various quotations that extol the power and the virtue of books. One, for example, by Thomas Carlyle, says: "In books lies the soul of the whole past time."

This is the kind of worshipful tone with which we have revered the book, as a medium and as an institution. Books have played a dominant role in human education since the development of movable type. A large part of that education has been self-help, or self-instruction, for which the book has been indispensable. Books have also provided entertainment. And now books are becoming journalistic media by presenting timely information and interpretation.

In spite of the advent of the popular press and the electronic media, books continue to play an important role in society. The reason, perhaps, is that the book is still the most convenient and most permanant way to package information for efficient storage, rapid retrieval, and individual consumption. When we compare the book with the newer media, we can recognize the special qualities of the book as a valuable communication tool.

HISTORICAL PERSPECTIVE

Books have a long history. As far back as 2400 B.C., clay tablets about the size of shredded-wheat biscuits were used as we use books today. In Babylonia, these clay tablets were inscribed with cuneiform characters to record legal decisions or financial accounts. In 700 B.C., an entire library of literary works written on such tablets existed in Nineveh in Asia Minor.

Technical Advances

The development of paper was the first great technical advance in book production. The earliest form of paper was papyrus, believed to have been used as a writing material in Egypt as early as 4000 B.C. In the second century B.C., finding papyrus difficult to procure because of conflict with the Egyptians, the king of Pergamon sought improvements in the prepara-

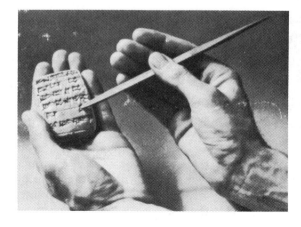

Figure 2.1. Cuneiform characters get their distinctive triangular shape from the reed stylus that is used to impress lines and wedges on wet clay, which is then baked so it can be preserved.

tion of animal skins for writing purposes, leading to the perfection of parchment. Parchment became the chief medium for writing until the tenth century A.D., when a writing material made from linen pulp was introduced.

Developments in bookbinding were also important. The earliest form of paper books, called *volumen,* consisted of rolls of papyrus or parchment, wound around a wooden rod. Such scrolls were difficult to handle and impossible to index or shelve for ready reference. In the fourth century A.D., the Romans developed a form of binding called *codex,* in which scrolls of paper were cut into sheets tied together on the left side between boards, forming the kind of book we still use. Codex binding opened a new world for books: readers could leaf through books and find the passages they wanted; they could begin to compare passages of books; they could set up a table of contents and an index and put material into some logical order.

The Development of Printing

The most important single innovation for book publishing was the invention of the printing press and movable type. The Chinese were the first to develop printing, in the first half of the ninth century A.D., and the oldest known printed book is *The Diamond Sutra,* printed in China in 868 and made up of seven sheets pasted together to form a 16-foot scroll. But the Chinese did not carry their invention much further. In Europe, books were hand-copied until the fifteenth century, when Johannes Gutenberg, in Mainz, Germany, put together a wine press and movable type to make a usable printing system.

The craft of printing spread rapidly in Europe, and more than 30,000 books were produced during printing's first 50 years. Most of these books were religious or ancient classics, printed in Latin or Greek. As more people came into contact with books and learned to read, printers slowly began to produce crude versions of these classics in vernacular languages, and they began to publish books on more popular subjects, such as history, astronomy, and supernatural phenomena.

The first printed books looked much like the hand-copied volumes produced during the Middle Ages. The style of type was Old English, which resembled the handwriting of the monks who had copied manuscripts in florid letters. Because this typeface was not easy to read, it was not useful as a conveyor of information. The spread of the printed word caused new type styles to be designed, and families of type began to grow. As more people began to read books, type style itself began to be "vulgarized," or simplified. Gothic type, characterized by black, bold, square letters, was easier to read than was ornate text type. This new type expressed a feeling of simplicity and directness. Roman type was a combination of Old English and gothic, with some ornateness and some simplicity in the design of the letters, much like the type styles in most use today.

Each development in the production of books—whether in paper,

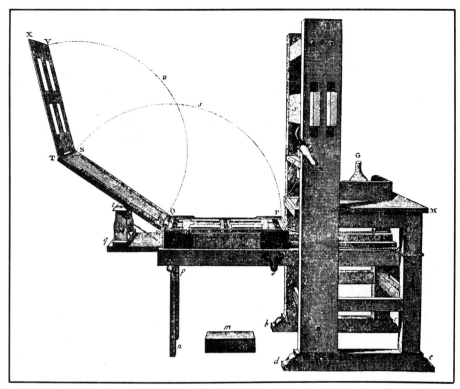

Figure 2.2. The earliest printing presses were simple wooden machines, and books were hand-printed and hand-bound in a complicated and time-consuming process. Books were expensive and available to only the privileged few. (Picture Collection, The Branch Libraries, The New York Public Library.)

binding, printing, typography, or broader distribution through popular translations—brought the book closer to the common person, and each development further paved the way for the eventual production and dissemination of the book as a mass medium.

Books in Early America

Books were, of course, important to the development of the United States. They allowed explorers to pass along their discoveries, and they accelerated the accumulation and distribution of this knowledge.

Nineteen years after the Pilgrims set foot at Plymouth Rock, Stephen Daye became the first printer in North America, establishing himself at Cambridge; and a year later, in 1640, he published his first book, *The Whole Book of Psalms*. The first American Bible was published in 1663; it was soon translated into the languages of the Massachusetts Indians for use in missionary work.

Popular works gradually made their appearance. The most famous of these was *Poor Richard's Almanac,* published by Benjamin Franklin every year from 1733 to 1758. Franklin wrote the almanac under a pseudonym, Richard Saunders, and filled the books with wise and witty sayings that were set between meteorological reports. In 1731, Franklin started the first subscription library in America, the Library Company of Philadelphia. One of the first American inventors, a scientist as well as an eminent statesman, Franklin was also one of America's pioneer mass communicators, as we have seen, making important innovations not only in book publishing, but in magazine and newspaper publishing as well.

Until the nineteenth century, books were relatively scarce, and the elite and affluent were most likely to possess or read them. A family's library was often a mark of its place in society. The aristocrats of Virginia, for example, prided themselves on their leather-bound volumes of classics. One of the best collections belonged to one of the greatest statesmen among them, Thomas Jefferson; his personal library was purchased by Congress in 1815 to start the Library of Congress.

Development into a Mass Medium

For the first 350 years of printing, the production of books changed very little. The type was set by hand; the paper was handmade; and the wooden press was hand operated. At the beginning of the nineteenth century, such slow production did not matter, because only about 10 percent of the population of the United States was able to read. But by the end of the nineteenth century, 90 percent of Americans had become literate. As literacy increased, the demand for books soon exceeded the supply. During the nineteenth century, mass-production techniques came to the book business.

The first technological innovation was the invention in France in 1798 of a machine that could make paper in a continuous roll rather than in single sheets. Press innovations were made about the same time, with the development in England of an iron press (to replace wood) and the use in Germany of steam power (to replace hand production) and a cylinder that pressed the paper against the type (to replace the flatbed press). It was not until 1846 that an American invented the rotary press, in which the type also was put on a cylinder. In 1865, another American put paper rolls together with a rotary press for the first high-speed printing. Type continued to be hand set until 1884, when Ottmar Mergenthaler of Baltimore perfected the Linotype to set type by machine.

These developments in technology were accompanied by rapid change in the editorial side of book publishing. To meet the rising demand for books that could be produced quickly and cheaply, book publishing became a more organized business. A few major publishers began to emerge, and they sought writers to produce books quickly for the new market.

Figure 2.3. The Linotype, perfected in Baltimore in 1884, is a typesetting machine that casts solid lines of type from dies, speeding the process and reducing the cost of the product. (Photo: Picture Collection, The Branch Libraries, The New York Public Library.)

The nineteenth century saw the emergence of the popular book, a cheaply produced and often sensational treatment of some popular theme, either fictional or nonfictional. The development of fast printing methods and cheap paper in the 1840s opened the way for the "dime" novel. Thus the world of books—which had been devoted primarily to works of philosophy, religion, literature, and science—also became inhabited, during the latter half of the nineteenth century, by popular heroes of adventure, romance, the wild West, and Horatio Alger success stories. Books came to be judged by the book industry not so much on their literary merit as on their popularity: How many copies were sold? How much money did they make? This best-seller concept would become basic to all mass media.

The Book in the Twentieth Century

Until the end of World War II, book publishing in the United States remained essentially the same kind of industry that it had been in the late nineteenth century. Most firms were still relatively small, family-owned publishing houses, usually specializing in one type of book, such as adult trade books, professional books (for example, books for medicine, law, or science), or textbooks for elementary or secondary schools or for colleges.

In the twentieth century, changes began to take place that resulted in the sustained growth of book sales. From 1952 to 1970, the book industry grew at a rate of more than 10 percent each year. In the 1970s, the industry grew by 16.5 percent a year. By 1980, the gross sale of books had exceeded $6.6 billion a year, with textbooks accounting for the lion's share of the market.

The growth in book publishing over the past 50 years can be attributed to four specific developments within the industry and American society: (1) the development of book clubs, (2) the emergence of paperback books, (3) changes in the organization of publishing firms, and (4) the boom in American education.

Unlike magazines and newspapers, books cannot depend on subscription sales, which guarantees that the consumer will purchase and receive issues of a publication over a regular period. The purchase of a book is usually a one-time transaction to fill a specific need. The book club helped change that process and became a new distribution technique that revitalized book publishing. Book clubs began to develop in the 1920s, providing a kind of automatic subscription for books and regular ordering each month through the mail, in a habit-forming pattern. In the late 1970s, more than $350 million was grossed annually by the industry through book-club sales.

A second element in the growth of book publishing was the emergence of the paperback book. Europeans were the first to publish cheaply

Figure 2.4. The paperback book has been one of the reasons for the continued success of the book-publishing industry, despite newer mass media. (Photo: Brendan Beirne.)

bound books on a large scale, giving readers access to a much broader range of books than they could otherwise afford. The growth of American paperback publishing spurted during World War II, when millions of servicemen needed inexpensive reading material that could easily be carried in their pockets. Today, paperback books are a staple item at almost every newsstand, drugstore, corner grocery, supermarket, bus depot, train station, and airport. Paperbacks are no longer limited to the 75-cent variety; the average trade paperback costs more than $6.

A new dimension was added to book publishing in the mid-1970s: the development of the managed book. Publishers began to put books together in the same way that movie producers and magazine executives assemble their products. A managed book begins in editorial board rooms, not in an author's imagination. Editors and publishers look at demographic charts and opinion polls and decide what kind of book is needed and what will sell. They then contract for various pieces of the work in order to get it

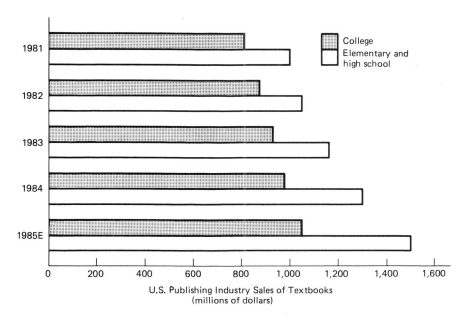

Figure 2.5. *The textbook has been a major product of the book-publishing business, and its sales have continued to grow as education has grown in the United States.*

done rapidly. Good examples of this type of publishing are the books produced by Time-Life Books.

The growth of the industry has been marked by important changes in the organization of publishing firms. Many are now large public corporations with wide distribution and public listing on the stock market. These corporations have often diversified their publishing activities into a broad range of books, including trade, juvenile, elementary-school, secondary-school, college-textbook, scientific, and technical-book publication. In addition, these corporations have been steadily merging into giant conglomerates, which often include other media as well.

But the most important development in the growth of book publishing has been the boom in American education. Textbooks now account for more than one-third of the total gross sales of books; in 1945, they accounted for only one-fifth. If we added together all books falling generally within the educational category, including encyclopedias and professional books, they would account for more than one-half of the book industry's sales. Among the mass media, the book has a particular usefulness for informing as well as for entertaining. As a tool of education, it is still far superior to other media, and this fact has been an essential element in the growth of publishing in the United States (see Figure 2.5).

BOOKS AND THE MASS MARKET

Aside from textbooks and educational books, which students are obligated to buy, what kind of book achieves mass circulation in America? An analysis of best-selling books is useful in understanding the publishing industry; it is also revealing of American society and culture. The list of best-selling books throughout our history does not include many books written by Nobel Prize winners or acclaimed by literary critics. Most best-selling books are self-help books. The top three best-selling hardcover books from 1895 to 1975 were cookbooks, and the best-selling paperback of all time is a book on baby and child care. Not far behind the cookbooks and child-care books are the sex manuals: *The Sensuous Woman, The Happy Hooker,* and *Everything You Always Wanted to Know about Sex but Were Afraid to Ask* have sold more copies in paperback than has any hardcover book other than the *Better Homes and Gardens Cook Book.*

One publishing phenomenon that should be noted is the work of Dr. Seuss. Five of his children's books are among the top ten best-selling hardcover books. Their titles ring with familiarity for almost all of us: *Green Eggs and Ham; One Fish, Two Fish, Red Fish, Blue Fish; Hop on Pop; Dr. Seuss's ABC;* and *The Cat in the Hat.*

One of the latest mass-market book genres is the lush, sexy paperback romance, called by the industry the "bodice-ripper." In 1971, Avon Books tested the historical-romance market with the publication of *The Flame and*

"I, for one, don't see how Herman Melville relates to our life style."

Figure 2.6. Cover of a bodice-ripper novel.

the Flower. It sold 3 million copies, and soon every paperback publisher was in the "bodice-ripper" business. These romances became the second-largest mass-market paperback sellers (after general fiction) in the mid-1970s. By the mid-1980s, the major paperback publishers were estimating that romance books constituted a large share of their total sales.

THE SCOPE OF BOOK PUBLISHING

Book publishing is smaller than the newspaper and magazine industries, but it is growing. From 1970 to 1980, book publishing grew at a slightly greater rate than did newspaper publishing—165 percent growth for books compared with 153 percent for newspapers. American publishers currently produce about 40,000 titles yearly.

There are about 1,750 book publishers in the United States, but the industry is dominated by a few large publishing houses. The larger publishers are conglomerates with many different imprints. Many venerable companies have merged with conglomerates: Harper & Row is now part of Rupert Murdoch's News Corp.; Scott, Foresman and Little, Brown are now part of Time, Inc.; New American Library is now part of Penguin; and so on.

The book-publishing industry has traditionally been headquartered in New York City, which still is the home of one out of three of the large publishers. The number of publishers in New York is declining slightly, however, and substantial growth is taking place in the West, particularly in California, and in the South. New York publishers account for about 45 percent of the industry's total receipts.

THE BOOK AUDIENCE

The average American does not spend as much time reading books for pleasure as does the average European. A survey completed in 1978, however, indicates that 55 percent of Americans read some books; of those, 25 percent had read 10 or more books in the past 6 months and were considered moderate to heavy book readers. Six percent of Americans read no books.

Generally, women read more books than men; 60 percent of American women are book readers, whereas only 49 percent of men are. Young people read more books than old people. In fact, book reading declines steadily with age, whereas newspaper and magazine reading seems to increase with age. Textbook reading in school undoubtedly plays a major role in these statistics. Education also plays a role: the more education a person has, the more he or she is apt to read books.

THE STRUCTURE AND ORGANIZATION OF BOOK PUBLISHING

The book publisher is essentially an intermediary between author and reader. In most small firms, the publisher contracts for all the services necessary for the production and distribution of the publications—including the work of artists, designers, copy editors, paper dealers, printers, binders, sales representatives, and distributors. Even some of the largest book publishers use outside services for some production aspects, and only a handful of major publishers have their own printing facilities.

The publisher operates at the center of a large number of services and specialists between the author and the reader. Generally speaking, says book publisher Henry Z. Walck, ''No more than forty to forty-five percent of the publisher's staff work is in the editorial, manufacturing, advertising, and selling departments. The shipping clerks, invoice clerks, accountants, yes, the top executive officer, frequently find their particular operations not much different from those in a plumbing business or that of selling cornflakes."[1]

The larger the firm, the more specialized each individual's function must become. Editors themselves have increasingly specialized tasks. Executive editors are responsible for planning publishing programs. These editors are decision makers, deciding what books to publish, which authors should write the books, and how the product should be packaged and promoted. Production editors are technicians rather than planners, performing the technical steps necessary to convert a manuscript into a finished book. This includes such tasks as copy editing, rewriting if needed, proofreading, and indexing.

The other jobs in book publishing are also specialized, whether in selling, promoting, distributing, or producing. Artists, designers, advertising copywriters, and promotion specialists are of increasing importance and concern. There are many different and challenging jobs in book publishing, and, as Walck says, "The qualifications necessary for many of these positions are not unique to publishing; they are the same as required by most other business enterprises for similar jobs. Book publishing is a business, and as such it offers opportunity to almost anyone who has a business skill or professional talent."[2]

THE TYPES OF BOOK PUBLISHING

Today we speak of book publishing in terms of three broad types of books: general, professional, and educational.

General Books

General books are also often called "trade books" because most of them are sold to the public by the trade, meaning bookstores. Trade books include reference works, children's books, "how-to" books, fiction, poetry, humor, biography, and religion. Children's books, or "juveniles" or "junior books," represent a rapidly growing segment of the trade field. Ideas or completed manuscripts often come from free-lance writers, except in the reference-book field. The typical large publisher may annually receive up to 25,000 unsolicited manuscripts or book outlines and ideas, only a fraction of which will be published. Trade books are generally sold through bookstores and to libraries for general readership. Reference works and

---

[1] Quoted in Daniel Melcher, *So You Want to Get into Book Publishing* (New York: Bowker, 1967), 10.

[2] Ibid.

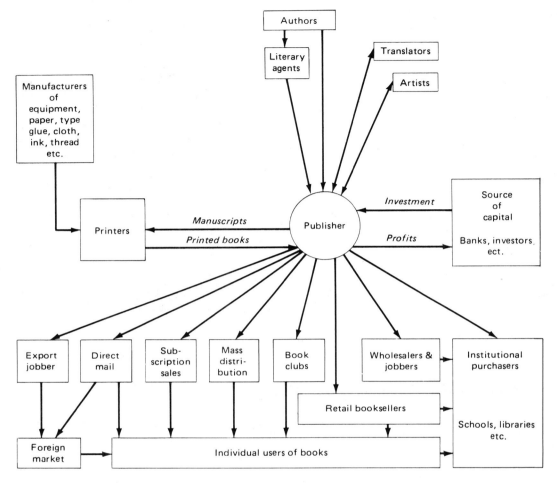

Figure 2.7. An organizational chart for a typical book-publishing house. (Reprinted from *A Guide to Book Publishing*, with permission of the R. R. Bowker Company. Copyright © 1966 by Xerox Corporation.)

encyclopedias are more often sold by subscription, through the mail, or by house-to-house sales representatives.

Professional Books

Professional books have become increasingly important because of our constantly changing and rapidly developing society. The professional person, no matter what the occupation, must keep up with the changes in his or her field or run the risk of obsolescence. Hundreds of books are published each year for lawyers, doctors, engineers, scientists, business executives, and teachers. Professional books are most often written by specialists in the various professions and are often produced at the suggestion of a book editor who is familiar with the occupation. Such books are usually sold through direct mail or in special technical or campus bookstores, and almost always at prices higher than those of trade books.

Educational Books

Educational books make up the largest area of publishing. There are more than 50 million students in primary and secondary schools; about 11 million students in colleges, universities, and technical institutes; and more than 25 million adults enrolled in evening courses, on-the-job training, or home-study programs. This represents a giant audience for textbooks, workbooks, supplementary materials, reference works, and laboratory manuals.

Most of these books are written by teachers, college professors, or specialists. As with professional books, they are often written at the suggestion of a particular editor or publisher who sees the need for a text. Ideas for educational books also come from educators who have developed new materials or new ways of looking at old subjects. The essential element of distribution for educational books is the "adoption." Textbooks are not selected by the individual student but are usually adopted by the instructor for an entire class. In some cases, a book is adopted for a local school, a group of local schools, or even the statewide school system.

THE BOOK AS A JOURNALISTIC MEDIUM

The book is becoming an important medium of journalism and has been rediscovered by journalists. Because of improvements in the speed of production, books are increasingly being used to present timely news and interpretation, especially when a subject needs more in-depth development than can be given in a newspaper or magazine.

This has stimulated the relationship between literary writing and journalism. Novelist Truman Capote, for example, used the techniques of the journalist to write *In Cold Blood*, a factual work of literary merit that was the forerunner of many similar books. And journalists have increasingly used literary techniques to bring color and action to their books—for example, Theodore H. White's *Making of the President*, a series of books about recent presidential elections. Using the book as their medium, journalists can add dialogue, description, and dramatic pacing that bring factual events to life.

Bob Woodward and Carl Bernstein, the *Washington Post* reporters who broke the Watergate story, turned to books to tell the full story of the events that led to the downfall of the Nixon administration. *All the President's Men* and *The Final Days* are journalistic books that read like fiction. The authors were criticized for having overdramatized, for having imagined scenes, for having avoided sufficient attribution, and for having failed

Figure 2.8. Books have become a journalistic medium for the in-depth reporting and analyzing of timely topics.

to document their sources fully. These are all journalistic sins; but by using these novelistic techniques, in book form, the writers were probably able to show the whole Watergate episode better than could other media.

The work of such writers as Robin Moore represents another dimension in the new role of books in journalism. Moore is the author of *The French Connection, The Green Berets,* and *The Washington Connection.* He employs a team of investigative reporters to research all the facts about a current public problem or situation—in the books mentioned, drug addiction, combat elites, prostitution, and political scandal. He then puts all the facts together in the form of a novel. Moore says his form of journalism is "faction."

Books can now be produced almost as rapidly as newspapers and magazines, which enables the book to be a news medium. Within a week after the return of the 52 hostages from Iran, for example, a publisher was selling a major book called *444 Days.* Paperback publishers were able to bring out copies of the Pentagon Papers in book form within hours after the Supreme Court had ruled that the government could not stop their publication. Within several days after the crash of the space shuttle *Challenger* in January 1986, several books were on the market providing complete treatment of the accident.

Figure 2.9. The book permits the author to develop a subject; and new technologies and the science of marketing allow the publisher to reach a small audience with a specialized topic and still make a profit. (Photo: Brendan Beirne.)

THE FUTURE OF BOOKS

The book has always been a very personal medium, but the new technologies will make books even more personalized. In the past, the high costs of older printing processes and of mass advertising needed to reach an intended audience meant that publishers could produce only books that would have relatively high sales. But the new technologies allow the publisher to use market research to find a specific or specialized audience, computers to alphabetize and zip code that audience so it will be easily reachable, and less expensive printing processes to produce highly specialized books for a smaller number of readers at affordable prices.

Publishers can also use word-processing equipment to further reduce costs and to produce more books. Authors can become their own typesetters by doing their writing on a personal computer, and the disk or tape that is produced can generate the computer composition of camera-ready copy needed to make the plates for printing. In addition, readers can now publish their own books. Information stored on microfilm or microfiche can be retrieved by computer and assembled into a customized book.

THE CHARACTERISTICS AND ROLES OF BOOKS

Books are marked by several distinguishing characteristics. They are the only medium to which we attach some permanence. We throw away magazines and newspapers. The sounds of radio and the visual images of television pass immediately, although this is changing somewhat with the increased use of home video recorders. Phonograph records are a bit more permanent, but they wear out, break, become dated, and are difficult to store. Movie film is also difficult for the private individual to store. But any person can put together bookshelves and keep books for a lifetime. The permanent storage of books has been institutionalized through libraries. All this gives books a reuse rate higher than that of the other media. The book can be retrieved, referred to, and reused better than can other forms of communication.

More than most other media, the book is personal. One can sit alone with a book, at leisure, whenever the mood strikes. One can read a book at one's own speed—can stop and start at will—can leaf through the book, and can find a special passage. There is no need for speed; time is of little concern; so the author of a book can develop a subject much more completely than can the originator of any other mass communication medium.

The book carries with it an aura of more dignity and respect than most other media, perhaps because it is so closely identified with education, intellectual activity, and the recorded wisdom of humankind. People who would not think twice about wrapping their garbage with ''The Week in Review'' section of the *New York Times* might keep on their bookshelves a superficial romance bound in book form. We tend to have a reverence for the book that transcends our reverence for all the other media.

SUMMARY

Books have gone through development stages from elite to mass to specialized forms. Technological developments since the invention of movable type have made the mass production of books possible, enabling many to become best-sellers. But while best-selling books may reflect the tastes of the masses, they may not be the most influential books published.

The book industry is usually organized around a publisher, who is a contractor for a variety of services—writing, editing, designing, promoting, advertising, printing, distributing, and selling. Book publishing is divided into three basic types—general, professional, and educational—and educational books constitute the largest segment of the industry.

Increasingly, books are becoming journalistic media because they can be produced and marketed rapidly, and they provide the journalist with the ability to deal with a subject with drama and depth. The new computer technology is increasing the book's ability to serve the personalized needs of individual communicators and readers.

Books are probably more individualized than all the other media, not only because they are produced in great variety, often for small numbers of readers, but also because the book-reading experience is personal. We read books alone, not in groups, and immerse ourselves more deeply in the process. The reader often experiences a sense of personal communication with the author, more than is achieved by any other mass medium.

BIBLIOGRAPHY

Book Production Industry. 425 Huehl Road, Building 11B, Box 368, Northbrook, Ill. 60662.

Books in Print. New York: Bowker, annual.

Dessauer, John P. *Book Publishing: What It Is, What It Does.* New York: Bowker, 1974.

The First One Hundred and Fifty Years: A History of John Wiley and Sons, Incorporated, 1807–1957. New York: Wiley, 1957.

Hiebert, Ray Eldon. *Books in Human Development.* Washington, D.C.: American University and the Agency for International Development, 1964.

Mott, Frank Luther. *Golden Multitudes: The Story of Best Sellers in the United States.* New York: Macmillan, 1947.

Paperbound Books in Print. New York: Bowker, annual.

Petersen, Clarence. *The Bantam Story: Thirty Years of Paperback Publishing.* 2d ed. New York: Bantam Books, 1975.

Publishers Weekly. 1180 Avenue of the Americas, New York, N.Y.   10036.

Uhlan, Edward. *The Rogue of Publishers' Row: Confessions of a Publisher.* New York: Exposition Press, 1960.

The U.S. Book Publishing Industry. Commack, N.Y.: Business Trend Analysts, 1982.

U.S. Book Publishing Yearbook and Directory. White Plains, N.Y.: Knowledge Industry Publications, annual.

Wallis, Philip. *At the Sign of the Ship: Notes on the House of Longman 1742–1974.* London: Spottiswoode, Ballantyne, 1974.

Writer's Digest. 933 Alliance Road, Cincinnati, Ohio 45242.

3

Newspapers

The mass media have generally followed a fairly typical pattern in their development. As John Bittner has analyzed in his textbook, *Mass Communication*, new communication means usually are introduced for a small elite. Then they become a mass medium. And finally they develop into more specialized, segmented media. Eric Barnouw some years ago showed that mass media also followed a fairly typical pattern in the ways in which their functions developed. They were often started to serve a business function, then developed an entertainment function, and finally took on a news and information function. Most mass media have, in general, followed this pattern, and newspapers were the first to go through the full cycle of development.

Although television has become the dominant mass medium in our society, newspapers were the first to become a true mass medium; and in many ways, they still are the most important. Newspapers occupy a special place in democratic societies. Indeed, newspapers and modern democracies grew up together, and it is doubtful that democracy could exist without free newspapers. Each day, more than 100 million Americans rely on newspapers to provide accurate, timely, and useful information to help them plan their daily lives. Newspapers provide the facts and analyses that allow informed citizens to make effective and responsible decisions, not only in coping with the complexities of modern living, but also in protecting the rights and liberties of a free society.

From the earliest days of newspapers, monarchical and authoritarian governments were challenged when newspapers spread information to the people. Information has always been powerful, and as people acquired more information, they gained more power over their own destinies, weakening their ruler's power over their lives. So newspapers have often been suppressed by authorities.

The Founding Fathers, hoping to establish a democratic society, knew that the free flow of information was essential to citizens who were seeking their rights and freedoms. They knew that newspapers were the key to the free flow of information, so they insisted on the right of newspapers to pursue the truth and publish it, whether or not the government agreed with the truth. Thomas Jefferson summed up his political philosophy when he said:

> The basis of our government being the opinion of the people, the first object should be to keep that right; and were it left to me to decide whether we should have a government without newspapers, or newspapers without a government, I should not hesitate a moment to prefer the latter. But I should mean that every man should receive those papers and be capable of reading them.[1]

HISTORICAL PERSPECTIVE

The regular publication of news goes back more than 2,000 years to at least 59 B.C., when the Romans posted public news sheets called *Acta Diurna*. The word *diurna,* meaning "daily," has been an important part of news ever since. The words *journal* and *journalism* have their roots in the same word, *day,* and the daily, current, or timely aspect of news has always been an essential factor in newspapers.

For much of the past 2,000 years, the communication of news has been carefully guarded. Through most of the years of the Roman Empire and the Middle Ages, the distribution of news came under the strict control of both secular and ecclesiastical authorities. Even after the development of the printing press in the mid-fifteenth century, it took another 150 years before the political climate changed sufficiently to allow the beginnings of the modern newspaper.

The Development of the Newspaper

In Europe during that 150 years (and long thereafter), printers had to fight monarchs for the right to publish. William Caxton, the first English printer, set up his press in 1476 and worked in relative freedom until his death 15 years later, largely because he did not print any news. When Henry VIII came to the throne of England, he feared the power of the press; and by

---

[1] Thomas Jefferson letter to Edward Carrington, 16 January 1787, in *A Jefferson Profile as Revealed in His Letters,* ed. Saul K. Padover (New York: John Day Co., 1956), 44–45.

Figure 3.1. Even though the earliest printing presses were simple, the words printed on them were so powerful that they often struck terror in the hearts of kings. (Photo: Picture Collection, The Branch Libraries, The New York Public Library.)

1534, he had established strong measures to control printing. For more than 100 years after that, the British authorities maintained repressive restrictions on printers; some were hanged, and many were imprisoned for defying the authority of the monarch.

As Edwin Emery points out in his history of journalism, *The Press and America*, "It is significant that the newspaper first flourished in areas where authority was weak, as in Germany, at that time divided into a patchwork of small principalities."[2] The first prototype newspaper, a rudimentary version to be sure, was published around 1609, probably in Bremen, Germany. In that year, a primitive newspaper appeared in Strasbourg, and in 1610, another was printed in Cologne. By 1620, simple newspapers were being printed in Frankfurt, Berlin, Hamburg, Vienna, Amsterdam, and Antwerp.

The first English prototype newspaper was printed in London in 1621. From that year to 1665, various *corantos* and *diurnals* ("current" and "daily" forms of publication) made their appearance. These often were tracts and broadsides in format, rather than newspapers. Their production accompanied a growing freedom from governmental control, climaxed by the ringing declarations of the poet John Milton. In 1664, in his essay, "Areopa-

---

[2] Edwin Emery, *The Press and America* (Englewood Cliffs, N.J.: Prentice-Hall, 1972), 5.

gitica," he expressed the basic rationale of a free press in a democratic society:

> [T]hough all the winds of doctrine were let loose to play upon the earth, so truth be in the field, we do injuriously by licensing and prohibiting to misdoubt her strength. Let her [truth] and falsehood grapple; who ever knew truth put to the worse, in a free and open encounter?[3]

In 1665, the first true English-language newspaper, in form and style, was published in Oxford, then the seat of English government. It was called the *Oxford Gazette*. When the government moved to London some months later, the newspaper moved, too, and became the *London Gazette*. Thirty-seven years later, in 1702, the first daily newspaper, the *Daily Courant*, was published in London. In those 37 years, English printers of newspapers had won many rights, including the freedom to publish without a license.

These early newspapers, in both Europe and, later, North America, were primarily journals of commercial and business information, printed for the elite of the mercantile class.

The Development of the Newspaper in the United States

Newspapers in Early America. In the colonies of British North America, where people did not have full British citizenship, printers did not yet enjoy the rights and freedoms that their counterparts had won in England. Thus the first newspaper in the colonies, *Publik Occurances, Both Forreign and Domestick,* published on September 10, 1690, was banned after the appearance of its only issue because its printer, Benjamin Harris, did not have an appropriate license from the British authorities.

Fourteen years later, the *Boston News-Letter* was started, published under the authority of the Massachusetts governor. Nevertheless, in its lifetime, from 1704 to 1776—when it ceased publication because of the outbreak of the American Revolution—it was rebuked by the government on many occasions, and publication was suspended several times.

Most early colonial newspapers, like their European counterparts, existed primarily for the purpose of spreading information about business and commerce. Produced by printers, not journalists, they contained some local gossip and stories, but many of them were concerned chiefly with advertising and often had the word *advertiser* in their title. They told about ship comings and goings, and gave market information, import and export news, and trade tips. But the colonial printers who published these newspapers could not help but inject stories about political conditions that af-

---

[3] John Milton, "Areopagitica," quoted in *Prose of the English Renaissance* (New York: Appleton-Century-Crofts, 1952), 766.

fected their businesses, and they expressed their opinions on such political matters. As they smarted under their second-class British citizenship, they began to express in their editorials their bitterness over the policies of the king of England.

In 1721, James Franklin, a colonial printer, began publication of the *New England Courant*. When he published a sarcastic comment about the British governor of Massachusetts, he was thrown into jail; his 13-year-old brother, Benjamin, took over the printing of the newspaper. This started Ben Franklin on a lifetime of writing, printing, and publishing. Later Franklin went to Philadelphia to start his own print shop and newspaper, and before he was 40, he had become the first "press lord" in America, having founded a chain of print shops and newspapers in which he held partial ownership.

Another colonial printer who ran afoul of the British authorities was John Peter Zenger, printer of the *New York Weekly Journal*. In 1734, Zenger was thrown into jail for having libeled the British governor of New York. But a jury of colonists ultimately freed Zenger when a shrewd Philadelphia lawyer, Andrew Hamilton, made a convincing argument that Zenger's facts had been true and that people should be free to print the truth, even if damaging.

The case eventually led to the legal interpretation that newspapers can print anything, even attacks on the follies and abuses of government, if

Figure 3.2. The trial of John Peter Zenger in 1735 proved to be a landmark case in the fight for freedom of the press, because it established the right to print the truth, even if it is damaging to rulers and authorities. (Photo: Courtesy of the State Library of New York.)

they can prove that their criticism is based on facts. This has given journalists an unprecedented power in the modern world.

The Zenger case emboldened the colonial newspapers to take up the attack against the colonists' status as second-class citizens. Increasingly, political activists used the pages of the colonial newspapers to arouse public opinion against the abuses of British authority, leading finally to the Declaration of Independence and the Revolutionary War.

Historian Arthur M. Schlesinger, Jr., in his book *Prelude to Independence: The Newspaper War on Britain, 1764–1776*, demonstrates clearly that colonial newspapers were powerful weapons in the battle for freedom from England. Some of the Founding Fathers were newspaper writers and "press agents" who fought for independence through the pages of the colonial press. Among them were Samuel Adams, Thomas Paine, Thomas Jefferson, John Adams, John Dickinson, Benjamin Franklin, and Richard Henry Lee.

After the Revolution, the newspapers again served to encourage social action, helping to persuade the citizens of the newly independent nation to ratify the Constitution and adopt a democratic form of government. Another historian, Allan Nevins, in his essay "The Constitution Makers and the Public, 1785–1790," describes how James Madison, Alexander Hamilton, and John Jay sent letters to the newspapers urging support for the Constitution. Today, we know those "press handouts" as *The Federalist Papers*. It was, says Nevins, "the greatest work ever done in America in the field of public relations."[4] Little wonder, then, that newspapers were so important to the new nation of America.

The Penny Press: The First Mass Medium. Although the first American "daily" newspaper, the *Pennsylvania Evening Post and Daily Advertiser*, was started in 1783, it was not until half a century later that newspapers began to reach a truly mass audience. Until the 1830s, newspapers were fairly high priced and aimed at a relatively elite group of merchants and influential politicians. They were politically affiliated, often functioning as organs for a particular political party or viewpoint.

Technical advances in printing in the early nineteenth century made communication for the masses more feasible. Most important was the replacement of the flat-bed press with the cylinder press, which speeded the printing process enough to allow for mass production. One New York printer, Benjamin Day, used the new, faster press to begin a trend in journalism. In 1833, he started the *New York Sun* and sold it for a penny rather than the usual 6 cents. By hiring newsboys to hawk the newspapers on the streets, he succeeded in making up in volume what he lost in individual sales. The *New York Sun* became the publishing success of jour-

---

[4] Allan Nevins, "The Constitution Makers and the Public: 1785–1790." *Public Relations Review* (Fall 1978): 5–6.

Figure 3.3. The *Boston Gazette and Country Journal* was one of several dozen colonial American weekly newspapers that inspired the struggle for independence by printing information and opinions about British rule.

nalism and started the era of the "penny press," the first mass-circulation medium.

In order to sell penny papers on a mass basis, the newspapers had to contain material of interest to many people. This economic factor led to the development of the profession of news gathering. The man most responsible was James Gordon Bennett, a printer like Day, who started the *New York Herald* in 1835, two years after Day had started the *Sun*. Both Day and Bennett realized that to sell newspapers on the streets of New York, they had to have good stories and interesting headlines.

Figure 3.4. James Gordon Bennett can be said to have fathered mass communication when in 1835 he founded the *New York Herald,* which he sold on the street for a penny a copy, thus making the newspaper available to the average person.

Bennett started the practice of hiring writers to go out and find the stories, and the modern news reporter was born. He sent men to police stations to get stories about crime, to city hall for stories about politics. He sent reporters into New York harbor in boats to meet ships coming in from Europe, so that his paper could be the first with foreign news. And when the telegraph came into use in the 1840s, he was the first newspaper publisher to station a correspondent in Washington, D.C., to telegraph to New York City stories about Congress and government.

The penny press proved to be a great business success. Only 15 months after Bennett's *Herald* was born, it had a circulation of more than

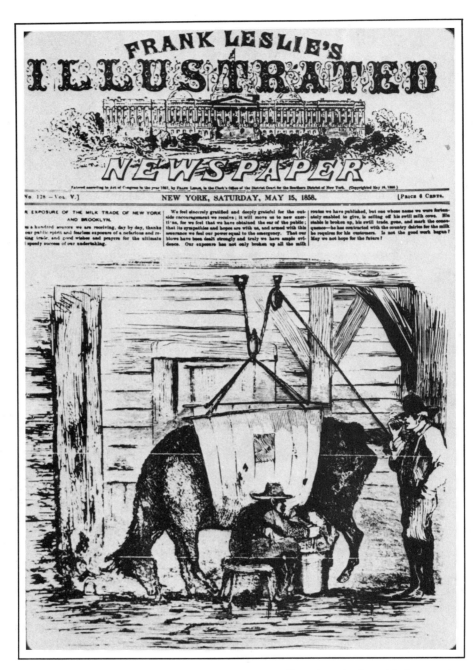

Figure 3.5. *Frank Leslie's Illustrated Newspaper,* like others in the mid-nineteenth century, used line drawings and woodcuts to help illustrate the news and attract readers.

40,000, and the number of readers grew steadily. Other newspapers, such as Horace Greeley's *New York Tribune* and Henry Raymond's *New York Times*, were started. With circulation ultimately reaching the hundreds of thousands, these papers and their editors became powerful forces in mid-nineteenth-century society, playing an influential role in the Civil War, the industrial revolution, western expansion, and urbanization. Similar newspapers soon were launched in cities across the country.

Yellow Journalism and Muckrackers. Mass-circulation newspapers had become big business by the end of the nineteenth century. The papers were highly competitive, for the most part independent, and no longer tied to any one political party or group. Circulation was built largely through sensational news coverage or interesting features, with bold headlines and extra editions carrying the latest news.

"Newspaper barons"—men who had built journalistic empires through aggressive promotion—emerged toward the end of the nineteenth century. Joseph Pulitzer developed the strong *St. Louis Post-Dispatch* and then bought the *New York World* in 1883. The *World* had a circulation of 20,000 when Pulitzer took it over; less than a decade later, by 1892, he had raised its readership to 374,000. Pulitzer stressed sound news coverage combined with crusades and stunts to win his readers; in 1889, he sent a young reporter with the pseudonym Nellie Bly around the world to beat the record of the fictitious Phineas Fogg, hero of Jules Verne's *Around the World in Eighty Days*. Nellie completed her trip in 72 days, and circulation of the *World* soared as readers kept up daily with her reports.

Another businessman, William Randolph Hearst, entered journalism as the student business manager of the *Harvard Lampoon* and then received the *San Francisco Examiner* as a gift from his wealthy father. In 1895, he purchased the *New York Journal* and copied many of Pulitzer's techniques to compete with the *New York World*. Knowing that headlines would sell papers, Hearst not only reported news, but also sometimes created news to get banner stories. Some historians have accused Hearst and the *Journal* of fomenting the Spanish-American War in 1898 to get more exciting stories and thus more subscribers.

In 1889, the same year that Nellie Bly circled the globe, Pulitzer's *World* produced the first regular comic section in a Sunday paper. It later was printed in color. The most popular cartoon was a strip called *The Yellow Kid*, a feature that gave the name "yellow journalism" to the whole era of sensational newspaper practices. Comic strips became extremely important in building newspaper readership and circulation, especially among immigrants who used the picture stories to help them learn English.

According to newspaper historian Frank Luther Mott, yellow journalism was based on sensationalized coverage of crimes, scandal and gossip, divorces and sex, disasters, and sports. Its distinguishing features were scare headlines, sensational pictures and photographs, stunts and faked

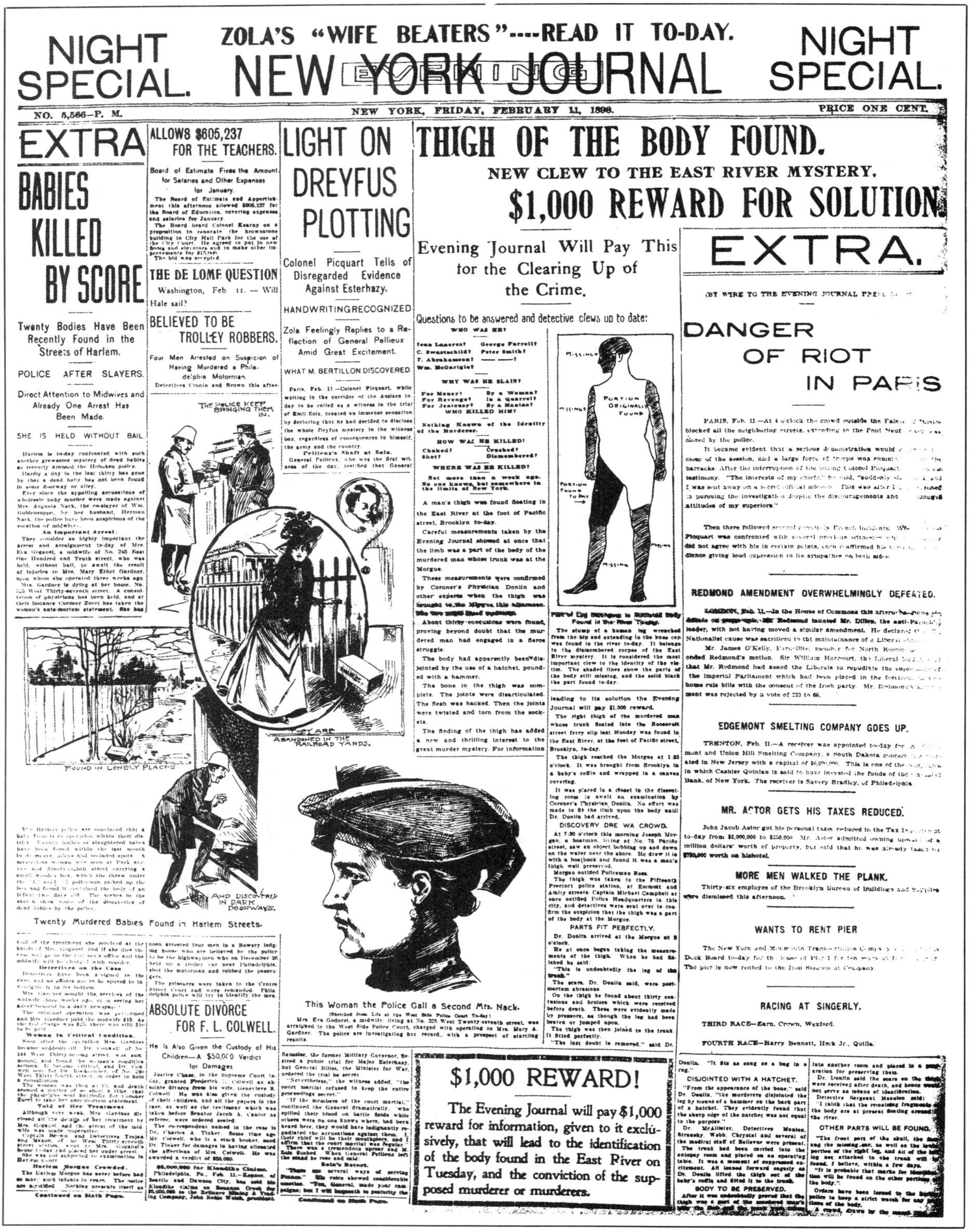

Figure 3.6. William Randolph Hearst's *New York Journal* typified the yellow journalism of the 1890s. As this issue illustrates, to build circulation, Hearst treated the discovery of a dismembered corpse as a mystery game whose solution would be rewarded with a prize. Later, his reporters caught the murderers. (Photo: Courtesy of the Bell & Howell Company.)

stories, comic strips, Sunday-supplement features, and crusades for the downtrodden and the lower classes. Similar elements often have been part of other new mass media.

The crusading element was most important. The yellow press, with hundreds of thousands of regular readers, exercised great influence on public opinion. By exposing graft and corruption in society, newspapers found that they could not only sell more papers, but also perform a service to society. A new breed of reporter began to develop, one who was interested in investigating the sins of society and the hidden perversions of power. These men, to use Teddy Roosevelt's expression, "raked the muck of society."

The so-called muckrakers did much social good. For example, writer Lincoln Steffens exposed graft and corruption in city governments and helped bring about municipal reform. Ida Tarbell's exposé of the Standard Oil Company helped strengthen antimonopoly laws. Samuel Hopkins Adams's investigation of the patent-medicine business led to federal food and drug regulations. These writers worked in the magazine and book fields as well as on newspapers, but they typified a new breed of newspaper journalist.

By the beginning of the twentieth century, the daily newspaper had become a power for good and evil in society. It was the first and most influential mass medium.

The Modern Newspaper. In the twentieth century, the American newspaper has grown more mature and responsible. During the first 30 years of the new century, some of the newspaper giants of the nineteenth century declined and fell, including the *New York World* and the *New York Sun*. In *The Compact History of the American Newspaper*, John Tebbel says this marked "the transition from propaganda and personal journalism to the conservative newspapermaking of a new generation of businessmen soon to rise."[5] In the twentieth century, corporate caution replaced individual newspaper flamboyance.

One of the reasons for the change was economic. James Gordon Bennett had started the *New York Herald* in 1835 with an investment of $500. By 1900, it would have taken $1 million to start a New York newspaper, and by mid-century, at least $6 million. The amount of investment required for a large metropolitan newspaper plant today is usually counted in the tens of millions of dollars. The *Los Angeles Times*, for example, estimates that it has more than $100 million invested in printing equipment alone. Enterprises with that sort of money at stake cannot afford to be reckless.

One consequence of rising costs and big-business operations has been the death of many newspapers and the merger of others. In New York

---

[5] John Tebbel, *The Compact History of the American Newspaper* (New York: Hawthorne Books, 1969).

Figure 3.7. The publication of the modern newspaper requires a gigantic printing press, with computers for typesetting and control and more than 1 million moving parts for printing. A huge room is needed just to store rolls of newsprint. (Courtesy of The Austin Company—Consultants—Designers—Engineers—Constructors.)

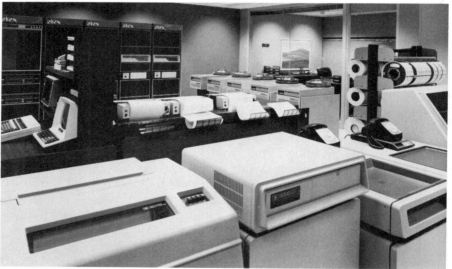

City, most of the giants of the nineteenth century merged, becoming the *New York World, Telegram,* and *Sun,* the *New York Herald Tribune,* and the *New York Journal-American.* And all these newspapers ultimately merged in the 1960s into the *New York World-Journal Tribune*—and then died. The same happened, although perhaps less dramatically, in other American cities.

Sensational journalism did not disappear completely in the twentieth century. An important manifestation of it was the so-called jazz journalism

of the 1920s, marked by the rise of tabloid newspapers, which are smaller than regular "blanket" newspapers. These papers usually make extensive use of photographs and are dominated by the headlines of one or two major stories. Such a paper is the *New York Daily News;* started in 1919, it grew swiftly in the 1920s, with sex and sensation as its basic news content. Its circulation became the largest in the country, a rank it held until the 1980s.

In the twentieth century, daily newspapers have had to face rising

Figure 3.8. The number of daily newspapers in the United States has been declining; about 1,675 were being published in the late 1980s. Those that have survived compete not only with other media, but also with other newspapers—as these vending machines testify.

competition from many sides. The new mass media—radio, television, and motion pictures—have grown to challenge the premier position of the newspaper as mass communicator. The automobile revolution, the suburban exodus, the death of the inner city, and growing leisure time for sports, recreation, and entertainment have also changed the place of the newspaper in the daily life of the twentieth-century American.

Today, a number of great American newspapers are economically sound, politically independent, and socially responsible, despite competition and high costs. For almost a century, the *New York Times* has maintained its reputation as the newspaper of record. (It is kept in libraries as the official record of the day's events.) Two other great newspapers that claim a national audience are the *Wall Street Journal* (the largest circulation daily in the mid-1980s) and the *Christian Science Monitor*, both of which have won wide respect for their coverage of important news and their penetrating analysis of events. The *Washington Post* rose rapidly during the 1950s and 1960s to challenge the *New York Times*, as did the *Los Angeles Times*, under the dynamic leadership of Otis Chandler.

The newest national newspaper is *U.S.A. Today*, which was started in

1982 and has grown rapidly. The newspaper is edited in the Washington, D.C., area, but is owned by the Gannett chain of newspapers and is printed by Gannett's printing plants around the country. The content is transmitted to the printing plants by satellite, with regional issues containing some regional content. By the mid-1980s, *U.S.A. Today*'s total daily circulation was more than 1 million, making it the newspaper with the third largest circulation in the country. Gannett has also begun the publication of European and Pacific editions in an attempt to make *U.S.A. Today* an international newspaper.

THE "ALTERNATIVE" PRESS

The "alternative" press has become a medium of communication that has a direct and personal appeal to select subcultures within our society. The newspapers are not "underground," as they are sometimes called, since they are publicly available. They came into vogue during the 1960s, and by the end of that decade, several hundred were in existence.

Today, there is considerable flux in the fortunes of the alternative press. Many of the newspapers—started during the rebellious years of the 1960s by flower children, hippies, Vietnam War protestors, social and sexual reformers, and university activists—have since died. Others, such as *Rolling Stone* and the *Village Voice*, have become so successful that they can hardly be considered alternatives anymore; they are now part of the establishment press.

These papers are usually printed by inexpensive offset methods, are often sold on the street rather than by subscription, and usually deal with sensational materials—either sexual, social, or political.

The alternative press appears to satisfy a need that is not fulfilled by the usual news media. Their editors often argue that traditional "objective" reporting is impossible and, indeed, that subjective reporting should be the norm. Although some of the content is designed simply to shock, much of the "news" in these papers simply cannot be found in regular newspapers. The success of some of these papers cannot be discounted. Alternative papers have been found on some military bases, on college campuses, and even at high schools.

THE SUBURBAN
AND THE SPECIALIZED PRESS

The development of inexpensive printing technologies have made the publication of small newspapers for specialized audiences economically feasible since the 1970s. The result has been the growth of small weekly newspapers to serve the local community and specialized weekly newspapers to

Figure 3.9. The *Los Angeles Times* and the *Washington Post* have grown since World War II to become major newspapers. This is how the *Times* covered the end of the war in 1945 and, on page 57, how the *Post* covered the landing on the moon in 1969. (Figure 3.9a, copyright 1945, Los Angeles Times. Reprinted by permission.)

The Weather

Today — Showers, thunderstorms, high in 80s. Tuesday — Fair, less humid. Chance of rain, 30% today. Winds variable, 10-15 m.p.h. Temperature range: Today, 72-88. Yesterday, 76-68. Details, Page D5.

The Washington Post

Times Herald

92d Year   No. 228   © 1969 The Washington Post Co.   **MONDAY, JULY 21, 1969**   Phone 223-6000   10c

Index   36 Pages   4 Sections

Amusements B 8	Fed. Diary C 3
Calendar B 4	Financial C 6
City Life B 5	Movie Guide B 7
Classified A 5	Obituaries C 4
Comics D 4	Sports D 1
Crossword D 4	Style B 1
Editorials A14	TV-Radio B 3

'The Eagle Has Landed'—
Two Men Walk on the Moon

Neil Armstrong and Edwin Aldrin plant the American flag on the surface of the moon. The flag is kept "flying" on the airless moon by a spring device.

'One Small Step For Man ... Giant Leap for Mankind'

By Thomas O'Toole
Washington Post Staff Writer

HOUSTON, July 20—Man stepped out onto the moon tonight for the first time in his five-million-year history.

"That's one small step for man, one giant leap for mankind," declared pioneer astronaut Neil Armstrong at 10:56 p.m. EDT, the giant leap for mankind.

Just after that historic moment in man's quest for his origins, Armstrong walked on the dead satellite and found the surface very powdery, littered with fine grains of black dust.

A few minutes later, Edwin "Buzz" Aldrin joined Armstrong on the lunar surface and in less than an hour they put in a show that will long be remembered by the worldwide television audience.

American Flag Planted

The two men walked easily, talked easily, even ran and jumped happily as it needed. They picked up rocks, talked at length of what they saw, planted an American flag, saluted it and talked by radiophone with the President in the White House, and then faced the camera and saluted Mr. Nixon.

"For every American, this has to be the proudest day of our lives," the President told the astronauts. "For one priceless moment in the whole history of man, all the people on this earth are truly one."

At 1:10 a.m.—2 hours and 14 minutes after Armstrong first stepped upon the lunar surface—the astronauts were back in their moon craft and the hatch was closed.

In describing the moon, Armstrong told Houston that it was "fine and powdery. I can suck it up loosely with my toe.

"It adheres like powdered charcoal to the boot," he went on, "but I only go in a small fraction of an inch. I can see my footprint in the moon like fine grainy particles."

Armstrong found he had such little trouble walking on the moon that he began talking almost as if it didn't want to leave it.

"It has a stark beauty all its own," Armstrong said. "It's like the desert in the Southwestern United States. It's very pretty out here."

Amazingly Clear Picture

Armstrong shared his first incredible moments on the moon with the whole world, as a television camera on the outside of the stingless Eagle landing craft sent back an amazingly clear picture of his first steps on the moon.

Armstrong seemed just like he was swimming along taking big and easy steps on the airless moon despite the cumbersome wide pressure-suit he wore.

"There seems to be no difficulty walking around," he said. "As we suspected, it's even easier than the consualt. It that we did in simulations on the ground."

One of the first things he did was to scoop up a small sample of the moon with a long-handled spoon with a bag at its end like a small butterfly net.

"Looks like it's easy," Aldrin said, looking down from the Lem.

"It is," Armstrong told him. "I'm sure I could push it in farther but I can't bend down that far."

Guides Aldrin Down Ladder

At 11:11 p.m., Aldrin started down the landing craft's ten-foot ladder to join Armstrong.

Backing down the nine-step ladder, Aldrin was guided the entire way by Armstrong, who stood at the foot of the ladder looking up at him.

"Okay, Armstrong said, 'watch your step' PLSS, for portable life support system) from underneath. Drop your pliss down. You're clear. About an inch clear on your plss.

"Okay," Aldrin said. "You need a little arching of the back to come down."

When he stepped onto the first rung of the ladder, Aldrin went back up to the Lem's front porch to partially close the Lem's hatch.

"Making sure not to lock it on the way out," he said in rover fashion. "That's our home for the next couple of hours and I want to make sure we can get back in."

Aldrin reported it was a "very simple matter to hop down from one step to the next." To make the last and longest step, he said he put both hands on the fourth rung up and leaned back with his feet foot first.

"Beautiful," said Aldrin when he met Armstrong on the lunar surface.

"Isn't that something," said Armstrong. "It's a magnificent sight out here."

See APOLLO, A8, Col. 1

Moon Walk Yields Data for Science

By Victor Cohn
Washington Post Staff Writer

HOUSTON, July 20—The human eye spotted the moon and within minutes became the sole scientist on the moon.

Edwin "Buzz" Aldrin was also making man's first look on the lunar surface from their command planetary posts.

From the moment to see a city building around the lunar surface of every shape, explosion in endless variety, and fresh. And "quite a few interesting things."

This, probably of the Physical Sciences, may be paraphrasing for the 1st Geological Survey, working to see of the science eye-lab's team here is its pack.

They've hit a good start to be collecting.

Even Neil Armstrong, on the craft for the moon in fact, He, eager astronomy, parallel on those tones, on surfaces—to began the first scientific "watching on earth's oldest satellite.

The mere fact that he did it and did it well immediately answered a vital question.

May can function on the moon.

One of the first things he said was "The NASA came were all right."

That was the "intelligence and equipment storage in earth)—a trunk in the side of the Lem—that held him a television camera and scientific equipment.

He was quickly giving details on the information about the nature of the lunar surface than they have gained in all their recent years of peering at it with unmanned probes.

"The lunar footpads (are) only depressed in the surface about one inch or two inches and I sink in to a fraction of an inch—the surface was remarkably cohesive.

"The surface appears to be very fine grained as you get close to it. It's almost a powder, very fine. ... It's soft powdery probably because of the constant 'gardening' by meteorite bombardment over the ages.

See SCIENCE, A13, Col. 4

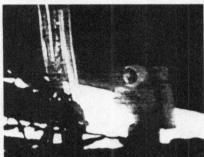

Armstrong takes his first steps on the moon. At left is the Eagle, the lunar landing craft.

'Squared Away and in Good Shape . . .'

The following is a condensed transcript prepared by UPI of the conversation showing man's first walk on the moon among astronauts Neil A Armstrong, Edwin E (Buzz) Aldrin and Michael Collins, ground commander, the Bruce McCandless and Mission Control astronaut John McLeish.

Armstrong—That's one your's way for man, one giant leap for mankind.

Armstrong—The descent

on the ground. I can see some evidence of rays emanating from the descent engine but a very insignificant amount.

Armstrong—OK. Buzz, ready to bring down the camera.

Aldrin—All ready. It looks to be all squared away and in good shape.

Armstrong—It's quite dark in the shadow and a little hard for me to see but I have good footing. I'm well

McLeish—Confirmation on first step 10:56:20.

Armstrong — Looking at the Lem. I'm standing in settle in the shadow now looking as at Base in the windows—and I can see everything quite clearly. The light is sufficiently back-lighted to the front of the Lem so that everything is clearly visible.

Aldrin—OK. I'm going to change ...

Data is good, the crew is doing well. 30 and a half way side of PLSS (are expected) slow.

Armstrong—Right.

McCandless—OK. Buzz, this is good.

Armstrong — It's very interesting. It's a very soft surface but here and there where I dung with the toe, tropnary surgeon I can into a very hard surface.

Aldrin—OK. the handle is off. It makes about my up

Apollo Liftoff Schedule

Apollo 11's key activities, cued for today:

1:55 p.m.—(Lunar module's ascent engine fires, lifting the module's upper stage off the moon and leaving the descent stage behind)

5:35 p.m.—Lunar module and command ship dock

9:20 p.m.—Lunar module is jettisoned

No key television is scheduled until 9:42 p.m. EDT

Millions Follow Moon Landing Around the World, Except in China

By Robert C. Jensen
Washington Post Staff Writer

Man's first journey to the moon was hailed in nearly every part of the world today. The exception was China, where one-fifth of the world's people live.

The Communist rulers at Peking decided to withhold the news that the Americans

said in a dispatch from Peking that no word of the landing or any part of the Apollo mission was mentioned to China.

In Russia, the news agency Tass announced the moon landing in a 52-word dispatch. And the reports were carried routinely in the Soviet television and radio broad-

Americans. "It's a great day," one shouted.

Much the same reaction was voiced by Vice President Humphrey, who beamed: "What a day to be human." Humphrey had returned from a briefing trip with Gov. Sergei C. Sokolov, first deputy defense minister. Humphrey brought

Figure 3.10. *USA Today* revolutionized the appearance of newspapers through its extensive use of color, photographs, and graphics and its streamlined writing style. Launched on September 15, 1982, it quickly grew to become one of the highest circulation newspapers in the United States.

serve distinct ethnic, cultural, or professional groups. In fact, the suburban press has been one of the fastest growing forms of journalism since the 1970s.

As people have moved out of the central city and into the suburbs, they have sought smaller newspapers with news about their local communities. In the typical suburban communities of Washington, D.C., for example, dozens of weeklies emerged in the 1960s and 1970s. One company, the Army Times Publishing Company, by using a central plant with automated equipment, was able to start five suburban weeklies in the Washington area in a short period of time—the *Montgomery Journal, Prince Georges Journal, Alexandria Journal, Arlington Journal,* and *Fairfax Journal*—each of which serves a specific Washington suburb with news about the local community that could not be provided by the *Washington Post*. With the closing of the *Washington Star,* the suburban *Journal* newspapers decided to publish five days a week to provide better community and suburban coverage for the Washington, D.C., area. Newspaper companies in other suburban areas have followed similar patterns.

Other specific groups in our society have been able to develop their own newspapers. Foreign-language papers—in Spanish, German, even Korean—are flourishing. Newspapers serving specific ethnic groups are also thriving. One company in Colorado is publishing the Soviet newspaper *Pravda* in an English version that duplicates the layout and graphics of the original Russian edition; the paper has already found a sizable audience of Americans who are interested in the Soviet version of the day's news.

Even within a community, the lowering of publication costs has made possible the proliferation of specialized publications. This is true within a corporation, an association, a university, and other institutions. At the University of Maryland, for example, until the mid-1960s, the campus was served by only one newspaper, the *Diamondback,* a student daily. Since then, cheaper printing has brought into existence several campus newspapers, each of which is read by a specialized audience. The faculty and administration have their weekly newsletters; the black students have a weekly newspaper; the fraternities and sororities, the commuter students, some of the dormitories, and some schools and departments regularly produce publications.

A rapidly growing type of specialized newspaper is the sensational, often sexually explicit national tabloid. Examples are the *National Enquirer,* the *Globe,* and the *Star.* These newspapers are often sold in supermarkets and on the newsstands. They thrive on exaggerated gossip about movie and rock stars, politicians, the rich, and the famous, as well as on tales, sometimes tall, of freaks and unfortunates and extraterrestrials. They constantly push the scandal that is their stock in trade to the limits of libel and slander, but make up for the legal suits they inspire by the money they make from the millions of readers to whom they appeal.

Special-interest groups are also producing newspapers for mass circulation, carrying the news from their perspective rather than from a general, objective point of view. For example, in the 1980s, a daily newspaper called the *Washington Times* was started in Washington, D.C. It is published by a group with backing from Sun Myung Moon, the Korean religious leader who has stimulated a religious movement. The *Washington Times* is a professional-looking newspaper with news stories, color photographs, editorials, features, and some advertising, but its general slant is toward Moon's philosophy.

THE BLACK PRESS

An exception to the growth of the specialized press has been the black press, which has been declining in circulation. Nevertheless, in the 1980s, it is still a potent voice. The black press was started in the United States 160 years ago when John B. Russwurm and the Reverend Samuel E. Cornish published the first issue of *Freedom's Journal* in 1827.

Before the Civil War, more than 40 newspapers were published for blacks. Many of them were short-lived; all suffered extreme pressures. The most prominent was the *North Star,* founded and edited by Frederick

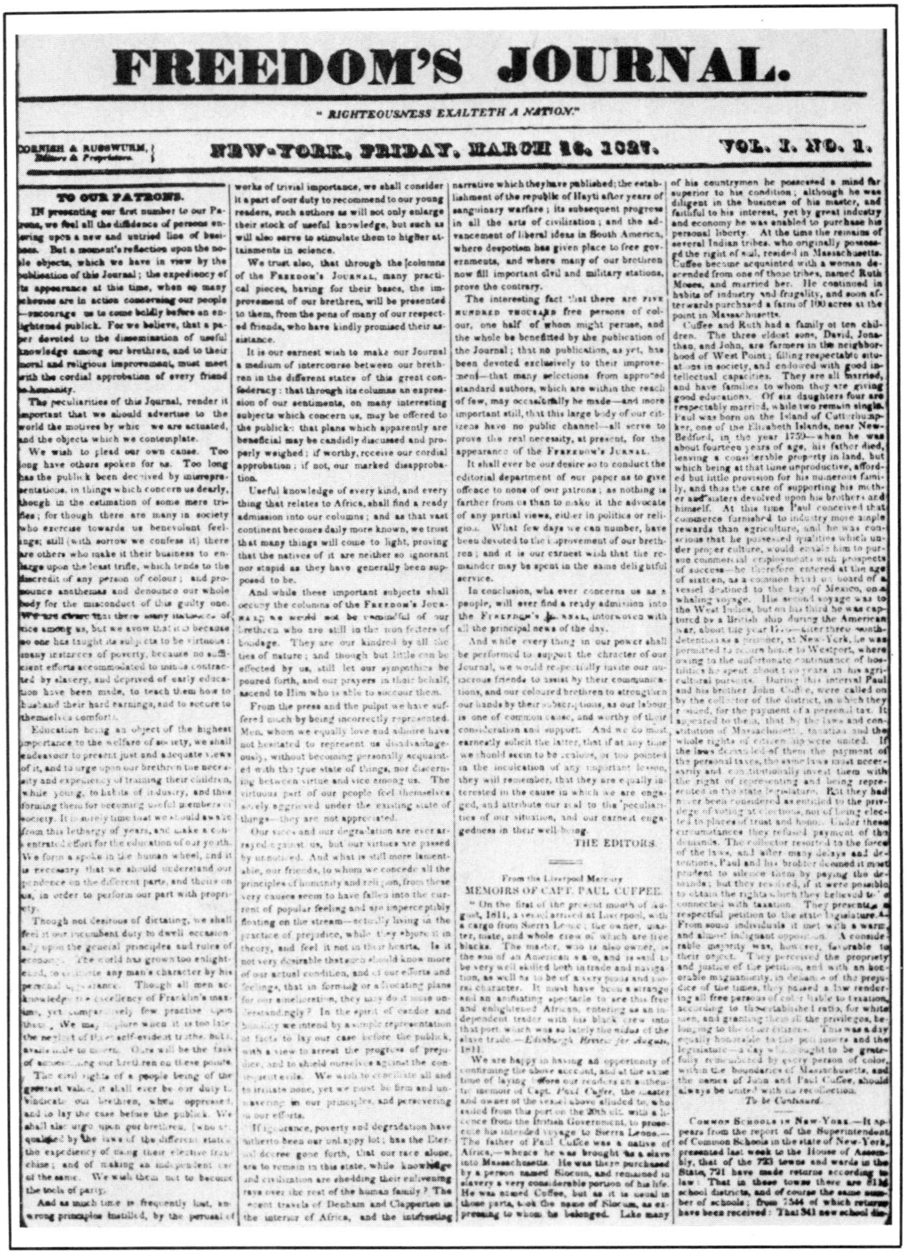

Figure 3.11. *Freedom's Journal,* established in 1827, was the first black newspaper published in the United States. It played an important role in the antislavery movement before the Civil War.

Figure 3.12. The *New York Amsterdam News* has the largest circulation of any black newspaper in the United States.

Douglass, to "attack slavery in all its forms." By 1890, there were 575 black newspapers in America.

Since the first publication of *Freedom's Journal*, more than 3,000 black newspapers have been founded in the United States. Many of them became great voices of the black community, especially such newspapers as the *Chicago Defender*, the *New York Amsterdam News*, the *Baltimore Afro-American*, the *Washington Afro-American*, the *Milwaukee Courier*, the *San Francisco Sun*, the *Columbus Times*, and the *Los Angeles Sentinel*. Only 220 are still being published, but most are financially strong, with a total circulation of about 4 million. Advertising linage is growing, although it is still a minor fraction of advertising space in the establishment newspapers.

The *New York Amsterdam News*, founded in 1909, is the largest paid-circulation black newspaper, with about 100,000 readers. Seven of the black newspapers in history have been dailies, and five, including the *Amsterdam News*, are still in existence. Others are the *Atlanta Daily World*, launched in 1932, and the *Chicago Daily Defender*, started in 1956. The *Columbus Times* and the *New York Challenge* were started in the 1970s.

The black press established its own organization in 1940: the National Newspaper Publishers Association. But the black press declined in the decades after World War II, as blacks became increasingly assimilated into white culture. James D. Williams, former director of communications for the National Urban League, presently with the NAACP in Baltimore, in a booklet *The Black Press and the First Amendment*, wrote that

> there were other factors that also began to operate against the black press; the general decline in newspaper readership as more and more people turned to television; the dispersal of black persons outside the central city where the black papers were available; the continued indifference of major advertisers to black media . . . and a decline, in some instances, of the quality and quantity of the reporting.[6]

THE SCOPE OF NEWSPAPERS

Although the number of daily newspapers in the United States in the mid-1980s has declined to 1,657, the survivors are financially strong, and overall circulation has grown. The peak number of newspapers was reached just before World War I in 1914, when 2,250 dailies were published. In 1984, newspaper circulation in America had grown to an all-time high of more than 64.6 million copies printed each day (Table 3.1).

After a period of decline, the number of weekly newspapers is beginning to rise again. In 1960, there were 8,138 weeklies in America, but that number had dropped to 7,466 by 1977. By the mid-1980s, about 7,700

---

[6] James D. Williams, *The Black Press and the First Amendment*. New York: National Urban League, 1976.

TABLE 3.1 TOP 25 DAILY NEWSPAPERS

Daily	Total daily circulation for 6 months ending March 31, 1986	Gain/loss over same period last year
1. Wall Street Journal (m)*(national edition)	1,985,559	−4,466
2. New York Daily News (m)	1,275,268	−115,687
3. USA Today (m)(national edition)	1,168,222	+5,616
4. Los Angeles Times (m)	1,088,155	+18,591
5. New York Times (m)(national edition)	1,035,426	+22,225
6. Washington Post (m)	781,371	+10,118
7. Chicago Tribune (m)	760,031	−15,633[1]
8. Detroit News (all day)	650,445	−16,031
9. Detroit Free Press (m)	645,266	−1,210
10. Chicago Sun-Times (m)	631,808	−7,379
11. Long Island Newsday (e)*	582,388	+40,315
12. San Francisco Chronicle (m)	554,611	−368
13. Boston Globe (m)	514,097	+3,530
14. Philadelphia Inquirer (m)	492,374	−27,247
15. Miami Herald (m)	458,759	−5,986
16. Cleveland Plain-Dealer	454,042	−10,209
17. Newark Star Ledger	452,148	+17,344
18. Houston Chronicle (all day)	425,434	−7,946
19. Dallas Morning News (m)	390,275	+21,592
20. Minneapolis Star & Tribune (e)	382,499	−1,158
21. Boston Herald (m)	358,725	−9,302
22. Baltimore Sun (combined m and e)	356,927	+7,026
23. Portland Oregonian (m)	335,162	+25,767
24. Phoenix Arizona Republic (m)	331,491[2]	+5,814
25. Denver Rocky Mountain News (m)	320,441	−8,940

* m = morning newspaper; e = evening newspaper.
Source: James L. Rowe, Jr., "Chains Seen Buying More Papers," *Washington Post*, 1 June 1986, F2.

weeklies were being published. Weekly newspaper circulation has shown steady growth over the past 20 years, from 21 million in 1960 to more than 49 million in the mid-1980s. Average circulation also rose to its highest level ever—more than 6,300 per newspaper.

Although the number of newspapers and their circulation have been relatively stable, newspaper advertising, both national and local, has grown enormously. In the mid-1980s, ad revenue reached an all-time high of more than $25 billion, more than $5 billion more than television's advertising revenue. Newspapers also received the largest share (26.4 percent) of the advertising dollar, while television was second (21.9 percent).

Chain ownership of newspapers is a twentieth-century phenomenon that developed to offset rising costs and growing competition from other

TABLE 3.2 U.S. NEWSPAPER GROUPS
Ranked by Daily Circulation

	Daily circulation	Number of dailies	Sunday circulation	Number of Sundays
Gannett Co. Inc.	5,508,000	90	4,737,000	60
Knight-Ridder Newspapers	3,626,700	27	4,374,500	22
Newhouse Newspapers	2,932,600	26	3,613,600	20
Tribune Co.	2,638,300	8	3,443,500	7
Dow Jones & Co. Inc.	2,469,600	23	400,200	10
Times Mirror Co.	2,448,300	8	3,188,600	8
News America Pub. Corp.	1,947,200	4	1,147,500	3
New York Times Co.	1,693,300	26	2,258,100	15
Scripps-Howard Newspapers	1,615,500	21	1,652,100	9
Thomson Newspapers	1,452,400	90	938,900	45
Cox Enterprises	1,209,800	19	1,501,400	16
Hearst Newspapers	1,125,100	15	2,068,400	11
Capital Cities Communications Inc.	932,900	8	821,100	4
Freedom Newspapers	892,300	29	880,300	20
Central Newspapers Inc.	809,100	7	890,500	4
Washington Post Co.	790,900	2	1,106,300	2
Copley Newspapers	730,800	12	690,400	6
Donrey Media Group	692,500	53	668,400	47
Chronicle Publishing Co.	598,500	2	762,400	2
Ingersoll Newspapers	569,400	24	359,700	12
Lee Enterprises	554,500	18	669,200	15
Media General	545,400	4	606,100	3
Morris Communications Inc.	542,100	14	556,700	6
McClatchey Newspapers	541,400	7	609,100	5
Harte-Hanks Communications Inc.	540,200	26	553,200	20

Source: James L. Rowe, Jr., "Chains Seen Buying More Papers," *Washington Post,* 1 June 1986, F2.

media. In chain ownership, a number of newspapers are owned by one company, thus gaining the advantage of considerable management and economic efficiencies. In 1910, only 13 groups owned a total of 62 newspapers. But by 1986, 146 companies owned more than 1 newspaper; together they owned 1,217 papers, or 73 percent of all American dailies (Table 3.2). Only 489 newspapers were still individually owned. Daily newspapers are published in 1,534 cities in the United States, and 47 cities still have 2 or more newspapers, but the number of cities with competing newspapers has steadily declined.

A typical metropolitan daily newspaper averages 72 pages on weekdays and 265 pages on Sunday, including inserts. This makes Americans

Figure 3.13. Some of the newspapers and magazines published by Newhouse Newspapers, which is the third largest chain of newspapers in the United States. (Photo courtesy the *Columbia Journalism Review*.)

by far the largest consumers of newsprint, the paper on which newspapers are printed. Americans use 42 percent of the world's newsprint. The second largest consumer is the Japanese, who account for less than 10 percent of the world's total.

Newspapers are profitable businesses on the whole. *Fortune* magazine's analysis of the top 500 manufacturing industries in 1979 showed that newspaper, broadcasting, and motion-picture production and distribution companies had an average profit of 9.6 percent, higher than that of many industries. Of newspaper expenses, 37 percent went to employees. Another large share of costs, 28 percent, went to buy paper, a cost that has been rising sharply in the past decade.

Newspapers are one of American's largest manufacturing employers (behind only the steel, auto-manufacturing, and auto-parts-manufacturing industries). Newspapers employ about 461,000 people. Most newspaper employees, 48 percent, work in production and maintenance, including printing. Editorial personnel make up only 15 percent of the newspaper's total work force. The number of women working in the business has increased and now represents more than 40 percent of the total work force.

Newspaper salaries have grown, too. In 1987, the minimum salary for a *New York Times* reporter who had served his or her apprenticeship was $929 a week, or about $48,400 a year. That same reporter would have made $120 a week, or $6,240 a year, in 1950.

THE NEWSPAPER AUDIENCE

Newspapers reach 138 million Americans every day. Two out of 3 adults read a newspaper every day, and 9 out of 10 adults read at least 1 newspaper every week. An average of 2.2 people read each newspaper delivered to a household. The average newspaper reader is more likely to be male than female, to be "mature" rather than either young or old, to be a college graduate rather than a high-school dropout, to have a higher income rather than a lower one, to be white rather than nonwhite, and to be stable rather than mobile.

Newspaper-reading habits usually develop in early adolescence and continue to grow until the retirement years. The average reader picks up a newspaper 1.9 times a day and reads 1.2 different papers. Almost everybody reads a newspaper sooner or later. Only 9 percent of Americans have

"It's not just me, Doctor. He's been turning away from the New York 'Times' as well."

(Drawing by Lorenz; © 1986 The New Yorker Magazine, Inc.)

not seen a weekday paper in the past week or a Sunday paper in the past month. In the five weekdays, 52 percent read a paper every day, and 84 percent read a paper on at least one weekday. More newspaper reading occurs in the afternoon than in the morning, but newspaper reading falls off dramatically after dinner, perhaps because people are turning on their television sets.

Children's reading of newspapers grows with age. The 9 minutes of newspaper reading a day by 6- to 8-year-olds stretches to 19 minutes a day for 15- to 17-year-olds. But 19 minutes is only a small fraction of the time that children and adolescents spend watching television each day. Nevertheless, as children's newspaper reading increases, their television watching decreases.

One of the most-read parts of the daily newspaper is the comics section; 6 out of every 10 readers read the comics every day. More than 100 million people read the Sunday comics section. A major strip may appear in more than 1,000 papers around the world. Almost every paper has a comics section supplied by the syndicates. The business is dominated by 25 syndicates led by King Features, which handles about 65 of the available 300 strips. *Punk,* a Sunday comics section, has a multinewspaper circulation of 14.5 million.

THE STRUCTURE AND ORGANIZATION OF THE NEWSPAPER

Like all the other mass media, the newspaper is a highly structured, carefully organized, and exceedingly complex mechanism. Literally millions of words come into the large metropolitan daily each day, from many sources. These words must be sorted, selected, checked, evaluated, edited, rewritten, set in type, laid out, made up into pages, printed, and distributed to readers, all in less than 24 hours. In order to accomplish this task with a maximum of reader interest and a minimum of error, the newspaper mechanism must work like a well-oiled machine, with each part running in its place and operating in a smooth relationship to the next.

The operation of a newspaper is usually divided into three parts: editorial, business, and production. Although the most important of these, for our purposes, is the editorial side, the newspaper could not function without the other two. The business manager is in charge of both classified and display advertising. The business manager is also in charge of selling or promoting the newspaper and is responsible for getting it properly distributed, through a circulation department, which is usually made up of independent distributors and a network of newspaper carriers. Finally, the business manager is in charge of the bookkeeping and accounting for the entire organization.

The production manager is in charge of the printing plant, which

Figure 3.14. Newspapers can get the news out very quickly because of their highly organized staff. The *Charlotte Observer* had an ''extra'' edition on the streets within hours of the tragic explosion of the space shuttle *Challenger* on January 28, 1986. (Photo by Jeff Willhelm, courtesy of the *Charlotte Observer*.)

usually includes composing or typesetting, engraving or photographic-plate making, stereotyping or casting of type into curved plates to fit on the cylinders of the press, and, finally, printing itself, usually on a gigantic press with more than 1 million moving parts.

The editorial side of the typical daily newspaper with a circulation of 100,000 has about 75 full-time editorial staff members. The main function of the editorial department is to gather information, judge its importance, evaluate its meaning, write and display it in ways that will attract and hold the attention of readers, and put it through the cycle of production until it reaches the printed page.

The process requires a complex organization for the typical newspaper. The important decisions are often made in committee. The editors meet at the start of each news day to draw up a list of assignments based on their knowledge of events that have taken place or will soon occur. As the reporters complete their assignments, they and the editors meet in conferences during the day and develop the way in which the news and opinions will be played in the newspaper. This kind of constant team effort is an essential aspect of newspaper work.

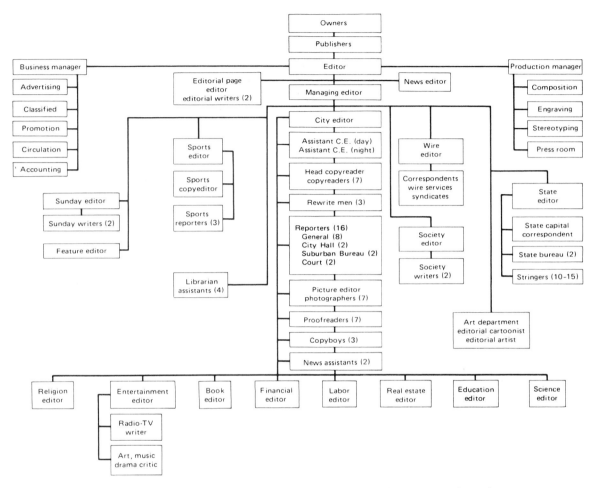

Figure 3.15. An organizational chart for a typical average-size daily newspaper. (Based on *The Structure and Layout of Editorial News Departments,* ANPA Research Institute Bulletin 1008, January 26, 1970.)

THE TECHNOLOGICAL REVOLUTION

A series of technical and electronic developments in the past few decades has brought about a revolution in the editing and production of the newspaper. By the mid-1980s, almost every daily newspaper was being printed by photo-offset lithography, a technique of printing from photo-sensitive plates rather than with raised letters. Type was being set by simple photo composition rather than by casting with hot metal on a Linotype machine. Optical character readers were being used to scan letters on a page or video

Figure 3.16. Newspapers have quickly taken advantage of the technological revolution by using computers in all departments—editorial, business, and production.

screen and to set the material in type automatically. The computer was being used to automate many of the functions of composition and printing, to store and retrieve material, and to transmit copy directly into an automated system. Word processors are bringing about a significant change. Most major newspapers have already revolutionized their newsrooms with the new equipment. Many other papers use computers for circulation, accounting, and advertising tasks as well.

In a word-processing system, the reporter types the story on a personal computer rather than on a typewriter. Editing on the screen can be done much faster than editing on paper because a reporter can add or delete words, sentences, or paragraphs with one push of a key. The reporter transmits the story to the memory bank of a central computer, from which it can be retrieved by the copy editor for further editing. The story then goes to the automatic typesetter, which can produce camera-ready copy, in the prescribed typeface and size, with a headline, to be pasted up for a negative, from which the final plates are made for printing. Systems are already being used to automate page layout and pagination as well.

THE CHARACTERISTICS AND ROLES
OF THE NEWSPAPER

With the development of new media in the twentieth century, the role of the newspaper in society has changed. The newspaper is no longer the fastest medium, and its responsibility for carrying the bulletins and headlines of the day has been taken over by radio and television. The "extra" edition, which typified newspaper publishing through World War II for any major news story, has all but vanished. Radio and television can do a better job of skimming the surface of events around the world and of providing hourly "extra" editions of the news.

But the newspaper has the advantage of being a better display case or bulletin board of news. At a glance, readers can survey the layout of the newspaper and quickly know what is happening. They have better control over the elements of news on which to spend their time. Readers can be more selective, choosing items that are important and pursuing them as far as time will allow.

Daily and weekly newspapers play an essential role in the community, providing the small details of day-to-day and week-to-week information that sew together the fabric of society. They announce births, marriages, and deaths; tell what is for sale; explain laws and customs; help citizens form opinions about issues close to home; and lighten the day with feature stories about local personalities and events.

Newspapers are turning more and more to investigative and interpretive reporting, forms of journalism that are not as adaptable to radio and television. Newspaper stories are getting longer and are going into greater depth; increasingly, newspapers let radio and television serve the function of providing spot news and headlines.

For the newspaper of the future, the key role will increasingly be local community reporting, specialized and in-depth coverage, and information and advertising display.

SUMMARY

The newspaper is the oldest mass medium and still one of the most important, particularly to the maintenance of a democratic society. Newspapers have gone through stages of development typical of most mass media, starting as business and commercial media for elite audiences, then gradually becoming mass media for popular audiences, and finally specializing for segmented audiences.

Although the number of newspapers has declined in the United States, circulation has risen. Fewer cities have competing newspapers, and more newspapers are owned by chain newspaper companies, making the business more efficient and profitable. Newspapers still have the largest amount of gross advertising revenue, in spite of the growth of television. And newspapers employ the largest number of workers of all the mass media.

With the rise of other media, newspapers are changing. They are less concerned with publishing news bulletins and more concerned with interpretating and analyzing the news. But newspapers will always have the advantage of being a display case for news, a local bulletin board for the community, and the investigator of ills that affect society.

BIBLIOGRAPHY

Ayer Directory of Newspapers, Magazines, and Trade Publications. New York: Ayer and Sons, annual.

Bernstein, Carl, and Bob Woodward. *All the President's Men.* New York: Simon and Schuster, 1974.

Bryan, Carter R. *Negro Journalism in America before Emancipation.* Journalism Monographs 12. Lexington, Ky.: Association for Education in Journalism, 1969.

Chalmers, David Mark. *The Social and Political Ideas of the Muckrakers.* Secaucas, N.J.: Citadel, 1964.

Compaine, Benjamin M. *The Newspaper Industry in the 1980s.* White Plains, N.Y.: Knowledge Industry Publications, 1980.

Editor and Publisher. 575 Lexington Avenue, New York, N.Y.   10022.

Editor and Publisher Yearbook. New York: Editor and Publisher, annual.

Eisenstein, Elizabeth L. *The Printing Press as an Agent of Change.* Cambridge, Eng., and New York: Cambridge University Press, 1979.

Emery, Edwin. *The Press and America.* Englewood Cliffs, N.J.: Prentice-Hall, 1972.

Hiebert, Ray Eldon. *The Press in Washington.* New York: Dodd, Mead, 1966.

Internal Control and Audit for Newspapers. New York: Institute of Newspaper Controllers and Finance Officers, 1965.

Jackson, Charles L., Harry M. Shooshan III, and Jane L. Wilson. *Newspapers in Videotex: How Free a Press?* St. Petersburg, Fla.: Modern Media Institute, 1981.

Journalism Quarterly. Association for Education in Journalism and Mass Communication, University of South Carolina, Columbia, S.C.   29208.

Merrill, John C., and Harold A. Fisher. *The World's Greatest Dailies.* New York: Hastings House, 1980.

Mott, Frank Luther. *American Journalism.* New York: Macmillan, 1964.

Newspaper Research Journal. Department of Journalism, Memphis State University, Memphis, Tenn.   38152.

New York Times Index. New York: New York Times, annual.

Presstime. American Newspaper Publishers Association, 11600 Sunrise Valley Drive, Reston, Va.   22091.

Reintjes, J. Francis. *Copy-Processing Systems for Small Newspapers.* Cambridge, Mass.: MIT Press, 1979.

Rivers, William L., William B. Blankenburg, Kenneth Starck, and Earl Reeves. *Backtalk: Press Councils in America.* San Francisco: Canfield, 1972.

Schlesinger, Arthur M. *Prelude to Independence: The Newspaper War on Britain, 1764–1776.* New York: Random House, 1965.

Schudson, Michael. *Discovering the News: A Social History of American Newspapers.* New York: Basic Books, 1978.

Shover, William R. *Promoting the Total Newspaper.* Washington, D.C.: International Newspaper Promotion Association, 1973.

Smith, Anthony. *Goodbye Gutenberg: The Newspaper Revolution of the 1980's.* New York and Oxford, Eng.: Oxford University Press, 1980.

Tichenor, Philip J. *Community Conflict and the Press.* Beverly Hills, Calif.: Sage, 1980.

Udell, Jon G. *Economic Trends in the Daily Newspaper Business: 1946 to 1970.* New York: American Newspaper Publishers Association, 1970.

Weaver, David H. *Videotex Journalism.* Hillsdale, N.J.: Erlbaum, 1983.

Woods, Allan. *Modern Newspaper Production.* New York: Harper & Row, 1963.

4

Magazines and Periodicals

Magazines and periodicals, including comic books and newsletters, have gone through stages of development similar to those of newspapers and the other mass media. They started in the eighteenth century as publications for the elite few. In the late nineteenth century, because of advances in print technology and the rise in literacy, magazines began to reach mass audiences. Indeed, while the newspaper was a mass medium, but limited to local and regional audiences, the magazine became the first medium to reach a national audience. But by the mid-twentieth century, large general-interest magazines were declining in number and in circulation, replaced by a growing number of periodicals aimed at specialized and segmented readers.

Magazines come in all sizes and shapes. Their pages are usually printed on heavier and higher quality paper than newspapers and are stapled or glued between soft covers. About 10,000 magazine titles are published in the United States, many of them under chain ownership. Magazines have a broader range than newspapers, both in subject matter and in geographical distribution, but are designed to reach more specialized audiences.

The word *magazine* means "storehouse;" it comes from the French word *magasin,* which means "store" or "shop." Indeed, the earliest magazines, appearing in France, were really catalogs of booksellers' storehouses. These were issued periodically, and essays, reviews, and articles eventually were added. The names of early magazines, often called "museums" and "repositories," reflected their nature as collections of varied items of general interest.

HISTORICAL PERSPECTIVE

From the beginning, magazines have often been started by young persons with new ideas and little money. The first English publication of magazine type was really a cross between a newspaper and a magazine; called the *Review,* it was published in London starting in 1704. It had four small pages in each issue and was printed as often as three times a week for nine years. Daniel Defoe, a Dissenter who went on to become one of the great men of British letters, was the author, editor, and publisher. Defoe wrote and published news, articles on domestic affairs and national policy, and essays on literature, manners, and morals.

In 1709, the fifth year of the *Review's* publication, an imitator was started, testimony to the fact that Defoe's idea had been a good one. The *Tatler* was produced by Richard Steele, who was later joined by Joseph Addison; together, they also published the *Spectator.* They printed political, international, and theatrical news, coffeehouse gossip, and moralistic essays. They also carried advertising, a feature that was to become a necessary aspect of almost all magazine publishing. The *Tatler* and the *Spectator* provided some of the first magazine contributions to English literature as well—the informal essay and the short story.

The first publication whose name included the word *magazine* was started in 1731; this was the *Gentlemen's Magazine,* founded by Edward Cave. He produced varied reading fare, but perhaps his most important contribution was his publication of reports of debates in Parliament. Eventually, Cave hired Dr. Samuel Johnson, a well-known lexicographer, critic, and poet, to write these reports; Johnson ultimately used this experience to found his own magazine, the *Rambler* (1750–52). By 1750, the *Gentlemen's Magazine* had the amazing circulation of 15,000 copies, and a number of imitators were being published in London. Half a century after the first magazine appeared, more than 150 periodicals were being printed in England.

The Development of the Magazine in the United States

Magazines in Early America. About 35 years after the first English magazine was published, the new medium appeared in the American colonies. Benjamin Franklin was, again, one of the pioneers. In 1740, he announced his plans to publish the *General Magazine and Historical Chronicle, for All the British Plantations in America.* Another printer in Philadelphia, Andrew Bradford, seizing on Franklin's idea, rushed his own magazine into print and beat Franklin by three days. Thus American magazine journalism was born in a state of competition that has marked it ever since.

THE
Royal *American* Magazine,

OR UNIVERSAL
Repository of *Instruction* and *Amusement*.

For JANUARY, 1774.

CONTAINING,

With the following EMBELLISHMENTS, viz.

No. I. A VIEW of the TOWN of BOSTON, with several Ships of War in the Harbour.
No. II. The THUNDER STORM, an affecting historical Piece, very neatly engraved.

BOSTON: Printed by and for I. THOMAS, near the MARKET.
Sold by D. FOWLE, in Portsmouth, New-Hampshire; THOMAS & TINGES, in Newbury-Port; S. and E. HALL, in Salem; J. CARTER, Providence; S. SOUTHWICK, Newport, Rhode-Island; E. WATSON, Hartford; T. and S. GREEN, New-Haven; T. GREEN, New-London; J. HOLT, New-York; T. and W. BRADFORD, Philadelphia; A. GREEN, Maryland; R. WELLS, and C. CROUCH, in South-Carolina.

Figure 4.1. The *Royal American Magazine* was typical of the early attempts at magazine publishing in the North American colonies. It contained articles on a wide variety of subjects. (Photo: New York Public Library Picture Collection.)

Bradford's *American Magazine, or a Monthly View of the Political State of the British Colonies* lasted for only three issues; Franklin's *General Magazine,* for only six. But they inspired more than a dozen other magazine efforts in colonial America. No American magazine published before 1800 lasted for more than 14 months, and advertising support was scarce. The average circulation was about 500 copies, although each issue was passed among many readers. Magazines covered a wide range of general topics, including religion, philosophy, natural science, political affairs, and literature. These magazines were a unifying force in the new nation, and they numbered among their authors and editors many of the great names of early America, including Franklin, Noah Webster, Philip Freneau, and Thomas Paine as editors; and George Washington, Alexander Hamilton, John Jay, Benjamin Rush, John Hancock, and Richard Henry Lee as authors. Paul Revere was the foremost magazine illustrator of the day.

After the turn of the nineteenth century, magazines blossomed into a national force, and some were started that would last a century and a half. They influenced education, spreading the new nation's ideas and culture, building literacy, and shaping public opinion. In the 1820s, 1830s, and 1840s, magazines played the same role that radio would play in the 1920s, 1930s, and 1940s. "This is the age of magazines," wrote a poet in the *Cincinnati Literary Gazette* in 1824. Edgar Allan Poe, magazine editor, writer, and poet, wrote in the 1830s: "The whole tendency of the age is Magazineward. The magazine in the end will be the most influential of all departments of letters."

Most famous among these magazines was the *Saturday Evening Post,* founded in 1821 (although it claimed lineage back to 1728 and Benjamin Franklin's *Pennsylvania Gazette*). It was published until the late 1960s, when it became a victim of high production and mailing costs and of competition from specialized magazines. Another was the *North American Review,* founded in 1815. It was published until 1938 and numbered among its contributors the literary figures of the nation.

As literacy spread during the nineteenth century, magazines became a literary force, building a national literature of fiction, poetry, and essays. *Harper's Monthly* and the *Atlantic Monthly,* both founded in the 1850s, were among several dozen widely influential literary magazines. These publications provided the launching pad for most American literary giants of the nineteenth century, including Henry Wadsworth Longfellow, Washington Irving, Ralph Waldo Emerson, Henry David Thoreau, Mark Twain, Henry James, Nathaniel Hawthorne, John Greenleaf Whittier, and Oliver Wendell Holmes.

The Magazine as a National Medium. With the outbreak of the Civil War, magazines played an increasingly journalistic role, informing citizens and influencing public opinion. Magazines were widely used by antislavery groups to spread information about slavery and to mold public opinion on the issue. Most famous among them was William Garrison's *Liberator*, which had been started in 1831 and ceased publication in 1865, when its goal of emancipation had been attained.

Magazines became reporters and interpreters of the social and political scene, increasingly dealing with public affairs. *Harper's Weekly*, founded in 1857 (sister publication to *Harper's Monthly*), got its great chance to further magazine journalism during the Civil War. It sent a staff of writers and artists to the battlefields for firsthand coverage of the war. Among them was photographer Matthew Brady, whose Civil War pictures are still regarded as among the best in photojournalism. During Reconstruction, magazines were in the forefront of the fight against political corruption, led by such publications as the *Nation*, whose militant editor, E. L. Godkin, shaped his magazine into a leading commentator on current affairs and a fighter for democratic principles.

After the Civil War, magazines—particularly those for special-interest groups—began to reach a national audience. Farming magazines had already emerged as a separate publishing field. Among them was the *Tribune and Farmer*, published by Cyrus H. K. Curtis, who would go on to establish one of the largest magazine empires in history. Magazines for women also came into their own, particularly with the founding of the *Ladies' Home Journal*, published by Curtis and edited by Edward Bok, one of the great innovative editors in magazine history. Other women's magazines that grew to nationwide circulation by the end of the nineteenth century were *Good Housekeeping*, *Woman's Home Companion*, *McCall's*, *Harper's Bazaar*, *Vogue*, and *Vanity Fair*.

By the end of the century, magazines were a mass medium. Improvements in printing, especially the automatic typesetting machine invented by Ottmar Mergenthaler in 1884, dramatically increased production speed. Prices were lowered, and the "nickel magazine" became a counterpart to the penny press and the dime novel. The number of magazines increased by almost 500 percent in a 20-year period, going from 700 in 1865 to 3,300 in 1885. By 1900, there were at least 50 well-known national magazines, many of which had circulations of more than 100,000. One, Curtis's *Ladies' Home Journal*, had a circulation of over 1 million. By 1908, another Curtis publication, the *Saturday Evening Post*—which he had taken over when it was failing—had also reached a circulation of 1 million copies per issue.

With a nationwide audience, magazines became a vital political and social force. Nowhere can this be better seen than in the socially conscious magazine writing of the muckrakers. Magazines eventually moved ahead of newspapers in using their pages to expose crime and corruption, fraud and manipulation. Chief among such publications was *McClure's Magazine*, founded by S. S. McClure in 1894. He used his pages to expose oil monopolies, railroad injustices, political corruption, and life-insurance fraud (among others). He was so successful, both in winning audiences and in reforming society, that other magazines—including *Cosmopolitan*, *Munsey's*

Figure 4.2. *Harper's Weekly* was one of a number of American magazines whose staff covered the Civil War, sending illustrations and photographs as well as written accounts from the battlefront. (Photo: Courtesy of *Harper's Magazine*.)

Figure 4.3. The *Ladies' Home Journal* was the first American magazine to reach a circulation of 1 million. Indeed, women were one of the first groups targeted for specialized magazine publishing.

Magazine, Collier's, and *Frank Leslie's Popular Monthly*—followed McClure's example.

Between 1894 and 1904, the American magazine came of age as a mass medium and proved itself to be a powerful institution in society.

The Magazine in the Twentieth Century.   Magazines have continued to change and to enlarge their scope in the twentieth century. Innovation in the magazine field seems to have come particularly from individual genius, often the vision of the young with new ideas and fresh talent.

The digest has become a major publishing phenomenon of the twentieth century, sharing with all the mass media one basic purpose: saving people time by giving them a synopsis, providing logical organization, and making it easy to read. None has achieved this better than the *Reader's Digest,* which by the mid-twentieth century had the largest circulation of any magazine in the world. *Reader's Digest* was the product of a young man, DeWitt Wallace, and his wife, Lila, both children of poor ministers. In 1922, while still in their twenties, the Wallaces borrowed the necessary funds to try their idea. In the 1980s, their magazine was being sent each month to almost 18 million subscribers in the United States alone, and other editions were sent to millions more subscribers all over the world.

Even more important than the popularity of the digest has been the emergence of the news magazine as a national force. Another far-from-wealthy son of a missionary, Henry Luce, founder of *Time, Life, Fortune,* and *Sports Illustrated,* must be given much of the credit for having built the weekly news magazine into a viable journalistic medium. Luce was a young man just out of Yale in 1923 when he and Britton Hadden founded *Time.* Like the *Reader's Digest,* it has not changed much since its early

Figure 4.4. *Time* was the first weekly news magazine, but it soon had imitators, such as *Newsweek* and, later, *U.S. News & World Report.*

Figure 4.5. *Life* and *Look* swept to national popularity using a new form of news coverage—photojournalism. But neither magazine survived the age of television in its original weekly format.

editions. And its imitators, including *Newsweek* and *U.S. News & World Report*, have generally followed its format.

Luce was also a pioneer in modern photojournalism, founding *Life* to report news through pictures. *Life* was not the first picture magazine, but it was the first to use photography as a regular journalistic tool to inform, entertain, persuade, and sell. *Life* had imitators, too, including magazines such as *Look*. Both the original *Life* and *Look* became casualties of the rising costs in the magazine business in the early 1970s.

The city magazine, once the only form of magazine, has come back into its own in the twentieth century. The most successful and most influential of these has been the *New Yorker,* founded in 1925 by former newspaperman Harold Ross. He built it into a magazine that has lived up to his original prospectus, which described it as a sophisticated "reflection in word and picture of metropolitan life." "It will be human," Ross wrote at the beginning. "Its general tenor will be one of gaiety, wit, and satire. . . . The *New Yorker* will be the magazine which is not edited for the little old lady in Dubuque."[1] It has not reached the circulation heights of some magazines that are edited for more average tastes, but it has influenced scores of other metropolitan magazines. Today, the *New Yorker* has a read-

[1] See James Playsted Wood, *Magazines in the United States* (New York: Ronald Press, 1956), 242, 255.

Figure 4.6. *Metropolitan Detroit* is typical of the city magazine, which is becoming increasingly popular.

ership well beyond New York City and is no longer considered only a city magazine; it is now categorized as *sophisticated.*

By the early 1980s, the city magazine was enjoying unusual growth. By the mid-1980s, every major city, and many states and regions, had their own magazines—some more than one. For example, in the Washington, D.C., area alone, a half-dozen city magazines were flourishing.

The twentieth century has seen the rise of magazines devoted to higher culture, too. Some of these magazines, in their articles on art, science, history, philosophy, and current affairs, are similar to some of the earliest magazines. Chief among these are *National Geographic, American Heritage,* and *Smithsonian. Smithsonian,* in fact, has been a major magazine success story of the 1970s and 1980s, growing in a few years to enjoy one of the largest circulations in the industry.

Other trends in the twentieth century should not be overlooked. True-confession and movie-fan magazines reach an enormous audience, as do specialized publications, from *Farm Journal* and *Presbyterian Life* to *Hairdo & Beauty.* The "little magazine" of poetry and criticism is another twentieth-century phenomenon, as are such esoteric or scientific journals as *Biotechnology & Bioengineering* and *Journal of Applied Polymer Science.* The association magazine, the trade journal, and the house organ are growing types of twentieth-century magazine journalism.

Figure 4.7. *Michigan Living* is representative of a new breed of state and regional magazines.

Perhaps the most remarkable development has been the increasing growth and success of specialized magazines aimed at a target audience. Ethnic groups are increasingly being served by their own magazines, such as *Ebony* and *Sepia* for blacks. Magazines have been started for Italian-Americans, German-Americans, and other ethnic groups. Special groups of many kinds have turned to magazines as a means of providing communication among those with similar interests, including such magazines as *Advocate,* the largest and most influential news magazine for the gay community, and *High Times,* a slick magazine for members of the American counterculture.

Among the most successful magazine types started after World War II are sexually explicit men's magazines. *Playboy* was founded by Hugh Hefner when he was only a few years out of the University of Illinois, with some experience at *Esquire. Playboy* ushered in an era of hedonism in American popular culture, with stress on sophisticated food and drink and on frank sexual pleasure. Begun in 1953, *Playboy* reached a circulation of almost 6 million before it began to decline in the early 1980s. *Playboy* had a profound influence on other men's magazines, such as *Penthouse* and *Hustler.*

In the 1970s, a new kind of women's magazine emerged, edited for the "independent woman." Unlike earlier magazines for women, such as *Good*

Figure 4.8. *Ebony,* one of the most popular magazines for blacks, is just one of the periodicals published for black readers by the Johnson Publishing Company of Chicago. (Photo: Courtesy of *Ebony.*)

Housekeeping and the *Ladies' Home Journal,* these new periodicals do not carry articles on cooking, homemaking, sewing, housecleaning, and child rearing. Instead, they publish articles on politics, career development, and sex. Some, like *Playgirl,* an imitation of *Playboy,* have centerfold pictures of nude men. Others, such as *Ms.,* spread the news of the women's movement. Among these new magazines for women are *Working Woman, New Woman, Self, Savvy,* and *Woman's World.*

SPECIAL PROBLEMS

In the 1950s and 1960s, television threatened to capture advertising dollars from the general magazine, causing some to predict that the mass-circulation magazines would die. Magazines fought back by playing what they called "the numbers game," building circulation figures to compete with television for national advertising. Some magazines turned from their traditional newsstand sales to concentrate on subscription sales. They hired

Figure 4.9. *Collier's* and the *Saturday Evening Post,* once among the most popular magazines in the world, could not survive the competition from television—not for lack of readers but for lack of advertisers.

high-powered subscription-sales organizations to attract subscribers at any cost. These organizations often used young people for door-to-door, high-pressure selling campaigns, offering long-term bargain prices or package deals of many publications for the price of one. The sales organization owned the subscription, collected the money from the subscriber, and sold the subscription to the magazine publisher.

In effect, such magazines were buying subscribers in order to produce a large number of readers to attract advertisers. They earned little money from the subscriber; indeed, they often had to pay to get the subscriber. And they had to lower their price far below value to keep the subscriber. In 1968, the average magazine cost the buyer 54 cents, but it cost the publisher perhaps four or five times that amount to produce each magazine. The publisher hoped to make up the difference through revenue from large advertising sales.

Such economics ultimately put some of the large mass-consumer magazines out of business. *Collier's,* the *Woman's Home Companion,* and the *Saturday Evening Post* failed in the 1950s and 1960s. They did not go under for lack of readers, however. When the *Saturday Evening Post* died, it had more than 4 million regular subscribers. But the magazine did not have the right audience (young, with discretionary income) to attract advertisers, who were not interested in reaching older, more conservative people.

Figure 4.10. *Parade* and *USA Weekend* are Sunday supplements, inserted into the Sunday edition of newspapers. Because they are not sold separately, these magazines are not included in lists of magazine circulation, but they are among the most widely read in the United States.

In spite of these failures, the magazine field is not by any means dying. Between 1962 and 1971, 160 magazines went out of business. But in the same 10-year period, 753 magazines were born. By the mid-1980s, magazine circulation and advertising revenue were at an all-time high. Magazine publishers were no longer selling their product cheaply to attract masses of subscribers in order to get advertising.

One reason for advertising growth was that advertisers acknowledged what the publishers call *media imperatives*. The publishers divided the adult population into four segments: (1) the heavy magazine reader and the light television viewer (the *magazine imperative*); (2) the light reader and the heavy viewer (the *television imperative*); (3) the heavy reader and heavy viewer; and (4) the light reader and light viewer. Through audience research, publishers demonstrated that the "magazine imperative" group was better educated, more affluent, and more apt to buy the products advertised than was the "television imperative" group. Obviously, then, it was in the advertisers' interest to place more advertising in magazines.

Publishers also encouraged single-copy sales, which have a larger margin of profit than do subscriptions. A copy of *Newsweek*, for example, costs $2 at the newsstand in 1987, with 52 issues a year; this is almost twice as much as the annual subscription rate of $58.24. More people buy magazines on a single-copy basis when they are available, not just at corner newsstands, but in drugstores and supermarkets as well. Supermarket sales turned out to be remarkably profitable, so much so that magazine distributors have developed "family reading centers" in stores. Some magazines are sold only as single copies. *Family Circle* and *Woman's Day*, for example, both of which are among the top-ten largest circulation magazines in the country, are sold primarily in grocery stores and supermarkets; there are few mail subscriptions. Other magazines are moving in this direction.

Another reason for encouraging single sales has been the rising cost of postage. The U.S. Postal Service started a phased increase for second-class mail in 1970; by the mid-1980s, publishers were paying three to four times more for mailing than they had paid in 1970. Naturally, publishers must look to other means of selling and distributing products.

Increasingly, magazines are using computers and new demographic data to make their advertising and editorial content more selective. For example, a magazine's production and circulation can be coordinated, so that circulation can be broken into 25 megamarkets, 50 megastates, and a group of top-spot zip-coders. Advertising can even be placed according to selected geographical regions to reach any one or any number of predetermined markets. For less money, the advertiser is able to reach a more appropriate market for the product, on either a regional or a reader-interest basis.

Time, for example, now has the technology to customize its editorial content to the extent of giving the reader at least one article per issue that meets one of his or her preselected interests. Thus the same issue of *Time* might bring to a sports fan an article on professional football, while the neighbor next-door, a science buff, will get an article on electronic engineering. Such magazines can have both mass and selectivity, with wide appeal to advertisers as well as consumers.

The ability to target one's audience also has made possible the controlled-circulation magazine. Such magazines are sent only to certain types of people—sometimes on application by the reader, sometimes on identification by the publisher. For example, two magazines in Washington, D.C., *Regardie's* and *Washington Dossier*, are sent free to households and businesses targeted by market-research and demographic studies as "active" and economically successful. These are the spenders that advertisers are anxious to reach—and the magazines are full of ads—even though the addressee has never indicated an interest in the publication.

One of the best examples of this new kind of magazine publishing is *Nutshell*, with which many college students are familiar. By the mid-1980s, millions of copies of *Nutshell* were being distributed free at hundreds of

Figure 4.11. Magazines are getting started all the time; all a potential publisher needs is a new idea, a mailing list, and some money. A promotion for a new publication, *Bathroom Journal,* was sent out in 1986 to test the market for a magazine that would appeal to those who like to read while relaxing in the tub.

colleges and universities across the country. The magazine carries ads wrapped around more than a dozen student-oriented features about campus fashion, college football, film schools, and draft registration.

Nutshell is only 1 of 10 such magazines published by the 13-30 Corporation of Knoxville, Tennessee. It is another success story of young people in the magazine field. The corporation was started by Philip Moffitt and Christopher Whittle, who had met as undergraduates at the University of Tennessee in 1967. The numbers "13-30" represent the age limits within which the corporation seeks its audience for its advertisers.

THE SCOPE OF MAGAZINES

More than 11,320 magazines were published in the continental United States in 1986. (Table 4.1) This total included only those magazines that were publicly available and did not count private, institutional, or in-house publications. The 11,320 figure represented a significant growth since 1979, when 9,700 magazines were published. More magazines—over 4,000—

Figure 4.12. *Singlesminded* was started in the mid-1980s as a controlled-circulation magazine sent free to young, upper-middle-income single professionals in the Washington, D.C., area. Readers could not subscribe to it but received it if they fit the demographics.

were published on a monthly basis than on any other basis. Magazines were published in every state of the Union in 1986, but almost one-third of them were published in New York.

Magazine ownership is spread broadly, and the largest publishers in the United States do not produce many different magazines. Time, Inc., publishes six magazines; Reader's Digest Association puts out only one; Triangle Publications, which publishes *TV Guide*, issues two; and the Washington Post Company publishes one magazine, *Newsweek*.

Magazine sales in general were lower in the mid-1980s than they were in the early 1980s. *TV Guide* had a weekly circulation of more than 19 million copies in 1984 and was in first place. By 1986, it had fallen to 16.8 million. *Reader's Digest* was in second place, with a monthly circulation of 16.6 million in the United States (and another 12 million in foreign countries, making it the biggest seller overall); most of its circulation (better than 90 percent) comes from subscription sales. *National Geographic* in 1986 had a circulation of 10.7 million, almost all of it by subscription; the magazine is rarely sold on the newsstands. Sixty-seven magazines in 1986 had circulations of 1 million or more; they represent only 13 percent of the total consumer magazines but account for more than 66 percent of the sales (Table 4.2).

**TABLE 4.1 NUMBER OF MAGAZINE
TITLES PUBLISHED IN THE UNITED
STATES, 1985 AND 1986**

	1985	1986
Daily	187	186
Tri-Weekly	21	19
Semi-Weekly	76	77
Weekly	1,367	1,383
Bi-Weekly	529	519
Semi-Monthly	272	270
Monthly	4,088	4,066
Bi-Monthly	1,361	1,387
Quarterly	1,759	1,895
Variants	1,430	1,526
Total	11,090	11,328

Source: The *IMS Directory of Publications*. Fort Washington,
Pa.: IMS Press, 1986, viii.

Magazine growth and decline provide an interesting index of Americans' changing interests and life styles. Two magazines that have grown rapidly from the mid-1970s to the mid-1980s are *Modern Maturity* and *NRTA* (National Retired Teachers Association) *Bulletin,* both of which are aimed at retired readers and are now in the top five among American magazine circulations. From 1984 to 1986, *Playboy* declined in circulation by 1.6 percent, *Penthouse* declined by 15.9 percent, *Playgirl* declined by 5 percent, and *Hustler*'s fall was so dramatic that it was no longer counted among the top 200 in 1986, although it had been in the top 50 in 1984. During that same period, *Money* increased in circulation by 12.3 percent, *Country Living* increased by 15.2 percent, *New Woman* increased by 20.2 percent, *Gourmet* increased by 49.1 percent, *50 Plus* increased by 40.7 percent, and *Sun* increased by 61.4 percent.

Since World War II, magazines have been growing faster than newspapers. From 1950 to 1980, magazines grew in circulation by 81 percent, while newspapers grew by only 16 percent. Magazine-advertising revenue has also continued to increase; in 1985, it reached a record high of over $5 billion.

On the expense side, the biggest item for magazine publishers is personnel. Unlike newspapers, most magazines do not own expensive printing equipment, but contract out that part of the production process. A large share of magazine costs goes to sales promotion and magazine distribution, including 13 cents on every dollar for postage.

Salaries in the magazine industry are about the same as salaries in the newspaper business for comparable work. A general editor at *Newsweek*

TABLE 4.2 TOP FIFTY MAGAZINES PUBLISHED IN THE UNITED STATES

1986 Rank	1985 Rank	Publication	Average total paid circulation	1986 Rank	1985 Rank	Publication	Average total paid circulation
1	2	TV Guide	16,800,441	26	26	Field & Stream	2,007,479
2	1	Reader's Digest	16,609,847	27	27	VFW	1,951,004
3	3	National Geographic	10,764,998	28	34	Money	1,862,106
4	4	Better Homes & Gardens	8,091,751	29	30	Seventeen	1,853,314
5	5	Family Circle	6,261,519	30	28	Popular Science	1,843,067
6	7	Woman's Day	5,743,842	31	31	Workbasket	1,779,463
7	9	Good Housekeeping	5,221,575	32	32	Parents	1,721,816
8	6	McCall's	5,186,393	33	42	Life	1,718,726
9	8	Ladies' Home Journal	5,020,551	34	29	Ebony	1,703,019
10	10	Time	4,720,159	35	37	Motorland	1,692,501
11	11	National Enquirer	4,381,242	36	35	Popular Mechanics	1,634,930
12	13	Redbook	4,009,450	37	40	Country Living	1,619,121
13	14	Star	3,706,131	38	33	Globe	1,600,963
14	12	Playboy	3,477,324	39	36	Elks	1,577,302
15	16	Newsweek	3,101,152	40	38	1001 Home Ideas	1,540,428
16	18	People	3,038,363	41	41	Outdoor Life	1,520,915
17	20	Sports Illustrated	2,895,116	42	46	Sunset	1,442,478
18	17	Cosmopolitan	2,873,071	43	43	American Hunter	1,412,723
19	19	Prevention	2,820,748	44	39	True Story	1,405,087
20	21	American Legion	2,648,627	45	45	Changing Times	1,379,781
21	23	Glamour	2,386,150	46	44	American Rifleman	1,362,225
22	15	Penthouse	2,379,333	47	48	Woman's World	1,348,098
23	24	Smithsonian	2,310,970	48	50	Bon Appetit	1,341,047
24	25	U.S. News & World Report	2,287,016	49	70	Discover	1,328,534
25	22	Southern Living	2,263,922	50	47	Boy's Life	1,306,172

Source: The Gallagher Report XXXV, No. 8, 23 February 1987, special supplement.

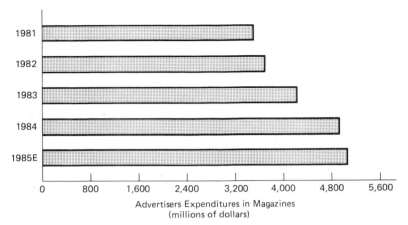

Figure 4.13. *Magazine advertising has continued to grow, in spite of competition from the other media. In 1985, advertisers paid more than $5 billion for space in magazines.*

makes a lower minimum salary ($775 a week, as of June 1986) than a *New York Times* reporter makes after an apprenticeship ($929 a week).

A magazine issue is read longer and by more people than a newspaper issue; however, a book is read longer and by more people than either a magazine or a newspaper. The average magazine copy is read by 3.8 adults, and each adult reads the magazine over a period of several days. Magazine reading varies with the seasons; less reading is done in the summer than in the colder months. Most magazines are read in the home, and most reading takes place after dinner. Women read slightly more magazines than do men, and magazine readership rises with income and education. Children are reading more magazines these days, and an increasing number of them have their own subscriptions.

Surveys of magazine readers' actions suggest that readers tend to take more action as a result of their reading than is taken by consumers of other media. A relatively large percentage of magazine readers discuss what they read with others and seek information about advertised products.

THE STRUCTURE AND ORGANIZATION OF MAGAZINES

Because magazines come in different sizes and shapes and are aimed at different kinds of readers, no one organizational or operational pattern fits them all. Each magazine develops its own way of organizing and operating to get its special job done. Some magazines—those that deal heavily in news and timely subjects—are organized in much the same manner as newspapers. Others that deal in less time-bound material are set up much like book-publishing firms.

Because they do not have to worry about daily printing schedules, magazines do not have to make an expensive investment in printing equipment but can contract with established printers. Some magazines, even famous ones such as the *Atlantic Monthly,* operate out of a small office, with a few editorial employees, a small number of typewriters, some furniture, and a supply of typing paper. Everything else, including production and distribution, can be handled by outside contractors.

The editorial staff of a magazine usually includes an editor as chief executive, who has overall responsibility for establishing policies and making final decisions. The managing editor or executive editor carries out the editor's policies and runs the day-to-day operation. Staff editors head various departments within the magazine or handle various functions, such as picture editing, copy editing or layout and production. Staff writers on magazines are often called editors.

Many magazines have contributing editors, who work either full time or part time in the office or out in the field; they often are specialists in certain fields and help the magazine discover material, find appropriate writers, approve the authenticity of the writer's copy, or do some writing themselves.

Another distinguishing feature of many magazines is the editorial board, a fixture not used by newspaper or book publishers to the same extent. The editorial board is often composed of leaders in the field to which the magazine is directed. They help to give the magazine direction and authority.

In the past, magazines depended largely on free-lance contributions for their editorial content. The editor waited for the mail and then published the best of what contributors sent in. There are literally hundreds of thousands of people who would like to be free-lance writers for magazines, and many of them try. *Harper's,* for example, receives more than 20,000 unsolicited manuscripts each year, even though the magazine does not publish unsolicited material. While many free lancers can supplement their incomes from part-time magazine writing, only a handful of professionals make a substantial salary from full-time free-lance writing.

Increasingly, magazines are using staff-developed and staff-written material. Schedules are too demanding and story development is too complicated to allow the editors to depend on volunteer contributions. Editor and staff determine the audience they are reaching, the type of material the audience needs and wants, and the subjects available for development into appropriate magazine articles and stories. Then they produce the material to make sure it fits their needs and their time schedules.

Even the *Reader's Digest,* ostensibly a selection of the most interesting articles from other magazines, in reality cannot depend on other magazines to produce all the material it needs to fulfill the demands of its readers. The *Digest* editors often produce the magazine's material, sometimes placing it in other magazines and then "borrowing" it for the *Reader's Digest*, or sometimes writing an article for a famous person and then "buying" it from that person for *Digest* publication.

TYPES OF MAGAZINES

Generally, magazines are divided into consumer (or general interest) and specialized (including children's, professional, and trade publications) magazines.

Consumer magazines are usually broken down further into at least 13 categories, including women's (for example, *Redbook*), men's (*Esquire*), sophisticated (*New Yorker*), quality (*Atlantic Monthly*), romance (*Modern Screen*), news (*U.S. News & World Report*), sports (*Sports Illustrated*), travel (*Holiday*), exploration (*National Geographic*), humor (*Mad*),

Figure 4.14. In the United States, many magazines are for sale at public newsstands. (Photograph by Harvey Wang.)

shelter (*Better Homes and Gardens*), class (*American Heritage*), and city (*Washingtonian*).

Specialized magazines can also be broken down into different kinds of publications: juvenile (for example, *Boy's Life*), comic (*Superman*), little literary (*Prairie Schooner*), literary (*Paris Review*), scholarly (*Journalism Quarterly*), educational (*College & University Journal*), business (*Nation's Business*), religious (*Christianity Today*), industrial or company (*Western Electric World*), farm (*Farm Journal*), transportation (*Railway Age*), science (*Scientific American*), and discussion (*New Republic*).

The specialized magazines, which aim their editorial fare at particular reading audiences, have been growing at a rapid rate. A 20-year survey of this group showed that entertainment guides grew in circulation by 256 percent; sports publications, by 247 percent; and business magazines, by 76 percent. According to *Advertising Age,* publishers themselves believe that the future of specialized magazines is the best of any industry group.

The business-publication field is one of the fastest-growing specialties in magazine journalism. Some magazine-publishing houses have developed large groups of such magazines, serving various trade and business groups, from automobile dealers to zoo keepers. Many such magazines are distributed to a prime list of readers, some free of charge. The publisher makes a profit by selling advertising to merchants who want to reach these specific groups.

THE COMICS

One popular form of mass communication that deserves special consideration is the comic book. Five classes of comics serve mass communication functions:

1. The single-picture (panel) newspaper feature, such as *Grin and Bear It*, *The Family Circus*, and the cartoons in the *New Yorker*, *Playboy*, and other magazines.
2. The black-and-white multipanel, daily-newspaper comic strip, such as *Dick Tracy*, *B.C.*, and *Mary Worth*.
3. The multicolor Sunday supplement, which is a collection of strips that either continue the daily newspaper feature's story line or tell a separate story. (Almost all strips are both daily and Sunday features, but many papers carry more comic strips on Sunday than during the week.)
4. The multipage color narrative in magazine form, which is issued monthly, bimonthly, or quarterly and is called a comic book (*Action Comics*).

5. The anti-Establishment, social-political-economic commentary comic, or underground comic book, which is usually published irregularly in black and white (*Zap, Despair,* and the like).

Two newspaper press lords—Joseph Pulitzer and William Randolph Hearst—battled to create newspaper comics. Richard Outcault's *Down Hogan's Alley* appeared in Pulitzer's *New York World* in the early 1890s and featured a nightshirted ragamuffin who was involved in unsavory lower-class goings-on. In 1896, the newspaper experimented with the use of yellow ink on the ragamuffin's nightshirt. The color test became a regular feature—*Down Hogan's Alley* became *The Yellow Kid.* Hearst hired Outcault away from Pulitzer, and both Pulitzer's *New York World* and Hearst's *New York Journal* ran *Yellow Kid* comics. Hearst printed the first comics section in 1896. The daily strip format emerged in the first decade of the twentieth century as the comics became a strong circulation builder.

Between 1914 and 1929, syndicates such as King Features emerged, supplying publications with a large selection of syndicated strips by a stable of creators. Nearly every newspaper in the country carried a comics section, and "funny papers" were a major part of the industry. During this period, most of the strips emphasized a humorous view of family life and its problems. In 1925, the *New Yorker* began its now-famous one-line panels of cartoons. Today, such cartoons appear in many general-reader magazines.

In the 1930s, three major creators began careers: Milton Caniff's *Terry and the Pirates* and later *Steve Canyon* featured characters who participated in and sometimes predicted political and military events; Al Capp's *Li'l Abner* became a sharp satirical comment on American society—nothing was sacred—and his attacks were savage; and the Walt Disney organization contributed two great characters to American pop culture—Mickey Mouse, a gentle, helpful, playful, and somewhat inept caricature of Americans, and Donald Duck, a satirical picture of the rascally, distempered, and ornery man, constantly attacking his fate.

The comic book emerged during the Depression. First came strip reprints in a format called *Funnies on Parade. Detective Comics* (1937) was the first to structure its content on one theme. Then in 1938, the most popular superhero of all time, *Superman,* appeared in *Action Comics.* By 1940, there were more than 40 comic-book titles; in 1941, 168 titles. At U.S. Army posts during World War II, comic books outsold all other magazines 10 to 1.

Like many other Americans, comic characters went to war, contributing to the propaganda effort. Some of the strips' heroes even entered the war before the United States did, joining the Royal Air Force or the Flying Tigers. In this way, comics may have helped psychologically to prepare the American public to support the war effort and glorify the American fighting man. There appeared special "war" strips, including *Male Call, G.I. Joe,*

Figure 4.15. *The Yellow Kid* and *Buster Brown's Blue Ribbon Book of Jokes and Jingles* were two of the first comic books published. Both appeared in the late 1890s.

Sad Sack, and *Johnny Hazard.* Possibly the most important comic characters of the war years were Bill Mauldin's "dogfaces," Willie and Joe. These characters depicted the tragicomic life of the average American soldier and earned Mauldin the 1945 Pulitzer Prize.

The most spectacular comic of all time is *Peanuts* (1950) by Charles Schulz. Schulz's creations seem to speak to the anxieties of twentieth-century Americans through the eternal loser, Charlie Brown. He and his friends may be the best literary explanation of American life styles in the

1960s. *Peanuts* also is the all-time success story in the comics business—a $150 million-a-year empire. The cartoon appears in more than 1,400 newspapers around the world, and it has generated hundreds of books in a dozen languages, a Broadway play, a line of greeting cards, seasonal television specials, and an entire products industry that includes sweatshirts, baseball caps, dolls, bed sheets, tie clips, stuffed animals, and calendars.

More than 100 comic-book companies publish 300 titles and sell in excess of 250 million copies annually. Pass-along readership of these comics is estimated to be three readers to every buyer. A company usually prints about 200,000 copies of an issue; but *Classics Illustrated,* which contained skeletal versions of important literary works, remained on the stand indefinitely, and most titles sold 1 million copies or more. The most avid readers of comic books are children aged 7 to 14, and they tend to be good readers rather than poor ones.

THE NEWSLETTER

The rise of the newsletter is another twentieth-century journalistic phenomenon, even though the newsletter is one of the oldest forms of journalistic communication. Letters were used for news and general communication in the ancient Greek and Roman civilizations and during the Middle Ages. The Fugger newsletters, produced in several German city-states in the fifteenth and sixteenth centuries by the Fugger banking house, were among the forerunners of the modern newspaper. Written in letter form, they contained financial and economic information that helped spread the mercantile revolution among the merchants and businessmen who read them. The modern newsletter is often used for a similar purpose.

The father of the modern newsletter was probably Willard M. Kiplinger, who started the *Kiplinger Washington Letters* in 1923. A Washington reporter for the Associated Press, Kiplinger was hired by a New York bank to produce reports on government information vital to banking and business interests. Kiplinger put this information in a letter that he regularly sent to the bank. He reasoned that he might sell the information in his letter to other banks and to business people, too.

He typed the four-page letter on his own typewriter and had it mimeographed and, later, printed by offset, without any fancy make-up or advertising. Underscoring and capitalization were used to provide some graphic effects, but Kiplinger was primarily interested in distilling information to its essence. Each typewritten line carried a complete thought. He wrote so that each line would be easy to read and remember. He did not feel constrained to follow normal journalistic restrictions of objectivity and attribution to sources. Kiplinger made analyses and predictions for his readers, taking them into his confidence.

In reality, Kiplinger was writing a personal letter to each of his subscribers, giving each his interpretation of the facts. He opened his letter with "Dear Reader" and closed it with his signature, printed in blue ink. This feature alone cost him thousands of dollars in postage because he had to send his letter by first-class mail, rather than by the second-class rate available to news publications. But the extra cost was worth it to Kiplinger because he wanted to have a form of communication that was warm, personal, and intimate. The *Kiplinger Washington Letters* have been widely

Figure 4.16. *Social Science Monitor, Hi-Tech Alert,* and *Video Monitor* are examples of specialized newsletters aimed at select audiences—in this case, public relations professionals.

imitated. Others preceded them, and others followed them; but none have been as successful or as widely copied.

By the mid-1980s, more than 4,000 commercial newsletters were being published. A commercial newsletter, as defined by the Gale Research Company, publisher of the newsletter directory, is a publication that is usually reproduced as a typewritten page, without elaborate make-up or printing. It does not carry advertisements, since its essential feature is the personal relationship it attempts to develop between author and reader, without any intermediary to sponsor or subsidize the communication. Thus the commercial newsletter must charge a subscription, and sometimes the rate may be very high. Some newsletters cost as much as $1,000 a year, if there are few subscribers and the information is of vital importance. The *Kiplinger Washington Letters* cost about $36 a year, an average for the field.

Not counted in the 4,000 commercial newsletters are the many thousands of subsidized newsletters used to promote or persuade, or internal organs of communication within an organization or a group. Almost every member of Congress today uses some form of newsletter to communicate personally with constituents. Newsletters are used by professional associations, church groups, factory workers, fraternal organizations, university administrations, alumni associations, labor units, and most other organized units in our society.

Newsletters have become so well established that there is now the *Newsletter on Newsletters* and the Newsletter Clearinghouse. In 1977, a group was founded in Washington, D.C., the Newsletter Association of America, to serve the special interests and needs of those who write, edit, and publish in this special medium.

A typical newsletter publishing company is Phillips Publishing of Washington, D.C. Started by Thomas Phillips in 1974, only six years after he graduated from journalism school, the company now publishes more than 20 newsletters. Phillips started with consumer newsletters offered at a relatively low subscription rate and aimed at a large general audience. He soon discovered that there was another, and perhaps better, market for the professional newsletter, with a relatively high subscription rate, aimed at a small specialized market. He decided to enter both markets. Thus some of his newsletters are aimed at the general consumer in finance, travel, and government affairs. They range in price from $27 to $39 a year. The others are aimed at professionals in the telecommunications industry and are priced at $127 to $247 a year.

The newsletter is quick, inexpensive, simple to produce, and useful. Just about anybody with a typewriter, a copying machine, and a mailing list can get into the newsletter business. Succeeding at the business is not so simple, however. Many newsletters have short lifetimes and make only a fleeting impression.

THE CHARACTERISTICS AND ROLES
OF MAGAZINES

Of all the media, magazines are produced by the largest number of separate owners. They require the least investment of organized business and the smallest budget to operate. "Find me a list of names and I'll create a magazine for it," said one bold magazine entrepreneur. He was not far off base. Magazines have been published for almost every group in our society.

In addition to this sort of selectivity, magazines have greater flexibility than all media other than books. The magazine publisher can create a package in almost any size, shape, or dimension and can achieve change and variation with ease.

Magazines have advantage of a greater intensification than newspapers, radio, or television can usually manage. With a longer lead time and less-pressing deadlines, magazine editors can afford to take a longer look at issues, to penetrate problems more deeply in order to do a better job of interpretation and analysis.

Magazines have an advantage over books in that they are usually timely enough to deal with the flow of events. And they have the power to sustain a topic over a period of time in a series of issues, achieving a cumulative impact, while books must settle for one impression.

One of the primary advantages of magazines as mass media is their ability to custom-tailor mass communications. Magazines, unlike other media, are ideally suited to small groups, whether they are organized by culture, race, religion, geography, or subject. Even mass general-consumer magazines, as we have seen, are finding ways to target their product for a specific region or interest group.

Magazines do not have the permanence of books, but they are not as temporary as newspapers and not as fleeting as broadcast messages. While the newspaper's lifetime is usually one day, weekly magazines often last for two or three weeks; monthlies for several months; and quarterlies are often bound and kept permanently.

SUMMARY

In spite of growing competition from other mass media, particularly radio and television, magazines have continued to remain influential and financially strong by specializing for segmented audiences.

Unlike most of the mass media, magazines can be started with a very small initial investment, and they can be produced by a very small staff.

Overall circulation of magazines declined somewhat in the mid-1980s, but the number of magazine titles has continued to grow. The decline and growth of individual magazine circulations provide a good index to the changing interests and life styles of American readers.

Comic books and newsletters are two important types of periodicals that have developed in the twentieth century, each reaching audiences of mass proportions—one primarily for entertainment, the other primarily for information and interpretation.

BIBLIOGRAPHY

Anderson, Elliott, and Mary Kinzie. *The Little Magazine in America: A Modern History*. Yonkers, N.Y.: Pushcart Press, 1978.

Ferguson, Rowena. *Editing the Small Magazine*. New York: Columbia University Press, 1963.

Flippen, Charles C. *Liberating the Media: The New Journalism*. Washington, D.C.: Acropolis Books, 1974.

Folio: The Magazine for Magazine Management. 125 Elm Street, P.O. Box 4006, New Canaan, Conn.   06840.

Ford, James L.C. *Magazines for the Millions*. Carbondale: Southern Illinois University Press, 1970.

Hollstein, Milton. *Magazines in Search of an Audience: A Guide to Starting New Magazines*. New York: Magazine Publishers Association, 1969.

Laird, Ruth Burton. *Magazines as Classroom Teaching Tools*. New York: Magazine Publishers Association, 1969.

Lawler, Philip F. *The Alternative Influence: The Impact of Investigative Reporting Groups on America's Media*. Lanham, Md.: University Press of America, 1984.   •

Lubars, Walter, and John Wicklein. *Investigative Reporting: The Lessons of Watergate*. Boston: Boston University School of Public Communication, 1975.

Magazine and Book Seller. 328 Eighth Avenue, New York, N.Y.   10001.

Magazine Design and Production. 4551 West 107th Street, Overland, Kans.   66207.

Magazine Newsletter of Research. 575 Lexington Avenue, New York, N.Y.   10022.

Mott, Frank Luther. *A History of American Magazines*. 5 vols. Cambridge, Mass.: Harvard University Press, 1957.

Nelson, Roy Paul. *Visits with 30 Magazine Art Directors*. New York: Magazine Publishers Association, 1969.

Peterson, Theodore. *Magazines in the Twentieth Century*. Urbana: University of Illinois Press, 1964.

Reddick, DeWitt C. *Literary Style in Science Writing*. New York: Magazine Publishers Association, 1969.

Smith, Donald L. *The New Freedom to Publish*. New York: Magazine Publishers Association, 1969.

Taft, William H. *American Magazines for the 1980s*. New York: Hastings House, 1982.

Tebbel, John. *The American Magazine: A Compact History*. New York: Hawthorn, 1969.

Wolfe, Tom. *The New Journalism.* New York: Harper & Row, 1973.

Wolseley, Roland E. *Understanding Magazines.* Ames: Iowa State University Press, 1965.

Wood, James Playsted. *Magazines in the United States.* 2d ed. New York: Ronald Press, 1956.

Writer's Market; Cincinnati: Writer's Digest, annual.

5

Motion Pictures

It is very difficult to characterize modern motion pictures. Traditionally, movies have been identified with eras or styles, such as silent comedy, films of the 1930s, musicals, Westerns, or horror films. But contemporary films refuse to be typecast.

Part of the problem is the absence of historical distance. Compounding it is the speed with which much of the change has taken place. Instant trends have been the norm over the past 20 years of motion-picture making. With the exception of James Bond and an assortment of sharks, space travelers, and Jedi warriors, very few film cycles of any length have been established. In 1964 and 1965, with the huge success of *My Fair Lady, Mary Poppins,* and *The Sound of Music,* musicals were in. Two years later, with such disasters as *Star* and *Dr. Dolittle,* musicals were out. Following *The Graduate* (1967), *Easy Rider* (1969), and *Alice's Restaurant* (1969), youth films were booming. Two years later, with Elliot Gould and others leading the way in such films as *Getting Straight* (1970) and *The Landlord* (1970), the youth-film boom was busted. Old-fashioned love was flowering once again in 1970 with *Love Story,* but less than two years later, *The Godfather* exhibited a different form of affection. *The Exorcist* (1973) started a brief occult cycle, but *Jaws* (1975) replaced it with a monster of a different kind. *Halloween* (1978) continued the horror cycle, but the industry soon jumped on an outer-space/adventure bandwagon generated by the phenomenal success of *Star Wars* (1977). This has proved to be the most enduring cycle, as box-office receipts for *E.T.* (1982), *Return of the Jedi* (1983), *Superman III* (1983), and *Indiana Jones and the Temple of Doom* (1984) have documented. However, with the success of *Beverly Hills Cop* (1984), *Ghostbusters* (1984), *Back to the Future* (1985), *First Blood* (1982), *Rambo* (1985), and *Rocky IV* (1985), the industry was again searching for a cycle of some endurance. All of this serves to illustrate the number of directions in which American films have been traveling. Hollywood's search for a lost audience, the next successful formula, and a return to past glories has continued unabated throughout the 1960s, 1970s, and 1980s.

Changes in the industry, in content, and in the overall pattern and structure of American motion pictures began in the late 1940s. The large studios, for years symbols of power and prestige, are now primarily financing and distributing organizations, with production a somewhat secondary activity. Indeed, in 1985, independent companies had 225 production starts compared with 105 by the major studios. Production companies are set up for individual films, and while the independent film is here to stay, it bears little resemblance to the low-budget films of a decade ago. Both *Indiana Jones and the Temple of Doom* and *Star Trek III: The Search for Spock* were independent productions; but in form, style, and content, they are little different from the blockbusters churned out by the studio system for decades. Motion pictures today in some sense resemble what they were at their beginning—products of individual taste and concern reflecting both what the audience wants and what individual communicators want to say. This, of course, was not always so and brings us to the beginning of our discussion—a brief historical overview of the medium.

HISTORICAL PERSPECTIVE

The motion picture is the child of science. Many traces of antiquity, such as cave drawings and shadow plays, are evidence of the universal quest to re-create motion. Very early, this quest was taken up by the scientist as well as the artist.

The Prehistory of the Motion Picture: 1824–1896

A number of discoveries, inventions, and theories occurred with some regularity throughout history and demonstrated a continued fascination

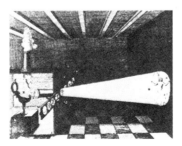

Figure 5.1. Kircher's magic lantern, shown in this seventeenth-century illustration, provided a crude form of projection.

Figure 5.2. The praxinoscope, a nineteenth-century parlor toy, provided the illusion of figures in motion. Circular strips of drawn figures in various stages of motion were inserted and were viewed in the mirrors at the center.

with reproducing motion. A variety of camera-projection devices were developed, including Leon Alberti's *camera lucida,* Giambattista della Porta's use of Leonardo da Vinci's *camera obscura,* and, most important, Athanasius Kircher's magic lantern. Nevertheless, none of these devices went beyond the ability to project drawn pictures of still life. There was no photography and no motion.

Before motion pictures could exist, therefore, several major discoveries had to take place. The following, all of which occurred in the nineteenth century, formed the scientific base of cinematography: (1) the discovery of the persistence of vision; (2) the development of photography; (3) the invention of the motion-picture camera; (4) the development of motion-picture projection techniques; and (5) the integration of motion, projection, and photographic concepts into cinematography.

This final evolutionary process began in 1824 with Peter Mark Roget's presentation of his theory of the persistence of vision. Roget demonstrated that through a peculiarity of the eye, a visual image is retained on the retina for a fraction of a second after it actually appears. Motion pictures are simply a series of motionless images (still frames) presented before the eye in rapid succession. Persistence of vision allows these still images to blend, creating the illusion of motion.

Soon after Roget published the results of his findings, a variety of motion devices incorporating his discovery were invented. Although they carried such imposing names as the stroboscope and the phenakistiscope, they were basically parlor toys in which drawn figures were animated.

The next required component was a system of projection. Projection in a crude form had existed for some time in the form of Kircher's magic lantern (1646), but it was not until 1853 that Baron Franz von Uchatius projected moving images visible to a large number of people. In the 1890s, the motion-picture projector as we know it today developed out of experiments by Thomas Edison and Thomas Armat in the United States and August and Louis Lumière in France.

Despite advances in projection, the pictures used to simulate motion were still being drawn. The next step was the invention of photography and, from this, the development of motion-picture photography. Still photography resulted from the efforts of Nicephore Niepce and Louis J. M. Daguerre, who presented copperplate photography to the public for the first time in 1839. Subsequently, photographs, rather than drawings, were used in projection devices.

In order for these developments in motion, projection, and photography to be integrated, special cameras, film, and projectors were needed. A camera that could take pictures faster than the still camera was essential. A number of attempts were made to solve this problem, including Eadweard Muybridge's famous demonstration in 1877 of the gait of a galloping horse. A more successful step came in 1882, when Dr. E. J. Marey developed what he called a "photographic gun," which could take a series of pictures in rapid succession. But his camera still used individual plates. Flexible-roll film was necessary for the complete development of a motion-picture camera.

An American preacher, Hannibal Goodwin, invented roll film, but George Eastman became its greatest promoter with the development in 1888 of his Kodak camera. He was not concerned with cinematography, however, and did nothing to develop motion-picture film.

It remained for William Dickson, an assistant of Thomas Edison, to perfect the first motion-picture camera using roll film. There is some confusion about exact dates, but it appears that by 1889, Dickson and Edison were taking moving pictures. In 1891, Edison applied for patents on the kinetograph as a photographing camera and the kinetoscope as a viewing apparatus and soon afterward began producing short film strips.

Edison's kinetoscope was a "peep-show" device that allowed viewing by only one person at a time. Edison was, in fact, slow to realize the importance of projection. At least a dozen other men began working on projection, including the Lumière brothers in France. In 1895, they demonstrated their projection device, the cinematographe, and shortly after began producing films. Edison soon realized his shortsightedness and, taking advantage of the efforts of the Lumières and of American inventor Thomas Armat, developed the Vitascope projector. On April 23, 1896, in Koster and Bial's Music Hall in New York, Edison's Vitascope projector was used for the first public showing of motion pictures in the United States.

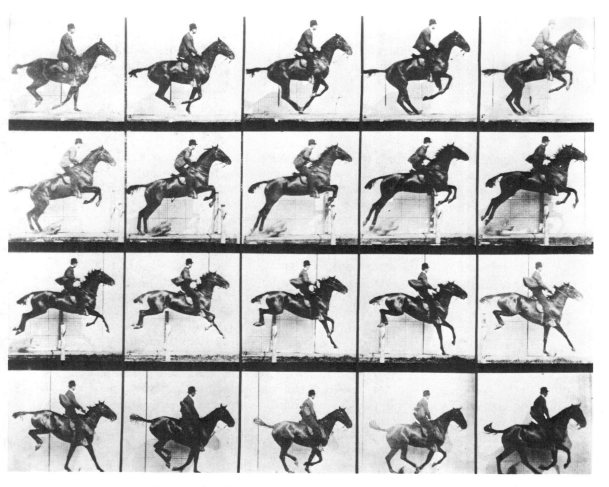

Figure 5.3. Eadweard Muybridge produced a series of what he called "motion studies" in the late 1870s and early 1880s. These demonstrated a crude form of motion picture. (Photo: Museum of Modern Art/Film Stills Archive.)

Beginnings and Narrative Development: 1896–1918

The first subject matter of the newly developed art of motion pictures was simple pictorial realism. Such films as *Arrival of the Paris Express, Venice Showing Gondolas, Kaiser Wilhelm Reviewing His Troops,* and *Feeding the Ducks at Tampa Bay* emphasized the camera's ability to record reality. Few of these films ran for more than 1 minute, and they were often run backward to pad the presentation and amaze the audience.

Despite the initial excitement, people soon tired of various versions of Niagara Falls and fire engines racing down a street. Motion pictures began to develop themes involving a story and sustained narrative. An important

Figure 5.4. A kinetoscope arcade in San Francisco, circa 1899. Viewers dropped their money into a slot and viewed a one-minute film. (Photo: The Bettman Archive, Inc.)

factor in this rapid development was that film, unlike some of the more traditional art forms, had the solid traditions and skills of photography and the theater behind it. In addition, when a new technique was discovered, it was quickly imitated by other filmmakers.

As early as 1896, the French filmmaker George Meliès began to create motion pictures with a story line. Meliès discovered new ways of seeing, interpreting, and even distorting reality. He contributed much to the development of many standard optical devices, such as the dissolve, split screen, jump cut, and superimposition. Meliès's most important contribution, however, was in using film to tell a story, not simply to record reality. Unfortunately, he was unable to move beyond his theatrical and magical background. His films, such as *Cinderella* (1899) and *A Trip to the Moon* (1902), were always a series of artificially arranged scenes shot from the fixed view of a spectator in a theater.

Developments in England and the United States soon propelled the motion picture into its unique means of expression. In America, Edwin S. Porter is credited with the initial development of narrative film. In two films, *The Life of an American Fireman* (1902) and, more important, *The Great Train Robbery* (1903), he demonstrated the power of editing as a means of film construction. The significance of *The Great Train Robbery* lay not only in

Figure 5.5. George Meliès was the first artist to incorporate dramatic narrative into filmmaking, as illustrated in his movie *A Trip to the Moon* (1902). (Photo: Museum of Modern Art/Film Stills Archive.)

its technique of building up an effective continuity of action through editing, but also in the timeliness of its arrival. Despite the camera trickery of Meliès, audiences had begun to tire of films that simply moved. *The Great Train Robbery* presented a new approach and offered the public excitement.

The years between 1906 and 1916 were the most important period of artistic development in motion-picture history. It was the time of the feature film, the first film star, the first distinguished director, the first picture palaces, a place called Hollywood, and, above all, the development of film as a unique and individual means of expression.

Some historians have aptly labeled these 10 years "the age of Griffith." It was David Wark Griffith who took the raw material of film and created a language, a syntax, and an art. His contributions were many, but more

Figure 5.6. Edwin S. Porter explored the techniques of film editing to provide dramatic continuity in several key films of the early twentieth century, including *The Great Train Robbery* (1903). (Photo: Museum of Modern Art/Film Stills Archive.)

than anything else, Griffith made film into a dynamic medium. Beginning with *The Adventures of Dolly* (1908) and culminating with *The Birth of a Nation* (1915) and *Intolerance* (1916), Griffith freed the motion picture from strictly theatrical bounds. He pioneered a more natural acting style, better story organization, and, most important, a true cinematic style. Rather than simply use film as a moving photograph or portable theater, he developed a language that emphasized the unique characteristics of the film medium, such as editing, camera movement, and camera angle.

To say that these years were the age of Griffith is not to deny the emergence of other notable film styles and important artists. Mack Sennett and his Keystone company developed their unique brand of slapstick comedy. Charlie Chaplin went beyond Sennett's slapstick into humor with a deeper, more philosophical edge. William S. Hart made realistic Westerns, and Mary Pickford was the screen's most popular personality.

The businessman also played an important role. Since most inventors of cinematic devices did little to exploit their devices commercially, it remained for individual entrepreneurs like B. F. Keith, Major Woodville Latham, and Thomas Talley, among others, to bring showmanship to the motion picture. The early commercial development of motion pictures began in vaudeville houses. Films started out as "headliners" but ended up

Figure 5.7. D. W. Griffith (seated at right) pioneered most modern filmmaking techniques. (Photo: Museum of Modern Art/Film Stills Archive.)

as "chasers," which moved patrons out of the theater between shows. Motion pictures then moved to slightly more permanent homes when projectors were installed in empty stores and music halls. There were also a number of traveling film shows, "electric theaters" as they were called. In 1905 appeared the first permanent motion-picture theater, the nickelodeon—so named because a nickel was the price of admission. By 1907, there were more than 3,000 of these small theaters, and by 1910, over 10,000 nickelodeons were scattered throughout the eastern half of the country.

Making motion pictures became a prosperous and thriving enterprise. Between 1905 and 1910, narrative films grew longer and more costly, and more popular and profitable. Edwin S. Porter's *Dream of a Rarebit Fiend* (1906), for example, cost $350 to make and grossed more than $350,000. The Vitagraph Company which started in 1896 with capital of $936, showed profits of over $900,000 by 1912. The trappings of an industrial empire were not yet apparent, however. There was no star system, no $1 million salaries, no Hollywood. These would all come about as a reaction against a monopoly called the Motion Picture Patents Company (MPPC). Formed in 1909 through the pooling of 16 patents, it controlled virtually every aspect of motion-picture production, distribution, and exhibition in the United States for more than three years.

Figure 5.8. The epic scale of D. W. Griffith's *Birth of a Nation* (1915) and other feature-length films of the time ushered in an age of motion-picture grandeur. (Photo: Movie Star News.)

The final stage of early economic development included a savage war between the MPPC and independent and foreign producers. It was a battle with one of these producers, Adolph Zukor, that precipitated the final development stage. Zukor acquired the rights to the French film *Queen Elizabeth* (1912), starring Sarah Bernhardt. In order to exhibit it, he had to apply to the MPPC for permission. It refused, and so he went to an independent exhibitor. The picture was a success, and the experience led Zukor to form his own company, Famous Players in Famous Plays—the forerunner of Paramount Pictures. Heartened by Zukor's stand, other independent producers began showing films without the permission of the MPPC. Pressure was applied by the MPPC, and as a result, many individuals moved west to escape its control. The move to California came gradually, but by 1914, the state had attracted such men as Cecil B. De Mille, Jesse Lasky, and Zukor. Some prospered, and many failed. Nevertheless, most of Hollywood's major studios trace their origins back to the independents who between 1910 and 1914 fought the MPPC.

By 1917, the MPPC had been dissolved by the courts. Even though brief, the MPPC fight produced lasting results, including the establishment

Figure 5.9. This still from the German expressionist film *The Cabinet of Dr. Caligari* (1919) dramatically illustrates the bizarre and visually striking set design that was characteristic of this genre. (Photo: *Museum of Modern Art/Film Stills Archive.*)

of Hollywood as the center of motion-picture production, the introduction of feature-length films, the rise of the star system, and the construction of elaborate motion-picture theaters. For obvious financial reasons, the MPPC had limited all films to one reel and had blocked actor identification. For the independents, longer films and stars became an effective way of attracting customers. To accommodate the influx of star-studded, feature-length films, new theaters were constructed.

International Awakenings: 1919–1929

By the time of the outbreak of World War I, motion pictures were firmly established as an artistic and economic reality. The war further strengthened America's position in the international film market because virtually all the major film industries of Europe either were shut down or had their production severely curtailed. By 1919, 80 percent of the world's motion pictures were made in southern California. By 1920, average weekly movie attendance in the United States was 40 million and growing rapidly.

Following World War I, there was a great deal of international development in film. The war-ravaged film industries of Germany, Russia, and

Figure 5.10. The unforgettable images in Sergei Eisenstein's *Potemkin* (1925) achieve most of their impact through his use of editing coupled with striking composition. (Photo: Museum of Modern Art/Film Stills Archive.)

France were quickly reconstructed and began producing films. Movements in these three countries were especially important because of the contributions they made to film theory and aesthetics. In Germany, for example, two types of film emerged: expressionistic and street films. Street films brought to film a new sense of naturalism and realism. The camera was also used with a new sense of personal perspective and movement. Important films of these two movements included *The Cabinet of Dr. Caligari* (1919) and *The Joyless Street* (1925).

The Russians, most notably Lev Kuleshov, Sergei Eisenstein, and V. L. Pudovkin, contributed greatly to the theory of film editing. The Russian concept of montage—the creation of meaning through shot juxtaposition—had a significant impact on Russian film and was used by Eisenstein and Pudovkin, especially, to produce films of stunning force and deep meaning. Key films here were Eisenstein's *Potemkin* (1925) and Pudovkin's *Mother* (1927).

In France, motion pictures displayed abstract and surrealistic forms through the work of intellectuals and creative filmmakers such as René Clair, Jacques Feyder, and Luis Buñuel. In such films as *Entracte* (1925) and *Un Chien Andalou* (1929), these men extended the boundaries of film beyond narrative into a world of deep symbolism and pure form.

All this foreign energy had a distinct yet diffused impact on the American film industry. Few of the actual film forms and theories were incorporated by Hollywood; however, the talent that produced them was absorbed. Not long after they had achieved international reputations, such directors and film stars as Emil Jannings, F. W. Murnau, Greta Garbo, and Marlene Dietrich came to the United States to make films. The result was the gradual weakening and ultimate destruction of most of the foreign movements.

Hollywood in the 1920s: 1920–1928

Meanwhile, Hollywood was busy producing films that were a reflection of the roaring twenties. Companies became studios, which grew in size and power. Salaries rose, huge stages were constructed, and many backlots contained entire towns. By the mid-1920s, 40 percent of a film's budget went for studio overhead.

Three kinds of films dominated the decade: the feature-length comedy, the Western, and the comedy of manners. In this era, many critics believe, film comedy reached its zenith. Comedic styles moved away from the broad, farcical slapstick of Mack Sennett toward a more subtle, sophisticated format, characterized so brilliantly by, among others, Charlie Chaplin, Harold Lloyd, and Buster Keaton. In such films as Chaplin's *The Gold Rush* (1925), Keaton's *The General* (1926), and Lloyd's *The Freshman* (1925), silent comedy reached the pinnacle of artistic film achievement.

The Western matured with the development of the ''big'' feature, which was best represented by John Ford's *The Covered Wagon* (1923), James Cruze's *The Iron Horse* (1924), and William S. Hart's *Tumbleweeds* (1925). The ''B'' Western, especially the romantic melodramas that starred Tom Mix, also became prominent, providing contrast to the spectacular Westerns of Ford and Cruze and the stark realism used so effectively by Hart.

The third film form was a direct result of the social conditions of the time. The mores of the country were more free and more open than at any time in its history. The comedy-of-manners film was a reflection of this increased sophistication, since it concentrated on high society, glittering wealth, and personal freedom. Such films as Cecil B. De Mille's *Male and Female* (1919) and *Why Change Your Wife?* (1920) appealed directly to this new sense of freedom.

The Arrival of Sound: 1927–1930

The 1920s were years of increased prosperity for the motion-picture industry. However, the end of the decade found Hollywood in trouble. As a result of a series of major scandals in the early 1920s, a motion-picture-code office was formed to police both the content of films and the behavior of the people who made them. The increasing popularity of radio and the automobile created attendance problems. In order to win back the lost audience, something new was needed.

Figure 5.11. Buster Keaton—seen here in his most famous film, *The General* (1926)—was one of silent film's true artists and most popular stars. (Photo: Museum of Modern Art/Film Stills Archive.)

Warner Brothers was a small studio on the verge of bankruptcy in 1926. Having little to lose, it invested its remaining capital in a new sound system called Vitaphone. On October 26, 1927, it presented the first talking feature—*The Jazz Singer,* starring Al Jolson. The motion-picture industry, reluctant at first to abandon silent films completely, soon recognized the public's acceptance of talkies as permanent and moved to total sound production.

The effect of sound on motion pictures was profound and lasting. Sound's impact on content was evident from the start. The more a film talked, sang, or shouted, the better it was. Swept aside in the rush were many unique forms, most notably silent comedy.

Individual stars were also greatly affected. Buster Keaton, Charlie Chaplin, Harold Lloyd, and other silent comics, whose basic style was visual, were hampered. In addition, many stars found that their voices were displeasing to audiences. The careers of such major silent-film stars as Charles Farrell and Norma Talmadge were greatly limited because of unsatisfactory vocal quality.

The impact on audiences was most important. In 1927, an average of 60 million people attended motion pictures every week. By 1929, this figure had risen to over 110 million. This success gave the industry a tremendous financial boost and helped it over the worst years of the Great Depression.

The expense of making sound films also brought financial domination in the form of such companies as Western Electric, RCA, and their respective financial backers, Kuhn-Loeb and the First National Bank of New York. RCA, which made sound equipment, bought a film company and theater corporation and set up a powerful new studio, RKO. The eastern banking interests gained a significant hold on the entertainment industry and its products. Despite Hollywood's domestic success, its dominance of the world market diminished because sound films—unlike silent films, which speak a universal language—required expensive dubbing of foreign languages for overseas distribution.

The Golden Age of Hollywood: 1930–1946

Like other institutions of the time, film reflected the tensions, crises, and deepening social awareness in the United States. One reaction was the documentary film, beginning with Robert Flaherty's work in the early 1920s and continuing under John Grierson's influence in England. Filmmakers in the United States initially failed to exploit the documentary's potential, but in 1936, Pare Lorentz produced *The Plow that Broke the Plains*. Lorentz was soon appointed as the head of the United States Film Service and, along with other directors, such as Willard Van Dyke, created several powerful films, including *The River* (1937), *Ecce Homo* (1939), and *The Power and the Land* (1940). For a variety of political reasons, however, the service was legislated out of existence in 1940, and it took the catastrophe of World War II to revitalize the documentary film.

Another response to the time was the social-consciousness film. Such films as *The Public Enemy* (1931) and *I Was a Fugitive from a Chain Gang* (1933) asked their audiences to view people and their actions as a part of or the result of the social conditions of the time. A third response was escapism. As the economic depression deepened, the studios turned toward more musical and comedic themes in an attempt to provide their audiences with another reality. Hollywood produced a wave of Busby Berkeley (*Footlight Parade* [1933], *Gold Diggers of 1935* [1935]) and Fred Astaire and Ginger Rogers singing-and-dancing spectacles (*Flying Down to Rio* [1936]). These musicals were soon joined by "screwball" comedies, such as *It Happened One Night* (1934), directed by Frank Capra, and *The Thin Man* series starring William Powell and Myrna Loy.

The 1930s were also the golden age of the studio system. Production was almost completely centered in seven dominant companies: MGM, Paramount, Warner Brothers, RKO, Universal, Columbia, and 20th Century-Fox. Each studio had its own stars and unique style.

Toward the end of the 1930s, with war imminent in Europe, American

Figure 5.12. Fred Astaire and Ginger Rogers—seen here in *Flying Down to Rio* (1934)—were major stars of the golden age of movies in the 1930s. (Photo: Museum of Modern Art/Film Stills Archive, Courtesy RKO Studios.)

studios began to produce strongly patriotic films, and some cautious steps were taken in portraying future allies and enemies in such films as *Foreign Correspondent* (1940) and *The Ramparts We Watch* (1939). Until the bombing of Pearl Harbor, however, the United States was technically a neutral nation, and most film companies were wary of economic reprisals by the Axis governments.

After the United States entered the war, Hollywood began to produce patriotic war films in which Japanese and Germans immediately became stock, stereotyped villains. The image of the American fighting man was equally stereotyped. American audiences did not want realistic war dramas that detailed the horrors they read about in newspapers or heard about on radio. As the war continued to wear on, the studios turned to more and more escapist fare. More than one-half of the 1,300 films produced from 1942 to 1944 had themes unrelated to the war. As a result of a war-weary civilian population seeking escape, the studios enjoyed enormous success and earned their highest profits ever.

Postwar Decline: 1946–1962

The story of film in the years following World War II is essentially a chronicle of decline and frustration for Hollywood and the major studios but of rebirth and growth for foreign and independent films. After the war, American studios resumed standard operating procedures, producing a steady supply of films designed for the mass public's tastes and habits. Soon, however, four events occurred that forced major changes in the traditional Hollywood structure: (1) the rise of television; (2) the hearings before the House Un-American Activities Committee (HUAC); (3) the Supreme Court's divorcement ruling; and (4) the emergence of a vigorous international film movement.

The advent of network television in 1948 diverted much of the audience from its traditional twice-a-week motion-picture habit. Between 1950 and 1960, the number of TV sets in the United States increased by 400 percent, while motion-picture attendance fell by 50 percent.

The fear of Communism in the United States, labeled the Red Scare, had a number of effects. The most devastating was the blacklist, in which many talented craftsmen and artists were labeled as Communists because of alleged left-wing activities and were banned from the motion-picture industry. Experimentation and initiative in content were discouraged, and producers either fell back on old patterns or grasped at experimental technological straws.

The third blow was the decision of the Supreme Court in the *Paramount* case (1950), which forced the Hollywood studios to end vertical integration—by which one corporation produced, distributed, and exhibited films. Film companies were forced to divest themselves of one of the three operations. Most major companies sold off their theater chains and stayed in production and distribution. This, in effect, caused the collapse of the basic industry monopoly and ended the absolute control that the major Hollywood studios had held on the American film market for 30 years.

Coincidental to these domestic happenings, and to a certain extent because of them, a strong international film movement emerged. Beginning with neorealism in Italy, vital national cinemas developed in the late 1940s and early 1950s. In 1951, Akira Kurosawa's *Rashomon* won the Venice Film Festival award for Japan, and American audiences suddenly became aware of non-Hollywood sources of motion pictures. Foreign films were available not only from Japan, but also from England, France, Italy, Sweden, and India. With this availability, yet another aspect of studio monopoly was undermined.

Motion pictures in the United States were no longer the mass medium, and in the 1950s, their future as a mass medium looked shaky. Attendance figures dropped off sharply. The industry frantically responded with such technological innovations as stereophonic sound, wide screens, and 3-D effects. These attractions were built on passing fancies, however, and the basic fact of a changing audience was ignored. Attempts to inject new vigor or new themes were fought consistently. This is clearly illustrated by Otto Preminger's unsuccessful fight to obtain the industry's seal of approval for two films: *The Moon Is Blue* (1953), an innocuous comedy about adultery, and *The Man with the Golden Arm* (1956), a film about drug addiction.

Hollywood tried to win back its lost audience and to regain some of its former prestige by emphasizing size. The spectacle had been a part of

Figure 5.13. In one of several attempts to attract a declining audience, the motion-picture industry introduced 3-D motion pictures in 1953. Although this large audience seems to be entertained, the need to wear cumbersome glasses and the poor quality of the films made 3-D a passing fad. (Photo: J. R. Eyerman, *Life* Magazine, © Time Inc.)

Figure 5.14. Julie Andrews as Maria in *The Sound of Music* (1965). *The Sound of Music* was one of the biggest box-office successes in the history of film, but most of the big-budget spectacles of the late 1960s and early 1970s were financial disasters. (Photo: Billy Rose Theatre Collection. The New York Public Library at Lincoln Center. Astor, Lenox and Tilden Foundations.)

Hollywood ever since *The Birth of a Nation* (1915), and in the 1960s, the form was looked on as the savior of the Hollywood system. *Cleopatra* (1963) should have been a warning signal; it was the most expensive and most publicized film made to this time, and it was a monumental box-office failure. But two years later, *The Sound of Music* (1965) became one of the biggest box-office successes in history, earning more than $80 million in rentals. The major studios, with their confidence bolstered, set into motion a series of spectacles, among them *Dr. Dolittle* (1968), *Star* (1969), *Goodbye Mr. Chips* (1970), and *Tora! Tora! Tora!* (1971). All were failures that plunged many of the studios to the point of bankruptcy and led to their eventual takeover by non-Hollywood business interests.

Cracks began to appear in Hollywood's façade. One change was the

Figure 5.15. The success of the low-budget film *Marty* (1955), which starred Ernest Borgnine, encouraged United Artists and other independent producers to continue making films outside the established studios. (Photo: New York Public Library at Lincoln Center, Courtesy United Artists Corporation.)

reorganization of United Artists. Originally organized in 1919 as an independent outlet for the films of D. W. Griffith, Charlie Chaplin, Douglas Fairbanks, and Mary Pickford, United Artists was revamped in 1951 to provide again distribution of independently produced films. With such films as *The African Queen* (1951) and *Marty* (1955), United Artists began to provide new hope for the independent filmmaker. From this beginning, the roots of the "new American cinema" emerged.

The Film Revolution: 1963–1975

In the 1960s, Hollywood and its traditional picture values declined even further. A new cinema emerged to take its place; a cinema that is difficult to characterize except, perhaps, in terms of what it rejected. The films of the

1960s and early 1970s were the products of a changing society, a society in which *relevance, awareness,* and *freedom of expression* became watchwords. Motion pictures no longer existed exclusively as a product to be passively consumed by a mass audience. New filmmakers were searching for new audiences, which, in turn, were seeking a new kind of involvement in the film experience.

Hollywood did not die in the 1960s, but it did experience radical change. Perhaps the most important force at work was the so-called new American cinema, which was essentially the surfacing of what used to be called underground films. There have always been films produced away from normal sources. They have been regarded as art, avant-garde, experimental, "new wave," or even pornographic films. Perhaps the major film trend of the 1960s was that such motion pictures acquired a legitimacy that allowed them to be exhibited virtually without restriction. Essentially, what happened was a juncture of the art-experimental film with the underground film through the normal channels of production, distribution, and exhibition.

One of the first underground features to surface and receive wide public distribution was Shirley Clarke's *Connection* (1961). This film was soon followed by Jonas Mekas's *Brig* (1964) and Kenneth Anger's *Scorpio Rising* (1966). By the late 1960s, this movement, coupled with the troubles of the major studios, had catapulted the independent filmmaker into a position of prominence. Dennis Hopper's *Easy Rider* (1969) was the watershed of this trend, for it finally convinced the major studios that a low-budget ($370,000) independently produced film could be a blockbuster (over $50 million in rentals).

The significance of *Easy Rider* was not in its artistic merits, although it certainly possessed them, but in the fact that talents outside the Hollywood mainstream (Dennis Hopper, Peter Fonda, Jack Nicholson, and Karen Black) could produce and star in a small-budget film that had wide audience appeal. It showed a new way to mine gold in the American audience.

There was a great deal of talk in the late 1960s and early 1970s of a new film generation, of an audience that was sophisticated and would demand more from films than entertainment. An indication of this was the expanding film curriculum in high schools, colleges, and universities. This new awareness, coupled with formal instruction in film production and consumption, produced an audience that was more perceptive and more knowledgeable about film than ever before. People went to a movie; they no longer went to the movies.

New audiences are basic to a new cinema. They were and are the driving force behind it. Motion pictures were no longer appealing to an audience composed of a cross section of the American population. Almost 75 percent of the film audience of the 1970s was between the ages of 16 and

Figure 5.16. Dennis Hopper (at left) and Peter Fonda, on the road in *Easy Rider* (1969). *Easy Rider* was an important film in the emergence of the "new American cinema." (Photo: Museum of Modern Art/Film Stills Archive, Courtesy Columbia Pictures Industries, Inc.)

30, and its effect on motion pictures was dramatic. On the one hand, many moviegoers demanded that film do more than simply provide escape; it should make statements, take sides, and promote causes. On the other hand, they were using film as escape, as pure entertainment.

They Shoot Horses Don't They? (1969), for example, revealed the sordid side of the often fondly remembered dance marathons of the 1930s. The outstanding success of such films as *Tell Them Willie Boy Is Here* (1969), *Five Easy Pieces* (1970), *Z* (1969), *Joe* (1970), *M*A*S*H* (1969), *Little Big Man* (1970), *Dirty Harry* (1971), *The Last Picture Show* (1971), *A Clockwork Orange* (1972), and *Cabaret* (1972) pointed to an increased awareness of film as a medium for social comment.

Nevertheless, what was thought to be a permanent trend turned out to be simply another cycle. The social-consciousness film movement that had begun with *Easy Rider* quickly faded. By 1973, a new cycle of films had appeared—the disaster film. Headed by *The Poseidon Adventure* (1973), this cycle dominated film production for two years with such films as *Airport 1975*, *Earthquake*, and *The Towering Inferno*. This trend was short-lived, however, as audiences grew tired of being guinea pigs for ambitious special-effects artists who filled vapid plots and surrounded dull acting with all sorts of magic tricks. Aside from this minicycle, 1974 was a year of great diversity, with such films as Francis Ford Coppola's intense character study, *The Conversation*; Sidney Lumet's witty *Murder on the Orient Express*; Roman Polanski's searing picture of the 1930s Los Angeles underworld in *Chinatown*; Art Carney's wistful portrayal of the problems and beauty of

Figure 5.17. Princess Leia (Carrie Fisher) places a message for help in Artoo-Detoo. The record-breaking profits from *Star Wars* (1977) established a new blockbuster trend in the film industry. (Photo: The Bettmann Archive, Inc.)

old age in *Harry and Tonto;* and John Cassavetes's continued exploration of the human condition in *A Woman under the Influence.*

Industrial Merger and Creative Conformity: 1976–Present

With *Jaws* in 1975, the era of the mega-rental film began in earnest, and in 1977, *Star Wars* exploded previous box-office records into outer space. *Star Wars* was *the* film of 1977 and of film box-office history. The success of this film immediately revived the long-dormant science-fiction genre, and a new cycle began. The new cycle was less one of content or style and more one of formula and financial success characterized by the obsessive use of sequels and reissues. The blockbuster psychology of the studios made it almost impossible to be offbeat and personal. The 1980s continued with more of the same, resulting in fewer films and bigger budgets, especially for advertising and publicity, as hype often substituted for quality.

In addition to *Star Wars,* 1977 saw the birth of two other "sequel sires": *Rocky,* starring Sylvester Stallone, and *Smokey and the Bandit,* starring Burt Reynolds. As the second and third most popular rental films of the year, they inspired (some would say "conspired to") a succession of baby *Rocky*s and *Smokey*s that is still going strong. *Grease* was the big film of 1978,

Figure 5.18. In 1982, *E.T.* headed the list of Steven Spielberg successes. In that year, three of his films made the "top 20" (box-office gross). *E.T.* remains the top box-office film of all time. (Photo: Movie Star News, Courtesy Universal Studios.)

followed, in turn, by *Close Encounters of the Third Kind* (actually released in late 1977) and *Animal House*. *Jaws II* and a reissue of *Star Wars* made the top-10 box-office list as well. *Superman* led the way in 1979 and was quickly followed by the Steven Spielberg–George Lucas dynasty, beginning in the 1980s. *The Empire Strikes Back* more than doubled the box-office rentals of the number-two film, *Kramer vs. Kramer*, in 1980; *Raiders of the Lost Ark* and *Superman II* held forth in 1981. The year 1982 starred *E.T.*, as well as *Rocky III*, *Star Trek II: The Wrath of Kahn*, a reissue of *Raiders of the Lost Ark*, and Spielberg's third film in the top 20, *Poltergeist*.

Feature-film follow-ups began to exert an extremely potent box-office appeal. In 1981 and 1982, sequels and follow-ups to major films (9 and 11 titles, respectively) accounted for 12 percent of all domestic rentals in each of those years. This is a startling performance, given that over 500 new and reissued pictures are released each year. The sequel syndrome appears to be a continuing phenomenon. *Return of the Jedi*; *Superman III*; *Octopussy*; *Jaws 3-D*; *Porky's II*; *Smokey and the Bandit, Part 3*; and *Psycho II* dominated

box-office statistics in 1983. However, some cracks began to appear because both *Jedi* and *Superman III* generated less return revenue (people
seeing a film twice and even three and four times) and met with decidedly
less than universal critical acclaim than had their originals. In 1984, 1985,
and 1986, however, series and sequel films continued to do well—*Indiana
Jones and the Temple of Doom; Star Trek III: The Search for Spock; Cannonball II;
The Muppets Take Manhattan; Oh God You Devil; Friday the 13th, Part 4; Rocky
IV; Rambo: First Blood, Part II; Karate Kid II;* and *Poltergeist II.*

Despite these minitrends, the real profile of the American feature film
in the 1980s has been one of isolated success. As several contemporary
critics noted, among the Hollywood studios and independent production
companies, strategy in production has replaced style, and the emphasis in
commercial filmmaking is focused almost totally on the mega-box-office
success. In four of the last five years of the 1970s, one huge box-office
success spawned a host of attempts at duplicating that success (*Jaws* in
1975, *Star Wars* in 1977, *Grease* in 1978, and *Superman* in 1979).

When one looks at films today, the only word that comes to mind is
conformity—not so much in style, as in the attempt to duplicate what has
proved commercially successful. One of the significant effects of this trend
has been the decline of the foreign film. The 1960s saw a tremendous surge
in foreign films, but by 1972, Ingmar Bergman's *Cries and Whispers* could
not find an American distributor. Today, the foreign film that successfully
cracks the American theatrical market is a rare commodity. Most illustra-
tive of this trend is the history in recent years of films made in France and
Italy, traditionally two leading suppliers of import films to America. None
of the films starring such French superstars as Jean-Paul Belmondo that are
popular in France have shown up on American marquees, as have few, if
any, of the many comedy hits coming from Italy. The current practice of
major American distributors is to concentrate on importing primarily European art films or fantasy and sex films, letting the middle range of popular
hits remain at home.

The key to understanding the conformity and noticeable absence of
individuality in American films of the 1980s is simple economics. As the
average cost of producing a feature film has risen from $1 million in 1972 to
over $16 million in the late 1980s, the small film—financed, made, and
distributed outside the major studios—has become all but obsolete.

Filmmaking today is controlled by a few major studios that are, in
turn, controlled by conglomerate owners. The individuals who run these
and other film conglomerates, such as MCA and Transamerica, have decided to devote their money to blockbuster films and to eliminate small
films. If one looks at top-10 box-office films of 1985, this pattern becomes
obvious. The top film, *Back to the Future,* represented some originality with
glimmers of early Steven Spielberg shining through. *Rambo: First Blood,
Part II* and *Rocky IV* as numbers 2 and 3 speak for themselves. *Beverly Hills
Cop* was primarily a vehicle for the run-to-the-bank humor and appeal of

Eddie Murphy. *Cocoon* was a charming offbeat comedy fantasy, but it was vaguely reminiscent of Ron Howard's previous hit, *Splash. The Goonies,* following the success of *The Gremlins,* was simply another Spielberg formula. Rounding out the top 10 were two sequels, *Police Academy 2—Their First Assignment* and *National Lampoon's European Vacation,* and the latest James Bond adventure, *A View to Kill. Witness* was perhaps the most original film to crack the top 10.

As the cost of making films has risen, the stylistic and thematic freedoms of the early 1970s have given way to the action-dominated and star-populated conformity of the 1980s. While small, personal films like *The Elephant Man* (1980), *Diner,* (1982), *Local Hero,* (1983), and *Mask* (1985) are still made, they represent a dying breed. The current trend is toward content-theme cycles of increasingly shorter duration; there are almost "seasons," as on television. The key is to start a new trend or get on the bandwagon quickly, before the audience gets bored.

There is no guarantee of success any longer. Previous "guarantees" included studios such as MGM; stars such as Gable, Cooper, Tracy, Newman, McQueen, and Hoffman; directors such as Ford, Bogdanovich, Peckinpah, Altman, and Kubrick; and audience habits such as going to the movies regularly.

The feature film of the 1980s bears little resemblance to its counterpart of the late 1960s. Part of the reason for this is the motion-picture industry's rating system, which no longer censors films but simply suggests suitable age levels for audiences of particular films. These ratings, administered by the Motion Picture Association of America (MPAA) and begun in 1968, are G for general audiences; PG, parental guidance suggested; PG-13, special guidance for children under 13; R, restricted to individuals at least 17 years old or those accompanied by a parent or guardian; and X, no one under the age of 17 admitted.

Freedom from industry censorship has led to a dramatic increase in the sexual and violent content of motion pictures. Sex and violence have been a part of motion pictures from the beginning; but industry codes, state and local laws, or both always checked excesses. The ratings and changes in society have led to new standards in treating sex and violence in films. For example, in earlier days, actual sexual activity was suggested, not shown. In 1972, a movie entitled *Deep Throat* rejected the norms, and "hard-core" sex films appeared. By the end of 1972, an estimated 700 theaters were showing "porn" films exclusively. This, too, was a cycle that quickly faded. The lasting results are not to be found in the occasional hard-core film that makes the national circuits but in the more open and free treatment of sex as a theme and an activity in most contemporary films.

Much the same could be said regarding violence. Although violence has had a long history in films, there used to be rules that governed its magnitude. These rules were graphically broken in the late 1960s by such films as *Bonnie and Clyde, Bullitt, The Wild Bunch,* and *The French Connection.* Violence became explicit; audiences saw bullet holes, blood, and torn flesh. The horror films of the late 1970s and early 1980s, which began with *Halloween* (1978), totally shattered most of the broken rules. No taboos were too sacred. Heads were severed, eyes were gouged out, stomachs were split open; in general, the human body was subjected to every imaginable form of mutilation until the effect became almost comic.

Whether audiences would "buy it" was, and is, the real issue. As long as the public is willing to accept violence, filmmakers are going to produce it. Some, such as Samuel Z. Arkoff, former board chairman of American International Pictures, may demonstrate a social conscience and set "a limit on the number of blood bags used." But the attitude of most seems to be that if psychiatrists don't have the answers, why should they?

Film and Television

In the mid-1970s, the relationship between film and television begun in the 1950s intensified and solidified. As motion-picture attendance decreased and the number of TV homes increased, the competition between the two media became cooperation and, ultimately, coexistence. What once appeared to be a destroyer has turned out to be a savior. Without television, Hollywood would not have survived, even in its diminished existence. Of the approximately 20,000 jobs in Hollywood, 10,000 are in television. While the number of theatrical motion pictures shown on the networks has declined, the number of made-for-television movies has increased. Motion pictures make up a significant part of television prime-time programming.

Television has become the new "B" movie and provides the function for the motion-picture industry that "B" movies have always provided—a substantial, reliable, steady income. New markets in cable and pay television hold great potential, and it is clear that television and motion pictures are firmly and permanently linked.

As Figure 5.19 illustrates, less than 50 percent of a movie's gross revenue comes from the theatrical box office, with the remaining dollars coming from some form of television and/or video source. In 1978, 80 percent of a film's total earnings came from theaters; by 1985, the box-office take was at 43 percent and heading downward. In 1980, studios collected $20 million from worldwide sales of videocassettes; in 1985, nearly $2 billion. Films that do poorly in theaters now enter the home-video market as soon as three months after their release. However, because studios can collect a fee only when they sell a cassette and because 90 percent of all videocassette transactions are rentals, the studios will continue to aggressively market pay television, pay cable, broadcast networks, and syndication. The syndication market is especially strong, since the number of independent TV stations has soared from fewer than 100 in 1978 to over 225 in 1985. Because they are not network affiliated, they need "product," and theatrical film packages fit their needs.

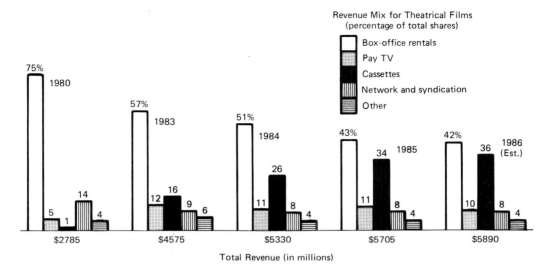

Figure 5.19. This chart illustrates how the mix of revenue earned by theatrical motion pictures has shifted in recent years. Although the average movie's revenue has shifted strongly toward videocassettes, all the "windows" (except pay TV) have gained in dollar amounts.

A clear shift has occurred in motion-picture revenue. Studios no longer depend on income from theatrical distribution alone; they have broadened their base to include various forms of distribution and exhibition.

It is difficult to say where motion pictures stand at the present; they are ultimately in the hands of the people who make them and the people who view them, and, as we have seen, both ends of the continuum have changed considerably. As Will Tusher reported in *Variety*:

> Will it really matter whether Ted Turner runs MGM instead of Kirk Kerkorian, whether Rupert Murdoch instead of Marvin Davis calls the shots at 20th Century Fox, or whether Coca-Cola performs a bottling industry marketing transplant at Columbia Pictures.
>
> In a nutshell—to a town occupationally petitioning for miracles—not very likely. Happy endings are more easily contrived on screen than off screen. In the real Hollywood, the only sure thing remains uncertainty.
>
> More than ever before, Hollywood is a game of multiplying operations. VCRs and videocassette rentals are not a passing fad. Erosion of the value of the commercial television selloff is matching the steady erosion of the primetime network audience. The market is more diffused than ever, the competition more intense than ever.
>
> Regardless of the vicissitudes in ownership, the motion picture industry remains an impossible effort to make a predictable business of an unfathomable art. Since the public itself is fixed to no preconceptions, how can

those in the business of guessing public taste hope to master reliable pre-conceptions of their own?

The public knows before the first gulp what a Coke or Pepsi is going to taste like. No such certainty can be attached to a movie. No two movies—however much alike some are—are so much alike that it follows that if the public buys one of a kind, it will buy more of a kind.

No one knows. No one will know. That is the nature of the lottery that is moviemaking. It is an art—or a business—unmoved by the self-pro-claimed omniscient or omnipotent.[1]

THE SCOPE OF MOTION PICTURES

The motion picture continues to be a primary recreational outlet, although it is not nearly as significant as it was 40 years ago. The industry peaked in 1946, with estimated box-office receipts of $1.7 billion from 4.1 billion ad-missions. The decline in admissions was precipitous until 1962, when it leveled off. Admissions have been relatively stable, at about 1.2 billion, for more than 20 years. In 1985, however, admissions declined by 11 percent to 1.06 billion (Figure 5.20).

Despite declining admissions, box-office receipts rose dramatically in the first four years of the 1980s because of the increase in ticket prices. In 1984, the motion-picture industry had its most successful year ever. Total theater receipts exceeded $4 billion for the first time. But in 1985, domestic box-office returns declined by 7 percent to $3.75 billion.

Increases in ticket prices continued unabated in 1985. The average composite ticket price in 1985 was $3.60, up 20 cents from 1984. In New York, the admission fee at first-run theaters went to $6 from $5.

Seasonal swings in the domestic theatrical-film box office have long been a fact of industry life, despite a lot of wishful thinking to the contrary. An analysis of week-to-week fluctuations throughout the year, created by industry analyst A. D. Murphy and published in *Variety* (Figure 5.21), shows a remarkably steady and recurring annual profile of film attendance within the United States. Weekly data compiled over a 15-year period were utilized, and ticket-price inflation has been removed in order to eliminate distortion. A "normal" 52-week year has been used for standardized com-parisons.

The overall analysis shows that business tends to slide in January by approximately 40 percent and then tends to stabilize until the Washing-ton's Birthday weekend upturn in February.

Next comes the slack period in late winter until the spring school-vacation season, when business perks up again to a slightly higher level than at Washington's Birthday.

---

[1] *Variety*, 8 January 1986, 6.

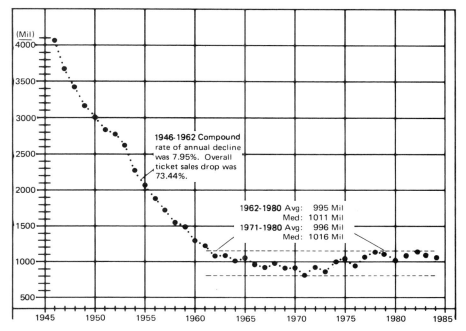

Figure 5.20. Theatrical film admissions in the United States (1946–1985). An unbroken decline in ticket sales occurred from 1946 to 1962. Since 1962, admissions have stabilized at around 1 billion a year.

The post-Easter weeks represent another, and deeper, box-office sag. Over Memorial Day weekend, business soars. But admissions then rapidly (although briefly) decline until the waves of summer-vacation school closings and business holidays propel business to another relative high for the year around July 4.

After July 4, business experiences a slight midsummer decline before rising again in late July and early August, followed by another mild sag until the Labor Day–weekend climax of that season.

The sharp September slump bottoms out late in that month, followed by a stable, slightly rising trend through October and November. But just before Thanksgiving week, there's a tapering off before the holiday upturn.

Next come the worst weeks of the year—early December, when business falls to its lowest relative point. This situation changes quite markedly as Christmas approaches, with box-office levels tripling between the second week of the month and New Year's week. As the graph indicates, the box-office barometer for 1985 paralleled Murphy's 14-year composite.

Major Hollywood producers and independents produced 452 feature motion pictures in 1985, a decade-high total. Feature-film production by the major studios, however, declined from 140 in 1984 to 135 in 1985.

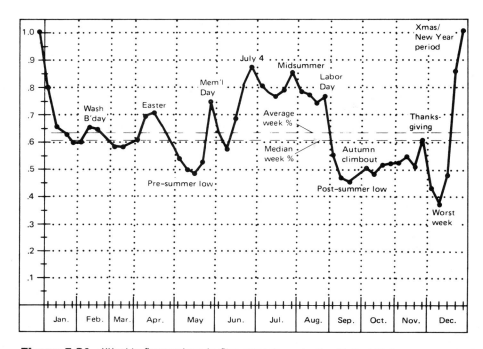

Figure 5.21. Weekly fluctuations in film attendance in the United States (1969–1983). The graph shows the ratio of weekly film attendance to a base reference—the final week of a year—given an arbitrary value of 1.0. The time base used is 1969–1983. Evidently, the idea of an "average" week is specious, given the wide fluctuations in a year. (Data source: MPAA, *Variety.* Chart © 1984 A. D. Murphy.)

The average cost of producing a feature film by the major American companies has increased many times since the beginning of World War II. In 1941, average cost per feature was $400,000. By 1949, the cost had risen to more than $1 million. The average production cost of theatrical films in 1972 was $1.89 million. In 1982, it reached $11.3 million; in 1985, $16.7 million. The average production budget is divided as follows:

Story costs	5 percent
Production and direction costs	5 percent
Sets and other physical properties	35 percent
Stars' and cast salaries	20 percent
Studio overhead	20 percent
Income taxes	5 percent
Contingency fund	10 percent

There were an estimated 20,200 theater screens in the United States in January 1985: 17,368 of them indoors, and 2,832 drive-ins. This compares with 14,732 indoor screens and 3,308 drive-ins at the end of 1981. The increased number of indoor screens reflects the continuing demolition of older theaters and their replacement by multiplex theaters with up to 12 screens. The decline in drive-ins is a result of the growing value of real estate and rising property taxes as well as the limited number of films available for showing on an increasing number of indoor screens.

California, still the world capital of motion-picture production, notwithstanding the proliferating level of runaway filming, is also the world champion in moviegoing, with the number of screens per state as the measurement. It is far out in front, with Texas in second place, followed by New York, Florida, Ohio, and Pennsylvania.

The average number of full- and part-time employees in the industry in 1983 was 218,000, up from the 214,000 registered in 1982. But it was down from the 220,000 in 1979, 1980, and 1981 and up only slightly from the 192,000 in 1960. In fact, unemployment in the motion-picture industry is at an all-time high.

The nature of the motion-picture audience has changed considerably over the past 20 years. What was primarily an adult audience has now become a youth audience. Almost 70 percent of the motion-picture audience is under 30 years of age, and 85 percent of the total annual admissions are generated by moviegoers under 40.

Some 60 percent of American moviegoers attend a neighborhood theater; 65 percent prefer single features to double bills; 80 percent consider the subject matter of a film important in deciding what to see; 30 percent consider the actors in a film important in deciding what to see; 70 percent prefer American films to foreign films; 83 percent prefer color films to black-and-white films; 39 percent are influenced by movie critics; 47 percent of drive-in admissions are from the suburban market; and 87.5 percent of moviegoers are aware of the MPAA ratings.

Even though greatly diminished as a mass medium, motion pictures continue to maintain a strong and vigorous presence in the mass communication system of the United States. Admissions to motion-picture theaters in 1985 accounted for over 45 percent of the spectators' total expenditures for amusement (compared with 82 percent in 1946). The total number of moviegoers was 120 million in 1985, with total admissions over 1 billion. The difference, of course, is caused by frequent moviegoers, who represent 37 percent of all moviegoers aged 12 and up and account for 84 percent of admissions.

THE STRUCTURE AND ORGANIZATION OF THE MOTION-PICTURE INDUSTRY

The film industry is divided into three major parts: (1) production—the making of films; (2) distribution—the supplying of films to markets; and (3) exhibition—the displaying of films to the public. In the past, all three functions were performed by one company. But, as noted earlier, in the late 1940s, the Supreme Court ruled that the practice of vertical integration (control of production, distribution, and exhibition by one company) re-strained free trade. Today, most companies only produce and distribute films; exhibition is controlled by individual theaters or by chains.

Production

The making of films is a complex operation that involves the talents of many people, including directors, cinematographers, producers, editors, lighting and sound crews, designers, musicians, costumers, make-up crews, choreographers, and actors. The size of a film crew is one of the key reasons that production budgets are high.

In recent years, the industry's unions, long one of the prime contribu-tors to exorbitant production costs, have relaxed some of their require-ments to allow skeletal crews and lower minimum wages for low-budget films. This shift in policy was forced on the unions by economic conditions. If Hollywood was to survive, labor costs had to be reduced. Still, personnel costs account for well over 50 percent of an average feature film's produc-tion budget, and for major features, unions are a major cost element. As Timothy Noah, writing in the *Washington Monthly,* observed:

> What is most distinctive about Hollywood's unions is the sheer number of locals and, consequently, work rules.
>
> The proliferation of unions complicates work arrangements in two ways. The first is that each local demands minimum staffing levels. For example, Local 659, the cameramen's union, tells producers that they must hire for each film a director of photography, a camera operator, a first assistant photographer and a still photographer. (The presence of the latter is required for taking publicity shots, even though the studios use much fewer of these than they used to.) In a pinch, all of these functions can be performed by one person. In non-union features, they often are. But if a producer is to honor the IATSE [International Alliance of Theatri-cal Stage Employees] agreement—and he must if he shoots at a major studio—then he must hire all four.
>
> The second problem is that once all these people are present on the set, they must not be permitted to seem superfluous. Thus it is a violation of the IATSE agreement to allow, say, a production assistant to move a stool three feet; he instead must ask a grip to move it for him. The IATSE agreement also defends turf lines among various locals. A grip, for exam-ple, may not move a lamp used to light the set; that job is performed by the "gaffer," the stagehand responsible for lighting. This past summer the producers negotiated an agreement to make these jurisdictional lines more flexible.
>
> Needless to say, this thick web of work rules drives up costs. So do various work rules that apply to all IATSE locals—for example, a provi-sion that says all overseas air travel must be first class. Finally, there are the wage rates. These can be hard to estimate, owing to elaborate provi-sions for "overtime," "night premiums," and "golden time" (a special overtime rate for long workdays that can be up to five times the normal rate), but the average basic rate for blue-collar workers—without any

extras—is $16 an hour. As assistant property master hired on a weekly basis starts out with a guarantee of $1,050. In other words, the *minimum* wage rate, even before you figure in bonuses, comes out to the yearly equivalent of more than $54,000.[2]

Because of rising personnel costs, filmmakers have been forced to cut back their nonproduction expenses. In the 1940s, almost 40 percent of a film's budget went to cover studio overhead, which involved the upkeep of the back lots and equipment and an extensive bureaucracy of production and nonproduction personnel. Today, a typical independent production company's permanent staff consists of a small secretarial pool, a good accountant, and the producer. Studio overhead currently accounts for barely 20 percent of production costs.

The heart of the motion-picture business in the 1980s lies beyond the studio gates. More and more films are being shot on location in the United States and Europe rather than on Hollywood back lots. In fact, few such back lots exist, with most being part working lot, part tourist attraction, such as at Universal Studios. In 1980, 60 percent of all American feature films were made in the United States. In 1985, the number dropped to 49 percent. With the advent of portable equipment, location shooting is much easier and less expensive than in the past. For most films, the sound stage has become unnecessary, especially since the development of the Cinemobile Mark IV in the 1960s. This studio-bus contains dressing rooms, bathrooms, space for a large crew, and a full complement of lightweight equipment.

The key word today in film production is *conglomerate.* Currently, six major film studios account for over 75 percent of all American films. On the surface, this does not seem to be any different from the production patterns of the 1930s and 1940s, but there is a basic change in the production structure of the major studios. These studios are now primarily financing and distributing agencies; the actual production is done by hundreds of individual corporations that are put together or packaged specifically for one film.

Much of this change took place in the late 1960s, when such non-Establishment filmmakers as John Cassavetes, Andy Warhol, Dennis Hopper, Peter Bogdanovich, and Francis Ford Coppola proved to Hollywood that magical names on the marquee were not necessary for success. With 75 percent of box-office revenue coming from an audience under the age of 30, it was the independent talent, often young itself, that was succeeding. As these filmmakers succeeded, they began to achieve financial independence. Directors such as Coppola, Robert Altman, Martin Scorsese, Steven Spielberg, and George Lucas formed their own production companies, and the studios became the bank and the distribution system. Because of indi-

---

[2] *Washington Monthly,* October 1985, 14. Reprinted with permission from *The Washington Monthly.* Copyright by THE WASHINGTON MONTHLY CO., Washington, D.C.

vidual successes, such as Michael Cimino's *Deer Hunter* (1979), many directors persuaded the studios to allow them almost total artistic and budgetary control. With Cimino's $30 million disaster *Heaven's Gate,* however, *accountability* once again became a key word. Ultimately, filmmakers who do not make money do not make films, as Peter Bogdanovich so successfully demonstrated. The studios, with their moguls, have been replaced by corporate presidents and boards of directors. Despite many industry people's feelings about such men as Harry Cohn, Jack Warner, and L. B. Mayer, not everyone agrees that growth of the conglomerate is a positive trend. As Will Tusher wrote in *Variety:*

> The more conglomerates take over, the more likely that Hollywood will rely increasingly on audience and marketing research, less on instinct or taste. A new takeover-era corporate conceit appears to be taking hold— the notion that high tech readings of the public pulse make it possible to know what the public wants.
>
> Corporate takeovers and consolidations dominated the motion picture industry during 1985.
>
> In a general climate of seemingly *laissez-faire* policy by the government towards business combinations, many entertainment companies were engaged in vertical and/or horizontal integration or expansion of their divisions.
>
> This contrasted with the era of the 1960s when large conglomerates bought up several film companies to become relatively small cogs in their corporate rosters: Avco Financial Services buying Embassy Pictures; Gulf & Western buying Paramount Pictures; Transamerica purchasing United Artists and Kinney buying Warner Brothers/7 Arts.
>
> In each case, the acquired motion picture company was in a different line of business than the new parent outfit.
>
> Another round of takeovers began in 1981–82 with oilman Marvin Davis buying 20th Century Fox and taking the company private; MGM buying UA from Transamerica; Coca-Cola Co. buying Columbia Pictures Industries; Orion buying Filmways (which earlier had swallowed up American Intl. Pictures); and from TV, Norman Lear and Jerry Perenchio purchasing Embassy from Avco.
>
> During 1985, major takeovers and mergers involved entertainment companies consolidating or expanding their interests. Transplanted Aussie media baron Rupert Murdoch bought out Marvin Davis' interest in 20th Century Fox. Ted Turner and his Turner Broadcasting System sealed an agreement to buy MGM/UA for $1.5 billion and in turn resold a revamped version of United Artists. The new entities MGM and UA would continue to run the distribution company MGM/UA as a joint venture.
>
> Coca-Cola purchased Embassy Communications. It promptly sold off the Embassy library and film distribution arm to Dino De Laurentis, who renamed it Dino De Laurentis Entertainment Group and disclosed plans to enter domestic theatrical distribution personally with a full slate of 1986 releases.
>
> Other horizontal expansions included Columbia merging into itself the

Walter Reade exhibition chain (to remain an autonomous unit of the parent company), making it the first of the U.S. majors to move in this direction since the Dept. of Justice had signalled in 1981 that it was reviewing the 1948 Paramount Consent Decrees divorcing distribution from exhibition for the larger companies. Columbia is not a party to the original consent decrees.

However, the Department of Justice said it would not seek to modify or terminate the consent decrees after all.[3]

This trend has given rise to new financial arrangements in which stars and directors take a percentage of a film's potential profit rather than a high salary, making them partners in a collaborative enterprise. Of course, only major stars can command such a contract.

Today, the package rules American filmmaking. The package rather than the idea is the key to getting a film made. The idea is a starting point, but preferably it should be presold to the widest possible audience. The idea should have a director, screen writer, and star who have solid track records; and if a successful marketing plan can be developed for the idea, the film may receive the necessary financial backing. *Grease* (1978) is a perfect example of the packaged product: it was presold through a record-breaking Broadway run, starred hot box-office draws Olivia Newton-John and John Travolta, appealed to a broad audience, and was marketed through a nationwide media advertising campaign that cost over $5 million.

Distribution

As indicated, the primary distributors of motion pictures are the major studios, which traditionally produced films. Most independent producers release their films through one of these established studios in two major markets, foreign and domestic.

The foreign market is important because it can account for over 40 percent of the annual revenue for many American films. In a great many nations of the world, American films dominate both the exhibition schedule and the box-office receipts. The popularity of American films is so great that most European nations limit the number of weeks that these films may be shown in local theaters. Rights to American films shown abroad are normally retained by the parent company. This contrasts with the practice of foreign film producers, who sell American distribution rights to their films.

Domestic distribution of films involves the normal channels that are used to move any product from producer to consumer. Six major studios dominate film distribution in the United States: Columbia, MGM/United Artists, Warner Brothers, 20th Century–Fox, Paramount, and Universal. A

---

[3] *Variety*, 8 January 1986, 6.

group of minor studios is also important, especially in the distribution of low-budget independent films. These include Embassy, Filmways, Cinerama, Allied Artists, and National General. The majors and minors account for 80 to 90 percent of annual film revenue in the United States.

Film-distribution operations involve the booking of films into theaters. Licenses between the distributor and the exhibitor include both price and nonprice agreements. The process of block booking—requiring theaters to buy groups of films rather than individual films—has been outlawed, and so every film is leased separately.

Local theater owners bid competitively for films. This usually involves a specific guaranteed minimum against a percentage of the gross receipts. For example, the theater owner pays an amount ($1,000 a week) or a percentage of the gross receipts (60 percent of one week's ticket sales), whichever is higher. This procedure saves the exhibitor from losing too badly if the film is a flop and helps the distributor if the film is a major success.

In the motion-picture business in the 1980s, the distributors are still the major risk takers because distributors are the prime borrower of funds to produce films. They finance or provide the collateral for 9 of every 10 films. If the cost of the movie exceeds production estimates, the distributors provide the necessary capital to complete it. Because of this, the distributors receive their return before the producers do. One-third of the distribution gross (total receipts minus the exhibitors' share) is retained to cover distribution costs; the remainder goes to the bank to retire the standard two-year loan. Before the producer earns any sizable sum, the film must earn roughly 2.5 times its production costs. Thus a film like Cimino's *Heaven's Gate,* with a cost of approximately $30 million, would have to earn over $75 million before the producer realized any profit. In effect, interest and distribution costs of a film run about 150 percent of the production costs. Marketing costs in film are among the highest—if not *the* highest—for any major consumer product. The risk in film is increased by the fact that the economic life of a film is extremely short; for most motion pictures, about 25 weeks account for two-thirds of the total gross revenue. Maximum gross in the shortest time is a critical aspect of film distribution.

Exhibition

The local theaters and drive-ins are the final link in the structure of the motion-picture industry. As with production and distribution, concentration of ownership is dominant. More than 50 percent of the theaters in the United States are owned by 700 theater chains. Some 70 percent of an average film's gross revenue comes from 1,000 key theaters. These bookings in major population areas mean the difference between financial success or failure for a film. The larger theaters (over 400 seats) account for 80 percent of the total dollar volume of most features. Nine of every 10 large houses are owned by the theater chains; the largest chain, ABC-Paramount, owns more than 500 theaters, most of which are in metropolitan areas.

Films are exhibited in either roadshow, popular-release, or four-walling patterns. Roadshow is used for only blockbuster films, such as *E.T.*, *The Empire Strikes Back*, and *Return of the Jedi*. It requires a large marketing investment and must have a good long-run potential. Tickets are usually sold at only one theater per market. If the film does not do well in this hard-ticket exhibition, it is immediately changed to popular release, in which the film is booked in as many theaters as possible. The trend today is away from roadshow exclusive releases and toward limited popular release and, in most instances, saturation booking. Several years ago, studios typically released their movies to 900 theaters across the country. But when revenues declined, they adopted a new strategy, "bursting," under which films are distributed to more theaters (1,200) for shorter periods of time. With marketing costs for a new film having jumped from $4 million to nearly $10 million since 1978, studios want to ensure a high return. One consequence of this saturation exposure has been the slow strangulation of second-run and drive-in theaters.

A more recent trend in exhibition patterns is four-walling, whereby the film's producer by-passes normal distribution channels and contracts directly with the local theater owner. For low-budget, limited-audience-appeal films, this is a popular method because the money usually given to the distributor is put into local advertising.

Success in film exhibition depends on a number of factors, including trade advertising, word of mouth, critical reviews, the weather, local publicity, previous box-office receipts, the season of the year, the number and quality of competing films in the area, the content of the film, and the film's rating by the code of authority. Thus the predictability of a film's success is difficult to assess until the film is released for public appraisal, and the exhibitor often assumes great risk. As Marvin Goldman, president of K-B Theatres in Washington, D.C., explained in *Variety*: "The business has gone from a buyer's market in the '40s and '50s to a seller's market today. Then, on the biggest film, the exhibitor, or movie theater owner, paid the distribution company 50 percent of the gross over a certain time period, and the average movie called for 30 to 35 percent."[4] Today, with approximately 100 movies being made each year—compared with 500 during the 1940s and 1950s—the companies can be choosy. And they command a large amount of money from theater owners to show their films.

In the mid-1970s, the studios inserted the "90–10" clause in most contracts involving the exhibitors' leasing of films. Under the clause, if a theater realizes gross revenue of $10,000 during the first week a movie is shown, an agreed-on deduction of $4,000 is retained by the theater to cover

---

[4] *Variety*, 8 January 1986, 79.

house expenses. Of the remaining $6,000, the movie company gets 90 percent, or $5,400, and the theater receives only $600.

The industry later instituted the "70-floor" clause, which guarantees at least 70 percent of the house's weekly gross. The film company has a choice of that arrangement or the 90–10, whichever offers more money. Using the same $10,000 example, the distributor would choose 70 percent, or $7,000 of the $10,000 gross. "Ninety-five percent of the movies we buy today—and that applies to every studio—have one or the other clause in effect," says Goldman.[5]

When it comes to bidding for a new picture, the distribution companies also have the upper hand. Only 23 states do not permit the practice of blind bidding. As the term implies, under this system, a theater owner must bid for, and subsequently lease, a film without first seeing it. In the 1960s, less than 10 percent of the films offered were the result of blind bidding. In the late 1970s, the percentage rose to 85.

THE CHARACTERISTICS AND ROLES OF THE MOTION PICTURE

The role and function of motion pictures has changed greatly in the past 30 years. Once a major source of recreation, motion pictures now serve as a primary source of content for another medium—television. Before the advent of videotape recording in the mid-1950s, TV reruns were possible only when theatrical films were used or when filmed kinescopes were made of a live performance. In the early 1970s, most dramas shown on the networks in the evening were filmed. Feature films made up an important block of network schedules, with all three networks running multiple "nights at the movies" and "movies of the week." Today, motion pictures are made with not just one eye, but with both eyes clearly focused on television or video as a source of income.

Newer movie theaters in the United States reflect the changes taking place in our society. They are often twin theaters or multicinemas with 200 to 500 seats per theater and are located in peripheral shopping centers or malls; the theaters are leased rather than owned. A new theater often seeks identification with the shopping area, has few parking problems, gains maximum traffic and exposure, and does not face inner-city problems. The multitheater operates with one lobby, one concession stand, and one projection booth to cut costs. Important movies can be run in both theaters, or the theaters can cater to two audiences by showing different films. A key trend in contemporary exhibition patterns is that concessions account for over one-half of the revenue in most theaters. The average mark-up for popcorn, soda, and candy is 600, 175, and 100 percent, respectively. Thus

---

[5] Ibid.

Figure 5.22. Multiplex theaters are often located in or near suburban shopping malls. By combining (in this case) 10 screens under one operating umbrella, the exhibitor achieves maximum cost efficiency for overhead. (Photo: Brendan Beirne.)

theaters can still make money by charging $1.50 for "twilight" screenings, as long as they charge $2.50 for the popcorn.

Audiences go to a movie rather than to *the movies*. Nevertheless, despite increased competition from television, motion pictures hold a unique position in American leisure patterns. Many singular elements make the motion picture attractive. The film experience is of a high technical quality that stimulates strong involvement. The picture is a large, high-definition, colored visual image. The sound is also of high quality. The theater is designed to encapsulate the viewer: it is dark; the chairs are comfortable; there are relatively few interruptions; and food is available. Every aspect of filmgoing is designed to heighten the impact of film experiences and to create viewer involvement.

The motion picture is perhaps the most international of the media. The primarily visual symbol system and easily dubbed sound of the motion picture make the entire world a film marketplace. Film has become a selective medium that caters to the tastes of an audience that is young, is relatively undiscriminating, and was brought up on television. The industry is youth oriented, and contemporary film themes reflect this audience's ambitions and tastes.

In summary, motion pictures have changed greatly over their relatively short history. But they still function as they always have, providing entertainment to a large number of people in a unique and involving way.

SUMMARY

The place of motion pictures in contemporary society, although diminished, remains strong. The motion-picture medium has experienced significant change in its almost 100-year history.

The development of motion pictures can be divided into several periods. From 1824 to 1896, the many discoveries, inventions, and theories demonstrated a continuing fascination with reproducing motion. This period of intense experimentation culminated, in the late 1880s, in Thomas Edison's invention of a motion-picture camera. During the period from 1896 to 1918, the first subject matter of motion pictures was developed, the first artists began to experiment with the medium, and D. W. Griffith emerged as a pioneer of the motion-picture art. An industry developed to produce, distribute, and exhibit motion pictures.

From 1919 to 1929, intense artistic and creative experimentation occurred in Russia, France, and Germany, resulting in significant films and movements that affected the course of motion-picture history. Concurrent with this international movement was development in the United States, primarily in Hollywood in the 1920s. During those years, the American film industry became firmly established and American film forms—particularly the feature-length comedy, the Western, and the comedy of manners—began to emerge as dominant genres.

The next significant period in motion-picture history occurred with the arrival of sound. From 1927 to 1930, the motion-picture industry underwent a great upheaval—sound film quickly and permanently replaced silent film, resulting in a significant impact on content, individuals, and the industry.

The golden age of Hollywood—1930 to 1946—was a period of intense industrial and creative development in American film, characterized primarily by the work of seven major studios and the artists working for them. World War II did little to diminish the structure of the industry, as Hollywood entertained audiences, both military and civilian, with great success. Following World War II, the American film industry went into a period of decline. This decline, from 1946 to 1962, was significant and resulted primarily from four events that forced changes in the traditional Hollywood structure: (1) the rise of television, (2) the hearings before the House Un-American Activities Committee, (3) the Supreme Court "divorcement" ruling, and (4) the emergence of a vigorous international film movement. By the early 1960s, the American film industry was experiencing significant declines in admissions, the number of films produced, and the number of theaters.

Following this period there emerged, both in America and internationally, a strong film revolution. From 1963 to 1975, films began to express the needs of a changing society, a society in which relevance, awareness, and freedom of expression became watchwords. Motion pictures were no longer a product to be consumed passively by a mass audience; they became vehicles by which creative artists could experiment and communicate messages of depth and intensity. The most recent period of film history, from 1976 to the present, is identified primarily by industrial merger and creative conformity. Films have become more expensive to produce and the corporate structure of the film industry has been collapsing; film companies have been absorbed by other corporations. The creative ferment of the 1960s and early 1970s began to fade. The last ten years have been characterized primarily by fewer films with bigger budgets and an emphasis on creating financial success through creative conformity.

The scope of motion pictures, although diminished, continues to be significant. The motion picture remains a primary recreational outlet. Despite declining admissions in the mid-1980s, box-office receipts have risen dramatically, primarily because of ticket price increases. Fewer feature films are produced than ever before and the average cost per feature has risen to over $16 million. California, specifically Hollywood, remains the capital of motion-picture production. The American film audience has changed considerably, with almost 70 percent of the audience under 30 years of age.

The motion-picture industry is divided into three major parts: (1) production—the making of films; (2) distribution—the supplying of films to markets; and (3) exhibition—the displaying of films to the public. The organization of these three aspects of the industry has changed considerably in the past 30 years. Originally, all three occurred within one company, but now production, exhibition, and distribution are handled by a variety of industrial units.

The motion picture today has several characteristics and roles, which have changed considerably over the past 30 years. Once a major source of recreation in themselves, motion pictures now serve as the primary source of content for another medium—television. But despite increased competition from television, motion pictures continue to hold a unique place in American leisure patterns. Films have high technical quality that demand strong involvement. The motion picture remains the most international of mass media. It is a selective medium, catering to the tastes of a young audience, and contemporary film themes clearly reflect this audience's ambitions and tastes.

BIBLIOGRAPHY

Balio, Tino, ed. *The American Film Industry.* Madison: University of Wisconsin Press, 1976.

Bohn, Thomas, and Richard Stromgren. *Light and Shadows: A History of Motion Pictures.* 3d ed. Palo Alto, Calif.: Mayfield, 1986.

Bordwell, David, Janet Staiger, and Kristin Thompson. *The Classical Hollywood Cinema: Film Style and Mode of Production.* New York: Columbia University Press, 1985.

Brownlow, Kevin. *The Parades Gone By.* New York: Knopf, 1968.

Cook, David. *A History of Narrative Film.* New York: Norton, 1981.

Ellis, Jack, Charles Derry, and Sharon Kern. *The Film Book Bibliography, 1940–1975.* Metuchen, N.J.: Scarecrow Press, 1979.

Everson, William K. *American Silent Film.* New York: Oxford University Press, 1978.

Jacobs, Lewis. *The Documentary Tradition.* 2d ed. New York: Norton, 1979.

Jowett, Garth, and James M. Linton. *Movies as Mass Communication.* Beverly Hills, Calif., and London: Sage, 1980.

Kerr, Walter. *The Silent Clowns.* New York: Knopf, 1975.

Lloyd, Ann. *Movies of the Sixties.* London: Orbis, 1983.

Mast, Gerald. *A Short History of the Movies*. 4th ed. Indianapolis: Bobbs-Merrill, 1984.

Monaco, James. *American Film Now: The People, Power, Money, Movies*. New York: Oxford University Press, 1979.

Perkins, V. F. *Film as Film*. New York: Pelican/Penguin, 1972.

Salt, Barry. *Film Style and Technology: History and Analysis*. London: Starward, 1983.

Sklar, Robert. *Movie Made America*. New York: Random House, 1975.

Stephenson, Ralph, and J. R. Debrix. *The Cinema as Art*. London: Penguin, 1969.

6

Radio

See You on the Radio[1]

See you on the radio . . . I say that every week.
A peculiar phrase, some people think, for anyone to speak.
I've got a piece of mail or two, up on my office shelf.
Complaining that the sentence seems to contradict itself.
"Dear Mr. Osgood," someone wrote, "That sign off is absurd.
Radio is for the ear . . . the song or spoken word.
The medium for seeing is, without a doubt, TV.
We therefore call it 'video.' That's Latin for 'I see.'
So please don't say that any more. You really should know better."
That's a gentle paraphrase of what was in this viewer's letter.

"Dear Sir," I then wrote back to him, and this was my reply:
I do believe that you are wrong, and let me tell you why.
I've worked some years in radio, and television, too.
And though it's paradoxical it nonetheless is true

That radio is visual, much more so than TV.
And there's plenty of good reason why that paradox should be.
You insist that on the radio there are no pictures there.
You say it's only for the ear . . . but I say "au contraire."
There are fascinating pictures on the radio you see
That are far more picturesque than any pictures on TV.

---

[1] Speech by Charles Osgood (CBS News, CBS Radio Network), NAB Convention, 1984.

No television set that's made, no screen that you can find,
Can compare with that of radio: the theatre of the mind.
Where the pictures are so vivid, so spectacular and real,
That there isn't any contest, or at least that's how I feel.
The colors are more colorful, the reds and greens and blues
Are more vivid yet more subtle than television's hues.
The dimensions of the radio are truly to be treasured
Infinite the size of screen diagonally measured,
With resolution so acute TV cannot compare.
We can whisper in the listener's ear and take him *anywhere*.
And you tell me that I cannot see the audience I touch?
Let me tell you now a secret . . . my experience is such
That although the room I work in may be very plain and small . . .
In a way that's quite miraculous, it isn't small at all.
I am there inside the radio, the one beside the bed.
And its me you hear when it goes off . . . come on now sleepy-
     head.
I can see you in the morning . . . I can see you coast to coast
As you sip your glass of orange juice and bite into your toast.
I am with you as you brush your teeth and as you shave your face.
You may think you are alone but I am with you everyplace.
And I see the lines of traffic stretching endlessly for miles.
Not a hundred or a thousand miles . . . A million there must be.
And I'm riding along with them. This is radio you see.
And I'm on the Jersey Turnpike, on the throughway and the Hutch,
And the Eisenhower expressway helping people keep in touch,
And the California freeways and the Houston traffic funnel.
I may lose you for a little while as you go through the tunnel.
But suddenly I'm there again, some episode to tell,
To nobody's surprise, because they know me very well.
For my voice is with them every day, and when it disappears,
They know it comes right back again, it's been that way for years.
I've been riding with them every day for such a long, long time
They are willing to put up with me when I resort to rhyme.
And that may be the ultimate and quintessential test
That proves beyond the slightest doubt that radio is best.
A friend will always stick with you . . . though your poems may
     not scan.
I'll see you on the radio . . . I can, you see, I can.

There are now over 8,300 radio stations. FM radio has grown from an experimental toy into the dominant programming vehicle in contemporary radio. Radios are in 99 percent of American homes and 95 percent of American cars. The average household has 5.5 radio sets, and persons 12 years old and over spend more than 3 hours daily listening to the radio.

Radio is a flexible, adaptable, individual, personal medium. Although it functions primarily as a medium for playing recorded music, it is as dynamic and popular as it was 30 years ago. Radio experienced one golden age, but unlike most mass media, it grew and changed to experience another. How it got to that point is the subject of history, and it is with the history of radio that we begin.

HISTORICAL PERSPECTIVE

Early History: 1840–1919

Radio developed out of scientific advances made in the fields of electricity and magnetism. The first transmission of an electromagnetic message over wire was made in 1844 by Samuel F. B. Morse, and by 1861, a transcontinental, high-speed, electric communication system was signaling coded messages across the United States. The first transatlantic cable was laid in 1858, and by 1870, a web of underseas cables linked the Western world and its economic outposts. The replacement of Morse code with voice transmission occurred in 1876, when Alexander Graham Bell used undulations in electric current to produce vocal communication by wire. The telephone's ability to code, transport, and decode voice transmissions personalized electric communication in a way that was impossible with the telegraph.

During the same period that the telegraph and the telephone were demonstrating and perfecting long-distance communication by wire, James Clerk Maxwell predicted (1864) and Heinrich Hertz demonstrated (1887) that variations in electric current produce waves that can be transmitted through space *without wires* at the speed of light. These theories stimulated much experimentation, the most successful being Guglielmo Marconi's work in the late 1890s. Marconi received a patent for his wireless telegraph in 1897 and by 1901 was sending wireless dot–dash transmissions across the Atlantic. Through the work of such men as Reginald Fessenden and Lee De Forest, high-quality wireless voice communication carried by electromagnetic waves became possible, thus setting the stage for radio broadcasting.

Radio broadcasting required more than technology, however. Two individuals talking back and forth is not broadcasting. The intellectual retooling needed to transform radio *telephoning* into radio *broadcasting* had to wait until people thought in terms of one person talking to a mass audience.

From 1910 to the outbreak of World War I, radio amateurs brought new sounds to the night as they chattered to one another from their basements and attics. It was a time of neighborhood experimenters who pieced together radio sender-receivers in order to carry on conversations with others of the same inclination.

During this period, the U.S. government passed two major laws con-

Figure 6.1. *Guglielmo Marconi in 1896, at the age of 22, seated behind his first wireless receiver. (Photo: 1895, The Bettman Archive, Inc.)*

cerning the use of radio. The first was the U.S. Wireless Ship Act of 1910, which required all passenger ships to carry radio-transmission equipment. The second was the Radio Act of 1912, which required all radio operators to be licensed by the Secretary of Commerce. The 1912 act was the first comprehensive attempt to regulate all phases of radio communication. When the United States entered World War I in 1917, the federal government took over all radio operations, and the medium marked time until the end of the war.

Nevertheless, the stage was set for the development of broadcasting. Public and industrial appetites were whetted. One of the visionaries of the medium was a young man named David Sarnoff. In 1916, he wrote a memo to his boss at American Marconi proposing a new use for radio.

> I have in mind a plan of development which would make radio a ''household utility'' in the same sense as the piano or phonograph. The idea is to bring music into the house by wireless. . . . The receiver can be designed in the form of a simple ''Radio Music Box'' and arranged for several different wave lengths.[2]

Sarnoff's foresight would eventually result in his emergence as president

---

[2] Quoted in Archer Gleason, *History of Radio to 1926* (New York: American Historical Society, 1938), 85.

Figure 6.2. Coverage of the returns of the presidential contest between Harding and Cox on November 2, 1920, by KDKA in Pittsburgh gave birth to modern broadcasting. (Photo: Courtesy of Westinghouse Broadcasting and Cable, Inc.)

of the Radio Corporation of America (RCA) and one of the most powerful leaders in broadcasting.

The Formation of the American Radio System: 1920–1928

After World War I ended, an organized attempt was made to develop radio broadcasting as opposed to point-to-point communication. With fewer than 1,000 radio sets in the entire nation, regular radio programming began with the broadcast of the returns of the 1920 presidential election (Warren G. Harding versus James M. Cox) over KDKA in Pittsburgh on November 2, 1920. Almost overnight, hundreds of stations were started and began to broadcast music, sports, drama, and vaudeville. By the end of 1922, almost 600 stations had been licensed. By 1923, over 1 million people were listening to programs broadcast from concert halls, theaters, and athletic fields.

As programming expanded, the public bought more radio sets. Additional hours of programming became available, and audiences grew more discriminating. Listeners' tastes soon forced broadcasters to provide a greater variety of entertainment.

As the broadcast industry developed, the revenue from the sale of

Figure 6.3. A radio broadcasting studio of the early 1920s. Hanging drapes on the ceiling and walls and placing a carpet on the floor were attempts to "deaden" the studio and reduce voice and music echoes. (Photo: The Bettman Archive, Inc.)

radio sets proved insufficient to support radio's mass-entertainment and information services. A new method had to be found to pay radio's bills. To solve this problem, two developments occurred: radio stations were linked into networks so that the increased cost of expanded programming could be shared by several stations; and merchants were asked to support the system by advertising their goods and services on the stations. The American Telephone and Telegraph Company (AT&T) and set manufacturers formed a network in 1923 to provide expanded program-distribution service. AT&T withdrew from program distribution in 1926, and a new corporate giant, RCA, took over. Formed in 1919 as a sales outlet for radio manufacturers, RCA soon became the dominant force in broadcasting. Following AT&T's departure, RCA immediately consolidated its position and formed the National Broadcasting Company (NBC). In 1927, William S. Paley formed the Columbia Broadcasting System (CBS), and network broadcasting was off and running.

With radio becoming big business, something had to be done about the chaotic state of signal transmission so that broadcasting could more efficiently serve the public and economic interests. In 1926, a series of court cases ruled that Secretary of Commerce Herbert Hoover did not have legal jurisdiction under the Radio Act of 1912 to regulate broadcasting. As more and more stations went on the air, they began to interfere with one another's signals. It was obvious that legislative action was needed if broadcasting was to survive.

The basic problem was that broadcast media are physically limited by the number of channels or spaces available in the radio spectrum. The Berlin Conference (1903) and the Havana Treaty (1925) established international rules for using radio frequencies, but internal domestic use of the allocated channels was left to individual governments. A growing awareness that the airwaves were a natural resource that belonged to the public also began to affect the legal decision-making process.

Congress passed the Radio Act of 1927, which created the temporary Federal Radio Commission (FRC) to straighten out the radio mess. The FRC was made permanent in 1929. Congress then passed the Federal Communications Act of 1934, which expanded and clarified the 1927 act and established the Federal Communications Commission (FCC) to regulate telephone, telegraph, and radio communication systems, in the public's interest, convenience, and necessity. This act remains in effect, modified, of course, by prevailing political, social, and economic conditions.

The Golden Age of Network Radio: 1929–1945

With its technical problems solved, radio was free to grow almost unrestricted. By the late 1920s, the medium had achieved a high degree of program sophistication and financial stability and was on the verge of entering a new stage of development. One of the major areas of growth was broadcast advertising. The increased economic stability provided by advertising set the stage for the advent of the golden age of network radio.

During the first half of the 1930s, a number of new types of radio programs evolved. Network programs drew increasingly large audiences as living rooms became the entertainment centers of a nation locked in the squeeze of the Great Depression. Despite the economic crisis, advertising revenue increased during this period, rising from over $25 million in 1930 to more than $70 million in 1940.

Indeed, the network economic picture was so good in 1934 that a fourth radio network, the Mutual Broadcasting System (MBS), was formed to challenge NBC-Red, NBC-Blue, and CBS. (NBC-Red and NBC-Blue were two separate systems, each with its own affiliates. Legend has it that their names derived from the color of the string that was used to map out the two systems.) By 1935, MBS had 60 affiliates competing with the 80 to 120 affiliates of the other networks. As network competition intensified and program costs increased, broadcasters needed to know more about the size of their audience. By 1935, a number of research organizations were providing data on the size and composition of radio audiences. With more than 22 million American radio homes, programming successes became advertising bonanzas.

The second half of the 1930s was a time of refining and polishing established formats. The networks continued to dominate, especially in advertising revenue and program production. More than 50 percent of all radio advertising dollars went to the four national networks (compared with 1 percent today).

Two major legal actions also occurred at this time. In 1935, the American Bar Association, in Canon 35, ruled that at the discretion of the presiding judge, broadcast journalists could be prohibited from using radio equipment in courtrooms to cover trials. In 1941, the FCC's "Mayflower decision" forbade broadcasters to editorialize. These two actions reflected to some extent the media bias of society, which identified print as information media and radio (and later, television) as entertainment media. The Mayflower ruling was overturned later in the decade, and broadcasters may now editorialize, although few actually do so. There is also increased, but by no means universal, radio and TV coverage in courtrooms.

Of the 850 stations on the air in 1941, 700 were affiliated with one of the four major networks. Only three corporations made up the network oligopoly at that time, however, since NBC had both a Red and a Blue network. The Federal Communications Commission, recognizing the long-range consequences of the situation, forced NBC to sell one of its networks. NBC sold its Blue-network operation to a group that formed the American Broadcasting Company (ABC) in 1943.

World War II brought domestic production of radio equipment to a standstill. Despite the decline in the number of radio receivers during the war years, advertising revenue continued to climb. The public's demand for war information doubled the number of news programs in the first half of the war, but as war weariness set in, entertainment programs began to squeeze news out of time slots as Americans sought escape from reality.

Significant among the many program types of this period was radio drama. Produced live (the networks banned recordings until the late 1940s), the form flourished with such series as "The Mercury Theater of the Air" and "Columbia Workshop" and produced several memorable programs, including Orson Welles's famous 1938 Halloween presentation of "The War of the Worlds." In addition, playwrights such as Norman Corwin and Arch Obler wrote material specifically for radio.

The Decline of Radio: 1946–1959

When World War II ended, radio broadcasting quickly resumed its prewar pace. During this time, however, television viewing began its phenomenal rise to preeminence as America's major leisure-time activity. By 1948, television was here to stay, and the handwriting was on the economic wall.

Other changes were also taking place that would affect radio. The first

Figure 6.4. The broadcasting of the radio series "Gang Busters" illustrates how live radio drama was created. The entire cast gathered around one microphone while the sound-effects men fired safety pistols. (Photo: The Bettman Archive, Inc.)

change made FM frequencies available for commercial use, and by 1948, over 600 FM stations had been licensed. With the growth of television, however, FM was put on hold until 1958, when the number of FM stations again began to expand. The second change adjusted the distance required between AM stations to allow for multiple use of frequencies previously used by clear-channel stations (stations that operated on an exclusive "clear" frequency). As a result, when the four-year "freeze" on TV's growth was removed by the FCC in 1952, radio's economic situation was further strained by the fact that 3,000 stations were now competing for audiences and revenue. Network domination of radio ended because network programming lost its economic base as reduced audience size brought in fewer advertising dollars. Also, the networks were busy establishing themselves in TV programming, and radio was quickly moved to the back burner. By 1960, the last of the networks' major programming forms, the daytime soap opera, went off the air. The only major network programming innovation of the period was NBC's "Monitor" weekend service, which was basically a modification of the disc-jockey format for a national audience.

Local stations quickly moved into this vacuum, mostly out of necessity. Nevertheless, once the reality of having to provide local programming and still make money became appreciated, local-station programming rapidly developed, primarily around a disc jockey, a stack of records, and a skeletal news and sports operation. Total advertising revenue stumbled along from 1953 to 1960 as local salespeople attempted to make up the slack created by the continued slide of network revenue, which hit an all-time low of $35 million in 1960. Despite the network crash, additional AM stations plunged into the business, so that by 1960, 3,500 AM stations were on the air. More than 1,000 stations reportedly lost money from 1956 to 1960. The number of FM stations grew to almost 700, but they were used primarily as an auxiliary service that simulcast AM programming.

The Renaissance of Radio: Since 1960

Despite the extensive and swift decline in network radio, the 1960s were a period of great economic growth for radio. More than 150 million radios were sold at a retail value of $6 billion. Advertising revenue totaled more than $8 billion during the decade. Network radio stabilized, and revenue increased slowly.

FM radio grew at a phenomenal rate from fewer than 700 stations in 1960 to almost 2,500 in 1970. Currently, there are 5,106 FM stations on the air. There are many reasons for this growth. In 1961, the Federal Communications Commission permitted FM stereo broadcasting, and by the mid-1960s, more than 50 percent of all FM stations were stereo operations. In 1965, the FCC ruled that AM–FM combinations in cities of over 100,000 population could no longer duplicate more than 50 percent of either station's programming. This "50-50 ruling," as it was called, affected approximately 330 stations and greatly opened up the FM market. As a result, a wide variety of station formats appeared in the late 1960s. There were and are stations that broadcast nothing but classified ads, stations with programming for the blind, stations that play only "golden oldies," all-talk stations, and all-news stations. As the number of FM stations, receivers, and listeners increased, FM's financial status improved enormously. Today, advertising revenues for FM have greatly surpassed those for AM.

Since 1960, AM radio has grown, too, but more slowly than FM, partly because of a freeze on new AM license awards from 1962 to 1964 and from 1968 to 1973. As a result, the differences in AM and FM listenership have steadily diminished, and in the top 10 markets, the FM share of the radio audience has tripled, from 20 percent to almost 60 percent. The battle between AM and FM is more like a rout, with FM the winner. Table 6.1 shows the breakdown of listening preference according to age group.

Today, industry observers offhandedly discuss the likelihood of AM's "survival." However, technology is creating opportunities for AM radio.

TABLE 6.1 PREFERENCES OF LISTENERS ACCORDING TO AGE GROUP

Age	FM	AM
12–24	84%	16%
25–34	73%	27%
35–49	59%	41%
50+	44%	56%

More than 200 AM stations are now broadcasting in stereo. In addition, digital systems will offer even clearer signals to both AM and FM radio.

Network radio has made a slow but steady climb out of the abyss of the late 1950s. A major innovation occurred in 1968, when ABC Radio developed four separate radio services for affiliates. Recognizing that the audience for radio had become increasingly segmented by age group and life style, ABC offered radio stations both news and public-affairs features that were fine-tuned to particular audiences.

Currently four major networks—ABC, NBC, CBS, and Mutual—dominate the field. Leading the pack is ABC, with seven network services and over 1,800 affiliates. Each network offers multiple programming services, in effect creating internal multiple networks. In addition, hundreds of smaller networks—such as Satellite Music Network, CNN Radio, and Transtar—have come into existence. As Walter Sabo, vice president of ABC Radio Networks, said, "The key to success for any network is to provide stations with services they can't do themselves."[3] Network radio will continue to exist as long as it lives by this idea. Rather than *broad*cast, radio networks now *narrow*cast, linking specific audiences with programs that speak their "language."

In the mid-1950s, few people would have predicted even moderate success for radio. But, 30 years later, radio has emerged from the ashes of its golden age to assume a new identity as a tough hybrid capable of not only competing with television, but also, in many cases, surpassing it.

When we compare contemporary radio with radio 30 years ago, we see several major differences. Four such differences stand out:

1. *Organizational and Industrial Structure.* Radio has gone from a national-network system with a wide range of programs (most with national sponsors) to a local operation with limited, if any, network service.

---

[3] *Variety,* 8 January 1986, 196.

(Drawing by Ziegler; © 1983
The New Yorker Magazine,
Inc.)

2. *Style.* In terms of codes and style, radio has moved from narrative, linear, dramatically structured 15- to 30-minute "programs" to nonnarrative, nonlinear, 20-second to 3-minute content units.

3. *Content.* Thirty years ago, radio's content was made up of stories, including soap operas, situation comedies, mystery and surprise, Westerns, drama, and variety. Today, radio's content is primarily recorded music and disc-jockey talk.

4. *Function.* Radio has changed from an in-house, sit-down, immobile storyteller to a nonhome, mobile, take-with-you informer, entertainer, and companion.

THE SCOPE OF RADIO

A statistical profile of radio in the mid-1980s reveals a strong, vigorous, and dynamic medium that meets a wide variety of listener needs and interests. There are more stations on the air, more sets in use, and more listeners than ever before.

Statistics, however, reveal more than simply a profile of contemporary strength. They also provide a picture of remarkable transition over the past

30 years, from a national-network-dominated, prime-time medium that broadcast comedy, drama, and variety programs to a local, selective, highly personal medium that serves many listener needs.

Perhaps nowhere else is radio's growth and change more evident than in the size and composition of the basic media units, or stations. The number of radio stations has almost doubled in the past 20 years—from 5,495 to 9,824. Contributing most significantly to this unprecedented growth is the remarkable growth in FM stations. AM stations have increased by fewer than 700 in the past 20 years. However, FCC rulings regarding so-called clear-channel stations have provided room in the AM portion of the electromagnetic spectrum for more growth in the future.

The financial outlook for the radio industry is basically good, with a few noticeable exceptions. In 1985, radio advertising grew by 12 percent over 1984 and closed the year with more than $6.5 billion in sales. This marked three banner years in a row. Revenues broke down as follows:

1. Local: $4.9 billion (+11.7 percent)
2. Spot: $1.3 billion (+11.4 percent)
3. Network: $327 million (+13.6 percent)

Of the radio dollar, 1 cent comes from network, 22 cents from spot, and 77 cents from local. FM-station revenue continued to increase more rapidly than that for AM stations. However, one out of every three radio stations lost money in 1984, indicating some definite "holes" in the overall picture. Costs in radio break down as follows:

Technical	7 cents
Sales	23 cents
Programming	28 cents
General administrative	42 cents

As we noted at the beginning of this chapter, radio is a widespread medium. It is in 99 percent of all American households and 95 percent of all cars. Fifty-seven percent of adults have radios at work. There are an estimated 510 million radio sets in the United States.

Radio's weekly cumulative audience is 183 million, or 95 percent of the total United States population. Ninety-six percent of men 18 years of age and older listen every week, as do 93 percent of women 18 years of age and older and 100 percent of teen-agers 12 to 17 years old. However, the amount of time that people listen to radio continues to decline, from 3 hours and 4 minutes a day in 1985 to 2 hours and 58 minutes a day in 1986. Speculation on reasons for this decline (albeit, a small one) range from the popularity of cable TV and videocassettes to the increased number of women in the work force.

FM radio dominates most of this data. As Figure 6.5 dramatically

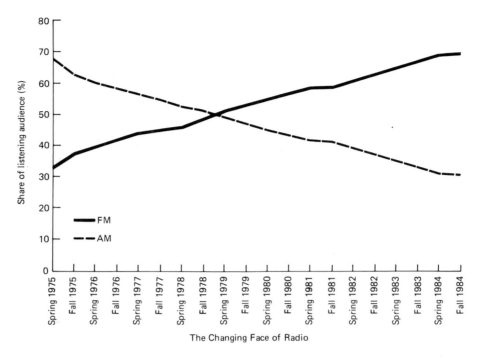

Figure 6.5. This graph dramatically shows the growth of FM radio and the decline of AM radio as measured by the share of the listening audience each received from 1975 to 1984.

illustrates, the world of radio has changed significantly over the past 10 years. FM radio's share of the audience is now 70 percent, with AM radio at its lowest listening level (29.4 percent) ever. On a weekly cumulative basis, AM radio reached 54.6 percent of the population in 1985, down from 57 percent in 1984. In contrast, FM radio reached almost 81 percent of the population. Of the approximately 3 hours a day spent listening to radio, 2 hours and 10 minutes are spent with FM and only 50 minutes with AM.

There are a wide variety of sounds, formats, and styles that make up contemporary radio programming. As our analysis of radio formats will indicate, the formats are fluid and rise and decline in popularity with almost volatile frequency.

In summary, a statistical profile of radio reveals a mass medium with a mass audience. Radio is local, however, rather than national in terms of stations, content, audience, and source of income. Radio-listening habits are personal, and stations program selectively to satisfy individual needs within a relatively homogeneous group. Above all, the data clearly demonstrate the health and strength of radio today as it has adjusted with remarkable speed and accuracy to meet the needs of a new audience in new times with new programming.

THE STRUCTURE AND ORGANIZATION OF RADIO

A variety of factors affect radio's structure and organization. The local radio station is the basic media unit responsible for almost all content, but several media service units are deeply involved in radio programming. The recording, or music, industry provides the majority of most stations' programming at little or no cost for the records, although stations are charged an annual fee for music rights by Broadcast Music, Inc. (BMI), and the American Society of Composers, Authors, and Publishers (ASCAP). Closely allied with the music that most stations play are syndication and format companies that supply a variety of program services, primarily play lists and specific musical formats or schedules. Networks provide a service of national news and features. The wire services (Associated Press and United Press International) provide the bulk of the news information for most stations.

Station organization varies greatly, depending on the size of the station, type of programming, size of the market, and amount of competition. At very large stations, specialized tasks and departments exist in the news, sales, and programming areas. At medium-size stations, announcers double as newspeople, salespeople, or engineers, as well as entertainers. At small stations, the program manager may also be the sales manager; there is often no news staff, and, usually, all announcers are licensed engineers.

New technology has had a revolutionary effect on radio, as it has had on every other form of contemporary life. Increasingly, stations are looking for ways to control costs and to program more effectively and efficiently. The use of satellites for program distribution, the rise of automated broadcast technology, and the widespread use of computers have added programming options and have improved stations' ability to improve operations and control costs. Approximately 15 percent of AM and 16 percent of FM stations are fully automated.

Radio stations are highly competitive, especially in big markets, and pay scales reflect this competitiveness and the size of the station's market. High salaries and specialized roles exist in only very large stations, however. The vast majority of people working for radio stations earn what at best can be termed modest salaries.

Kinds of Radio Stations

Technically, there are two kinds of radio stations: amplitude-modulation (AM) and frequency-modulation (FM). The standard bank of frequencies (535–1,605 kilocycles) is used for AM broadcasting, while FM broadcasting

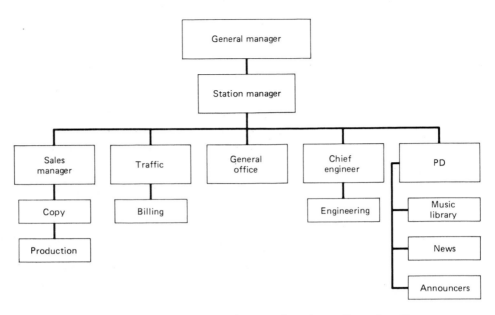

Figure 6.6. An organizational chart for a small-market radio station. (Source: Federal Communications Commission.)

occurs on frequencies between 88 and 108 megacycles (1,000 kilocycles equals 1 megacycle).

Because over 4,800 AM stations are licensed for broadcast on 107 channels, an intricate system of accommodation has been established based on three major variables: power, signal direction, and hours of operation. AM stations are divided into four classes within three channels:

1. Clear-channel stations operate on limited access frequencies, usually with 50,000 watts of power. These stations are designed to serve remote rural areas as well as large urban populations. There are 45 authorized clear channels, with one 50,000-watt station (Class I) and two to several dozen medium- and low-power stations (Class II) on each channel.
2. Regional channels that accommodate 30 to 50 stations (Class III), each with power ranging from 1,000 to 5,000 watts.
3. Local channels on which small stations operate with a maximum power of 1,000 watts during the day and 250 at night. There are six local frequencies, each used by 100 or more stations (Class IV).

To further lessen interference problems, most AM stations are required to direct their signal in a specific pattern and to operate within assigned hours. With increasing demand for more stations and additional hours of operation, especially in the AM group, the FCC has in recent years "opened up" the AM frequency. Specifically, the United States has signed agreements with Mexico and Canada that will permit additional hours of operation for certain daytime AM stations as well as establish AM openings on clear and adjacent·channels. The FCC has also cleared the way for more than 1,000 new commercial FM stations.

Three classes of FM stations are in operation today; they are defined primarily by power and antenna elevation. The maximum combination of power and antenna height is 100,000 watts and 2,000 feet. Class A stations have an effective coverage area of 15 miles; Class B stations cover 30 miles; and Class C stations broadcast up to 60 miles. The reason for the exceptionally high antennas and power is that FM signals are direct signals that reach only to the horizon, unlike AM signals, which encompass both ground and sky waves.

Part of the reason that FM listening has increased so dramatically in recent years is the quality of its signal. Because of its location in the VHF band, the FM signal is almost totally free of static. The FM signal can also reproduce sounds with greater cycle range than can the AM signal and has a larger dynamic range than the AM signal. Because the FM signal is 20 times the width of an AM channel, stereophonic sound is possible through multiplexing. Over 93 percent of FM stations now broadcast in stereo. AM stereo became reality in 1982, and two competing AM stereo systems are fighting it out in the marketplace to determine which one will become the de facto industry standard. Almost 15 percent of AM stations currently broadcast in stereo.

Radio stations in the United States are identified by call letters beginning with K or W. Except for a few early stations, such as KDKA in Pittsburgh, stations east of the Mississippi River have call letters beginning with W, while K is assigned to stations west of the Mississippi. Most early broadcast call signs used three letters, but they were quickly exhausted; today, most stations have four-letter call signs.

One additional classification for radio stations is as commercial and noncommercial or educational. Of the more than 1,100 educational radio stations today, only 24 are AM; they date from the early years of radio. In 1945, the FCC reserved 20 FM channels between 88 and 92 MHz for noncommercial educational stations. Since then, the number of noncommercial stations has grown slowly but steadily to over 1,400.

Kinds of Networks

There are many commercial national networks, including CBS, NBC, Mutual, and ABC. These networks provide a national news service to their affiliates and a few sports programs, features, and commentaries. Only a limited number of affiliated stations receive payments from the networks, and those that do receive only a nominal sum. At ABC, for example, the majority of affiliates pay the network for the services it provides. In 1985,

58 percent of all commercial radio stations were affiliated with one or more networks—the networks' best showing ever.

In 1970, National Public Radio (NPR) began the development of a network-radio service designed to provide programming for noncommercial educational stations. Funded through the Corporation for Public Broadcasting (CPB), NPR has expanded rapidly in the past 10 years to almost 250 affiliates. At one time, educational radio was little more than a classical jukebox, but today it provides a unique alternative to commercial radio. The NPR affiliates face an uncertain future, however, as President Reagan's economic plan calls for a 50 percent cutback in federal funding by 1990. This loss of revenue, coupled with management problems, has created a diminished role for NPR. With the exception of two premiere news programs, "All Things Considered" and "Morning Edition," NPR network programming is virtually nonexistent. Many of the program innovations of the 1970s have been eliminated or severely reduced because of finances.

In addition to the major national networks, hundreds of smaller regional or specialized program networks either interconnect stations for a specific program (a football game) or provide various special programming (black news or religious information).

Most radio stations broadcast a blend of music, news, talk, commercials, and special content, such as sports. The average FM station programs 4 minutes of news an hour; AM stations program almost 6 minutes an hour. The average number of commercial minutes an hour on FM is almost 10, with AM at 11 minutes. Sports programming is heard on 72 percent of AM stations, while on only 44 percent of FM stations.

STATION PROGRAMMING

Most radio programming (primarily music) is based on format broadcasting, in which a station selects a segment of the audience (those aged 18 to 24, for example) and attempts to reach that segment throughout its entire schedule.

An important term in radio programming is *audience fragmentation*. Much in the same manner as the magazine, radio is now a medium of specialization. Programmers, taking into account factors ranging from age to income to geographical location, are targeting their product at specific audience "cells."

Targeted broadcasting is further linked to a "life-style" concept. Knowledge of a listener's life style—interests, tastes, attitudes, habits, and values—can be attributed to media research organizations' ability to profile the psyche of listeners with startling accuracy and reliability. The result of this kind of research is an uncovering of irritants and, frequently, a restructuring of a station's program mix to appeal directly to a specific life-style.

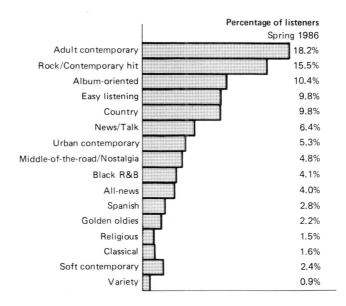

Figure 6.7. The graph illustrates the variety of radio formats in today's marketplace. The figures are from Arbitron's spring 1985 ratings gathered from the 100 largest AM- and FM-radio markets.

Radio Formats

A direct by-product of targeted radio has been the advent of formats. *Broadcasting* magazine lists over 60 program formats or sounds, but most stations fall into the following major categories: (1) adult contemporary (A/C), (2) contemporary hit radio (CHR), (3) album-oriented rock (AOR), (4) easy listening, (5) country, (6) news/talk, (7) urban contemporary (UC), (8) oldies/nostalgia, (9) ethnic, (10) religious, (11) classical.

These 11 formats are somewhat misleading in that they represent a much wider variety of individual sounds and styles. For example, AOR can mean a number of sounds, ranging from hard rock to classic rock to new wave. As a result of this format's volatile nature, it is constantly undergoing change. Radio formats are fluid and reflect current trends in music. Country-western music, for example, has fluctuated widely in popularity, and there has been a tremendous growth in recent years of progressive or urban contemporary music.

Adult Contemporary. Adult contemporary (A/C) is the most-listened-to radio format in America. Its popularity may be due in part to confusion as to what constitutes "adult contemporary." At some stations, the format is merely a convoluted top-40 presentation; other stations have developed a full-service product featuring everything from meteorologists to financial experts. The audience target for this format is the 25 to 49 age group, and it is especially effective in attracting female listeners. The music is usually pop standards by such artists as Barbra Streisand or Neil Diamond and is generally presented in uninterrupted sweeps of 10 to 12 minutes in length.

Contemporary Hit Radio. Also known as top 40, contemporary hit radio (CHR) plays only the current best and fastest selling records. The target audience is the 12- to 18-year-old. The format is characterized by a tight, fast pace with little, if any, "dead air." Disc jockeys often play an important role in this format, although in recent years, program consultants such as Bill Drake have deemphasized the disc jockey's presence in favor of a consistent flow of music.

Album-Oriented Rock. Considered by many to be the most volatile of all formats, album-oriented rock (AOR) features a steady diet of rock 'n' roll. Successful stations with this format carefully research music and are aggressive promoters. AOR has been very effective in reaching the 18- to 34-year-old male, but has done poorly with female listeners. Like adult-contemporary music, it is broadcast in sweeps, and the disc jockey's "presence" is not significant. Typical artists include the Rolling Stone, Bruce Springsteen, and David Lee Roth.

Easy Listening. Call it dentist-office music, if you will, but "beautiful music," as it is also called, remains one of the most popular formats in America. Utilizing instrumentals and light vocals assembled in blocks of about 15 minutes, these stations usually feature minimal talk. Many are computer operated, thus eliminating the need for live announcers and other operational costs. Typical artists include Ray Conniff, the Hollywood Strings, Frank Sinatra, and Sergio Mendes. The target audience is the 25 to 54 age group, and the stations boast a devoted audience. Almost 50 percent of the stations use syndicated material, and almost 75 percent are automated to some extent.

Country. Country may be the AM format of the 1980s. Programmers throughout the nation are opting for country formats. Some offer a citified music selection, stretching the criteria to include artists ranging from Dan Fogelberg to Linda Ronstadt. Others offer a mainstream blend concentrating on "pure" artists, such as Willie Nelson and Conway Twitty. Stations frequently offer a mix of news and other information services. Country's target audience is primarily the 25 to 50 age group, and the format has always been particularly popular with blue-collar workers. Since the 1960s, the country format has been adopted by more radio stations than any other.

News/Talk. This is a generic format that covers several variations, such as news, talk, and news/talk. As all-news, it is easily the most expensive format to run and so is confined primarily to AM outlets in major markets. The all-news format is highly structured, with frequent time checks, weather forecasts, and story repetition. The news/talk format is a less expensive hybrid of all-news in which stations concentrate their news efforts to morning and afternoon drive time and fill in the midday and evening periods with talk. The target audience varies according to the specific blend of news and talk, but generally falls in the 25 to 54 age group.

Urban Contemporary. Some have called urban contemporary (UC) the "melting-pot" format; others, "disco radio grown up." UC is the logical extension of contemporary hit radio with accessible dance music. The format is especially viable in metropolitan areas with large, heterogeneous ethnic populations. It generally features a broad play list and stresses strong disc jockey personalities. The target audience is aged 18 to 34.

Oldies/Nostalgia. The play list of oldies/nostalgia stations concentrates primarily on pop tunes of the 1950s and 1960s. The format was executed in its most finely tuned manner in the late 1970s by Al Ham, having been introduced in the 1960s by Bill Drake and Chuck Blore. Oldies is a highly syndicated format that is programmed primarily by AM stations. The target audience, quite understandably, is adults 40 years old and over.

Ethnic. Hundreds of ethnic stations exist in the country, but black and Hispanic stations dominate. Over 300 stations are classified as black formated, with Hispanic formats a close second. Both formats began in 1947 and have steadily increased ever since. Many other stations devote a significant portion of their schedules to ethnic programming—primarily foreign language—including more than 20 stations that broadcast exclusively to American Indians and Eskimos.

Religious. Over 600 stations currently broadcast a full-time religious format. The format breaks down into stations that broadcast music and those that do not. Primarily an AM outlet, religious broadcasters claim that their messages reach almost one-half of the American radio audience.

Classical. Although there are fewer than three dozen full-time classical music stations in the country, no other format can claim a more loyal audience. Because of classical's up-scale audience, prestige blue-chip accounts find the format an efficient buy. This is exclusively an FM format that programs to a 25- to 49-year-old age group, college educated with high income.

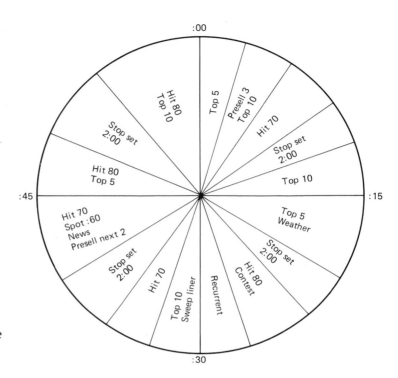

Figure 6.8. A typical morning-drive-time CHR program clock illustrates the tight structure of radio formats.

Program Scheduling

Regardless of the format, few program and/or music directors entrust the selection and scheduling of music and other program elements to disc jockeys or other on-air personalities. In most cases, a program director carefully constructs each hour of programming, including not only what type of music, but when news, features, and commercials are to be slotted. To help them, program directors have developed program wheels or format disks. These carefully designed "clocks" ensure the effective presentation of on-air elements. Figure 6.8 presents a typical morning-drive-time CHR clock. It reflects a 9-minute commercial load per hour and very detailed "instructions" about what to play when. Stations often have many program wheels, each of which represents specific content. Figure 6.9 is a news clock for WICB-FM in Ithaca, New York. It provides instructions from the news director in concert with the program director on how to format the news to achieve the best integration of news with the other program elements. In all such clocks or wheels, balance is the key.

As radio has become even more competitive in recent years, and as musical formats have become more specialized, the program wheel has become less a local program director's option and more a syndicated formula backed by extensive research and testing. Companies such as Cen-

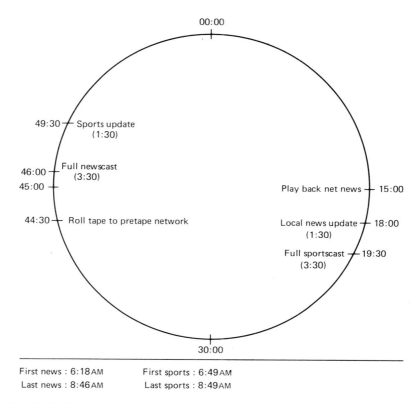

First news : 6:18AM   First sports : 6:49AM
Last news : 8:46AM   Last sports : 8:49AM

Figure 6.9. A typical morning-drive news and sports schedule.

tury 21, Churchill Productions, and Drake-Chenault Enterprises market tapes of selected music cuts that are programmed up to 24 hours in length. The tapes are programmed hourly and provide different moods, rhythms, and styles. They even incorporate seasonal changes. Figure 6.10 illustrates the variety of syndicated formats available from Century 21.

Formats are basically an economic issue. Stations want the most effective and efficient programming possible, and syndicators promise, at least, to take the guess work out of such efforts. As Century 21's Dave Scott says, "An exact clock is tailored for our client station after our market study. The format we provide will perfectly match the station in tempo, style, music mix, announcing, promos, news, weather and commercial load. Then the programming is professionally positioned to maximize our clients, sales, ratings and profits."[4]

Fees for syndicators' services vary according to a sliding scale based on

[4] Quoted in Michael C. Keith and Joseph M. Krause, *The Radio Station* (Boston: Focal Press, 1986), 238.

Eighteen Successful Sounds: One's Right For You

The Z Format.
Since 1973, Century 21's contemporary hit Z Format has delivered the best track record in the business!

The Hot Z Format.
Today's hottest hits give you the most popular music, so your station will be the most popular in your market!

Album Oriented Z.
Century 21's album rock format is available either unannounced or uniquely custom-voiced.

The A-C Format.
Adult contemporary music goes hand-in-hand with a big, responsive audience.

Good Ol' Rock & Roll.
Here are the top hit oldies of the 50's, 60's & 70's that still sound good today.

SUPER-COUNTRY.
You can choose from our *three* different formats: modern, traditional, or pop/cross-over country.

The C-C Format.
This Country-Crossover Format blends country with adult contemporary music.

The E-Z Format.
Century 21's E-Z Format moves "middle-of-the-road" music into *your* lane.

MORE BEAUTIFUL.
MORe Beautiful blends middle-of-the-road vocals with the finest instrumentals.

Simply Beautiful.
Beautiful music is the favorite format of broadcasters seeking trouble-free, stable operations.

MEMORY MUSIC.
Here's the ideal mixture of M-O-R and nostalgia. Music vintages are tailored to your station.

SACRED SOUNDS.
Century 21 delivers four Christian formats: beautiful, adult contemporary, traditional & country gospel.

The Jazz-Z Format.
As either a full- or part-time format, Century 21's Jazz-Z sound gives your station unique popularity.

Figure 6.10. A sample of syndicated formats from Century 21.

a station's revenue for a particular market. The range for syndicated-format fees falls between $600 and $18,000 a month. Over 83 percent of all radio stations, both FM and AM, are using syndicated satellite-delivered music and talk programming.

THE CHARACTERISTICS AND ROLES OF RADIO

At present, radio is a mass medium with a highly fragmented audience and revenue base. Radio is a local rather than a national medium, in terms of both its audience and its income. Radio-listening habits are personal, and stations program selectively to satisfy individual needs within a relatively homogeneous group. Radio, adapting to the nature of our society, has used technological advances to become mobile. People listen to radio as a secondary activity to accompany the work or play of the moment, and advertisers use radio to supplement the primary medium in their advertising mix.

Local

Radio is a local medium in terms of sources of audience and of income. Localness has normally applied to content, as well. However, with some 83 percent of all stations using syndicated material, *local* is an adjective with relative meaning. Until the 1950s, radio was the prestige mass medium, controlled by national advertisers and networks. Network affiliation ensured affiliated stations of extensive programming, audience, and revenue.

In the 1980s, local stations attract the audiences, earn the revenue, and, until recently, provided much of the programming. Syndicated- and network-program services have assumed much of the local stations' programming role. Local disc jockeys, news announcers, and other personalities operate within a local frame of reference; but program sources in radio are increasingly national.

Fragmented and Selective

In the mid-1950s, radio broadcasters were in the position of needing more programs but having less money to pay for them. Since both talk and music were relatively cheap, radio rebuilt its programming around music and news. What evolved has come to be called formula, or format, radio.

Very quickly, AM and FM broadcasters realized that general radio was dead. The more variety a specific station offered, the more its audience dwindled. Television had assumed the role of general entertainer. Stations began to develop program specializations, based on types of recorded music. Audience research indicated that certain formats attract select segments of the available audience. Top-40 stations, for example, hold a vir-

TABLE 6.2. AM–FM RADIO, WASHINGTON, D.C.

AM Radio Stations			FM Radio Stations		
Dial	Format	Call Letters	Dial	Format	Call Letters
570	Classical Music	WGMS	88.1	Progressive Music	WMUC
630	Pop Music/Talk (ABC Information)	WMAL	88.5	Arts/Information (NPR)	WAMU
730	Continuous Country Music	WRMR	89.3	Jazz Community Radio (Pacifica)	WPFW
780	Religious/Sacred Music	WABS	90.1	Jazz/Information	WDCU
900	Adult Contemporary	WLMD	90.9	Arts/Information (NPR)	WETA
950	Christian Music	WCTN	91.9	Educational/Cultural	WGTS
980	News/Talk (NBC)	WRC	93.9	Urban Contemporary	WKYS
1050	Beautiful Music	WGAY	94.7	Adult Contemporary	WLTT
1120	Gospel: Talk/Music	WUST	95.5	Adult Contemporary	WPGC
1150	24-Hour Comedy	WJOK	96.3	Progressive Black Music	WHUR
1220	Inspirational/Devotional	WFAX	97.1	Up-Tempo Familiar Music	WASH
1260	Personality/A/C (RKO)	WWDC	98.7	Country	WMZQ
1290	Popular Music	WAGE	99.5	Beautiful Music	WGAY
1310	All-News	WEEL	100.3	Album Soul	WOOK
1340	Inspiration/Information	WYCB	101.1	Album Rock	WWDC
1390	Big Band/Swing	WEAM	102.3	Progressive Music	WHFS
1440	Country	WVBK	103.5	Classical Music	WGMS
1450	Adult Contemporary (SBN)	WOL	104.1	Hit Oldies	WXTR
1460	Contemporary	WPRW	105.1	Album Rock	WAVA
1500	All-News (CBS)	WTOP	105.9	Continuous Country Music	WPKX
1530	Country, Gospel	WPWC	106.7	Adult Contemporary	WEZR
1540	Contemporary Latin Music/News	WMDO	107.3	Contemporary Music (ABC-FM)	WRQX
1560	Hit Oldies	WXTR			
1580	Adult Contemporary	WPGC			
1600	Oldies (Mutual)	WINX			

tual monopoly on the teen-age and subteen groups, while country-western stations have strong appeal not only in the South and the Southwest, but also for vast numbers in large northern metropolitan areas. Broadcasters began to program selectively to serve one portion of the population. The FCC granted licenses for racially and ethnically oriented stations, which specifically set out to establish themselves as radio services for minority groups within the community.

Stations today seek to create a distinct personality based on a program formula. Radio stations program selectivity in order to corner a special segment of the listener-consumer market. Then, if an advertiser wants to reach the black market, the teen-age market, or the young housewife market in a given area, that advertiser must deal with the station that programs selectively for the audience in question. Table 6.2, from the Washington, D.C., market, graphically illustrates this diversity.

Personal

Closely allied to radio stations' selective programming is the fact that listening to radio has become a personal activity. No longer does the family gather around the console radio to be entertained as a group. People tend to listen to the radio as individuals, and radio-station announcers attempt to develop "personal" listening relationships with radio audiences. How many times have you heard a disc jockey single out specific individuals for attention? "I'm sending this song out to Tom and Donna and to Don and Karen." The talk-show host builds a loyal audience of individuals with whom he or she disagrees. Entire formats are now built around the talk-show concept.

Much of radio's personal orientation is possible because of the number and variety of radio sets available. In kitchens, radio is listened to for weather reports in order to send children off to school properly dressed. Upstairs, teen-agers tune in to hear the latest number-one hit in the country. On the way to work, people listen to traffic reports on the automobile radio. The jogger tunes out the outside world and tunes in on his or her Walkman radio. In all these cases, the individual listens in relative isolation, seeking to gratify a personal entertainment or information need of the moment.

Mobile

The United States has been called a "society on wheels," and radio has the ability to get out and go with its American audience. This ability to participate in the individual's daily routine has been made possible by radio's mobility.

The phenomenal increase in radio sales in recent years results in great measure from the production of three specific kinds of radio receivers: the car radio, the portable radio, and the clock radio. Home radios, usually small AM–FM sets, constitute little more than 15 percent of all radio sales.

The trend toward increased mobility began immediately after World War II, although the production of car radios had been an important part of total radio production as early as 1930. By 1951, auto-set production exceeded that of the home-receiver class for the first time, and car radios have continued to be the leading type of set manufactured for the past 15 years.

During the 1950s and 1960s, portable-radio production also topped home-receiver production, excluding clock radios. The tremendous surge in portability was made possible by the transistor, which reduced the size and cost of sets. Today, manufacturers seem obsessed with making radios smaller and more portable. Several companies are producing credit-card-size radios weighing 1 ounce. Sony has taken its Walkman under water,

Figure 6.11. The development of the transistor made radio a portable medium. The Walkman radio represents maximum portability, since it literally goes where the listener goes.

where it can be submerged for up to 30 minutes and still play your favorite tune.

Secondary and Supplementary

The final characteristics of radio are its use as a secondary activity by listeners and as a supplementary medium by advertisers. Radio is used as background while driving a car, studying, jogging, or relaxing at the beach. Radio listening is no longer a primary entertainment activity, and with the added mobility of radio, it goes along as a companion for the activity of the moment. An automobile radio is secondary to the prime function of the car itself—to go somewhere. We need traffic reports to get there, and radio provides them. Another development that enhances radio's usefulness as a secondary item is the clock radio. It does not jolt you awake; it sings or talks you out of bed and into the day. Its primary function is not to entertain or to provide information; it is basically an alarm clock.

National and local advertisers with sizable budgets use radio to supplement the major medium of an advertising campaign. Most local advertisers use newspapers primarily, but keep the campaign supported with radio ads. Major national advertisers usually spend only a small portion of their total budget on radio. Nevertheless, Radio Advertising Bureau studies have shown that radio can effectively and efficiently reach consumer prospects that television misses. Most of the nation's top advertising agencies spend less than 10 percent of their national clients' budgets on radio. The major exceptions to the rule are the automobile and related industries, which extensively use "drive time" to hit the available audience going to or coming from work.

Radio has clearly survived the competition from television and has evolved into a new and remarkably solid medium. Radio is now a companion medium, fine-tuned to meet almost any need. This unique ability will continue to provide it with the audience and revenue needed to sustain future expansion.

SUMMARY

Radio has gone through several major changes in its 70-year history. It has experienced growth, decline, and rebirth. Today, it is a massive medium, providing entertainment and information to all segments of American society.

The development of radio can be divided into several periods. The years from 1840 to 1919 were characterized by a number of scientific advances and inventions in the fields of electricity and magnetism. These experiments culminated in the late-nineteenth-century work of Marconi, which gave us the wireless telegraph. The early years of the twentieth century witnessed intense amateur experimentation in both code and voice transmission.

The second major period of radio development—the formation of the American radio system—occurred from 1920 to 1928. Regular radio broadcasting began in 1920 when presidential election returns were broadcast over KDKA in Pittsburgh. Almost overnight, hundreds of stations were started, broadcasting music, sports, drama, and vaudeville. It was during this period that the industry developed and networks were formed. Laws were passed to govern the industry and the economic structure of radio was established.

The golden age of network radio were the years 1929 to 1945. A number of new program types evolved and network radio assumed a dominant position in American society.

Radio experienced a period of decline from 1946 to 1959. The decline was primarily in network radio, as network television quickly took over the prime-time evening programming function. Local stations began to develop original and profitable formats based primarily on the playing of recorded music. Since 1960, however, radio has become revitalized and has experienced great economic growth.

A current statistical profile of radio reveals a strong, vigorous, and dynamic medium, meeting a variety of listener needs and interests. There are more stations on the air, more sets in use, and more listeners than ever before. FM programming and stations dominate radio broadcasting.

There are three major components in the structure and organization of radio: (1) the local station, (2) the networks, and (3) program suppliers, primarily the recording industry. Stations are categorized by FM and AM frequencies, by commercial and noncommercial status, and by signal strength and signal location. There are a variety of radio networks providing an array of program services, including music, sports, features, and commentary.

Most radio programming today is based on format broadcasting, in which a station selects a segment of the audience and attempts to reach that segment throughout its entire schedule. There are a wide variety of radio formats but we have identified 11 as being most important: (1) adult contemporary, (2) contemporary hit radio, (3) album-oriented rock, (4) easy listening, (5) country, (6) news/talk, (7) urban contemporary, (8) oldies/nostalgia, (9) ethnic, (10) religious, (11) classical. A number of companies specialize in various formats and provide radio stations with music services targeted to a specific audience.

Contemporary radio has a number of characteristics and roles. It is a local rather than national medium in terms of audience and income. Radio listening habits are personal and stations program selectively in order to satisfy individual needs. Radio is a mobile medium. People listen to radio as a secondary activity, to accompany the work or play of the moment, and radio is used by advertisers to supplement their advertising mix.

Radio has clearly survived the competition from television and has developed into a new and aggressive medium. Radio is a companion medium fine-tuned to meet a variety of audiences' needs.

BIBLIOGRAPHY

Browne, Donald R. *International Radio Broadcasting: The Limits of the Limitless Medium.* New York: Praeger, 1982.

Duncan, H. James, Jr. *Duncan's Radio Market Guide: 1986 Edition.* Kalamazoo, Mich.: Duncan's American Radio, 1986.

Fornatele, Peter, and Joshua E. Mills. *Radio in the Television Age.* Woodstock, N.Y.: Overlook Press, 1980.

Hilliard, Robert L., ed. *Radio Broadcasting: An Introduction to the Sound Medium.* 3d ed. White Plains, N.Y.: Longman, 1985.

Leinwoll, S. *From Spark to Satellite: A History of Radio Communication.* New York: Scribner, 1979.

MacDonald, J. Fred. *Don't Touch that Dial! Radio Programming in American Life, 1920–1960.* Chicago: Nelson-Hall, 1979.

Routt, Edd, James B. McGrath, and Frederic A. Weiss. *The Radio Format Conundrum.* New York: Hastings House, 1979.

Shane, Ed. *Programming Dynamics: Radio's Management Guide.* Overland Park, Kans.: Globecom, 1984.

Terrace, Vincent. *Radio's Golden Years: The Encyclopedia of Radio Programs, 1930–1960.* San Diego: Barnes, 1981.

Whetmore, Edward Jay. *The Magic Medium: An Introduction to Radio in America.* Belmont, Calif.: Wadsworth, 1982.

7

Television

Cap Cities and ABC; Turner and MGM; Viacom and MTV; Murdoch and Fox; KKR and Storer; Tribune and KTLA; GE and RCA.

These pairs represent just some of the possible, proposed, and actual media mergers in 1985 and 1986. More important, they represent some of the extensive and fundamental changes sweeping through the television industry in the United States. Much like radio, television is feeling the heat of intense competition in the marketplace, and, as radio did in the 1950s, television is searching for a new identity and function. By television, we mean the traditional structure of stations and networks (mainly ABC, CBS, and NBC) linked in the function of providing broadly based entertainment programming to a national audience.

In a speech before the International Radio and Television Society in January 1986, CBS/Broadcast Group president Gene Jankowski talked about the changes affecting television, and in doing so spoke of the "three ages of television."

The first age was from 1950 to 1975 and was a period of uninterrupted growth dominated by two networks: CBS and NBC. As Jankowski notes, "It was a space in which movement was easy to track; in which competitive gains and losses were traded directly by the participants and in which the driving forces remained constant. The business grew larger, but its dynamics did not change."[1]

---

[1] Speech by Gene Jankowski, 15 January 1986.

The second age, between 1975 and 1980, was one of competition among three networks, as ABC became a full-time player. Although lasting only five years, it was a period of intense competition, with massive promotion, advertising, and marketing efforts. There were second and even third seasons, and "sweeps" became network programming contests. Costs escalated rapidly but were basically absorbed by an inflationary economy.

Television's third age, since 1980, introduced structural change identified most closely with new technologies and deregulation. The marketplace changed rapidly, and, as Jankowski pointed out, television's "maturity" as a medium and business was open to question and interpretation.

All of this serves as notice that television, despite its dominant position in our lives, is a young medium—still growing, still developing, still becoming. The three ages of television span fewer than 40 years. This brief history is important not only in looking back to see what was, but also in looking ahead to see what may be.

HISTORICAL PERSPECTIVE

Prehistory: 1884–1925

As did radio, television grew out of the intense experimentation with electricity in the late nineteenth century. Basic research in electromagnetic theory by James Clerk Maxwell and Heinrich Hertz led to more practical experimentation, which culminated in the work of Guglielmo Marconi. Coincidental with this research in wireless communication in the 1880s was the work of Paul Nipkow, who experimented with mechanical scanning-disc methods of sending pictures by wire. Most of the early experiments in television employed the mechanical method, including work in the 1920s by Charles Jenkins in the United States and John Baird in Britain. Television research slowed down after the tremendous surge of radio. Nevertheless, work on an electronic TV system was begun in the United States by Philo T. Farnsworth and Vladimir K. Zworykin. Both men contributed basic inventions, including, most singificantly, Zworykin's camera tube, the iconoscope, which he patented in 1928.

Early Development: 1925–1947

Barely three years after radio broadcasting became a reality, a crude, all-electronic TV system was available, although much of its early use was not successful. The first real transmission of television occurred in 1925, using Jenkins's mechanical method. Zworykin's method of electronic scanning was simpler, however, and eventually produced a better picture. Experiments with electronic television were conducted throughout the world in the 1920s. The Federal Radio Commission (later the Federal Communications Commission [FCC]) granted the first experimental license for visual broadcasting to the Radio Corporation of America's (RCA) station W2XBS

Figure 7.1. Vladimir K. Zworykin demonstrates the cathode-ray television system that he developed at Westinghouse in 1929. (Photo: The Bettman Archive, Inc.)

in April 1928. That same year, the General Electric Company broadcast the first TV drama over W6X in Schenectady, New York.

Experimentation continued throughout the 1930s, chiefly by Zworykin and his team of engineers working at RCA; by 1937, 17 stations were operating under noncommercial experimental license. The first major public demonstration of television occurred at the 1939 World's Fair in New York City, with President Franklin D. Roosevelt's appearance on television the hit of the fair.

Commercial TV operations were scheduled to begin on September 1, 1940, but the FCC rescinded its original authorization. The delay was ordered by the commission because it felt that RCA had indulged in an unwise promotional campaign to sell its transmitting and receiving equipment that would retard further TV research and experimentation.

In January 1941, the National Television System Committee (NTSC) suggested TV standards to which the FCC reacted favorably, and the start of commercial telecasting was rescheduled for July 1, 1941. On that date, both the DuMont and the CBS stations aired programs. But it was RCA's station WNBT that ran the first commercial (Bulova Watch Company) and the first sponsored programs, including Lowell Thomas's news program (Sunoco) and "Uncle Jim's Question Bee" (Lever Brothers). By the end of 1941, some 10 commercial stations were serving 10,000 to 20,000 television homes, half of them in New York and half in Chicago, Philadelphia, and Los Angeles.

World War II interrupted TV's growth and delayed its national appearance. Commercial telecasting ended in early 1942, although experimental telecasts on six stations continued on an irregular basis. Advertisers were encouraged to use the facilities free of charge. Although the war was detrimental to the immediate evolution of television, it had some positive effects. Chief among them was the development of better electronic techniques and equipment, the most important being the image-orthicon tube.

During the war years, the single most important event affecting TV's future was a duopoly ruling in 1943 that forced NBC to divest itself of one of its two radio networks. This decision created ABC, another economically strong national radio operation that enabled the ABC-TV network to evolve and survive during its early years.

Following World War II, the development of television was further retarded by problems involving the placement of television in the electromagnetic spectrum and the $1 million price tag attached to building and equipping a TV station. In 1945, there were 6 commercial stations on the air, and by 1947, only 11 more had been added. At this time, many broadcasters thought that FM radio would be the next important medium.

By March 1947, however, the FCC had set aside Channels 2 to 13 in the very-high-frequency (VHF) band, and more and more receivers were appearing on the market. By this time, too, AT&T had begun to install intercity coaxial cable, making possible network interconnection. The rush for TV facilities was on. There was a definite need for more stations because people were buying the high-priced sets as fast as they were being produced. More than 1 million sets were sold in 1948 at an average price of $400. By early 1948, 19 stations were on the air, 81 stations had FCC authorization, and 116 applications were before the FCC. It became obvious that the commission would have to reevaluate TV broadcasting to prevent station interference, since only 12 VHF channels were available to serve the total system.

The Formation of the American Television System: 1948–1952

Between 1948, and 1952, three major factors significantly affected the future of video broadcasting: (1) the Federal Communications Commission's "freeze" on TV station allocations; (2) the development of TV networks; and (3) the evolution of video-programming formats.

The Freeze. By the fall of 1948, there were 36 TV stations on the air in 19 cities and another 73 licensed in 43 more cities. In order to solve technical-interference problems, provide for the increased demand for licenses, and study color-television systems, the Federal Communications Commission froze allocations for new stations from September 30, 1948, to July 1, 1952. During these years, the RCA compatible-color system was adopted, ultra-high-frequency (UHF) Channels 14 to 83 were added to VHF Channels 2 to 13, and 242 station allocations (frequencies on which stations broadcast) were reserved for educational television. This third class of stations—public, noncommercial, and educational—was established through the efforts of Commissioner Frieda B. Hennock, despite the lack of support from most educators and universities.

While the freeze was on, 108 of the 109 commercially licensed stations went on the air, and TV homes jumped from 1.5 million to 15 million. Between 1948 and 1952, one of every three American families bought a TV set at an average cost of $300. Although no new licenses were being granted, growth was possible during this period because almost every major population area was being served by at least one TV station.

The Networks. The generally accepted date for the inauguration of national television networking is the 1948/1949 TV season. In January 1949, the Midwest and the East Coast were linked by coaxial cable. The West Coast link-up occurred in September 1951. Since not every station was able to carry live feeds, however, many new stations had to depend on kine-scopes (films of electronically produced pictures) for network programming.

The birth and survival of the television networks depended on four factors: (1) a financially sound parent company that could survive the lean years of television development; (2) ownership of key stations in the largest population centers to provide local revenue and to guarantee that the network's series would be aired in those markets; (3) expertise in national radio operations that provided both financial support and a ready-made line-up of affiliates to carry programs; (4) a backlog or quick development of talent and programs that would attract large audiences for national advertisers.

ABC, CBS, and NBC were able to meet these criteria, and they survived. The key, of course, was financial strength. NBC lost over $18 million in its first four years of network-television operation. The Mutual Broadcasting System, which did not own any radio stations, was the weakest national radio operation and was never able to develop the resources necessary to enter television. The DuMont Television Network, owned by Allen B. DuMont Laboratories, an early pioneer in TV operations, did not have a radio network, financial strength, station ownership, or programming experience; despite early promise and some limited performance, it ceased operations in 1955.

Programming. In these early years of network and station development, most of the content of television came from radio-programming formats. The quiz shows, suspense programs, Westerns, variety shows, soap operas, and comedies were direct descendants of programs on radio. Indeed, most of TV's early hits were exact copies of radio series transposed intact to television, such as "Suspense," "The Life of Riley," "The Aldrich Family," "The Lone Ranger," "Break the Bank," and "Studio One." Television's first stars were radio personalities, including Red Skelton, George Burns and Gracie Allen, Arthur Godfrey, Jack Benny, and Edgar Bergen. The networks also adopted other traditional radio programs, such as newscasts, sports events, and live coverage of special events—for example, the 1948 and 1952 political conventions and election returns.

Local stations provided programming to fill the gaps left in the network schedules. Much of it was of poor quality, however, and as a result, the syndicator emerged early as an important source of TV content. In 1950, the first package of theatrical films found its way into the local marketplace.

The financial base of television was clear from the start. The public was acclimated to radio commercials and accepted them as the means of paying for their programs. Also, the networks had contractual agreements with sponsors. Structurally, TV economics was simply an extension of radio economics, and because of this, television developed much faster than expected.

Despite its affinities to radio, television was still a new medium. Its particular pattern of adoption in society, coupled with its unique properties, were prime factors in the rapidly changing pattern of programming. Television, like newspapers and radio before it, was initially not a household medium. As newspapers were first read in coffeehouses, television was first viewed in local bars and taverns. This pattern and television's inherent visuality were strong reasons that sports programming made up as much as 30 percent of all sponsored network evening time in 1949. As the TV set became more of a household item, children's and women's programming became more important, as did such family entertainment as variety shows.

In 1952, the FCC issued its Sixth Order and Report. The report did more than end the freeze. It was essentially a master plan for TV development in the United States. Television viewing was on the brink of fulfilling its destiny as the dominant leisure-time activity for most Americans.

The Golden Age of Television: 1952–1960

This slice of television history contained the most fantastic growth spurt ever experienced by a mass medium. By 1955, there were 439 stations on the air. The 15 million TV homes in 1952 expanded to 26 million in 1954, 42.5 million in 1958, and 45 million in 1960. During these eight years, the percentage of TV-equipped homes in the United States grew from 33 to 90.

Station and network profits kept pace with this growth, as gross industry revenues increased from $300 million in 1952 to $1.3 billion in 1960.

The dominant networks were CBS and NBC, primarily because of their network-radio experience, available capital assets, top-quality talent, and large number of affiliated stations. ABC had many problems, primarily the lack of affiliates. The death of the DuMont Television Network in 1955 eased to a limited degree ABC's need for more affiliates. The merger of ABC with United-Paramount Theaters also helped increase its competitiveness, but throughout the 1950s, it ran a poor third to CBS and NBC.

The FCC's Sixth Order and Report was designed to ease problems that faced the industry, but the implementation of these changes took considerable time. Seventy channels were opened in the UHF band, but since most TV sets were built to receive only VHF signals, special adapters and antennas had to be purchased in order to receive UHF stations. Although 120 UHF stations were operating in 1954, they were in an extremely poor competitive position; as a result, their number fell to only 75 in 1960. This situation continued until 1962, when Congress passed legislation that required that all TV sets produced after January 1, 1964, be capable of receiving both UHF and VHF signals.

Color television in the form of RCA's electronic system began to emerge slowly following FCC approval in 1953. The first color sets were manufactured in 1954 and sold for about $1,000. The high cost of both receivers and broadcast equipment dictated a slow growth, however. The season of 1954/1955 was the first color season, with NBC programming 12 to 15 hours a week.

Several factors were responsible for the public's slow response to color television:

1. The price of color-television sets was extremely high.
2. ABC and CBS refused to move into color programming because such a move would have given NBC the competitive edge, since most compatible-color patents were held by NBC's parent company, RCA.
3. The electronics industry already had a thriving business in black-and-white sets, and it, too, would have had to do business with RCA. Many manufacturers chose to experiment with, rather than produce, color sets, and so as late as 1960, there were no color series on ABC or CBS.

By 1966, however, all three networks were running a complete color, prime-time schedule. This growth in available color programming led to a boom in sales of color sets, and by 1972, 50 percent of American homes with television had color receivers. Today, over 80 percent of American TV homes have a color-television set. What is equally important, people with

Figure 7.2. The popularity of Milton Berle (seen here dancing with Beatrice Lillie) in his variety show of the early 1950s earned him the nickname "Mr. Television." (Photo: Movie Star News.)

color televisions watch their sets approximately 20 percent more than do people with black-and-white televisions.

Another important technical development that occurred in the 1950s was the move toward film and videotape programming. With the development of videotape in 1956, live telecasting, with the exception of sports events, specials, and some daytime drama, soon became a thing of the past. By 1960, virtually all network prime-time programming was on film or videotape. Two reasons for the rise of recorded programming were:

1. Errors can be corrected before a show is broadcast, thus improving the artistic quality of the program.

2. The program can be rerun, cutting the skyrocketing costs of program production.

Programming in the 1950s continued the trends of the early years with a mixture of sportscasts, family situation comedies, and variety-vaudeville shows. The variety-vaudeville–show format was led by "Mr. Television"—Milton Berle. Beginning in 1948, Berle captured the screens of American households on Tuesday night as host and star of "Texaco Star Theater." Ed Sullivan, with the "Toast of the Town" (later "The Ed Sullivan Show"), represented a saner and more broadly entertaining show that lasted for more than 20 years. One of the most creative comedy-variety shows of the time and a classic of television's golden age was "Your Show of Shows," starring Sid Caeser and Imogene Coca. Family situation comedy was a format taken directly from radio, with such series as "The Goldbergs," "The Life of Riley," and "Our Miss Brooks." However, it was "I Love Lucy," first broadcast in 1951, that set the standard for this type of comedy. Children's programs were very popular. They were led by "Howdy Doody" featuring Buffalo Bob Smith and a host of puppets, and Burr Tillstrom's more adult "Kukla, Fran, & Ollie," starring Fran Allison. Two important program additions were the adult Western, starting with

Figure 7.3. Lucille Ball (seen here with stage and, then, real husband Desi Arnez) helped develop the genre of television situation comedy with her program "I Love Lucy." (Photo: Movie Star News.)

Figure 7.4. "Robert Montgomery Presents" was one of many live television dramatic series that flourished in the mid-1950s. (Photo: The Bettman Archive, Inc.)

"Gunsmoke" in 1955, and the big-prize game shows, beginning with "The $64,000 Question" in 1956. Westerns reached their peak in 1959/1960, with 32 Westerns aired in prime time, but gradually declined until, by the mid-1970s, none were on network schedules. The quiz scandals in 1959 revealed that some participants had received answers prior to their appearance on the shows or had been coached in their responses to heighten tension. This notoriety killed off the prime-time big-money quiz shows, although game shows continue to be a staple of daytime and early-evening programming.

"Live" drama reached its zenith in the mid-1950s, with such programs as "Studio One," "Playhouse 90," and "The Armstrong Circle Theater." But television's voracious appetite for new material soon made it impossible to sustain high artistic standards. The form began to blend with other dramatic types and gradually faded from the scene. Today, with the exception of "The Hallmark Hall of Fame," British Broadcasting Corporation (BBC) imports on public television, and limited network specials, quality drama on television is rare.

Program experimentation began to dwindle as network competition heated up. In the late 1950s, Westerns, situation comedies, and crime-detective dramas accounted for over 50 percent of all prime-time programming. Producers seemed to be jumping on various bandwagons, duplicating whatever was popular at the moment.

The TV quiz scandals in 1959 seemed to herald an end to the age of euphoria. According to the Tenth Annual Videotown Report, which was published in 1957 by Cunningham & Walsh, television had become accepted as a routine part of life and had lost much of its novelty and excitement. A public-opinion poll taken by Sindlinger in 1959 revealed a sharp drop in the public's estimation of television following the quiz scandals. Congress began a series of investigations that focused particular attention on the relationship among advertisers, agencies, and broadcasters. Much of this concern was strikingly capsulated by FCC chairman Newton Minow in 1961, when he criticized television and called it "a vast wasteland."

Figure 7.5. Jack Barry reads a question for contestant Charles Van Doren, who is in the booth behind him. Barry's quiz show "Twenty-One" was taken off the air when Van Doren confessed that he had been given answers in advance. (Photo: Picture Collection, The Branch Libraries, The New York Public Library.)

The 1950s were a time of experimentation and change for television. A whole new generation of programs, stars, and techniques came into being. By 1960, the trial period was over. Television was ready to settle down and grow up. The tensions created by these two trends would highlight TV's maturing years.

Growth, Progress, and Criticism: 1961–1980

Growth and progress were television's two most dominating characteristics in this period. Criticism of television also became popular as politicians, educators, social scientists, members of minority groups, and parents took turns attacking the medium. Of particular public concern was television's role in the violence in the United States in the 1960s and 1970s. Countless studies focused on TV's effects, especially on children.

Television's impact on the political process became apparent in the 1960s, beginning with the Nixon–Kennedy debates in 1960, continuing in

Figure 7.6. Television helped bring American presidential campaigns into the home through such events as presidential debates. In this photo from an NBC monitor, Jimmy Carter and Ronald Reagan prepare to face each other and a national television audience in 1980. (Photo: AP/Wide World Photos.)

1968 with TV's coverage of the Democratic National Convention in Chicago, and highlighted by the Carter–Ford debates in 1976, the Reagan–
Carter debates in 1980, and the Reagan–Mondale debates in 1984. The role
of television in the political-campaign process grew tremendously and
stimulated concern about packaged candidates and election by commercial
slogan.

Networks continued their domination of programming. By 1969, they
provided almost 64 percent (77.5 hours a week) of their affiliates' programming. As revenue and profits increased, criticism seemed to keep pace.
The FCC proposed a plan whereby 50 percent of all prime-time programming would have to be non-network originated, but this proposal was
never implemented. In the 1971/1972 season, however, the FCC instituted
a rule cutting network prime-time programming from three and one-half to
three hours an evening in the 7:30 to 11:00 p.m. (EST) time block.

As 90 percent of American homes became equipped with television
sets and viewing levels reached 6 hours a day in the average TV household, a great deal of concern was generated over programming. Violence
on television was attacked following the assassinations of President John F.
Kennedy, Martin Luther King, Jr., and Robert Kennedy. An overhaul of
Saturday-morning cartoon shows occurred in the 1970/1971 season to appease critics, although this area of programming remains heavily criticized.
Perhaps the most dramatic and effective action came against the cigarette
industry by the Surgeon General's office, with its claims that cigarette
smoking is dangerous to a person's health. Pressure by the Surgeon General resulted in all cigarette advertising being taken off the air on January 2,
1971. A "family hour" was implemented in 1975/1976 in which the first
hour of prime-time programming was limited to material suitable for the
entire family. The result was a mishmash of weak comedies and variety
programs that proved to be poor lead-ins for later programs, and it was
phased out in 1976.

Any historical overview of television in the 1960s finds itself overwhelmed by the sheer number of events, people, and issues in the TV
spotlight. In this decade, three events stand out: the Vietnam War, the
assassination and funeral of President Kennedy, and the *Apollo 11* moon
landing. All three are competitors for the label of TV's finest hour. Instead
of simply hearing or reading about the war, the president's funeral, or the
moon walk after they happened, the American public was able—through
television—to witness and participate in these events as they were happening. At times, this witnessing was inspiring, as when television went to
the moon. At times, it was frightening, as when suspected presidential
assassin Lee Harvey Oswald was murdered by Jack Ruby in full view of the
nation, or when a captured Vietcong soldier was shot in the head as cameras recorded the scene. At times, it was illuminating, as when dogs and
water hoses were turned on civil-rights demonstrators and when police

Figure 7.7. All cigarette advertising, such as this Old Gold live commercial, was taken off television in 1971. (Photo: Picture Collection, The Branch Libraries, The New York Public Library.)

fought with protesters in Chicago during the 1968 Democratic National Convention. (Many people remember the protesters chanting, "The whole world is watching" as they were pummeled by the police.) The 1960s were anything but peaceful, and television was on hand to provide dramatic witness, perhaps even dramatic stimulation, to the turmoil. Much of the world was watching and was being changed in the process.

Whatever else television was in this period, it was programs; shown primarily on the networks, motion pictures became a major part of prime-time fare. The ABC network broke new ground by showing *The Bridge on the River Kwai* in 1966, and by the 1970s, the networks were engaged in a furious bidding war for recent and successful motion pictures.

Situation comedies formed the single strongest genre of the period. "I Love Lucy" dominated the 1950s and set the standard for others to follow. The 1960s were populated by a variety of programs, including "Hazel," "The Andy Griffith Show," "The Beverly Hillbillies," "The Dick Van Dyke Show," and "The Donna Reed Show." Most of these were good-natured domestic situations that had little relationship to the reality of the turbulent decade.

Figure 7.8. Television allowed millions of viewers to share in the thrill of astronaut Ed Aldrin's moon walk while it was happening, during the *Apollo II* moon landing in July 1969. (Photo: *The Bettman Archive, Inc.*)

However, the 1970s witnessed an abrupt and dramatic shift in the situation comedy to more "adult" themes and topics. It started in 1971 with "All in the Family" and proliferated throughout the first half of the decade until it made up over 25 percent of the network's prime-time schedule in 1976/1977. Such programs as "Maude," "Soap," "Sanford and Son," "Alice," "Mary Hartman, Mary Hartman," and "Three's Company" regularly used abortion, premarital sex, narcotics, bigotry, and adultery as comic material. The producer Norman Lear was responsible for many of the decade's biggest series, including "All in the Family," "Maude," and "The Jeffersons." Other popular sitcoms of the 1970s that were less realistic in tone included "The Mary Tyler Moore Show," "The Bob Newhart Show," "Happy Days," and "Laverne and Shirley." However, the most dominant sitcom of the period and a classic in the genre to rival "I Love

Lucy" was "M*A*S*H." Critics and audiences loved the program, which wove the delicate threads of realism and humor into a rich, touching, intelligent, and very funny picture of life in a combat surgical unit during the Korean War.

Westerns, with the exception of a few major long-running hit shows, declined in the period. Only "Gunsmoke," "Bonanza," and "Little House on the Prairie" were able to survive the gradual shift in network television programming toward what might be called "adult modern."

Variety programs started strongly, but by the late 1970s had all but disappeared. Interestingly, this genre also "grew up" in the 1960s. "The Ed Sullivan Show" carried on through 1971, showcasing a remarkable variety of talent—from Elvis Presley to the Beatles to opera stars Robert Merril and Roberta Peters to animal acts, comics, and acrobats. Imitators of Sullivan included Perry Como, Dinah Shore, and Andy Williams. The big break with the Sullivan tradition occurred with such programs as "The Smothers Brothers Comedy Hour," "Rowan and Martin's Laugh-In," and "That Was the Week that Was." Not only was the content adult, often satirical and political, but also, especially with "Laugh-In," the style changed dramatically from that of the vaudeville stage to an edited style that emphasized rapid pacing and strong visual appeal. The visuality of such comedy-variety programs as "Carol Burnett," "Sonny and Cher," and "Donny and Marie" often compensated for the absence of major guest stars or creative skits.

Finally, the genre evolved into its last (to date) stage with "Saturday Night Live." Because of its late-night time period, the success of "Saturday Night Live" was due to its controversial topics as well as to its genuine and occasionally unique talent. The Not Ready for Prime Time Players cast of Dan Aykroyd, Chevy Chase, Bill Murray, Gilda Radner, and John Belushi ultimately became a program into itself, and all of the actors ultimately left the show to assume star status on their own.

Prime-time drama has gone through several stages since the golden age of live drama in the 1950s. The form became less theater and more television with such programs in the 1960s as "Alfred Hitchcock Presents," "Perry Mason," "The Defenders," "Dr. Kildare," "Ben Casey," "Peyton Place," and "The Twilight Zone." The 1970s were dominated by "The Waltons," but as the decade wore on, more realism and adult themes began to appear in such programs as "Lou Grant." However, the major trend in prime-time drama was in bringing the daytime soap-opera format and content to nighttime television. "Dallas" is the prime example of the form, with "Dynasty," "Knotts Landing," and a host of others following suit. The 1980s brought stronger realism in the form of such programs as "Hill Street Blues" and "St. Elsewhere." A "Hallmark Hall of Fame" major event, such as the presentation of *Death of a Salesman* in 1985, provides an occasional dramatic peak, but in general, prime-time drama is formula-bound, cliché-ridden mass entertainment.

Not to be outdone by their prime-time counterparts, daytime soap operas assumed major cult status in the late 1970s and early 1980s. Daytime soap operas have been a broadcast staple since the early 1930s. Television simply picked up the form from radio and continued the pattern. Targeted primarily at women, soap operas achieve remarkable viewer loyalty; note the 30-year life span of such programs as "As the World Turns." The major trend in soap operas of the past five years has been the "heating up" of content. Dialogue, situations, and scenes that would have been unthinkable 20 years ago are standard fare. Soap operas have always dealt with romance and love, much of it traumatic and suggestive. Today, however, the soaps "suggest" very little and "reveal" a great deal—from a man's bare chest to an "active" bedroom scene. Murder, adultery, and rape, while not exactly everyday events, occur with startling regularity and in fairly graphic detail. Soaps have become a strong source of revenue for the networks and have tightened their hold on the American viewer.

Like talk shows on radio, "talk TV" has emerged as a strong form, primarily in syndication during the daytime. "The Phil Donahue Show" is a good example of the standard formula of host, guest(s), and audience. The key to the success of such programs is the host's manipulation of the relationship among guest, audience, and host. The only successful nighttime version is, of course, "The Tonight Show." Johnny Carson masterfully orchestrates his audience and guests into a classic and enduring program that is unlikely to be duplicated. Much as Ed Sullivan did, Carson "defines" the genre.

There are other genres and other program forms: children's programs, game-quiz shows, action-adventure. We do not have the space to analyze them all. But two forms require at least passing attention because of their special, almost symbiotic, relationship to television: sports—primarily football—and the miniseries. Professional football became the national TV pastime as the Green Bay Packers, Dallas Cowboys, and Pittsburgh Steelers became a variation on America's team. The Super Bowl stopped being a football game years ago and is a media event in its own right, with all the accompanying ritual. The miniseries is another made-for-television format that emphasizes the medium's serial and episodic structure. With the broadcasting of "Rich Man, Poor Man," "Roots," "Holocaust," and "The Thorn Birds," the miniseries became a strong programming factor that, coupled with ratings "sweeps," threatened to alter television's long-standing seasonal structure built on 13- and 26-week series.

Network and local news also took on an enlarged and more important role. Network news on television began in 1948 with a 15-minute program on CBS, "Douglas Edwards with the News." This program length remained the standard until 1963, when all three networks expanded to a 30-minute newscast. Along with the increased time devoted to it, news grew in prestige and as a source of revenue. A star system soon developed in network news, led by the anchors for the network-news evening program.

Figure 7.9. CBS News anchor Dan Rather prepares copy for his nightly newscast. Network news and the people who deliver it have become an important part of network-television competition, resulting in "star" billing for many people like Rather. (Photo: CBS News.)

Walter Cronkite of CBS became the dominant broadcast journalist of the 1970s and—along with David Brinkley, John Chancellor, Dan Rather, and many others—became a network star.

On the local level, the commercial success of news programs led to a show-business style aptly dubbed "happy talk." News became choreographed and packaged, like any other entertainment program, much to the chagrin of critics and journalists.

The Age of Technology: Since 1980

Television today must come to grips with its past and confront new technologies that threaten the basic structure of the industry. James Rosenfield of CBS made this position very clear in 1985 when he stated that television is facing its fourth major trial—the "trial of technology." Indicating that television had survived three previous trials—acceptance as a medium, cultural integration, and maturity—he expressed deep concern about what he called "unregulated competitors" for the TV audience.

The major changes in television in the 1980s have not been in programming but in the manner in which programming is distributed to and received by the American public. The technological developments of the 1960s and 1970s, together with broadcast-industry deregulation, have spawned a new era in program-delivery systems that involve satellites, cable television, and videocassette and videodisc players. What is occurring today is the simultaneous activity of programming, new technologies, and regulatory actions, creating an unpredictable marketplace. As Gene Jankowski of CBS remarked:

A good symbol for this new order might be the "double helix"—the famous model of the DNA molecule. It looks like a spiral staircase without the steps. We still have discrete industry segments—stations, networks, production companies, agencies, clients and so on at the core, but the functional elements of our business no longer relate themselves to these segments in the traditional manner.[2]

What is clear from all this is that the television industry of the future will not resemble the one familiar to most of us for the past 30 years. The three networks will no longer dominate television, and the mix of entertainment and information carried over our television receivers will be more varied, more fine-tuned, and influenced by more viewer's needs and demands than ever before.

Satellites. When the Communications Satellite Act was passed in 1962, the United States officially got into international television. The first satellites, *Telstar* and *Relay*, were launched in 1963 and provided intercontinental coverage of the funerals of Pope John XXIII and President Kennedy, among other events. In 1965, the first commercial satellite, *Early Bird*, was launched by COMSAT. By 1969, satellite usage had increased, much of it for coverage of the Vietnam War via *Lanai Bird*, the Pacific counterpart of *Early Bird*. By 1971, a full-scale international communication system existed, with three synchronous satellites in fixed positions over the Atlantic, Pacific, and Indian oceans, as well as a large network of earth stations.

The United States began domestic satellite transmission in 1973, when RCA leased time on Canada's *ANIK II* to relay signals between the East and West coasts. In 1974, ABC Radio began transmitting service to its four radio networks via satellite.

As network distribution costs via AT&T land-based long lines increased steadily in the 1970s, the use of domestic satellites increased as well. In 1976, KPLR-TV in St. Louis was granted an FCC license for a satellite receiver, and other stations soon followed suit. In 1977, the Public Broadcasting Service (PBS) began construction of a satellite-interconnect system that eventually would provide direct satellite-to-earth-station distribution for all PBS television stations and National Public Radio (NPR) radio stations. By the early 1980s, satellite distribution of programs was being used by a wide variety of networks, production companies, and even local stations. Ted Turner's station WTBS-TV in Atlanta, Georgia, began to distribute its local programs to cable systems by satellite in 1979. By the early 1980s, Turner had developed the Cable News Network (CNN), a news service sent to cable systems across the country, opening the way for a number of special networks that fed programs to cable systems.

Twenty-three years after the launch of AT&T's *Telstar,* the boom in satellite communications shows no sign of abating. In the mid-1980s in the

---

[2] *Ibid.*

Figure 7.10. This satellite earth station at Raisting, Upper Bavaria, is one of the largest in the world. Satellites and dishes such as this one have transformed international communication and helped make Marshall McLuhan's vision of a "global village" a reality. (Photo: Courtesy Siemens AG Communications.)

United States, the Federal Communications Commission authorized the launch of two dozen more satellites for domestic service and a dozen more for international service. Australia, Brazil, and Mexico sent up their first satellites.

These satellites are a far cry from the tiny *Telstar*: bristling with antennas and packed with electronics, each weighs a ton or more and typically costs $100 million to build, launch, and insure. Some of them relay telephone conversations to ships and airplanes; others transmit television to compact earth stations; still others provide telecommunications services to remote areas. Currently there are two dozen purely domestic American satellites in service, relaying cable-television programs, digital data, and voice traffic to more than 1 million earth stations. More than 20 local television stations in the United States have equipped themselves with satellite-transmitting dishes mounted on trucks, with which they relay remote news feeds to their studios. NBC has over 50 such systems for regional news gathering. Almost every American station has a dish for picking up network and syndicated programs.

The key to satellite distribution of programs is not simply the satellite itself, but two other elements: a ground-based transmission station, known as an "uplink" and a receiving dish, or "downlink." The uplink sends a signal to the satellite, which amplifies and retransmits the signal to the downlink, which, in turn, feeds a cable system, a local station, or, in the case of direct broadcast satellite (DBS), a home. As earth stations become technically, economically, and legally easier to construct, the possibilities of direct satellite-to-home distribution become more obvious, allowing DBS to by-pass the station or cable delivery system. The number of home satellite dishes sold in the United States has increased dramatically in the past three years and shows no signs of slowing down.

These developments are causing concern, however. Satellites compete directly with AT&T's ground networks and, in the case of direct transmission to individual receivers, with local stations and cable systems. The economic consequences of direct satellite-to-home transmission, especially, are great. Nevertheless, the potential for expanded program service at a reduced cost makes the risk worthwhile.

Cable Television. Cable television, CATV (Community Antenna Television), has made even more dramatic strides than the use of satellites (Table 7.1). In 1960, there were only 640 operating systems in the United States, with a total of 650,000 subscribers. By 1970, cable had grown to almost 2,500 systems and 1.3 million subscribers. In 1986, over 6,500 systems were serving more than 41 million TV households, or 47.4 percent penetration.

Pennsylvania has the most systems (351); California, the most subscribers (2.6 million). The average monthly fee (basic service) is $8. An estimated 3,250 systems originate programming in their own studios, at an average of 23 hours weekly. Over 700 systems (14 percent of all systems) accept advertising on their local origination channels (excluding automated channels), with rates from $2 to $400 for a 30-second spot. Most cable systems receive less than 5 percent of their gross revenue from advertising.

What began in the late 1940s as simply a master receiving antenna for

TABLE 7.1 THE GROWTH OF CABLE TELEVISION IN THE UNITED STATES

Year	Cable subscribers (thousands)	Household penetration (%)	Pay subscribers (thousands)
1965	1,760	3.3	Unavailable
1970	4,498	7.5	Unavailable
1975	9,197	13.2	Unavailable
1980	17,671	22.6	7,599
1981	23,219	28.3	11,842
1982	29,341	35.0	17,311
1983	33,794	40.5	21,151
1984	37,291	43.7	22,375
1985	38,700	45.3	
1986	41,000	47.4	

Source: Cabletelevision Advertising Bureau.

isolated communities has grown to the point where it clearly poses an
economic threat to local broadcasters. Cable television is a major programming force in today's TV environment. It no longer exists simply to serve
rural areas or even to bring a local or regional station's signal into individual homes. Cable has developed a programming life of its own by aug-
menting its local-station service with distant-signal imports (such as Atlanta's WTBS-TV), local origination programs, and special services (such as
Home Box Office [HBO]). With FCC deregulation of cable in the early
1980s, especially the decision in 1986 by the Supreme Court in *Quincy Cable
TV Inc.*, which left standing a lower court decision stating that must-carry
regulation was a violation of the First Amendment, cable is now free to
compete in the open marketplace for audiences and advertising dollars.
Growth in cable penetration and programming is occurring at a consistently strong rate.

Major cities, among them Dallas, New Orleans, Cincinnati, Pittsburgh, and Boston, are being wired and added to the cable universe. This
expansion is adding subscribers to the industry roll at a rate of 250,000 per
month.

Cable operators are building supersystems in the new markets. Many
will offer 50 channels, and some more than 100, although about 30 channels seems to be the maximum at present. The cable operators are also
upgrading existing cable systems and expanding channel capacity to 20 or
more channels to increase services and revenue and to make the systems
less vulnerable to competition.

The widespread introduction of satellite-delivered pay television revolutionized the industry in the latter half of the 1970s, providing an enormous leap in revenue without significant additional capital investment.
Multipay, the selling of two or more pay services to the same home, has
proved viable and is counted on to fuel the construction and operation of
the high-capacity urban systems. Pay-per-view pay television (PPV) and
advertising are regarded as the most immediate sources of additional revenue. And the so-called two-way services—videotext, security, teleshop-
ping, telebanking—although slow in developing, promise new revenue for
the future.

Cable has become the medium of choice. Operators (and, ultimately,
subscribers) have a panoply of programs to choose from, all delivered
conveniently to their backyards by satellites. A survey by *Broadcasting* in
1986 found no fewer than 47 program services—35 basic and 12 pay—with
15 others in the wings.

In 1975, RCA's *SATCOM I* satellite was sent into space, enabling HBO
and, later, two smaller rivals, Showtime and the Movie Channel, to transmit movies to local cable systems. Since then, the living room has rapidly
been supplementing the theater as an arena for watching motion pictures,
and the amount of money collected from home viewers has soared. The
fees paid by subscribers for a monthly diet of movies has increased signifi-

cantly in the past five years, to revenues in 1985 of almost $3 billion, as compared with $3.5 billion at the conventional theater box office.

Programming on pay cable typically includes first-run motion pictures and sports events. A greater variety is emerging, however, including X- and R-rated films on "adult cable" and cultural programs provided primarily by the BBC over cable rather than through its traditional American outlet, the PBS stations. Prices for pay TV vary according to the system, but most subscribers pay $10 to 15 a month for Home Box Office programming or similar services.

Over-the-air pay TV, or subscription television (STV), has had mixed success in the past five years. As a result of FCC deregulation in 1977, STV finally got off the ground with two stations, one in Los Angeles and one in New York. By the early 1980s, more than 25 stations were operating, all of which were located in large urban areas. Programming on STV is similar to that on cable, but because STV can offer only one channel to a subscriber (versus the tiered service possibilities of cable), many feel that its future is limited to areas that do not have cable. Indeed, by mid-1983, STV subscribership had slipped from a high of 1.4 million to 1.1 million. The Entertainment Channel, a pay-TV network created by RCA, folded in 1983 after only nine months of operation and more than $80 million in losses. The problems of STV merely underscore the challenges facing other pay-TV delivery systems, such as multipoint-distribution services (MDS) and direct broadcast satellite (DBS).

The formula for success in pay television is no longer simply offering people the latest *Star Wars* or *Indiana Jones* blockbuster. Instead, "made-for-pay" series and sports events are being bought on an exclusive basis by the pay networks. Further development of pay television includes pay-per-view television, and, as a result, pay cable services will need to offer viewers more variety and choice in order to compete.

Many factors cloud the future of cable, the most important being financial. While cable's rapid expansion into a $5-billion industry has secured a foothold in TV's future, the growth has strained resources on every level. Advertising revenue is coming in more slowly than expected, since advertising agencies are experimenting with cable instead of investing in it. Production costs of original cable programming have risen, and local cable operators are squeezed between programmers who are demanding higher prices for their product and subscribers who are demanding more service for the same fee. Most of the problems have originated with cable's high hopes for itself. To support the promise of something for everybody, many companies promoted market projections to unrealistic levels. They estimated and developed revenue levels on the basis of 60 to 70 percent penetration when 45 percent was more realistic. The phenomenal increase in VCRs has also reduced cable's promise—especially the promise of pay cable, with its basic "uncut-movie" premise.

It seems clear that cable will succeed only to the extent that it provides a strong alternative to existing programming. If cable chooses to utilize its potential for minority-interest programming, two-way transmission, multichannel programming, and "custom-tailored" programming, it will not only survive, but also prosper. If it chooses merely to relay existing signals, performing the role of conduit, it will most likely fail. The "shakeout" period is now cable's reality.

Low-Power Television. Low-power TV (LPTV) is a new kind of television station, licensed to broadcast over a geographic area between 10 and 15 miles in radius. A full-power station covers about 80 miles. Low-power stations are inserted on the VHF and UHF spectra, but emit signals that are so weak that they do not interfere with full-power stations on the same channels in nearby cities. Before low power, for instance, Stillwater, Minnesota, couldn't use Channel 5, which is allocated to St. Paul. Now a broadcaster in Stillwater can send out a low-power signal over Channel 5 without impinging on the larger station's signal.

Low-power stations are modeled on the "translator," or repeater, stations that were used for some time in rural areas to pick up and rebroadcast remote signals. Translator operators were forbidden to originate their own material until 1981, when the FCC lifted the restriction.

The nation's first LPTV station was Channel 26 in Bemidji, Minnesota, and despite some early promise, growth has been slow. The primary problem is financial. To survive in the localized form for which they were intended, LPTV stations have to carry a high volume of ads. Advertisers, even in small communities, want the largest and best audience for their dollar, and so the pressure is on most LPTV stations to supply popular off-network and/or syndicated programming. This ultimately defeats the intent of LPTV, and the future of the medium may ultimately be with large corporations, such as Park Communications, which have applied for a large number of LPTV licenses and which have the financial resources to acquire programs and stay in the market over the long haul. In 1986, there were 383 LPTV stations on the air—242 VHF and 141 UHF. Another 210 had received construction permits.

Teletext and Videotex. Teletext and videotex are two distant but potentially bright stars on the horizon. By linking the power of the computer to the television set, they have the ability to transform an entertainment medium into an information-age appliance.

Videotex uses a telephone line, or two-way cable, to connect the TV set to a central computer, and thus is interactive. A popular and simplified version of on-line computer time sharing, videotex allows thousands of individuals to communicate with one computer in order to retrieve information or conduct transactions. For a monthly subscription fee plus telephone charges, the videotex subscriber uses a small keyboard to bank, shop, play games, do research, and conduct a variety of other transactions.

Figure 7.11. This videotex "page" is typical of the format, style, and content of most videotex systems. (Photo: Courtesy AT&T Information Systems.)

Teletext is a one-way technology that delivers textual and graphic information to TV sets as part of the standard broadcast signal. Digital data are "inserted" into a few lines of the TV picture called the "vertical blanking interval."

The information is presented on "pages," which viewers can call up on their screens by punching a number on a decoder. Most teletext "magazines" contain about 100 pages of information, typically including news headlines, weather reports, sports scores, video games, and stock prices. Teletext is generally supported by advertising and is free to anyone who buys a decoder. Thus teletext promises to be more widely available than videotex, even though it cannot do as much.

As with other forms of new technology, videotex and teletext are media seeking an audience. Those companies who were quick to enter the videotex and teletext market, such as Knight-Ridder and Times Mirror, have pulled the plug on their services. The reasons for these failures included technology that was too expensive and difficult for the consumer to use and a lack of understanding of what services consumers wanted. Although many have touted the demise of some systems as a major setback to videotex, there are many indicators that lead others to believe in the vitality of the medium.

A number of successful system operators and services are currently not only in households, but also in businesses and public areas (for example, banks and shopping malls). Examples of these include CompuServe, Dow Jones/News Retrieval, and The Source. Further evidence of the potential success of videotex comes from the *Wall Street Journal*'s recent projection that 20 percent of all households will subscribe to a videotex service within the next 10 years. Those who are in videotex seem to be willing to wait until the right combination of price and services triggers a profitable market for electronic message sending, home banking, shopping, and database retrieval.

Videocassette and Videodisc. The late 1970s witnessed a tremendous surge in new forms of video technology, including home videocassette and videodisc systems, video games, and use of the TV set with home computers and multiband cable systems.

Figure 7.12. The Sony Betamax, introduced in 1975, was the first videocassette recorder available for home use. The VHS format, however, has far surpassed Sony's Beta format in popularity. (Photo: Courtesy Sony Corporation of America.)

The 1980s have carried this surge to the point of a media revolution, a revolution in technology centered on delivery and distribution. While satellites and cable television have been steadily encroaching on the traditional network long-line–distribution structure, their progress has been measured and, in many instances, encouraged by the networks. The revolution involving videocassettes, videodiscs, and home computers has been neither measured nor encouraged by the networks.

Home video recording dates back to the 1960s, but it was not until 1972 that Sony produced the first videocassette recorder (VCR) for business and education. In 1975, Sony introduced the Betamax for home use. In 1977, the market expanded with the introduction of the VHS system. Today, VHS captures almost 85 percent of the home video-recorder market. A new format—8mm—is just emerging.

The VCR "revolution" has been an extraordinary one. VCR unit sales increased by 250 percent to 2 million in 1982, and sales in 1983 doubled to over 4 million units. These figures were merely a prelude to the numbers for 1984 (7.4 million) and 1985 (12 million). In fact, VCR sales for the first 23 weeks of 1985 exceeded those for *all* of 1983. VCRs have been installed in over 40 percent of all American households and have become an integral component of the home-entertainment system. Households with at least one VCR use it an average of 6 hours a week for recording and more hours a week for playing cassettes. In 1985, Nielsen developed the first report on the impact of VCRs on network programming. The ratings company found that VCR recording did not significantly influence network ratings. Forty percent of prime-time programs showed no change, 42 percent had a negligible (0.1–0.2%) change, and 70 percent of daytime programs had no change. Movies, soap operas, and younger adult programs ("Miami Vice," "Moonlighting," "Cheers") are most heavily recorded.

The VCR boom is being fed by lower prices and added features that increase the versatility of the basic machines. Many models feature two-week advance programming, remote-control tuning, and "scanning," which gives the viewer the ability to "fast forward" the picture to avoid commercials. Other features permit "zapping," the elimination of the commercial altogether. Also fueling this expansion is the growth of the "software," or programming. Surveys indicate that over 80 percent of VCR owners buy or rent prerecorded programs, mostly movies. An estimated 10 million prerecorded videocassettes were sold in 1985, and for every sale, there are approximately 10 rentals—bringing the total to 100 million rentals.

The videodisc, once thought of as the shining star of the video revolution, has been essentially the story of great promise unfulfilled. After four years of "hard sell," RCA pulled out of the field in 1984, leaving the laser system developed by Pioneer and North American Philips with the market to itself.

The videodisc may, after all, ultimately play the lead role in the video revolution. The disc can turn a TV set into an interactive instrument with multiple uses. The key to the videodisc's role in shaping the future of television lies not so much in its ability to provide an alternative means of distributing a series such as "Dallas" or a movie such as *Top Gun*, but in its power and potential as an information-processing and -storage medium. When linked with a home computer, the videodisc can perform myriad functions, ranging from interactive teaching lessons to vicarious traveling, in which an individual can tour a foreign country through programmed response patterns.

The immediate future of videodiscs rests with the concept of "video publishing," in which videodisc programs are marketed much like books or records. Corporations like RCA, with its SelectaVision disc system, are releasing catalogs of movies and selected TV series for home consumption. The networks themselves are also bidding to program this market.

All these new technologies have ultimately had their impact on the home receiver. Now being described as a "home video terminal," the set of tomorrow here today has incorporated special input and output jacks for video devices, higher resolution tubes and circuitry to accommodate computers and teletext, and built-in tuners that substitute for the cable-TV converter box. In addition, such features as stereo amplifiers and speakers, remote-control channel selectors, and giant screens have spurred record sales of color-television receivers–over 16 million in 1985.

THE PUBLIC BROADCASTING SERVICE

After languishing for over a decade, educational television (ETV) began to flex its muscles in the 1960s. The pivotal event in ETV's growth was the passage of the Public Broadcasting Act of 1967, which ranks with the 1952

Sixth Order and Report as one of the most important documents in the history of educational television. In effect, the 1967 act provided for the first interconnected network of ETV stations. Most important, it provided educational television with the financial support necessary to become a creative force in American life. Without the 1967 act, many ETV stations would never have been built or modernized.

The act established the Corporation for Public Broadcasting (CPB), which, in turn, established the Public Broadcasting Service (PBS) in 1970. After a lengthy and damaging struggle between CPB and PBS for control of the system, PBS emerged in 1973 as the creative controller of the system, with CPB continuing its role as program funder. PBS manages TV programming, production, distribution, and station interconnection, which is primarily by satellite. The most important single programming development during the early years of the PBS system was the creation of the Children's Television Workshop (CTV), producer of "Sesame Street" and "Electric Company," among other programs. An independent nonprofit corporation, CTV's only ties to public broadcasting are partial funding by CPB. Another important programming source is the British Broadcasting Corporation, which has supplied such series as "Civilization," "The Forsyte Saga," and "Upstairs, Downstairs." In 1980, however, the BBC entered into a 10-year agreement to sell its programs in the United States to a cable network, threatening one of PBS' best sources of prestige programming.

Financing is at the heart of public broadcasting's future role. Throughout the Nixon administration, there was controversy resulting primarily from CPB's increasing development of public-affairs programming, including several controversial programs and series. Legislation passed under President Ford provided for a federal matching plan and five-year financing. This $634 million bill became law in 1976 and ensured public broadcasting of a relatively stable financial base for the first time in its history.

TABLE 7.2 SOURCES OF PBS PROGRAMMING FUNDS*

Business	28.5%
Public television stations:	25%
CPB	14.5%
Other federal agencies	12%
Independent producers	11%
Individuals, state and local government, educational institutions	5%
Foundations	4%

* Based on 1982 budget

However, the Reagan administration's cuts have clouded the future of public television, and PBS is continually seeking new sources of revenue.

As Table 7.2 indicates, a funding shift has occurred in recent years, with private business rather than the federal government as the major source of funds. Second on the list are the local stations, which raise money through program underwriting, membership drives, auctions, and other promotions. Many stations are pushing membership drives and local fund-raising efforts to the saturation point and, as a result, are beginning to explore other means of obtaining operating revenue, including limited sale of time and programs. In 1986, there were 300 educational TV stations on the air—114 VHF and 186 UHF.

NONBROADCAST TELEVISION

Most of us know only the world of television that comes through our TV sets every day. We are at least vaguely familiar with networks, stations, and cable systems. However, there is a world of nonbroadcast television that is rapidly expanding.

Nonbroadcast television has many names: corporate video, instructional television, small-format video, and industrial television. In many ways, it is a profession in search of an identity.

Who is using these forms of video? Today, almost every type of organization is using video to communicate both internally and externally.

Educational institutions were among the first users of nonbroadcast television, and despite some misguided concepts and uses continue to be an important consumer. However, business and industry are the major users of nonbroadcast video. The applications fall into three categories: training, employee communications, and public information. Production facilities range from one portable video unit stored in an office to elaborate video centers rivaling many TV stations. Annual expenditures for just the audiovisual part of corporate training exceed $2 billion, with a large portion of that allocated to video.

Government agencies, social-service agencies, professional organizations, medical and health organizations, religious groups, production houses, and consultants are just some of the many users of nonbroadcast television. The Federal Bureau of Prisons, for example, conducts staff training by video. Rather than take officers away from their duties, videotapes are sent to each federal prison. The Red Cross has studios in Washington, D.C., where it produces a variety of tapes on such topics as blood donation and disaster relief. Hospitals, clinics, medical schools, and individual physicians use video in numerous ways. Plastic-surgery technology is documented by a hospital in Springfield, Illinois, for distribution to other hospitals and surgeons.

The examples are endless. The use of nonbroadcast video has expanded at the rate of about 40 percent a year. Why this expansion? Diane Gayeski, in her book *Corporate and Instructional Video,* provides some insight by listing 10 factors she believes account for this rapid growth:

1. Video is an effective communications tool.
2. Travel is becoming more expensive.
3. Organizations are becoming larger.
4. Video equipment is becoming cheaper and more portable.
5. Video is cost effective.
6. People like to watch television.
7. Video allows for self-paced learning.
8. Video programs, unlike people, do not get tired or bored.
9. Video is immediate.
10. We are learning how to use the medium.

Careers in nonbroadcast television are growing also. While not as glamorous as some positions in broadcast television, jobs in nonbroadcast video are very satisfying and rewarding. There are few set formats, and clients change regularly. Most producers are responsible for the whole production rather than for simply one part. Also, the salaries are competitive, especially at the entry and middle-management levels.

THE SCOPE OF TELEVISION

Despite the continuing avalanche of criticism about television, the number of households with television sets and the prime-time television-network audiences have continued to grow. TV viewing, however, recorded its first drop in history in 1984/1985 from 7 hours and 8 minutes to 7 hours and 7 minutes a day. However, viewership in February and July (typically the high and low months) increased significantly.

Prime-time programs broadcast on Sunday night attract the largest audience. Thursday night is second, followed by Monday, Tuesday, Wednesday, and Friday nights; Saturday night receives the least attention.

Television viewing increases through the day, hitting a peak between 8:00 and 10:00 P.M. The 8:30 to 9:00 P.M. half-hour is the most viewed time, and women account for the greatest share of viewing during prime time.

In terms of total viewing, women 55 years and older do the most TV viewing—41 hours and 13 minutes a week in November. That's 10 hours and 34 minutes more than average. Female teen-agers watch the least—24 hours and 16 minutes a week. Pay-cable households view significantly more television than non-cable households; and houses with children view significantly more than houses without children.

As Table 7.3 shows, the number of TV households is also increasing every year. TV households exist in virtually every area of the country, but

TABLE 7.3 GROWTH OF TV HOUSEHOLDS IN THE UNITED STATES*

	1959	1965	1970	1975	1980	1985
TV households	43,950	52,700	59,700	70,100	79,900	85,900
% of all households	85.9	92.6	95.2	97.5	98	98
Color-set households	250	2,810	27,800	51,500	67,915	78,600
% of all households	0.7	4.9	39.2	70.8	83.0	91.5
Multiset households	4,200	10,225	19,700	31,500	40,749	48,393

* In thousands
Source: A. C. Nielsen.

the top six markets—New York, Los Angeles, Chicago, Philadelphia, San Francisco, and Boston—are considered to be the most important, since they constitute over 24 percent of all TV households.

As Table 7.4 indicates, the number of TV stations, although limited by spectrum space and frequency allocation, continues to grow, primarily in the UHF band.

Television continues to prosper financially. A major study by the Broadcast Financial Management Association released in 1986 revealed that net revenues earned by the three networks jumped by over 62 percent from $4.1 billion in 1980 to $6.7 billion in 1985. The survey also found increases of 44 percent over the same 5 years in the consolidated revenues of the commercial stations in 9 of the top 10 markets (the exception was Dallas–Fort Worth). For the networks, prime time was the principal source of revenue, followed by sports and then daytime.

In addition, the American public spent over $8 billion in 1985 for TV sets, representing a cumulative expenditure since 1948 of approximately $125 billion.

As these data show, television continues to grow and prosper, despite criticism and competition. However, the pattern of growth is changing as new technology continues to have an impact.

TABLE 7.4 TV STATIONS ON THE AIR

	VHF	UHF
1976	511	190
1978	515	201
1980	516	218
1982	517	260
1984	539	357
1986	540	401

Source: *Television & Cable Factbook* (Washington, D. C.: Television Digest, 1986).

Any financial summary of television must include the tumultuous events of 1985 and 1986, which saw the greatest economic restructuring of the broadcast industry since the early 1950s.

The deregulation of the industry by the Federal Communications Commission, the growing realization that broadcast properties were more valuable than the stock market recognized, and the emerging specter of hostile bids from corporate suitors—all converged to turn 1985 into a time of takeovers.

In February, Taft Broadcasting Company purchased six TV stations and eight radio stations from Gulf Broadcasting Company for $755 million.

In March, Capital Cities Communications bought the American Broadcasting Company for $3.5 billion—at the time, the largest merger in the United States outside the oil industry and the first time in more than 30 years that a television network had been sold.

In April, cable-television entrepreneur Ted Turner filed a plan with the Securities and Exchange Commission to purchase two-thirds of CBS, Inc., using "junk bonds"—high-interest, high-risk debt—as well as stock in his Turner Broadcasting System Company.

In May, Australian media mogul Rupert Murdoch, along with oilman partner Marvin Davis, bought Metromedia's seven television stations, making him the nation's largest independent television broadcaster.

Meanwhile, the Tribune Company, owner of television stations in New York City and Chicago, paid a record $510 million for KTLA in Los Angeles—making Tribune the most potent rival to Metromedia, renamed Fox Broadcasting.

And finally, in the biggest merger of the year, General Electric acquired RCA and its NBC-TV network.

THE STRUCTURE AND ORGANIZATION OF TELEVISION

The structure of television is composed of five major groups: (1) networks; (2) local stations; (3) syndication companies; (4) network-owned-and-operated stations (O&Os); and (5) station groups. Television's basic function is programming, however, and the ways in which programs are produced, distributed, and exhibited are the basis for the organization of the TV industry.

Program production is the responsibility of networks, stations, and program-production companies. Distribution is the critical function of the networks, using the ground facilities of AT&T and satellite transmission. The exhibition of programs is the primary role of local stations. The structure of television in the United States can be analyzed best by discussing the two critical participants in programming: the networks and the local stations.

The Networks

At the present time, the primary forces in commercial-television programming are the three national networks: the American Broadcasting Company (ABC), the Columbia Broadcasting System (CBS), and the National Broadcasting Company (NBC). These three commercial networks generate over 40 percent of commercial TV's total income.

The networks are organized much like stations into four main areas: programming, sales, engineering, and administration. Within each of these major divisions are many units, such as news and sports, each with a separate administrative structure. At CBS, for example, the CBS/Broadcast Group has six major divisions: CBS Radio, CBS Television Stations, CBS News, CBS Television Network, CBS Entertainment, and CBS Sports. Within the CBS Radio Division, there are 15 discrete units, among them Engineering, Program Practices, and Network Sales.

Networks exist only to the extent that they provide a service to stations through an affiliation contract. This contract sets the terms by which the network pays the station for the right to use the station's time to program its offerings. Stations, in effect, *clear* time from their own schedules and sell it to the networks for a price based on the individual station's local rate for one hour. Rates range from $10,000 an hour at the network-owned stations in New York City to under $100 at stations in small markets.

The key function of the TV networks is to provide their affiliated stations with programming that will be viewed by a large aggregate audience. The network makes its money by selling this aggregate audience (measured by ratings) to advertisers. Without successful programs, the networks would not survive. Like local stations, the networks get most of their programming from outside production organizations. Approximately 90 percent of the networks' prime-time schedule is produced cooperatively with these program-production agencies. For an annual program season, more than 30 separate production companies prepare programs for the networks, which spend in excess of $1 billion a year for the right to broadcast the programs.

The networks currently provide about 65 percent of all programming hours broadcast by their affiliates during the four blocks of time that make up the TV week. The rest is filled by the local stations with local or syndicated programs.

The most important time period in television is called *prime time* (8:00–11:00 P.M. EST) and is dominated by the three networks. By FCC regulation, the networks may provide up to 3 hours of programming per night. During these hours, the most expensive and elaborate programs are aired, and the TV audience is the largest.

The dominant forms of prime-time network programming are action-adventure series, situation comedies, and movies. Specials and miniseries are also prominent, as the networks continue to experiment with various strategies to win the audience-rating race. The only "live" programs—

transmitted at the time of the event—are various sports events, such as ABC's "NFL Monday Night Football," and certain news programs. All other programs are either filmed or videotaped. The one innovation in the past 10 years has been to tape programs before a live audience and try to achieve a certain degree of spontaneity. Programs such as "Cheers" utilize this process. All programs are telecast in color.

The second most important time for television networks is *weekday daytime* (7:00 A.M.–5:00 P.M., Monday to Friday). This time is taken up with quiz and game shows, news shows like NBC's "Today" and ABC's "Good Morning America," reruns of networks' series, and soap operas. Programming philosophy assumes that the audiences are composed primarily of women and children. At one time treated lightly by the networks, daytime programming has become increasingly important to network success because of the relatively low production costs of the shows and the rather constant audience.

Weekend daytime (7:00 A.M.–5:00 P.M., Saturday and Sunday) has also taken on greater importance for the networks in recent years as the audiences for children's programming and for sports have increased in size and purchasing power. Even Sunday morning, the traditional "dead zone" of broadcasting, is now programmed heavily with network news and public-affairs shows as well as with syndicated religious programs.

Fringe time (5:00–8:00 P.M. and 11:00 P.M.–1:00 A.M.) is the fourth time period for TV programming and consists primarily of network and local news, syndicated programs, talk shows, and movies. As the demand for TV time by advertisers has increased, fringe time has become more important to the networks. ABC began programming nightly news updates during the Iranian hostage crisis in 1980 and subsequently developed its popular late-night network news program, "Nightline." The contract negotiations and manipulations involving Johnny Carson and his late-night talk show also demonstrate the value of the late-evening audience.

In addition to exercising production control, the networks assume economic responsibility for distributing programs, using the coaxial cable and microwave facilities of AT&T and the satellites. This cost alone amounts to over $75 million a year.

Each network owns VHF stations in major metropolitan areas. These network-owned-and-operated stations (O&Os), along with the other 700 affiliates, provide for the exhibition of network TV programs. The dominance of the networks in programming is further strengthened by the fact that successful network series often turn up in syndication programming carried by the local stations.

In addition to the national networks, numerous regional and special-program networks, such as CNN and ESPN, offer programs for local broadcast and on cable systems. These networks service national, regional, and local advertisers and are becoming increasingly important in sports, religious and news programming.

The Stations

The local station is the key element in the total structure of broadcasting. The actual broadcasting, or airing, of programs is done by stations in each market. Although all stations are local, most are affiliated with one of the three networks. Stations enter into an affiliation contract with a network in which they agree to carry the network's programs in exchange for payment. Network payments are not made for most sports, news, and late-night programs. In addition, a specific number of advertising slots in these programs, usually at station breaks, are left open for local sales.

The schedule of the local network-affiliated station generally consists of 65 percent network shows, 25 to 30 percent syndicated programs, and 5 to 10 percent locally produced shows. The syndicated programs are dominated by feature-movie packages, old network series, game shows, and talk shows. Locally produced programming consists primarily of the six o'clock and eleven o'clock news, noon and morning talk shows, plus a local children's series, such as "Romper Room."

The local station's role, then, is primarily as an exhibitor of programs created by someone else. Administrative personnel of a station seldom preview the episodes of a series before they are aired, and, in effect, stations have little control over many of the programs that they telecast. Despite this fact, the station assumes responsibility for the content of all the programs that it broadcasts and is held legally accountable for the content.

No two TV stations are exactly alike, but certain basic functions are common to most commercial stations. In a typical TV station, there are four primary activities: programming, sales, engineering, and management. The organization of a noncommercial station is the same, except for the replacement of a sales operation by an underwriting and grants operation. The general manager performs the overall supervisory function for a station, but no one category is most important. Programming incorporates the greatest diversity of any of the units because it includes on-air personalities, writers, producers, directors, and editors, among others. The sales function in a large station is handled by a sales or advertising department, which employs a sales manager and a number of salespeople. In a small station, one person may constitute a whole department or may handle programming in addition to sales. Engineering involves all personnel used to run cameras, slides, and film projectors, as well as those used to maintain technical engineering standards. The typical television station employs 70 people. Of its operating budget, 35 percent is spent on administration; 25 percent, on programming and production; 14 percent, on sales; 12 percent, on engineering; 12 percent, on news; and 5 percent, on advertising and promotion.

Unlike radio stations, all TV stations are classified as local outlets. As local outlets, they can be typed according to several classifications: technical, market size, or network affiliation.

Technically, TV stations are grouped according to where their signal falls in the electromagnetic spectrum. The two bands into which all TV signals are placed are very high frequency (VHF) and ultrahigh frequency (UHF). Channels 2 to 13 are VHF. Channels 14 to 83 are UHF. This technical classification is very important because stations located in the VHF band reach a greater geographical area with less power and a clearer signal than do stations in the UHF band. Thus almost without exception, VHF stations are more powerful, better established, and more profitable than are their UHF counterparts.

Another important classification of TV systems is market size, or the number of households a TV station reaches. In order to be consistent, advertisers use the Arbitron Area of Dominant Influence (ADI) to define market size. The ADI concept divides the country into 209 markets, each made up of the counties that cluster around the signal of a particular TV station. Generally, there are three basic market-size groups: (1) major, the 100 largest ADIs in the country; (2) secondary, ADIs with populations ranging from 50,000 to 125,000 (3) small, ADIs with less than 50,000 population. Market size is vital in TV broadcasting. National advertisers buy time on stations according to market size; stations in major markets get most of the national advertising dollar, while stations in small markets must depend heavily on local advertising.

The third important basis for TV-station classification is whether the station is independent or network affiliated. While most TV stations want network affiliation because networks are capable of providing the more popular types of programs and therefore of attracting a larger audience, the number of independent stations has grown significantly—from 73 in 1972 to 230 in 1985. And because of changes in marketing and programming, even long-established independents have experienced increases in ratings. In 35 large markets surveyed by Nielsen, the independents' share of the 24-hour viewing audience has increased from 17 to 22 percent since 1972, while the network share has dropped from 75 to 63 percent.

The independents have made their headway in the face of an economic mismatch. Networks have the money to underwrite programs that will attract the largest audience. Independents have to shop for every program and then shell out money for the rights. Network affiliates have "availabilities"—commercial slots—that are presold to advertisers. Independents must go out and hustle to fill their accounts. And the 85 percent of independent stations that broadcast on the weaker UHF frequencies suffer the additional disadvantage of lesser audience reach.

Given these problems, how did the independents manage, by 1985, to build up as much combined audience share as a network? Part of the answer is that they specialize. Many independents with specialized formats also emphasize local flavor. Especially in small markets, they feature local news and concerns.

Meanwhile, independents are relying less and less on off-network reruns and movies. Cheap satellite transmission offers an unprecedented variety of material, while serious and costly efforts by independents to create original programming have won over advertisers as well as viewers.

THE CHARACTERISTICS AND ROLES OF TELEVISION

Television today is huge, complex, costly, continuous, and competitive. It is a mass entertainer, mass informer, mass persuader, and mass educator.

Television is universal; more than 98 percent of America's homes have TV sets, and viewing television is the dominant leisure-time activity in our society, occupying over seven hours a day in the average household.

Watching television is an in-home activity, and although multiset homes are increasing, TV usage is still a family or small-group activity rather than an individual or large-group experience. The content of the medium is dominated by national organizations that seek to provide general programming for extensive, heterogeneous audiences, although special content for limited, homogeneous minorities is increasing.

The medium is the costliest of the electronic media because of the demand placed on it by the 18-hour daily schedule of most stations. Only television among the advertising media has sight, sound, motion, and color. This makes it the most dynamic sales tool available. The appeal of television accounts for the fact that it costs advertisers an average of $150,000 for 30 seconds to advertise on network prime-time television.

As we have pointed out, the primary role of the magazine is the custom-tailoring of mass communication. Television's primary role is just the opposite. Television specializes in the mass distribution of mass communication. It is the channel through which stream mass-produced messages for the widest possible dissemination. With virtually the entire population having access to television 18 hours a day, 365 days a year, it is the mass medium for reaching most of the people most of the time. Because of this, television is perhaps the least flexible of the mass media. While it can and does provide instant coverage of many important national and international events, the majority of TV time is taken up with programs and schedules that have been put together a year or two in advance.

In a more critical sense, television has a number of primary social roles, two of which stand out—reflecting society and evaluating society. It has been observed that television's most common role is as one of many windows through which we observe, transmit, and reflect society to one another. But television has been criticized strongly for assuming this primarily passive role in society. Too often, critics say, television is simply a conduit, neutral to a fault and rarely engaging and challenging its audiences.

Television has another role, however, and on occasion plays it. Despite its essentially passive nature, television, at times, does act in its own right and uses its power of communication not merely to convey other people's images but also to make its own statement. Many people feel that the TV coverage of the assassination and funeral of President Kennedy and of the *Apollo 11* moon landing were times when television did create genuine statements, perhaps not so much because of its particular design or structure, but merely because of its ability to record the event as it was happening.

The future of television seems to rest in the ability of audiences to control and use it for their own purposes. The technological revolution will have a major impact on traditional broadcasting. Broadcasting as we have traditionally defined it may be replaced with *narrow*casting, in which producers will send out messages to small clusters of demographically linked groups, who, in turn, will manipulate and "massage" the content for their own purposes. The television marketplace is in transition, reshaping its four major segments: the three national networks; independent stations; basic cable; and pay-cable TV. At the end of 1986, the networks' share of the viewing audience was 71 percent; independents' was 18 percent; basic cable's was 4 percent; and pay cable's was 7 percent. By 1990, the networks' share will probably not be more than 60 percent of the viewers; the independents' share could grow to 23 percent; basic cable might have about a 9 percent share; and pay-cable TV's share could reach 11 percent.

The new technologies offer many opportunities for producers and consumers alike. Many industry people, however, fear that greed and failure to take risks will waste the expanded opportunities. As Les Brown, editor-in-chief of *Channels*, noted:

> In the end the revolution may not be technological in nature but cultural. The lag is classic: The delivery systems have arrived well ahead of the product. And in the long run the art of communication, rather than any of the technological miracles, may shape the electronic landscape.[3]

SUMMARY

Television today, much like radio, is searching for a new identity and function. Despite its dominant position in American society, television is still a young medium, growing and developing.

The development of television, also, can be divided into several distinct periods. From 1884 to 1925, basic research in electromagnetic theory led to more practical experimentation with radio waves and, ultimately, with television signals. From 1925 to 1947, there were experiments in television transmission, and in 1940 commercial television operations began.

---

[3] *Channels* 5, no.4, November/December 1985. 4.

World War II, however, delayed the commercial development of television.

From 1948 to 1952, three factors significantly affected the future of video broadcasting: the FCC's "freeze" on television station allocations, the development of television networks, and the beginning of video programming formats. The golden age of television occurred in the years from 1952 to 1960. During this time television developed into a mass medium. Color television and videotape were invented and most of the major program forms were developed.

Next came a period of growth, progress, and criticism—1961 to 1980. Television took on a major role in American society, with network television, especially, assuming dominance as a mass medium. Viewing levels exceeded six hours per day and strong criticism began to emerge concerning television's impact on and role in society. Television program forms continued to evolve. Network and local television news became more important.

The 1980s have been a time of intense change and competition in the television industry. Much of this change is technological and threatens the basic structure of the industry, especially the distribution and transmission of content by satellites, cable television, low-power television, teletext and videotext, videocassettes, and videodiscs.

Public television has continued to grow but is experiencing increasing financial problems. Nonbroadcast television is expanding rapidly and the world of corporate video is emerging as a major communication medium.

The television industry is composed of five major groups: (1) networks, (2) local stations, (3) syndication companies, (4) network-owned and -operated stations, and (5) station groups. The ways in which programs are produced, distributed, and exhibited are the bases for this organization. The two primary forces are the networks and the stations. The networks provide most of the commercial television programming seen by Americans, and the actual broadcasting is the function of the stations in each market. Most local stations are affiliated with one of the three major networks and receive the bulk of their programming from that network. However, other programming sources and independent stations not affiliated with networks are becoming more important in television programming.

Despite increasing competition and criticism, television today is a huge, complex, costly, continuous, and competitive medium. It is society's mass entertainer, mass informer, mass persuader, and mass educator. It is a universal medium. More than 98 percent of American homes have television, and television viewing is the dominant leisure-time activity in American society. Television is the costliest of all the electronic media.

The future of television rests on the ability of audiences to control and use it for their own purposes. The television marketplace is in transition and is being reshaped by a variety of technological and social forces.

BIBLIOGRAPHY

Adler, Richard P. *Understanding Television: Essays on Television as a Social and Cultural Force*. New York: Praeger, 1981.

Arlen, Michael J. *Thirty Seconds*. New York: Farrar, Straus & Giroux, 1980.

Baldwin, Thomas F., and D. Stevens McVoy. *Cable Communication*. Englewood Cliffs, N.J.: Prentice-Hall, 1983.

Barnouw, Erik. *A History of Broadcasting in the United States*. 3 vols. New York: Oxford University Press, 1966, 1968, 1970.

————. *Tube of Plenty: The Evolution of American Television*. New York: Oxford University Press, 1975.

Brooks, Tim, and Earle Marsh. *The Complete Directory to Prime-Time Network TV Shows: 1946–Present*. 3d ed. New York: Random House (Ballantine Books), 1985.

Brown, Les. *Les Brown's Encyclopedia of Television*. New York: Zoetrope, 1982.

Charren, Peggy, and Martin Sandler. *Changing Channels: Living (Sensibly) with Television*. Reading, Mass.: Addison-Wesley, 1983.

Comstock, George. *Television in America*. Beverly Hills, Calif.: Sage, 1980.

Eastman, Susan Tyler, Sydney W. Head, and Lewis Klein. *Broadcast Programming: Strategies for Winning Television and Radio Audiences*. 5th ed. Belmont, Calif.: Wadsworth, 1985.

Esslin, Martin. *The Age of Television*. San Francisco: Freeman, 1982.

Gitlin, Todd. *Inside Prime Time*. New York: Pantheon Books, 1985.

Goethals, Gregor T. *The TV Ritual: Worship at the Video Altar*. Boston: Beacon Press, 1981.

Gross, Lynne Schafer. *The New Television Technologies*. Dubuque, Ia.: Brown, 1983.

Himmelstein, Hal. *Television Myth and the American Mind*. New York: Praeger, 1984.

Kaminsky, Stuart M., and Jeffrey H. Mahan. *American Television Genres*. Chicago: Nelson-Hall, 1985.

Levinson, Richard, and William Link. *Stay Tuned: An Inside Look at the Making of Prime-Time Television*. New York: St. Martin's Press, 1981.

Linsky, Martin. *Television and the Presidential Elections*. Lexington, Mass.: Lexington Books, 1983.

McNeil, Alex. *Total Television: A Comprehensive Guide to Programming from 1948 to the Present*. 2d ed. New York: Viking Penguin, 1984.

Marc, David. *Demographic Vistas: Television in American Culture*. Philadelphia: University of Pennsylvania Press, 1984.

Newcomb, Horace, ed. *Television: The Critical View*. 3d ed. New York: Oxford University Press, 1982.

Quinlan, Sterling. *Inside ABC: American Broadcasting Company's Rise to Power*. New York: Hastings House, 1979.

Rose, G. Brian, ed. *TV Genres: A Handbook and Reference Guide*. Westport, Conn.: Greenwood Press, 1985.

Smith, F. Leslie. *Perspectives on Radio and Television: Telecommunication in the United States*. New York: Harper & Row, 1985.

Sterling, Christopher, and John Kittross. *Stay Tuned: A Concise History of American Broadcasting*. Belmont, Calif.: Wadsworth, 1978.

Turow, Joseph. *Entertainment, Education and the Hard Sell: Three Decades of Network Children's Television*. New York: Praeger, 1981.

8

Recordings

No mass medium has had a more volatile or unsettled history than the recording industry.

No mass medium has meant more to the youth revolution than the record business.

No purchase by a young adult has been more costly, more time-consuming, and more important than the ultimate stereo—except for an automobile, which must have an AM–FM cassette deck, an equalizer, and a compact-disc (CD) player with speakers fore and aft.

No piece of media equipment is influencing "the business end of the business" more than the videocassette recorder—the night out at the movies for middle-aged shut-ins.

No self-respecting middle-class family can live the American dream without the ubiquitous home-entertainment center, including turntable, CD player, dual tape deck, equalizer, stereo receiver, and cable-ready TV monitor wired to a pair of powerful speakers.

DEFINITION OF TERMS

The use of the term *recordings* is generic and refers to a variety of reproduction systems, including cylinders, records, reel-to-reel tapes, cartridges, cassettes, video recordings on VHS, Beta, and 8 mm formats, laser compact discs, and videodiscs. Like other electronic media, recordings require machines to record and play back the content; unlike the others, consumers of recordings have direct control over what they use. Individuals buy, rent, and play them, when and where they want. Recordings stop time in the sense that the event can be repeated because it is stored on records, tapes, and laser discs.[1]

HISTORICAL PERSPECTIVE

There are five major periods in the history of the recording business.

Invention, Experimentation, and Exploitation: 1877–1923

Research by Leon Scott de Martinville and F. B. Fenby, who is credited with having coined the word *phonograph* (from the Greek word for "sound-writer") preceded the actual "invention" of practicable recording machines. Two men working on different continents contributed to the birth of the phonograph. In April 1877, Charles Cros filed a paper with the French Academy of Science that described a system of sound reproduction, but the French physicist never produced a working model. In the United States, Thomas Edison and his machinist, John Kruesi, actually built in December 1877 a functional device that recorded and played back sound. This phonograph used a hand-cranked metal cylinder wrapped in tin foil for recording purposes, but Edison applied for patents on a disc system as well as on the cylinder. The Edison Speaking Phonograph Company, formed in 1878, built several hundred machines, and salesmen hit the vaudeville circuit. Audiences flocked to hear the demonstrations, but without practical application, there were few sales and the crowds disappeared. The novelty wore off quickly, and the company suspended business.

In 1885, Alexander Graham Bell, working with Chichester Bell and Charles Tainter, patented a device called the graphophone, which used cardboard cylinders coated with wax. It had little volume but better quality sound than Edison's phonograph. Edison, in 1886, then developed the phonogram, a reusable wax cylinder that ran for 2 to 4 minutes. Both the Bell-Tainter and the Edison patents were bought by Jesse H. Lippencott's North American Phonograph Company in 1888. Lippencott's dream was the development of a business device to replace hand transcription of

---

[1] We have chosen to discuss videocassette recordings in this chapter as well as in the television and motion-picture chapters for a variety of reasons. Although VCRs are used primarily to record television shows for later viewing and to screen movies rented from the local video outlet, these uses of VCRs, along with the music-video phenomenon, make both the viewer and listener and the "new" industry more like the traditional sound-recording and music business than like those of any other medium. And, perhaps more important, the basic technology is the same for both video and sound recording. Whether sight or sound, it is a recorded recording. If the video revolution continues, it may well become an independent mass medium.

dictation. The dream collapsed as a result of poor sound quality and resistance from male stenographers who feared the loss of their jobs.

In 1889, Edison issued the first commercial recordings, and the Automatic Phonograph Company's nickelodeon appeared as an entertainment machine in arcades. Lewis Glass, in 1890, electrified a nickelodeon that played material aloud after the insertion of a nickel, and the public became enthralled with a forerunner of the jukebox. Many machines installed in a lobby or an arcade offered a wide variety of choices. By the mid-1890s, the phonograph was in the parlors of many American homes, but it was too late. North American Phonograph was bankrupt, and Edison was in court, so years passed before production was resumed. The Columbia Phonograph Company stepped into the void and from profits bought existing patents and marketed a hand-cranked model that used wax cylinders.

During this same period, another American, Emile Berliner, was experimenting with a system that used flat discs instead of cylinders. Berliner's spring-wound gramophone, patented in November 1887, used a governor to control the speed. The disc had four advantages over the cylinder.

1. The disc could be mass-produced from an etched negative master, whereas each early cylinder had to be an original.
2. The shellac record was harder and more durable than the wax cylinder.
3. The disc was more easily stored than the cylinder.
4. The disc produced greater volume and better quality from a simpler machine.

In 1901, Berliner and Eldridge Johnson formed the Victor Talking Machine Company and started selling "Red Seal" one-sided recordings made by opera stars. In 1906, the Victrola was born; its distinguishing feature was a speaker horn. Columbia used the Odeon two-sided discs (introduced by Germany's Odeon Company in 1905) for its music. The disc business, with 10,000 outlets, became profitable and thus respectable. Edison, who refused to accept "platter reality," continued with his work on wax cylinders and thus faded from the field that he had invented. Assets for Victor grew to over $30 million by 1917, with Americans buying 25 million two-sided discs a year. As prices came down, audiences increased. After an initial coolness toward the medium, famous artists turned to the phonograph as a means of expanding their audiences, and millions of their records were sold. Enrico Caruso did more than any other artist to legitimize the medium, and over the years, fans rewarded him with more than $5 million, tax free, from sales of his records. The industry became worldwide, as interlocking patents permitted the sale of records everywhere.

From 1905 to 1923, few significant technical changes took place in

records and only minor changes were made in the recording device. Although the speaker horn of the Victrola was soon enclosed in the cabinet, the scratchy quality persisted. Many musical instruments could not be used to make recordings because they did not record well. Artists stood in front of a huge bell or horn and shouted their songs onto masters. It was a far cry from the concert hall. Nevertheless, in 1921, 100 million records were sold. Exclusive patent rights had lapsed during World War I, and a variety of new companies started to compete in the record business. Things went quite well until the radio came along to end the "golden age" of tenors.

Technical Improvement but Financial Disaster: 1924–1945

Economically, the 1920s were expected to be a boom time for the recording industry. Low-cost, reliable phonographs were available, and people had the money to buy them. Although developments in electronic-radio technology (microphones and speakers) led to significant improvements in the technical quality of the phonograph, the public acceptance of radio created an economic recession for the recording industry. Radio broadcast "live" rather than recorded music, produced a better sound, and best of all, provided the music for free. The recording business was rapidly disintegrating. Then Western Electric patented an electrical-recording process and demonstrated the system for Victor. Eldridge Johnson, however, declined to participate in a project that had anything to do with radio, the medium that was destroying his business. Finally, in financial desperation, the phonograph industry moved into "radio recording."

The first commercial, electrically produced recordings were marketed by both Victor and Columbia in 1925. The new process opened an entirely new aural dimension. The electrical-recording process expanded the frequency range, could be played back louder with "blast," allowed musicians to work in a studio setup that approximated the physical arrangements of live performances, and improved the home phonograph with a dynamic loudspeaker. That same year, the Brunswick Company marketed a low-cost electric phonograph with speakers of brilliant quality compared with the quality of earlier mechanical horns. By 1926, whole symphonies and operas were being recorded on albums of up to 20 discs.

Despite the technical progress, the medium continued to lose ground—first to radio, then to talking pictures. In 1928, RCA purchased

Figure 8.1. Thomas Edison (above) poses with the tin-foil cylinder phonograph that he invented in 1877. The photograph was taken by Civil War photographer Mathew Brady in Washington, D.C., on April 18, 1878. Emile Berliner (below) poses with the gramophone that he developed in 1887, using flat discs and a turntable. These two men were the two keys that unlocked sound recording for generations to come. (Above: Photo courtesy of the Edison National Historic Site; below: Photo courtesy of the Smithsonian Institution.)

Victor and discontinued the production of record players in favor of that of radio receivers. Edison had stopped all phonograph production in 1927. The Great Depression hit the recording industry harder than it did any other medium. Record sales dropped to one-tenth of what they had been, and few playback devices were marketed. In 1932, only 6 million records were sold and 40,000 phonographs produced. The phonograph seemed headed for extinction. The end of Prohibition led to the one bright spot in the record business. In the new bars and clubs of the 1930s, the jukebox found a home and turned gathering places into "juke-joints." By 1940, more than 250,000 "jukes" were using 15 million records a year made by bands of the "swing era." Despite this public consumption of popular music, the record business was still dominated by classical music, limited by drained financial resources, and hindered by unimaginative marketing.

Several business changes stimulated the medium's growth. Jack Kapp and E. R. Lewis bought and reorganized U.S. Decca. They produced 35-cent records to compete with the 75-cent versions of their major competitors. By 1939, Decca was the second-ranking company (behind RCA Victor) and sold 19 million records. In 1940, RCA and Decca sold two of every three records.

Columbia, in serious financial difficulty, was purchased by CBS in December 1938. Edward Wallerstein, a former RCA executive, was hired to rebuild Columbia's fortunes. Wallerstein signed a large number of successful pop musicians and almost cornered the popular-music market. He cut the price of Columbia's classical albums to $1; overnight, sales jumped by 1,500 percent. By late 1941, a revitalized Columbia helped the industry sell 127 million discs. Radio–phonograph combinations were also selling well. RCA Victor was selling a record player for less than $10. Music helped by big bands and the "swing era" was back in business.

Then the Japanese bombed Pearl Harbor. World War II destroyed all hope for the industry's immediate rebirth. Shellac, required for disc production, became unavailable, and electronics manufacturers turned to war work. And on July 31, 1942, the American Federation of Musicians (AFM), headed by James Caesar Petrillo, refused to allow its members to cut any more records. The AFM was concerned that "canned" music would cut back employment opportunities for musicians. The record companies initially refused to negotiate, but a year later, economic pressure forced both Capitol and Decca to allot up to 5 cents per record sold to the AFM's funds for unemployed musicians. Decca needed to bring out the first original

Figure 8.2. Two major factors significantly influenced the music business in the 1930s: radio and the coin-operated jukebox. Radio technology improved the sound quality of recordings and of live music that was broadcast but syphoned off audiences. The jukebox helped offset drops in home sales and thus supported the industry during its roughest years. (Above: Cacophonous Quintet Copyright © 1935, renewed 1963, by the Conde Nast Publications Inc., courtesy *Vanity Fair* Magazine. Below: AP/Wide World Photos.)

Broadway cast album, *Oklahoma*. In mid-1944, RCA and Columbia accepted similar terms. The AFM gains were wiped out in 1947, however, when the Taft-Hartley Act made it illegal to collect royalties in this fashion.

The Renaissance of Records: 1946–1963

Following World War II, five major forces revolutionized the phonograph industry: (1) technical achievements in electromagnetic recording; (2) improvements in records and playback systems; (3) changes in marketing procedures; (4) television's destruction of radio's old format; and (5) a dramatic change in the content of the medium.

Electromagnetic Recording. Electromagnetic recordings had been experimented with as early as 1889, when a Danish engineer, Vladimir Poulsen, produced a recording on steel wire. Later, paper was used; later still, plastic tape.

In July 1945, John T. Mullin, then in the Army Signal Corps, came across a sophisticated magnetic tape recorder in a Radio Frankfurt station in Bad Nauheim, Germany, where the American Armed Forces Radio Network was supervising a German staff. This magnetophone was a truly superior sound system, without the background noise so typical of phonograph recordings. Mullin brought 2 machines and 50 rolls of tape to the United States and in May 1946, demonstrated the system at a meeting of engineers. In June 1947, Mullin and a partner were invited to show the system to Bing Crosby and the staff of his ABC Radio show. Mullin was hired by Crosby, Ampex duplicated and improved the machines, and the 3M Company started producing tape.

Tape recording revolutionized the record business. Real-time performances gave way to multitrack, engineered-time performances, with Capitol and Decca the first record companies to take advantage of the new system. By 1949, most major studios were using noise-free tape recordings for masters, which were then edited and transferred to discs.

The 1950s saw extensive use of reel-to-reel tapes, and technical experiments during these years led to a tape bonanza in the 1960s. Today, there are three basic tape systems.

1. Reel-to-reel systems, which can be edited and have both playback and record capability. High-quality units are fairly large even in portable models.
2. Cartridge systems, which were introduced in 1958. These are compact, have great selectivity in 8-track models, but do not usually have record capability.[2]

---

[2] For all practical purposes, production of prerecorded music on 8-track cartridges ceased in 1983, and manufacture of the playback systems is at a standstill. The hardware has gone the way of all obsolete electronic gear: first to the basement, then to the garage sale, next to the junk pile, finally to the collector.

3. Cassette systems, which were introduced in 1964. These are portable but cannot be easily edited. They have record capability, however, and dubs can be cheaply made on inexpensive blank tape.

The introduction of tape-improved sound quality provided detailed aural separation of instruments, allowed for the most minute editing (for example, deleting coughs and miscues), and led to the engineer's becoming a vital force in the "mixing" of the final product. Modern production methods are increasingly using the direct-to-disc process, eliminating the tape-to-disc transfers. Computers and digital recording are being used with great frequency, further enhancing the quality of recorded sound.

Record and Record-Player Improvements. In 1948, Columbia introduced the microgroove $33\frac{1}{3}$-rpm long-play (LP) record, which had been developed by Peter Goldmark. This was far superior to the 78-rpm shellac record. The $33\frac{1}{3}$ could accommodate almost 25 minutes of music a side because of its slower speed, larger size, and narrower grooves, whereas the 78 produced only 3 to 5 minutes of music. The $33\frac{1}{3}$ records were made of plastic "biscuits" and were so resilient that they were called "unbreakable."

Rather than submit to a coup by Columbia, RCA Victor, in 1949, brought out its 7-inch 45-rpm records in both single and extended-play (EP) versions. The center hole was far larger than that on either the 78s or the $33\frac{1}{3}$. This meant that the consumer needed both a larger spindle and a lower player speed to adapt to the 45s.

The "battle of the speeds" lasted for two years, and both Columbia and RCA[3] spent a great deal of money promoting their products. RCA produced record players for their 45s and sold them for less than cost. By 1950, when the speed war ended, record sales had dropped to $50 million below the 1947 level. The consumer, uncertain as to which of the two systems would be adopted, bought neither. The companies reached a compromise that established the $33\frac{1}{3}$ LP album as the vehicle for recording classical works and collections by pop artists; the 45-rpm record was for pop singles. By 1955, 78-rpm records were no longer in production.

During this period, significant improvements were made in the sound quality of record players, and high-fidelity recordings became possible with advances in electromagnetic recording-studio techniques. The hi-fi boom lasted for nearly 10 years. Stereophonic, or multichannel, sound systems, demonstrated in 1957 and marketed in 1958, made monaural systems obsolete. An equipment boom has continued for phonograph manufacturers. Today, all LPs produced by the major companies are hi-fi stereo albums, and even the 45 is a total stereo production.

---

[3] Columbia was sustained in the battle with the resounding success of its LP version of *South Pacific* in an album format. RCA captured the jukebox market with a tiny, sturdier, and better-sounding record because the large-holed 45 rpm was easily adapted to the machine.

Figure 8.3. Following World War II, the "battle of the speeds" raged between Columbia (33 1/3 rpm) and RCA (45 rpm). In the late 1940s, this record player was sold at less than cost to spur sales. All was resolved when the RCA format became the standard for singles and the Columbia format, the standard for albums. (Photo: Courtesy RCA.)

The home sound-recording unit of today may be composed of a variety of playback units, including a stereo phonograph, a cassette or cartridge or reel-to-reel tape system, and an AM–FM radio, with speaker sets throughout the house. In addition, tape units have become important accessories in automobiles. The component system is now a major part of the international electronics business.

Marketing Procedures. At the end of World War II, the major companies controlled the industry and released 40 to 100 records each week. Local dealers marked up the records by about 40 percent. There was a "straight-

line" marketing system from manufacturer to distributor to retailer to consumer. It was a tight, profitable system for everyone except those outside
the system.

Soon, however, independent producers began to produce records,
and they made stars of unknown performers. This development meant
that small retailers were faced not only with the speed war and with pricing and stock-duplication headaches, but also with an increasing number
of "off brands." The widening variety of musical types forced retailers to
make larger investments or suffer the consequences of an inadequate inventory. In addition, promotion people replaced salespeople. The promotion staff worked with radio stations, and retailers were left to their own
devices.

The real crack in the majors' armor was the profit motive. The majors
controlled the talent and the music, the studios and the manufacturing, as
well as the distribution. They were secure, and so they rented studios to
the independents. These were the only studios that the producers of the
new labels had access to, and even though they paid high rent—it was the
only game in town—it taught them the tools of the trade. In order to
"cover" hits (record a song first issued by another company with your
artist) of the independents, each of the majors set up a subsidiary: RCA
(Bluebird), Columbia (Okeh), Decca (Brunswick), and so forth.

The patterns of selling records changed in the mid-1950s as (1) discount outlets (low-margin retailers) offered significantly reduced prices on
all popular records; (2) the major record producers, noting the success of
small record societies, started their own record clubs; and (3) rack jobbers
rented space in dime stores, drugstores, grocery stores, and anywhere else
one would be likely to buy a record on impulse. All these marketing innovations hurt the traditional retail-sales outlets—record and department
stores. But business was so brisk that the traditional dealers' complaints
carried little weight with the record companies. Today, rack jobbers and
national record-store chains dominate retail record sales.

The Dawn of Television and the Death of Network Radio. From 1948 to
1952, television began to emerge as the dominant mass entertainment medium. Both radio and films had to adapt in order to survive economically.
After the Federal Communications Commission lifted the "freeze" on
local-television-station allocations in 1952, there was no holding back video
broadcasting. Financial conditions forced network radio to cut back operations, and local radio stations had to develop a new source of programming. The music, news, talk, and sports format evolved as the program
policy of most American radio stations. Music was the dominant element
in the mix. Since the recording industry is based on popular music, the
phonograph record became the content of radio. This provided free exposure of the record industry's products to a huge, affluent young audience

of potential buyers, and the boom was on. It is ironic, considering their history, that the radio and recording industries are such good "bedfellows" now.

The Birth of Rock 'n' Roll. Popular music in the United States reflects the diversity of America's "melting-pot" culture. Thirty years ago, this was not the case. The four major (RCA Victor, Columbia, Decca, and Capitol) and three emerging companies (MGM, Mercury, and London) produced essentially three kinds of music: white popular, classical, and show (theatrical). Each company had an all-powerful artist-and-repertoire (A&R) person, who was, in effect, the company's record producer. This individual selected all the songs to be recorded and all the artists to record them. Performers were told what they would record and when a "take" was acceptable. Each major also told its artists which potential hits on the other labels they would "cover." In effect, a very small number of people controlled the music industry. It was the independent record producers who generally spearheaded new musical trends. As a result, they were responsible for many structural changes in the business.

In the early 1950s, these independents created a musical form that shook the music industry to its foundations. Nowhere was the cultural gap between young and old so evident as in the controversy over the sound that Cleveland disc jockey Alan Freed named rock 'n' roll. Rock has never been rock *and* roll. Grammar is not its forte.

Rock music is the only musical form that is indigenous to the electronic media. In fact, rock is the only music whose recording is the original and whose live performance is the imitation. *Rock 'n' roll* has been defined best by music expert Richard Penniman (Little Richard), in his hit song "Tutti Frutti," as *Awopbopaloobopalopbamboom*. Translated, this means there is no satisfactory definition of this musical form. But we can identify its characteristics.

1. Rock is a *heavy beat*.
2. Rock is *loud*. It is tactile and insulates listeners from problems.
3. Rock is *electric* music. It is plugged in and we are turned on.
4. Rock is traditionally *simple* (but not simple-minded).
5. Rock is *crude*.
6. Rock is *blatant*. It is the most sexually up-front of any musical form.
7. Rock is a *rejection* of adult sensibilities, an assault on the status quo, and a sign of alienation.
8. Rock is *committed* to social change. It was, and is, the voice of the young during times of war, recession, and cultural upheaval.
9. Rock is *people music*. It is the most "pop" of pop cultures.
10. Rock is *young*. The young make it, buy it, and listen to it; every teen-ager is a potential star.

Figure 8.4. The "King," Elvis Presley, reigned supreme at the dawn of rock music. He made crossovers from country and Western, through rock-a-billy, back through country rock to white pop. He could do it all. He is the universal symbol and the single most influential talent in the history of the musical form. (Photo: *Photoplay Presents.*)

11. Rock is *color blind*. A major part of the civil-rights movement, it desegregated the young as well as their music.
12. Rock is *unpredictable*. Who knows what will be popular tomorrow?
13. Rock is *immediate* music that depends on high turnover. Today's hit is tomorrow's "golden oldie."

14. Rock is *international* and has fans worldwide.
15. Rock is very *big business.*
16. Rock is *dance* music.

Rock comes out of five traditions in American music.

1. *Rhythm and blues* (R&B) provided the horns, the black beat, and a frank approach to the sexual experience. R&B was rural music that became urbanized for southern blacks who had migrated to northern cities. The form was influenced by jazz, boogie, and the blues. Gospel traditions of "rocking and reeling" were critical in its development. The independents were the major source of R&B records because it was considered to be "race" music by the majors. Chess, Atlantic, King, Imperial, and others cut the R&B originals, which were "whitewashed" by the majors that covered their records. But it still introduced whites to the black R&B sound.

2. *Country and western* (C&W) provided the first "stars," the basic instrument (the guitar), and "songs of life and pain." Jimmy Rodgers, "the father of country music," fused the blues with country. Then western swing bands took the "hillbilly" out of country music. The music spoke to the lower class (now the middle class) about poverty, a hard life, and the sadness of "sneakin' around." It held to traditional values and was slow to change.

3. *White popular* ("pop") music provided sentimentality, the "crooner" sex symbol, and industrial know-how. "Pop" was money, power, status, and respectability. It was the music for most Americans until the rock 'n' roll revolution.

4. *Folk* provided the tradition of untrained writers who performed their own music, the participation of the audience, and the rebellion against those in power. Folk music was "people" music, by and for them. It held that the "amateur" professional had to be close to his "roots." For years, folk had been integrated with the blues, country, and gospel traditions.

5. *Jazz* provided high-quality, trained musicians, improvisation, and a tradition of racial integration. Jazz moved up-river from rural southern America. It developed from a fusion of both black and white musical traditions and innovations that spawned "swing," "bop," "cool," and so forth.

All five forms remain integrally involved in the rock mainstream, as well as independent musical forms.[4]

---

[4] A sixth influence new-waved in from England and out of Jamaica: Reggae. The form was the Carribean version of rock 'n' roll. It brought with it complete, syncopated rhythms, a gentle determination to right political wrongs, and the dress and spirit of carnival. Bob Marley became a rock star. Perhaps reggae will become a permanent part of rock 'n' roll music.

Money and Politics: 1964–1978

Today, middle-aged America looks back on these 15 years as the golden age of rock 'n' roll. Some artists make movies (*The Big Chill*) and TV series (Michael Mann's "Crime Story") that hark back to that musical time. To set the record straight, the golden age of rock 'n' roll is whenever *you* become aware of the music; rock is what makes puberty, high school, and parental mistakes bearable. As childhood gives way to adulthood, each of us goes through the rites of passage that in middle-class America are getting a driver's license and buying a stereo.

In the mid-1960s, several factors rocketed the record business into the economic stratosphere: (1) the increasing popularity of FM radio; (2) the potential to earn big money; and (3) the politicization of music.

The FM Phenomenon. Radio stations in the FM band had faced tough sledding until they married themselves programmatically and, therefore, economically to rock 'n' roll. In 1964, the British invaded America, led by the boys from Liverpool—the Beatles. Rock music flowered, and FM became economically viable with the new, energized multifaceted sounds of top 40, album-oriented rock (AOR), urban contemporary, soft rock, country rock, folk rock, soul, and fusion. FM stations sold demographics and because of their inherent sound quality, ran roughshod over their AM brethren. And radio—FM radio—was selling millions of records and tapes.

Economic Excesses. Everybody in the music business was making big money. The major companies bought up the independents, whence the innovative music had always come. Rockers earned big money and became stars. Stars made bigger money and became superstars. Everyone thought that the boom would go on forever. So when the record companies bid against one another for stars, contracts got out of hand. Enormous salaries were paid to stars who had lost their audiences, and a lot of new talent failed to get noticed and promoted because the radio stations were locked into tight formats with limited play lists. And the independents were not out there pounding on doors. When rock musicians counted their money, they knew they were important; and they wanted audiences to listen to their music, not dance to it. The kids were persuaded to stop dancing. When the kids stopped dancing, they sat down and listened to the radio. The business, and the audience, got old quickly and did not even realize that it was in trouble.

In 1964, with little fanfare, the cassette was introduced. Unlike the 8-track-cartridge machines, the cassette has recording capability. Nobody noticed because rock money was growing on trees. Who cared that the audience was home listening to the music—an album at a time on AOR radio. However, they were also taping it. And the boom times were about to end.

Figure 8.5. The Beatles, Bob Dylan, and Motown were significant forces in the rockin' 1960s. The Beatles, inspired by Elvis, stormed ashore in 1964. Bob Dylan typified the protest movement of the Vietnam War era. Motown artists did as much as anyone to integrate pop music and the young people of America. Rock 'n' Roll remains a significant cultural, economic, and political force today. (Photos: Above, The Bettman Archive, Inc.; below, Movie Star News.)

Cultural Involvement. There was also the Vietnam War. Young people, for the most part, did not like the war, and their music reflected their dislike. Rock was a vital part of the antiwar movement. Rock music became a marching song and a call to political action, righting cultural wrongs. Theatrical movies and TV dramas avoided mention of the war. Newspapers, books, and magazines were controlled by the Establishment. The only medium to which youth had access was the recording industry, and they sang their polemic loud and clear. Protest songs, acid rock, heavy metal, and the rest became committed. The music was a part of the protests covered by TV news, which showed the protesters in open rebellion and dying at Kent State University. After the war, there was Watergate. Then the music died a little. It was less fun. It had gotten self-righteous. Who can dance when they are self-righteous. And if you can't dance to it, maybe it ain't rock 'n' roll.

In 1978, there were more gold (193) and platinum (102) albums than ever before. The industry sold 726.2 million recordings for $4.1 billion. The music business was in the big time. It was making lots of money. The FM stations were in format heaven.

Recession, Hi-Tech, and MTV: Since 1979

And then the bottom fell out.

The Recording Recession. Since the late 1970s, the United States has been going through an economic and cultural recession. America lost much of its creative leadership and innovativeness in the rock-music business to the Europeans, especially to the second British invasion of punk, new-wave, and new-music bands. Europeans had been out in dance clubs nurturing new musicians and styles, while Americans were home listening to "Stairway to Heaven" for the umpteenth time or taping one another's old records. Or watching the Iranians tweak the nose of a nice, sincere man—President Jimmy Carter.

The economic recession was also a hard reality in the music business. In 1978, the music business had reached its zenith in terms of units sold. In the decline from 1979 to 1982, the industry raised prices dramatically to shore up profits, and home cassette taping increased dramatically in an effort to save money. In 1983, unit sales stabilized, due in large measure to one album, Michael Jackson's *Thriller;* 1984 was very strong because of the rejuvenation of the business via music videos (MTV); 1985 was down again, despite the sale of 22.6 million compact discs. Substantial increases in record prices and the inflated prices of CDs ($15) were critical to maintain the status quo. CDs are the only major growth market in the music business, up 291 percent in units sold and 277 percent in dollars earned in 1985. The music business seems stable, with $4.3 billion in revenue, and will remain so if enough CDs can be produced in the late 1980s. The good

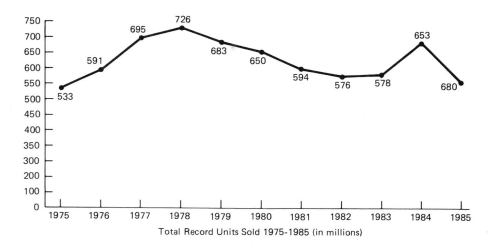

Total Record Units Sold 1975-1985 (in millions)

Total Record Dollar Volume 1975-1985 (in millions)

Figure 8.6. These two graphs visualize unit sales of and dollars generated by record sales. Tremendous growth occurred through 1978. Then unit sales dipped sharply until they bottomed out in 1982. However, the industry staved off losses by raising unit prices until total earning in 1984 finally edged past the 1978 level. Today, economic growth is being sustained by music-video promotions and by sales of CDs with inflated prices. As the American population ages, the recording industry faces numerous challenges in order to maintain recordings' share of the market. The sound-recording industry has the lowest growth potential of any mass medium, but video recording will support itself, the film industry, and, hopefully, the music industry as well. (Data source: Recording Industry Association of America.)

times will roll again. (See Figure 8.6 for a detailed look at unit sales and dollar income over the past decade.)

The industry, in effect, is healthy, but not really growing. A number of factors are contributing to this condition, including high prices, pirating and home taping, the recession, the aging of America, and a kind of dormancy in musical innovation. Music videos have been a real shot in the arm for the music business, and they continue to be the major influence on most pop-music record or tape purchases. They constitute the major marketing tool of its industry in the 1980s.

In general, the number of specific releases continues to decline. Table 8.1 shows both short-term and long-term patterns for new releases in terms of recording format.

1. *Singles.* Although new single releases, on 45-rpm records, were up by 11 percent in 1985, the pattern from 1978 to 1985 indicates that today's singles are being released at only 74.6 percent of the 1978 level.

2. *Dance Remixes.* Digitally remixed club or dance singles were up by 29 percent in 1985, and have shown growth each year over the entire eight-year period for total growth of 562.5 percent in terms of new releases.

3. *CDs.* Data are limited to the 1983 to 1985 period of their issue. Although 1985 showed no growth (0.4 percent), that was due to lack of production capacity rather than to lack of consumer demand. New releases grew by 305.3 percent in three years, and CDs are destined to become an increasingly important factor in new releases and as sales of CD-players increase.

4. *LPs.* Only 2,360 LPs were released in 1985, compared to 4,170 in 1978–a decrease of 76 percent.

5. *EPs.* Extended-play discs and cassettes are not significant factors and are being phased out as the $33\frac{1}{3}$ dance-remix format grows.

6. *Cassettes.* Cassettes remain the number-one format in terms of new releases (2,395 in 1985), but down to 78.5 percent of 1978 release level.

7. *8-Tracks.* In 1984, 8-tracks stopped being released. As you can see, the descent into obsolescence was dramatic—new releases went from 2,450 in 1978 to 0 in 1984.

It is evident that the music business had contracted substantially in terms of the number of new releases available to the public. It is much more difficult for a new group to get exposure than it was in the halcyon days of the past decade. This is directly attributable to the reduction in the number of independent producers. And even with all the product cutbacks, 84 percent of all pop and 95 percent of all classical recordings do not break even.

TABLE 8.1 RELEASE PATTERNS FOR MAJOR RECORDING TYPES: 1978–1985

	1978	1979	1980	1981	1982	1983	1984	1985	1984–1985* (%)	1978–1985† (%)
Singles (7-inch)	2,950	2,800	3,370	2,315	2,285	2,105	1,980	2,200	(+11)	(−74.6)
Dance remixes (10-inch and 12-inch)	160	550	305	335	460	610	700	900	(+29)	(+562.5)
CDs‡	—	—	—	—	—	380	1,155	1,160	(+0.4)	(+305.3)*
LPs	4,170	3,575	3,030	2,810	2,630	2,300	2,170	2,360	(+9)	(−56.6)
EPs‡										
Disc	—	—	—	40	235	150	70	50	(−29)	(−33.3)*
Cassette	—	—	—	10	50	150	70	50	(−29)	(−33.3)*
Cassettes	3,050	3,025	2,725	2,465	2,710	2,065	2,400	2,395	(0)	(−78.5)
8-Tracks	2,450	2,075	1,525	985	400	60	0	0	(0)	—

* Growth loss is expressed as a percentage of added growth.
† Growth loss is expressed as a percentage of remaining growth.
‡ Computations for CDs and EPs use 1983 as the base year.
SOURCE: Data from the Recording Industry Association of America.

Space-Age Technology. The synthesizer is revolutionizing rock music. "Digital synths" are replacing guitars as the lead instrument, and the percussionist is being usurped by a "drum box." Eliminated are entire string, woodwind, and brass sections. New music requires new sounds and new colorations of old, familiar sounds.

It all began with the invention of what came to be called "the moog," a modular synthesizer developed by Robert Moog and Donald Buchla. The moog was intended for classical music and was popularized by Wendy Carlos in the film *A Clockwork Orange.* Rock innovators—the Moody Blues and Emerson, Lake, and Palmer—used it early on. Synthesized music was further developed by Kraftverk and by Tangerine Dream and then went through "techno pop" with Gary Newman and Ultravox. Its widest popular acceptance was in disco. It is also widely used to score commercials and, by Vangelis, Giorgio Moroder, and others to make motion-picture sound tracks. Jan Hammer has made "Miami Vice" the prototypical synthesized video score. Computer-software programs became available in 1983 and allow home computers to double as basic synthesizers, and the Korg Vocoder is close to reproducing vocals.

Now, one artist, working alone and at home, without the special acoustics of a recording studio, can create music that goes straight from the synthesizer through a computer to a digital recorder using an electrical code. The sound-to-microphone step is no longer necessary. Northeastern Digital's Synclavier is part of the new wave of instruments that actually can add harmonics to the sine wave. Precise sounds can be called up from memory and repeated ad infinitum. Timbre, vibrato, and attack can be duplicated to resemble almost any instrument. The more complex the computer, the more exact the sound that can be replicated. Synclavier has 16 tracks and will soon be able to be hooked to a printer in order to print out complete scores in up to 16 parts. The cost is between $30,000 and $70,000, depending on auxiliary equipment. Even complete systems of multiple instruments costing $200,000 can pay for themselves over a short period by eliminating the cost of studio rental and studio musicians.

Digital technology not only has revolutionized the production process, where its pulsed code eliminates the noise that is often on analogue recordings, but also has entered the home as the compact disc (CD). The CD produces a high-quality sound, very clean and distinct even at high volume levels. Sony CD players were introduced in Japan in October 1982, and in the autumn of 1983, marketing began in the United States. The digital code is read by a laser beam without loss of sound quality. There is no record wear, and damaging CDs in normal circumstances is very difficult. Portable versions are now available; they plug into car as well as stereo systems. Disc demand currently exceeds manufacturing capability, and prices are artificially inflated because of inadequate supplies. Present plant capacity is being expanded, but the manufacturing must be done in a super-clean environment.[5] CDs represent the next boom area of the music business, with the 2 percent of homes equipped with CD players now accounting for 5 percent of all music sales. The CD owner is a heavy user and is buying all new products to use in the CD player. The CD player sells for $100 to $200, with portable battery-powered units available.

Music Videos. Rock music on television is not new. Both Elvis Presley and the Beatles appeared on "The Ed Sullivan Show." "American Bandstand" featured rock 'n' roll. Ricky Nelson rocked in his parents' series "Ozzie and Harriet." There have been videotapes of rock concerts on pay cable for years, and concept video albums began with "Blondie" in the 1970s.

But music television is different. It is more like radio with pictures, 24 hours a day.

Music videos first flowered in Europe's dance clubs, where state-operated radio and TV limit pop-music performances in broadcasting. The European record companies used videos to expose consumers in clubs to new artists and to new songs by established artists. The videos then flowed

---

[5] Compact discs are produced in a dust-free environment. A laser beam etches pits in a glass master; then the master is silver coated and electroformed to make a nickel negative. From the negative are made multiple positives, which, in turn, are used as stampers in the molding process. Under heat and pressure in a vacuum chamber, the disc is molded and metalized with an extremely thin, reflective aluminum layer. The disc then is lacquered while spinning and has its hole carefully aligned, labeled by direct printing, packed in a plastic box, packaged, and shrink-wrapped.

through corporate channels to the United States, where publicity departments sent copies to cable outlets to be used as fillers between movies and by pay services like HBO's "Video Jukebox."

In August 1981, Warner-Amex put Music Television (MTV) on the satellite, which bounced it into cable homes. The pictures were accompanied by an FM stereo signal that could be connected to sophisticated home sound systems. MTV, a 24-hour basic cable service, has revolutionized music merchandising by introducing new music[6] to the hard-to-reach American heartland and has single-handedly broken the sterile grip that album-oriented radio (AOR) stations had on musical taste in America. When FM radio was young and hungry, it married itself to rock music. As FM radio became profitable, it became cautious and musically entrenched. Broadcasters looked at their profit-and-loss statements and their ratings and stopped listening to innovative music, the lifeblood of rock 'n' roll. New artists and new musical styles could not get exposure. Radio sells "numbers" and "demographics" to advertisers that could not care less about rock music. Stations have narrow play lists with heavy rotation of "charted" songs within tight schedules. Air time is not available to the new musical ideas being tried out in cities, at free college concerts, and on music video. AOR stations were the rage in the early 1980s, and their personnel smugly assumed that they knew what rock music sounded like; their audience (predominately young white males) would always listen to Led Zeppelin's "Stairway to Heaven." In the summer and fall of 1983, some of the new music made the charts, and top-40 stations made it on the radio. The AOR and other "old" formats got trounced in the ratings. Stations made wholesale changes in music formats to play the songs heard on videos. The same songs that listeners had phoned in to request and that had been rejected were now staples. Radio began to ape rock 'n' roll television. After MTV hit New York and Los Angeles cable services, the record companies believed what retailers in the Midwest had been saying—MTV sells records. The British and European groups that played new-wave music and whose videos were in constant rotation on MTV were selling. At the same time, American artists on radio were in the doldrums. Video-promotion departments now compete for slots for American groups to get into rotation on MTV, which has visualized the music business and revolutionized youthful fashions à la Madonna's layered ragamuffin-doll look and Cyndi Lauper's secondhand, gaudy, wrestler look and everybody's 501 jeans. Music-video styles were rapidly adopted by advertising and are a staple of TV ad-campaign style today.

Production costs for early music videos averaged $10,000 per cut. By 1983, the average cost had risen to the $25,000 to $30,000 range; Billy Joel

---

[6] Video clips had been used widely in European music and dance clubs. Because European acts had a ready supply of videos, they were the first to take advantage of music television. That generated immediate, widespread interest in and demand for what came to be called simply new music.

Figure 8.7. *Flashdance,* starring Jennifer Beals, was the first of the MTV-inspired spate of musicals that have done well at the box office and spectacularly in videocassette sales (over 350,000) and rentals. Rock was dancing again on the big screen, on the small screen, on the cable screen, and in the industry's cash registers.

and Paul McCartney music videos ran into the hundreds of thousands. In late 1983, John Landis directed Michael Jackson in the title cut from *Thriller* at a cost of $1 million. It was packaged with "The Making of *Thriller*" and premiered on MTV in December 1983. The $29.95 videocassette sold 550,000 copies and generated over $16 million in retail revenue—let alone stimulating additional sales of the album, which was already multi-platinum. The lid was off, and the rush was on.

Video promotions, at almost any cost, are cheap when compared with the cost of mounting a concert tour. And, at present, video promotions are more effective than tours in generating record sales. They even create a demand for tickets for tours that are mounted.

Increasing production values are driving up production costs. Most music videos are shot in 35mm film, transferred to tape, and edited digitally on video with all the "bells and whistles."

Originally, video-production costs were absorbed by the record companies and budgeted as promotions. Today, contracts call for videos to be paid for out of joint profits, and new groups sometimes pay the entire video bill. MTV is not the only game on television. Cinemax and HBO run "Pop Spots" and "Video Jukebox" as fillers. "Video Soul" is on the Black Entertainment Network cable feed. "Night Tracks" is on Ted Turner's superstation WTBS-TV. The "Nashville Network" plays country-and-western videos on cable channels throughout America, and NBC has "Friday Night Videos" and was the first to offer token royalty payments in 1983. But record companies do not want to kill the golden goose that may lead the recording business back into the black. Only BMI and ASCAP seem concerned about royalty payments at this time. MTV is offering to pay for exclusive rights to music videos during their initial release.

Long-form music-video albums are not yet a major economic force in videocassette sales, but most companies expect them to be in the near future. "Thriller" is the only music video in the all-time top-20 videocassette sales list, where it is number 4. But two music-video-inspired feature-length films are represented: Prince's *Purple Rain* (number 5) and *Flashdance* (number 13). Rock hit sound tracks are part and parcel of MTV's rotation and are promoting both the albums and the films by integrating film clips and artist performances à la *Top Gun*.

By 1983, an industry study indicated that MTV was more influential in determining record purchases than were all the radio stations in America. Record companies now coordinate new releases with MTV premieres. Given the state of the industry, video clips are going to be a part of the business for quite a while.

THE SCOPE OF THE RECORDING INDUSTRY

A variety of factors are at work in the marketplace that are having a significant impact on the recording industry: (1) the problem of piracy and illegal taping of copyrighted materials; (2) the advent of video recording in home entertainment; and (3) the changing nature of audiences.

Piracy and Home Taping

The record and motion-picture industries lobbied mightily in the early 1980s for surcharges on sales of blank tape to offset the loss of revenue from home taping, for which 80 to 90 percent of all blank tape is used to duplicate copyrighted material. This effort was unsuccessful because of the combined lobbying efforts of video stores, tape suppliers, and equipment manufacturers. The problem is serious in both the sound-record and the video-record areas.

It is estimated that the home duplication of music (from other tapes, records, and radio broadcasts) and the pirating of copyrighted music by organized crime reduces record and tape sales by as much as 50 percent. Data suggest that perhaps 75 percent of all tapes sold in Asia and Latin America are "pirated" copies. Upward of 80 percent of all blank tapes sold are used for illegal tapings; that is equivalent to 500 million lost sales units worth $2 billion annually.

The end of governmental regulation of home taping, at least temporarily, was signaled by the Supreme Court decision in the *Sony Betamax* case (1984) that home taping is not a copyright infringement. This killed the royalty on blank tapes, at least in the near future.

The Advent of Videocassette Recorders

Both the television and motion-picture industries have been greatly affected by videocassettes. Therefore, some review and analysis of videocassettes is appropriate in the chapters devoted to those industries. But ultimately, videocassettes belong to the larger, generic world of recordings. In

November 1985, VCRs celebrated their tenth birthday. They are the fastest growing item in recent electronics history and are much more widespread than either color TVs or stereos were at their 10-year mark. Even though the economy has been sluggish, VCR sales accelerated to 4.0 million in 1983, 7.4 million in 1984, and 12 million in 1985. In 1986, more than 1 in 3 American homes had a VCR, and nearly 1 in 10 owned 2 recorders. Penetration is expected to reach 55 percent by 1990, because VCRs can now be purchased for as little as $200.

Three formats compete for business: Beta, VHS, and 8mm. The VHS (Matsushita patents) formats outsell Beta (Sony patents) four to one, and the new 8mm (Sony patent) is just beginning its initial exposure. Of the 70 brands competing in the market, nearly all are made in Japan, but Korea entered the low-end VHS market in 1986. None of the three configurations is compatible with either of the other two at this time. All systems now promote improved picture and sound systems and home videography camcorders, with recorders within the camera itself.

It is the software end of the business, however, that is now in the public eye because of the impact that VCRs are having on the movie studios, on low-budget video production, and on a burgeoning retail cassette-rental industry. Americans use VCRs to "time shift" TV programs (50 percent of VCR homes tape programs for later viewing at least once a week) and to show movies that they rent from a retail outlet (40 percent of VCR homes do this at least once a week). Record companies are betting that long-form music videos will become a profitable item as soon as stereo TV sets become widespread and more and more people plug television monitors into home-entertainment centers.

There are more than 25,000 video stores in the United States, with an equal number of other types of merchants who have tape-rental counters. In most towns, it seems as though there is a video store on every corner. The average video store has 3,000 tapes of 1,900 titles. Tape rentals generate $4 of every $5 for video retailers, who must rent a tape 25 times to cover the purchase and store overhead. Industry sources indicate that an outlet needs at least 1,000 regular customers to make ends meet. The rental of erotic (X-rated) films remains a major source of income for retailers, who normally charge more than $4 or $5 for this material. However, the video retail business is going through a shake-down period, and some stores will probably go out of business in the next few years.

Most first-run feature films are marketed in the $69.95 to $79.95 price range because the film studios do not share in the profits generated by tape rentals. Producing a cassette of a feature-length film costs between $6 to $8, depending on packaging; it is sold for $40 to $50 to distributors, who mark it up by $5 to $10 for the retailer, who sells it at list price. The price is kept artificially high because of the "first-sale doctrine," which means that if a store buys a tape, it can rent it as often as it likes.

The doctrine also means that the film company makes money only when it sells the tape, so prices remain high until a film's rental life expires; then prices are lowered. In December 1986, every major film company ran a promotion for gift giving with tapes in the $29.95 to $39.95 range, which has traditionally included the biggest sellers: *Beverly Hills Cop* (1.4 million copies), *Raiders of the Lost Ark* (1 million copies), *Purple Rain* (450,000 copies), and *Star Trek III* (450,000 copies). The high price of prerecorded tapes and the low cost of blank tapes are the major reasons that cassettes are copied (the same reasons that music is illegally taped by consumers).

The retailer's problem is that everyone wants to rent the "hits" when they come out; the store hopes that consumers will rent another tape if the specific film they are looking for is not available. Competition has driven rentals as low as $1 a night, not a profitable level for the average video store. Retailers gamble every time they place an order; they must guess which tapes will move and how many they should order.

The studios would prefer to be paid per rental, but since they can now earn more from tape sales than from theater box-office receipts, they are not rocking the boat.

THE RECORD AUDIENCE

There is no accounting for taste. What is hot today is passé tomorrow. Today's hit is tomorrow's "golden oldie." What will the audience buy? And what will it tape? Who is buying it where? And why are they buying it now? Are there target audiences for different types of music? Do tastes change as the record buyer ages or moves to another part of the country?

What do we know about you as record consumers?

1. We know that you spend over $4 billion a year for more than 650 million records.
2. We know that you buy more cassettes than albums. In fact, you spend twice as much for tapes as for albums.
3. We know that you want to buy more CDs but cannot always find what you want and wish the price would go down—not only for CDs, but for all formats.
4. We know that you are dancing again because dance remixes are doing well.
5. We know how you allocate your money:

Singles	6 percent
Albums	27 percent
Cassettes	56 percent
CDs	10 percent
8-Tracks	1 percent

This means that cassettes are truly dominant but that CDs are going to be very profitable if enough can be produced.

6. We know that you make 52 percent of your purchases at record and tape outlets and that one in four purchases is a gift for someone else.

7. We know that the music audience is aging and was spending significantly less money on rock and more on pop and easy listening in the first five years of the 1980s, both in retail purchases and through record clubs.

8. We know what you buy by age, race, sex, and region of the country. For example, 64 percent of rock music is bought by consumers aged 24 or younger; 96 percent, by whites; 58 percent, by men; and 57 percent, by northeasterners and southerners. The rock target consumer profile is young, white, male, and living on the East Coast. On the contrary, country-music customers are older (70 percent over 25), white (97 percent), female (54 percent), midwesterners and southerners (57 percent). Table 8.2 outlines these and other consumer characteristics. It has very broad categories and breaks down the target audiences for nine styles of recording. This type of consumer profile is done in much greater detail— perhaps as specific as zip code and last record purchases—by marketing departments in order to reach specific target markets not only for general types of music, but also for specific artists.

9. We know that when you make a purchase, you, on the average, buy two recordings at a cost of $14.

10. We know that you are often an impulse buyer and love to be the one who gets a record first and that you let your best friends make a tape of it and hope it comes back to you in playable condition.

THE STRUCTURE AND ORGANIZATION OF THE RECORDING INDUSTRY

Before a record can be a success, several groups must support it: (1) the creative element; (2) the business element; (3) the information and distribution element; and (4) the consumer element. No single element can create a hit or prevent one.

The Creative Element

The artist-musician creates the material. Many successful rock performers write as well as perform their own material. The engineer-mixer-technician manipulates the inherent qualities of the medium to create recorded music. Performers are aided, guided, and supervised by a business consultant, generally called an agent. Performers also have managers to handle details

TABLE 8.2 RETAIL AND DIRECT-MARKETING CONSUMER PROFILE (% 1984 dollars spent)

	Total[1]	Rock	Country	Pop/Easy Listening	Black/Dance	Classical	Gospel	Children's	Jazz	Soundtracks/Shows
Age										
10–14	5%	9%	2%	4%	4%	0%	1%	0%	0%	4%
15–19	13%	22%	6%	13%	16%	5%	3%	1%	3%	7%
20–24	26%	33%	22%	27%	27%	16%	16%	18%	14%	24%
25–34	24%	20%	24%	24%	35%	19%	24%	47%	40%	23%
35+	32%	16%	46%	32%	18%	60%	56%	34%	43%	42%
Race										
White	89%	96%	97%	86%	48%	95%	90%	95%	73%	94%
Nonwhite	11%	4%	3%	14%	52%	5%	10%	5%	27%	6%
Sex										
Male	52%	58%	46%	49%	51%	63%	39%	18%	63%	56%
Female	48%	42%	54%	51%	49%	37%	61%	82%	37%	44%
Region										
Northeast	23%	26%	14%	26%	20%	31%	9%	20%	27%	24%
North central	23%	24%	23%	22%	24%	18%	18%	21%	23%	33%
South	34%	31%	45%	33%	42%	22%	48%	35%	29%	29%
West	20%	19%	18%	19%	14%	29%	25%	24%	21%	14%

[1] Survey group represents cross section of population according to United States census figures.
SOURCE: Recording Industry Association of America, *Inside the Recording Industry: A Statistical Overview* (New York: Recording Industry of America, 1985), p. 7.

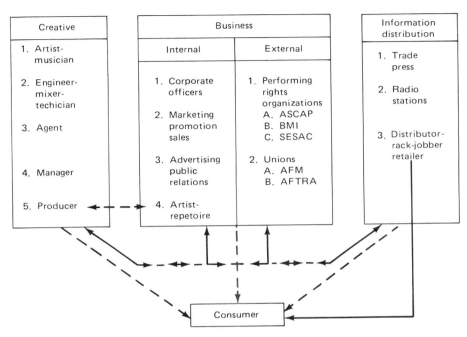

Figure 8.8. This model lays out the structural components of the music industry and identifies the various participants in each segment. All three groups must be aware of the audience, its tastes, and its willingness to buy the product.

and to run concert tours. Both agents and managers are paid a percentage of the performer's income, usually 10 percent. Artist-and-repetoire (A&R) people serve a similar function for production companies. The record producer often also serves an A&R function, although his or her task is not to select the groups but to get them taped in a satisfactory manner.

The Business Elements

There are two subcategories: internal, individuals within the record company; and external, groups outside the record company that have a significant impact on the music business.

Internal. Decisions to exploit the creative element are made by high-level corporate officers who approve the financial appropriations that are considered to be essential to the successful marketing of the record. They provide the capital and reap the greatest portion of the profits. The marketer-promoter-sales representative devises the best way to get visibility for the record. If an established star or group makes a record, there is less difficulty than if it is made by an unknown. The field representative can promote only what the company puts out, and there is no way to force radio stations to play the company's product. Since all the company's records cannot be pushed with equal effort, the field representative must promote one unit in preference to another. The advertising and public-relations staffs prepare trade announcements for radio stations, distributors, and retailers, as well as consumer advertisements for the general public. Most of the effort and money is spent on trade materials. In effect, records are "pushed" through the distributor-retailer by the trade press and air play, rather than "pulled" through by consumer demand. The A&R person is a talent scout who seeks the next "stars" in the field. Other A&R people, not associated with established companies, act as go-betweens for the artist and the producer.

External. Publishing-rights organizations collect performance payments, which come primarily from radio and TV stations. Under the copyright law of 1976, each jukebox pays an annual tax in order to play records. The three organizations that handle publishing rights are the American Society of Composers, Authors, and Publishers (ASCAP), which has about 18,000 members and collects 67 percent of the fees; Broadcast Music, Inc. (BMI), which has over 21,000 writers and 9,500 publishers as clients and accounts for 32 percent of all fees; and SESAC, a small, family-owned company that does about $2 million in business annually for its 200 publishers and 375 catalogs. Broadcasters normally subscribe to both ASCAP and BMI.

The two major labor unions in the recording business are the American Federation of Television and Radio Artists (AFTRA) and the American Federation of Musicians (AFM). Record companies are closed shops, in that vocalists and musicians must join a union in order to record. Union-scale wages are set for every aspect of the business—from studio sessions to club appearances to concert tours. The unions are a real power in the music business.

The Information and Distribution Element

This area has three participants: the trade press; radio-station programmers; and distributors, rack jobbers, and retailers.

The Press. The trade press serves as a general information and evaluation source. Five major publications serve this function. *Billboard, Cashbox,* and *Record World* are reliable sources of business and creative information helpful to the retail industry. The radio industry uses another publication extensively—*Radio and Records,* which publishes the play lists of 250 selected contemporary hit radio stations in large (P-1), medium (P-2), and smaller (P-3) markets. These play lists document the songs that are getting air play and the heaviness of their rotation (the number of plays daily). *Rolling Stone* concentrates on creative evaluation and has a wide public as well as trade readership. All five periodicals aid in the selection process by featuring articles on those records that are expected to be successful. These "trades" cover industry news, trends, and new releases.

There are also tipsheets, such as *Album Network*, the *Brennerman Report*, *Friday Morning Quarterback*, and the *Hard Report*, which anticipate break-outs and report what is going to happen rather than what is currently popular. Fringe music and new artists are covered by the *Contemporary Media Journal* and *Rookpool*, which help with data on specialty and college markets.

The Programmers. Radio-station programmers greatly affect the sales performance of many records. If the local disc jockeys do not play the records, the public cannot become acquainted with them, and audiences are less likely to buy them. Stations must choose a limited number of songs each week to add to their play lists. Only a handful of the 200 singles and 100 LPs received each week ever get extensive air play, which is more valuable than any advertising. Stations are serviced by independent record promoters who are paid fees or commissions by the record companies for their success in getting new songs on the air. In the mid-1960s, "NBC Nightly News" broadcast a story that money was paid by the independents to radio program directors for adding new songs to their rotation and reporting these additions to *Radio and Records*. The scheme was called *papering* when the program directors reported adding a song but did not actually play it. After the report, many record companies distanced themselves from the independents, but rumors persist of payoffs in the form of cash, drugs, and favors to disc jockeys to gain airtime.

As we indicated before, MTV and other video services have replaced radio as the primary influence on consumers' decisions regarding music purchases, thus resulting in the rise of new music from Europe and the rebirth of visual heavy-metal style.

The Distributors. The distributors, rack jobbers, and retailers are also crucial to the recording industry. If a record is not in stock, it cannot be bought. And since the life of popular music, especially singles, is short, it is crucial that the record be available immediately on public demand.

The Consumer Element

Ultimately, there is the omnipotent audience, the consumers who purchase records, cassettes, CDs, and videos. The record buyer decides whether a group will become stars or a record will become a hit. The Recording Industry Association of America certifies gold, platinum, and multi-platinum records.

1. A gold album must sell 500,000 albums, cassettes, and CDs or generate $1 million in wholesale sales at one-third of the list price. Gold

singles must sell 1 million copies. (Sales of 45s and of 12-inch dance remixes are added together. The 12-inch records count as two single sales in the computation, which means that a record could sell 500,000 45s and 250,000 dance singles and be certified gold.)

2. A platinum album must sell 1 million copies or generate $2 million in wholesale income. Platinum singles must sell 2 million copies using the same formula for 45s and dance remixes.

3. A multi-platinum album must sell 2 million copies or generate $4 million in wholesale income. Singles must sell 3 million copies.

The audience can select from only those recordings that are available. Each element can block or hinder the recording communication process. Nevertheless, even if the industry elements all support a given record, the public can, and often does, prefer to buy something else.

"FLOW" IN THE RECORDING INDUSTRY

In order to understand how records get into the hands of consumers, the flow chart illustrated in Figure 8.9 is helpful. Record companies send copies of records to the trade press and to radio stations for publicity and air play. They also take out ads and get stories about artists printed and broadcast. Performers hit the road to push their recordings. These road shows or concert tours are covered by the press and stations and are attended by consumers. And, most important, music videos are produced and sent to broadcast and cable outlets. Records are distributed by the companies' distribution system or by general distributors to rack jobbers, who sell their units in non-record-store outlets, record-store chains, and one-stops, which service jukebox operators as well as consumers. In the industry, there are both large, self-distribution companies, such as Columbia and RCA, and independent-label companies, which usually specialize in one kind of music and use regional distributors and national networks to sell their product to retailers and then consumers. New movements like early rock 'n' roll and today's "rap" and street music are usually independent projects because they adapt to changes rapidly. As this music is popularized, independents are often bought out by larger groups when specialized music tastes become part of the mainstream. Record clubs are another source of sales for the company.

The consumer is influenced by concerts, music heard on the radio and in jukeboxes, and the press; he or she then buys records from clubs, one-stops, chains, and low-margin retailers. Each year, the consumer makes selective purchases from the thousands of 45s, dance remixes, and LPs released annually by the record companies.

Sound recording is a tough, competitive business in which 8 of every 10 recordings do not make money. In the classical field, 95 percent of the

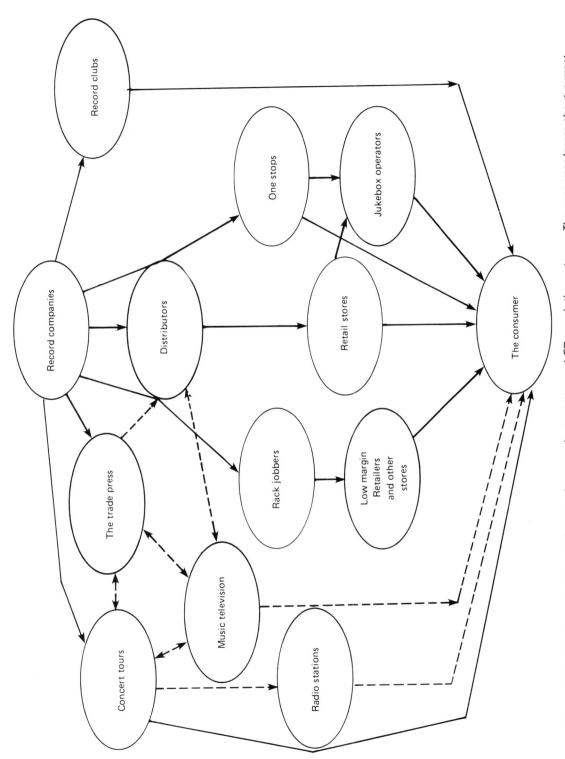

Figure 8.9. This flow chart shows the way that records, cassettes, and CDs reach the customer. The consumer learns about current music by attending concerts, reading the trade and regular press, listening to radio, and, most important, watching MTV. Product flows from a variety of retail outlets via rack jobbers, one-stops, and distributors, as well as directly from the record company through its own record clubs.

TABLE 8.3A MANUFACTURERS UNIT SHIPMENTS (MILLIONS)
(net after returns)

	1973	1974	1975	1976	1977	1978	1979
Singles	228.0	204.0	164.0	190.0	190.0	190.0	195.5
LPs/EPs	280.0	276.0	257.0	273.0	344.0	341.3	318.3
COs	—	—	—	—	—	—	—
Cassettes	15.0	15.3	16.2	21.8	36.9	61.3	82.8
8-tracks	91.0	96.7	94.6	106.1	127.3	133.6	104.7
Total	614.0	592.0	531.8	590.9	698.2	726.2	701.1

TABLE 8.3B MANUFACTURERS DOLLAR VALUE ($ MILLIONS)
(at suggested list price)

	1973	1974	1975	1976	1977	1978	1979
Singles	$ 190.0	$ 194.0	$ 211.5	$ 245.1	$ 245.1	$ 260.3	$ 275.4
LPs/EPs	1,246.0	1,356.0	1,485.0	1,663.0	2,195.1	2,473.3	2,136.0
COs	—	—	—	—	—	—	—
Cassettes	76.0	87.2	98.8	145.7	249.6	449.8	604.6
8-tracks	489.0	549.0	583.0	678.2	811.0	948.0	669.4
Total	$2,001.0	$2,186.4	$2,378.3	$2,732.0	$3,500.8	$4,131.4	$3,685.4
*Average price per unit	$3.26	$3.69	$4.47	$4.62	$5.01	$5.69	$5.25

* $\dfrac{\text{Total dollar value}}{\text{Total units sold}}$ = Average price per unit

SOURCE: RIAA market research committee.

albums lose money; this field is literally subsidized by the government and foundations in their grants to orchestras. Big new hits and the work of established artists pay most of the company overhead.

To break even, a single must sell about 50,000 copies; an album, 145,000 copies. When an artist has a hit, the individual group can earn a royalty of from 5 to 15 percent on the list price. Under the 1976 copyright law, songwriters get 2.75 cents for each sale. A single that sells 1 million copies, therefore, can earn a writer over $30,000.

The economics of the industry work out so that the producer earns from 40 to 50 percent of the retail price; distributors get from 15 to 25 percent; the retailer gets the remaining 20 to 30 percent, depending on the mark-up. The rack jobber pays the record company 40 to 50 percent, and the retailer pays a flat fee of 10 to 15 percent of total sales, which means that the jobber keeps 35 to 40 percent of every record he or she markets.

1980	1981	1982	1983	1984	1985	1984– 1985 (%chg)	1978– 1985
164.3	154.7	137.2	124.8	131.5	120.7	(−8)	(−64)
322.8	295.2	243.9	209.6	204.6	167.0	(−18)	(−51)
—	—	—	0.8	5.8	22.6	291	
110.2	137.0	182.3	236.8	332.0	339.1	2	+453
86.4	48.5	14.3	6.0	5.9	3.5	(−40)	
683.7	635.4	577.7	578.0	679.8	653.0	(−4)	

1980	1981	1982	1983	1984	1985	1984– 1985 (%chg)	1978– 1985
$ 269.3	$ 256.4	$ 283.0	$ 269.3	$ 298.7	$ 281.0	(−6)	+8
2,290.3	2,341.7	1,925.1	1,609.0	1,548.8	1,280.5	(−17)	−52
—	—	—	17.2	103.3	389.5	277	
776.4	1,062.8	1,384.5	1,810.9	2,383.9	2,411.5	1.2	+436
526.4	309.0	49.0	27.9	35.7	25.3	(−29)	
$3,862.4	$3,969.9	$3,641.6	$3,014.3	$4,370.4	$4,387.8	.4	
$5.65	$6.25	$6.30	$5.22	$6.43	$6.72		

The individual artist or group is usually advanced money to produce an album. The advance must also cover touring expenses, which, for groups, can cost $7,000 a week. For example, say that a group gets $100,000 for an album. Production costs are roughly $50,000 for audio and $30,000 for a video clip, which leaves $20,000 to tour for an average of 10 weeks. If the group is new, it can expect to earn only $1,000 to $3,000 a week. If the album sells 100,000 copies, the group's royalty is $63,000, which the company keeps to cover part of the advance. This leaves the group in arrears $37,000 for the advance, in debt for the tour, and in need of money to produce a second album. The company does a bit better. At 94 cents an album, it earns $94,000 on album sales plus $63,000 in artist royalty, for a total of $157,000, which gives it $57,000 above the advance. The economics of the recording industry notwithstanding, rock superstars earn from $2 million to $6 million each year from song royalties, concerts, singles, albums, promotions, and tours.

THE CHARACTERISTICS AND ROLES
OF THE RECORDING INDUSTRY

Dramatic changes have occurred in the recording industry in the past 10 years. What we are really talking about is the home-entertainment industry, where consumers determine when and where they will listen to or view materials on their own systems. There are four basic components to the home-entertainment consumption pattern.

1. The music industry, which supplies records, cassettes, and CDs for personal consumption. This is the traditional element in the home-entertainment mix.
2. The time-shifting use of VCRs, whereby off-air and off-cable television programming is recorded for later viewing. This remains the number-one use of videotape technology in the home.
3. The rental and/or purchase of theatrical motion pictures on videotape for home use, which is on its shake-down cruise at present. The first sale or rental royalty issue is still up in the air, but movie rental is very strong at the bargain $1 to $2 price range currently in vogue. Until the price of taped film drops below $20, sales primarily will be to video stores.
4. New product (self-help, travel, educational materials, long-form music videos) are available and will grow as profit potential improves. "The Jane Fonda Workout" and "The New Jane Fonda Workout" tapes are number 3 ($850,000) and number 15 respectively ($300,000) on the all-time sales charts. There are also films and series being produced specifically for home-VCR consumption.

The business is massive; the music industry sells over 650 units annually for more than $4 billion. VCR tape sales now generate substantially more for film companies than do box-office ticket sales.

Recordings are the primary source of content for radio and music-television programming. Long-form music videos are on the horizon as a creative entity.

The medium is international in scope. American music is heard everywhere, and English sounds are sold throughout the United States. The industry is more international than is any other mass medium, even film, but the VCR is a factor here.

Culturally, sound recording is highly selective. It has to be because the music is multifaceted, appealing to many specialized tastes. Pop music is dominant, with rock and pop accounting for 53 percent of all sales.

Traditionally, a youth medium, the audience for recordings is aging. Those aged 24 and under account for only 44 percent of all dollar sales. Sound recordings and films still cater to the youth market more than do other media.

Figure 8.10. Bob Geldof, shown here starring in *Pink Floyd the Wall,* led the first of the recent music industry's fund-raising campaigns to ease world hunger. Geldof's British effort, Band Aid, was matched by Lionel Richie and Michael Jackson's ''U.S.A. for Africa'' recording and then Willie Nelson's Farm Aid concert and album. The industry remains committed to causes that benefit humanity. (Photo: Courtesy MGM/UA.)

The medium is more portable than ever. Miniaturization and excellent quality in headphones have made the Sony Walkman and portable CDs real successes, with up to two hours of listening on the tape. Nearly one-quarter of all new cars sold are cassette equipped.

The phonograph is a high-technology, high-quality medium. New compact discs and digital recordings are a significant improvement over what were already high standards. This new technology also makes the product more durable; the content ages before the record wears out. The Japanese dominate the technology as well as the sales of home-entertainment equipment.

The sound-recording medium is a major instrument in the socialization process, especially of the young. It is dated to, danced to, touched to, and fallen in love to. But parents worry, perhaps unduly, about a decay of moral values.

The recording business remains committed to the causes of the young artists and consumers whom it serves. Politicians should be wary of its power.

Sound recording has the highest turnover of talent and content of any medium. Like the book, it is a storehouse of our heritage. It makes for easy retrieval of that cultural force.

SUMMARY

The recording industry includes video as well as audio reproduction on records and magnetic tapes and on laser discs. They are all part of the home-entertainment environment, which gives consumers direct control over *what* they view or listen to and, most important, *where* and *when* they do the listening and viewing.

The history of recording breaks down into five major historical periods: (1) 1877–1923, when the basic experiments, inventions, and exploitation occurred; (2) 1924–1945, when the technical improvements, financial disasters, and consumer ambivalence occurred–all in relation to the new radio medium; (3) 1946–1963, when network radio died and records became the content of local stations; the technology and marketing of recordings were radicalized; and rock 'n' roll and its audiences came alive; (4) 1964-1978, when FM came to dominate radio; the music industry lost all sense of fiscal responsibility; and the music became a cultural force and political instrument; and (5) since 1979, when the bottom fell out of the industry and the United States lost its leadership in pop music; the VCR and music video came forth and gave direction to a floundering medium; and space-age technology was married to the recording.

The current music industry evolved through these periods to become a complex industrial structure that integrates creative processes with the business and the information and distribution systems to serve the consumer. This structure has many participants, with sub-industries and other media involved in the recording communication process. All play important specialized roles.

The recordings flow to the consumers through a variety of channels that participate economically and facilitate the growth and success of the home-entertainment conglomerate. This industry is trying to deal with a number of serious situations: (1) the problem of piracy and home taping, which syphons off nearly 50 percent of the industry's potential sales and thus limits growth; (2) the advent of a new recording industry around the VCR and the dominance of that industry not by the music business and its retail outlets, but by movie studios and a new retailer—the "mom-and-pop" video store; and (3) the changing nature of a music and video audience that is aging and whose tastes and buying habits are somewhat unpredictable.

All of this leads to a medium that can be described as massive, in both the music ($4 billion) and the video ($3.5 billion) areas; the primary source of content for radio and music-video cable services; international in scope (Japan leads in technology, Europe in music, and the United States in consumption); dominated by youth; portable, yet of high-quality; a major socialization instrument committed to social causes; and having extremely high turnover of talent and content.

Of all the media, it is the most difficult to discuss because it is changing the fastest and will be more powerful in the future than it has been in the past and because it puts control of content and time in the hands of the consumer.

BIBLIOGRAPHY

Bronson, Fred. *The Billboard Book of Number One Hits.* New York: Billboard Books, 1985.

Clark, Dick, and Richard Robinson. *Rock, Roll, and Remember.* New York: Crowell, 1976.

Dranov, Paula. *Inside the Music Publishing Business.* White Plains, N.Y.: Knowledge Industry Publications, 1980.

Eberly, Phillip K. *Music in the Air: America's Changing Tastes in Popular Music, 1920–1980.* New York: Hastings House, 1982.

Gelatt, Roland. *The Fabulous Phonograph: 1877–1977.* New York: Collier Books, 1977.

Hirsh, Paul. *The Structure of the Popular Music Industry.* Ann Arbor: Institute of Social Research at the University of Michigan, 1968.

Home Video Marketplace, 1985–1986. White Plains, N.Y.: Knowledge Industry Publications, 1985.

Inside the Recording Industry: An Introduction to America's Music Business. New York: Recording Industry Association of America, 1985.

Inside the Recording Industry: A Statistical Overview. New York: Recording Industry Association of America, 1985.

Marsh, Dave. *The First Rock and Roll Confidential Report.* New York: Pantheon Books, 1985.

Shemel, Sidney, and William M. Krasilorsky. *This Business of Music.* 5th ed. New York: Billboard Books, 1985.

Sklar, Rick. *Rocking America.* New York: St. Martin's Press, 1984.

The Video Age: Television Technology and Applications for the 80's. White Plains, N.Y.: Knowledge Industry Publications, 1985.

Video Cassettes: Production, Distribution, and Programming for the VCR Marketplace. New York: Practicing Law Institute, 1985.

The Videocassette Recorder: An American Love Affair. Washington, D.C.: Television Digest, 1985.

Weissman, Dick. *Music Making in America.* New York: Ungar, 1982.

Whitburn, Joel. *The Billboard Book of Top 40 Hits.* New York: Billboard Books, 1985.

What Do Mass Media Communicate?

9

News and Information

Now that we have described the seven major mass media, we have to discuss what they do. For what do we use the media?

In many ways, the use of the mass media to give news and information is most important, so we will start there. It is not the oldest use; most media were usually used initially for some selling or business purpose. Nor is it the most widespread; most of us use the mass media primarily for entertainment. In fact, the communication of news and information in the past was often an incidental function of mass media. People spent time and money on mass media as part of their leisure acitivity, and if they got some news and information in the process, that was merely a side benefit.

Today, however, news and information are vital to the sustenance of a complex civilization. We turn to the news every day, not only because we want to be entertained, but also because the events that transpire and the facts that are communicated have direct consequences on our lives and on the actions that we must take to survive.

Indeed, news has become a commodity that sells by itself. It does not always have to be wrapped in a cloak of entertainment in order to capture the interests of the masses. But most people are still most interested in news that has some immediate reward for them, as we shall see.

One of the most consequential phenomena for the mass media of modern times is the increasing blame placed on them for the ills of society. And it is mostly the news function that has caused the criticism. The bearer of bad news is often blamed for the news. In ancient times, the messenger who brought news about a defeat in battle was slain as punishment for the bad tidings he bore.

Figure 9.1. Reporters at work in the famous City News Bureau of Chicago in the 1920s. ("City Room—No Place for a Nice Girl," Painted by Dean Cornwell, is reprinted with permission of the Chicago Press Veteran's Association, to whom this painting was given by the artist.)

For the most part, however, the media do not cause the events that become news. They merely record them, interpret them, or express opinions about them. Other forces in society—political, economic, sociological, meteorological, or even personal—cause events to happen. Media react to those events. As human beings acquire greater control over their environment, they can also exercise greater control over communication by manipulating people, events, and environment to make news.

Of course, the media are not simply passive agents manipulated by other forces. By making judgments about which of the millions of daily events are newsworthy, about what is important or unimportant, about what is true or false, reporters and editors in the mass media play a role in shaping the course of events. But no one has yet fully substantiated the precise impact of that role.

THE CATEGORIES OF NEWS

News covers a surprising range of subject matter. A national survey by the American Newspaper Publishers Association found more than 40 general categories of news in daily newspapers. The survey found that more space

is devoted to sports than to international news, more space
crime than to cultural events and reviews, and more space is a
news of interest to men than news of interest to women.

Different media emphasize different categories of news. Newspapers
give more coverage to news of crime and justice than do local and national
television. National TV gives more coverage to news of government and
politics than do newspapers or local television. National TV also gives
more coverage to foreign affairs, whereas newspapers give more space to
domestic policy. Local TV gives more coverage to economic and social
issues and to human-interest items than does national network television.

WHY DO WE NEED NEWS?

The need for information is basic to almost all human beings. Even in
primitive societies, someone acts as a watchman for the tribe. The best
climber is dispatched to climb the tallest tree and look out over the horizon
for rain or fire, for game or enemies. The tribe depends on such reports in
order to survive.

America is an information-hungry society. We need information of all
kinds in order to thrive in our complex world. News and information are
commodities that we must have and are willing to pay for. Increasingly,
the most successful mass media are those that provide the most information, not just the most entertainment.

In modern society, we sometimes employ private informers, such as
detectives or investigators, to supply us with information. But for the most
part, we depend on the mass media to keep us aware of dangers and
opportunities on the horizon. We need journalists to provide a check on
government and business. The journalist is, indeed, a tree climber, a person who knows how to get the broadest view of what is happening in the
world in order to report the important news and information to a particular
audience.

In the terminology of the journalist, news is that which an individual
is willing to pay for with time or money in order to read or hear or watch.
In other words, news must have some intrinsic value to the individual.
News is different from information. A great deal of information about
many subjects is available in the world, but information does not become
news until a journalist selects it for presentation via news media.

Before information can become news, it should fit the quality—objectivity, accuracy, balance, and fairness—and the criteria—timeliness, proximity, prominence, consequence, and human interest—of news.

The selection and evaluation of events depend on many factors, not
the least of which is the nature of the group to which the journalist is
reporting. We might say, then, that news is that which reporters and
editors decide should go into the stream of communication on any given
day, based on what the audience is willing to read, hear, or watch. Today's

Figure 9.2. Connie Chung gives news-hungry Americans their early morning news on "NBC News Sunrise." Chung started her career in broadcast journalism as an intern at a local TV station while she was a university journalism student.

news may not be relevant tomorrow, and news for one person may not be news for another, because news values are relative.

THE NEWS AUDIENCE

Various factors—including sex, age, race, education, culture, and socio-economic status—affect the way in which we read news. For nearly every-one, however, news about accidents, disasters, and natural phenomena holds intense interest. Women read less sports news than do men, and men read more business news than do women. Older people read more obituaries than do younger people, while younger people read more enter-tainment and Hollywood news than do older people.

Children develop an interest in news gradually; 6- to 8-year-olds look to newspapers mostly for comics. By the time they are 12 years old, chil-dren read newspapers more for sports news than for comics. Interest in general news, local news, and editorials grows with age, while interest in comics declines.

Children's news knowledge grows with age, too. During President

Jimmy Carter's administration in the late 1970s, more children aged 6 to 8 could identify television and singing stars Donny Osmond and Marie Osmond than could identify Carter. Even teen-agers had difficulty identifying some not-uncommon elements in the news, such as inflation, the Equal Rights Amendment, and the SALT talks.

Immediate and Delayed Rewards

News in American journalism is usually selected by reporters and editors because it fulfills some audience need. The basic criterion is: Will it sell? Will people pay attention to it? Do they want it and need it? Wilbur Schramm, formerly a professor of communication at Stanford University, categorized news as fulfilling either an "immediate reward" or a "delayed reward" to a felt need.

Immediate-reward news provides instant satisfaction for the recipient, who laughs, cries, sympathizes, thrills, or muses. Schramm places in this category such news as crime and corruption, accidents and disasters, sports and recreation, and social events.

Delayed-reward news has an impact that does not affect the consumer until later. Such news includes information about public affairs, economic matters, social problems, science, education, weather, and health. Often, delayed-reward news may bring an unpleasant consequence for the reader, listener, or viewer, while the immediate reward can bring instant gratification. Schramm concludes that most news consumers spend more time with, find more satisfaction in, and give greater attention to immediate-reward news than to delayed-reward news.

THE ELEMENTS OF NEWS QUALITY

Although the American Constitution guarantees the right of anyone to operate a news medium, the "profession" of news reporting in the United States has acquired certain standards by which to judge the quality and the reporting of news. It should be noted that not all societies share these standards.

Objectivity

Perhaps the most dominant principle of news in the United States is the concept of objectivity. News is supposed to be a factual report of an event as it occurred, without the bias of the reporter or an attempt on the part of the journalist to make any one view more influential than another. In the United States, the journalist usually plays a nonpartisan role—taking the part of a teacher, passing on facts for their own sake, allowing the individual to draw conclusions and make interpretations. The journalist is supposed to disavow the role of promoter, which is to pass on information in order to persuade or influence an audience.

Objectivity is a difficult quality to measure and a difficult standard to attain. Journalists can never wholly divorce themselves from their work; their emotions and opinions are apt to be tied into their perceptions of facts and events, whether they think they are or not. Moreover, no journalist ever sees the whole of any situation; and as events become more complex in our complicated world, the journalist necessarily sees a smaller portion of any set of facts.

A growing school of thought in American journalism argues against the principle of objectivity for these reasons. This "new journalism" is devoted to the idea that reporters should be more than messengers delivering a message; "new" journalists say that their reporting will be better if they openly and honestly admit their biases and clearly label their reports as their views of the situation.

In any case, the goal of most news operations is supposed to be to keep people informed about vital events and information, knowledge of which is essential to full citizenship in a democratic society. The people have a right to know—that is a basic tenet of a free society—and news ought to provide the necessary factual basis for forming sound opinions. The reporter who wishes to fulfill this responsibility through objective reporting is supposed to work at it diligently.

Objectivity is enhanced by proper attribution of facts and opinions. An

(Drawing by Ed Fisher; © 1986 The New Yorker Magazine, Inc.)

"President Reagan said today—and I probably misquote . . ."

objective report is supposed to attribute to an authority—an eyewitness, an official, a participant, an expert—anything that is not routine and is not readily verifiable knowledge.

Accuracy

Accuracy of reporting is another basic quality of news. Reporters are supposed to train their eyes to see and their ears to hear as accurately as possible. They are supposed to be constantly vigilant for detail and perpetually skeptical of those who would deceive or exaggerate in order to twist and distort the truth.

Balance and Fairness

Balance and fairness in reporting are crucial standards by which the quality of news is judged in the United States. Telling all sides of the story is so much a part of American journalism that reporters sometimes seem to be unpatriotic, unwilling simply to accept the pronouncements of presidents or bureaucrats as the only statements on a matter. In war, this becomes particularly difficult for leaders to understand, since the press and the electronic media seem bent on reporting the successes of the enemy as well as the failures of compatriots. But the journalist is supposed to be dedicated to the proposition that only from balanced reporting of both sides of a story will the people be able to discover the whole truth.

THE CRITERIA FOR NEWS SELECTION

On what basis do journalists for the mass media make judgments about people and events that turn information into news? In mass communication, where millions of people depend on the information that journalists decide to publish and broadcast, the decision about what is news and what is not is supposed to be made as rationally as possible. In the future, journalists may well use computers as well as experience in making these judgments. Meanwhile, we depend on a few standard bases of news judgment.

Timeliness

Certainly one of the most important criteria for news is its newness. We say that "nothing is as old as yesterday's newspaper," but actually the length of time for which a piece of information continues to be newsworthy depends on the medium. For radio, a story may lose its timeliness after an hour. Television news may have a slightly longer lifetime, from an hour to a day. Daily-newspaper news has a day lifetime; after that, the story must be rewritten with new information. Weeklies have a week, monthlies, a month; and so on.

ʀʀoximity

Geographical factors are also important to news judgment. Relatively speaking, the nearer an event occurs to the people who read or hear about it, the more newsworthy it is. The election of the governor of New York is much more important to New Yorkers than it is to Pennsylvanians, who live in the state next door. A two-car accident in which two local people were killed might be more significant to the audience in their community than a major earthquake in Peru that took the lives of thousands on the same day.

Prominence

The more widely known the participants in an occurrence, the more newsworthy the event. If the president of the United States hits a hole-in-one on the golf course, it could be national news. If the mayor does the same, it probably would be news only in his town. If the golf pro does it, it might be news only for the newsletter at the country club. Actually, prominence has a snowball effect on newsworthiness, since the mass media make famous people more prominent through constant reference to them.

Consequences

The consequences of an event have a direct bearing on its newsworthiness. The earthquake in Peru might be more newsworthy to the small community where the two-car accident occurred if the tremor will cause a shortage of Peruvian tin at the local factory.

Human Interest

Finally, we can identify a criterion that we refer to only vaguely as human interest—matters that catch and hold our attention because of physical and emotional responses that are built into human beings. A number of elements provide human interest, including adventure and conflict, humor, pathos and bathos, sex, the odd and the unusual, and self-interest. A high percentage of each day's news is selected on the basis of these factors.

THE CONSEQUENCES OF NEWS SELECTION

Judgments about news may constitute the most important decisions made in our society, with wide significance and deep consequences. It is important to examine the problems that have arisen in the past and that loom on the horizon of the future as a result of news selection.

First, since news decisions are consumer oriented, news often overemphasizes immediate-reward types of information in order to sell media. Crime and violence almost always outweigh and outdraw stories of good deeds, constructive action, peaceful progress, and even orderly dissent. Sex is not as large an element in news as it is in advertising, but it is

"Today, in all aspects of life losses outnumbered gains."

(Drawing by Dana Fradon; © 1986 The New Yorker Magazine, Inc.)

nonetheless a significant factor. The aberrations of society—the odd, the unusual, the unique—are more often the subject of news than are the normal events.

One result can be a distorted or gloomy view of the world. Dr. Glenn T. Seaborg, Nobel-Prize-winning nuclear scientist and former chairman of the Atomic Energy Commission, warned that the last decades of the twentieth century may usher in a worldwide doomsday depression. People, he said, are so constantly reminded of evil and corruption in the world by the news media that they may sink into a hopeless morass of gloom and despair, not realizing that the world is still a beautiful place with much more good about it than bad.

Indeed, fright and hysteria can sometimes result from a small detail of news. The famous Orson Welles broadcast in 1938 brought such a reaction. The Welles radio program, called "War of the Worlds," was a dramatization of a science-fiction story about Martians invading the earth, told in the form of a news program, with bulletins interrupting a music show. Dr. Hadley Cantril, a psychologist who studied the event, summarized his findings in his book, *The Invasion from Mars*:

> Long before the broadcast had ended, people all over the United States were praying, crying, fleeing frantically to escape death from the Martians. Some ran to rescue loved ones. Others telephoned farewells or warnings, hurried to inform neighbors, sought information from newspapers or radio stations, summoned ambulances or police cars. At least six million people heard the broadcast. At least a million of them were frightened or disturbed.[1]

As a result, the code of the National Association of Broadcasters (NAB)

---

[1] Hadley Cantril, *The Invasion from Mars* (Princeton, N.J.: Princeton University Press, 1947), 2.

adopted a resolution forbidding dramas to be presented as news programs. Yet legitimate news stories also have such an effect. A massive publicity effort by the federal government to tell people that smoking might cause lung cancer had the effect of sending thousands of smokers to their doctors to be examined for imagined ailments.

One news reader in Washington, D.C., expressed the feeling of many consumers when she wrote to the *Washington Post*:

> Isn't there such a thing as *good news* any more? Every morning after read-ing the newspaper (yours) I am left depressed for the rest of the day. Is it that I am too weak to cope with the cruel realities of the world or is it that *you* are too weak to deny the sensationalism that brings your paper its profit and salaries? Can you never print just *one* happy or amusing or heart-warming story on the front page? Or for that matter, on *any* page? Even the food advertisements on Thursdays are psychologically devastat-ing, but that, in short, is not your fault—I guess none of it is. I guess, too, that you are just printing things as you seem them.
>
> It's a vicious cycle, though: the world is sick, which makes the people sick, which makes the sick people make a sicker world. If everybody gets as depressed as I do after reading or seeing the news, there's only one destiny for all of us—an insane asylum.[2]

Journalists have traditionally defended the publication of "bad" news and "unusual" information by saying that people prefer to read such sto-ries and that exposing evil and corruption does more good for society than praising constructive action. But here, too, greater balance is desirable.

A second consequence of news selection is the distortion caused by the attempt to be objective and fair. The unprincipled person can tell a lie to make news and have it reported with the same weight as the honest person who tells the truth.

Perhaps the best historical example of this problem involves Senator Joseph McCarthy of Wisconsin, who in the early 1950s used the exposure of Communists in government for his own political ends. The senator made charges, most of which he was never able to substantiate, that some-times ruined people's careers and lives. The news media objectively re-ported the fact that Senator McCarthy had charged Mr. A with being a Communist, and Mr. A, if available, denied the charges. Both sides of the story were told, so the news media were giving a fair and balanced cover-age of news. But the reporters could not inject their opinion that the sena-tor was lying, and thus irreparable public damage was done to the accused.

Ultimately the truth will win out, if we believe John Milton's theory about putting truth to the test in the open marketplace of ideas. And ultimately, in the case of Senator McCarthy, it was the news media that continued to give him coverage until his distortions became so apparent that his colleagues in the Senate finally censured him.

---

[2] Letters to the Editor, *Washington Post*, 4 July 1970.

"News brief: Trouble all over the place. Now, back to our movie."

(© 1985; Reprinted courtesy of Bill Hoest and Parade Magazine.)

In the end, we must say that news is a two-edged sword that cuts both ways. Those who would use it purposely to deceive the world will, sooner or later, be exposed by the same media that allow them expression. The consequences of news, however, are enormous, and no one should undertake to deal with news who does not want to accept the awesome responsibilities for making such decisions.

HOW NEWS DECISIONS ARE MADE

Of the millions of events that occur in the world each day, and of the thousands of people who do something interesting, who decides what goes on the front page of the newpaper or which will be the top story on the 11 o'clock TV news?

The executive editor may have the last word but usually has a lot of help in reaching a decision. At most newspapers and television stations, news decisions are made in regular conferences among reporters, editors, news directors, and producers.

At the *New York Times* and the *Los Angeles Times* news conferences, the managing editor begins by conducting an informal inquiry of editors from the metropolitan, national, foreign, and financial departments. There are generally two such inquiries: an early one involving primarily assistant editors, and a later one involving senior editors. From the two conferences and from conversations before and between them, a consensus gradually emerges on the day's major stories, and an executive news editor sketches in the actual placement of the stories on a dummy (a layout form of design) during the second conference. The dummy is often distributed to all the major desks and bureaus of the newspaper, and the editors are encouraged to challenge it. At the *Washington Post*, the managing editor goes over the

Figure 9.3. After the news copy is set in type, it is "pasted up" on cardboard sheets that are sized to the exact dimensions of the newspaper page. When all articles, headlines, photos, and graphics have been pasted on the sheet, it is photographed, and a plate for printing the page is made from the negative.

dummy at a final news conference, asking the appropriate editor to comment on each story already tentatively sketched in. The editors may suggest changes, and late-breaking events can force additional changes throughout the day.

Different editors and different publications and broadcast operations make different judgments about the news. *Time* and *Newsweek* often come up with the same cover story, perhaps because they are aiming at the same general audience or because it is relatively easy to arrive at a consensus on the number-one national story of the week. Such consensus is much rarer from one metropolitan newspaper to the next, and even from one TV newscast to the next.

A study of the front pages of the *New York Times, Los Angeles Times,* and *Washington Post* reveals great differences in judgment, interest, style, scope, and tone among the papers. Only 28 times over a 155-day period did the newspapers agree on the most important story of the day. On 56 days (one-third of the time), each paper had a different lead story. On 33 days (one-fifth of the time), there was not a story that appeared on the front pages of all 3 papers. Only on 32 days did the 3 front pages have more than 2 stories in common.

Another study of newspapers in more than a dozen cities on 50 selected days showed an even greater diversity in front-page selection. Local stories generally dominated the front pages, leaving room for only one or two, if any, national or foreign stories.

NEWS SERVICES AND NEWS GATHERING

Most news media have a network outside their local communities for gathering news. Some employ homemakers or students as part-time stringers in suburban communities or outlying towns. Some have bureaus in the state capitals or county seats to report local governmental news. A few large stations and publications have bureaus in New York City, primarily to report business and financial news. An increasing number of media of all sizes have correspondents or bureaus in Washington, D.C., which is often regarded as the news center of the world. And the larger media have their own foreign correspondents. For most newspapers and broadcast stations, however, the processing of local news is their primary purpose.

No one newspaper (not even the *New York Times*) and no radio or television station or network (not even NBC, CBS, or ABC) could provide worldwide coverage of news on an efficient basis. Increasingly, the news media have turned to independent news services or wire services for such coverage.

News services are the primary news gatherers and processors for newspapers and broadcast stations. The largest American services are the Asso-

Figure 9.4. Part of a large news room, typical of a news service, where reporters and editors produce the news copy on word processors after gathering the facts in the field.

ciated Press (AP), a cooperative that sends teletype news and features to the more than 8,500 newspaper, magazine, TV, and radio media units that are members of the association; and United Press International (UPI), a private association that has more than 7,000 media-unit subscribers. The Associated Press is the older service, founded in 1848. UPI is an amalgam of the former Hearst International News Service, begun in 1909, and the Scripps-Howard United Press, started in 1907. These organizations, or wire services, as they are also called, produce material only for media units, not directly for the public. Both AP and UPI are active in more than 100 countries around the world. Together, they employ more than 12,000 full- and part-time journalists, who operate nearly 400 bureaus. Together, they lease more than 1 million miles of telephone wire and make extensive use of radio-teletype circuits and transoceanic cables. They transmit nearly 10 million words a day, thousands of pictures, and hundreds of special broadcast reports. The mass media are dependent on them largely for national and international news and information and for regional news features.

News services today are the world's news brokers, providing the vast bulk of national, international, and regional news for most media. By the mid-1980s, about 75 percent of all the news that most Americans read and heard was provided by the Associated Press and United Press International. Many countries and regions have their own news agencies. For example, the Pan African News Agency (PANA) serves the news media in many African countries. But besides AP and UPI, only three other news agencies have worldwide impact: in England, it is Reuters; in France, Agence France-Presse; and in the Soviet Union, TASS, which is part of the government.

News services provide a variety of coverage, such as a national wire, a state wire, a local wire, or a special radio wire written for broadcast. They charge their subscribers a fee based on circulation or station size. A small newspaper of 25,000 circulation may pay from $100 to $400 a week, while a large metropolitan daily might be charged as much as $6,000 a week. Both AP and UPI have annual budgets in excess of $50 million.

The news services are staffed by seasoned reporters who work out of bureaus that are organized much like the city staff of a daily newspaper, with researchers, reporters, copyreaders, and editors. Almost every state capital, all major cities, and most foreign capitals have news-service bureaus. New York City is the headquarters and houses the largest operation for both AP and UPI.

The news services provide an excellent training ground for news work. The top minimum salary at a news-service job in 1987—a weekly $675 at AP and $585 at UPI—is higher than the salaries at newspapers in many American cities. Only reporters for major newspapers have a higher top minimum.

THE STYLE AND STRUCTURE OF PRINT NEWS

Since the purpose of news is to transmit information as efficiently as possible, it must have a style and structure that permit quick and effective communication. Language must be clear, simple, and to the point. Syntax must be direct and concise. Organization must be logical. The writing must have clarity and brevity.

The news story must be organized and written in such a way that others can work on it easily; it might be compared to a racing car with easily accessible parts that allow for rapid repair by all mechanics at the pit stop. Copyreaders, announcers, editors, directors—all must be able to work with the news copy quickly and cooperatively.

In newspaper news, the "inverted-pyramid" structure is usually used to organize the story. Inverted-pyramid organization places the most important part of the story at the beginning, the less significant material in the middle, and the least meaningful at the end. Newspaper stories usually are not told chronologically or dramatically because the most important things usually happen at the end of an event or a drama, not at the beginning. If we were writing fiction about a baseball game, we might start our story with a description of the weather and a discussion of the butterflies in the stomach of the pitcher. But a newspaper article will begin with the final score of the game.

This method of reporting serves two important functions. First, it gives the hurried newspaper reader the most important information immediately. Readers need not learn more about the event unless they have the time or a special interest in the story. Second, it allows the editors to cut a story at the end, if there is competition for time or space (as there usually is), without losing the essential facts of the story.

Since the beginning of the story is the most important, the lead, or opening paragraph, is usually used to summarize the significant facts of the event. In the past, reporters spoke of the five *w*s and the *h*: who, what, when, where, why, and how. If these questions about each event were answered in the lead, the main points of the story would be summarized. Today, there is less emphasis on the five *w*s and the *h*, and yet the basic principle remains—that the first few paragraphs must summarize the most important elements of any news situation.

Investigative News Reporting

One of the most important developments in news and information has been the increase in investigative reporting. Indeed, investigative reporters such as Robert Woodward and Carl Bernstein, the *Washington Post* team that cracked the Watergate story, have become the modern heroes of American journalism. Others, such as Don Bolles of the *Arizona Republic*, have been assassinated by the enemies they created in uncovering inside

Figure 9.5. Jack Newfield is an investigative reporter for the *Village Voice* in New York City who takes his work very seriously. His articles have led to major investigations of political corruption in Manhattan. (Photo by Janie Eisenberg, courtesy of the *Columbia Journalism Review.*)

information. Investigative reporters make news by going beneath the surface situation to find the real cause or purpose of an event. At times, they are almost a combination of police detective, spy, and gossip columnist. In their book *All the President's Men,* Woodward and Bernstein gave an unusual glimpse of the world of investigative reporting: wheedling secrets from confidential sources, talking their way into private homes and offices in the hope of getting new facts, meeting contacts in dark parking garages to glean morsels of information, and building a case, piece by piece, until a larger picture is formed.

To satisfy the journalistic need for speed and thoroughness, investigative reporting is often done best by teams of reporters. Jack Anderson, who bills himself as an investigative reporter in Washington, employs a small staff of aides who serve as researchers and investigators for his column. A number of newspapers have set up investigative teams, as have the news services.

RADIO AND TELEVISION AS NEWS MEDIA

The number of people who depend on the broadcast media for their news has risen steadily; today, the majority of the people in the United States fall into this category.

The major broadcast networks have large news operations, with correspondents covering the world in somewhat the same way the news services do, although much less extensively. The networks concentrate their news coverage on major news centers, such as Washington, D.C., New York City, Los Angeles, and a few foreign capitals.

Figure 9.6. The Cable News Network (CNN) has become a major news service for people all over the world. Chris Curle and Don Farmer anchor CNN's "Primenews."

Local radio and television stations have increased their news operations as well. Indeed, providing local news has become one of the most important functions of individual stations.

Both network and local stations have been increasing the amount of time devoted to news. Although radio usually provides news in only short bursts—5 minutes on the hour—the number of radio stations has increased to more than make up for the loss of the 15-minute newscasts.

Only one radio network in the mid-1980s was doing extensive news on radio, with in-depth reports using correspondents stationed around the world for documentaries and news-magazine features. That network was National Public Radio (NPR), a service of the Corporation for Public Broadcasting, serving as a national production-and-distribution center for some 270 noncommercial, mostly FM, radio stations across the United States. NPR produces more radio programming than does any other network, and its listenership grew rapidly in the first half of the 1980s. NPR produces "Morning Edition," which provides its network stations with 3 hours of news each morning; "All Things Considered," a 1½-hour news magazine that is broadcast in the evening and is probably the most influential news program on radio; and "Weekend Edition," a Saturday and Sunday news magazine. The growing popularity of these programs indicates the revival of radio as an important medium for news and interpretation.

Television news has settled into a format of network news in the morning, some local news at noon, local and network news in the evening,

Figure 9.7. Electronic news gathering has increased the flexibility of broadcast journalists. The minicam, used by KOCO-TV, Oklahoma City, has made it easier to tape reports from news locations.

and local news in the late evening. A recent trend that expands the news day is late-evening network news, such as ABC's "Nightline."

Electronic News Gathering

One of the most important developments in broadcast news has been the introduction of electronic news gathering—or ENG, as it is called in the trade. ENG is possible because of the perfection of minicams—miniature hand-held television cameras. Minicams can be used either for videotape or for live transmission, doing away with the time-consuming jobs of developing and editing movie film.

Electronic news gathering enables a television station to send out a crew for live coverage of a news event—say, a fire. The crew travels in a van that has a microwave relay dish on top of it. They use the minicam to get a video picture of the fire and maybe an interview with the fire chief or a fire victim. The relay dish on the van sends the signal directly to the TV station, and the station, in turn, puts the live picture on the air. The television viewer can see the fire while it is happening and listen to the reactions of persons on the scene.

Figure 9.8. This Skylink mobile satellite transmission unit, used by WXIA-TV in Atlanta, enables a reporter to broadcast live from any location. The signal can also be sent instantly to other television stations owned by WXIA-TV's parent company, Gannett.

ENG is greatly changing the nature of television news. For one thing, it is expanding the television news day. When stations were limited to the use of movie film, which involves setting up elaborate equipment, a TV station could cover events from only, say, 10:00 A.M. to 2:00 P.M. Because ENG involves a minimum of setup time and no film-development time, the news day can run from early morning to late at night. ENG poses some new problems for broadcast journalism, too, such as the ethical problems of live coverage. When ENG reporters go on the air live, they have no editors to judge the news for the viewers. Whatever happens live happens on the screen as well. This is the excitement but also the danger of this new kind of news presentation.

MEDIA DIFFERENCES IN THE PRESENTATION OF NEWS

News is not treated in the same way by all the mass media. Communication that is designed to be viewed must be structured in quite a different way from communication that is designed to be heard or read.

In writing for the print media, an important principle is that the eye is

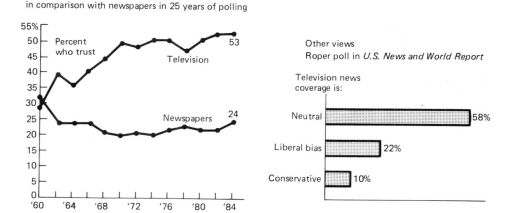

Figure 9.9. Television news is perceived by the American public to be more credible and more neutral than newspaper news. (Courtesy of *USA Today,* June 13, 1986.)

likely to be attracted to the first part of the page or the story or the paragraph or the sentence; the eye then is attracted elsewhere. Thus the most important element is usually placed at the beginning. A newspaper lead would begin, "Ronald Reagan has won the election, according to the latest figures."

Unlike the eye, which focuses immediately, the ear needs time to become accustomed to sound. So news copy for radio and television generally backs into a story, giving the ear time to listen for the important element of the sentence. Our lead for radio or television might begin, "According to the latest figures, Ronald Reagan has won the election."

In addition, the print media have more space to develop stories in-depth, while the broadcast media usually have time only to skim the surface of the news. Broadcast news must use fewer words and transmit fewer stories than print news. A 15-minute newscast contains only about 1,800 words and about 25 stories. An average daily newspaper has more than 100,000 words and dozens of different news items. Radio must tell the news in terms of effective sound. Television must tell the news in terms of vivid visual images. These principles obviously affect the nature of news transmitted by each medium.

In the future, media news coverage may become even further differentiated, with the media complementing one another through various types of coverage rather than competing for the same facts and using the same methods. The print media will no doubt increasingly stress in-depth coverage, interpretation, explanation, and analysis, while the broadcast media will assume the headline and spot-news responsibilities, the extra editions, and perhaps more of the light, dramatic, and human-interest elements of the news.

SUMMARY

News is one of the most important functions of the mass media. As our world grows more complex, we depend more and more on information about what is happening around us in order to function in society. The news media can place themselves in a position to get quicker and more complete and accurate news than can the ordinary citizen.

News, however, is relative to the interests of the audience. What is news for one person may not be news for the next. We do expect certain qualities in all news, including objectivity, accuracy, balance, and fairness. Journalists use certain criteria—including timeliness, proximity, prominence, consequences, and human interest—to select news that they believe to be of interest to their audiences.

News interests vary with age and socioeconomic status. However, most people are usually more interested in information that gives them some immediate satisfaction than news whose consequences are less obvious. Since sensational news is usually of more interest than nonsensational news, news can actually distort reality by overemphasizing the weird and evil in society. Even objective and balanced reporting can be distorted by those who wish to manipulate the news, and both news reporter and news audience must be constantly vigilant about the sources of information.

Decisions about what is news on any given day are usually not made by individuals but by teams of reporters and editors. The major news services—AP, UPI, Reuters, Agence France-Presse, and TASS—are the principal news gatherers for the world. The style and structure of news varies from medium to medium. Investigative reporting is becoming more important to print media, while electronic news gathering (ENG) is an essential new element of television news. The differences in the style and structure of news provided by the various media may increase in the future as each medium develops its own way of presenting news and information.

BIBLIOGRAPHY

Abel, Elie. *What's News: The Media in American Society.* San Francisco: Institute for Contemporary Studies, 1981.

Adams, William, and Fay Schreibman. *Television Network News: Issues in Content Research.* Washington, D.C.: George Washington University, 1978.

Altschull, J. Herbert. *Agents of Power: The Role of the News Media in Human Affairs.* New York: Longman, 1984.

ASNE Bulletin. American Society of Newspaper Editors, Box 1350, Sullivan Trail, Easton, Pa.   18042.

Cannon, Lou. *Reporting: An Inside View.* Sacramento: California Journal Press, 1977.

Chancellor, John, and Walter R. Mears. *The News Business.* New York: Harper & Row, 1983.

Columbia Journalism Review. Columbia University, 700 Journalism Building, New York, N.Y.   10027.

Diamond, Edwin. *The Tin Kazoo: Television, Politics, and the News.* Cambridge, Mass.: MIT Press, 1975.

Epstein, Edward Jay. *News from Nowhere: Television and the News.* New York: Random House, 1973.

Fang, Irving E. *Television News, Radio News.* St. Paul, Minn.: Rada Press, 1980.

Friendly, Fred W. *Due to Circumstances beyond Our Control.* New York: Random House, 1967.

Gans, Herbert J. *Deciding What's News: A Study of CBS and NBC News, "Newsweek" and "Time."* New York: Pantheon Books, 1979.

Hartley, John. *Understanding News.* London: Methuen, 1982.

Hofstetter, C. Richard. *Bias in the News: Network Television Coverage of the 1972 Election Campaign.* Columbus: Ohio State University Press, 1976.

Journalism Quarterly. Association for Education in Journalism and Mass Communication, University of South Carolina, Columbia, S.C.   29208.

Mott, Frank Luther. *The News in America.* Cambridge, Mass.: Harvard University Press, 1952.

Quill. 35 East Wacker Drive, Chicago, Ill.   60601.

RTNDA Communicator. 1735 DeSales Street, N.W., Washington, D.C.   20036.

Rucker, Bryce W. *The First Freedom.* Carbondale: Southern Illinois University Press, 1968.

Schiller, Dan. *Objectivity and the News: The Public and the Rise of Commercial Journalism.* Philadelphia: University of Pennsylvania Press, 1981.

Smith, Nelson, and Leonard J. Theberge. *Energy Coverage—Media Panic: An International Perspective.* New York: Longman, 1983.

Tuchman, Gaye. *Making News: A Study of the Construction of Reality.* New York: Free Press, 1978.

Washington Journalism Review. 2233 Wisconsin Avenue, N.W., Washington, D.C.   20007.

Westin, Av. *News-Watch: How TV Decides the News.* New York: Simon and Schuster, 1982.

10

Analysis and Interpretation

During the Vietnam War, the American government often gave a daily "body count" of the North Vietnamese soldiers killed in action. The next day, the news media duly reported the government's "body count" as an objective fact. The impression left with the American people was that we were killing more of their men than they were of ours, so we must be winning the war. It took some time for Americans to realize that we were not winning the war. The objective reports of the facts released by the government did not alone provide all the information needed for the people to know what was going on.

It is essential to have facts, but facts often have to be interpreted. The man who climbs the highest tree and looks out over the horizon may send back an accurate and objective report, yet he may not be communicating all the information that his tribe needs to know. A black cloud may turn out to contain locusts, not rain. Friendly looking visitors may prove to be hostile. A promising supply of fruit or game may not be edible. As we have seen in Chapter 9, even the fair and objective account of an occurrence may be misleading.

During World War II, it became apparent that objective news reports about the war were often influenced by Allied and Axis propaganda activities. American concern about the effects of international propaganda prompted the establishment of a high-level group to study the problems of free communication in modern society. The Commission on Freedom of the Press carefully investigated and analyzed the passive objectivity of news reporters and concluded, among other things, that "it is no longer enough to report *the fact* truthfully. It is now necessary to report *the truth about the fact*."[1]

Many indications from the world around us confirm the notion that straight reporting of the facts, while essential, may not always be sufficient. At no time in American history was this better illustrated than during the years of student unrest and political protest over the Vietnam War. Many groups practiced manipulation of the news media to serve their own political purposes. The term *media event* was coined to describe a "happening" staged to attract maximum media coverage. As dissenters became increasingly street smart in dealing with people and savvy about what reporters and broadcasting crews looked for in a news story, they orchestrated confrontational events—demonstrations and sit-ins in places that were normally considered to be off-limits, such as the office of a university president or the lanes of an interstate highway. These tactics usually attracted throngs of reporters, whose cameras and microphones recorded the activity and usually the comments of an activist spokesperson.

Today, such techniques are used by those who demonstrate against capital punishment and the manufacture and deployment of nuclear weapons, among other things. Since an execution can be witnessed only by those required or invited to be present, editors usually do not send many reporters or much equipment to a prison for coverage. But now that executions are preceded by vigils outside prisons, more coverage is being given to them. Antinuclear activists have also attracted more attention to the deployment of weapons by conducting themselves in a way that will ensure the interest of the media: chaining themselves to fences at weapons' depots and military installations, using their bodies as roadblocks, conducting "street-theater" performances that predict disaster—all behaviors that are designed to force the media to discuss feelings as well as facts in a story.

Those who wish to express a particular point of view, from the right to the left, from the old to the young, can use the news function of the media to communicate their ideas. To balance the use and abuse of news, the media must also be used to fulfill the need for analysis and interpretation— to put facts into perspective, to tell what an event means, to explain, to argue, to persuade, to express expert opinion about what happened, and to provide a forum for the expression of conflicting opinions.

Actually, the role of persuader, the act of molding opinion, came earlier in the historical development of media than did the role of informer. Early newspapers and magazines were often more a collection of editorials and advertisements than of news stories. It was not until the mid-nineteenth century that news assumed great importance in mass communication.

---

[1] Zechariah Caffee, Jr., *Government and Mass Communication* (Chicago: University of Chicago Press, 1947), 50.

Figure 10.1 Activists have discovered that they can influence news coverage by staging events to attract attention to their point of view. A group of antinuclear activists chain themselves together in an attempt to block the delivery of a component to a power-plant site. Cameras and reporters record the event, and it dominates the evening television news and and the next morning's front page. [Photo by Tom Sobolik, courtesy of the Concord (N.H.) Monitor.]

THE SEPARATION OF FACT AND OPINION

When news became a part of American journalism, the tradition grew that news and opinion should be communicated separately. The reporter has been taught not to editorialize, not to express ideas and opinions and feelings about what happened, but to tell simply what happened. This practice is not followed by journalists in all countries. In many European countries, journalists are expected to bring their interpretation to the news they report.

The usual practice among American newspapers is to place editorial comment and opinion on a separate editorial page, often printed toward the end of the first section of the paper, and to leave the front page and first inside pages for the publication of "straight" news. Another practice is to label clearly intepretative analysis or comment. A newspaper often publishes an objective news account of a major story on page 1, followed by an interpretative report as a sidebar feature, either on the same page or on the inside pages. An editorial might then be written, on the same day, but more often on succeeding days, telling what the newspaper management's opinion is about the occurrence.

Much criticism is frequently directed at the news media for injecting editorial remarks into the presentation of news. The political affiliation of a newspaper or the bias of its staff may sometimes seem to affect its "objective" political news coverage. News magazines such as *Time, Newsweek,* and *U.S. News & World Report* have a particular problem because although they conceive of their mission as a weekly "interpretation" of the news, their stories are not individually labeled as interpretation, and many readers accept these stories as unbiased news accounts. The blurring of fact and opinion in the news media has become an increasing problem, requiring more critical attention on the part of the consumer.

Radio and television also have a special problem in being used for interpretation and analysis. For many years, the Federal Communications Commission prohibited editorializing on the somewhat nebulous ground that broadcasting is such a powerful medium that it should not be allowed to influence opinion; it should only report facts. Happily, that situation no longer exists, but the FCC still regulates the editorial function of broadcasting, particularly through the so-called Fairness Doctrine. The Fairness Doctrine requires that when a station presents one side of a controversial issue of public importance, a reasonable opportunity must be afforded for the presentation of contrasting views. For example, when KURT in Houston, Texas, expressed the opinion that the John Birch Society engaged in "physical abuse and violence" and "local terror campaigns against opposition figures," the FCC ruled that the station must give the John Birch Society equal opportunity to express its views. Many such rulings have been made.

HOW THE MEDIA INTERPRET AND ANALYZE

It is useful to examine the variety of ways in which the mass media are used to provide interpretation and analysis of the world in which we live.

Interpretative and Background Reports

An increasing emphasis is being placed on reporting that attempts to tell more about an occurrence than the fact that it happened today. Historical background and perspective are needed. Many facts need further explanation, amplification, and clarification. The news media are increasingly developing specialists among their reporting staffs, people who know as much about their subjects as the experts and who, in reporting about a complex or controversial matter, can add their own expert opinions to give their audiences a fuller understanding of the situation.

Even the wire services, long the staunchest defenders of straight, objective news reporting, are making more use of background and interpretative reports. The Associated Press employs teams of special reporters who carry out in-depth investigations of complicated yet vital concerns and practices. They are under no deadline pressures that would force them to write a quick and superficial report of the facts. They can get behind the facts, explore the ramifications and meanings of the facts, and reveal the "truth about the facts."

Editorials

Editorials have become a standard feature on the editorial pages of American newspapers and in some magazines and on television programs as well. At times, they are placed on the front page when they concern an issue that is extremely important to the publisher, but the responsible practice is to put the editorial in a box, set it in larger type, or in other ways make it appear separate from news coverage.

Generally, editorials do not have by-lines. They are written by writers who represent the medium's management. The editorial-page staff begins each day by deciding which issues require editorial statements. Members of the editorial staff discuss the general treatment of these issues and, with guidance from management on crucial issues, determine the stand that the newspaper will take. Others also may write editorials, including the editors, the publisher, and reporters who may have strong opinions about the news they are covering and feel compelled to make a relevant editorial judgment.

Unlike the print media, which have long enjoyed freedom of expression in the United States, the broadcast media have not yet unanimously embraced their right to air their opinions. A survey by the National Association of Broadcasters (NAB) indicated that only slightly more than one-half of the stations in the country (57 percent of radio and 56 percent of television) regularly broadcast editorials (following the NAB's definition of an editorial as an on-the-air expression of the opinion of the station licensee, clearly identified as such, on a subject of public interest).

But the editorial function is growing in broadcasting. The larger stations are more apt to editorialize, which bears out the journalistic theory that the stronger the medium, the more courageously it accepts its responsibilities. Four out of 10 television stations now put editorials on the air every day; 2.5 out of 10 radio stations do the same.

Weekly Summaries and Interpretations

Weekly news magazines, Sunday-newspaper supplements, and some weekly newspapers also fulfill the need for interpretation and analysis. News magazines, particularly *Time, Newsweek,* and *U.S. News & World*

Figure 10.2 Newspapers generally keep their opinions about the news on the editorial or opinion page, which is usually clearly labeled as such, as it is in *USA Today*.

286

Report, have had a major impact on interpretative journalism. They regard their role as weekly summarizers and explainers, putting the news of the week into historical, political, or scientific perspective in order to express the meaning in the news. *Time,* especially, has perfected the technique of "group journalism," in which facts are sent to New York headquarters by many different reporters who cover many different angles on a given story. These facts are scrutinized by editors and specialists, who then put together a final summary that synthesizes, interprets, and analyzes the facts from a broad perspective.

Most major metropolitan newspapers publish special weekly reviews for their Sunday editions in which news for the past week in various fields—politics, education, finance, culture—is reviewed and interpreted. A few publications, printed in weekly-newspaper format, have been started for this purpose alone. One is *Barron's,* a national weekly financial review that is published by Dow Jones & Company.

Editorial Cartoons

The editorial cartoon may be the most widely communicated interpretation or analysis. It has been a force on the American editorial page since 1754, when the first cartoon appeared in the *Pennsylvania Gazette,* accompanying an editorial written by Benjamin Franklin. It pictured a snake, cut into 13 pieces, representing the British colonies, and it was entitled "Join or Die."

Effective editorial cartoons use the art of caricature, employing a few swift lines to exaggerate a character, personality, or feature to make a point. Bill Mauldin's "G.I. Joe" came to represent the attitudes and feelings of servicemen for an entire generation, and a few strokes of the pen could

Figure 10.3 An editorial cartoon from a colonial American newspaper. (Facsimile from *Pennsylvania Gazette.*)

(Reprinted by permission of
United Feature Syndicate, Inc.)

Shaping the young mind.

communicate much meaning. Herblock's grim, five-o'clock-shadowed hydrogen bomb expressed widely shared opinions about banning nuclear weapons. The economies of time and space that are permitted by the editorial cartoon give it particular force for mass communication; but by the same token, the editorial cartoon is often a superficial and exaggerated statement about people or issues.

Documentaries

The broadcast media have combined interpretive reporting, analysis, and even editorial comment into the documentary, one of the best vehicles for getting at the truth behind the facts. The documentary has often been a powerful force for the interpretation and analysis of events that often cannot be better communicated in any other way. The documentary, using historic film footage and current interviews, can provide a vehicle to review recent history and put confusing events into clearer perspective. In 1983, ABC produced "Vietnam: A Television History," a 13-part series shown on prime-time that interpreted and analyzed a war in American history that was difficult to report on objectively while it was happening.

Some intepretative programs and documentaries have been "tucked away at unwanted hours" of Sunday mornings or afternoons, the so-called

Sunday ghetto of broadcasting, says William S. Small, former news executive at CBS and NBC, in his book, *To Kill a Messenger: Television News and the Real World.*

The networks use special documentaries that preempt regularly scheduled shows whenever an event of major consequence occurs—an earthquake, a space launch, a riot, or the death and funeral of a great person. Using sight and sound, television has been able to probe, capture, and communicate such events with great effectiveness. When the space shuttle *Challenger* exploded shortly after lift-off in January 1986, the networks devoted many hours to specials and documentaries and panel discussions, replaying the scene in slow motion, investigating the probable causes, and examining the event from every angle for the fullest interpretation possible at the time.

The same techniques have been used to probe, analyze, and interpret great issues. The networks have produced documentaries on race relations, drug addiction, court procedures, political campaigns and elections, espionage, island invasions, and war. Local news staffs of both radio and television stations have used the documentary to expose local police corruption, poverty, hunger, housing, shortages, and education problems.

The documentary can have a powerful effect because it can use sounds and pictures together to move people. Small describes one of the most impressive CBS News efforts, the 1968 documentary "Hunger in America," an hour of emotional broadcasting that opened with film of a baby actually dying of starvation in front of the camera. "The broadcast had tremendous impact," says Small,

> particularly on the then Secretary of Agriculture, Orville Freeman, who bitterly attacked it and demanded equal time. He called it "shoddy journalism" that blackened the name of the Agriculture Department. Even as Freeman attacked, he was taking official steps that CBS interpreted as conceding the broadcast's main points: The Department abandoned its ceiling on food stamp programs, sharply expanded the number of counties with such programs, enlarged the quantity and variety of surplus food and sought (and won) Senate approval for an additional $200 to $300 million for food programs.[2]

In 1971, CBS's "The Selling of the Pentagon," a documentary on the public-relations efforts of the military, became an editorial issue in its own right. Supporters and detractors used the media to praise or attack the production. The program's format eventually caused an attempt by the House Commerce Committee, chaired by Harley O. Staggers, to issue a contempt citation against CBS president Frank Stanton. Stanton refused to submit "out-takes" (film not actually used in the program) for committee analysis. The committee was concerned that two personal interviews

---

[2] William S. Small, *To Kill a Messenger: Television News and the Real World* (New York: Hastings House, 1970), 39.

Figure 10.4 An in-depth documentary on the space shuttle *Challenger's* tragic explosion on January 28, 1986.

shown in "The Selling of the Pentagon" may have been used out of context. Eventually, the issue about whether Congress should become the arbiter of what is *truth* in programming was settled. The FCC ruled that the program had met all the criteria under the Fairness Doctrine. Some cynics regarded the criticism of the documentary as an attempt by Pentagon supporters to cloud the issue or prevent future media disclosure of military-industrial activities for fear of reprisals.

Crusades

In some ways, the print-media counterpart to the broadcast documentary is the crusade. A newspaper may undertake a crusade for or against an issue on which it feels public interpretation and analysis is vital. The *Washington Star* undertook a crusade against fraudulent used-car sales practices and forced the government to improve regulations. The *Washington Post* crusaded against deceitful savings-and-loan bank operations that helped bring about legislation curbing such activities. Crusades have been the hallmark of courageous journalism and often have led to media prizes.

A crusade often starts with a news story that uncovers some problem in society that the editors feel should be exposed. A reporter or a team of researchers and writers may be assigned to dig into the facts. After the newspaper editors know the facts, they decide how they will treat the story; they may publish the material in a series of news stories or interpretative reports, sometimes follow up with sidebars and features on various aspects of the problem, and conclude the crusade with an editorial or a series of editorials in which the newspaper presents its conclusions and recommendations.

Columnists and Commentators

The media provide an opportunity for experts and specialists to analyze and interpret public problems in their fields on a regular basis through the column, a by-lined feature. Many newspapers and magazines have staff columnists who write on local or special interests. But most columnists are handled by national syndicates, to which the publications subscribe. Columnists have great latitude to handle material in their own way, with a light or heavy touch, with sarcasm, satire, or humor.

A typical newspaper publishes an amazing variety and number of columns. On an average Sunday, the *Washington Post* published the opinions of about two dozen columnists, who covered a wide range of topics. Among them were four nationally syndicated political columnists who represent a variety of political viewpoints: Joseph Kraft, liberal; George F. Will, conservative; David S. Broder, moderate; and Jack Anderson, investigative. A fifth, Henry Fairlie, a British journalist, wrote on international topics. The *Post* also ran a variety of columns on cultural subjects, including Sander Vanocur writing about television; Paul Hume, music; Joseph McLellan, records and paperback books; and Norman Eisenberg, stereo equipment.

Syndicated columnists also dealt with personal problems in the *Post*: Ann Landers's advice on sex, love, marriage, and almost anything else (the modern version of the old "advice to the lovelorn" columns); Dr. Jean Mayer and Dr. Johanna Dwyer's advice on nutrition; and Dr. Timothy Johnson's advice on health. In this particular issue, the *Post* also carried four columns on a variety of sports: two on local sports, one on motor

'Shoe'   **By Jeff MacNelly**

(Reprinted by permission: Tribune Media Services.)

sports, and one on outdoor sports. Sports columnists' coverages vary from day to day, taking in almost every sport.

Other columns dealt with hobbies and helpful hints, and in this particular issue, there were columns on stamp and coin collecting, needlepoint, gardening, and consumer problems. Columns on humor and "just plain easy reading" were also carried. This issue of the *Post* carried Art Buchwald's "Capitol Punishment," a column of Washington satire that often has more political bite than does the work of some writers who do not use humor.

The Sunday *Washington Post* also contained special sections with news

(GRIN AND BEAR IT by Fred Wagner © Field Enterprises, Inc., 1972 by permission of North America Syndicate.)

"He's a distinguished comentator, Roscoe, and he certainly has better reasons than you for guessing wrong!"

reports and comments, including book-review, business, and travel sections; *Parade*, a national Sunday-supplementary magazine; *Potomac*, a local magazine; a TV guide for the week; and 16 pages of comics in color.

Radio and television also utilize commentators who play a similar role for audiences of the broadcast media. The format of 15-minute radio commentaries by strong personalities has vanished: individuals with strong political commitments, such as Gabriel Heatter, Raymond Gram Swing, and Fulton Lewis, Jr., or persons with strong interpretative-reporting talents, such as Elmer Davis, H. V. Kaltenborn, and Edward R. Murrow, are gone and have not been replaced.

Most stations now use a variety of reporters and correspondents, some of whom might comment on and analyze local news, but often not as personalities. The networks have commentators, but they, too, are more likely to be reporters than persuaders—anchors such as CBS's Dan Rather, NBC's Tom Brokaw, and ABC's Peter Jennings. Paul Harvey, on radio, still falls into the category of the strong personality with definite political commitments.

Criticism and Reviews

The mass media assume a responsibility to provide critical analysis of public performances, particularly in the popular arts. Books, movies, concerts, recordings, and dramas are public performances that need to be

Film Critic

(Drawing by Handelsman; © 1986 The New Yorker Magazine, Inc.)

reviewed. Reviews help a potential audience find the right performance and the performer play to the right audience, aiding the artist in perfecting a craft and the public in making decisions.

In the past, most mass media commentaries on the popular arts were reviews rather than criticisms; they were reports of what happened, and only sometimes were they critical reports. The reviewers were more likely to be news reporters who had been given the book beat, the movie beat, or the music beat. There is now a general trend on the larger newspapers, at the networks, and certainly among national magazines for these reviewers to be critics, expert and trained judges of literary, dramatic, or artistic performances who can make authoritative evaluations.

Letters to the Editor

Finally, it is the responsibility of the mass media to provide a forum for the expression of audience opinion. This function increases in importance as the ability of citizens to communicate publicly decreases because of the rising costs of printing and broadcasting. The people who write letters to the editor do not represent a true cross section of the public, nor can the media publish or broadcast all the letters that come into their offices. As in all other phases of mass communication, selection and judgment are key elements in communicating the public's opinions.

PUBLIC ACCESS

The analysis and interpretation of information raise the issue of the right of access to the mass media by the public. Do only media analysts and interpreters have a right to comment and pass judgment on facts and events and ideas? What rights do outsiders have to express their opinions in the mass media? The mass media are privately owned institutions, but do they have an obligation to make their air time and pages available to non-owners who want to express themselves?

Public access to mass media has become a critical issue. Some forceful pressure groups advocate open access to the media. In his book *Freedom of the Press vs. Public Access*, Benno C. Schmidt, Jr., describes some of the rights claimed by those who advocate access: the right of political candidates to advertise or appear in the media in which their opponents appear; the right of a person to respond to an attack or criticism; the right to advertise competing goods, services, or ideas in a medium that accepts advertising; or the right of anyone to have his or her views published or news covered on subjects about which the medium has carried its views or news.

In broadcasting, FCC regulations such as the Fairness Doctrine and formerly the equal-time provision have made access a fact of life. In 1969, *Red Lion vs FCC*, the ruling of the Supreme Court not only upheld the notion that broadcasters should provide reasonable opportunity for contrasting views to be heard on a subject, but also supported the idea that all media have an obligation to preserve an uninhibited marketplace of ideas.

The FCC regulations on cable television, adopted in 1972, required each new cable system in the top 100 markets to keep available an access channel for use by the general public, educational institutions, and local government. This channel was to be available without charge at all times on a first-come, first-served nondiscriminatory basis. Live studio presentations of less than 5 minutes were to be subsidized by the cable system, but other production costs were to be paid by the user. The public-access channel caused some problems in cities where it was in use, such as New York, where the programs tended to appeal to narrow and special-interest groups, such as homosexuals or transcendentalists, and the channel had trouble attracting audiences and financing.

In the late 1970s, in an effort to reduce restrictions on the growth of cable television, the FCC removed the open-access-channel regulation for cable-television systems. Now, no mass medium must provide access to outsiders to its properties. No one can walk into a radio or TV station and demand to go on the air with his or her version of the news or opinions. And no one can demand that any newspaper, magazine, or book publisher accept his or her ideas and put them into print.

The access philosophy once accepted by the FCC for cable television has been suggested for other media, but it has not been implemented. Further definitions of access rights came about as a result of the most celebrated access case of the 1970s, *Miami Herald Publishing Co. v. Tornillo*. In 1972, the *Miami Herald* ran an editorial that opposed the candidacy of a Florida union leader who was running for the state house of representatives. The candidate, Pat L. Tornillo, Jr., wrote a reply, which the *Herald* refused to publish. The case ultimately reached the Supreme Court, which ruled that the newspaper did not have to publish the reply. The Court's decision in the *Miami Herald* case was a firm rejection of the idea that anyone has a constitutional right to force a publisher to print something against the publisher's will. The Court held that such a ruling would do greater damage to freedom of the press than access would help freedom of expression.

Nevertheless, the mass media have an obligation to encourage uninhibited public dialogue and freedom of expression for everyone. And today, the mass media voluntarily accept this responsibility in larger measure than ever before. For example, newspapers are providing more space for letters to the editor. Some newspapers, such as the *Salt Lake City Tribune*, have a "common carrier" column for outsiders and pay a community panel to screen the contributions. Bill Monroe, former executive editor of NBC's "Meet the Press" and former Washington editor of the "Today" show, has advocated a "letters-to-the-editor" feature for radio and television stations as well, and a growing number of stations are moving in this direction. The reporters on "60 Minutes," the popular CBS investigative news program, conclude the show each week by reading letters of reaction to earlier shows. Other media have appointed ombudsmen to deal with readers' and listeners' complaints. Many newspapers are giving greater visibility to their published corrections than they used to. These are all signs that mass media leaders are concerned about public access at the same time that they enjoy their essential rights to use their own franchise freely.

SYNDICATES

As news services provide for the centralized gathering and distribution of news and information, so syndicates serve as central agencies for the analysis and interpretation function for the media. More than 400 agencies sell feature and editorial material to the media, both print and electronic. Small, independent weekly and daily newspapers or radio and television stations are the most likely customers for syndicated material.

Syndicates hire writers and commentators and market their work to individual media. Like wire services, they charge the media on the basis of circulation or size. A widely syndicated columnist like political humorist Art Buchwald can earn well over $250,000 a year through syndication.

Editor and Publisher's Yearbook lists more than 2,500 features that can be purchased from syndicates in the following categories: astrology, automotive, aviation, beauty, books, bridge, business-financial, cartoons and panels, checkers, chess, farming, health, history, household, maps, motion pictures, music, nature, patterns, photography, puzzles-quizzes, radio and television, religion, science, serials, short stories, special pages, sports, stamps, travel, veterans, and women's pages. These are main features. Other classifications include agriculture, bedtime stories, dogs, foreign news, labor, manners, politics, questions and answers, schools, and verse.

THE IMPACT OF ANALYSIS
AND INTERPRETATION

Finally, we must ask the question: How effective are the media in fulfilling a role as interpreters and analysts in our society? Most readership studies show that more people read comic strips than editorials.

In its study of the impact of broadcast editorials, the National Association of Broadcasters concluded that awareness of and actual exposure to editorials are more prevalent among men, young adults, and college-educated people. The NAB's survey showed that about 66 percent of the public felt that broadcasting stations should editorialize. A large majority of those who have seen or heard editorials (83 percent for television, 73 percent for radio) remembered instances in which an editorial made them think more about a particular issue. And about half (54 percent for television, 47 percent for radio) reported that these editorials helped them make up their minds about issues.

Do editorials change minds? Probably not as much as editorial writers would like. During political campaigns, editorial endorsement of political candidates does not seem to make a great impression on voters, according to most studies. Frank Luther Mott's analysis of the power of the press in presidential elections showed that candidates who had been supported by newspapers were beaten more frequently than they triumphed.

But there is much tangible evidence of the immediate impact of the mass media's analysis and interpretation, from editorials, columns, commentaries, crusades, and documentaries, including legislation passed, injustices corrected, individuals aided, tasks completed, and political victories won.

Well-informed citizens, who alone can make democracy work, require news, information, analysis, and interpretation. They should get their facts, and the truth about the facts, from as wide a selection of media as possible. They should not depend on any one radio or television station or any one newspaper or magazine. They should have access to as many different reporters and interpreters for any given event or issue as possible. Otherwise, they will be like the blind men who touched only one part of the elephant and falsely interpreted it as the whole.

SUMMARY

The analysis and interpretation functions of mass media, although not given as large a role as news and information or entertainment and advertising, are nevertheless important and may be becoming more so with the growing complexity of modern life. Many studies have shown that facts can be manipulated and news can be distorted. The media have an obligation to provide a fuller interpretation of the truth.

The American tradition has been to present fact and editorial opinion separately. Newspapers follow this format for the most part, but news magazines usually do not pretend to provide facts without their own interpretation and analysis. Radio and TV have not been as active in expressing editorial opinion, in part because the FCC formerly regulated against it.

Today, the media present analysis and interpretation in a variety of forms: interpretative and background reports, editorials, weekly summaries and interpretations, editorial cartoons, documentaries, crusades, columnists and commentators, criticism and reviews, and letters to the editor.

Increasingly, the public is concerned about its own ability to express a variety of opinions in the mass media. Recent Supreme Court decisions have interpreted our laws to mean that the broadcasting media have some obligation to present opposing points of view on issues that are broadcast, while the print media do not have such legal constraints. Nevertheless, a growing number of mass communicators agree that such an obligation exists for all mass media.

Syndicates are the chief means whereby newspapers and, to a lesser extent, broadcasting can provide interpretative and analytical material on a broad range of subjects. In the end, however, studies show that even though interpretation and analysis are vital to the public's complete understanding of events, people do not read editorials as much as they read news and entertainment, and the opinions expressed by the mass media have not often been as persuasive as communicators might hope them to be.

BIBLIOGRAPHY

Block, Herbert. *Straight Herblock*. New York: Simon and Schuster, 1964.

Brown, Lee. *The Reluctant Reformation: On Criticizing the Press in America*. New York: McKay, 1974.

Ethridge, Mark F. *The Editorial Writer: Facing Today's Issues in the White Tradition*. Lawrence: University Press of Kansas, 1968.

Hulteng, John L. *The News Media: What Makes Them Tick?* Englewood Cliffs, N.J.: Prentice-Hall, 1979.

———. *The Opinion Function: Editorial and Interpretive Writing for the News Media*. New York: Harper & Row, 1968.

———. and Roy Paul Nelson. *The Fourth Estate: An Informal Appraisal of the News and Opinion Media*. New York: Harper & Row, 1971.

Kreighbaum, Hillier. *Facts in Perspective: The Editorial Page and News Interpretation*. Englewood Cliffs, N.J.: Prentice-Hall, 1964.

———. *Pressures on the Press*. New York: Crowell, 1972.

Lewis, Jerry D. *The Great Columnists*. New York: Collier Books, 1965.

Liebling, A. J. *The Press*. New York: Pantheon Books, 1975.

Masthead. National Conference of Editorial Writers, P.O. Box 34928, Washington, D.C. 20034.

Murray, J. Edward. *The Editor's Right to Decide*. Tucson: University of Arizona Press, 1969.

National News Council. *In the Public Interest*. New York: National News Council, 1975.

Pool, Ithiel de Sola. *Talking Back: Citizen Feedback and Cable Technology*. Cambridge, Mass.: MIT Press, 1973.

Rivers, William L., William B. Blankenburg, Kenneth Starck, and Earl Reeves. *Backtalk: Press Councils in America*. San Francisco: Canfield Press, 1972.

Routt, Edd. *Dimensions of Broadcast Editorializing*. Blue Ridge Summit, Pa.: Tab Books, 1974.

Shaw, David. *Journalism Today: A Changing Press for a Changing America*. New York: Harper's College Press, 1977.

Stein, M. L. *Shaping the News: How the Media Function in Today's World.* New York: Pocket Books (Washington Square Press), 1974.

Vainowski, Robert. *In Our View: Broadcast Editorials.* Belmont, Calif.: Tresgatos, 1976.

Weiner, Richard. *Syndicated Columnists.* 3rd ed. New York: Richard Weiner, 1979.

White, David Manning, and Robert H. Abel. *The Funnies: An American Idiom.* London: Collier-Macmillan, 1963.

11

Persuasion
and Public Relations

Public persuasion through the mass media has become one of America's fastest-growing activities. In Bethesda, Maryland, a government official at the National Institutes of Health approves a news release, announcing a discovery in cancer research, that will be sent to the mass media. In New Brunswick, New Jersey, a corporate officer at Johnson & Johnson calls a press conference to tell reporters about a new tamper-proof container for Tylenol. In Dallas, Texas, at the national headquarters of the Boy Scouts of America, an audiovisual specialist puts the finishing touches on a 30-second filmed public-service announcement, encouraging community support for the scouting movement, that will be sent to TV stations.

All over the country, day in and day out, thousands of people are engaged in the business of shaping messages for the mass media that will further their cause, whatever it might be. The media, as we have seen, are used to inform and interpret. But they are also used to promote causes, to persuade others to act or believe or accept or understand.

It is important to make a distinction at this point between information and education, on one hand, and persuasion and propaganda, on the other. Education is the communication of facts, ideas, and concepts for their own sake, because they have an intrinsic value to the receiver of the message.

Teachers should be interested in passing information on to students, regardless of how students use that information. News-media reporters and editors, in providing news, information, interpretation, and analyses for their audiences, should inform their readers, listeners, and viewers without regard to the uses of that information. Teachers and journalists should attempt to provide a balanced, fair, objective, and accurate presentation of the facts, from which receivers can make up their own minds and take their own action.

Propaganda, on the contrary, is the communication of facts, ideas, opinions, and concepts, not for their intrinsic merit or for the sake of the audience, but for the benefit of the communicator, to further the communicator's purposes, whatever they might be. The word *propaganda* has had many definitions; it comes from the Latin word *propagare*, which referred to the gardener's practice of pinning fresh roots into the earth in order to reproduce new plants. The Roman Catholic Church took this meaning when it established its College of Propaganda in 1622, considering its mission to be that of propagating the Christian religion.

Most specialists accept the definition of *propaganda* given by the Institute for Propaganda Analysis in the 1930s and inspired by Harold Lasswell: "Propaganda is the expression of opinions or actions carried out deliberately by individuals or groups for predetermined ends through psychological manipulation."[1]

Any attempt to persuade another person is propagandistic, whereas any attempt to inform is educational. Of course, propaganda contains a good deal of information, and there is much persuasion in education. People's minds are changed by both education and propaganda; the difference between the two lies in the purpose of the communicator.

THE RIGHT TO PERSUADE

Human beings are more often persuaders than teachers. Most of us communicate only when we want someone to do something for us. Early in life, babies communicate to get their diapers changed or have someone bring food or warmth. Most private communications are purposive. In most democratic societies, it is a basic right of individuals to express themselves freely so that they can get others to serve their needs or believe in their ideas.

Each of us has the right not only to his or her point of view, but also to a *different* point of view. We are all conditioned by different cultural, psychological, physical, and informational frames of reference. As the world grows more populated and more complicated, the variety of points of view multiplies and difficulty in achieving agreement on the truth increases.

---

[1] Harold D. Lasswell, "The Strategy of Soviet Propaganda," in *The Process and Effects of Mass Communication,* ed. Wilbur Schramm (Urbana, Ill., University of Illinois Press, 1954), 538.

THE ROLE OF PUBLIC RELATIONS

Because it is increasingly difficult to get one's point of view expressed in a mass society, experts and specialists have come into existence to aid that process. In fact, a profession has developed to provide counsel on communication between parties with differing perceptions, differing languages, and differing cultures. That profession has become known as public relations.

Public relations professionals are experts in relating one public to another through communication. The techniques of public relations provide ways to adjust relationships between individuals and groups with different points of view, especially when those differences can lead to misunderstanding, disagreement, or even hostility.

Public relations professionals are interpreters or translators. They must take the viewpoint of one group and restructure it or translate it so that it can be understood by another group. Newspaper editor Walter Lippmann commented on this phenomenon in American society in his book *Public Opinion:*

> The development of the publicity man is a clear sign that the facts of modern life do not spontaneously take a shape in which they can be known. They must be given a shape by somebody, and since in the daily routine reporters cannot give a shape to facts, and since there is little disinterested organization of intelligence, the need for some formulation is being met by the interested parties.[2]

Public relations is a profession devoted to getting others to see the world as one sees it. Public relations systematizes the persuasive efforts of individuals and organizations because access to mass media requires expert techniques and knowledge. Public relations is necessary because in a democratic society, it is essential to win public acceptance, for nothing can succeed without the approval of the people.

The public relations person is an advocate of an idea or a point of view, much as an attorney is an advocate for a client. Public relations practitioners have a right and responsibility to defend their client's point of view before the court of public opinion as much as attorneys have a right and an obligation to defend their client's actions before a court of law.

In this book, we are concerned primarily with the media or communication functions of public relations. But public communication is only one part of the work of public relations, just as courtroom activity is only one part of the role of a lawyer; and in both professions, the public work may be the smaller role. As do lawyers, public relations professionals spend

---

[2] Walter Lippmann, *Public Opinion* (1922; reprint, New York: Free Press, 1965), 218.

Figure 11.1 The American government began to develop mass propaganda for the first time during World War I. Posters such as this were part of a national campaign to inspire Americans to buy bonds to support the war effort.

time giving advice, helping guide the client in ways that will be acceptable to the court of law or the court of public opinion.

THE DEFINITION OF PUBLIC RELATIONS

Public relations is a difficult term to define because it has often been mis-used. In 1976, Rex Harlow, a social scientist and public relations practi-tioner, used a survey of professionals in the field to devise the following definition:

> Public relations is a distinctive management function which helps estab-
> lish and maintain mutual lines of communication, understanding, accep-
> tance, and cooperation between an organization and its publics; involves
> the management of problems of public opinion; defines and emphasizes
> the responsibility of management to serve the public interest; helps man-
> agement keep abreast of and effectively use change, serving as an early
> warning system to help anticipate trends; and uses research and sound
> and ethical communication techniques as its principal tools.[3]

Organizationally, public relations is perhaps best conceived as the
total public communication effort of an operation, the overall umbrella
under which comes advertising, marketing, promotion, publicity, employee communication, community relations, press relations, public affairs, and other such functions, including public relations counseling. Of
course, not all organizations follow this formula.

Advertising, for our purposes, should be defined as a very specific type
of communication effort, one that is based on purchasing time or space in
the mass media in order to send out a message. Institutional advertising,
which promotes the total institution rather than individual products, plays
an important role in public relations.

Publicity should be defined in specific terms as free time or space in the
communication media to send out a message. In order to get free space in a
newspaper, for example, the message must contain some element of news
or human interest. To get free time on radio, for instance, the message
must contain some element of news, human interest, or public service
because of a long history of public service requirements for radio and
television stations by the FCC.

The main difference between advertising and publicity is that since
advertisers pay for the time or space they use, they have more control over
what is said. In publicity, since the message is free, the final shaping of it is
left in the hands of the media reporters and editors. Of the two, publicity
may be more effective because it carries the tacit endorsement of the media
and thus may seem to have more credibility.

Promotion means the use of both advertising and publicity over an
extended period of time to communicate a specific point. We speak of
"promotional campaigns," implying that a relatively long period of time is
involved over which message senders wage efforts to get their views into
the public consciousness.

Public, for our purposes, has two meanings. There is, of course, a
general public, meaning all the human beings in the universe. But more
often, we use the term to mean a particular public, such as American
citizens or, more specifically, employees, stockholders, and customers.

---

[3] Rex Harlow, "Building a Public Relations Definition," *Public Relations Review* 2 (Winter 1976): 34–42.

Some public relations professionals have identified hundreds of kinds of publics, each with a different kind of concern about the problem at hand.

THE PROCESS OF PUBLIC RELATIONS

Public relations as a process consists of three basic parts: management, communication, and publics. Management involves administrating, dealing with public opinion, and evaluating effectiveness. Communication includes six primary methods: person-to-person, publicity, printed materials, audiovisual materials, advertising, and special events. Finally, the process requires knowledge of the publics—and, of course, these publics vary from case to case.

Public relations should best be conceived as a circular process. The practitioner starts with a problem or a case; then defines the problem and determines solutions; then develops the themes, ideas, and facts that have to be communicated; then chooses the appropriate methods to communicate in order to reach the appropriate publics to achieve the desired results, which then must be evaluated through feedback to determine the extent to which the problem has been solved (see Figure 11.2).

THE ORGANIZATION OF PUBLIC RELATIONS

Today, most large business concerns, corporations, associations, and institutions with in-house public relations activities have a person in charge of these activities at a high level in the organization, often equivalent to that of a vice president. This person's job is to help the organization with its communication, making use of mass media whenever possible. Communication with and between employees is an essential element, of course, and so the person in charge of public relations often has a staff of people who specialize in internal communication, producing employee newspapers and magazines or other house organs. Public relations directors are also concerned with the owners or principals of their organizations, for whom they may produce stockholders' reports or an annual report. The larger the organization, the more publics the directors must deal with, and the more they need specialists on their staffs to deal with these publics or the special media needed to communicate with them (see Figure 11.3).

Perhaps most important, the public relations executive is concerned with the public at large—the customer, consumer, voter, and other people who make up "public" opinion. Reaching this audience means using publicity, institutional advertising, promotional materials, and special events to establish communication channels to the mass public. In this task, public relations makes its greatest use of mass media.

To use the media, public relations experts must put the intended mes-

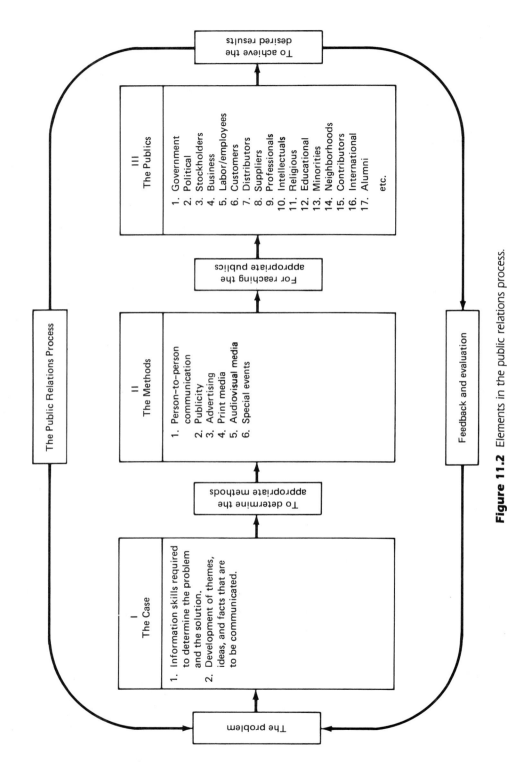

Figure 11.2 Elements in the public relations process.

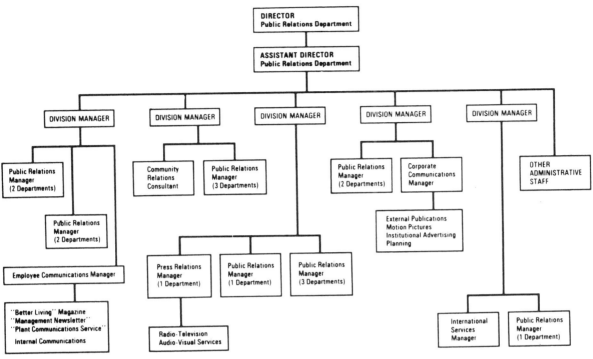

Figure 11.3 An organizational chart for a large public relations department. (Source: IPRA Exhibition, London, 1978.)

sage into terms that are useful for the media; that is, they must make the message newsworthy, compellingly vital for human interest, or of public service for the broadcast media. The public relations person puts messages in the form of news releases and public service announcements or finds other means to get messages into the mass media.

The other side of public relations is the external public relations counsel. Counseling firms, like legal firms, exist to provide independent advice on public relations problems for clients. Some of these firms undertake the entire public relations effort of their clients, producing their internal communications as well as providing direction for achieving their public image.

We have discussed here primarily the public communication aspects of public relations, the "outbound" communications. But there is also a very large "inbound" communication aspect, in which the public relations practitioner is concerned with public attitudes, opinions, and conceptions, and it is a large job to report these to the client. This part of the task involves analysis of the media as well as analysis of public opinion, through polls, surveys, and other measurement instruments.

THE GROWTH OF PUBLIC RELATIONS

J. A. C. Brown, in his book *Techniques of Persuasion,* shows how the development of the printing press enhanced the ability of people to persuade others. The first printed books, Bibles and missals, were used not only to win souls, but also to reform and revolutionize the church. Printed tracts were used to persuade Europeans to migrate to the New World. Early newspapers quickly became organs of propaganda for economic, religious, and political causes, persuading people of the New World to break with the Old, to revolt, and to adopt a democratic form of government. When the mass magazine appeared in the United States in the late nineteenth century, it was quickly put to use to persuade readers of the ills of society.

The forerunner of the modern public relations practitioner was the nineteenth-century press agent, publicity stunt man, and promoter. His job was to get information about his clients into the newspaper. He promoted ideas, gimmicks, schemes, gadgets from the assembly line, land-speculation deals, theater personalities, and carnival freaks. Press agents were men like P. T. Barnum, the circus entrepreneur who got newspaper publicity for his circus acts, thus making Tom Thumb and Jenny Lind, the Swedish Nightingale, into public sensations. They were men such as Buffalo Bill, who got newspaper coverage of the exploits of ruffian cowboys and thus made them seem to be the heroes of the Wild West.

The first professional public relations man was Ivy Ledbetter Lee, a former *New York Times* and *New York Journal* reporter. In 1904, he opened a publicity firm which was involved not simply in promoting his clients, but also in guiding their total public communications. He saw an analogy between the court of law and the role of public opinion, and he saw himself as a new kind of lawyer, one who would represent his client before the court of public opinion by counseling the client on its public communications. He regarded his job as one of "adjusting relationships between clients and their publics"; he spoke of "public relationships,"[4] and so the phrase *public relations* came into use. Ivy Lee counseled such important men and groups in America as John D. Rockefeller, the Pennsylvania Railroad, Standard Oil, Bethlehem Steel, Chrysler, the American Red Cross, and Harvard and Princeton Universities.

Before long, many others were engaged in similar practice. During World War I, the United States government officially recognized, for the first time, that it had to organize persuasive efforts on its behalf in order to win the war. It had to use communication to advocate its position before the American public and the world. President Woodrow Wilson employed a Colorado newspaper editor, George Creel, to head the Committee on Public Information. Creel's committee advertised, publicized, and promoted America's role in the war.

---

[4] Ray Eldon Hiebert, *Courtier to the Crowd* (Ames, Iowa: Iowa State University Press, 1966), 13.

Figure 11.4 Ivy Ledbetter Lee is often regarded as the father of modern public relations. He opened the first firm devoted exclusively to advising clients about their public relationships and how to improve them. His clients included some of the wealthiest families and largest corporations in the United States.

Although Creel's committee was disbanded after the war, America's increasing role in international affairs led to the realization that the nation needed to defend itself before the world court of public opinion, to express its national views to other countries of the world. Nothing of this sort was done, however, until after the United States had entered World War II. The government then established the Office of War Information, headed by Elmer Davis, a radio news commentator.

After World War II, the Office of War Information evolved into the United States Information Agency (USIA), the official public relations organization for the U.S. government in its relationships with other nations and foreign peoples. The Voice of America (VOA) was also established as an external broadcast service, using shortwave to beam information, news, and persuasion about America around the world.

Between World Wars I and II, private public relations firms multiplied and grew to maturity in the United States. Chief among those who pioneered in the maturation of public relations during this period was Edward Bernays, a nephew of Sigmund Freud. Bernays attempted to take public relations out of the realm of art and make it systematic and scientific. He wrote a pioneering book on public relations, calling it the "engineering of consent."[5]

Systematic and scientific persuasion required accurate measurement of public opinion. In the 1930s and 1940s, the practice of public opinion polling emerged, pioneered by such men as George Gallup, a former journalism professor, and Elmo Roper, a social scientist. Polling not only provided a mechanism for the media to obtain feedback from their messages, but also became a necessary adjunct to communication efforts by those who used the media to persuade the public.

In the 1950s and 1960s, public relations professionals turned increasingly to social and behavioral scientists to help measure public attitudes and test the effects of different ideas and messages on public opinion. Yet most public relations activities in the 1970s and 1980s still centered on communication efforts and utilized basic communication skills, using the mass media to send messages to persuade millions.

THE SCOPE OF PUBLIC RELATIONS

Englishman J. A. R. Pimlott, in his 1951 book, *Public Relations and American Democracy*, wrote:

> "Public relations is not a peculiarly American phenomenon, but it has nowhere flourished as in the United States. Nowhere else is it so widely practiced, so lucrative, so pretentious, so respectable and disreputable, so widely suspected and so extravagantly extolled."[6]

By the mid-1980s, more than 100,000 people were directly engaged in public relations in the United States. Several hundred independent public relations consulting firms provide advice to clients (Table 11.1). Most of them are headquartered in New York, often with branch offices in other large American and foreign cities. But almost every sizable organization in America—whether business corporation, labor union, political party, educational institution, or religious group—has it own public relations representative; show-business personalities and other influential public figures also utilize the services of such representatives. Governments, too, at the local, state, and national levels, employ public relations experts to help get government facts and opinions expressed in the mass media, since the government does not own the mass media in the United States.

The Public Relations Society of America (PRSA), an association of about 13,000 professional members, maintains a program of accrediting public relations practitioners through a series of written and oral examina-

---

[5] Edward Bernays, *Public Relations* (Norman, Okla.: University of Oklahoma Press, 1952).

[6] J. A. R. Pimlott, *Public Relations and American Democracy* (Princeton, N.J.: Princeton University Press, 1951), 3.

TABLE 11.1 50 LARGEST U.S. PUBLIC RELATIONS OPERATIONS, INDEPENDENT AND AD AGENCY AFFILIATED FOR YEAR ENDED DECEMBER 31, 1985

	1985 net fee income	Employees as of Oct. 15, 1985	% change from 1984 income
1. Burson-Marsteller*	$104,667,000	1,792	+28.0
2. Hill and Knowlton*	78,000,000	1,297	+12.0
3. Carl Byoir & Associates*	32,285,946	611	+4.0
4. Ruder Finn & Rotman	20,000,000+	325	—
5. Daniel J. Edelman	17,910,464	360	+24.0
6. Manning, Selvage & Lee*	16,788,000	272	+28.0
7. Ogilvy & Mather PR including Dudley-Anderson-Yutzy*	—	275+	—
8. Gray and Co. Public Communications Int'l	15,621,000	186	+36.0
9. Fleishman-Hillard	14,604,000	167	+32.0
10. Ketchum Public Relations*	14,196,000	217	+14.0
11. Regis McKenna	10,973,000	139	+43.0
12. Rogers & Cowan	10,351,000	159	+5.0
13. Doremus Public Relations*	—	140	—
14. The Rowland Company*	8,620,202	95	+13.0
15. Needham Porter Novelli*	8,244,552	136	+44.5
16. Creamer Dickson Basford*	7,900,000	108	—
17. Booke and Company	—	100+	—
18. Howard J. Rubenstein Assocs.	—	100	—
19. Robert Marston and Assocs.	7,223,000	70	+3.0
20. Bozell & Jacobs PR*	7,050,000	96	+38.0
21. Cohn & Wolfe*	5,340,000	94	+114.0
22. Adams & Rinehart	5,300,000	77	—
23. Financial Relations Board	4,850,006	69	+16.0
24. Kekst and Company	—	50	—
25. Richard Weiner Inc.	4,520,000	83	+22.0
26. Dorf & Stanton Communications	4,443,038	80	+28.0
27. Aaron D. Cushman and Assocs.	3,902,000	62	+9.0
28. Ayer Public Relations*	3,865,005	47	—
29. Anthony M. Franco Inc.	3,843,205	70	+32.0
30. Lobsenz-Stevens	3,450,000	56	+22.0
31. Hill, Holliday, Connors, Cosmopulos*	3,321,900	43	+9.1
32. Gibbs & Soell	3,164,756	46	+20.0
33. Padilla and Speer	3,073,000	39	+22.0
34. The Kamber Company	3,039,000	71	+39.0
35. Baron/Canning and Co.	—	40	—
36. Hank Meyer Associates	2,774,083	30	+10.0
37. Kanan, Corbin, Schupak & Aronow	—	30	—
38. The Stoorza Company	2,712,942	34	+20.5
39. Brum & Anderson	2,677,000	50	+40.0
40. Simon/McGarry Public Relations	2,634,330	33	+21.0
41. Franson & Associates	2,582,000	53	+22.6
42. Geltzer & Company	2,410,265	33	+19.0
43. Earle Palmer Brown Cos.*	2,410,000	32	+25.3
44. Edward Howard and Co.	2,178,199	32	+28.0
45. Hesselbart & Mitten/Watt*	2,173,232	20	+58.0
46. The Hannaford Company	2,162,011	24	+14.5
47. Dorn Swenson Meyer	2,134,405	35	+26.9
48. Creswell, Munsell, Fultz & Zirbel*	2,001,726	26	+33.8
49. The Rockey Company	1,945,000	33	+12.9
50. Public Communications	1,943,795	34	+30.0

* Ad agency subsidiary

Source: O'Dwyer's Directory of PR Firms, 1986. Copyright 1986 by the J. R. O'Dwyer Co., Inc., New York.

tions on the body of public relations theory and practice. Another organization, the International Association of Business Communicators (IABC),
also with about 13,000 members, represents those people who work in
communications within organizations. Both organizations maintain a code
of ethical and professional standards. Such programs have increased pro-
fessionalism in the field.

OTHER WAYS
TO COMMUNICATE PERSUASION

Some tools of communication are used extensively in public relations.

Direct Mail

The personal letter can be used as a form of communication to persuade.
Direct mail is based on sending a message through the postal system to
potential readers who have something in common. The gathering of mailing lists of the names of such readers has become a big business, and one
can rent or buy lists of names from a mailing-list company to reach almost
any desired audience.

In the past, direct mail letters were printed and sent to anonymous
recipients. But today, with sophisticated computer capability and the development of the word processor and printer, letters can be individually
addressed, with personal messages inserted at key points in the letter.
Also, the letter can be signed with pen and ink by a signature machine,
which can produce an exact copy of an original handwritten signature.
Letters from the president, members of Congress, or business and con-
sumer-group officials are now often handled in this manner, with thousands of letters sent to individuals; they appear to be personal letters but,
in fact, are mass-produced by machine (see Figure 11.5).

Members of typical senator's or representative's staff, having received
a heavy volume of mail on a political issue, might program into the computer a half-dozen stock replies; each incoming letter is simply marked for
one of those responses. Names and addresses and any variations can be
inserted in the program, and the computers automatically do the rest, even
signing the legislator's name.

Pamphlets, Brochures, and Graphic Materials

Printed matter other than books and periodical publications is also increasing in volume. These are not new media, but they are being put to new
use. They include tracts, leaflets, flyers, pamphlets, brochures, and booklets. Their proper distribution has always been a problem; the government
alone produces many thousands of such printed materials each year, ranging from booklets on legislative actions to leaflets on rat control in inner-
city slums. But in the past, many of these materials remained on literature

MUTUAL FUND FORECASTER

A Service of The Institute for Econometric Research
3471 North Federal Highway, Fort Lauderdale, Florida 33306

Saturday morning

A SYSTEM TO BEAT THE SYSTEM

Dear Investor:

Now you can profit from a new approach to stock market investing. After 15 years of exhaustive investigation, one of America's leading investment research organizations has developed what may be the ultimate winning market system.

Mutual funds are known to one and all. Most can be bought and sold with no commissions. You can start with as little as $100. The best mutual funds have soared more than ten-fold over the past decade, while the Dow Jones Average has only doubled.

Money Magazine says mutual funds are "the surest, safest way to invest in a surging market." And Nobel Prize winning MIT economist Paul Samuelson warns, "Anyone with a portfolio of, say, under $100,000 is unlikely to do as well investing his own money as he can do in a mutual fund."

But until now, the total investment potential of mutual funds has been untapped. The key to successful mutual fund investing is owning the right fund at the right time. MUTUAL FUND FORECASTER has developed a system using sophisticated computer technology to make sure you own the right fund at the right time.

Are you a short-term trader? A long-term investor? Do you prefer penny stocks? Or gold? Are you an international investor? If you answer "yes" to any of these questions, you will improve your investment performance with our unique system.

Higher Profits — Less Risk

The system begins with a Profit Projection for every major equity mutual fund in America, including nearly 500 load and no-load funds. This is a scientific forecast of each fund's performance for the coming twelve months.

The second step is a Risk Rating, an objective assessment of the risk of loss for every fund. We then combine the Risk Rating and the Profit Projection to select those very few individual funds that will give you maximum profit with minimum risk.

Many surveys tell you which mutual fund did best last year. What you need to know is which funds will do best in the future — and this is exactly what MUTUAL FUND FORECASTER will do for you. You can profit in both good and bad markets.

Our uncannily accurate forecasting models have been helping investors make more money for years. Now, with this new service, they will enable you to buy the mutual funds most likely to reward you with the largest gains — both short and long-term. And

Figure 11.5 A direct-mail letter.

racks in post offices or stored in government warehouses. The use of direct mail techniques to distribute these reading materials to people named on appropriate mailing lists has vastly increased their utility.

Use of display graphics, one of the oldest forms of communication, is increasing. Earlier societies used wall posters and notices tacked on bulletin boards to inform and persuade. Many countries, particularly China and the Soviet Union, still use wall newspapers and posters, as well as outdoor radios and television sets, to inform and exhort their citizens. In the United States, posters have experienced a rebirth and revitalization; poster publishing companies have come into existence to produce eye-catching posters in volume for decoration and information. Billboards have been a fixture in graphic display for as long as America has had highways and automobiles. Equally ubiquitous but even more effective, according to research findings, are exterior and interior car cards on streetcars, subways, and buses. Even the automobile bumper sticker carries a message, often political, and so can matchbook covers and even restaurant menus.

Figure 11.6 The American Cancer Society uses poster graphics to communicate information on cigarette smoking and health. (Courtesy of the American Cancer Society.)

The National Institute of Mental Health, a U.S. government agency that is fighting drug use among young people, decided to tell its message about the abuses of drugs not through the traditional media, but through display graphics. As a result, it produced brilliant posters for the bedroom as well as the classroom, eye-catching billboards, striking car cards and bumper stickers, and even clever matchbook covers. These media carried a message to many people who might not otherwise have been reached.

Audiovisual Materials

Audiovisual materials are now widely used for persuasion. Most of the equipment is built for small-group usage. But the equipment is standardized, and programs are being mass-produced to the extent that audiovisuals almost qualify as mass media. Yet they retain their personal intimacy and allow for easy and inexpensive production of audiovisual presentations, even by amateurs.

Most audiovisual displays use still photographs, slides and film strips, and motion pictures. Audio materials for sound reproduction include disc recordings, audiotape recordings, and videotape recordings. Videotape, of course, includes sound and picture. Most sound reproduction is now made to synchronize with visual presentation, even with slides and film strips, and simple systems are now available to program, synchronize, and mix sound and sight. The development of stereo tape and tape cassettes has also enlarged the potential of the entire audiovisual field, providing compact and convenient packages of sound that rival the convenience of books for storage, retrieval, and easy access.

Closed-circuit broadcasting is another form of audiovisual presentation, one that is finding increased use in offices for employee communication, at conventions, and in educational institutions to augment the communication process. Closed-circuit radio and television are being used in home and office and in shops and factories.

Mixed-Media Presentations

Since person-to-person communication is still the most effective way to send a message, eyeball-to-eyeball confrontation has become institutionalized in our mass society. It has long been the dominant form of communication in the classroom, church, synagogue, or town hall. Now person-to-person meetings are widely used and fairly standardized in format to persuade.

Meetings, seminars, conferences, and institutes have become such successful media for communication that they are now regularized affairs for most groups. Most convene on an annual basis, although some are semiannual; some, quarterly; others, monthly or weekly; and, not inconceivably, some, even daily. Most such meetings bring together people from diverse geographical locations for personal communication; hotels have become common meeting grounds, and new hotels are equipped with the latest audiovisual apparatus.

Sometimes the message rather than the audience is moved from place to place for different meetings. The display and exhibition have become new communication media for such a purpose. They provide for direct confrontation with their audience and lend a personal approach to the message. The traveling display or exhibition has been used effectively for communicating across cultural barriers. The United States makes wide use of such shows in its overseas information programs. The Soviet Union made effective use of this technique in a traveling exhibition of photographs, including hundreds of black-and-white and color pictures of life in Russia. This exhibition was displayed in hotels in major cities around the United States and received an enthusiastic public response.

In many of these person-to-person communication efforts, mixed-media presentations are used to enhance the effectiveness of the communication. But nowhere is the mixed-media presentation so varied as at a fair, with its color, lights, sound, pictures, sights, people, smells, and even tastes—all designed to send a persuasive message.

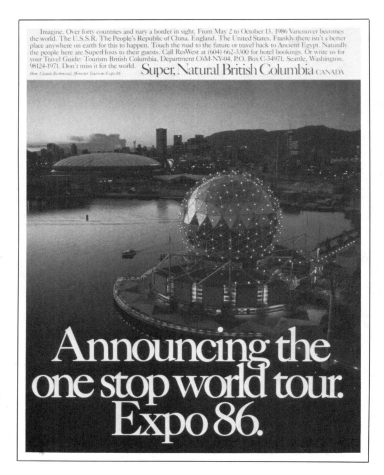

Imagine. Over forty countries and nary a border in sight. From May 2 to October 13, 1986 Vancouver becomes the world. The U.S.S.R. The People's Republic of China. England. The United States. Frankly there isn't a better place anywhere on earth for this to happen. Touch the road to the future or travel back to Ancient Egypt. Naturally the people here are SuperHosts to their guests. Call ResWest at (604) 662-3300 for hotel bookings. Or write us for your Travel Guide: Tourism British Columbia, Department C6M-NY-04, P.O. Box C-34971, Seattle, Washington, 98124-1971. Don't miss it for the world.

Hon. Claude Richmond, Minister Tourism/Expo 86

Super, Natural British Columbia CANADA

Announcing the one stop world tour. Expo 86.

Figure 11.7 Expo 86, which was held in Vancouver, was a good example of the use of the world's fair as a vehicle for communicating persuasive information.

The grandest expression of multimedia presentation is probably a world's fair. Here, nations and cultures communicate with one another—through sight and sound and smell and touch—the way neighboring farmers might at a county fair. New forms of multimedia presentations, developed at world's fairs, have furthered the techniques of effective communication. Such presentations have ranged from posters and brochures to light-and-sound shows, from multimedia-screen projections to complicated, all-encompassing exhibits through which one rides in a car fitted with audiovisual, olfactory, and sensory mechanisms to massage all the senses and provide for total communication.

The communication techniques developed for world's fairs have had wide application in other areas, including higher education and popular entertainment, from the multimedia center at the University of Texas to Disneyland in California and Walt Disney World in Florida.

PUBLIC RELATIONS AND POLITICS

Nowhere is public relations more important than in American politics. Politicians are most often persuaders of public opinion, and increasingly they employ the mass media to influence the electorate. They often use the techniques of public relations, and they sometimes hire professionals to help them win elections and guide their relationships with constituents.

The process of legislation itself requires publicity and promotion through the mass media. Bills that cannot capture the attention of the public through mass communication rarely reach the floor of Congress or of state legislatures. Former Senator Joseph Tydings of Maryland expressed a growing sentiment when he charged that members of Congress who could win media publicity were more likely to get their bills signed into law than were those who were ignored by the press.

Extensive use of public relations has also been made in the process of electing public officials. Consultants who specialize in political persuasion have tried to make election campaigning more sophisticated, systematic, and scientific. They use survey research and polling to determine voters' interests, to gauge the popularity of issues, and to test the public image of their candidates. They use computers to analyze the research and to aid in targeting the audience for the candidate's message. They advise the candidate, on the basis of research data, on the platforms to adopt and the personality aspects to emphasize or conceal. And they prepare the messages—through speeches, television commercials, press conferences, and news releases—to reach the voter.

Interestingly, these new techniques of political persuasion can make the election process more democratic. Politicians can take their candidacy directly to the people through the mass media, particularly through television. They can by-pass the traditional party structure, the political boss, and backroom politics. The public can be brought more directly into political decision making.

Unfortunately, however, the new public relations techniques in electioneering require money and a new kind of talent. The costs are high for public relations advice, polling, computers, advertising preparation, and media time and space. More than $400 million was spent on such electioneering in the 1972 presidential campaign. But expenses were far less in 1976, 1980, and 1984, as a result of federal laws that limit the amount of money that can be contributed to and spent on a political campaign. For a time in the 1960s and early 1970s, much concern was expressed that the "new politics" of public relations campaigning through the mass media would result in only very wealthy candidates being able to run for political office. But the election of Jimmy Carter, a farmer of relatively modest wealth from rural Georgia, proved that the new campaign-reform laws were working and dispelled many fears.

A new kind of political talent is often required, too. Politicians who

"Well, at least we can say he's not a media candidate."

use media—particularly television—to reach the voter must have a certain charisma. They must be able to captivate the audience through the media. For example, Jimmy Carter used a low-key, common-folks' approach to television that did not feel out of place or unwelcome in millions of American homes. Ronald Reagan spent most of his professional life in front of the cameras as an actor. Few could argue that he has not used his acting skills to exercise political leadership through the persuasive mechanism of mass media.

In the Carter–Reagan debate in 1980, Carter was the more authoritarian, more aggressive of the two men. He tried hard to seem decisive and presidential, qualities that his critics felt were often lacking during his administration. Reagan appeared softer, easier, and less aggressive. He seemed to know and use the medium better than did Carter. A telephone survey conducted by ABC immediately after the debate showed that more than two-thirds of the people who responded felt that Reagan had won the debate. Later, election analysts often agreed that the Carter–Reagan debate was a crucial factor in Reagan's victory.

In the 1984 presidential election, the televised debates between Reagan and Walter Mondale again proved to be a pivotal point in the campaign. Almost all the experts agreed that Reagan had simply made better use of the media. Indeed, Reagan's two terms in the White House may prove to be a turning point in American politics, where the ability to persuade through the mass media may be the key to all future election

"*According to this survey, you've become credible, though not quite electable.*"

(Drawing by Stevenson; © 1985 The New Yorker Magazine, Inc.)

victories and to the exercise of political power. Reagan's background as a former radio sports announcer and movie actor may have equipped him for the new era of politics far better than would the study and practice of law, which traditionally has been the principal route to political office. However, Reagan's failure to hold the public's trust after the Iran arms scandal and subsequent questions about his management style have brought concern about his qualifications for leadership.

In sum, the new politics requires a thorough understanding and effective use of mass media. The public relations adviser who can help a political candidate win elections will increasingly be part of the American political scene.

GOVERNMENT AND NONPROFIT PUBLIC RELATIONS

Although public relations is often viewed in terms of corporate and business interests, most areas of our society use public relations as a way of maintaining and adjusting relationships with their various publics, including local, state, and federal governments; hospitals; schools; religious organizations; the arts; the sciences; and even the mass media themselves. The federal government increasingly uses public relations people and techniques. By the mid-1980s, more than 10,000 federal government employees were directly involved in the practice of public communication.

Figure 11.8 World War II stimulated the growth of the American government's information and persuasion apparatus. Without the techniques to communicate the seriousness of the war, it is doubtful that the United States could have been victorious. Since World War II, the government has been engaged in persuasive communication on a grand scale.

There is a long-standing tradition in America that government should not be directly involved with public communication. The government does not own or publish any daily newspapers or own and operate any radio or television stations in the United States. The philosophy has been that government employs public relations practitioners, both to counsel gov-society. Rather, the media should be privately owned and unrestricted, so that they can report the activities of government and keep the bureaucracy from growing too powerful.

Nevertheless, it has become increasingly clear that even the government in a free society must communicate vital information to the public and must be sensitive to the attitudes and opinions of the people. So government employs public-relations practitioners, both to counsel government on its public relations and to inform people through the media, by using press releases, press conferences, media events, films, brochures, magazines, newsletters, and any other means that prove effective.

At the federal level, government has not permitted the use of the term *public relations* because some politicians and legislators still feel that government should not be engaged in "propaganda" and that only elected officials should be in direct contact with the public. The executive and judicial branches should only carry out the laws created by Congress; they should not be responsive to their publics. So the public relations function in the executive branch of the federal government is called "public information," and public information personnel are supposed to "inform the public," not persuade the public.

RIGHTS IN CONFLICT

Unfortunately, not all that is sent to the mass media from public relations offices is legitimate news or genuine human interest material. Much of it is puffery, self-promotion, or a cover-up of damaging facts. One cannot blame public relations people for putting their clients in the best possible light. That is their job. And the desire of the client is not only a natural human tendency; it is a human right. We cannot expect public relations practitioners to have the objective judgment about their messages that journalists should have.

Even more unfortunately, however, journalists often fail in their role as objective judges of the competing messages of various vested interests. Too often, the public relations professional's news release provides an easy way out for reporters or editors. It gives them a story for which they do not have to do extensive interviewing and research. Lazy journalists, hurried journalists, untrained journalists too often fall victim to the messages of public relations.

How much of today's news starts in a public relations office? No authoritative answer has been given to that question. Obviously, the answer depends on the medium. Newspapers and news broadcast offices that maintain large, well-trained, and well-paid staffs are less likely to depend on the messages of outsiders than are small, economically weak, and marginal news operations. Studies of some media have shown that more than 50 percent of the editorial matter originated in press releases or promotional material.

Clearly, two rights are involved and are sometimes in conflict here. One is the right of each individual or group to express its point of view and tell its version of the truth. The other is the right to know, the right of individuals and groups to have access to accurate information about any subject of immediate concern. When these two rights are in conflict, it is difficult to know which has supremacy over the other. Perhaps the best that can be done in a democratic society is to maintain a balance between the two; the tension resulting from the effort to maintain such a balance should help preserve a healthy society.

THE FUTURE OF PUBLIC RELATIONS

Without doubt, the role of public relations will grow more important in the late 1980s and beyond. As the population of the world grows and as the size of the planet shrinks (with supersonic jets and instantaneous global electronic communication), the relationships among people will become more crucial.

Communication, indeed, is essential to world peace. Understanding is essential to satisfactory relationships. Increasingly, more people in the world will need expert advice on how they can make themselves understood, or how they can change their ways to make themselves acceptable. This can be and should be the work of public relations, making use of mass media for persuasion, through two-way communication, to achieve consensus and accord.

SUMMARY

In a democratic society, everyone has a right to persuade others about their points of view. As media have grown more massive and society has grown more complex, individuals have found it increasingly difficult to exercise that right. This has led in the twentieth century to the development of a new profession called public relations. The public relations professional serves to persuade public opinion in much the same way that the legal professional works to persuade the court of law.

In the effort to persuade the public through the mass media, public relations uses advertising, publicity, and promotion. It also uses a variety of media other than the traditional seven mass media, including direct mail, pamphlets, brochures, graphic materials, audiovisual materials, and mixed-media presentations.

Public relations is best seen as a circular process with a problem, ideas to solve the problem, methods to communicate the ideas to the appropriate publics, and evaluation and feedback to determine the results. The profession has grown up mostly in the United States, but is now practiced in democratic countries throughout the world.

Persuasion through the techniques of public relations has become essential to modern American politics, but it is also important in government, business, education, religion, health care, the arts and sciences, and every other area of public life.

Public persuasion through the mass media involves two rights that are in conflict. One is the right of everyone to express him- or herself, whether the expression is honest or not. The other is the right of everyone to know the truth. Journalists are essential in solving the conflict between these two rights. The problems of such conflict will grow in the future, and solving these problems may well be the key to peace and prosperity for humankind.

BIBLIOGRAPHY

Aronoff, Craig E., and Otis W. Baskin. *Public Relations: The Profession and the Practice.* St. Paul, Minn.: West, 1983.

Bernays, Edward, L. *Biography of an Idea: Public Relations Counsel.* New York: Simon and Schuster, 1965.

———— *Public Relations.* Norman: University of Oklahoma Press, 1952.

Bloom, Melvyn H. *Public Relations and Presidential Campaigns: A Crisis in Democracy.* New York: Crowell, 1973.

Cantor, Bill. *Experts in Action: Inside Public Relations.* New York: Longman, 1984.

Center, Allen H., and Frank E. Walsh. *Public Relations Practices: Case Studies.* 2d ed. Englewood Cliffs, N.J.: Prentice-Hall, 1981.

Chase, W. Howard. *Issue Management.* Stamford, Conn.: Action Publications, 1984.

Cutlip, Scott M., and Allen H. Center. *Effective Public Relations.* Rev. 5th ed. Englewood Cliffs, N.J.: Prentice-Hall, 1982.

Diamond, Edwin, and Stephen Bates. *The Spot: The Rise of Political Advertising on Television.* Cambridge, Mass.: MIT Press, 1984.

Druck, Kalman S., and Ray E. Hiebert. *Your Personal Guidebook: To Help You Chart a More Successful Career in Public Relations.* New York: Public Relations Society of America, 1979.

Dunn, S. Watson. *Public Relations: A Contempory Approach.* Homewood, Ill.: Irwin, 1986.

Gordon, George N. *Persuasion: The Theory and Practice of Manipulative Communication.* New York: Hastings House, 1971.

Grunig, James E., and Todd Hunt. *Managing Public Relations.* New York: Holt, Rinehart and Winston, 1984.

Hiebert, Ray Eldon. *Courtier to the Crowd: The Life Story of Ivy Lee and the Development of Public Relations.* Ames: Iowa State University Press, 1966.

————, Robert F. Jones, John d'Arc Lorenz, and Ernest A. Lotito. *The Political Image Merchants: Strategies for the Seventies.* 2nd ed. Washington, D.C.: Acropolis Books, 1976.

Jamieson, Kathleen Hall. *Packaging the Presidency: A History and Criticism of Presidential Campaign Advertising.* New York: Oxford University Press, 1984.

Lang, Gladys Engel, and Kurt Lang. *The Battle for Public Opinion: The President, the Press, and the Polls during Watergate.* New York: Columbia University Press, 1983.

Lerbinger, Otto. *Designs for Persuasive Communication.* Englewood Cliffs, N.J.: Prentice-Hall, 1972.

Lesly, Philip. *Lesly's Public Relations Handbook.* 3d ed. Englewood Cliffs, N.J.: Prentice-Hall, 1983.

Linsky, Martin. *Television and the Presidential Elections.* Lexington, Mass.: Lexington Books, 1983.

Lippmann, Walter. *Public Opinion.* New York: Free Press, 1965.

McGinniss, Joe. *The Selling of the President, 1968.* New York: Pocket Books, 1970.

Newsom, Doug, and Alan Scott. *This Is PR: The Realities of Public Relations.* 2d ed. Belmont, Calif.: Wadsworth, 1981.

Nimmo, Dan D., and James E. Combs. *Medicated Political Realities.* New York: Longman, 1983.

———, and Keith R. Sanders. *Handbook of Political Communication.* Beverly Hills, Calif.: Sage, 1986.

Pimlott, J. A. R. *Public Relations and American Democracy.* Princeton, N.J.: Princeton University Press, 1951.

Public Relations Journal. 845 Third Avenue, New York, NY   10022.

Public Relations Quarterly. Box 311, Rhinebeck, NY   12572.

Public Relations Review. 10606 Mantz Road, Silver Spring, Md.   20903.

Raucher, Alan R. *Public Relations and Business, 1900–1929.* Baltimore: Johns Hopkins University Press, 1968.

Roll, Charles, W., and Albert H. Cantril. *Polls: Their Use and Misuse in Politics.* Cabin John, Md.: Seven Locks Press, 1980.

Sabato, Larry J. *The Rise of Political Consultants: New Ways of Winning Elections.* New York: Basic Books, 1981.

Seitel, Fraser P. *The Practice of Public Relations.* 2d ed. Columbus, Ohio: Merrill, 1984.

Simon, Morton J. *Public Relations Law.* New York: Meredith, 1969.

Simon, Raymond. *Public Relations Management: Cases & Simulations.* Columbus, Ohio: Grid, 1973.

Stevens, Art. *The Persuasion Explosion.* Washington, D.C.: Acropolis Books, 1985.

Vermeer, Jan Pons. *"For Immediate Release": Candidate Press Releases in American Political Campaigns.* Westport, Conn.: Greenwood Press, 1982.

Voros, Gerald J., and Paul Alvarez. *What Happens in Public Relations.* New York: American Management Association, 1981.

Walsh, Frank. *Public Relations Writer in a Computer Age.* Englewood Cliffs, N.J.: Prentice-Hall, 1986.

12

Advertising

Advertising is a specialized form of persuasion. We must pay special attention to it because of the impact it has on our capitalistic economy and because of what the ads say about Americans and living in America. Advertising is truly a force to be understood and reckoned with if we are to be critical consumers.

Ads affect what we buy!

Ads affect the way we look!

Ads affect how others think about us!

Ads affect even those of us who claim to be totally oblivious to advertised products and services!

Advertising is the most measurably powerful of all the functions and roles of the mass media.

THE DEFINITION OF ADVERTISING

In order for a message to be classified as an advertisement, it must have the following characteristics:

1. A medium must be sued to transmit the message.
2. Money must be paid by the advertiser to the medium for carrying the message.
3. The message must be directed at more than one person, preferably a large number of potential consumers.

Figure 12.1 After the break up of "Ma Bell," the American Telephone and Telegraph Company (AT&T) launched a campaign to retain the lion's share of long-distance customers. This message meets all the criteria required to make it an advertisement. It uses a medium—the magazine that was paid to carry the ad. It is directed at everyone who has telephone service and identifies the advertiser specifically as "AT&T—The right choice."

4. The message must identify the goods or services and/or the sender of the message.

These characteristics make advertising a different business communication from personal selling, sales promotion, publicity, or public relations.

Advertising supports commercial broadcasting entirely and pays for over one-half of the costs of newspapers and magazines. In turn, consumers pay for this advertising when they buy the goods and the services advertised. But rarely, if ever, are consumers' decisions based solely on an advertisement. Consumers are affected by price, by their needs, by their familiarity with the product, by their previous satisfaction with the product, by packaging, by the availability of the product, and by myriad other factors. Advertising can help create awareness of a product, a favorable attitude toward the product, and action in regard to buying the product.

Advertising decision making is based on many forces, inside and outside the client's organization, based on the marketing program. They include (1) distribution, pricing, and the number of brands a company sells; (2) the amount of personal selling involved; (3) the nature of the product, its competition, the demand for it, and the type of consumer who uses it; and (4) the budget available. You must remember, as advertisers do, that advertising is only one part of the total marketing mix.

The basic advertising convictions of most large advertisers in the United States are these:

1. *The advertiser's chief role is selling the consumer.* Ads emphasize the distinctive qualities of the product and reflect the overall cultural values of the society.
2. *Advertising creates markets.* Ads suggest new uses for old products and new products to solve old problems. Competition has created new technologies and made better products available in the marketplace.
3. *Advertising lowers costs to consumers.* Ads increase sales, and per unit production costs decrease because of this. The per unit savings far exceed the cost of the advertising, which the consumer eventually pays.
4. *Advertising spurs continual product improvement.* Ads cannot "resell" poor products, and the competition will overwhelm those products· that do not become "new and improved."
5. *Advertising forces competition.* Ads are necessary in today's marketplace, where price and quality are essentials in the marketing mix. The sales and distribution system is incomplete without advertising.
6. *Advertising and scientific research work hand in glove on a vast and amazingly productive scale.* Ads help the consumer profit from inventions by speeding up the diffusion of innovation process.

Many individuals have very strong attitudes about advertising as a result of some ad campaigns and the "pop literature" concerning the power and influence of the advertising industry. Advertising is neither the devil incarnate nor the savior of our economic system.

Advertising is an economic force to be reckoned with, because it accounts for 2 percent of the gross national product (GNP) and generates over $100 billion in economic value annually in the United States.

THE STRUCTURE OF THE ADVERTISING INDUSTRY

Four distinct industrial groups are involved in the process of advertising communication: (1) the advertiser or company that produces and/or sells the goods or services being advertised; (2) the advertising agency that represents the advertiser and creates advertisements; (3) the media representative, who has three essential duties—to sell a given medium in preference to another, to sell a given market area in preference to another, and to sell one basic media unit in preference to another; and (4) the medium that carries the advertisement.

The Advertiser and the Medium

In most cases, the local advertiser deals directly with the local media. Ads are usually prepared in one of three ways. First, the local merchant's advertising department can design them. This is done by most large department stores, such as Marshall Field & Company, Macy's, and Bloomingdales, all of which have outstanding advertising departments. Second, the local merchant can use advertisements provided by the national manufacturer of the goods it sells. Third, the medium can prepare the ad for the advertiser as a part of the total media service. In all these circumstances, there is considerable interaction between the advertiser and the medium (Figure 12.2).

The Advertiser, the Agency, and the Medium

Advertisers that use agencies to represent them seldom deal directly with the media. In this situation, the agency, the company's advertising expert, prepares ads for and recommends media to the advertiser. If the advertiser

Figure 12.2 In the simplest advertising transaction, the local advertiser, usually a retailer, deals directly with a local medium, most frequently (in terms of dollar volume) the local newspaper.

Figure 12.3 In this transaction, an intermediary, the advertising agency, works for the advertiser but, interestingly, earns a commission (traditionally 15 percent of the advertisement's cost) from the medium in which the ad is placed.

approves, the agency then deals with the newspapers, magazines, or broadcasting stations involved in the ad campaign. In this case, the agency initiates the action with both the advertiser and the medium (Figure 12.3).

The Advertiser, the Agency, the Media Representative, and the Medium

At another level of complexity, the media may also have advertising representatives. In this instance, the agency devises an advertising campaign and secures the advertiser's approval. Then the agency contacts the media representatives, who make the necessary arrangements with the media. Under this interaction pattern, the media and the advertiser are still further removed from one another, since the major negotiations are conducted between the advertising agency and the media representatives (see Figure 12.4).

As the advertising industry has grown more complex, advertising agencies and media representatives have become extremely important communication partners of advertisers and media in the sales-communication process. Each of the components of the advertising business has an impact on the number and kinds of goods and services that Americans purchase.

ADVERTISING IN CORPORATE AMERICA

Advertising is only one element in a company's overall marketing plan. It functions in relation to publicity, public relations, promotion, and sales considerations, which involve (1) introducing new services, hard goods

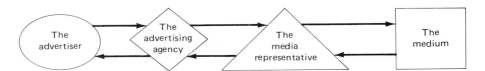

Figure 12.4 In this four-part interaction, the agency represents the advertiser, and the medium seeks advertising through the services of a media representative, who earns a commission on the advertising space or time sold to a national advertiser through its agency in a local medium (a TV or radio station).

(automobiles, furniture), soft goods (clothes, draperies), and package goods (ready-to-eat cereals, soaps); (2) building brand loyalty for established lines; (3) rejuvenating older product lines with refurbished contents and images; and (4) modifying overall consumer attitudes toward the company and its goods and services.

Besides advertising, the corporation must plan, package, price, promote, distribute, service, display, and work with franchisees and retailers. A general advertiser normally runs simultaneous national, regional, and local campaigns, which have to be coordinated. An advertiser may conduct industrial campaigns to gain business clients as well as consumer advertising while running trade advertising to bolster its image in its peer group and with the government, which is not unlike institutional ads for the general public.

Sales can also be increased by distributing samples, pricing, couponing, holding contests with rewards, giving premiums, participating in trade shows and public exhibitions, and conducting tours and plant promotions, in conjunction with ad campaigns. Remember that advertising is often the mortar that cements the total marketing mix into an integrated sales campaign.

The Place of the Advertising Department

The emphasis on and use of advertising by a company determines the place of the advertising department in the corporate structure.

1. The advertising department can report directly to the head of the company. This format gives advertising its strongest corporate role, on an equal footing with other functions (Figure 12.5).
2. The advertising department can be a part of the marketing area. This pattern is very common and emphasizes the importance of all three sub-elements of the marketing function (Figure 12.6).
3. The advertising department can report to the sales manager. This structure is dominant in corporations in which personal selling is an essential and in which advertising supports that effort through distributors and retailers (Figure 12.7).
4. Today's conglomerates and those companies with franchise operations may use a hybrid, in which there are two levels of advertising decisions (national and local) within the corporate structure; and each division or brand has its own decision-making apparatus. The format shown in Figure 12.8—separate brand apparatus—ensures creative independence and allows for specificity in ad development.

Figure 12.9 shows two layers of cooperative advertising, with the corporate advertising creating national awareness while coordination of regional and local franchise advertising campaigns generate immediate sales based on price and convenience.

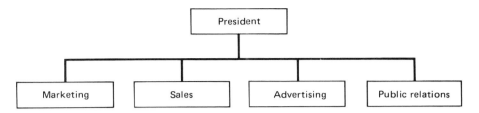

Figure 12.5

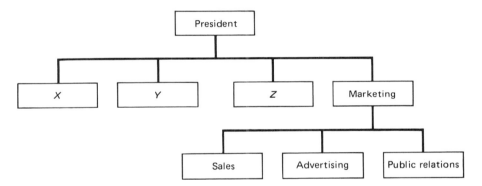

Figure 12.6

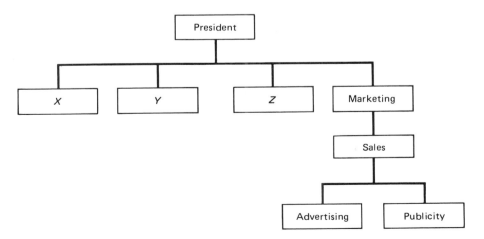

Figure 12.7

331

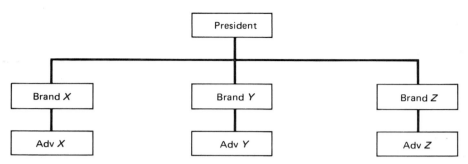

Figure 12.8

The Work of the Advertising Department

Within the advertising department, internal organization is usually based on market, brand, function, or medium. The advertiser's ad department has to work with the media, with media representatives, and, most important, with the advertising agency. The overriding consideration of the ad manager is to function effectively within the constraints of the advertising budget.

Perhaps the most important decision that an advertising department makes or advises the parent company to make is the selection of an advertising agency. A number of important considerations are involved:

1. The cost of creative talent is high; a good advertising agency can attract it and then spread the cost across a number of clients.
2. Media decisions are complex and specialized. Personnel in ad agencies are trained and equipped to deal with these problems.

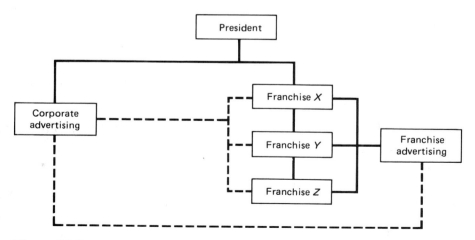

Figure 12.9

3. Agencies over the long haul can offer insights into the marketing, sales, publicity, and public-relations areas for little or no additional cost.
4. A good ad agency has close and good ties to suppliers (talent agencies, producers, specialty houses).
5. The most important element that an agency can offer is an additional voice that tends to be relatively uninfluenced by corporate politics.
6. The hows and whys of selecting a specific agency involve the following questions: Do we need an agency? Do we like a particular agency's work? Will we work well with its personnel, business style, and work patterns? Which of the "top" people in the agency will actually work on our account? Has the agency had experience with our type of goods and services, and does it now have a client in our product class or industry segment? Will we be a big or a small account in the agency, and is the size of billings an issue in determining the servicing of our account? How wide are the agency's specialized services, and how much do they cost? Where is the agency located? How long has it been in business? How big is it? How financially sound is it? What is its reputation among other agencies and with former clients? How much turnover is there in key personnel?

In the long run, the smooth functioning of the relationship between advertiser and agency is based on mutual trust and respect; open communication in all areas at all times; more than one contact person at both ends; clear-cut objectives and expectations; and correcting areas of disagreement quickly and positively.

THE ORGANIZATION AND SERVICES OF THE ADVERTISING AGENCY

Most advertising agencies are organized around the major services that they provide their clients. Figure 12.10 illustrates the four major functions of an advertising agency. Agencies are in business to solve their clients' problems in essentially four areas: research, creative, media, and client services. In addition, a large agency must perform its own administrative tasks. The organization of a typical large agency has four major divisions:

1. An administrative unit, which handles the day-to-day business details and corporate public relations.
2. A client services unit, which is staffed by account personnel who deal with clients' needs and meet directly with the advertiser as liaison officers.

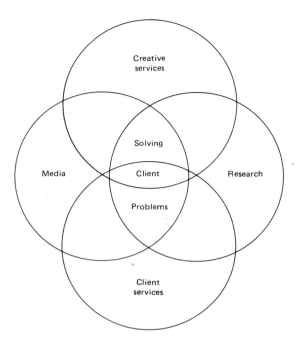

Figure 12.10 The four
major functions of advertising
agencies.

3. A marketing unit, which handles media decisions, sales promotion, and media research.
4. A creative unit, which is the heart of every agency because it is here that print- and broadcast-media campaigns are designed, tested, and executed.

Note that the research function reports to both the creative and the marketing units.

Research Services

Traditionally, creative research is an in-house operation, whereas media research is supplied by outside sources that survey print- and electronic-media audiences. The numbers in media research are important and have an impact on an agency's decisions. Agencies vary in the amount of research effort they support, but there is a trend toward decision making based on supportable facts, rather than on the old "seat-of-the-pants" approach. However, suspicion of the "numbers crowd" remains in some areas of the advertising business. The research department is involved in primarily three activities: (1) evaluating creative ideas and copy in the research workshop to identify and articulate problems early on, so that they can be corrected before huge financial investments are involved; (2) devising up-front market research and development funded from profits and not from the client's budget; and (3) evaluating government, private, or consumer research that might have an impact on the client's products.

Media research asks eight critical questions about target audiences.

1. Who are our potential customers in terms of demography?
2. Are there geographical differences in consumption? How much of the budget should be allocated to each market?
3. Are there seasonal differences in consumption? Should advertising weight vary across the year, or should it be constant?
4. What are competitive brands doing in terms of budget size and advertising strategy?
5. How do the consumers' demographic characteristics relate to their exposure to the various media?
6. Does the product's sales message lend itself to a particular medium?
7. Is exposure in one medium more valuable than in another in terms of impact on brand preference?
8. In terms of cost per 1,000 people in the desired target group exposed to the advertising, which media vehicles are the most efficient?[1]

All creative and media research seeks answers that will help enhance the advertising and marketing of the client's products and/or services. Research is the first step that the agency takes on behalf of the advertiser.

Creative Services

The process of creative decision making has one goal in advertising: to help the client, usually in the form of selling goods and services. Objectivity, avoidance of quick decisions to support cute or clever ideas, and simplicity are essential. Ads have to be simple and attractive in order to catch the eye and ear, pleasurable, and memorable. Above all else, the ad should sell the client's goods and services.

When an ad is being designed, many questions are asked.

1. Is this a good, simple idea?
2. Will the reader, listener, or viewer be left with the idea? What will he or she remember from the ad?
3. Is this a good technique for presenting the idea?
4. How will the audience feel about the product and advertiser? (Most consumers want to do business with people they like!)
5. Is the presentation talking to the right people—people who will buy the product?[2]

---

[1] *Training Manual for the Media Department* (Chicago: Leo Burnett Company, 1970), pp. 1–6.

[2] Interview with Dick Stanwood, of the Leo Burnett Company, Inc., Chicago, Illinois, December 1976.

The concepts, the ideas, and the ads have to come from writers, artists, art directors, musical talent, and other creative specialists in art, copy, and production. These creators must be able to conceptualize as well as write or draw or make up a storyboard. The development of ideas is the most valuable contribution that a creative individual can offer an agency. The members of the creative team must understand and appreciate every aspect of creative activity as well as their own specialty because the words of the writer must jibe with the visuals of the artist and the music of the arranger.

Creative ads depend on a select number of considerations in creative development.

Source. Who is the loneliest man in town? The *Maytag repairman*. Who sends you to the store to buy Starkist? *Charlie the Tuna*. Other product spokespersons are the *Jolly Green Giant*, the *Pillsbury doughboy*, the *Keebler elves*, and the ladies in the laundry room who use Cheer. Whether real or created, their attractiveness adds power to an advertisement.

Message. "The night belongs to Michelob." "Fly the friendly skies of United." "You're in good hands with Allstate." "Take the Nestea plunge." All these phrases focus the message, develop conclusions, and state the product's case. They are central to building up the brand image. The most difficult lesson for advertising students to learn is that they have to create messages that sell. If the messages are also witty and clever, all well and good, but selling is the important issue.

Production. The quality and style of an ad depends on the creative talents of those who produce it. The artists, copy editors, cartoonists, and others make good ideas work.

Copy strategy varies according to product conditions; in general, new brands seek to create awareness and promote a first purchase, whereas established brands seek to create unique images to expand their market share. The overall objectives of the marketing plan must guide creative work. Copy can characterize a product by creating an image, provide a description of the type and quality of functions the product performs, and serve as a physical description of the product. But ads must at some point increase sales by providing reminders that the product is available and that it has multiple uses. The recruitment of new consumers and the increased rate of consumption by current users are the two major ways to increase market share.

Media Services

The buying of space in the print media and time on the broadcast media has value only if an advertisement reaches the client's prospective consumers. The selection and buying of media space and time is a highly complex operation that is of necessity research based. Time and space buyers must be increasingly "on target" because the placement of ads has taken on new intensity as the costs of ads skyrocket.

Advertisers seek out target audiences who use or are likely to buy their products. Advertising research seeks to specify the characteristics of the target audience, to identify the basic media units that reach the target audience most efficiently, and to develop advertisements that persuade that target audience to purchase the product being marketed.

Consumers must work to sort out the thousands of product advertisements that compete for their attention, time, and money. It is estimated that Americans see or hear more than 1,500 ads each day, and as consumers, they have created psychological mechanisms that filter out those advertising communications that are of no value to them and have become increasingly aware of products for which they have an immediate need. That is why advertisers must ensure that their ads reach more of the right people and are better communications than are those of the competition.

The Print Media. Magazines are generally grouped by content, life style of consumer, workplace, or locale. The trend is toward greater selectivity in audiences, rather than general readership. This has proved to be an excellent development for the advertiser with a narrowly defined target audience that can be reached at a low cost per 1,000 readers. Regional runs of magazines have increased the flexibility of smaller national advertisers as well as larger local advertisers. Ads can now be run in some periodicals on the basis of zip-code references. Sales representatives for magazines sell space to advertisers at rates that decrease as advertising volume increases. The size of an ad, its position in the magazine, the use of color, and the number of copies in the run have an impact on the cost.

Newspapers are the backbone of retail advertising. The newspaper is the largest ad medium in the United States because it offers good geographical flexibility for advertisers seeking general audiences. National advertisers pay higher rates than do local advertisers, and this has led to cooperative, or co-op, advertising, by which the national advertiser pays most of the cost. Because the ad is placed by the local advertiser, the lower local rate is paid. Costs of advertising are based on rate systems that go down as annual ad volume goes up. The size of an ad, its position in the newspaper, the type of reproduction, and the use of color have an impact on the cost. Both national and local Sunday supplements are valuable vehicles for advertising and offer superior reproduction and environment. However, as with magazines, newspaper readership rather than circulation is a true measure of the medium's value. Like magazines, newspapers have primary readers, who purchase the newspaper, and pass-along readers, who peruse it if it is available, but do not have enough interest to buy it. In-home versus out-of-home readership also is important because the out-of-home reader is generally a short-term user of the newspaper, and the advertiser must depend on repeated exposure to make an impact.

The Broadcast Media. In television, cost to the advertiser is based on audience size and characteristics, production and distribution costs, and advertiser demand, which has accelerated dramatically. This increase in demand has increased the prices paid by national advertisers. Advertising on local TV is sold by commercial units to local advertisers and by audience units (Gross Rating Points) to national advertisers through local stations' media representatives. Most of the networks' advertising formats are packages or scatter plans, which provide a series of spots spread over a variety of shows at a group price. Full or partial sponsorship of programs and specials is relatively rare because of costs, risk, and demand. The national advertiser is very dependent on network television, and the high cost and unavailability of commercial times on the networks is generating considerable interest in the development of "fourth-TV-network" alternatives. The high cost of commercials shown on the networks has also increased interest in other advertising media by traditional heavy users of television time. Television ads are sold in time units of 60 seconds, 30 seconds, and, more recently, 20 seconds. The 60-second TV commercial was totally dominant until the late 1960s, either as a full 60-second spot for a product or as a "piggy back" (two 30-second halves for two products in a 60-second unit). By 1981, the 60-second ads accounted for only 1 percent of all TV spots, and 98 percent of TV ads were 30 seconds long. Today, because of costs, 20-second ads are the rage. In 1986, one in five ads was a 20-second spot, and that growth trend is expected to continue into the 1990s and may well become the dominant time unit.[3]

Radio is classified in the same way as television, but the medium is used in significantly different ways. Radio tends to supplement the media plans of most local advertisers, whose major focus is on newspapers, and of national advertisers, who emphasize television. Radio dayparts (e.g., drive-time 7-9 A.M., 4-6 P.M.) and program formats are key factors in audience size and composition, and because of this, the selectivity of radio audiences has become an advantage to the advertiser with a specialized target audience. The 60-second commercial remains the dominant time unit on radio, although shorter ads are used by some sponsors. But for most advertisers, the cost differential is so minimal that the 60-second format is preferred.

Other Media. Direct mail is the second-largest medium by dollar volume in the United States and is very selective because it is based on personalized messages sent to names on specific mailing lists. It is expensive but successful. It can include letters, stuffers, cards, brochures, and anything else that fits into an envelope. Many companies now include ads with their monthly billing statements; this is an excellent advertising format, which cuts postal costs because the bill has to be sent anyway.

---

[3] "Shorter Commercials," *Channels* 6 (September 1986): 80.

Outdoor ads take essentially two forms: the 24-sheet billboard and the painted spectacular (always lighted and sometimes animated). Boards have a life span of one to six months, on the average. Outdoor ads are not selective, have to be bought locally, and usually carry reminder messages. This is an excellent supplementary medium for ads that do not rely on extensive copy.

Other ad formats include car cards, displays at airports and sporting arenas, matchbooks, sky writing, shoppers' specials, sound trucks, and anything else from ballpoint pens to T-shirts. Media plans attempt to reach the greatest number of potential consumers as often as possible, to meet marketing objectives within tight fiscal controls.

Client Services

For the general public, the role of the account executive may be the most commonly recognized in the agency business. He or she is both the liaison and the policymaker who interprets the client's needs for the agency and presents the agency's solutions to the client. Client service personnel are in the middle and, on occasion, mediate the planning, coordination, and evaluation of the total ad campaign. Account group personnel are the generalists among the specialists who populate the agency business.

Client service personnel deal with a wide variety of client advertising departments, but five traditional approaches are common.

1. The client's advertising department may be organized by media. Under this arrangement, the advertiser has a television and radio manager, a newspaper manager, and an outdoor manager. The emphasis of specialization in this case is based on the unique characteristics of each medium.
2. The advertising department may be organized by product. At Proctor & Gamble, each of the company's brands has a complete team to service it, which leads to strong competition among teams as well as with other manufacturers.
3. The advertising director may have assistants for the South, Northeast, Midwest, and West. This geographical pattern of organization works well in companies that produce regional products or use specialized channels of distribution.
4. Some companies base their advertising operations on the kinds of users who buy their products and therefore have a farm manager, an industrial manager, an institutional manager, and a consumer manager.
5. The functional approach is used by many companies. This arrangement has an art manager, a copywriting manager, a media manager, and a production manager.

The client service department of the agency is literally a part of the

marketing staff of the advertiser. The account executive often has a counterpart—the brand manager—in the advertiser's organization, and they
are the working contacts or partners or links in the agency–advertiser
relationship.

Client service is, in effect, involved in everybody's else's business. It is
the account group's responsibility to bring to bear all the resources of the
agency to solve the client's problems intelligently and efficiently.

ADVERTISING CLASSIFICATIONS

Advertiser-communicators have developed labeling systems to clarify advertising processes. The four basic ways to classify advertising are by type
of advertiser; by message content, placement, and approach; by type of
medium; and by type of audience. These classification systems are important because they identify the who, what, where, when, and how in relation to advertisers' expenditures and media earnings.

Type of Advertiser

The two major categories of advertisers are general and retail. The general
advertiser is usually a national or regional producer or distributor of a
limited number of product classes. The company does not normally sell
directly to the consumer. Most general advertisers' campaigns are developed and executed by advertising agencies. Some corporations produce
competing brands in the same product class and therefore utilize the services of a different agency for each brand. Most general advertisers have
come to use television heavily, but also invest large sums in supplementary
advertising in magazines, on radio, and in newspapers.

The retail advertiser, by contrast, is normally a local or limited regional
operation that traditionally does not retain an advertising agency. The
retailer's ads are prepared or supplied by the retailer's advertising department, the media in which the ads are placed, or the general advertiser
whose products the retailer merchandises. The retail advertiser depends
most heavily on local newspapers and radio stations.

In terms of advertiser classification that has an impact on advertising
style, consider supermarket ads. Unquestionably, the overall advertising
style of food retailers is essentially the same: large pages in local newspapers that show multiple product lines, departments, sales, specials, cou-
pons, and so on. The consumer shops the ad as well as the store. This
format is valuable to both shopper and seller. Interestingly, attempts to
transfer this technique to fast-talking radio and flash-cutting TV ads are not
successful. In today's market and with today's prices, most consumers
want to comparison shop very deliberately.

The personality of the consumer often becomes involved with the
personality and the function of the product. The advertiser must know its

Figure 12.11 The advertisements for Marlboro cigarettes are placed by a general advertiser, Philip Morris, to increase retail sales of the product. The Marlboro man is the central character in the most widely recognized (in terms of recall) ad campaign ever created. (Reprinted by permission of Philip Morris.)

"place" in the market and then convince the consumers that they need to shop in that intellectual, emotional, physical "place"—the retail outlet. Store loyalty is more important than brand loyalty for supermarkets and similar advertisers.

Type of Message

The content, placement, and approach of advertisements are important because they designate the intent of the advertising communication.

The content of an advertising message may be institutional or product-oriented. Institutional ads refer to messages that develop the image of the advertiser. Institutional messages do not seek the immediate sale of specific products, but attempt to create an attitude of goodwill among the public toward the advertiser. Institutional advertising may also seek to correct a negative corporate image, align the company with specific national goals, or, more recently, place the company in the vanguard on a specific social issue, such as race relations. Many industries pool individual, corporate, and financial resources to improve the general image of the

Why do we buy this space?

For more than 12 years now, we've been addressing Americans with weekly messages in principal print media. We've argued, cajoled, thundered, pleaded, reasoned and poked fun. In return, we've been reviled, revered, held up as a model and put down as a sorry example.

Why does Mobil choose to expose itself to these weekly judgments in the court of public opinion? Why do we keep it up now that the energy crisis and the urgent need to address energy issues have eased, at least for the present?

Our answer is that business needs voices in the media, the same way labor unions, consumers, and other groups in our society do. Our nation functions best when economic and other concerns of the people are subjected to rigorous debate. When our messages add to the spectrum of facts and opinion available to the public, even if the decisions are contrary to our preferences, then the effort and cost are worthwhile.

Think back to some of the issues in which we have contributed to the debate.

• Excessive government regulation—it's now widely recognized that Washington meddling, however well intentioned, carries a price tag that the consumer pays.

• The folly of price controls—so clear now that prices of gasoline and other fuels are coming down, now that the marketplace has been relieved of most of its artificial restraints.

• The need for balance between maintaining jobs and production and maintaining a pristine environment—a non-issue, we argued, if there's common sense and compromise on both sides, a view that's now increasingly recognized in Washington.

Over the years, we've won some and lost some, and battled to a draw on other issues we've championed, such as building more nuclear power plants and improving public transportation. We've supported presidents we thought were right in their policies and questioned Democrats and Republicans alike when we thought their policies were counterproductive.

In the process we've had excitement, been congratulated and castigated, made mistakes, and won and lost some battles. But we've enjoyed it. While a large company may seem terribly impersonal to the average person, it's made up of people with feelings, people who care like everybody else. So even when we plug a quality TV program we sponsor on public television, we feel right about spending the company's money to build audience for the show, just as we feel good as citizens to throw the support of our messages to causes we believe in, like the Mobil Grand Prix, in which young athletes prepare for this year's Olympics. Or recognition for the positive role retired people continue to play in our society.

We still continue to speak on a wide array of topics, even though there's no immediate energy crisis to kick around anymore. Because we don't want to be like the mother-in-law who comes to visit only when she has problems and matters to complain about. We think a continuous presence in this space makes sense for us. And we hope, on your part, you find us informative occasionally, or entertaining, or at least infuriating. But never boring. After all, you did read this far, didn't you?

Mobil®

Figure 12.12 During the oil crisis, Mobil fought back with institutional ads that presented their views on the situation and justification for the course of action they were following. This ad is both informational and persuasive. It was placed in print media to improve the corporate image of Mobil as a public-spirited company. Mobil is widely recognized for its institutional advertising as well as its participation in public service. (Copyright © 1984 Mobil Oil Corporation. Used with permission.)

industry as a whole. In effect, this advertising message serves a function that is generally assigned to public relations. However, it is hoped that the long-range effect of institutional ads may lead to future sales by creating a positive image.

Product advertising seeks to generate sales of a specific commodity. The sales may occur immediately or at a later date when the consumer needs to replace or replenish a specific item. In terms of total dollars spent, product advertising overwhelmingly exceeds institutional advertising.

The placement category identifies the advertiser that is placing the message in a given medium. There are three designations of ad placement: national, spot, and local. National advertising refers to ads placed by general advertisers in national media (broadcast networks, magazines). Spot (or national spot) advertising identifies ads placed in local media by general advertisers. Local advertising specifies messages that retailers place in local media.

When the Oldsmobile Division of General Motors advertises on the NBC Radio network, that is national advertising. When Oldsmobile places an ad directly with WSB-TV, an Atlanta television station, that is spot advertising. When a Milwaukee Oldsmobile dealer buys space in the *Milwaukee Journal*, that is local advertising.

In terms of TV income, national advertising accounts for nearly 45 percent of every TV dollar; spot, 38 percent; and local, 17 percent. For radio income, local advertising accounts for 68 percent; spot, 29 percent; and national, only 3 percent.

A hybrid has emerged in this category: cooperative (co-op) advertising. *Co-op* refers to ads placed on a local station by general advertisers and their retail outlets in combination. They share the costs and reap the benefits of the lower local TV and radio spot rates. Co-op advertising also encourages retailers to do more national product advertising.

The content approach is another way of analyzing advertising messages. Advertisements may be direct and demand immediate action: "Sale, Today Only!" "Buy Now and Save!" The indirect approach is a "soft sell." It seeks action, but is calmer and more reserved; it may use whimsy, humor, and informality in its approach. "Now" is replaced by "soon" or "at your convenience" or "when the need arises."

Both approaches are effective, and when handled by experts, neither content approach is insensitive or offensive. But the indirect approach seems to be growing more dominant.

To be successful, advertisements must create awareness of the goods and services being advertised well enough to have them considered as an option, associate positive aspects of the product with consumers' needs (the unique selling points must be emphasized), emotionally involve consumers and make them identify with and desire the product, and produce action that influences potential consumers to become buyers and, eventually, committed heavy users.

Type of Medium

The classification by medium helps assess the relative strengths of the various media. Radio and television account for practically all advertising revenue for the electronic media, although a small amount is spent for consumer advertising in motion-picture theaters. Five media account for most of the revenue earned by print advertisers: newspapers, magazines, billboards, transit, and direct mail.

Every company's media plan begins with an analysis of alternative classes of media. There is no universal rule that stipulates which medium is best because each medium has advantages and drawbacks. More important, marketing objectives for most products require an advertising campaign that uses a "media mix" to provide the greatest degree of flexibility.

The medium remains a substitute for "the real thing" in advertising. The real thing, of course, is personal selling—what politicians call "pressing the flesh." All the TV ads for Chevrolet's Nova (built in cooperation with Toyota) and all the newspaper layouts ballyhooing the mileage estimates and rebates only get the potential buyer into the showroom. It is the salesperson's personal selling skills and the point-of-purchase advertising tools that clinch the sale. But in an ever-increasing number of product categories, the medium is replacing the salesclerk to some degree. The catalog showroom is a retailing fact of life, and in the near future, the video-display terminal in the home may replace the catalog. Shopping by television could eliminate personal selling altogether.

The media mix is essential to the success of an advertising campaign. Too often, beginners emphasize the more glamorous and expensive ad media and lose the impact that direct-mail, outdoor, transit, specialty-item, and point-of-purchase advertising can have.

Remember that media strategy emerges from and does not usually determine general marketing, advertising, brand, and creative strategy. The media mix involves selecting the medium (radio), selecting the medium vehicles (stations and networks), and scheduling the chosen medium (the number of spots, when they are run, and in what pattern they are run).

The overall media strategy is structured around marketing and sales objectives, creative style, target-audience coverage, budget constraints, cost efficiencies, timing and seasonality of consumption, competition strategy, and availability of media time and space.

The media element of the advertising mix is perhaps the most scientific aspect of the total process. It is quantifiable, and evaluation is rigorous.

Type of Audience

Two groups to whom advertisers seek to sell their goods and services are other businesses and consumers. Advertisers who seek industrial buyers, including other manufacturers, distributors, and retailers, are involved in business advertising. Most business advertising appears in the industry or

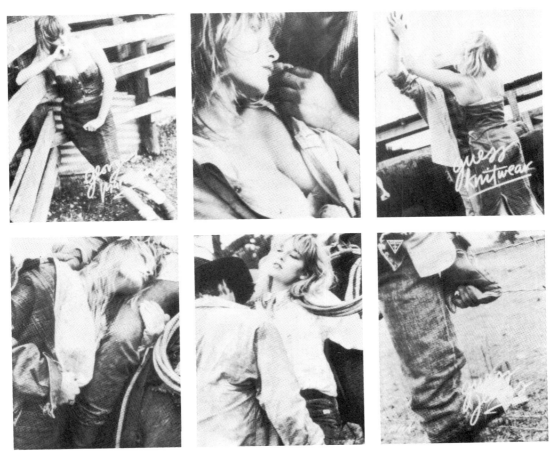

Figure 12.13 The target audience of this ad is the designer-jeans generation. The message is sexy. But the "designer-jeans wars" of the 1980s manage to do it in style. And it seems that the more controversial the ad, the more sensuous the headline, the more titillating the photograph—the better the sales. There is little need for copy in these ads. As they say, "A picture is worth a thousand words," and this six-page spread for Guess is the quintessential example of this style of photographic storytelling and jeans selling.

trade press and in specialized direct-mail campaigns. Advertisers that seek individual or individual-family buyers are involved in mass, consumer advertising. Consumer advertising uses all the available media to varying degrees, depending on the specific thrust of the ad campaign.

The target audiences of business and consumer advertising make significantly different demands on the advertiser, especially regarding the media plan and the number of buyers available. The business advertiser sells goods and services that are, in turn, converted into consumer goods and services. The advertiser of consumer goods sells items to be used directly by the people that buy them.

Advertising can benefit the consumer in a variety of ways:

1. Advertising is an important source of information if the consumer uses the data intelligently.
2. It saves time, and in today's world, it can save energy. Let your eyes and ears do the driving, as your fingers do the walking.
3. It eventually improves quality because it encourages competition.
4. It can lower the per-unit cost of products if it increases sales volume.

The sophistication of audience research has gone beyond demographics and now includes psychographic profiles of the likes, dislikes, and personality traits of the consumer. Advertising messages are beginning to reflect as well as create these preferences and tastes.

DIRECT AND INDIRECT CONTROLS
OF ADVERTISING

A variety of direct and indirect controls of advertising exist to protect the consumer and head off public criticism that could lead to more restrictive laws and a falling off in consumer confidence in industry practices. These controls come from three major sources: (1) regulation by government; (2) industry codes of self-regulation; and (3) public-interest and political-action groups that seek changes by influencing regulatory agencies and industry self-regulation organizations as well as specific advertisers.

Regulation by Government

The primary force in governmental regulation of advertising is the Federal Trade Commission (FTC), which was set up under the Federal Trade Commission Act of 1914 and bolstered by the Wheeler-Lee amendments of 1938. Since that time, a variety of laws have increased the FTC's role. Each new law has, in effect, been a compromise between the forces seeking stringent governmental controls and the industry, which feels that any additional legislation is unnecessary. This kind of compromise is characteristic of our society, which is in a constant state of flux.

Although the Federal Communications Act of 1934 and subsequent broadcast legislation have never given the Federal Communications Commission direct control over advertisers, the FCC can and does exert some influence over radio and television stations which it licenses, in advertising matters. In the case of cigarette ads, the commission had no jurisdiction over the tobacco companies. However, this agency forced radio and TV stations to refuse to accept cigarette advertising after January 1, 1971, but allowed them to accept ads for cigars and pipe tobacco.

In the end, however, it is the FTC that serves as the major federal watchdog over advertising practices. Most of the current laws and pro-posed legislation deal with seven basic problem areas:

1. Copyright laws protect expressions of advertising ideas from being exploited by anyone other than the creators or their agents.
2. The Lanham Trade Mark Act (1947) protects the use of distinctive product names, identifying symbols, and advertising exclusively by the creators and their agents.
3. An individual's "right of privacy" is protected, since the advertiser must obtain written permission for any use of a person's name or his or her endorsement in an advertisement.
4. A lottery is an illegal interstate activity and is outlawed in many states. Advertising contests must not contain these three elements: prize, consideration, and chance. If they do, they are defined as lotteries and are subject to gambling laws.
5. Obscenity and bad taste are difficult to identify because the morals of this country are continually changing. What is acceptable today would have been obscene 10 years ago. Some ads in *Playboy* could be thought to be in bad taste by some people if seen in the context of a magazine like *Boy's Life*.
6. Truth in advertising is generally agreed to be an absolutely essential item of an advertisement. An exact definition of truth is hard to come by, however. The FTC attacks untruths in advertising be-cause they are "unfair methods of competition."
7. Libel or defamation (the intent to harm a person's reputation) is a legally punishable offense, and advertisers take every precaution against it.

Most of the cases handled by the Federal Trade Commission originate with a business competitor or a consumer. Some cases originate from stud-ies initiated by the FTC or another agency. After investigation, a formal complaint may be issued; the advertiser is given an opportunity to respond in a hearing. If the advertiser is found guilty, a cease-and-desist order is issued, forcing the advertiser to end the practice.

Besides the FTC and FCC, the United Stated Postal Service, Food and Drug Administration, Alcohol Tax Unit, Patent Office, and Securities and Exchange Commission exert pressures, if not actual control, over advertis-ing at the federal level. In many cases, these indirect pressures are more effective in achieving a change in practices than is direct legislative author-ity or control.

Self-Regulation through Industry Codes

Public and governmental outcries over excessive amounts of advertising, special-product advertising (liquor), labeling, and other problems have led the industry to devise means for self-regulation. The general purpose of self-regulation is twofold: it helps protect the public from false advertising; and it heads off further governmental restriction of advertising.

Industry self-regulation of advertising practices comes from three sources: advertisers, advertising agencies, and media. Although this form of regulation is not legally binding, it is effective because internal pressures are applied by the industry on offenders.

Advertisers. Self-regulation occurs on both the local-retailer and the national-manufacturer levels. Retailers have organized Better Business Bureaus to investigate consumers' and competitors' advertising complaints before legal action becomes necessary. There are approximately 100 local bureaus associated with the National Better Business Bureau, which developed the "Fair Practice Code for Advertising and Selling." In addition, "The Advertising Code of American Business" has been adopted by both the Advertising Federation of America and the Association of National Advertisers.

Advertising Agencies. Self-regulation functions under the auspices of the American Association of Advertising Agencies. The "4As" endorses "The Advertising Code of American Business." This code's major concerns are truthfulness, responsibility, decency, and accuracy.

The Committee on Improvement of Advertising Content of the American Association of Advertising Agencies seeks to evaluate offensive ads and recommends changes in the offensive campaign to the agency that devised it. The advertisers individually or through trade associations police advertising practices.

Media. The media also review advertising and regulate the kinds of products and appeals that appear for public consumption. The stronger a given newspaper, magazine, or radio or TV station becomes financially, the less likely it is to permit marginally acceptable ads. The fleeting quality of the broadcast media makes radio and TV ads more difficult to review, but the National Association of Broadcasters has established a "code" for advertising and other member activities. Unfortunately, not all stations subscribe to the code.

Indirect Influence by Public Pressure Groups

The most effective form of advertising control is the consumer's refusal to buy the product—the action most feared by advertisers. When the course of action is organized, it can have a devastating economic impact on an advertiser. Political action groups and public pressure groups are very powerful influences on the marketing of goods and services.

The consumer's major success has been in group protests and information campaigns, such as that of the Consumers Union, which publishes *Consumer Report*. Occasionally, crusaders arise to take up the consumer's cause. Under the leadership of Ralph Nader, an increasingly successful group of dedicated people has committed itself to consumer protection.

Advertisers and the retail outlets of the advertisers' products are very sensitive to public pressures that not only cut back on sales of a specific product, but also reduce total traffic in the stores that carry the product.

Consumers, as individuals, do not realize the power that they could exercise. It is through organizational action that their political, cultural, and economic control over advertising and marketing becomes effective.

SUMMARY

Advertising has real power, and that power is constantly measured by what we buy. Ads pay for all the cost of commercial broadcasting and for most of the cost of the basic cable-television services, newspapers, and magazines. That activity accounts for 2 percent of America's GNP. Although advertising's primary focus is selling, it also helps create new markets, lowers costs of products and services, spurs product improvements, and improves competition. And in most instances, the consumer benefits.

The four basic partners in the advertising process are advertisers; their advertising agencies; the ad media and their representatives, all of which interact in varying combinations, depending on whether the campaigns are national, regional, and local; and the interaction of general and retail components.

Major corporations have advertising departments at varying administrative levels, depending on the emphasis placed on advertising within the marketing mix and in relation to other marketing activities: promotion, public relations, and sales. The advertising department's most important ally is the company's advertising agency, with which the ad department must work in concert.

The four major advertising-agency activities are research, creative, media, and client services. All of these work to solve clients' problems.

The ad campaigns developed by the ad agency and approved by the advertiser can be classified in terms of the type of advertiser (general or retail); the type of message content (institutional or product-oriented); the type of medium (primarily print, broadcast, direct-mail, outdoor, or specialty advertising); and the type of target audience (business or consumer).

Control over advertising practices is both direct and indirect, and that control involves government agencies, professional associations, and public-interest groups.

The key factor in the success or failure of advertising, regardless of control, is the purchasing power of the consumer. Buying or not buying is the ultimate feedback, when it comes to measuring the success of an advertising campaign.

BIBLIOGRAPHY

Alwitt, Linda F., and Andrew A. Mitchell, eds. *Psychological Process and Advertising Effects: Theory, Research, and Application.* Hillsdale, N.J.: Erlbaum, 1985.

Barr, David Samuel. *Advertising on Cable: A Practical Guide for Advertisers.* Englewood Cliffs, N.J.: Prentice-Hall, 1985.

Bellaire, Arthur. *The Bellaire Guide to Controlling Your TV Commercial Cost.* 2d ed. Chicago: Crain, 1982.

Bergendorff, Fred et al. *Broadcast Advertising and Promotion: A Handbook for Students and Professionals.* New York: Hastings House, 1983.

Book, Albert et al. *The Radio and Television Commercial.* 2d ed. Lincolnwood, Ill.: National Textbook, 1984.

Geis, Michael L. *The Language of Television Advertising.* New York: Academic Press, 1982.

Guernica, Antonio. *Reaching the Hispanic Market Effectively: The Media, the Market, the Methods.* 2d ed. New York: McGraw-Hill, 1982.

Neelankovil, James P. *Advertising Self-Regulation: A Global Perspective.* New York: Hasting House, 1980.

Pattis, S. William. *Opportunity in Advertising.* Lincolnwood, Ill.: National Textbook, 1984.

Surmanek, Jim. *Media Planning: A Practical Guide.* Lincolnwood,Ill.: National Textbook, 1985.

Ulanoff, Stanley M. *Advertising in America: An Introduction to Persuasive Communication.* New York: Hastings House, 1977.

13

Education

In 1982, the CBS-TV network and New York University announced the end
to one of TV's grand experiments in formal education, "Sunrise Semester."
After 25 years, the televised college course, on which some of the university's most distinguished professors reached an early-morning audience of
credit and noncredit students, was being canceled. The numbers told the
story: CBS indicated that in 1981, only 42 of its 200 affiliated stations carried
the program and only 47 students were enrolled for credit. Thus another of
TV's attempts to integrate formal education with broadcast function and
design came to an undistinguished end.

With the single exception of books, media and formal education have
had a checkered history. Each side is apt to blame the other for everything
from lack of vision to lack of money. In the case of "Sunrise Semester," the
problems were familiar ones to the media–education dialogue: primarily, a
minimal investment in production. The most articulate instructors could
not overcome this limitation. In addition, the university did not always
provide the more eloquent lecturers, who in the early years had given the
program much of its reputation. On camera, lectures without visual and
production support—mere "talking heads"—make for dull education.

In an age when government and industry have embraced new technologies as a fact of communication life and are increasingly using these
technologies in training and education, the American educational system
remains in a catch-up phase. Too often, schools have neither the resources
to acquire the technology nor the teachers to train students in its use.

The American educational system is still dependent on primarily one

351

mass medium—the book—whether it be a textbook, a workbook, a reader, a reference book, or an index. Teaching remains classroom- and library-based. The educational system, the school, the teacher, and the book have served this country well, regardless of education's current low estate. But technology may be passing education by. That could lead to learning suicide.

The most innovative uses of the communication revolution and instructional techniques are not in the "halls of ivy" but in the "real world" of work. Advanced uses of media learning are invading the home and the workplace before they are seen in school. Indeed, many secondary schools, colleges, and universities are only responding to the demands of students who come to school with advanced skills and knowledge acquired at home.

Some critics are saying that our schools are in jeopardy unless they can reorient and redirect themselves to meet future challenges rather than react to an obsolete past. The mass media surround us, and so it is important for schools and educators to understand the extent to which the media have become our tutors, both inside and outside the formal educational system. No less a group than the National Council of Teachers of English (NCTE) has recognized and endorsed this point of view. They note that media other than the printed word should be integrated into the English curriculum because communication demands the ability to understand, use, and control more complex symbol systems. Schools must teach "through" the new media in order to impart a complete understanding of how they function.

There are other hopeful signs on the horizon, perhaps none more significant than the Annenberg/CPB Project. Started in 1981 by an initial $150 million gift from *TV Guide* owner Walter Annenberg, the project has met with a great deal of acceptance in higher education. Since 1981, over 950 of the approximately 3,000 colleges and universities in the United States have offered PBS television courses, ranging from prime-time programming such as "The Brain" to more direct for-credit courses in mathematics or English.

However, the challenge in all the efforts to use communications technology in education is to develop effective methods to enhance the way faculty teach and students learn. Technology in higher education has started to move beyond the initial stage of haphazard, incidental use into a stage of institutionalization.

Before we examine some of these media and some of these trends, let us review the basic educational functions that the mass media perform. The mass media perform three major educational tasks: (1) socialization, in which media reinforce or modify cultural norms; (2) informal education, in which media supplement the education of the individual outside the school; and (3) formal instruction, in which media systematically impart specialized information and skills in a controlled, supervised environment, which occurs in school and, increasingly, the workplace.

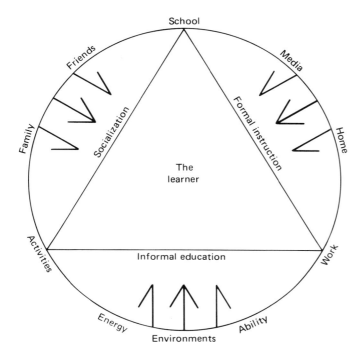

Figure 13.1 This model of the learning wheel illustrates the variety of interactions that determines learning. At the center of the wheel is the learner, the recipient of many factors that create a unique learning pattern for each individual.

The extent and mix of media in each individual's learning experience is different. Nevertheless, some general patterns are evident in the amounts and kinds of formal instruction, informal education, and socialization in which Americans participate. The learning wheel illustrated in Figure 13.1 indicates that a variety of contacts determine learning. A learner's ability, energy, health, work habits, home, peers, family, activities, schools, teachers, and media material form a part of his or her educational achievement.

SOCIALIZATION

Socialization is a most important learning process. It is how we gain membership in society. And communication is the primary means of socialization. In fact, socialization is impossible without communication. Interpersonal communication is usually more important than mass communication for most socialization, but as our media environment grows larger and more pervasive, media impact is becoming more significant and important to understand.

It is obvious that infants acquire many of their behavior patterns from the family and the immediate environment. Child psychologists tell us that children's concepts of themselves in relation to others are well established before they can even talk; their social values are well on the way to being established before they have sufficient social experiences to have any ra-

Figure 13.2 Television characters such as Big Bird have an important role in the socialization process. Here, Big Bird introduces children to the Great Wall of China on an NBC-TV special. (Photo: AP/Wide World Photos.)

tional perceptions of radio or television. And children usually have considerable formal instruction before they can read newspapers, magazines, and books. For young children, even those under two years of age, the media, especially television, are having an increasingly powerful effect on the socialization process. ''Mr. Rogers's Neighborhood'' and ''Sesame Street,'' for example, have a demonstrated impact on preschool children, not simply in learning to count to 10, but also in developing concepts such as friendship and emotions. The use of ''Sesame Street'' characters, such as

Big Bird, Oscar the Grouch, Bert and Ernie, and Cookie Monster, to teach, socialize, and even sell has become an established fact of media life for young children.

Television is the medium that contributes most to the socialization of Americans because it is the medium used by more people more of the time. Both commercial and public stations and networks contribute significantly to socialization as well as informal education.

For older children, the electronic media are significant in modifying attitudes and life styles. In order to understand this process better, it is useful to view socialization as consisting of different sorts of learning, some of which are more affected by mass media than others. Gerhart D. Wiebe, former dean of the School of Public Communication at Boston University, has sharpened the definition of socialization by breaking the communication process into three zones on a continuum. He refers to these as directive media messages, maintenance media messages, and restorative media messages.[1]

Directive messages command, exhort, instruct, persuade, and urge in the direction of learning and new understanding. They must, says Wiebe, come from authoritative figures and call for substantial and conscious intellectual effort by the learner. Most studies show that messages that intend to direct performance or change behavior do not succeed unless they tie in to a structured, face-to-face, teacher–pupil relationship. Since the mass media cannot provide this relationship, they are not important bearers of directive messages. They may supplement and enrich the direct learning process, but they cannot replace it. In classrooms from kindergarten to college, teachers have a direct relationship to students, one that cannot be replaced by books, TV sets, or computerized learning machines. As Wiebe says, "The printed Bible has not made the church obsolete nor has it reduced the role of the clergy."

Maintenance messages tell us what to do in the everyday business of living: where we can find food, what dangers we should avoid, when we should pay our taxes, how we can get a driver's license, and who we should regard as friend or foe. Such messages call for relatively little conscious intellectual effort. The mass media play an extensive role in sending maintenance messages through the communication of new information, analysis, interpretation, persuasion, and sales promotion. Wiebe maintains that three conditions must exist before communication messages will have an impact on maintaining social norms.

1. The audience must be predisposed to react along the lines indicated in the message.

---

[1] Gerhart D. Wiebe, "The Social Effects of Broadcasting," in *Mass Culture Revisited,* ed. Bernard Rosenberg and David Manning White (Princeton, N.J.: Van Nostrand, 1971), 154–168.

2. Social provisions must exist for facilitating such actions.

3. The message itself must have audience appeal.

Restorative messages renew and refresh the human capacity for productive social relationships. Restorative messages include fantasies, which allow us to escape the realities of life; humor, which allows us to relieve the tensions of the day; and drama and violence, which can provide catharsis for frustrations and anxieties. In their communication of restorative messages, the mass media play perhaps their most important role in the socialization process, not only in the dramas of pulp novels and soap operas, but also in escapist TV serials and televised sports events and the violence of news.

INFORMAL EDUCATION

All the mass media provide content that is neither socialization nor formal instruction. *National Geographic* specials on public television; recordings of children's literature; and a variety of other content are used for learning purposes in both the home and the school. Perhaps the most visible and successful examples of informal education are "Sesame Street," produced by the Children's Television Workshop, and "Mr. Rogers's Neighborhood."

Research in the area of informal education is limited, but all of us have learned about sharks, whales, seals, and other creatures of the sea from the televised programs of Jacques Cousteau. We have learned about the world we live in from books and magazines. Informally, we educate ourselves about food, wine, travel, and art by means of all media. In effect, our informal education occurs before, during, and after our school years. It is the means by which we stay intellectually and emotionally alive.

Motion pictures are used in informal education primarily through the documentary format. Documentary films were first developed as a conscious film form in the 1920s by filmmakers Robert Flaherty in the United States and John Grierson in England. Grierson defined the documentary as a creative treatment of actuality. He believed that the documentary should have a point of view, that it should be a vehicle for presenting and interpreting human problems and their solutions. Thus Grierson, Flaherty, and others developed the concept of the documentary as a socially significant film form rather than merely a vehicle for showing newsreel footage and "travelogue" material. The documentary flourished in the 1930s and 1940s, when it was used to communicate messages to a variety of audiences about the Depression and World War II.

Today, television has become the prime influence on the continuing development of documentary films. The commercial networks, primarily through their news departments, and the Public Broadcasting Service occa-

Figure 13.3 Television series such as ''The Undersea World of Jacques Cousteau'' are important to the informal-education process. The photo shows Cousteau (at the right) and his son Philippe on location in Mexico to film ''The Sea Birds of Isabela.'' (Photo: Courtesy Metromedia Producers Corporation.)

sionally produce and broadcast significant documentaries that are later released in 16mm-film form. Programs such as ''Vietnam: A Television History,'' ''The Selling of the Pentagon,'' ''Yo Soy Chicano,'' and the Jacques Cousteau and *National Geographic* specials are examples of outstanding TV documentaries that have wide use in education as 16mm films.

Almost all present-day documentaries contain a social or political message, stated or implied, and the evaluation of this message is, of course, part of the teaching and learning process. Normally, the documentary's point of view is not too difficult to ascertain. A relatively new development, however, the ''docudrama,'' has complicated the process. In general, the docudrama is a dramatization of current newsworthy events and trends, rather than creative reportage. Although the makers of docudramas insist that their films are dramatizations of fact, not fiction, the line between ''docu'' and ''drama'' may sometimes be difficult for the viewer to draw. The evaluation of the point of view may also be comparatively difficult.

The film *Death of a Princess,* a dramatization of the search by an English journalist for the truth behind published reports that a young Saudi Arabian princess and her lover had been publicly executed for adultery at the instigation of her royal father, is a prime example of the docudrama genre. Shown on PBS, the film generated considerable controversy. Did it document Saudi Arabian ruling-class mores and Islamic legal principles? Or did it dramatize them in such a way that fiction prevailed over fact?

The history of informal education by means of television is essentially the continued use of the documentary format inherited from film and the development of several outstanding programs and series on American public and educational television.

An example of television "enterteaching" is occurring with music videos. "ColorSounds" uses current hit records to teach such things as phonics, grammar, spelling, and reading comprehension.

Students using the ColorSounds system watch music videos whose lyrics appear at the bottom of the screen. Different vowel sounds, parts of speech, and grammatical structures stand out from the rest of the words with an identifying color—say, green for adverbs. The students are also provided with lyric sheets and crayons so they can practice and be tested on what they have learned using a similar color-coding system.

The music used by ColorSounds is carefully screened for vocabulary, grammar, diction, and suitability. It covers a wide spectrum of rock, pop, country, and soul—and such performers as Alabama, Donna Summer, Genesis, Diana Ross, The Stray Cats, Kool & the Gang, David Bowie, and Culture Club.

Motion pictures and television shows in recent years, especially, have become our history educators through docudramas on killer Gary Gilmore (*The Executioner's Song*) and the Civil War (*The Blue and the Gray*) and films on the life of Gandhi (*Gandhi*) and actress Joan Crawford (*Mommie Dearest*). In addition, the media teach us about World War II (*The Winds of War*), the Russian Revolution and the life of John Reed (*Reds*), political violence in Chile (*Missing*), the lives of British Olympic runners (*Chariots of Fire*), and the life of George Washington (*George Washington*).

All this activity is no accident. After the 1985 miniseries on the Civil War, *The Blue and the Gray*, scored well in ratings, network officials felt that audiences would respond to other historical subjects. "The American public likes to be taken into the landscapes of the past," said Marian Brayton, vice president–dramatic specials for CBS Entertainment. "After 'The Blue and the Gray' was well received, we wanted to do something else in American history." A quick check found that not much had been done on the Revolutionary War. "We thought if we could tell a deeply personal story about Washington, if we could show him as a man—living, breathing flesh—we thought the public would respond."[2]

CBS's line-up of historical specials especially improved its reputation among educators, members of the clergy, and others who are often critical of network programming. For example, the New York Archdiocese worked with CBS on *Pope John Paul II*. The Church officials were very cooperative and supportive of the project, and the archdiocese even encouraged Catholic churches in New York to run items in their Sunday

---

[2] *USA Today*, 3 March 1984, 12.

Figure 13.4 Feature motion pictures such as *Chariots of Fire* (1981) function as docudramas in the process of informal education, communicating the "facts" of historical events in a narrative-story format. In this photo, Ben Cross, who played the British runner Harold Abrahams, is seen winning his race in the 1924 Olympics. (Photo: Movie Star News, Courtesy Warner Bros., Inc.)

bulletins alerting parishioners that the movie would be broadcast on Easter.

Many educators hope that these television specials will encourage children to investigate the subjects further at the local library. Through its TV reading program, CBS sent out a teaching guide and classroom materials, including a list of suggested sources, to be used in conjunction with *George Washington.* Through its "Read More about It" program and its "CBS Television Reading Program," the CBS/Broadcast Group educational and community services department has provided millions of copies of teacher and student guides and book lists for several years. Although some critics tend to view such network public-service programs with disdain, believing that they are merely a ploy to take the heat off TV, Joanne Brokaw, vice president of the CBS/Broadcast Group department, disagrees. "We operate from as pure an educational posture as possible," she says.

Figure 13.5 Carl Sagan, host of "Cosmos," uses a giant model of the solar system to explain why the orbits of the planets are stable. "Cosmos" is a public television series devoted to describing astronomy and space explorations in the broadest human context. (Photo: Edwardo Castaneda, Courtesy Scott Meredith, Inc.)

"No one in the network ever tells us what to do and that allows us to maintain our credibility."[3]

CBS/Broadcast Group generates about four student–teacher TV reading programs every year. Additionally, the "Read More about It" program, which CBS runs in conjunction with the Library of Congress, provides reading lists for a greater number of network programs through the year. In the 1981/1982 TV season, for example, CBS provided reading lists for a diversity of programs, ranging from *A Charlie Brown Celebration* to *Skokie* and *Bill* to *The Magic of David Copperfield*.

The role of the Public Broadcasting Service in informal learning is even more significant than that of commercial stations. Especially important have been the exciting, well-made explorations of science, including "The Ascent of Man," "The Body in Question," "Connections," and "Cosmos." These TV series evaluate the cultural impact and the future implications of our uses of technology. "Civilisation," "Alistair Cooke's America," and "Nova" are other examples of media contributions to general learning.

Informal education is a critical educational force in the United States. It is the "high" culture of the electronic and print media. It has cultural impact and broadens the intellectual horizons of those who choose to use this content.

---

[3] Ibid.

FORMAL INSTRUCTION

In the United States, classroom instruction involves the more than 54 percent of our population that enrolls in formal instruction in nursery schools, kindergartens, elementary schools through senior high schools, four-year colleges and universities, junior and community colleges, professional schools, vocational and technical schools, correspondence schools, and continuing education. Over 70 million children and adults attend school every day. They are taught by over 2 million teachers. Another 11 million students go to colleges and universities.

Books

The most influential medium in formal instruction is the book, which also plays an important role in socialization and informal education. Books are successful largely because they adapt so well to the individual needs and habits of the students who use them.

Three crucial elements interact in the classroom: the student, the book, and the teacher. The book is often the central reference point for both students and teachers. For example, books may be the only intellectual experience that most white, middle-income teachers share with black, low-income pupils in ghetto schools.

A specialized form of the book has evolved in the school environment. The textbook, by definition, is a book prepared specifically for classroom use; it provides an exposition of one subject area and serves as the content core of a given class. Several other kinds of books are specifically designed for the classroom; they include teacher editions of the text, consumable workbooks (the student writes directly in the book) used in conjunction with the text, standardized tests to evaluate students' performance on the text, and manuals and trade books used to supplement and reinforce textbooks. The paperback, a softbound, less expensive form of trade book, is used for a variety of classroom purposes, largely in higher education. Two kinds of textbooks are of primary importance: authored books focus on a special topic within the general subject area; and edited books provide a general survey of materials written by a large number of specialists in their field of expertise.

Although most of the publicity goes to best sellers, much of the income in the publishing industry comes from the sale of textbooks and reference works. If you consider all the sales possibilities of books, more than 60 percent of all book sales are education related. In terms of textbooks sold to a particular audience, approximately 50 percent are sold to college students; 30 percent, to elementary schools; and 20 percent, to high schools. Textbooks cost Americans more than $3 billion annually and account for almost one-third of all book sales.

One of the major problems for textbook publishers is that elementary- and secondary-school enrollments are dropping. There are 10 to 15 percent fewer students in the 1980s than in the 1970s. College enrollments are also beginning to decline, which means that more schools are competing for fewer students in a time of severe cost increases.

Textbooks have a relatively low profit margin and are expensive to market. It costs well over $1 million to launch a new elementary-school series. For the individual high-school text, preparatory costs can run as high as $250,000; for one college text, $100,000. To compound the problem, many textbooks have lifespans of only three to five years before revisions are necessary.

Paperback editions and resales help hold down costs somewhat, but that is relative to the inflationary spiral that educational institutions and students now face. In the late 1980s, the average college student spends more than $150 a semester on books.

Societies have created a separate institution just to house their books. Libraries provide long-term storage and easy retrieval of information. In order to make efficient use of the information stored in the library, a separate class of books was developed. Reference books, despite their limited numbers, account for 8 percent of book revenue each year. This group includes general references, indexes, annuals, encyclopedias, handbooks, and other subcategories. The reference book is crucial to the retrieval of data from large, complex library systems.

The book is a useful learning device because it is compact, portable, low in cost, and reusable; it does not require special equipment to use; it does not disrupt nonusers; it allows for individualized learning, since people can set their own rate of learning; it has easy reference capacity. And the reader can reread portions of a book that were not mastered at the first reading.

Without doubt, the book is the best medium for many kinds of classroom instruction. Its inherent characteristics, and the school's predisposition to exploit them, make the book an important information source in the classroom, library, and bookstore. Books are important for providing insights into a variety of activities and skills.

Books, as a particular combination and structure of words on paper, are in transition as new technology has its impact on this oldest medium, particularly in education. Increasingly, the most economical way of storing and displaying words is electronically, rather than on paper. As the sociologist Ithiel de Sola Pool observed in his article "The Culture of Electronic Print": "Virtually all handling of text . . . and also publishing, will be done within computers. . . . Printing the text onto paper will be for the convenience of the reader alone." The storage of books is also being revolutionized by the computer, and the concept of the library is changing. As Pool indicates in the same article,

> The videodisc may be the most promising storage technology. Over 100,000 books can be stored on an optical-digital disc pack of six discs. At

$51,000 a pack, the cost of storing a book would be 40 cents. One hundred disc packs, or the total contents of The Library of Congress, would cost $5 million and would fit into a medium sized room.[4]

Just as important to the emerging electronic book is the method of publishing. Traditionally, the book is a fixed unit in which certain ideas are presented. Electronic publishing can alter this concept because a group of authors, such as the authors of this text, can write and edit on computer networks. Hiebert can type some comments at a terminal and give access to Ungurait and Bohn on the network. As each author modifies, edits, and expands the content, the text changes from day to day.

In addition, the teacher in the classroom could use the text in new ways. This text would be on-line and, although it is not permitted under current copyright law, theoretically the instructor could make modifications in the text. The student could also make modifications, and so reading would become an interactive dialogue with the teacher and authors. The notes that many students make in the margins could become part of the text and part of a growing dialogue.

Magazines

The *Standard Periodical Directory* lists more than 62,000 titles of periodicals other than newspapers. The educational system uses a wide variety of these magazines and other serials, but two kinds of periodicals are more important than the others: the 5,000 or more scholarly journals, which print the latest research and other information in a given field; and the 20,000 or more trade journals, which offer the latest information about the application of new research.

These two kinds of magazines are important learning tools, especially at the university level. As a field expands, the number of scholarly and trade journals proliferates as well. For example, almost 2,000 periodicals deal with education, about 1,000 cover library science, and more than 500 deal with media and media-related activities. It is almost impossible to stay abreast of the information in these fields, and so special reference services, which cover a given area, have emerged. For example, *Topicator* is a periodical guide to a select group of magazines that deal with radio and television.

The magazine plays a minor role in the primary grades of public schools because few magazines of the quality of *Highlights* are published for elementary pupils. Publishers find that subscribers outgrow their material rapidly, and it is too expensive to resell their product to each generation. Also, many classes of advertising are not considered suitable for children's fare. Most school libraries fill the void by subscribing to such general adult periodicals as *National Geographic, Popular Science,* and *Popular*

---

[4] Ithiel de Sola Pool, "The Culture of Electronic Print," *Daedalus* 3 (Fall 1982): 17–32.

Mechanics, which are used by children. Since few school libraries can afford to bind back issues, these periodicals are usually used for informal education rather than for instruction or research, however. Even in high school, when term papers become part of assignments, many students who want to search periodical literature use the public library.

Thus students making the transition from high school to college sometimes have difficulty adjusting to the increased emphasis placed on the magazine. Although the book is easier to find and use than the magazine, a large library's periodical collection can and should expand the amount of data available to researchers.

Magazines, even more than books, will come to be used in revolutionary new ways in education. Since scholarly journals are published more frequently than books, and since their purpose is to communicate the results of ongoing research, electronic publishing is more compatible with the structure and function of journals than with the structure and function of books. Rather than subscribe to a journal, an instructor will have on-line access to a database that "publishes" information in a format unique to that instructor. The whole concept of information input, storage, and delivery is changing rapidly, and although books, magazines, and newspapers will not die, their methods of publication will change the way in which they are used, especially in formal education.

Newspapers

Although the newspaper is heavily used in the socialization of members of society, especially for the communication of maintenance and restorative messages, it is the least used mass medium in formal instruction. Newspaper organizations are increasing their efforts to have newspapers used in classrooms, but barring a few exceptions, newspapers are not widely used.

Newspaper organizations increasingly think of themselves as educational institutions rather than as merely businesses. The editorial staff of a daily newspaper is essentially in the business of developing and communicating knowledge, researching facts, and packaging them for the paper's audience. Some newspapers approach this task with the same seriousness that universities bring to the development of knowledge, allowing their staffs sufficient time, freedom, and security to pursue knowledge and even establishing a sort of tenure and sabbatical-leave system for expert writers and specialists on the staff.

Without doubt, newspapers provide a wide variety of information necessary for carrying out day-to-day living, as well as an increasing number of facts and ideas to round out the informal education of a well-informed citizen. Newspapers have also become source materials for some academic disciplines, particularly the social sciences.

Although few people would predict the newspaper's death, new technologies are changing its form and function. Especially important are the distribution systems known as videotex and teletext. Transmitted over

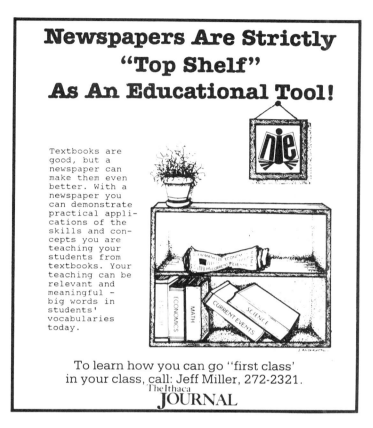

Figure 13.6 One example of how newspapers are trying to develop a more important role in formal education.

television frequencies or telephone and cable-TV lines, teletext is a one-way system that continually transmits information from which viewers can select what they want. Videotex is a two-way system that provides services such as at-home shopping and electronic mail.

Videotex has come a long way from what it started out to be—information sent on request through a cheap specialized terminal attached to the home TV set and telephone. The few videotex companies that started that way still use telephone lines but now transmit directly to customers' personal computers.

Videotex is taking various routes into the home. Three popular on-line database systems—Reader's Digest's Source, H&R Block's CompuServe, and Dow Jones News/Retrieval—together have more than 500,000 subscribers, who typically pay $10 or more a month for access to packages of news, entertainment, and electronic mail, as well as shopping and financial services.

Before analyzing the electronic media, it is important to understand that despite the potential educational impact of television, film, radio, and sound recordings in classroom instruction, there is little use of electronic media, compared with print media, in most classrooms. Six major issues have had a negative impact on the use of electronic media in schools.

1. Society's general attitude is that electronic media are for entertainment, not for education.
2. Teachers often are print oriented and have little free time to develop the skills and attitudes necessary to use electronic media in the classroom.
3. The decision to use electronic media in schools is often made at the administrative level and forced on teachers, who resent this imposition.
4. Most of the materials available do not exploit the inherent qualities of electronic media.
5. Electronic media are expensive unless they are used for a large number of students.
6. The software (content) of electronic media is a threefold problem:
   a. The traditional suppliers of materials have not moved vigorously to provide it.
   b. Local "in-house" materials do not reach the production standards that people have become accustomed to in commercial radio and in TV films.
   c. The content ages rapidly and is difficult to maintain professionally and economically.

Despite these conditions, however, the telecommunications revolution is beginning to have an impact on education, especially higher education.

After years of premature claims of a coming revolution in higher education and given many of the issues noted above, many teachers and administrators have been understandably hesitant about fully embracing the new communication technology for teaching and learning. But the steady penetration of telecommunications hardware into the homes and lives of Americans is opening the way to change. However, if education is to be a full partner in the new telecommunication systems, educators must get rid of their technological prejudice and egoism of being the original source of knowledge. They must establish institutional arrangements for providing and overseeing universal public education. Let us review some of the ways in which the electronic media interact with formal education in order to better assess the changes that are occurring and the directions being taken.

Radio

The formal-education function of radio in the United States is expensive and fairly ineffective. For a number of years, some of the more than 1,100 public radio stations served as little more than classical jukeboxes for an elite audience within the total society. National Public Radio, formed in 1969 and government and foundation subsidized, is attempting to change the educational-radio service. Attempts have been made to use educational radio as a means of formal instruction, but despite its potential, radio is rarely involved in classroom instruction.

Sound Recordings

Although radio as an educational medium has not been effective, audio-based courses and instruction are finding an increasing number of users, especially in higher education. In 1985, over 85% of all colleges and universities used some form of audio in their instructional programs. Complete audio-based courses were offered by 9 percent of the institutions.

Perhaps the most rapidly growing general use of audio media is for self-paced instruction and "mastery learning." The slow student can repeat segments of the lesson as often as necessary, since the recorder and playback machine can serve as a *very* patient tutor. The accelerated student can skip ahead or increase the pace of his or her instruction.

Prerecorded audio materials are available in a variety of subjects. For music classes, records and tapes can be used to introduce new material or to provide musical accompaniment. In preschool and primary grades, tapes and records can be used for developing rhythms, telling stories, playing games, and acting out stories. In social studies, tape and records can bring into the classroom the voices of people who have made history.

One special application of prerecorded audio media is "talking books" for blind or visually impaired students. The "Talking Books Program" has been set up by the American Printing House for the Blind to make as much material as possible available to the visually impaired. At present, over 11,000 book titles are available, along with recordings of several current periodicals.

Audiotapes can easily be prepared by teachers for specific instructional purposes. One of the most common uses of audio materials is for drill work. For example, the student can practice spelling vocabulary words that were recorded by the teacher on tape, working out multiplication tables, taking dictation or typing from a prerecorded tape, or pronouncing foreign-language vocabulary.

Students can also record themselves reciting, presenting a speech, performing music, and so on. They can then listen to the tape in private or have the performance critiqued by the teacher and/or other students. Initial efforts can be kept for comparison with later performances and for reinforcement of learning.

Audio material is also used extensively by business and industry. American corporations are using cassettes most often as extensions of sales training and for personnel development. An executive of the Gillette Corporation estimates that the company's sales representatives in rural areas spend the equivalent of 18 to 25 weeks a year in their cars. During that time, they can be receiving production information, sales leads, and customer information.

Many companies and individuals have found cassette tapes to be extremely useful for personnel development. Usually, the tapes are closely integrated with workbooks. Perhaps the most commonly used cassette programs are those that develop basic skills: reading improvement, writing-skills development, listening skills. Motivation programs are also popular.

Some companies have exploited the dramatic capabilities of the audio medium in management-training programs that deal with conflict resolution and stress management. The low price of cassettes compared with the cost of video or a series of seminars plays an important part in the decision to use audiotape.

Motion Pictures

Films are used in limited numbers in formal instruction today. This was not always so, however. Before the development of videotape and, more important, the small format (Beta or VHS) videotape recorder, 16mm and 8mm films were a familiar instructional tool for most primary- and secondary-school teachers. Films are still used extensively, but their future as an instructional medium is limited. As video projection reaches the point where large screen images are sharp and faithful in color rendition, the last major obstacle to using video rather than film in the classroom will have been overcome. Of course, by that time, videodisc may have replaced videotape as the most popular format. Because they can be mass-produced like phonograph records, videodiscs are considerably cheaper than videotape. Videodiscs are also a more versatile format for instructional purposes. Recorded moving images will always have a firm place in instruction. Motion pictures have proved their usefulness in just about every kind of educational situation. However, with the exception of certain types of instruction, such as film-history courses, instructor preference, or absence of appropriate video technology, film as an instructional medium will play a limited role in the future.

Television

Despite many efforts, the use of television in the classroom has been less than a complete success, especially when money spent and successful results are compared. Much of this limited success was due to the manner in which television was used and the forms that it assumed. Until the mid-1980s, television and formal instruction were, at best, unwilling and ineffective partners. Television was essentially a remote, expensive, restricted business whose primary interest and appeal was as a medium for the masses—"television of abundance," as it was called.

Television is now easily accessible for use in education not only through over-the-air broadcasts, but also by means of closed-circuit and cable-TV systems, all of which may by linked by satellite relays. Programs are now available on videocassette and videodisc, making TV materials nearly as available as audiotapes and records. Furthermore, portable video recorders enable instructors—and their students—to create their own materials.

Like film, TV can present color moving pictures with sound. As such, it shares many of the instructional advantages of film. But a major difference is that television can be transmitted long distances and its signals can be recorded and played back instantly. By means of television broadcasting, large audiences can be reached at a low cost per person. Viewers dispersed over vast geographical areas can see a live event simultaneously. Learners can be reached at home, making "open learning" a reality. At the same time, this mass medium is becoming an individual medium. The development of small, inexpensive home video recorders makes it feasible for students to view video materials on an individually prescribed basis.

The complex electronic technology that affords television so many of its advantages is also, in a sense, a disadvantage. The technology allows many possibilities for disruption of the communication flow. Programs may be poorly produced, even in sophisticated studio surroundings. Atmospheric conditions may disturb broadcast signals or satellite reception. Classroom receivers may malfunction. There is, in short, always the possibility that technical difficulties over which the instructor has little or no control will intervene between the lesson and the learner.

Costs are another limiting factor. Even basic equipment can be expensive. Sophisticated equipment, such as cable distribution systems and satellite reception setups, can cost a great deal of money. Hardward costs are only the most visible expenses, however. The human labor involved in production, distribution, maintenance, and utilization overshadow the original equipment costs. So unless a large number of learners is being served or unless TV is performing a vital teaching function that cannot be performed efficiently and effectively by less expensive means, these costs may be difficult to justify.

Perhaps television's most serious limitation as an instructional tool is that under typical conditions, it is a one-way channel of communication. A feedback loop can be provided by means of push-button student response systems or even "talk-back" arrangements. But in normal practice, one-way communication is still the rule. In the United States, television has become widely available as a resource to supplement and enrich the curricula of elementary and secondary schools. However, it is still not used in a systematic manner by a large proportion of teachers. The availability and use of Instructional Television (ITV) has been documented as a result of a series of surveys conducted by the Corporation for Public Broadcasting (CPB) since 1977. The CPB sent questionnaires to all school districts. According to the most recent (1984) survey, 70 percent of all school districts can receive broadcast ITV off-air from a public-TV station; 97 percent of all teachers have access to television sets; 81 percent of all teachers have access to video-recording and -playback equipment; and 29 percent of all teachers actually use at least one ITV series regularly. Average viewing time per week by their students is 1 hour and 45 minutes.

In higher education, the use of television for instruction appears to be widespread but quite conservative. More than 80 percent of colleges and universities used video for instruction during the 1984/1985 school year, according to a study by the Corporation for Public Broadcasting and the Department of Education. About 32 percent of schools offered telecourses, which make substantial use of video, in 1985. Although some institutions serve sizable enrollments of students in many different courses, only a few courses are usually offered via television, enrolling a total of about 100 students. Further, despite television's potential for extending the university's reach beyond the campus, only about 14 percent of the total college TV effort is devoted to off-campus course work.

It is clear that higher education is increasingly accommodating itself to the telecommunications revolution, but developments are serendipitous and generally undocumented. Educators realize that their lives are changing, but the environment is disorganized. It is difficult to keep pace with rapid new developments. The only information sources are the technology industries themselves. But no single source provides the educational and telecommunications communities with objective, reliable information about what the new technologies are, where they are being applied, and in what settings and for which learners particular technologies seem most effective.

The 1980s have brought with them some noticeable changes in the telecommunications environment of postsecondary education, however. Technology in higher education is starting to move beyond the initial stage of haphazard, incidental use into an advanced state of marked institutionalization. Evidence of this trend continues to be reflected in the centralization of efforts now under way through regional and national initiatives to provide programming services, to facilitate teleconferencing networks, to gather information on the use of telecommunications in higher education, and to assist colleges and universities in implementing technology within courses and curricula.

Since 1981, the PBS Adult Learning Service has involved over 800 institutions, and 85 percent of PBS stations enroll approximately 250,000 students in telecourses.

As we pointed out at the beginning of the chapter, the major reason for the demise of "Sunrise Semester" was money: money to create, money to produce, money to distribute, and money to promote. An even more ambitious experiment in televised learning also met an untimely death in 1982, the University of Mid-America's American Open University.

The open-university concept was inspired by the British Open University, which was started in 1971 with government financing, the expertise of the British Broadcasting Corporation, and a large, full-time faculty. The instructors not only develop radio and TV programs and extensive textbooks for home study, but also run a system of remote-control homework and examinations with the help of computers and tutors. The British program has reached hundreds of thousands of new students. In 1981, for example, it admitted 21,000 degree-seeking students. In its first 10 years, it had a graduation rate of nearly 60 percent more than 10 percentage points higher than America's on-campus colleges.

In 1979, the American Open University began to conduct in-depth feasibility studies and obtained the approval of the trustees of the University of Mid-America for plans to establish a nationwide, independent degree-granting institution of higher learning. Preparations included surveying existing correspondence courses, telecourses, and computer-aided instruction; hiring a staff with academic expertise; and assembling two sets of advisory faculties, one in the arts and sciences and one in business. Rejection of further financing by the National Institute of Education dashed all hopes for further operations.

The stage had been set, however, and in 1981, publisher and philanthropist Walter H. Annenberg announced his intention to donate $150 million over a 15-year period toward the improvement of telecourse programs. In collaboration with the Corporation for Public Broadcasting, the Annenberg/CPB Project invites proposals for innovative program ideas or other telecommunications applications. The most worthy are funded for implementation. In 1984, the first wave of Annenberg-funded programs began to be distributed in North America. It included the 26-program series "Congress: We the People," in which veteran TV journalist Edwin Newman hosts an inside look at how Congress works. Taped at the Capitol and in congressional home districts, the documentary-style series mixes videotape footage with commentary by leading members of Congress and political scientists as it considers such topics as elections, lobbying, party leadership, ethics, and congressional committees and staffs. A more "typical" telecourse is "The Write Course," a 30-lesson series consisting of video lessons closely integrated with textbook readings, study guides, and writing assignments. The series is, in effect, a one-semester college-level course in composition that covers basic writing skills, such as pre-writing, planning a composition, and composing effective sentences and paragraphs. In 1984, an estimated 100,000 tuition-paying students tuned into PBS telecourses.

At the opposite end of the mass-communication–personal-communication continuum from the telecourse is a relatively new concept—interactive video. Interactive video has become the latest "buzz word" in media instruction. The possibilities for branching, collecting data, using computer-generated text and graphics, and creating personalized message systems make this linkage between computer and video technology one of the most flexible mediated systems of instruction in use today.

Figure 13.7 Linking up a computer with videotape and videodisc playback gives learners the ability to interact with the content rather than simply be passive consumers. (Photo: Courtesy Control Data Corporation.)

As Diane Gayeski, a professor at Ithaca College, points out: "One of the simplest, but most powerful, techniques using the random accessibility of video segments is showing people what they're interested in. This can be done by providing a menu in print, through computer generation, or in the tape or disc itself, by which a participant can select a topic." [5]

One segment in a demonstration tape that Gayeski produced for Panasonic's Interactive Video Training System works like a databank; the section allows the student to learn how to use various reference tools (a dictionary, a thesaurus, industrial reference manuals, zip code directory). Using a menu, the user can go immediately to an explanation of just what he or she has to learn.

The difference between random access video and traditional linear video is like the difference between a book and a scroll. With a book or random access device, you can locate just the "page" or "chapter" you want, without having to "scroll" through the whole program.

Training and information can be provided by the branching capabilities of interactive video. By asking questions, the teacher can determine whether or not a trainee has grasped an important concept. If not, remedial segments can be shown that correct misunderstandings. People who un-

---

[5] Diane Gayeski and David Williams, "Interactive Video—Accessible and Intelligent," *E-ITV* (June 1984), 31–32.

derstand particular concepts quickly can speed through a program without becoming bogged down in more explanation than they need.

Systems that allow for multiple branching can "diagnose" a learner's particular misconceptions and address them with specific feedback. Rather than merely showing a segment over and over until the correct response is given (perhaps by elimination), such programs can present the information in different terms or can clarify the confusion indicated by the response. Many computer-based programs are able to keep track of patterns of responses and to branch to a specific style or level of explanation accordingly.

Other systems include print-out or record-keeping options, allowing an instructor to see exactly how students responded and how long it took them to respond. This record keeping provides useful information about the user's progress, as well as the program itself. Such hard copy can become a part of a students' record for documentation of skills learned or concepts mastered.

Interactive video can increase the effectiveness of testing and assessment, allowing for immediate scoring and/or feedback and supplementary instruction, if necessary, as part of the test. Instead of being limited to print or diagrams to present test items, video can present dramatized scenes, moving parts, and realistic sounds, adding to the scope and face validity of the assessment. Using one tape-based system, an instructor can even hook up a camera and microphone and record trainees' responses to questions.

As we pointed out in Chapter 7, the extent to which business and industrial organizations rely on television for job training and basic-skill instruction is rapidly increasing. Indeed, the vast majority of user organizations operate television "networks," sending their programs to seven or more viewing locations. Hundreds of corporations, among them IBM, Ford Motor Company, Coca-Cola, John Deere, Equitable Life Assurance, Norwich Laboratories, and Burlington Industries, operate "coroprate video networks" with more than 50 outlets. Most organizations produce their own programs. The total annual program output of corporate video is far greater than the combined output of the major commercial television networks, and total usage has increased each year.

Much of the excitement about these new technologies is centered on their potential to improve the quality of education for students both off and on campus. Collaboration is one key factor. Collaborative thinking about the content and how to teach it offers a chance that the quality of teaching will improve.

Second, the technologies have the potential to provide students with access to richer and more varied resources than is currently possible. With large databases to draw on, the student may be able to tackle problems and concepts as an undergraduate that previously were regarded as appropriate for only graduate students.

Third, embedded within the technologies is the potential for helping students to see ideas differently and to manipulate them more effectively. Some students, for example, find it difficult to visualize abstract mathematical or scientific concepts when aided by only static drawings and the printed page. But with computer simulations or video representations, some of which can be electronically manipulated so that the student can "see" the concept from different perspectives, the ideas can be made more comprehensible.

Many efforts are under way to explore these possibilities. For example, the Massachusetts Institute of Technology is currently developing a new generation of language-laboratory materials that use computer and videodisc technologies to create exercises that emphasize discourse as a key to acquiring language skills. They combine text-based instruction with video and audiodisc exercises to improve both comprehension and pronunciation within the context of conversation. In addition to providing a rich array of materials in French, Spanish, German, Russian, and English as a second language, the project will produce a package of authoring tools that will allow faculty members to develop their own language exercises.

The transformation of schools by technology, for good or ill, however, remains a long way off. As Marc Tucker, who is conducting a study on the use of information technology in education, remarks, "Society and schools and most students are not about to change. But it's easy to get smoke in your eyes."[6]

The smoke of high expectations, in fact, has obscured the vision of educational reformers throughout this century. The eduational-theory section of the library is a graveyard of would-be assaults on orthodoxy: teaching machines, for example, and individualizing instruction and the guided-design approach. Educational technology too often seems to constitute yet another entertaining diversion from the intractable problems of public education.

But the usual cynicism may not be justified at this time. The microcomputer will soon be a major household appliance, and it will not be banished from the schools, which already own more than 130,000 of them. The new forms of television appearing in the classroom—cable (especially two-way cable) and videocassette recorders—already are ubiquitous. The videodisc also has profound educational possibilities, if only a flickering existence now. The question is not, ultimately, whether the new technology will be deployed; it is whether the door that separates the dedicated and imaginative teachers, the brilliant psychologists, the human philosophers, and the creative software designers from the world of misuse, indifference, suspicion, and hostility will be unlocked.

As Marilyn Kressel, founder and former director of the Center for

---

[6] Hyman H. Field, "Issues in Financing Higher Education Telecommunications," *National Forum* (Summer 1986): 12.

Learning and Telecommunications of the American Association for Higher Education, stated in a recent article:

> The quality and evaluation of technology-based instruction continue to plague educators and policymakers. Software is being cranked out everywhere from obscure garage-top attics to high-tech production factilities. A critical analysis of what works and what doesn't work when delivered by television, radio, computer, telephone, or any other technology is simply unavailable. What is sound education vs. entertainment? What is a creditworthy telecourse vs. slick television? When is the computer-based course a skill-enhancer rather than a video gimmick? How does the educator know which packages to select for which students? How does the faculty member select a software package adaptable to his/her teaching style?
>
> While problems are apparent, the solutions are not. Who will support the next steps to create a forum to disseminate effective models, assist state planning efforts, and enhance the debate over quality criteria and methods of evaluation? Where might this entity be lodged?
>
> Will these systems address the issues of educational quality and thrive, or will they go the way of so many other innovations, fizzling into a footnote in educational textbooks? Might we be left with dormant, 1960-vintage university and college production studios and warehouses filled with obsolete PC's and bins full of floppy discs? Those of us who have seen the potential for technology to instruct and excite when integrated into educationally sound delivery systems would hate to be accused of such faddism. The scenario is preventable, but who will marshal the necessary resources to ensure good practice?[7]

As with most other aspects of society, the new communication technology is clearly affecting education. There are many problems to be solved, and the new communication technology cannot alone solve them. However, if the technology is intelligently developed and used by those in education, the marriage of technology and education may be a happy one yet.

SUMMARY

Mass media and formal education have had a checkered history. The American educational system is still primarily dependent on one mass medium, the book. However, new technologies and innovations, especially in the work place, are having a major impact on both formal and informal education.

The mass media perform three major educational tasks: (1) *socialization*, in which media reinforce or modify cultural norms; (2) *informal education*, in which media supplement the education of the individual outside

---

[7] Marilyn Kressel, "Higher Education and Telecommunications," *National Forum* (Summer 1986): 6. Reprinted by permission of *National Forum: The Phi Kappa Phi Journal*, Summer 1986.

e school; and (3) *formal instruction,* in which media systematically impart ecialized information and skills in a controlled, supervised environment.

e extent and mix of media and each person's learning experience is ᴜᴜferent. Nevertheless, some general patterns are evident in the amounts and kinds of formal instruction, informal education, and socialization in which Americans participate.

The media are an important factor in socialization through a series of messages: (1) *directed messages* command, exhort, instruct, persuade, and urge in the direction of learning and new understanding; (2) *maintenance messages* tell us what to do in the everyday business of living, such as where to find food and what dangers to avoid; and (3) *restorative messages* renew and refresh the human capacity for productive social relationships.

The media also participate in informal education—primarily through motion pictures and network television but the Public Broadcasting Service is becoming increasingly active in this area.

All the media are involved in formal instruction. Books, the most influential medium, are successful largely because they adapt so well to the individual needs and habits of the formal-instruction process.

Magazines are also used in formal instruction, especially the 5,000 or more scholarly journals that print the latest research and other information in specific fields.

Newspapers are one of the least used mass media in formal instruction. Videotex systems, however, are beginning to be used as a form of newspaper to communicate information directly into the home.

Radio is used little. Some public radio stations provide instruction, but, in general, the potential of radio for formal instruction has not been realized. However, audio-based courses using sound recording are finding an increasing number of users, especially in higher education. Prerecorded audio materials are used in a variety of settings, especially in "mastery learning." Cassette tapes are used extensively in education, business, and industry to communicate a variety of content.

As we have seen, motion pictures play a strong socialization role, but they are not used extensively in formal instruction. This was not always so, however. Before the development of videotape, 16mm and 8mm films were a familiar instructional tool for most primary and secondary school-teachers. They are still used, but video formats and television, have supplanted motion pictures as audiovisual media of instruction.

Television has unlimited potential for formal instruction. It is now easily accessible for education, not only through over-the-air broadcasts, but also with closed-circuit and cable-television systems, as well as programs available on videodisc and videocassette. Television's most serious limitation as an instructional tool is that, under typical conditions, it is a one-way channel of communication. However, through interactive video and other forms of new technology, television is being used more extensively. In recent years, a series of PBS telecourses is making creative and imaginative use of the medium as a formal-instructional tool.

The impact of new technologies on education has been significant but there are still many problems to solve and many questions to answer. Technology alone cannot solve the problems.

BIBLIOGRAPHY

Aldrich, Michael. *Videotex: Key to the Wired City*. London: Quiller Press, 1982.

Bretz, Rudy, and Michael Schmidbauer. *Media for Interactive Communication*. Beverly Hills, Calif.: Sage, 1983.

Budd, John F., Jr. *Corporate Video in Focus: Management Guide to Private TV*. Englewood Cliffs, N.J.: Prentice-Hall, 1983.

Dizard, Wilson. *The Coming Information Age*. New York: Longman, 1982.

Gayeski, Diane. *Corporate and Instructional Video*. Englewood Cliffs, N.J: Prentice-Hall, 1983.

———, and David Williams. *Interactive Media*. Englewood Cliffs, N.J.: Prentice-Hall, 1985.

Haney, John B., and Eldon J. Ullmer. *Educational Communications and Technology*. 3d ed. Dubuque, Ia.: Brown, 1980.

Hawkridge, David, and John Robinson. *Organizing Educational Broadcasting*. New York: Unipub, 1982.

Rice, Ronald E. *The New Media: Communication, Research and Technology*. Beverly Hills, Calif.: Sage, 1984.

Schramm, Wilbur. *Big Media, Little Media*. Beverly Hills, Calif.: Sage, 1977.

14

Entertainment and Art

Entertainment, whether or not the fact is appreciated by critics, may well be the single most important role of mass communication. And for an ever-increasing segment of Americans—especially the poor, the undereducated and illiterate, the unskilled and unemployed, the new migrants and established minorities, the children, and the elderly—it is electronic media, especially television entertainment, that are defining the nature and value of our culture.

For most of us, the day is filled with work, whether schoolwork, housework, or "jobwork." That work is often boring, stressful, exasperating, and exhausting. The pace, tension, and anxiety of the workplace is as real in basic minimum-wage jobs as it is in well-remunerated careers. To many young people, what looks like a glamorous career from the outside becomes simply a job, with all the attendant stresses, once they begin to work at it. Therefore, when the workday ends, most people look for relaxation, release, and enjoyment in their free time. Entertainment is the prime means to that end, and the mass media dominate the production and uses of entertainment.

This media entertainment also serves as the primary source of what has come to be called popular culture, which is the chosen art of the people. Entertainment as "pop art" is used to shrug off the world of work and refresh us at the end of the day, so that we can return to and cope with the work load ahead.

THE RELATIONSHIP OF ART
AND ENTERTAINMENT IN THE MASS MEDIA

In every culture, much of what came to be considered as art began as entertainment. New movements in art emerged out of a rejection or modification of the art that came before it. It always takes a period of time before any new art is accepted. New art forms are often enjoyed by audiences long before they are recognized by critics. So it is with the content of mass communication.

Not all mass media entertainment is art, but even the content that has artistic merit takes time to be recognized. Consider the Italian Renaissance and the dramatic literature that was produced during that period. It is not the stilted imitations of classical tragedies produced by the literati (the cultural elite of the day) that is remembered. We celebrate the low, vulgar, knockabout comedies of the streets, the commedia del l'arte, as the dra-

Figure 14.1 Commedia del l'arte, reviled by critics during the Italian Renaissance as vulgar street entertainment, is now considered to be the major theatrical art of the sixteenth to eighteenth centuries. In the seventeenth century, the commedia was a frequent subject of artists. (*Italian Comedians,* Antoine Watteau, 1684–1721; National Gallery of Art, Washington; Samuel H. Kress Collection, 1946.)

matic legacy from that time. Who can predict with certainty what will be remembered as the *high art* of the twentieth century? Yet it is safe to assume that some of it, perhaps much of it, will come from the ranks of what is now entertainment in the mass media. Perhaps Lieutenant Frank Furillo of "Hill Street Blues" or Indiana Jones or James Bond or the "crazies" that inhabited "Saturday Night Live" and now star in major feature films will become the dramatic characters of our time.

In the marketplace of popular entertainment and art, two forces are in tension: the demand for content and creative potential.

Demand for Content

The economic and physical need to fill the time and space of the mass media is very real. Enormous quantities of content produced at equally enormous costs are the facts of life in mass communication. Although quality and quantity are not theoretically impossible to produce in tandem, the timetable that producers set for themselves makes it a difficult feat to accomplish.

Creative Potential

All media artists wish to create the best work they can under the time limitations of the media. No director, novelist, editor, or designer sets out to produce a failure or, worse, trash. Creative people believe in their projects, but sometimes these storytellers, dancers, artists, or actors falter along the way in the execution of their vision. Every generation is blessed with only a limited number of significant artists—let alone a genius like a Shakespeare or a Mozart or a Nijinsky or a Van Gogh. If we are realistic in our expectations, the quality of mass media entertainment and art far exceeds that which we could possibly predict.

Two elements have a significant impact on the demand for quality content and also the creative ability to produce it: time and audience taste.

Time. As mentioned, time refers both to the amount of content that must be produced to fill the schedule and to the hours allotted to accomplish this task. Time also relates to the years it takes to recognize and truly appreciate the merit of a work of art produced as popular entertainment. Traditionally, entertainment is thought of as a diversion of the moment, whereas art is considered to be an expression of lasting beauty. Since media content is evaluated immediately on (and sometimes before) public exhibition, it cannot be expected that reviewers will be able to determine the critical value of a film after one or even a number of screenings. It takes time to make a *Citizen Kane,* and it takes time to reflect on its beauty. Many films that were undervalued by contemporaries are revered much later as objects of lasting

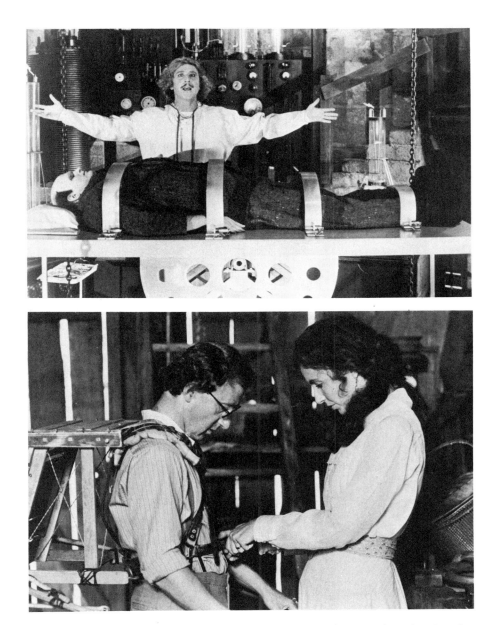

Figure 14.2 Comic genius is timeless, and humor seems, in general, to time travel better than more serious work. Mel Brooks's wonderful send-up of horror films, *Young Frankenstein* (above), seems to be heading toward classic status. Rather than any single film, the total body of work of Woody Allen (below) has the attendant marks of films that will have lasting value. His personal creations of wonderful, neurotic clowns and insights on the human condition make his films humane as well as humanistic. The comedies of both Brooks and Allen are artful entertainment. (Photos: Music Star News; *Young Frankenstein* courtesy of Paramount Pictures Corp. and *A Midsummer Night's Sex Comedy* courtesy of Orion Pictures Company.)

beauty. The films of Charlie Chaplin and Buster Keaton are prime examples. Only recently has the status of these men been elevated from media clown to film artist.

Audience Taste. The evaluation of media content as entertainment or art depends on the acquired taste of audience and critic alike. Perceptions of the value of both art and artist vary, depending on region and tradition and prior experiences with the style in question. For example, Jerry Lewis is a popular entertainer in the United States; in France, however, he is regarded as an artist, as the equal of Chaplin. Tastes change; in total honesty, the mass media have improved some cultural standards over the past century as well as expanding audiences for works of art. More and better novels, plays, films, short stories, graphic art, and music are being produced as a result of their widespread distribution via mass communication.

Figure 14.3 Jerry Lewis's position as a great comic, here in *The Nutty Professor*, is secure in the hearts of the French. But in the United States, he may be more revered as a humanitarian, for his annual Muscular Dystrophy Telethons, than as a great media clown. His recent comedy, *Hardly Working*, was a tremendous box-office hit in Europe but was not well received at home. Different audiences have different tastes, and Lewis may well be the proverbial comic "prophet in his own land." (Photo: Movie Star News, Courtesy Paramount Pictures Corp.)

MEDIART IN MODERN SOCIETY

Popular art is, in effect, folk art aimed at mass audience. It is a product of current technology. Tradition and originality are caught up in the speed of the times, and qualitative evaluation is difficult. Several basic conclusions can be offered, however.

1. Entertainment has long been the basis for art, and mediart does emerge from mass entertainment.
2. Mediart exists to be enjoyed by the largest possible audience because we live in a mass society.
3. To enjoy mediart fully, audiences have to learn to understand it.
4. Mediart exists for audiences as well as for artists and critics, and educated audiences should be and are sought.
5. There are various audiences for various media; it should not be necessary for every medium to provide every form of mediart at every cultural level. Trained audiences will find what is good.
6. Artists have always needed patrons, and the patrons of mediartists are big business and big audiences.
7. There will always be tension between mediartists and media audiences. The greater the originality, the greater the tension; but this tension leads audiences to "better" preferences in their future selection of media content.
8. Mediart is what you "like," and you learn to like it. Media appreciation can be learned, although it is difficult because audiences are so close to it. And, as always, there are levels of enjoyment.

Value judgments in mediart come from the paying customer. What we are willing to pay for now will determine the quality of the media entertainment and art that the mass media will provide in the future. The advance of culture depends on the education of the public.

The content of mass media will improve to meet the challenges that the audience provides. Over the long haul, both the media and their audiences have benefited—not in every case, but enough to keep us going on.

Always bear in mind that almost all mediart is immersed in entertainment. The TV play, film, recorded music, novel, or magazine is designed to entertain; but art through the ages has served this purpose. Michelangelo's *David* is entertainment; Aristophanes' *Birds* is entertainment; Beethoven's Symphony no. 9 is entertainment. All had audiences of various levels of understanding, but all, like mediart, were created to entertain.

Levels of Mediart

Considerable debate has taken place over the value and effects of mass media entertainment-art on our culture and society. Cultural anthropologists, sociologists, and critics have tended to group cultural artifacts into

Figure 14.4 The Milos Forman film *Amadeus* was adapted by Peter Shaefer from his play of the same name. But the film and the stage play are quite different from each other because the conventions and audiences of modern cinema and theater are dissimilar. But both film and play make superior use of the music of Wolfgang Amadeus Mozart. The music of Mozart has stood the test of time and is truly art. The film and the play, excellent by contemporary standards, must also stand the test of time until final judgment can be passed on their artistic merit. (Photo: Courtesy Movie Star News.)

three categories, which have been given various names. Van Wyck Brooks, a media critic, coined the terms *highbrow, middlebrow,* and *lowbrow* to describe these categories.

Highbrow, or high, *culture* is composed of cultural artifacts that can be appreciated by only an educated and intellectual elite. Examples include Shakespeare's plays, T. S. Eliot's poems, Beethoven's sonatas, Matisse's paintings, the *Economist, Daedalus,* and Ingmar Bergman's movies.

Middlebrow culture has pretensions of being refined and intellectual but also has wider human appeal. Examples include *Horizon* magazine, the *Washington Post,* Neil Simon's plays, Amedeo Modigliani's paintings, Ogden Nash's poems, and Norman Mailer's novels.

Lowbrow culture consists of those artifacts that have massive appeal to the largest possible audience, an appeal that is usually visceral rather than cerebral, emotional rather than rational, crass rather than aesthetic. Examples include soap operas, TV situation comedies, confession magazines, advice-to-the-lovelorn newspaper columns, sex and violence movies, and pulp novels.

There is in this analysis an elitism that verges on snobbery. It seems more reasonable to adopt a method of analysis that is more objective and a classification based on the medium used, the techniques used, the function of the content, and the success of the content.

Originality and tradition are in conflict in many works. *Barry Lyndon,* a brilliant film by Stanley Kubrick, based on a minor novel by William Makepeace Thackeray, goes against the grain of Kubrick's traditional films. His originality was misunderstood by his movie audience. The beauty, elegance, and grace of *Barry Lyndon* are a joy. The photography, sets, music, and acting are remarkable. But audiences were less responsive to the film because it lacks the story, the liveliness, and the hype of *2001: A Space Odyssey* or *A Clockwork Orange.* Mass audience rejection or acceptance of a film is not necessarily the measure of its worth. Beauty can be learned over time or, in some cases, realized instantly.

Interestingly, Kubrick turned back to a popular genre, the horror film, for *The Shining.* But this film depends less on shock treatments and the standard hype of this genre and more on an intense study of a character, played by Jack Nicholson, crumbling into insanity. High art for the lowbrow brought some grumbling from horror fans in need of their fix of stock scares. Perhaps Stanley Kubrick was ahead of his audience. Nonetheless, movies are made for a "now" box office and not for tomorrow's critical credos.

If we use the categories of highbrow, middlebrow, and lowbrow over a period of time to measure audience perceptions of film as a medium, its techniques, function, and success, motion pictures have moved from lowbrow in the 1890s to middlebrow in the 1940s to highbrow in the 1980s. The interaction of the mediartist, the mass medium and its techniques, and the audience create the film's worth.

Once again, the quality of the mediart produced depends on the interaction of the artist with the audience, using the tools and techniques of the medium. The audience must be an active participant. Great artists improve the tastes of audiences, but not all producers of media content are great artists. This dichotomy leads to both intense criticism of and defense of mass culture.

CRITICISM AND DEFENSE OF MASS CULTURE

On one side of the debate are those who argue that the purveyors of entertainment-art through the mass media are little more than panderers, catering to the lowest common denominator in the mass audience. These critics maintain that most mass media entertainment has a degrading effect

Figure 14.5 Jack Nicholson slides convincingly into insanity in Stanley Kubrick's *Shining* (based on Steven King's novel). This film ranks as one of the masterpieces of suspense, but it disappointed some of King's fans, because it downplayed the supernatural elements of the novel, and some horror-movie buffs, because it lacked gore, which has become "the stuff of life" in "horror flicks." Kubrick's vision creates an unending tension throughout the film, never allowing the audience to predict what's around the next corner. It is a magnificently made film despite the disappointment of specialized audiences. (Photo: Museum of Modern Art/Film Stills Archives, Courtesy Warner Brothers, Inc.)

on our culture. The mass media, these critics say, by emphasizing that which is popular and salable, ruin standards of style and taste, leading to a "cultural democracy" in which the "good," the "true," and the "beautiful" are decided by the vote in the marketplace of mass media audiences rather than by sensitive, refined, and knowledgeable authorities. Some critics take the position that the only antidote to mass culture is high culture. To the elitist, *high culture* refers to art and learning inaccessible to the masses. To the snob, *mass culture* is only for those persons suffering from severe brain damage. This position is unfortunate as well as inaccurate.

Popular culture, or popular arts, might best be regarded as current culture or current arts. These arts have mass audiences and therefore are rejected out of hand by some critics. The popular arts are designed to entertain and, one hopes, to earn large returns on the dollar investment. Popular culture is big business and therefore suspect, yet artists have always had patrons and tried to sell their work. The popular arts are democratic rather than elitist arts.

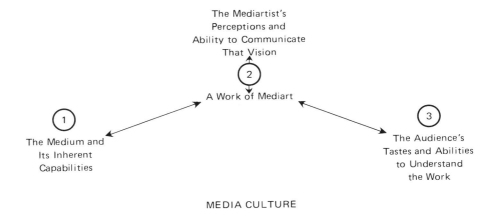

The Mediartist's
Perceptions and
Ability to Communicate
That Vision

②

A Work of Mediart

①
The Medium and
Its Inherent
Capabilities

③
The Audience's
Tastes and Abilities
to Understand
the Work

MEDIA CULTURE

Figure 14.6 This model suggests that mediart exists in a cultural framework and depends on: (1) the medium, (2) the mediartist's perceptions, and (3) the audience's tastes.

Traditionally, art criticism has been based on the value judgments of those trained in the art form being evaluated. Today's media critics tend not to be trained artists in film, music, or television, but people educated in English or journalism. Many of these "pop critics" have an inordinate impact on art forms in which they were not trained.

The crass statement of the mass-culture position is that of the media entrepreneur who says, "Give the fools what they want. If people will pay for comic books but not poetry, give them comics. If the audience demands burlesque and will not attend tragedy, give them Gypsy Rose Lee and not Lady Macbeth." Most media owners are, first and foremost, businessmen who must sell a product to as many customers as are necessary to make a profit.

But there is an intellectual side to this argument—that the content of the mass media is important to the overall soothing and comforting of an anxious and complex society. The mass media, of necessity, make news, information, and education digestible. Most people do not read comic books or watch situation comedies all day long. Even for those who do, their attention to the mass media helps involve them in other uses of media, which is culturally beneficial.

A similar but perhaps more meaningful argument in defense of mass culture maintains that both good and bad exist in "class" culture and in mass culture and that class and mass not only coexist in a society, but also enrich and enliven each other. There are pretentious elements of class culture, just as there are products of genuine quality that emerge from mass culture.

Because these art forms enliven and enrich each other, it is as important for students to study the popular arts as it is for them to give serious attention to sculpture, sonnets, and sonatas. This broadening of the critical perspective to include mass culture also has a potentially beneficial effect on classical studies.

"Class" products and artifacts that reach a mass audience through the mass media—Jacques Cousteau's TV documentaries, James Reston's newspaper columns, or Stanley Kubrick's films—prove that a growing number of people have a taste for quality at a price they can afford. By the same token, mass-produced or mass-communicated culture that acquires unexpected quality—Charlie Chaplin's little tramp, Red Smith's sports columns, the Beatles's rock recordings, or Rod Sterling's "Twilight Zone" TV series—proves that what moves the masses often has genuine and long-lasting quality.

THE RELATIONSHIP OF LEISURE, ART, AND ENTERTAINMENT

Three things are relevant to an understanding of the importance of entertainment and art in the mass media: (1) leisure, or free time from work or duty; (2) play, or nondirected, random, and spontaneous amusement; (3) recreation, or diverting pastime for relaxation and rejuvenation. Both art and entertainment are a combination of the mental, emotional, and physical acts that occur during leisure time in the form of play for enlightening and recreational purposes.

In order for artists to write, direct, and perform in plays, movies, TV series, operas, concerts, records, and the like, they need "free time" to be creative. It is difficult, if not impossible, to work all day at a job and then go home and be creative. Psychologist B. F. Skinner suggests that leisure time is a prerequisite for both the creation and the enjoyment of art. This does not mean that everyone who has time will use it to create art or that consumers will use their free time to enjoy that art. But without freedom from care or want, art is an unaffordable luxury.

Time to enjoy life or relax and prepare for the next work period is essential. Entertainment, whether self-produced or supplied by the mass media, requires leisure time. Think about the difference in your TV-viewing time at school during exam week and at home during winter break. During vacation, you have time to spend watching television. Only when you have it can you spend it.

A large segment of the media audience uses music, films, television, novels, and magazines to meet their need for art; this art literally improves the quality of life in our intense, crowded, increasingly urbanized society. Art brings "beauty" to humankind.

The New Leisure Class

Traditionally, the leisure class was composed of a wealthy and well-educated elite, which was expected to use its freedom from work to refine the culture and to use its money to encourage artists to improve life. For the rest of society, limited leisure was earned by working; "leisure" time often had to be used to prepare for future labors. Art has flourished under these conditions, as did entertainment in previous periods of history—the Renaissance, for example.

The modern world has forced us to change our attitudes toward leisure. Machines have taken over much of our heavy labor, shortening our workweek and leaving us with more free time. In 1900, the average workweek was 6 days (72 hours); by 1950, it had been reduced to 5 days (44 hours); by 1970, fewer than 40 hours a week was average; today, the 4-day workweek is becoming increasingly popular. One observer computed that the average workers in 1970 had 2,750 hours of "free" time each year— time not spent working, sleeping, or commuting. A large portion of those 2,750 hours was spent with attention focused on the media and the art and entertainment they provide. Consider the average weekday of 8 work hours, 8 sleep hours, 2 personal-needs hours, and 2 household-activity hours; that leaves 4 leisure hours a weekday, plus most of the weekend, for recreation.

In addition, life expectancy is increasing; the later adult years, which do not usually include a job, must be made worth living. The development of a leisure ethic could imbue individuals with confidence to use spare time. Leisure has worth in learning, self-expression, and personal well-being. A major challenge in this society has become what to do with free time. For too many Americans, free time has become a plague.

The Mass Media as Play

Americans used to have difficulty coping with play because our society was work-oriented. Those who followed the work ethic praised labor and achievement and condemned play and idleness. Play was considered worthwhile only when it was evaluated as the work of children. Entertainment and nonessential art were often suspect because they occupied time that could be better spent at work. For many Americans, work was the real business of life; the periods between labors were times of guilt. Much criticism of the mass media has been inspired by this work ethic, prompting the feeling that if readers or listeners or viewers are not being informed, enlightened, persuaded, or educated, their time is being wasted.

The Mass Media as Recreation

Today we recognize that recreation is vital to personal happiness and self-development. The human being needs to be restored and rejuvenated through diversion and relaxation. The pressures of society, the pace of modern life, the intensity of competition, and the anxieties caused by increasing change and mobility have made recreation more important than ever.

Much mass media fare has been designed specifically to provide recreation. Television situation comedies, newspaper advice-to-the-lovelorn columns, comic strips, magazine features, radio disc-jockey chatter, and the publishing bonanza of the romance (bodice-ripper) novels of Rosemary Rogers (*Sweet Savage Love*) and Kathleen Woodiwiss (*Shanna*) and others have often been criticized by segments of the intellectual community, but they have an important recreational function. They provide emotional escape, create fantasy, and allow for the physical catharsis necessary to the renewal of the human spirit.

Audience Use of Entertainment-Art

Americans are part of mass media audiences because they have free time. They spend this leisure both actively (engaging in hobbies and sports) as physical participants and passively (reading, listening, and viewing) as emotional participants. Physical activity shakes out the body's kinks and is good for health. Passive entertainment replenishes us emotionally, physically, intellectually, and spiritually. Both kinds are necessary.

Away from work, mental play is just as important as physical play. All of one and none of the other is unhealthy. The dumb jock is no better or worse off than the weak aesthete.

Recreation in the media environment is valuable because audiences are offered many kinds of entertainment and art. These audiences make conscious choices among various entertainments of varying levels of artistry. This choice is based on what audiences have learned to like; what their immediate physical, emotional, and intellectual conditions are; and what is available for the time and money they have to spend. The mass media provide both entertainment and art.

Entertainment: The Overlaid Function

Entertainment is an important element in almost all aspects of mass media. Artists, writers, journalists, teachers, and preachers have long known the value of drama, humor, entertainment, and art in the process of creating, reporting, educating, and promoting. We might speak of entertainment as an "overlaid" use of mass media because it is an aspect of almost all media content.

In fact, entertainment is vital because audiences are available to the media; they have leisure, which they use for play. In effect, we seek recreation in our use of news, analysis, propaganda, education, and advertising. When this process reaches its zenith, we call it an art.

News as Entertainment. Newspapers and news magazines often try to make the news as entertaining as possible. The layout of the page is designed to make information attractive and palatable. News content is often intermingled with humorous features, amusing sidebars, diverting human-interest stories, and clever fillers.

Sometimes news provides unexpected entertainment. One of the most interesting moments in news entertainment came during the NBC-TV broadcast of the 1964 Republican National Convention when John Chan-

Figure 14.7 The ultimate in news as entertainment is the popular syndicated show "Entertainment Tonight." Jeanne Wolf is one of a staff of reporters who works the "soft-news" entertainment-industry beat. The show is a fast-paced, super-hype version of the "happy-talk" news format.

cellor was carried off the convention floor in semi-arrest for allegedly blocking an aisle. As he was being taken away, he signed off with, "This is John Chancellor, somewhere in custody." It was news, and it said something about that convention; but it was also entertaining.

In preparation for the 1983/1984 TV season, the three major networks returned to the single-anchorman format in their evening news programs. The decision was based in large part on research that indicated that most viewers prefer one information source so that there is no confusion about who is really in charge of the news. Tom Brokaw (NBC), Peter Jennings (ABC), and Dan Rather (CBS) are "in the know." They are "news stars"—for as long as their ratings say they are. They have the charm and poise and style of movie actors of the highest rank. They are consummate entertainers as well as competent newsmen.

On local stations, it is sometimes difficult to determine where the "happy talk" ends and the news begins. The set is crowded with chatty and charming news, weather, and sports personalities. On sports pages in newspapers across America, the "coverage" of local sports favorites reads as much like public relations as it does news. And it is certainly entertaining—especially when the home team defeats their "bitterest" rival.

Analysis as Entertainment. Much analysis contains entertainment. Editorial cartoons take positions on issues, analyze and interpret events, but also entertain audiences. The humor in such cartoons helps attract the reader's attention and becomes important in the analysis of the problems involved.

The *Peanuts* comic strip, paperback books, TV specials, and feature motion pictures are blatant, unadulterated, good-natured fun. For many fans, *Peanuts* is the ultimate entertainment, and Charlie Brown is a child's version of Everyman. The philosophy of Charles Schulz (creator of *Peanuts*) is that a comic strip that does not say anything is valueless. Schulz analyzes, interprets, and editorializes as he entertains.

Persuasion as Entertainment. Entertainment is an ingredient essential to persuasion and propaganda. One must attract and hold public attention in order to persuade, and entertainment is often more effective than information in winning over an audience. Sometimes the most subtle propaganda is that which contains the least haranguing and the most entertainment—

Figure 14.8 The hit film *Top Gun* is a throwback to pre–Vietnam War days, when films were made in which American military personnel were the good guys and America's antagonists were the bad guys. (Photo: Courtesy Movie Star News.)

for example, a military concert to promote the Pentagon, or the programming of the Voice of America to promote the interests of the United States.

During World War II, hundreds of feature films supporting the war effort were made. They included *Across the Pacific, Bataan, Guadalcanal Diary, Lifeboat, Master Race, Mrs. Miniver,* and *They Were Expendable*. In each of these films, the enemy was depicted as evil and dehumanized; Americans and their allies, by contrast, were pure, tough, and right. Interestingly, few major films were made in direct support of America's military involvement in Vietnam. One was *The Green Berets,* which was entertainment that propagandized in a World War II fashion. The film was not very popular, suggesting that factors other than entertainment are involved in effective propaganda. Beginning in the late 1970s, however, American artist-propagandists released a series of antiwar films set in the Vietnam period; *The Boys in Company C, Coming Home, The Deer Hunter, Apocalypse Now,* and the 1987 Academy-Award winning *Platoon*. The successful persuasion came in the form of entertainment years after the war was over. It was as though the war needed to be purged from America's soul.

Figure 14.9 *Platoon* is recognized as one of the most powerful, personal reappraisals of the war in Vietnam. Its power lies, in part, in the face that virtually all of today's middle-aged Americans "fought" that war—either in the field or, through television, in their living rooms. The film is thought by some to be part of the "purging" of this war from the American soul. *Platoon* shows "war is hell" and uses entertainment to convey an important and powerful message. (Photo: Ricky Francisco. Copyright © Hemdale Film Corporation 1986.)

Education as Entertainment. Textbooks are written to hold a child's attention as they teach reading skills. Much English instruction in the United States is designed to teach youngsters to appreciate entertaining literature.

"Sesame Street" is an educational TV program that is also highly entertaining. The series was designed to teach preschoolers basic skills that are helpful when they enter kindergarten and first grade. In order to maintain attention, "Sesame Street" uses the most interesting qualities and techniques of film and television.

Films like *Pretty in Pink, Ferris Bueller's Day Off, Risky Business,* and *All Night Long,* as well as MTV Music Television or radio programming of rock music, are elements in the socialization of young people. All three media are concerned primarily with entertainment but play a role in commenting on interpersonal relationships and teaching acceptable or, in some cases, unacceptable behavior. This is one of the major concerns of convervative pressure groups in their campaigns to implement their perception of media decency.

Advertising as Entertainment. The primary purpose of advertising is to sell products, but to make sales requires audience attention. Entertainment is one way to get that attention; entertaining ads also sell. One of the best ad campaigns was the Volkswagen series. They were good advertisements because they helped sell VW "bugs" and "rabbits." And they were good entertainment because they were interesting, diverting, and amusing. Another campaign entertainingly sold the Miller Brewing Company's Lite beer by placing retired athletes in comic settings to argue about the ad campaign's two major selling points: that the beer is "less filling" and "tastes great." The Florida Department of Commerce produced an award-winning ad that sought to attract motion-picture production to that state by taking a humorous look at the famous "Hollywood" sign. Advertising makes more overt use of entertainment variables than does any other mass communication function other than entertainment itself. The entertaining advertisement is a way of life in ad media throughout the world.

MEDIA AND ENTERTAINMENT

Each medium has technical, cultural, and economic limitations that determine how much and what kinds of entertainment it can provide. Some media are essentially purveyors of mass culture; others, of elite culture. The media and the audiences tend to be selective and seek each other out.

The Electronic Media

Approximately 80 million American homes are equipped with at least one TV set that is used an average of more than 6.5 hours a day. Watching television has become one of Americans' major leisure-time activities. Peo-

Hollywood weather without Hollywood overhead.

California's weather is great for location shooting. So is Florida's. In fact, in Florida, you can produce as good a film as you could in Hollywood or New York. On a much better budget.

You don't pay a premium for more and longer days of good shooting light.

You don't pay more for the nation's third-largest pool of acting talent. Or for experienced, professional technicians or state-of-the-art equipment, facilities, or services.

You don't pay extra travel, shipping, and per diems to get to locations like jungles, plains, deserts, cities, seashores, New England village greens – just about everything except snow-capped mountains.

And you don't waste time and money coping with hassles and red tape, because those are about the only things we don't have here.

Call us for all the help you need in planning your next location shoot:

scouting, information on crews, equipment, facilities, you name it.

You'll bring back New York or Hollywood film in the can. On a Florida budget.

Ben Harris, Charlie Porretto or Ray Quinn, Motion Picture and Television Bureau, Suite WV4-1, Collins Building, Tallahassee, Florida 32301.

(904) 487-1100

Figure 14.10 This Florida Department of Commerce ad plays off recognition of the famous sign above Los Angeles. This advertisement seeks to emphasize the state's merits as a place to make feature films at reasonable rates. Most states actively promote themselves as film-location sites. Florida is now ranked third in feature-film production, behind California and New York, because of the aggressive promotion by local filmmakers as well as by state and local film offices. (Photo: Courtesy Florida Department of Commerce, Bureau of Motion Picture, Television and Recordings.)

ple use television to be diverted, interested, amused, and entertained. This does not mean that television provides no service to specialized audiences. It does mean that mass culture dominates the content of commercial TV. Network television provides filmed dramas and videotaped variety shows in prime time (8:00–11:00 P.M. EST). Daytime television consists of situation comedies, soap operas, and quiz shows. Local stations broadcast little more than a news block and syndicated series that were previously shown on the networks. To many critics, television seems to have been designed primarily to be a massive pop-culture machine catering to the entertainment needs of its audiences.

Unlike the pages in a book, which can be enlarged or increased, the cuts in a record album, the number of which could be increased, or the footage of a film, the length of which can be increased, the number of hours in a day, which is the broadcast media's physical limitation, cannot be increased. Television entertainment is time-bound. In addition, television is a limited resource—only a specific number of channels are available. Our society seems to have charted a course for television, and that course is entertainment. But not all TV content is popular, mass culture. Significant cultural programs are constantly available on the commercial networks as well as on educational channels and cable services.

The radio and recording media are closely linked in the entertainment function because recorded music constitutes the bulk of most radio stations' programming. A wide range of musical tastes is served, but most markets are dominated by a top-40 or a rock-music station.

The recording has great flexibility and provides almost any kind of music desired. Although classical music does not dominate radio programming, classical records continue to be produced, and most university towns and metropolitan areas are served by at least one FM classical "jukebox." The primary cultural thrust of these media, however, is to provide music for specialized audiences.

The masses who used to flock to movie houses now stay at home to watch television. Because of this loss of its general audience, the film medium has begun to turn to specialized entertainment films, which seem to come in topical waves, for minority audiences. Films try to provide content that is not available on television.

Of all the electronic media, the motion picture seems to serve specialized tastes most satisfactorily. It has been discarded by most general audiences, and criteria to evaluate films have been institutionalized. Nevertheless, although film is the most socially conscious of all the electronic media, it is still primarily an entertainment medium.

America is in the midst of a period of rapid social change. Motion pictures often reflect this state of affairs. Major trends in entertainment and social values are being exploited:

1. The market for films has become youth-oriented because some two-thirds of all movie tickets are bought by people under 30.

2. The presentation of content has become much more explicit, especially in terms of violence and sex.
3. The teen-age "life-style" films and the horror and science-fiction cycles have emerged.

Because of the "tastes" of youthful audiences for "skin and gore," the motion-picture industry may well face the closest scrutiny by groups seeking to change media content in the areas relating to violent and sexual entertainment.

Print Media

Of all the mass media, newspapers provide the greatest amount of information and perhaps the smallest amount of pure entertainment. But mass entertainment is an essential part of the daily-newspaper fare. The *Washington Post,* for example, which prides itself on being the equal of the *New York Times* as a national newspaper, for years published the largest number of comic strips of any newspaper in the country. It claimed that those comics helped build its circulation to make it the largest newspaper in the nation's capital. Almost every newspaper publishes comics and cartoons, as well as features and human-interest stories, to entertain as well as inform and instruct.

Magazines are able to provide a more specialized form of entertainment for select audiences. The comic book itself is a form of entertainment for a specific type of reader. The range of such entertainment in magazine form stretches as far as the imagination will allow, from the most mundane (such as comic books and titillating sex and violence magazines) to esoteric journals on jazz, poetry, folk art, and classical drama.

Books also seem, on the surface, to be a primary medium for an elite audience, useful more for education and art than for entertainment. But books also have entertainment uses. The paperback revolution has brought the book to the economic level of mass audiences, which has allowed books to be used for popular entertainment ranging from best-selling gothic romances to such entertainment as *The Joy of Sex.*

SUMMARY

Art and entertainment have always been closely entwined in Western civilization, and contemporary critics often fail to recognize those works of entertainment that will have lasting cultural value and will stand the test of time and eventually be considered as works of art.

In the mass media, popular culture and entertainment are influenced by the constant demand for more and more content and the limited creative potential to produce high-quality work. It usually takes time for media artists to produce good work and time for the audiences to acquire the taste for and the ability to appreciate new popular art. Without doubt, popular taste and media content have a symbiotic relationship, and the two improve in concert. The tension among media artists, their mediart, and audiences is natural, because audiences are trained by those artists to seek quality entertainment in the popular arts. This is essential because the audience is the economic patron of mediart.

Obviously, there are levels of quality of media content just as there are disagreements as to what is just entertaining and what has artistic merit. Traditionally, we have talked about lowbrow, middlebrow, and highbrow art, with the media's contribution relegated to the lowest level. But a more objective approach would be to evaluate content by medium, technique, function, and success of the approach used. Elitists are often disappointed in the ways that audiences vote with their dollars. But there is considerable historical evidence that people do support quality when they recognize it in their cultural democracy of entertainment.

Americans use the media as means of play and recreation in periods of leisure. Because of the stress and labor of the workplace, people need entertainment, and the entertainment they learn to like is what they consume. Nearly all media content—whether news, analysis, persuasion, education, or advertising—is part and parcel of the entertainment process. Entertainment is the *overlaid* function, and all electronic and print media provide a variety of content that has entertainment value. Some of it will eventually come to be considered the art of our time.

BIBLIOGRAPHY

Arts for Young Audiences: An ACT Handbook. Newtonville, Mass.: Action for Children's Television, 1982.

Cable and Children: An ACT Handbook. Newtonville, Mass.: Action for Children's Television, 1981.

Cantor, Muriel G. *Prime-Time Television: Content and Control.* Beverly Hills, Calif.: Sage, 1980.

Castleman, Harry, and Walter J. Podrazik. *Watching T.V.: Four Decades of American Television.* New York: McGraw-Hill, 1982.

Cosell, Howard. *I Never Played the Game.* New York: Morrow, 1985.

De Franco, Ellen B. *TV On/Off: Better Family Use of Television.* Santa Monica, Calif.: Goodyear, 1980.

Grote, David. *The End of Comedy: The Sit-Com and the Comedic Tradition.* Hamden, Conn.: Shoe String Press, 1983.

Himmelstein, Hal. *On the Small Screen: New Approaches in Television and Video Criticism.* New York: Praeger, 1981.

Johnson, Jerome, and James S. Ettema. *Positive Images: Breaking Stereotypes with Children's Television.* Beverly Hills, Calif.: Sage, 1982.

Kaminsky, Stuart M., and Jeffery H. Mahan. *American Television Genres.* Chicago: Nelson Hall, 1985.

Madsen, Alex. *"Sixty Minutes:" The Power and the Politics of America's Most Popular TV News Show.* New York. Dodd, Mead, 1984.

Patton, Phil. *Razzle Dazzle: The Curious Marriage of Television and Football*. New York: Dial Press, 1984.

Postman, Neil. *Amusing Ourselves to Death: Public Discourse in the Age of Show Business*. New York: Viking Press, 1985.

Real, Michael J. *Mass Mediated Culture*. Englewood Cliffs, N.J.: Prentice-Hall, 1977.

Tannebaum, Percy H., ed. *The Entertainment Functions of Television*. Hillsdale, N.J.: Erlbaum, 1980.

Toll, Robert C. *The Entertainment Machine: American Show Business in the Twentieth Century*. New York: Oxford University Press, 1982.

Turrow, Joseph. *Entertainment, Education, and the Hard Sell: Three Decades of Network Children's Television*. New York: Praeger, 1981.

————. *Media Industries: The Production of News and Entertainment*. New York: Longman, 1984.

Williams, Martin. *TV: The Casual Art*. New York: Oxford University Press, 1982.

PART III

How Does Mass Communication Work?

15

Communicators

When Fred Hirsch graduated from Ithaca College 14 years ago with a degree in communication, he immediately set out for New York City to climb the broadcast network ladder. Hirsch is still in broadcasting, but rather than being one of many radio newspeople at NBC, CBS, or ABC, he is the chief reporter and announcer at radio station WDME in Dover-Foxcroft, Maine. As the *Wall Street Journal* reported his story, Hirsch is the station's business manager, advertising salesperson, and promoter. He also cleans the station's bathroom. Hirsch does not mind all these duties because he *owns* the station. Fred Hirsch is a communicator.

The process of communication starts with a communicator. The mass communicator, however, differs significantly from the individual communicator in interpersonal communication. When messages are exchanged on a person-to-person basis, the sender and receiver are individual entities. In mass communication, the receiver may be flesh and blood, but an individual sender is more myth than reality.

The communicator, or sender, in mass communication rarely acts alone. Even Fred Hirsch is only the visible portion of a vast and complex network of people, Many people, not simply those we actually see or hear, help shape the media message. A mass communicator is somewhat like the conductor of a symphony orchestra. One message comes from many sources, and while the conductor may represent the orchestra, he or she is not the only communicator responsible for the message sent.

When Mike Wallace appears as a correspondent on "60 Minutes," for example, the audience may assume that Wallace is the person responsible

Figure 15.1 At home at radio station WDME in Dover-Foxcroft, Maine, station owners Vickie and Fred Hirsch represent the many individual communicators who make up part of the conglomerate mass communicator. (Photo: Courtesy Fred Hirsch.)

for the story. Actually, Wallace is primarily a performer on a program written and edited by many others, including its executive producer, Don Hewitt. Indeed, the general rule in TV news is that the longer the broadcast, the smaller the role of the on-camera correspondent.

In turn, the people who are called correspondents—Mike Wallace, Diane Sawyer, Morley Safer, Harry Reasoner, and Ed Bradley—often serve more as performers. They conduct the major on-camera interviews but do not participate in much of the research on their stories and frequently do not write their own scripts. Given the system, it could scarcely be otherwise. An average story for "60 Minutes" takes a producer six to eight weeks to complete, and each "60 Minutes" correspondent appears on three stories every four weeks.

"It's quite apparent that we can't do all, or even a lion's share of the reporting," says Wallace, who is generally credited with doing more of his own reporting than most. Wallace says that he serves an editor's role on his stories—reading material as it comes in, suggesting interviews, and

Figure 15.2 Mike Wallace represents the performing dimension of "60 Minutes," communicating the stories and often the words of other mass communicators, such as reporters and writers. (Photo: Courtesy CBS News.)

talking with the producer about the direction of the story. "By the time you arrive at the filming stage, you're pretty well prepared," he adds.

Along with several colleagues, Wallace points out that television is a collaborative process by nature. "I love the process of working with a producer and a camera crew and an editor. That's what television always was, and always will be, and I think in general the system works well."[1]

Therefore, even though Fred Hirsch and Mike Wallace are individual media communicators, they function as part of a complex organization. Individuals at times seem to function alone as mass communicators. The animated films of Norman McLaren, for example, are essentially the work of one individual. Because of McLaren's association with the Canadian Film Board, however, the characteristics of mass communicators, such as

---

[1] Stephen Zito, "Inside Sixty Minutes," *American Film* 2, no. 3 (December-January 1977): 37.

complexity, specialization, and organization, are evident when his films are marketed, promoted, and exhibited by others.

Performers or public personalities, then, are only one part of the conglomerate mass communicator. Too often, potential broadcasters, filmmakers, or newspaper reporters focus only on performance careers, not recognizing that mass communication is a *process* that goes beyond *performance*. Although performers are highly visible role models, they are often unrealistic or limited role models. Students of mass communication must recognize the vast network of media communicators that extends beyond performers.

A good example of this is Tom Brokaw, anchor for ''NBC Nightly News.'' Brokaw, in a recent interview, said:

> I love what I'm doing—who wouldn't? There's no heavy lifting, the hours are good, the pay is excellent. But the truth is, of my three titles—Anchorman, Managing Editor of NBC Nightly News, and Reporter—the one that means the most to me is Reporter. You can't be effective as an anchor unless you get out from behind the desk.
>
> I didn't get into journalism to put on make up and read out loud. If television hadn't been invented I'd be working as a newspaperman. I like being a reporter. I'm still excited when I get on to a good story. I like going face to face with people. I want to see events first hand, get the smell and feel of what's happening. There's nothing quite like it. And if you bring those same instincts to the anchor job, well, I think it shows.[2]

Brokaw is not unique in his feelings or in his multiple communicator roles. Most radio news directors spend more time gathering and reporting news, while their counterparts in television spend more time managing their operations, according to a survey conducted by the Radio-Television News Directors Association. The survey reports that 53 percent of the TV news directors questioned said that they spend more time as managers than as journalists, while 8 percent of radio news directors surveyed spend more time as managers.

THE CHARACTERISTICS
OF THE MASS COMMUNICATOR

Many features characterize the mass communicator in the United States.

Competitiveness

One of the most significant characteristics of the mass communicator is competitiveness. Mass communicators compete intensely for audiences and spend huge amounts of money to reach those audiences. In interper-

---

[2] Advertisement, *Electronic Media*, 21 March 1985, 19.

sonal communication, individuals compete for the attention of another person. Parents of small children are especially aware of this as they try to separate messages from the "I was talking first" cacophony. A busy signal on the telephone suggests communicator competition. All of this is minor, however, compared with the intense competition among mass communicators.

Competitiveness exists primarily because the media are trying to reach as large an audience (within geographical, socioeconomic, demographic, and such guidelines) as possible. The three national TV networks go head to head for essentially the same audience. Witness the intense competition among the three network evening news programs. As part of the conglomerate communicator of these programs, Peter Jennings, Tom Brokaw, and Dan Rather are, in fact, competing with one another to communicate with the largest audience possible. In the summer of 1986, *The Karate Kid II* and *Ruthless People* competed for the largest share of box-office revenues. *Time* and *Newsweek* compete for the larger circulation figures. Madonna competes with Sheena Easton for the larger number of records sold and most often played on radio.

This competition is fueled, of course, by media economics, in which the mass media also compete for advertising, subscription, and consumer dollars. Of course, in media systems that are essentially state-owned monopolies, such as in the Soviet Union and China, competition is not a significant communicator characteristic.

In order to measure this competitiveness accurately, the American mass media system relies on companies, such as A. C. Nielsen and the Audit Bureau of Circulation, to research the comparative standing of programs, magazines, advertisements, and networks. Competition, then, in mass communication is a major force that has great impact on the communicator.

Size and Complexity

Size and complexity are also important mass communicator characteristics. Successful mass communicators gain the opportunity to speak out; their weaker competitors lose that opportunity. The economic necessity to reach large audiences in order to survive normally requires a large organization. Size in this context requires some clarification, however. Certainly, Fred Hirsch's radio station is not large. The average TV station in the United States employs only 60 full-time employees. Of the approximately 1,800 book publishers in the United States, only 350 have more than 20 employees. Nevertheless, all media organizations, regardless of their internal size and structure, rely on networks of specialized people and organizations. Hirsch's radio station, for example, makes use of the vast resources and staff of the Associated Press news service. The smallest book publisher employs artists, copy editors, and other editorial personnel on a free-lance

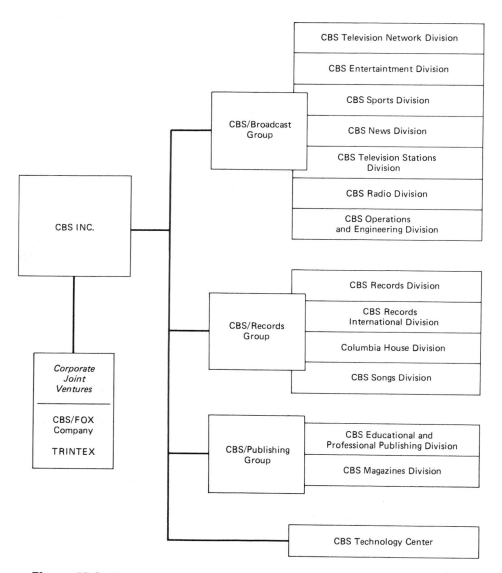

Figure 15.3 This chart illustrates the corporate and organizational complexity of CBS, Inc., yet another part of the mass communicator concept.

basis. Small newspapers use temporary reporters, called stringers, in the field. While not part of a paper's full-time staff, these people are a necessary part of the organization.

Complexity and size are closely related in mass media organizations. As size increases, complexity emerges. A large daily newspaper has many separate divisions, among them reporting, editorial, advertising, circulation, promotion, research, personnel, production, and management, to handle its work. CBS is known primarily as a TV network. But as Figure 15.3 indicates, the CBS/Broadcast Group is only one of three groups that include CBS/Records Group and CBS/Publishing Group. The Broadcast Group itself has seven subdivisions.

The number of people who receive on-screen credit for a motion picture can run into the hundreds. The 1986 movie *Ruthless People* had three directors and four writers. Behind the screen (or off) are thousands of other communicators, such as distributors, exhibitors, and promoters.

Industrialization

Competitiveness, complexity, and size form the base from which several other common mass communicator features emerge. Industrialization is perhaps the most obvious characteristic. A glance at the stock-market section of a newspaper reveals the extent of industrialization in the mass media. Many mass communication organizations are part of large industrial conglomerates. The National Broadcasting Company (NBC) is a small part of a corporate giant, the Radio Corporation of America (RCA), which, in turn, is owned by an even larger company, General Electric (GE). Almost all major film studios are subsidiaries of larger corporations. Gulf & Western owns Paramount; Warner Brothers films are a product of Kinney Leisure Services; and Columbia Pictures is owned by Coca-Cola. Traditionally, motion-picture studios were identified with their production executives—Harry Cohn of Columbia, L. B. Mayer and Irving Thalberg of MGM, Darryl Zanuck of Fox, and Jack Warner of Warner Brothers—or with the major stars in their pictures, who were employees under long-term contract. Today, motion-picture stars not only move easily among major studios, but often form their own companies, becoming conglomerate communicators in their own right. Studio production heads have been replaced by bankers, investment counselors, and corporate CEOs.

Book publishers are conglomerates with many different imprints: Random House is owned by Newhouse and within Random House are Vintage, Pantheon, Knopf, Ballantine, Villiard, and Times Books. Brown is part of the Time, Inc., media family. Most daily newspapers are part of large newspaper chains: Gannett, Newhouse, and Knight-Ridder are some examples. As with motion pictures, dominant personalities of print media, such as William Randolph Hearst, Henry Luce (of Time, Inc.), Joseph Pulitzer, and William Allen White, have been replaced by the less-well-known communicators associated with the major newspaper chains. To be sure, some editors, such as Ben Bradlee of the *Washington Post*, continue to function as public personalities, but the majority of newspaper editors are less interested in their public image and more concerned about their managerial style and productivity.

Specialization

Specialization is a mass communicator characteristic that represents internal fragmentation. This fragmentation is perhaps nowhere more apparent than in the motion-picture industry. Feature films usually credit between 50 and 60 people with performing the jobs required to produce a motion picture. Many of these jobs are subdivided by trade unions. For example, painters may include a foreman, a color mixer, a sign writer, and a marbelizer. An organizational chart of a typical daily newspaper reveals about two dozen areas of specialization, including three different subunits under advertising: display, national, and classified advertising. The photography department may have as many as 20 photographers, each one specializing in a different aspect of the job.

Representation

Still another mass communicator characteristic is representation. Representation is basically an external fragmentation of the mass communicator. Mass communicators have become so complex and must deal with so many different audiences that they often find it impossible to contact and make arrangements with all the individuals and organizations necessary to a smooth functioning of the organization. Mass communicator representatives include talent agents, managers, unions, program distributors, broadcast station representatives, and music-licensing services.

The impact of these characteristics on the mass communicator and, in turn, on the content is significant. The content and messages of mass communication are rarely the work of one individual. The *auteur* theory in motion pictures and the by-line concept in print journalism are attempts to create for some media content a feeling and sense of individual control. But, in fact, media messages are essentially *products* of a complex communication system that is manipulated and massaged by many people. As a result, the rhetoric of mass media is a corporate rhetoric, one shaped by economic competition. The "sequel syndrome" so common in the motion-picture industry is a good example of how economic competition fosters a corporate rhetoric based on repetition of a successful format—for example, *Rocky, Rocky II, Rocky III, Rocky IV*, ad infinitum. Critics of mass media content point to the negative consequences that intense economic competition has for mass communicators—lack of originality, reliance on "safe" themes, imitation, outright plagiarism, and the like.

THE BROADCAST MEDIA

The radio and TV industries have three basic groups of communicators: networks, independent production companies, and local stations. Within each group are individual communicators who perform a variety of tasks.

Networks

Networks are organizations that provide TV programming and a limited supply of radio news and special-information services. On network television, the idea for a program or a program series can, and often does, originate outside the network. By the time most programs or series are broadcast, however, they have come in contact with and have been influenced by many network people, all the way from stagehand to the chief executive of the network.

Production Companies

Today, the three major TV networks create few programs and concentrate on broadcasting news, sports, and some documentaries. Ninety percent of all TV network prime-time entertainment comes from program-production companies or package agencies working in conjunction with network programmers. The function of the package agency is to develop a program or a program series. Package agencies employ writers, producers, actors, and technical personnel. This team of creators does everything short of broadcasting the program. Some production companies produce a pilot program independently and then attempt to sell a series to a network on the basis of the pilot. A more common practice is to produce a feature-film pilot, with financial and creative support provided by the network on which the series is expected to appear. Showcases for this material have been developed by the networks, such as ABC's "Movie of the Week" and NBC's "World Premiere Movie." Package agencies also produce material directly for syndication on local TV stations. "Wheel of Fortune" and "Jeopardy" are sold on a station-by-station basis rather than to the network.

As the telecommunication delivery system has expanded into cable, videodisc, videocassette, and satellite transmission, the number of video communicators has increased. Despite changes in the way content is delivered to audiences, however, the nature of the video communicator does not change.

Although individual communicators vary from program to program, the process of production is similar for all programs. A writer creates a script, writing not only the performers' lines, but also descriptions of what the viewer will see. A producer takes the script and assembles a creative staff to produce the show. A director coordinates the artistic efforts of the actors and technicians, including editors, camera operators, soundpeople, set designers, and musicians. The performers add another dimension as they work with the total company.

Television-program syndicators are also broadcast communicators. They are both passive and active senders. They are passive to the extent that they take off-network programs or feature motion pictures and sell them to individual stations in a package. They do not sell programs as such, but merely the right to show the programs. They do not create programs, but simply distribute them. Some of the major program syndicators are the three networks and many of the package agencies, such as Viacom, which distributes such programs as "The Twilight Zone" and "The Cosby Show." Distribution is normally done by mail. In what is known in the industry as *bicycling*, each station, after airing a particular program, sends it to the next customer.

Local Stations

A local TV station generally employs its own staff to produce local programs. Staff sizes range from over 100 at major-market stations to fewer than 20 at smaller organizations. Figure 15.4 illustrates the organizational structure of a typical large TV station. Even large stations rely on outside senders, such as the phonograph industry, jingle-package agencies, syndicators, and the networks, for most of their program material. "Romper Room," for example, is a syndicated creative idea produced by local stations under guidelines established by the syndicator, which trains the local teachers who appear in the series.

Radio stations vary greatly in staff size. In New York, for example, WABC has over 50 employees, but more than half of all AM and FM stations employ fewer than 11 full-time people.

At the local level, radio stations depend on three outside creators for the bulk of their content: (1) the recording industry, which includes artists who write, arrange, and perform popular music and recording engineers who mix sound tracks to produce a master tape; (2) jingle-package companies, such as Music Makers of New York, which produce such items as station-break announcements, weather spots, and station identifications; and (3) format syndicators, which package and distribute specific music and news/information formats. The need to reach the right audience and attract the maximum possible number of listeners has led to extensive program-formula design in local radio. For a number of years, top 40 was one of the few formats for local radio; today, over 50 major formats exist. These formats are often the product of format syndicators. The major work of a format syndicator is the creation of what is referred to as a "customized sound hour."

Customized sound hours are designed for each format to ensure consistency and compatibility on the local-station level. The format is matched to the station in tempo, style, music mix, announcing, promos, news, weather, and commercial load. Audience and market research and analysis are conducted by syndicators before implementing a particular format.

Format-programming packages include hundreds of hours of music, as well as breaks, promos, and station identifications by major market announcers. Customized identity elements, such as jingles and other special format features, are made available by the majority of syndicators.

To stay in step with the ever-changing marketplace, syndicators routinely update the programming they provide to their subscribers. Many subscribers receive over 100 updates annually.

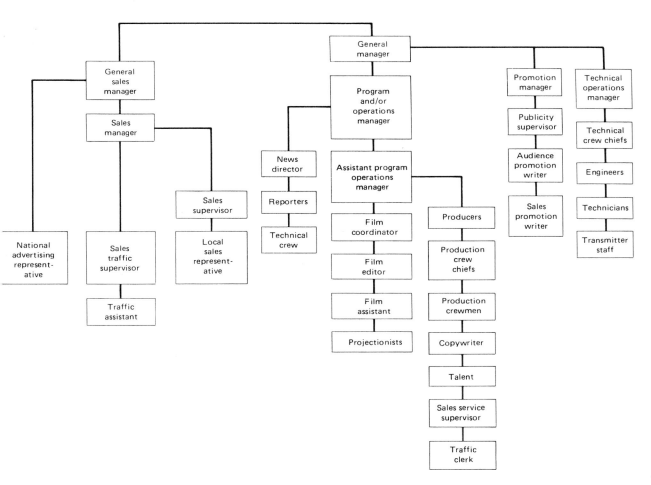

Figure 15.4 This organizational chart of a typical large-market television station illustrates yet another dimension of the conglomerate mass communicator. Radio stations, although somewhat less complex, still contain many of these same structural parts.

Syndicators assist stations during the installation and implementation stage of a format and train operators and other station personnel. Comprehensive operations manuals are provided to ensure proper format procedures. Such services add additional complexity and structure to the local station and, more important, further obscure the sense of an individual communicator.

One of the most significant local-station communicators in radio is the program director (PD). PDs supervise and, in effect, regulate all aspects of a station's programming. In addition to working closely with various disc jockeys and announcers, the PD pays careful attention to the general nature and quality of other ingredients. Music is, of course, of paramount importance. Songs must fit the format, and the quality of the artistry and the audio mix must meet certain criteria. A substandard musical arrangement or a disc with poor fidelity detracts from the station's sound. Jingles and promos must effectively establish the tone and tenor of the format, or they have the reverse effect of their intended purpose. Commercials, too, must be compatible with the program elements that surround them.

In all, the program director scrutinizes every program component to keep the station true to form. The PD helps maintain consistency. Erratic programming in today's highly competitive marketplace is tantamount to directing listeners to other stations.

Despite the increasing influence of format syndicators, radio still retains some attributes of a personal medium through the presence of the disc jockey, who is the bulwark of local-radio programming. The disc jockey represents the individual thread that weaves together the material supplied by other creative people. Often, his or her individuality is a major force in the station's popularity. Like the music, the role of the air personality is carefully designed. A good announcer sets the pace—he or she is the

Figure 15.5 Disc jockeys like Richard Neer of WNEW-FM, contribute a personal quality to the radio mass communicator. (Photo: Courtesy WNEW-FM.)

spirit of a radio station. The disc jockey provides the nonmusical muscle and showcases the product. For most radio stations, the disc jockey remains a key element in creating and executing the appropriate atmosphere for the desired audience. Today, with increased fragmentation and similar play lists on competing stations, the importance of personality is once again being stressed.

The announcer must develop a rapport with the audience. He or she must sound like a "real person," must speak the language of the listener. The day of the contrived, hype announcer has passed. Good disc jockeys possess an understanding of their audiences and the audiences' life styles. Their overriding message to the listener must be, "I'm one of you."

Undeniably, high-profile, identifiable personalities are an important element in cultivating listeners' loyalty to a station. Certain formats, notably talk shows, rely totally on the appeal of the personality. In most cases, morning radio also mandates a high-profile announcer. In certain formats, such as album-oriented rock (AOR), however, the air personality must not eclipse the music, which is the absolute "star" of the radio station. The announcer must complement the music, not dominate it. Again, this is a function of a particular format.

MOTION PICTURES

The communicator in motion pictures assumes many of the characteristics and performs many of the functions of the broadcaster. Indeed, the amount of TV production done by motion-picture studios adds to this similarity. Basically, the role of motion-picture communicators is not as complex as that of broadcast communicators because of the absence of such elements as networks and thousands of individual stations. Although theaters serve as the local exhibition outlet for film production, they are primarily passive outlets as contrasted with the more active involvement of stations in broadcast production.

Motion pictures have grown enormously in terms of production complexity. In the early twentieth century, production involved few people. Often one man—a Chaplin, a Keaton, or a Lloyd—conceived an idea, wrote the script, directed the film, and played the leading role. Only a camera operator and a few extras were needed. The emergence of studios in the 1920s changed this pattern. Huge organizations were built to produce an assembly-line product. Thousands of people became involved with the making of one motion picture.

The communicator role in motion pictures is perhaps the most specialized in all the mass media. Figure 15.6 reveals some of the major and minor communicators involved in the production of a feature motion picture. Each person has a specialized task. The producer is an organizer, creating a structure in which other communicators can work effectively. The screenwriter produces a working film script. The film editor reviews the raw footage from the director and assembles the film into a meaningful form. The director has overall artistic control of the film's actual production.

Motion-picture credits are becoming more specialized than ever. *Star Trek II: The Wrath of Khan*, for example, credited Marc Okrand for "Vulcan translation" and Thaine Morris for "pyrotechnics." *Dragonslayer* had a "Latin adviser," a "magic adviser," and several "dragon movers." *Creepshow* had "roach wranglers" to handle its 25,000 cockroaches.

Some Hollywood movies today have technical staffs six or eight times as large as their casts. Only 20 actors got their names on the screen for *Star Trek II*, but 127 behind-the-scenes personnel were credited. *Raiders of the Lost Ark* cited 232 technicians, with such esoteric specialites as computer engineering and electronic-systems design; *Tron* more than matched its 44 actors and stuntmen with nearly 300 people whose faces did not appear on the screen.

The credit lists have lengthened largely because of the sophisticated special-effects movies that have poured out since *Star Wars*. No longer is it enough to have a gaffer (the head electrician), a best boy (the gaffer's right-hand man), and a number of grips (the equivalent of stagehands). New categories, such as synthevision technology, computer-image choreography, and object digitizing, are evidence of the computer-generated imagery that is increasingly a part of moviemaking.

In addition, communicator complexity has increased because most major movie studios have become parts of large industrial conglomerates. No longer is the motion picture communicator a single studio with hundreds of departments and divisions. Instead, the overlay of an industrial conglomerate has created new levels of corporate structure that must be considered. Gulf & Western is the corporate parent of Paramount Pictures. In addition to Paramount, Gulf & Western operates Famous Music, Inc.; Desilu; Esquire, Inc.; Simon and Schuster; Madison Square Garden Corporation; and several other entertainment-based enterprises.

In the late 1960s, a relaxation of union rules governing the participation of various crafts in filmmaking permitted films to be made by fewer people. Such films as *Easy Rider* (1969) and *Billy Jack* (1971) were written, directed, and performed by small groups of people and formed what many regarded as a new wave in American film. For years, we had the individualistic (*auteur*) films of foreign directors like Ingmar Bergman, François Truffaut, and Akira Kurosawa. In this country, the experimental films of Andy Warhol, Jonas Mekas, and Kenneth Anger often involved little more than the creator and strips of film.

But major motion pictures, such as *Indiana Jones and the Temple of Doom* (1984), *Out of Africa* (1985), and *Top Gun* (1986), illustrate that American films are still the product of many people working together. The real change in motion pictures has been the deemphasis of the studio and the elimination of many elements of general studio overhead that at times

CAST

Heywood Floyd	Roy Scheider
Walter Curnow	John Lithgow
Tanya Kirbuk	Helen Mirren
R. Chandra	Bob Balaban
Dave Bowman	Keir Dullea
HAL 9000	Douglas Rain
Caroline Floyd	Madolyn Smith
Dimitri Moisevitch	Dana Elcar
Christopher Floyd	Taliesin Jaffe
Victor Milson	James McEachin
Betty Fernandez	Mary Jo Deschanel
Maxim Brailovsky	Elya Baskin
Vladimir Rudenko	Savely Kramarov
Vasali Orlov	Oleg Rudnik
Irina Yakunina	Natasha Shneider
Yuri Svetlanov	Vladimir Skomarovsky
Mikolai Ternovsky	Victor Steinbach
Alexander Kovalev	Jan Triska
Anchorman	Larry Carroll
Jessie Bowman	Herta Ware
Nurse	Cheryl Carter
Hospital Neurosurgeon	Ron Recasner
Dr. Hirsch	Robert Lesser
SAL 9000	Olga Mallsnerd
Commercial Announcers	Delana Michaels, Gene McGarr
Stunt Players	M. James Arnett, Jim Burk,
	Jim Halty, Robert Harman, Freddie Hice,
	John Meier, Gary Morgan, Mic Rodgers

CREDITS

Written for the Screen, Produced and Directed by	Peter Hyams
Based on the Novel by	Arthur C. Clarke
Director of Photography	Peter Hyams
Production Designer	Albert Brenner
Editor	James Mitchell
Visual Effects Supervisor	Richard Edlund
Music	David Shire
Casting by	Penny Perry
Costume Designer	Patricia Norris
Associate Producers	Jonathan A. Zimbert,
	Neil A. Machlis
Unit Production Manager	Neil A. Machlis
First Assistant Director	William S. Beasley
Second Assistant Director	Alan B. Curtiss
Set Decorator	Rick Simpson
Visual Futurist	Syd Mead
Film Editor	Mia Goldman
Assoc. Editors	Joanna Cappuccilli, Ross Albert
First Assistant Editor	Barbara Dunning
Second Assistant Editor	Greg Gerlich
Assistant Editors	Craig Herring, Ann Martin
Makeup Supervision	Michael Westmore
Script Supervisor	Marshall Schlom
Camera Operator	Ralph R. Gerling
Assistant Camerman	Don E. Fauntleroy
Second Asst. Cameraman	Michael Wheeler
Chief Lighting Technician	John Baron
Key Grip	Tom May
Still Photographer	Bruce McBroom
Production Illustrator	Sherman Labby
Sound Design	Dale Strumpell
Production Sound Mixer	Gene Cantamessa
Boom Man	Raul Bruce
Rerecording Mixers	Michael J. Kohut, C.A.S.,
	Aaron Rochin, C.A.S.,
	Carlos deLarios, C.A.S., Ray O'Reilly, C.A.S.
Supervising Sound Editor	Richard L. Anderson
Sound Editors	Warren Hamilton,
	David Stone, Michael J. Benavente,
	Donald Flick, James Christopher
Apprentice Sound Editor	John Pospisil
ADR Editor	Vince Melanori
Music Editor	William J. Saracino
Technical Advisor	Dr. Richard Terrile
Special Effects Supervisor	Henry Millar
Special Effects Assts	Dave Blitstein, Andy Evans
Flying Supervisor	Robert Harman
Hairstylist	Vivian McAteer
Propmaster	Martin Wunderlich
Men's Costume Supervisor	Bruce Walkup
Men's Costumer	Jim Kessler
Women's Costume Supervisor	Nancy McArdle
Transportation Coordinator	Randy Peters
Transportation Captain	Candace Wells
Stunt Coordinator	M. James Arnett
Production Coordinator	Katharine Ann Curtiss
Producer's Secretary	Barbara Allen
Production Controller	Steve Warner
Location Manager	Mario Iscovich
Unit Publicist	Don Levy
Effects Project Administrator	John James Jr.
Graphics	Arthur Gelb
Marketing Director	Elliot Fischoff

Visual Displays and Graphics
by Video-Image

Video Effects Supervisor	Greg McMurry
Video Playback Coordinator	Rhonda Gunner
Video Computer Graphics	Richard E. Hollander
Computer Graphics Supervisor	John C. Wash
Video Technician	Pete Martinez
Production Associate	Steven Jongeward
Marine Technical Advisor	Dr. Jay Sweeney

Entertainment Effects Group, Los Angeles

Visual Effects Art Director	George Jenson
Director of Photography	Dave Stewart
Visual Effects Editor	Conrad Buff
Matte Department Supervisor	Neil Krepela
Mechanical Effects Supervisor	Thaine Morris
Special Projects	Gary Platek
Model Shop Supervisor	Mark Stetson
Optical Supervisor	Mark Vargo
Chief Engineer	Gene Whiteman
Animation Supervisors	Terry Windell,
	Garry Waller
Chief Matte Artist	Matthew Yuricich
Production Advisor	Jim Nelson
Business Manager	Laura Buff
Prod. Supervisors	Michael Kelly, Lynda Lemon
Camera Operators	John Fante, John Lambert,
	Mike Lawler, Bill Neil
Motion Control Technicians	David Hardberger,
	Mike Hoover, Jonathan Seay
Camera Assts.	Clint Palmer, Pete Romano,
	Jody Westheimer, Bess Wiley
Assistant Matte Cameraman	Alan Harding
Still Photographer	Virgil Mirano
Optical Printer Operators	Chuck Cowles,
	Bruno George
Optical Line Up	Phil Barberio,
	Ronald B. Moore, Mary E. Walter
Animators	Peggy Regan,
	Richard Coleman, Eusebio Torres
Technical Animators	Annick Therrien,
	Samuel Recinos, Rebecca Petrulli,
	Margaret Craig-Chang,
	Wendi Fischer, Juniko Moody
Stop Motion	Randall William Cook
Matte Artist	Michelle Moen
Key Effects Man	Bob Spurlock
Key Grips	Pat Van Auken, Ben Haller
Gaffer	Robert Eyslee
Effects Technicians	Bob Cole,
	Robin Kolb, Larz Anderson
Visual Effects Editor	Arthur Repola
Assistant Effects Editors	Jack Hinkle,
	Marty November, Dennis Michelson
Miniatures Crew	Jarek Alfer, David Beasley,
	Gary Bierend, Leslie Ekker, Kent Gebo,
	Bryson Gerard, Patrick McClung,
	Thomas Pahk, Robin Reilly, Milius Romyn,
	Christopher Ross, Dennis Schultz,
	Nicholas Seldon, Tom Silveroli,
	Paul Skylar, Ken Swenson
Miniature Mechanical Effects	Bob Johnston
Chief Moldmaker	David Shwartz
Chief Model Painter	Ron Gress
Starchild Personnel	Jon Alberti,
	Lance Anderson, Jon Berg,
	Tom Culnan, Gunnar Ferdinandsen,
	Mike Hosch, Stuart Ziff
Artistic Consultants	Brent Boates,
	Adolph Schaller
Video Systems	Clark Higgins
Design Engineers	Mark West,
	Mike Bolles, Rick Perkins
Electronics Engineers	Jerry Jeffress,
	Robin Leyden, Bob Wilcox
Software Programmer	Kris Brown,
	Paul Van Kamp
Illustrator	Janet Kusnick
Cinetechnicians	George Polkinghorne,
	Mark Matthew, Ken Dudderar,
	Michael Nims, Joseph Ramos
Lab Technicians	Pat Repola,
	Brad Kuehn, Mike Lehman
Production Associates	Thomas Brown,
	Richard Johnson, Dan Kuhn, Sam Longoria,
	L. Mark Medernach, Laurel Walter
Production Accountant	Claire Wilson
Accountants	Kayte Westheimer,
	Leslie Falkinburg, Kim Ybiernas
Apprentice Matte Artist	Tanya Lowe
Addit. Miniatures Personnel	Adam Gelbart,
	George Pryor, Bob Wilson,
	Cynthia Czuchaj, Leslie Stetson
Prod. Administration	Jill Allen, Jamie Jardine,
	Mary Mason, Terry Platek
Digital Jupiter Simulation	Digital Productions
Addit. Display Material	Bo Gehring Associates
Prod. Assts.	Carl Brodene, Allen Cappuccilli,
	Dan Hutten, Brian Lee, Guy Marsden,
	Jon Schreiber, Harry Zimmerman
Projectionist	Don McLaren

Additional Optical Effects by Cinema Research

Filmed with a Louma Crane by Panavision, Inc.

The producers gratefully acknowledge the
following for their assistance:

The Very Large Array Radio Telescope,
an operating activity of the National Radio
Astronomy Observatory, which is sponsored
by the National Science Foundation

Marineland, Rancho Palos Verdes, California
Panasonic
Sheraton Hotels
Pan American Airlines
Ford Motor Company
Sanyo
3M Company
Adidas
Physio Control
Mag Instruments
Yamaha International
Lightning Sculpture by Bill Parker
Huffy
Carrera
Apple Computers, Inc.
Convergence Corporation
Calma G.C. Co.
Heartrate Incorp.
AT&T Systems
Aquarium World

Also Sprach Zarathustra!
by Richard Strauss
Lux Aeterna
by György Ligeti
Performed by
The North German Radio Chorus
Conducted by Helmut Franz
Courtesy of Deutsche Grammophon
a division of Polygram Classics

Electronic Music Produced by
Craig Huxley and David Shire
Synthesizer Programmed by Craig Huxley

Filmed in PANAVISION®

Titles and Opticals MGM

Prints in METROCOLOR®

Color Timer	Bob Kaiser

Figure 15.6 These credits for the feature motion picture *2010* demonstrate the degree of communicator specialization in the motion-picture industry. (Copyright © 1984 MGM/UA Entertainment Co. All rights reserved.)

cluttered and overburdened a film with too many communicators. However, there is a "down side" to the decline of the studio system. Critics today speak of the new vulnerability of motion-picture directors. They have to find their crew and then train it to their ways, whereas the best studio directors in the old school, such as Anthony Mann or Mitchell Leisen, had the advantage of a unit in which there were only occasional changes of personnel. They also had the studio's paternal administration, the cafeteria, pensions, and producers. From 1943 to 1963, every film that Vincent Minnelli made was at MGM; his decline coincided with the need to scout around town for work.

All those directors who fell by the wayside in the 1960s had been brought up in a system under which the studio carried the weight of hack work on a film. They were essentially free to direct. They had only to envisage the scene and handle the action. They did not struggle with the script, audition actresses, and fight over casting. They did not argue for time and money, negotiate with every actor over terms, worry about lunch for the extras, or have to handle anxious calls from investors in the company. Those tasks fell to the producer, whom the director was able to despise, resent, and blame—if need be.

More often than it might seem, however, directors do the work of producers. Since every film is now set up as a one-time deal, and since most films involve directors far earlier than was the case in the studio era, directors today have to be negotiators, businessmen, and managers.

The motion-picture communicator remains one of the most fascinating and complex media communicators.

THE PRINT MEDIA

For years, the "by-line myth" has dominated the concept of print-media communicators. Many people assume that because one person's name precedes or follows a particular article or story, that person alone is responsible for the content. The stereotyped visions of individual, entrepreneurial newspaper reporters created by such movies as *The Front Page* and *All the President's Men* have contributed greatly to this myth. In reality, the content of a newspaper, magazine, or even book is the result of the collaborative efforts of many individuals.

Print communicators work within large, organized, specialized, competitive, and highly expensive environments. Creative producers of print messages include researcher and reporters, who find basic facts; writers, who assemble material into effective messages; and editors, who create ideas, manage their production, and evaluate the results.

In the jargon of the newspaper profession, legmen are researchers whose main task is to get the facts. They might station themselves at a police headquarters and simply telephone leads into the home office. The reporter is both researcher and writer. In the magazine or book industry, the researcher is often a fact checker who verifies the authenticity of the work of reporters and writers.

Writers play the key creative role in the production of print-media messages. They often are the people with the original ideas, although some magazine and book writers are word technicians who take the ideas of others and dress them in effective language.

The editor—whether copy editor, assignment editor, or managing editor—is more an evaluator of communication than an originator. But editors are part of the sending process to the extent that they supervise the entire package of communication through imaginative management and evaluation.

The masthead from *Time* (Figure 15.7) indicates the many mass communicators who work on each issue. Like that of other mass media, the process of print mass communication involves hundreds of people.

THE RECORDING INDUSTRY

The recording industry also demonstrates many mass communicator characteristics. The performer on a record is just one of many communicators in the recording industry. For example, on the album *We Salute You* by the group AC/DC, in addition to the performers, the following communicators are listed: producer, recording engineer, mixing engineer, three assistant engineers, and master disc engineer. Similar and more extensive credits grace most record album covers. In addition, the conglomerate effect has been felt in the recording industry.

As Figure 15.8 indicates, ABBA was not only a hugely popular Swedish pop group but also part of a corporate conglomerate. The chart, prepared by *Variety*, is based on a rough diagram sketched by Lars Dahlin, vice president of Polar International AB, the holding company jointly owned by ABBA members and their manager, Stig Anderson. The chart doesn't necessarily reflect each and every one of ABBA and Anderson's holdings, but gives a representative sampling of the organization's scope.

THE INDIVIDUAL COMMUNICATOR

Given the enormous industrial complexity of today's mass media, the mass communicator has difficulty being an individualist. Nevertheless, complexity and size do not diminish the contribution of the many specialists who make up the conglomerate communicator. A corporate structure is not some sort of infernal machine that runs itself. It is run by individuals who are vital parts of the communication process at all levels. At times, the human dimension of even something as vast and complex as network

TIME

Founders: BRITON HADDEN 1898-1929 HENRY R. LUCE 1898-1967

Editor-in-Chief: Henry Anatole Grunwald
Chairman and Chief Executive Officer: J. Richard Munro
President and Chief Operating Officer: N.J. Nicholas Jr.
Chairman of the Executive Committee: Ralph P. Davidson
Corporate Editor: Ray Cave

MAGAZINE GROUP
President: Reginald K. Brack Jr.
Chairman: John A. Meyers
Group Publishers: S. Christopher Meigher III, Robert L. Miller

MANAGING EDITOR: Jason McManus
EXECUTIVE EDITORS: Edward L. Jamieson, Ronald Kriss
ASSISTANT MANAGING EDITORS: Richard Duncan, John Elson, Henry Muller
INTERNATIONAL EDITOR: Karsten Prager
SCIENCES EDITOR: Leon Jaroff
ADMINISTRATIVE EDITOR: Leah Shanks Gordon
SENIOR EDITORS: Charles P. Alexander, David Brand, Martha Duffy, William F. Ewald, José M. Ferrer III, Russ Hoyle, Walter Isaacson, Stefan Kanfer, James Kelly, Donald Morrison, Christopher Porterfield, George M. Taber, Robert T. Zintl
ART DIRECTOR: Rudolph Hoglund
CHIEF OF RESEARCH: Betty Satterwhite Sutter
OPERATIONS DIRECTOR: Gérard C. Lelièvre
PICTURE EDITOR: Arnold H. Drapkin
SENIOR WRITERS: Ezra Bowen, George J. Church, Gerald Clarke, Richard Corliss, Otto Friedrich, Paul Gray, Robert Hughes, Gregory Jaynes, John Leo, Ed Magnuson, Lance Morrow, Frederick Painton, Roger Rosenblatt, R.Z. Sheppard, William E. Smith, Frank Trippett
ASSOCIATE EDITORS: Patricia Blake, Tom Callahan, John S. DeMott, William R. Doerner, John Greenwald, William A. Henry III, Marguerite Johnson, Stephen Koepp, Richard N. Ostling, Jay D. Palmer, Sue Raffety, J.D. Reed, George Russell, Thomas A. Sancton, Martha Smilgis, Richard Stengel, Anastasia Toufexis, Claudia Wallis, Michael Walsh, Richard Zoglin
STAFF WRITERS: Janice Castro, Edward W. Desmond, Philip Elmer-DeWitt, Guy D. Garcia, Lloyd Garrison, Richard Lacayo, Jacob V. Lamar Jr., Michael D. Lemonick, Sara C. Medina, Jamie Murphy, Barbara Rudolph, Michael S. Serrill, Jill Smolowe, Wayne Svoboda, Susan Tifft, Nancy Traver, Amy Wilentz
CONTRIBUTORS: Kurt Andersen, Jay Cocks, Thomas Griffith, Pico Iyer, Charles Krauthammer, Melvin Maddocks, Jane O'Reilly, Kenneth M. Pierce, Richard Schickel, Mimi Sheraton, John Skow
REPORTER-RESEARCHERS: Rosemary Byrnes, Ursula Nadasdy de Gallo, Brigid O'Hara-Forster, Victoria Salès (Department Heads); Audrey Ball, Bernard Baumohl, Peggy T. Berman, Val Castronovo, Nancy McD. Chase, Oscar Chiang, Georgia Harbison, Michael P. Harris, Anne Hopkins, Naushad S. Mehta, Nancy Newman, Jeanne-Marie North, Susan M. Reed, Elizabeth Rudulph, Alain L. Sanders, Zona Sparks, William Tynan, Susanne Washburn (Senior Staff); Wilmer Ames Jr., David Bjerklie, Elizabeth L. Bland, Kathleen Brady, Richard Bruns, Robert I. Burger, Howard G. Chua-Eoan, Tom Curry, Nelida Gonzalez Cutler, Sally B. Donnelly, Andrea Dorfman, Helen Sen Doyle, David Ellis, Kathryn Jackson Fallon, Mary McC. Fernandez, Cassie T. Furgurson, John Edward Gallagher, Nancy R. Gibbs, Lois Gilman, Edward M. Gomez, Christine Gorman, Rodman Griffin, D. Blake Hallanan, Janice M. Horowitz, Jeanette Isaac, Carol A. Johmann, Sinting Lai, Daniel S. Levy, JoAnn Lum, Katherine Mihok, Emily Mitchell, Lawrence Mondi, Christine Morgan, Adrianne Jucius Navon, Jeannie Park, Michael Quinn, Barry Rehfeld, Theodore P. Roth, Megan Rutherford, Andrea Sachs, David Seideman, David E. Thigpen, Sidney Urquhart, Jane Van Tassel, Elsie B. Washington, Leslie Whitaker, Linda Williams, Linda Young
ADMINISTRATION: Daniel M. Rubin, Donald Sweet
CORRESPONDENTS: Henry Muller (Chief); B. William Mader, John F. Stacks (Deputies) **Washington Contributing Editor:** Hugh Sidey **National Political Correspondent:** Laurence I. Barrett
Senior Correspondents: Benjamin W. Cate, Frederick Ungeheuer
Washington: Strobe Talbott, Ann Blackman, David Aikman, David Beckwith, Gisela Bolte, Jay Branegan, Ricardo Chavira, Anne Constable, Patricia Delaney, Michael Duffy, Hays Gorey, David Halevy, Jerry Hannifin, Neil MacNeil, Johanna McGeary, Barrett Seaman, Elaine Shannon, Alessandra Stanley, Dick Thompson, Bruce van Voorst **New York:** Bonnie Angelo, Joseph N. Boyce, Sandra Burton, Mary Cronin, Jennifer Hull, Thomas McCarroll, Jeanne McDowell, Raji Samghabadi **Boston:** Robert Ajemian, Joelle Attinger, Melissa Ludtke, Lawrence Malkin **Chicago:** Jack E. White, Barbara Dolan, Lee Griggs, Harry Kelly, J. Madeleine Nash, Elizabeth Taylor **Detroit:** William J. Mitchell **Atlanta:** Joseph J. Kane, B. Russell Leavitt, Don Winbush **Houston:** Richard Woodbury **Miami:** Marcia Gauger **Los Angeles:** Dan Goodgame, Jonathan Beaty, Elaine Dutka, Jon D. Hull, Edwin M. Reingold, Michael Riley, James Willwerth, Denise Worrell **San Francisco:** Paul A. Witteman, Cristina Garcia
Europe: Christopher Redman **London:** Christopher Ogden, Steven Holmes **Paris:** Jordan Bonfante, B.J. Phillips, Adam Zagorin **Bonn:** William McWhirter, John Kohan **Rome:** Sam Allis, Erik Amfitheatrof, Cathy Booth **Eastern Europe:** Kenneth W. Banta **Moscow:** James O. Jackson **Jerusalem:** Roland Flamini **Cairo:** Dean Fischer, David S. Jackson **Nairobi:** James Wilde **Johannesburg:** Bruce W. Nelan **New Delhi:** Ross H. Munro **Bangkok:** Dean Brelis **Peking:** Richard Hornik **Hong Kong:** William Stewart, Bing W. Wong **Tokyo:** Barry Hillenbrand, Yukinori Ishikawa **Melbourne:** John Dunn **Ottawa:** Peter Stoler **Caribbean:** Bernard Diederich **Mexico City:** John Borrell, John Moody **Managua:** Laura López **Rio de Janeiro:** Gavin Scott
Administration: Suzanne Davis, Emily Friedrich, Demetra Kosters, Susan Lynd **News Desks:** Frances Fiorino, Waits L. May III, Jacalyn McConnell, David Richardson, Susanna Mary Schrobsdorff, Pamela H. Thompson, Diana Tollerson, Joanne Waugh, Ann Drury Wellford, Jean R. White, Mary Wormley, Arturo Yáñez
ART: Nigel Holmes (Executive Director); Dorothy D. Chapman, Anthony J. Libardi, Irene Ramp (Deputies); Arthur Hochstein, Leonard S. Levine, Billy Powers, Barbara Wilhelm (Assistant Directors); Angel Ackemyer, James Elsis, Carol March (Designers); Nickolas Kalamaras **Layout:** Steve Conley (Chief); John P. Dowd (Deputy); Stefano Arata, Joseph Aslaender, David Drapkin, Jay Petrow, Nomi Silverman, Kenneth Smith, Eugene Tick **Maps and Charts:** Paul J. Pugliese (Chief); Joe Lertola, E. Noel McCoy, Nino Telak, Deborah L. Wells
Special Projects: Tom Bentkowski
PHOTOGRAPHY: Michele Stephenson (Deputy); Peter J. Kellner, Rose Keyser, Julia Richer (Assistant Editors); Linda D. Vartoogian, Helen Eisenberg (Administration); Carmine Ercolano (Operations) **Researchers:** Dorothy Affa, Martha Bardach, Richard L. Boeth, Anne Callahan, Mary-Anne Golon, Paula Hornak Kellner, Gary Roberts, Carol Saner, Nancy Smith-Alam, Robert B. Stevens, Mary Themo **Photographers:** Eddie Adams, Terry Ashe, William Campbell, Sahm Doherty, Michael Evans, Rudi Frey, Dirck Halstead, Peter Jordan, Shelly Katz, David Hume Kennerly, Neil Leifer, Ben Martin, Harry Mattison, Mark Meyer, Ralph Morse, Robin Moyer, Carl Mydans, James Nachtwey, Matthew Naythons, Stephen Northup, Bill Pierce, David Rubinger, Antonio Suarez, Ted Thai, Diana Walker
MAKEUP: Charlotte J. Quiggle (Chief); Eugene F. Coyle (International); Leonard Schulman (Deputy); Peter J. McGullam
OPERATIONS: Sue Aitkin (Deputy Director); Susan L. Blair (Copy Chief); Stephen F. Demeter (Systems Manager); Gail Music (Production Manager); Judith Anne Paul, Joseph J. Scafidi, Shirley Barden Zimmerman (Deputies); Trang Ba Chuong, Theresa Kelliher, Suzi Romanik, L. Rufino-Armstrong, Lee R. Sparks (Supervisors); Ted Alban, Frances Bander, Robert L. Becker, Minda Bikman, Robert Braine, Bruce Christopher Carr, Silvia Castañeda Contreras, Barbara Collier, Kenneth Collura, Barbara Dudley Davis, Jonathan Elukin, Osmar Escalona, Dora Fairchild, Evelyn Hannon, Garry Hearne, Judith Kales, Sharon Kapnick, Kevin Kelly, Claire Knopf, Agustin Lamboy, Jeannine Laverty, Marcia L. Love, Janet L. Lugo, Peter K. Niceberg, Linda Parker, Maria A. Paul, Lois Rubenstein, Judy Sandra, Lamarr Tsufura, Maitena Z. Viani, Jill Ward, Amelia Weiss
LETTERS: Joan D. Walsh (Chief); Amy Musher (Deputy)
EDITORIAL SERVICES: Christiana Walford (Director); Peter J. Christopoulos, Benjamin Lightman, David E. Trevorrow, Beth Bencini Zarcone

PUBLISHER: Robert L. Miller
Associate Publisher: John J. Crowley Jr.
General Manager: Barbara M. Mrkonic
Assistant to the Publisher: Charles D. Hogan
Business Manager: Allen M. Barr
Public Affairs Director: Steve Cohen
Promotion Director: Katherine R. Erskine
Circulation Director: Katherine M. Bonniwell
Director of Administration: Rose L. Epstein
Production Director: Michael V. Dukmejian
Corporate Production Director: Robert D. McCoach
U.S. ADVERTISING SALES DIRECTOR: Richard Heinemann
Associate Sales Directors: Stephen W. Alexander, Franklin S. Roth

TIME, MARCH 2, 1987

Figure 15.7 As this list of credits illustrates, many individuals, not simply the by-lined writers, collaborate on the content of an issue of *Time*.

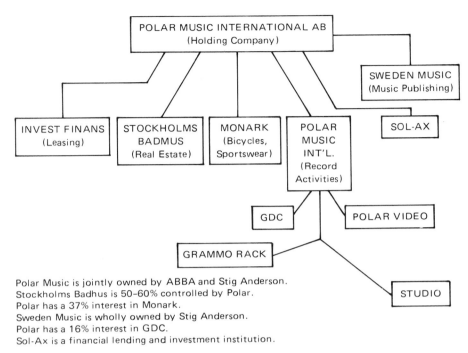

Polar Music is jointly owned by ABBA and Stig Anderson.
Stockholms Badhus is 50–60% controlled by Polar.
Polar has a 37% interest in Monark.
Sweden Music is wholly owned by Stig Anderson.
Polar has a 16% interest in GDC.
Sol-Ax is a financial lending and investment institution.

Figure 15.8 The conglomerate mass communicator is also present in the recording industry. This chart illustrates the corporate complexity of the recording group ABBA.

television rears its individualistic head, often in humorous ways. For example, in February 1979, during the showing of the NBC miniseries "Loose Change," a technician at the network inadvertently switched episodes, substituting Part 3 for Part 2. For 17 minutes, a national audience watched with puzzled expressions a drama that was out of synch with its internal reality.

Essential attributes of individual mass communicators are the abilities to think, to see things accurately, to organize their thoughts quickly, and to express themselves articulately and effectively. Mass communicators have to be curious about the world and about the people in it. Communicators are called on to make judgments, sometimes of vast importance, and they should be able to distinguish the significant from the insignificant, the true from the false. Mass communicators need to have a broad view of the world, but increasingly they must specialize in the communication field. Finally, they must know how to communicate. In mass communication, this seemingly simple act becomes exceedingly complex, requiring many kinds of talents, abilities, and specialties. Above all, the sender must understand and respect the medium in which he or she works.

The training and education necessary to become a part of mass media institutions and the personal attributes of mass communicators are often misunderstood. Many potential mass communicators believe that technical training is the key to understanding the process of mass communication. The technology of mass media often blinds students to the fact that the process of mass communication involves more than pushing a button or flipping a switch and that performers are but a small part of the mass media communicator.

In his book *The Information Machines: Their Impact on Men and Media*, Ben Bagdikian writes about "printed and broadcast news as a corporate enterprise."[3] He says that news is both an intellectual artifact and the product of a bureaucracy. Distinguished journalism, he writes, requires strong individual leadership; yet such journalism is often at odds with the demands of corporate efficiency. In a similar vein, Edward Jay Epstein notes in his excellent study *News from Nowhere: Television and the News:* "Before network news can be properly analyzed as a journalistic enterprise, it is necessary to understand the business enterprise that it is an active part of, and the logic that proceeds from it."[4] Both men point to the basic condition of the mass communicator: the ability and need of the individual to function as part of a complex environment—an environment that is competitive, specialized, usually very large, and very often industrialized.

One must add, of course, that our complex, specialized, and industrialized corporate media enterprises have produced more information and entertainment than any simple, individual, and altruistic effort could achieve. There is both good and bad in the system. But one cannot understand the mass communicator without seeing the individual as part of a much larger organism.

SUMMARY

The process of communication starts with the communicator. In interpersonal communication, however, mass communicators differ significantly from individual communicators. Mass communicators are characterized by (1) competitiveness; (2) size and complexity; (3) industrialization; (4) specialization; and (5) representation. The impact of these characteristics on mass communicators and, in turn, on mass-communication content, is significant. Mass communication messages are rarely the result of one individual. Media messages are essentially products of a complex com-

---

[3] Ben H. Bagdikian, *The Information Machines: Their Impact on Men and the Media* (New York: Harper & Row, 1971), 41.

[4] Edward Jay Epstein, *News from Nowhere: Television and the News* (New York: Random House, 1973), 216.

munication system, manipulated and massaged by many people. As a result, the rhetoric of mass media is a corporate rhetoric, one shaped by economic competition.

Each medium has a variety of communicator types. In broadcasting, there are three basic groups: (1) networks; (2) independent production companies; and (3) local stations. In television, the networks are the primary communicators, with local stations assuming a somewhat secondary role. In radio, local stations are the dominant communicators, backed up by the recording industry, jingle-package companies, and format syndicators. Local radio also has disc jockeys who perform a critical and important role as individual communicators.

The communicator in motion pictures assumes many of the characteristics and performs many of the functions of the broadcaster. The amount of television production done by motion-picture studios adds to this similarity. Basically, however, the role of the motion-picture communicator is not as complex as that of the broadcast communicator because of the absence of such elements as networks and thousands of individual stations. Theaters serve as the local exhibition outlet for film production, but they are primarily passive outlets, contrasted with the more active involvement of stations in broadcast production. Motion pictures have grown enormously in terms of production complexity and employ hundreds of people to produce feature motion pictures.

For years the "by-line myth" has dominated print-media communication. Many people assume that because one person's name precedes or follows a particular article or story, that person alone is responsible for the content. However, print communicators work within large, organized, specialized, competitive, and highly expensive environments. Communicators of print messages include researchers and reporters, writers, editors, managers, and a wide variety of syndicated content services.

The recording industry also demonstrates many mass communicator characteristics. On one album alone, in addition to the artists, there are producers, recording engineers, mixing engineers, assistant engineers, and a variety of artistic and technical communicators.

Given the enormous industrial complexity of today's mass media, the mass communicator has difficulty being an individualist. However, complexity and size do not diminish the contributions of the many specialists who make up the conglomerate communicator. Individuals still operate the mass communication system, and it is important for mass communicators to be well educated and possess a variety of critical personal and professional attributes in order to succeed.

Ultimately, the mass communicator is a combination of individual and corporate influence and impact. It is important for us to recognize the nature of that communicator and the impact that the mass communicator has on content.

BIBLIOGRAPHY

Allman, Paul. *Exploring Careers in Video.* New York: Rosen, 1985.

Blythin, Evan, and Larry A. Samovar. *Career Choices for Students of Communication and Journalism.* New York: Walker, 1985.

———, *Communicating Effectively on Television.* Belmont, Calif.: Wadsworth, 1985.

Collins, J. E. *She Was There: Stories of Pioneering Women Journalists.* New York: Julian Messner, 1980.

Compaine, Benjamin et al. *Who Owns the Media? Concentration of Ownership in the Mass Communication Industry.* 2d ed. White Plains, NY: Knowledge Industry Publications, 1982.

Costello, Marjorie, and Cynthia Katz. *Breaking into Video.* New York: Simon and Schuster, 1985.

Ettema, James S., and Charles D. Whitney, eds. *Individuals in Mass Media Organizations: Creativity and Constraint.* Beverly Hills, Calif.: Sage, 1982.

Grewe-Partsch, M., and G. J. Robinson, eds. *Women, Communication, and Careers.* New York: Sauer, 1980.

Marzolf, M. *Up from the Footnote: A History of Women Journalists.* New York: Hastings House, 1977.

Matusow, Barbara. *The Evening Stars: The Making of the Network News Anchor.* New York: Random House (Ballantine Books), 1984.

Newcomb, Horace, and Robert S. Alley. *The Producer's Medium: Conversations with Creators of American TV.* New York: Oxford University Press, 1983.

Turow, Joseph. *Mass Media Careers.* Chicago: SRA, 1984.

16

Codes: Symbols, Styles, and Formats

Ideas are without existence until they find expression. That is the essence of the art of mass communication.

The authors, journalists, copy editors, and other wordsmiths of the print media use symbols and develop styles within accepted book, newspaper, and magazine formats.

The creative partners in the electronic media use sounds and moving pictures as well as words to give voice to complex ideas, events, and emotions. Only after a message has been coded is there any chance that it will ever be understood and enjoyed, let alone acted on.

THE RELATIONSHIP OF THE CODE, MEDIUM, AND CONTENT

Obviously, the content of mass communication is important, but how the message is put together and is expressed, or coded, is equally as important. And every mass medium has its own unique, idiosyncratic syntax, traditions, and characteristics in terms of symbols, styles, and formats.

The content, the code, and the medium, interact to form the *message unit*. Those three elements are, in effect, stylistically inseparable. It is their interaction that gives rise to excellence or mediocrity. In the hands of expert media teams, this interaction leads to message units that have creative worth, value, and quality.

425

The content, then, must be wedded to the code of a specific medium. Exactly the same content, using the same *medium*, can be radically altered by the code. These three elements form *the message unit*.

1. *Content* is the data, the idea, the substance. It is the *communication*.
2. *Code* is the symbol system. The symbols, styles, and formats used have a significant impact on the content. It is the communication *language*.
3. *Medium* is the organizational structure, the framework on which the ideas are woven. The technology, the tools, the practices, and so forth make each mass medium's expression of the same content different. It is the *organization*.

Each mass medium adds its unique contribution to traditional language structure. The syntax of each medium's symbol system also depends on an audience's past experiences with all other media as well as the one currently in use.

Mass media codes add a new set of symbols to traditional language structure. In other words, books, newspapers, magazines, radio, television, film, and recordings employ new languages. Each codifies reality differently; each makes its own statement in its own way. Mass communication theorist Edmund Carpenter has pointed out that, like theater, film is a visual and verbal medium presented before an audience. Like ballet, film relies heavily on movement and music. Like a novel, film usually presents a narrative that depicts characters in a series of conflicts. Like painting and photography, film is two-dimensional, composed of light and shadow and, sometimes, color. But the ultimate definition of film lies in its unique qualities.

MASS MEDIA CODING SYSTEMS

Communication can occur only when both the mass communicator and the audience share a coding system (symbols, styles, and formats).

Symbols

Symbols are signatures, signs, or tokens that individually or in combination carry meaning between sender and receiver. The alphabet and the words created using its letters are sets of symbols. In film and broadcasting, the coding devices are sounds or images that transmit an idea or emotion. For example, the Scarecrow, Tinman, and Cowardly Lion, Dorothy's compatriots in *The Wizard of Oz*, serve as symbols for intelligence, love, and courage, when rewarded for their heroic deeds with a

Figure 16.1 Perhaps the most beloved symbols of intellect, emotion, and courage in the history of motion pictures are the wonderful bumbling heroes of *The Wizard of Oz.* The characters sing, ''If I only had a brain, a heart, the nerve . . . ,'' which serve as universal symbols that we all recognize and yearn to possess.

diploma, a heart-shaped clock, and a medal. These signs and characters carry meaning far beyond the words they speak. Movie audiences are exposed to, understand, and respond to these symbols emotionally as well as intellectually.

Styles

Styles are characteristic ways of putting symbols together in meaningful patterns. Styles conform to accepted patterns or fashions. Surrealism, a style of painting, influenced film artists, who made movies incorporating Surrealistic images and techniques. ''Miami Vice'' is often accused of being all style and no substance. The costumes, sets, editing techniques, and popular music of this series have developed a way of presenting material more like music videos than traditional police-action television shows. It has style as well as *a style.*

Formats

Formats are the frameworks that house stylistically similar and dissimilar content units. A format is the general plan or structure of a newspaper, magazine, or radio station. Music television (MTV) is tightly formatted in terms of which videos are broadcast, how often, when, and in what order. *Playboy* formats stories, features, and articles as well as putting the monthly "playmate" in the middle of the issue for ease of access and removal. Format shapes the substance of the mass medium in question.

Each medium, then, has unique ways of coding content and structuring reality. The key questions are these: What do the media add to communication codes that are not found in interpersonal exchanges? Are there commonly shared symbols among media and groups of media? Are today's audiences trained to interpret these styles? Is one format more effective than others with certain content?

To begin with, interpersonal communication uses all five senses:

1. We see messages (writing).
2. We hear messages (speech).
3. We touch messages (handshakes).
4. We taste messages (birthday cakes).
5. We smell messages (perfumes).

The mass media tend to depend largely on sight and sound. But the print media use different paper stocks—newsprint (cheap), magazines (slick), books (permanent)—to tactile advantage. Print ads and children's books have "scratch-and-sniff" patches for olfactory experiences. (In the 1950s, "smellovision motion pictures" with scent jets under the seats failed.) Taste remains the least-experienced sense. The edible-food advertisement may be around the next bend in the media road, however.

But for practical purposes, the mass media depend on sight and sound. Only film and television can be seen as well as heard. The print media are deaf; the phonograph and radio are blind.

Despite sensory handicaps, motion pictures offer such visually and aurally powerful experiences that it seems we can taste, smell, and touch scenes in some motion pictures.

CODING IN THE PRINT MEDIA

The content of print is "hard copy." It exists in space, unlike electronic content, which exists in time. Essentially, the print media depend on printed words and still illustrations. The print communicator attempts to make the words flow and the visuals move through a design concept wedded to the ideas being presented.

Linear Progression

The print media depend on a linear progression.

The book is the most rigidly ordered of the print media. Content is paged in exact order to facilitate a detailed analysis of significant amounts of information.

The magazine presents all or a major portion of a specific article or pictorial essay as a unit, with its conclusion often appearing in later portions of the magazine to give the advertising exposure. Magazines are less ordered than books but more ordered than newspapers.

The newspaper is an information supermarket for news shoppers. Readers are attracted by major stories on the front page or the first page of major sections. Readers may or may not finish reading the stories on following pages.

Basic Code Considerations

The style of the printed page has been influenced tremendously by major art movements: Cubism, Futurism, Surrealism, Art Deco, the Bauhaus movement, op art, and the rest. Print designs have their roots as much in graphic design as in information transfer. The overall language of a book, newspaper, or magazine (the *medium*) is to merge language (*code*) with the *content.*

The print-media designer has to fill the surface with meaning and pleasure for the eye of the reader. Whether in books, magazines, or newspapers, the basic "canvas" in print communication is the paper page. This two-dimensional space (height and width) is usually higher than wider and almost never square. In terms of page size, the general upward progression seems to be paperback book to hardback book to magazine to tabloid newspaper to blanket newspaper.

Some books rooted in visual design (art books) logically are larger than magazines, and some magazines go to extremes. *Reader's Digest, Jet,* and *TV Guide* are relatively smaller and *Rolling Stone* and *Billboard* are relatively larger than other magazines.

Page Design: Styles and Formats

Most page design in print is based on a grid principle. The layout for most word-based books is the simplest. Newspapers are the most predictable and magazines the most creative in their design practices. In terms of ideas, books and magazines are flowing space.

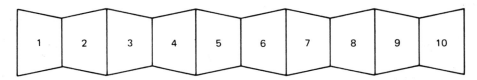

Figure 16.2 Print-media design is based on a format in which each page flows out of and into the preceding and following pages. And these pages tend to have a consistent design in keeping with the style of the newspaper or magazine.

Pages need to be intellectually and visually joined in the minds of the audiences. There is space, then, not only within pages but among pages.

Gatefolds extend the images even more satisfyingly. The most famous example is the *Playboy* "playmate" foldout, which comfortably represents the human form in a three-page vertical or horizontal format.

Someone—perhaps the editor or designer but normally not the reporter or writer—organizes the spatial elements of the page to conform with the overriding intent of the message. The "designer" gives the page.

1. *Symmetry*, whether symmetrical or asymmetrical
2. A sense of *proportion*
3. *Balance*, which gives a feeling of equilibrium
4. *Dimension*, or a sense of depth as well as height and width
5. *Contrast*, which is generated by sizes and shapes, lines and textures, values and colors, and signs and symbols that are recognizable to the reader
6. A sense of *movement*, which gives the eye *visual direction* through the page

All of this takes place within a basic design, called the *grid*, on the surface. This typographic grid is the systematic management of physical space. The surface (the page) is a constant within a given publication. But the arrangement of space is creatively variable within certain constraints: size of type; number and width of columns; number and size of visuals; amount of text in individual units; size of headlines; length of captions; and width of margins.

The Building Blocks of Print

Successful communication occurs because of the choice of words, the logical organization of ideas, and the expression of those ideas with a compatible typeface and layout that contains the right pictures, illustrations, graphs, charts, and tables in position to give visual reinforcement to the total message.

Specifically, the building blocks of print communication are (1) copy

Figure 16.3 These two advertisements illustrate the dynamic use of print space for a company actively involved in the business of communication. The single-page ad (right) utilizes vertical design principles, whereas the double-page ad (above) changes the inherent vertical shape of the magazine to horizontal by using two adjoining pages.

The single-page ad turns white space into black space, which draws the reader's eye into the visual of a man's face as a circuit board and humanizes technical advances. The copy emphasizes the importance that the company places on research. The ad introduces the parent company, Plessey Telecommunications, which, for some readers, is less familiar than Stromberg-Carlson.

The two-page spread draws the eye into the barbed wire in the upper-left-hand corner and then races it along the curved line into the optical fiber, which explodes into the headline "From Barbed Wire to a Beam of Light." The copy in the white space capitalizes on the history and achievements of Stromberg-Carlson as the newest member of the international corporation Plessey Telecommunications.

Both ads seek to impart a positive image of a company in the midst of the hi-tech revolution and its own corporate change. (Reprinted by permission of Stromberg-Carlson.)

set in columns; (2) headlines, headings, and titles; (3) photographs and illustrations; (4) charts, graphs, and tables; (5) captions; and (6) margins and white space.

Copy. Print media organize copy in columns because columns make the page easier to read and give it visual rhythm. Columns also allow for horizontal as well as vertical ads. The copy is built out of letters into words into sentences into paragraphs into pages into articles in newspapers and magazines and chapters in books.

The *word* is a "learned" combination of letters, which when spelled correctly serve as a symbol for an idea or a thing. The *line* is an optical arrangement of words with a spatial potential of less than to more than one sentence. The *sentence* is an action statement of words that normally includes a subject and verb. The *paragraph* is a complete idea, except in editorials and historical romances. The *column* is a series of ordered lines with width and height, which are the essential copy blocks and the central style element of the printed page.

Headlines, Headings, and Titles. Titles, headings, and headlines draw the eye's attention to and stimulate the mind's involvement with the information unit. They are the "come-on" for the material they announce. Headlines summarize and analyze the content of the story. They set a mood or tone for the piece. They also index the page for the reader.

Photographs and Illustrations. The key elements of a visual are size; cropping; position; bordered or bled; physical relationship to the copy format; intellectual and emotional relationship to the words; physical relationship to other visuals on the page; and direction in which they force the eye.

In any printed story, the purpose of the illustrations is to help carry the information load. The ideas presented by the visual must help the reader understand the content. The visual pleasure of a photograph must be a secondary consideration.

Charts, Graphs, and Tables. In a descending order of effectiveness, the chart is best; the graph is better; the table is good. All three graphic displays must present the minimum data and, if necessary, break down the data into multiple charts rather than one table (*simplicity*), force the eye to help the brain reach the conclusion (*effectiveness*), and isolate the major points from the lesser points (*clarity*).

Captions. The caption must be more than a label. Somewhere (and the closer to the visual, the better) the caption must explain or justify the visual if the visual is not self-explanatory or self-justifying. The problem with caption content is that it tends to be ignored by readers; points made in the caption often go unnoticed.

Margins and White Space. Blank areas set off and highlight all the other elements. Margins and white space are critical in most print-media designs.

Special Visual Displays

Print media use specific visual displays to aid the reader's satisfaction with the content.

1. The *title, logo,* and *masthead* identify the source. The *slogan* defines the focus.
2. The *table of contents* in books, magazines, and newspapers serves as a general guidepost. The *index* in books, periodical guides, and newspaper reference systems provides detailed access.
3. The *dateline* adds a historical footnote.
4. The *cover* provides the basic statement of purpose, the identification mark (the logo), the visual trademark (because cover design is based on graphic decisions), and the headlines. The best covers are simple, but when complexity is needed, the cover format must make the ideas easy to handle. The cover must be a visual greeting.

Type

Unquestionably, type is the single most important creative element in the design of print materials. The selection of type available is extremely large and getting larger.

Type is a tone of voice—the vocal quality of the silent eye. Headlines raise the voice; but shouting must be used sparingly, or it will be heard rather than listened to. One of the main principles in selecting the type for *Mass Media V* was readability. Will the pages be able to be read quickly and clearly? The type face used to set *Mass Media V* is Palatino. It has a no-nonsense, up-front, scholarly voice. The following examples illustrate the impact that type and design have on meaning.

Have you ever seen the word *1ne?* Do you understand what *1ne* means? Would it help to see that word in relation to similar ideas coded the same way? Look at the following list.

1ne
2wo
3hree
4our
5ive
6ix
7even
8ight
9ine
10n

Only in a series does this list have meaning. Alone, each line is meaningless, and so the type design has an "intellectual" flavor. Type elements include:

CAPITAL LETTERS
lowercase letters
1 2 3 4 5 6 (numbers)
P.u,n;c't:u?a(t''i''o-n) marks!
$+ - \div \times$ math signs
———————————— lines
ornamentation
Space   s p a c e d   s p a c i n g
Dir
    e
     c
      t
       i
        o
         n

Individual pieces of type or letters have shape, SIZE, **weight**, WIDTH, and *slope*.

1. Shape is the essential design of the face.
2. SIZE refers to measurement of height—for most purposes, from 6 points to 72 points. A point is about 1/72 inch.
3. **Weight** is the thickness of the stroke.
4. WIDTH is the horizontal space the letter takes up.
5. *Slope* is the angle, or lean, of the letter in italic, bold italic, or oblique form.

All creative designs and decisions in print are for reader satisfaction—and perhaps for writer, editor, publisher, and designer satisfaction as well. Legibility, instant communication, clarity, and simplicity lead to understanding and retention.

Individual Print Media

As Marshall McLuhan and others have pointed out, when writing was introduced, it did not simply record oral language; it was an entirely new language. It utilized an alphabet as its code. Nevertheless, bits and pieces of alphabets are meaningless in themselves. Only when these components are strung out in a line in a specific order can meaning be created.

Books. The book is basically an extension of the alphabetized code with an even more uniform linear order. Using this linear order, a book's code proceeds from subject to verb to object, from sentence to sentence, from paragraph to paragraph, from chapter to chapter. Events take place one after the other in books, rather than all at once, as they often happen. A football play involves an explosion of simultaneous action that books cannot adequately describe. To do so, a book must restructure the reality in linear form. Books present an organized, logical progression of words and pictures in a word-ordered world.

Because of its coded form, the book is an individual medium generally read silently and alone. A book is usually conceived of as a "serious" mass medium with a definite author or authority. The content is generally placed in some sequential order, either narrative, descriptive, or chronological. Thus a book tends to be read in a standard progression rather than selectively, as are most magazines and newspapers. The code by which a book is structured also enables the audience to consume content at its own pace, even to reread portions of the content. A book therefore can deal with complex ideas and plots involving many issues or people; its language and code are best able of those of the print media to handle this complexity effectively.

Newspapers. Instead of a line-by-line development of an idea, in newspapers there is an explosion of headlines and stories, all of which are juxtaposed and competing for attention. The front pages from the *New York Times*, the *Daily News*, and *USA Today* give some idea of this simultaneity of ideas. They also suggest that code systems can be manipulated in different ways to reach different readers with different information. The *Daily News* is coded to attract a different reader from the *New York Times* reader and to accommodate the kinds of news it prints. *USA Today* has redesigned the newspaper to fit Americans' new information life style, which seems to survive on "headline news." The colorful design style of *USA Today* uses extensive visuals as well as color photos and graphs and charts to illustrate the capsule news style. The overall newspaper code does not require se-

Figure 16.4 The front page of the *New York Times* is dominated by the major story of the day, but also contains coverage of a variety of other news. Banners and headlines draw the attention of the reader to the story in the standard, or blanket, page size format of this paper. The style of the *New York Times* is rather staid visually compared with the styles of many of its competitors. (Copyright © 1987 by the New York Times Company. Reprinted by permission.)

Figure 16.5 In contrast to the *New York Times,* the tabloid-page-size *Daily News* shouts at our eyes, galvanizes our attention, and focuses our mind on the story of the moment. This loud visual approach trumpets the brassy news style to come on the pages and in stories that follow. (Copyright © 1987 by the New York News, Inc. Reprinted by permission.)

Figure 16.6 *USA Today* is a national newspaper influenced by broadcasting "headline-news services." It does not cover stories or issues in-depth but offers succinct reports in a visually arresting and colorful style. *USA Today* is having considerable impact on the layout and display of news in many local newspapers. (Copyright 1987, USA TODAY. Reprinted by permission. USA TODAY and its associated graphics are federally registered trademarks of Gannett Co., Inc. Used by permission. All rights reserved.)

quential use but encourages selective reading by the audience. Through a balanced page make-up using multicolumn headlines with stories developed vertically beneath the headlines, the newspaper gives readers a choice.

Other noticeable code characteristics are evident in the newspaper. The inverted-pyramid style of writing a story is one. With this coding style, the important information is given first. Less important items follow in an order of descending importance. The reader can stop anywhere and still grasp the essence of the story. The editor can cut the story easily at any point without destroying its meaning.

Short paragraphs and narrow columns are also characteristic of newspaper codes. The format of the newspaper and the audience dictate this. Newspaper columns are narrow because a short line is easier to read than a long one. Short paragraphs are easier to read than long ones and aid readers in assessing meaning. By breaking up a story, short paragraphs permit an audience to skim and read selectively.

Another newspaper-code characteristic is the use of banners and headlines in different type sizes. Headlines in different sizes perform two functions: they indicate the importance of the articles; and they give the reader a quick summary of the contents.

This coding process and its characteristics—inverted-pyramid story structure, narrow columns, short sentences and paragraphs, and headlines in different type sizes—extend naturally from the way people read newspapers. They do not generally sit down with a newspaper for hours; instead, they read selectively for short periods of time on the subway, in the office, or over breakfast. Few people read a newspaper from front page to back page. Some people read only one or two sections, such as sports or the comics, the front page, or the women's section. Newspaper codes are a natural outgrowth of the uses that readers make of the medium.

Magazines. Magazines follow several formats that are dissimilar to that of the newspaper. Instead of presenting many stories to the reader simultaneously, magazines publish articles in a sequential plan according to the publication's philosophy. Most magazines print a table of contents, which demonstrates their use of sequential organization. On the page, however, magazines adopt a different style, demonstrating the creative use of juxtaposition—one story versus another, advertisements versus stories, photographs versus print, and color versus black-and-white.

Traditionally, the magazine reader makes five choices:

1. A reader who is familiar with the magazine will turn directly to *Time*'s movie reviews or whatever else has priority in his or her use of that issue.
2. If the cover of *Newsweek* instigated the purchase, the reader will often go directly to the cover story.

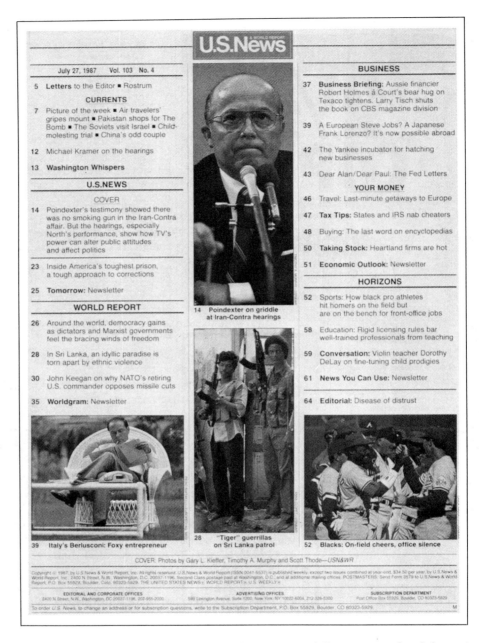

Figure 16.7 *U.S. News & World Report* is a "born-again" news magazine. It has recently jazzed up its visual style to compete with *Time* and *Newsweek*. Although it does not cover "soft news" (theater, literature, television, and films), *U.S. News* has shed its once-rigid, "no-nonsense" page make-up. It is full of color photos and graphic designs. News is defined narrowly on this Contents page: (1) U.S. News, (2) World Report, (3) Business, and (4) Horizons. However, the visual displays hint not only of the importance of the coverage, but also of the pleasure of becoming informed. (Copyright © 1987 U.S. News & World Report Inc. Reprinted by permission.)

Figure 16.8 *Time* has a writing style all its own—chatty, slick, and fun to read. Over one-quarter of *Time's* stories cover soft-news issues: people, science, law, medicine, art, show business, books, and sports. *Time* remains the most styled, if not the most stylish, of the three news magazines. (Copyright © 1987 Time Inc. All rights reserved. Reprinted by permission from TIME.)

3. The "professional" reader (researcher) will focus on the table of contents of *U.S. News & World Report*.
4. With a magazine structured around visuals, the reader will head straight for the centerfold in *Playboy*.
5. The reader who is "killing time" on an airplane or in an office or at the supermarket check-out line will riffle through *People* until something catches his or her eye and is read to fill the time.

In magazines, single pages are usually vertical, and the spread (two facing pages) is horizontal. But both should be laid out horizontally to get the best and most pleasing visual impression. In effect, layout breaks pages down into horizontal modules.

Because of the specialized nature of magazines, several design-code observations are important.

1. Although each issue's cover is unique, cover design is the visual signature of most periodicals.
2. Each issue has an overriding visual design, but special articles demand individual creative identity.

Figure 16.9 The covers of *Newsweek* remain photo-oriented, but designs also creep onto its covers. *Newsweek* is the most newspaper-like of the three major news magazines, perhaps because its parent company is in the newspaper business (the *Washington Post*). *Newsweek* is much closer to *Time* than to *U.S. News & World Report*, in terms of both its style and its coverage. It is strongly visual in terms of its format and the stories it covers. (Copyright © 1987 by Newsweek Inc. All Rights Reserved. Reprinted by permission.)

3. Pictorial features offer limitless possibilities and are an art form in and of themselves.
4. The typeface becomes the fabric of the periodical and creates an overall gray scale, or visual tone.
5. Lines and decorative elements (borders, indentations, and such) serve as fences to separate some ideas and as glue to join others.

Again, much of the particular code system comes from the kind of readership and the way the reader uses the magazine.

CODING IN THE ELECTRONIC MEDIA

The electronic media can be split into two combinations:

1. *Aural media.* Radio and sound recording are completely dependent on sound.
2. *Audiovisual media.* Motion pictures and television use all the sound techniques of aural media, all the design capabilities of print, and movement.

The Building Blocks of Sound

Sound is paramount in aural media, and in audiovisual media, sound must be wedded to the visuals. Orson Welles's training in radio and theater brought an aural dimension to *Citizen Kane* that has reverberated in films over the past 40 years. Sound is at least as important as sight in creating illusions and realities in motion pictures.

Essentially, sound can be categorized as (1) voice, (2) music, (3) sound effects, and (4) silence.

Voice. The voice can be that of singer (record), announcer (radio), actor (film), or narrator-commentator (television). All four media, of course, use all four vocal entities.

Figure 16.10 *Citizen Kane* is an audiovisual masterpiece. This motion picture's images and sounds remain as effective as they were when Orson Welles "raised Kane" more than 45 years ago. The beauty of the film is that its visual and aural techniques complement each other and advance the dramatic intent of the plot and theme. Orson Welles as Charles Foster Kane stands in front of his larger-than-life campaign poster at a political rally that becomes immense and yet rings hollow because of the sound techniques used. In this scene, the images and sounds contradict each other to dramatic effect. (Photo: Movie Star News, Courtesy of RKO Studios.)

Music. The music can be vocal or instrumental. The uses of music in mass media drama include

1. Main-title music over credits, which prepares the audience for the film as an overture does in musical theater
2. Music to identify characters, time period, and place
3. Music to support action
4. Music to establish mood
5. Music to state themes
6. Music to reinforce the visual style

Bernard Herrmann's score for *Psycho* does it all. It literally controls the emotions of the members of the audience and makes them fear for their lives. It is the "music," not Norman Bates's "mother," that slashes at the audience. It meets and exceeds every criteria for the film score: it is the mood, the action, the theme, and the characters. If you have the opportunity to view *Psycho* without sound, the point will be driven home.

The kinds of music used for backgrounds in film and TV drama are as varied as music itself. But film scores may well be the "classical" music of the twentieth century. Certainly, electronic music and modern symphonic scores have found their intellectual haven in motion-picture art.

Sound Effects. *Star Wars* revolutionized sound even more than it did special visual effects. Sound effects can be local, identified visually; background, accepted environmental source; and artificial, unique aural identity, as in *Star Wars's* lasers, spaceships, and so on.

Silence. The tension created by silence is often more effective than jarring sound. The film *2001: A Space Odyssey* is a textbook on the uses of silence.

The Building Blocks of Sight

All the visual techniques in television and film are built around *movement*, because both movies and television are *motion* pictures. The basic principles of still composition—balance, symmetry, line, value, shape, texture, color, dimension, contrast, and the rest—are developed around the basic concepts of movement.

There are essentially two classifications, or elements, in telecommunication and film communication.

1. *Intrashot elements.* This is movement within the shot and includes movement of the camera; movement of actors, animals, and things; and movement of the background.
2. *Intershot elements.* This is movement created by editing shots together. Literally, a visual rhythm is created between shots.

Figure 16.11 The *Star Wars* trilogy rethought the use of sound as well as special visual effects. The sound effects—from the voices of "droids" and aliens to the buzzes of light sabers and the roars of machines—do much to create the new space of *Star Wars, The Empire Strikes Back,* and *Return of the Jedi.* Here, our heroes are being brought to the grotesque Jabba the Hutt by his minions. We believe because we hear as well as see these delightful galactic adventures. (Museum of Modern Art/Film Stills Archive, Courtesy of 20th Century-Fox.)

Intrashot Elements. Composition is the overriding visual concern of every shot, and each movement in a shot of camera, actor, or background requires a recomposition of that shot. Several basic elements have an impact on the composition.

The *frame shape* has essentially three formats:

1. The regular film: screen ratio, which is 1.33:1, or 1.33 units of width to each unit of height.
2. Wide-screen formats, which range from 1.65:1 to 2.55:1.
3. Television has the 1.33:1 ratio, but the rounded corners of the tube and the scanning system have an impact on the composition of theatrical releases shown on television.

Camera angles determine the viewpoint and area seen by the audience. Basically, *objective* camera angles are the least emotional views of an unseen observer; *subjective* camera angles offer a personal viewpoint and involve the audience emotionally; *point-of-view* camera angles offer a specific character's viewpoint (as though the camera were the actor's eyes).

Subject size depends on the distance from the camera and on the lens used. In descending order, they are extreme long shot, long shot, medium shot, close-up, and extreme close-up.

The shots also involve more than one subject, and so there are two-shots (two characters), three-shots, and group shots. The shots also have foreground and background treatments.

The lens used also has an impact on size. Lenses fall into three general groups: *wide-angle* lenses see more than the eye can; *telephoto* lenses see less than the eye can and are used for close-ups at long distance (as is a telescope); *normal* lenses approximate the eye. These three lenses have fixed focal lengths. The zoom lens has a variable focal length and approximates visually all three of the above lenses and incorporates them with zooming in or out.

The depth of field (area in focus) also varies with each lens. It is greater with wide-angle (short) lenses than with telephoto (long) lenses.

Figure 16.12 Although some viewers of Stanley Kubrick's filmed version of William Makepeace Thackeray's novel *Barry Lyndon* were disappointed with its pace, few could be unimpressed with its dazzling visual beauty. The cinematography duplicates the look of eighteenth-century oil and watercolor paintings. Lenses and film stock were used that allow scenes to be shot by candlelight, so that the screen is filled with the passionate orange hues of that time period. Emotional qualities are generated that words alone cannot convey. Film's unique coding capabilities expanded the sensory experience of *Barry Lyndon.* (Photo: Museum of Modern Art/Film Stills Archive, Courtesy Warner Brothers, Inc.)

Lighting is to film what paints are to canvas. The cinematographer paints with four basic lights: the *key light* is the primary light source (the sun or a lamp); the *fill light* softens the effects of the key light by eliminating harsh shadows; the *kicker*, or *backlight*, separates the actors from the background; the *background light* adds depth to the composition.

Film stock is more than the difference between black-and-white and color. It has to do with contrasts (hardness, softness, hues) and the amount of light (speed) and filters and processing.

All these elements contribute to the overriding concern of the cinematographer: composition. The positioning of all the pictorial elements within the frame shape is the paramount consideration in filmmaking. Every shot must be a whole and contribute to the audience's understanding and enjoyment of the film's themes, ideas, and story lines.

Intershot Elements. The second category of movement in film (and television) is the movement created by linking one image to the next. The movement between shots, or intershot movement, is an editorial function. And for many critics, editing is the heart and soul of audiovisual art. A film's ability to be cut is the unique potential of the medium and may well be the most dynamic tool of the filmmaker's creative kit. The manipulation of a succession of visual and aural images generates both a kinetic and an intellectual energy, as well as moving forward the dramatic intent of the story line.

Editing manipulates both *real* time (the clock time the audience spends viewing) and *dramatic* time (the life length of the story and the characters that live the drama). Basically, editing moves the story line and facilitates action. *Continuity editing* is storytelling; it is slower and less frantic than *dynamic editing*, which is used in fast-paced action scenes. In both forms, editing controls time (speeding it up or slowing it down), establishes direction, controls pace and rhythm, generates spatial and emotional relationships of characters and locations, and reveals details of insights that the audience needs to know.

The building blocks of the art of editing are

1. The *frame*, which is a single photographic image (sound films are shot and shown at 24 frames per second).
2. The *shot*, which is an individual moving image or length of film exposed from the time the camera begins running until it ends.
3. The *scene*, which is a dramatic unit in one place at one time; it consists of one or more shots. If either time or place changes, a new scene begins.
4. The *sequence*, which is a major dramatic unit made up of scenes that completes exposition, character development, a theme, or a dramatic action.

Figure 16.13 In "The Odessa-Steps Sequence" from *Potemkin,* director Sergei Eisenstein used dynamic editing to expand time, which enabled him to explore the emotional content of rapidly occurring events. Yet by cutting abruptly from image to image (general to specific, realistic to symbolic, long shot to close-up), he manipulated the rhythm of the film so that the pacing seems to quicken, thereby accentuating the feeling of terror and panic implicit in the narrative. (Photos: Museum of Modern Art/Film Stills Archive.)

Frames, then, are edited into shots, shots into scenes, scenes into sequences, and sequences into films.

Editing "builds" the film, and the editor's function is the critical element in restructuring film and video drama. The editing of a scene must be compelling and coherent because the audience must be both involved and able to understand the film. The editor performs a series of creative steps.

First, he or she selects a specific shot from those available. Normally, only 10 to 20 percent of the available footage appears on the screen. Second, the selected shots are arranged so that the story line moves forward meaningfully. Third, each component shot is modified into a length that emphasizes the dramatic tone and action of the film.

The available footage is the raw material of the editor, who follows some general principles and some specific techniques to cut a film. For example, the techniques of editing includes *cuts* (one shot changes instantaneously to the next), *dissolves* (one shot gradually recedes as another gradually replaces it), *wipes* (a new shot shoves another off the screen vertically, horizontally, or diagonally), and *fades* (a shot goes to or comes from black). Traditionally, cuts are used between shots; dissolves, between scenes; and fades, between sequences. In principle, editing involves *matching* images so that image size, position, and direction match; *cutting* on movement of an actor, an object, or the camera; *using reactions* as well as actions, depending on what is being done versus the impact of that action; *parallel editing*, which keeps the audience up to date on simultaneous actions occurring at different locations. Editing must, of course, always be done so that it keeps the attention of the audience engaged.

As the editor moves from raw footage to rough cut to fine cut, he or she must edit not only image to image and sound to sound, but also image to sound. Synchronization of image and sound is the basic element (and "sync" was the toughest problem to lick in the development of motion pictures).

Visually, the five elements of an art form—line, shape, value, texture, and color—dominate print. Film and television add a sixth element—motion. The illusion of movement in television and film occurs because the eye is unable to see changes in the 525 electronic lines on the TV tube or the 24 still frames per second on the movie screen.

Aurally, the recording studio, with "sweetening" techniques, which improve the dynamics of the sound, and 16, 24, 35, 48, and ad infinitum tracks mixed down, can improve the live performance to an extent that the rock concert substitutes audience participation, "show-biz" staging, and volume for the studio-mixed sound-recording quality.

Although radio drama is in the doldrums, those of us old enough to remember will testify that in its heyday, network radio generated pictures in our minds. The mass media "intensify" visual and aural experiences. Color photography is more intense than color in the "real" world. The media codes generate a hyperreality that today is bigger and better and faster and more intense than ever before. We are willing to suspend belief while watching a fantasy like *Return of the Jedi* or the re-created reality of a docudrama like "Holocaust." Media codes transport us to new levels of experience. Certainly, a level of intense participation exists when the media environment, content, and mass communicator's handling of codes take us into the jungles of Vietnam with the "grunts" in *Platoon* or transport us through the pages of Tolkien's *Hobbit* or capsulate the week in *Sports Illustrated* or rock us to sleep with the newest images in music videos.

Audiences have learned to "decode" new media languages and adjust to new dialects as they emerge. The naïve movie audiences of the early 1900s have grown into a hardware-oriented generation of "film freaks" who want to know how the special effects work as well as experience the story line. Audiences have grown "more literate," which allows the film-maker to expand the lexicon of the medium. Audiences are not getting younger; they are getting better.

Both television and film attempt to fuse *form* and *content*. The form, or code, is neither identical to nor totally different from the content. The filmmaking process, for example, attempts to merge the medium, the code, and the content. This is what makes the creative process such a joy. The media are expanding human language.

SUMMARY

The process of coding in mass communication involves three essential elements: (1) symbols, which stand for things, ideas, and emotions; (2) styles, which are characteristic ways we put symbols together to generate meanings; and (3) formats, which are the overall structures or frameworks that organize mass media content.

Three parts of the HUB Model of Mass Communication interact as the message unit: codes, contents, and the mass media themselves. Since every mass medium is unique, with significantly different coding devices and traditions from any other medium, the same content will be a signifi-cantly different experience, depending on the medium code used to trans-mit the message or messages.

Codes of the print media vary from one another as well as from those of the electronic media. However, there are similarities in terms of the basic building blocks, if not in the ways the building blocks are manipulated. The print media proceed linearly from letter to letter, word to word, para-graph to paragraph, page to page, section to section. Design consider-ations on individual pages involve symmetry, proportion, balance, dimen-sion, contrast, movement. Undoubtedly, type is the key consideration in print coding, but the other building blocks (headlines, photos and illustra-tions, charts and graphs, captions, and margins and white space) are of prime importance in page design.

In the electronic media, sound and movement are added to the tradi-tional art elements (line, shape, value, color, and texture). Sound is of paramount importance in radio and sound recording, but is also an essen-tial element in the talking pictures of television and film. Voices, music, sound effects, and silence contribute to the aural style of a film. The camera, the actors and things, and the background move within a shot, and the total meaning of a scene is expanded by editing shots together in unique patterns. The cinematographer uses a variety of compositional tools: frame shape, angles, subject size, and depth of field, which are controlled by lenses, film stock, and lighting. The editor then builds frames into shots into scenes into sequences into a film.

Audiences have learned to understand media languages as well as their native tongues. The content of the mass media are made magical by the manipulation of each medium's symbols, styles, and formats. There is a language for each mass medium—its code.

BIBLIOGRAPHY

Baskettem, Floyd K., and Jack Sissors. *The Art of Editing.* New York: Macmillan, 1971.

Blum, Richard A. *Television Writing: From Contract to Contract.* 2d ed. Boston: Focal Press, 1984.

Blythin, Evan, and Larry A. Samovar. *Communicating Effectively on Television.* Belmont, Calif.: Wadsworth, 1985.

Bobker, Lee R. *Elements of Film.* New York: Harcourt Brace Jovanovich, 1979.

Breyer, Richard, and Peter Moller. *Making Television Programs: A Professional Approach.* New York: Longman, 1984.

Carlson, Verne, and Sylvia E. Carlson. *Professional Lighting Handbook.* Boston: Focal Press, 1985.

Dymytryk, Edward. *On Film Editing: An Introduction to the Art of Film Construction.* Boston: Focal Press, 1984.

Fielding, Raymond. *The Technique of Special Effects Cinematography.* 4th ed. Boston: Focal Press, 1985.

Kessler, Lauren, and Duncan MacDonald. *When Words Collide: A Journalist's Guide to Grammar and Style.* Belmont, Calif.: Wadsworth, 1984.

Miller, William. *Screenwriting for Narrative Film and Television.* New York: Hastings House, 1980.

O'Donnell, Lewis B. et al. *Modern Radio Production.* Belmont, Calif.: Wadsworth, 1986.

Pellegrino, Ronald. *The Electronic Arts of Sound and Light.* New York: Van Nostrand, 1983.

Routt, Edd et al. *The Radio Format Conundrum.* New York: Hastings House, 1978.

Shelter, Michael D. *Video Tape Editing: Communicating with Pictures and Sound.* Elk Grove Village, Ill.: Swiderski Electronics, 1982.

17

Gatekeepers and Regulators

When a word is "bleeped" off radio or television, do you know who is responsible for censoring it? When you were in your early teens and tried to see an R- or X-rated movie, do you know who kept you out of the theater? When the publisher of *Hustler* is tried in a Georgia courtroom for obscenity, do you know why?

In the first two examples, the media themselves are the censors; in the third example, a local government authority has power to regulate *Hustler*'s sale.

Many people simply assume that the federal government is responsible for these actions. In many national systems, the government *is* the chief censor and regulator of mass media. But in the United States, the government plays a relatively small role in media regulation. In fact, the United States government cannot *censor* the news media. Only local authorities have the right to censor, and the only medium they can censor is the motion picture. Along with other institutions in our society, however, government can apply pressure in some areas of mass communication to regulate and control quantity, quality, and direction.

Although many aspects of our lives are governed by statutes and ordinances, the Founding Fathers felt that certain liberties were sacred to the democratic process—freedom of speech, freedom of worship, freedom to assemble, and freedom of the press. The framers of our Constitution wrote in the First Amendment:

> Congress shall make *no* law respecting an establishment of religion, or prohibiting the free exercise thereof; or abridging the freedom of speech,

or of the press; or the right of the people peaceably to assemble, and to petition the government for a redress of grievances.

That guarantee has made mass media regulation in America different from media laws in most other societies, for few countries have such a sweeping declaration of press and speech freedom. However, it would be a mistake to think that mass media in America are absolutely free from any restraint or regulation.

We can identify six groups that, formally and informally, regulate the process of mass communication: (1) media gatekeepers, (2) government, (3) content source, (4) advertiser, (5) individual consumer, and (6) consumers joined together in pressure groups.

THE MEDIA GATEKEEPER AS REGULATOR

The mass media are regulated by forces inside the media and forces outside the media. Most media regulation starts internally, and media's self-regulation or even self-censorship can often be the most crucial. In fact, the media often submit to self-regulation simply because they do not want to offend their audiences or do not want a public outcry to encourage government to be more restrictive.

The internal regulators are known as media gatekeepers. They are the employees of mass media who exercise final authority over what gets published, broadcast, recorded, filmed, and distributed. They are editors, for the most part: personnel who review the creations and productions of communicators. But they are also directors, producers, publishers, and other managers who exercise final responsibility for the product. Some mass media, particularly the broadcast industry, employ internal censors whose sole responsibility is to review all out-going material to make sure it conforms to standards that those media have adopted for themselves. Gatekeepers can also be lawyers for media organizations who review communication content to make sure that messages will not get the companies into legal trouble, such as their being charged with libel or invasion of privacy.

Mass media organizations and individuals have joined together into associations to protect their rights, collect information, lobby for sympathetic laws, further their interests, and establish uniform codes of conduct to guide individual gatekeepers in performing their internal regulation. For example, newspaper owners, magazine and book publishers, broadcasters, and film producers belong to such associations. In addition to national organizations, such as the American Newspaper Publishers Association, media units often have state, county, or city groups, such as the Maryland–Delaware–D.C. Press Association and the Montgomery County (Maryland) Press Association.

In broadcasting, the National Association of Broadcasters (NAB) lobbies in Congress on behalf of broadcast stations. It also monitors stations' observance of the NAB radio and television codes. In the film industry, the Motion Picture Producers Association (MPPA) has a production-code division, which establishes film ratings (G, PG, PG-13, R, or X) for all films submitted by its members. The Recording Industry Association of America (RIAA) serves as an arbiter of production standards and controls for the sound-recording industry.

Media workers, too, have professional associations. The largest is the Society of Professional Journalists, Sigma Delta Chi, which has both campus chapters (at colleges where journalism and mass communication are taught) and professional chapters (for those working in the media). Other associations represent almost every communication professional, from editors and editorial writers to photographers, public relations people, advertisers, and cartoonists.

These associations were often started in response to public pressures to regulate or restrict media. For example, the comic-book industry, which grew rapidly during World II, found itself after the war facing growing public criticism linking comics to the rise in juvenile delinquency. The attacks led to the establishment of the Association of Comic Magazine Publishers (ACMP) in 1947. A code was drafted to safeguard children from comic books that presented nudity, torture, sadism, and frightening monsters. The code also banned racial, ethnic, and religious slurs; negative marital story lines; ridicule of law officers; profanity; and detailed descriptions of criminal acts. The ACMP later became the Comics Magazine Association of America (CMAA) and developed a 41-point code. By the mid-1980s, 90 percent of industry members were voluntarily submitting materials for code approval, allowing them to display the code seal on their products.

Gatekeepers are not legally obligated to accept codes of conduct that act as regulators of their actions. This is true in the United States more than in most other countries because the First Amendment prevents such codes from being legally binding on the communicator. In Sweden, for example, a journalist can be thrown out of the profession for violating a journalistic standard, but in the United States—since the Constitution guarantees anyone the right to practice journalism—such codes can be used only as voluntary guidelines. Examples of important professional codes are "A Statement of Principles" of the American Society of Newspaper Editors and the "Code of Professional Standards" of the Public Relations Society of America.

Self-censorship has long been an important concept in the motion-picture and broadcast media. A motion-picture code was adopted by the

Figure 17.1 A Statement of Principles, American Society of Newspaper Editors. (Adopted by the ASNE board of directors, Oct. 23, 1975.)

PREAMBLE

The First Amendment, protecting freedom of expression from abridgment by any law, guarantees to the people through their press a constitutional right, and thereby places on newspaper people a particular responsibility.

Thus journalism demands of its practitiones not only industry and knowledge but also the pursuit of a standard of integrity proportionate to the journalist's singular obligation.

To this end the American Society of Newspaper Editors sets forth this Statement of Principles as a standard encouraging the highest ethical and professional performance.

ARTICLE I—RESPONSIBILITY

The primary purpose of gathering and distributing news and opinion is to serve the general welfare by informing the people and enabling them to make judgments on the issues of the time. Newspapermen and women who abuse the power of their professional role for selfish motives or unworthy purposes are faithless to that public trust.

The American press was made free not just to inform or just to serve as a forum for debate but also to bring an independent scrutiny to bear on the forces of power in the society, including the conduct of official power at all levels of government.

ARTICLE II—FREEDOM OF THE PRESS

Freedom of the press belongs to the people. It must be defended against encroachment or assault from any quarter, public or private.

Journalists must be constantly alert to see that the public's business is conducted in public. They must be vigilant against all who would exploit the press for selfish purposes.

ARTICLE III—INDEPENDENCE

Journalists must avoid impropriety and the appearance of impropriety as well as any conflict of interest or the appearance of conflict. They should neither accept anything nor pursue any activity that might compromise or seem to compromise their integrity.

ARTICLE IV—TRUTH AND ACCURACY

Good faith with the reader is the foundation of good journalism. Every effort must be made to assure that the news content is accurate, free from bias and in context, and that all sides are presented fairly. Editorials, analytical articles and commentary should be held to the same standards of accuracy with respect to facts as news reports.

Significant errors of fact, as well as errors of omission, should be corrected promptly and prominently.

ARTICLE V—IMPARTIALITY

To be impartial does not require the press to be unquestioning or to refrain from editorial expression. Sound practice, however, demands a clear distinction for the reader between news reports and opinion. Articles that contain opinion or personal interpretation should be clearly identified.

ARTICLE VI—FAIR PLAY

Journalists should respect the rights of people involved in the news, observe the common standards of decency and stand accountable to the public for the fairness and accuracy of their news reports.

Persons publicly accused should be given the earliest opportunity to respond.

Pledges of confidentiality to news sources must be honored at all costs, and therefore should not be given lightly. Unless there is clear and pressing need to maintain confidences, sources of information should be identified.

These principles are intended to preserve, protect and strengthen the bond of trust and respect between American journalists and the American people, a bond that is essential to sustain the grant of freedom entrusted to both by the nation's founders.

The members of the Radio Television News Directors Association agree that their prime responsibility as newsmen—and that of the broadcasting industry as the collective sponsor of news broadcasting—is to provide to the public they serve a news service as accurate, full and prompt as human integrity and devotion can devise, To that end, they declare their acceptance of the standards of practice here set forth, and their solemn intent to honor them to the limits of their ability.

ARTICLE ONE

The primary purpose of broadcast newsmen—to inform the public of events of importance and appropriate interest in a manner that is accurate and comprehensive—shall override all other purposes.

ARTICLE TWO

Broadcast news presentations shall be designed not only to offer timely and accurate information, but also to present it in the light of relevant circumstances that give it meaning and perspective.

This standard means that news reports, when clarity demands it, will be laid against pertinent factual background; that factors such as race, creed, nationality or prior status will be reported only when they are relevant; that comment or subjective content will be properly identified; and that errors in fact will be promptly acknowledged and corrected.

ARTICLE THREE

Broadcast newsmen shall seek to select material for newscast solely on their evaluation of its merits as news.

This standard means that news will be selected on the criteria of significance, community and regional, relevance, appropriate human interest, service to defined audiences. It excludes sensationalism or misleading emphasis in any form; subservience to external or "interested" efforts to influence news selection and presentation, whether from within the broadcasting industry or from without. It requires that such terms as "bulletin" and "flash" be used only when the character of the news justifies them; that bombastic or misleading descriptions of newsroom facilities and personnel be rejected, along with undue use of sound and visual effects; and that promotional or publicity material be sharply scrutinized before use and identified by source or otherwise when broadcast.

ARTICLE FOUR

Broadcast newsmen shall at all times display humane respect for the dignity, privacy and the well-being of persons with whom the news deals.

ARTICLE FIVE

Broadcast newsmen shall govern their personal lives and such nonprofessional associations as may impinge on their professional activities in a manner that will protect them from conflict of interest, real or apparent.

ARTICLE SIX

Broadcast newsmen shall seek actively to present all news the knowledge of which will serve the public interest, no matter what selfish, uninformed or corrupt efforts attempt to color it, withhold it or prevent its presentation. They shall make constant effort to open doors closed to the reporting of public proceedings with tools appropriate to broadcasting (including cameras and recorders), consistent with the public interest. They acknowledge the newsman's ethic of protection of confidential information and sources, and urge unswerving observation of it except in instances in which it would clearly and unmistakably defy the public interest.

ARTICLE SEVEN

Broadcast newsmen recognize the responsibility borne by broadcasting for informed analysis, comment and editorial opinion on public events and issues. They accept the obligation of broadcasters, for the presentation of such matters by individuals whose competence, experience and judgment qualify them for it.

ARTICLE EIGHT

In court, broadcast newsmen shall conduct themselves with dignity, whether the court is in or our of session. They shall keep broadcast equipment as unobtrusive and silent as possible. Where court facilities are inadequate, pool broadcasts should be arranged.

ARTICLE NINE

In reporting matters that are or may be litigated, the newsman shall avoid practices which would tend to interfere with the right of an individual to a fair trial.

ARTICLE TEN

Broadcast newsmen shall actively censure and seek to prevent violations of these standards, and shall actively encourage their observance by all newsmen, whether of the Radio Television News Directors Association or not.

Figure 17.2 Code of Broadcast News Ethics, Radio Television News Directors Association.

industry in the 1920s in an effort to avert government censorship. The code was extremely restrictive: one could not show on film the udder of a cow, a woman's body in profile, or the inside of a bathroom. But codes tend to reflect public interest, and as Americans became less squeamish about sex in the 1950s and 1960s, administration of the strict movie code became more relaxed. In 1968, the movie industry adopted a more lenient form of voluntary self-censorship, a rating system that allows people to determine for themselves the type of movie they wish to see. G (family), PG (parental guidance), R (restricted to those under age 17 without an accompanying parent), and X (restricted to all under age 17) are ratings that are not required by government but are made by the industry itself.

A recent joke explains the rating system according to hat colors: In a G- or PG-rated movie, the guy in the white hat gets the girl. In an R-rated movie, the guy in the black hat gets the girl. In an X-rated movie, everybody gets the girl. Sometimes the public does not agree with the ratings. When *Indiana Jones and the Temple of Doom* and *Gremlins* were released in 1984, they were rated PG. But critics and parents reacted negatively to the amount of intensity of violence in both films. A new rating, PG-13, was instituted in 1984. It was designed to warn parents to use extra caution in allowing children to see some films that are sexually innocent but contain much violence.

Filmmakers often object to the ratings received by their productions because such ratings can affect box-office receipts, and producers can appeal the rating. The producers of *Ryan's Daughter* threatened to pull out of MPPA when the film was rated R because they said that the rating would limit the audience of the expensive production. Under this pressure, the rating was changed to PG. *Midnight Cowboy*, rated X when it came out in 1969, was re-rated to R without change to the film. *A Clockwork Orange*, originally rated X, became R after a few seconds of violence were cut out. Steven Spielberg's appeal to change the rating of *Poltergeist* from R to PG was granted without any fanfare, but Brian De Palma had to fight long and hard and cut some violent scenes to prevent his *Scarface* from getting an X rating.

In all media, editors play an important gatekeeping function. In some mass media, that function is growing simply because the production process is getting more complex. For example, movie directors use to be careful during the shooting of each scene, and the editor merely had to assemble the footage. Now directors tend to retake scenes dozens of times and shoot far more footage than can ever be used, giving the editor a much more creative role. Editors can affect pacing, atmosphere, and use of reaction shots. They can make a comedy funnier, increase the suspense in a thriller, double the excitement in a war picture. Good editing can enhance a weak film, and poor editing can ruin an otherwise fine picture. The same problems, of course, occur in the print media.

In the broadcast media, the editor may not be as important as the internal censor. Each network, for example, has a division of lawyers and managers who must approve all material in advance. They are the final arbiters of what goes on the air. Prime time is particularly sensitive, and each prime-time show has its own internal censor, who reads scripts, watches dailies—the raw footage of that day's shoot—and can request changes. If a producer is unhappy about a change, he or she can battle it out with the lawyers and managers, but the latter have the last word.

As society changes, the networks change, says NBC's vice president in charge of standards and practices. A TV writer, Dick Guttman, says, "The networks are responding to where the country is going and the fact the public now has an alternative in cable, which is far more explicit."[1] In 1985, Guttman's CBS-TV movie *Passion Flower* was allowed to include 22 minutes of love scenes. Back in the 1960s, CBS censors refused to let the stars of "The Dick Van Dyke Show" sleep together, even though they played a married couple. Twenty-five years later, husbands and wives—as well as lovers—not only share beds, but make passionate love on the air. In a 1985

---

[1] Jefferson Graham, "How Much Vice Can 'Miami' Show," *USA Today*. 3 December 1985, 3D.

Figure 17.3 Media gatekeepers have become much more liberal in their interpretation of public morals in the 1980s. "Hill Street Blues" ushered in an era of more lenient standards, although its first season saw many battles with the network gatekeepers. (Photo: NBC, *USA Today*, Dec. 3, 1985.)

episode of NBC's "Miami Vice," a bare-chested Philip Michael Thomas rolled around in bed with his bare-chested girlfriend, Pam Grier, on prime time.

The networks employ many people to perform the gatekeeping function. NBC's broadcast-standards department numbers more than 40 people. Since television views itself as a family medium, it has usually adopted stricter standards than the movie industry, with the result that as television broadcasts more movies, it has more work to do in censoring various aspects of these movies. In 1976, for example, when CBS showed the movie *Smile*, a satirical comedy about young women embroiled in a California beauty pageant, it had to remove certain scenes and words. A scene in which a plucked chicken gets smooched by hooligans at a fraternal initiation was cut by CBS. The words *sanitary napkin* were censored from a scene in which plumbers are complaining about discarded sanitary napkins clog-

Figure 17.4 "The Equalizer," starring Edward Woodward as a secret agent turned agent of justice, was a bold departure into more explicit sex and violence on prime-time television for CBS, which had conservative standards for its gatekeepers. (Photo: CBS, *USA Today*, Dec. 3, 1985.)

ging the pipes. By the mid-1980s, however, such prudishness would have seemed ridiculous.

In the early 1980s, the so-called family-viewing policy of the NAB provided an interesting example of government interference in professional codes. "Family viewing" was pushed by Congress and the Federal Communications Commission. It stated that prime-time-television periods should be restricted to programs that are appropriate for a general family audience, including children. Hollywood writers, actors, and program producers were upset, claiming that the concept of "family viewing" limited their freedom of expression. A district court in California agreed, ruling that "family viewing" violates the First Amendment and need not be enforced or followed by networks or stations.

THE GOVERNMENT AS REGULATOR

In American society, devoted to the twin freedoms of press and speech, government is the only agency capable of protecting those guarantees of freedom. Most American government regulations, but by no means all, are more concerned with maintaining an environment of free communication and with protecting the individual's rights in the communication process than they are with restricting communication and freedoms.

Freedom of the press is the result of a long struggle for individual rights and freedoms under Anglo-Saxon law. The way was paved by such

Figure 17.5 A drama about incest, "Something about Amelia," broke all the taboos that had been maintained by the gatekeepers at ABC. The success of the show highlighted the changes that had taken place in the public mind. (Photo: Courtesy The Leonard Goldberg Company.)

documents as the Magna Carta of 1215, the Petition of Rights of 1628, the English Bill of Rights of 1689, and the American Declaration of Independence of 1776. In the New World of the American colonies, where both communication and independence were important, freedom of speech and of the press became key elements in the sociopolitical fabric.

The First Amendment to the Constitution does not define the *limits* of freedom. Judicial and legislative decisions have defined the meaning of that amendment, usually in the light of current trends and social conditions. The Constitution, as it is interpreted by the courts and lawmakers, controls the regulators and determines which of their actions are permissible under the American system.

Censorship

Censorship, meaning prior restraint or suppression of communication by the government, has been held to be unconstitutional in all its many forms except one—motion pictures. Government agencies, both local and national, have from time to time attempted to censor communication, sometimes for the best motives. The Minnesota state legislature, for example, passed a "gag law" in the 1920s aimed at restricting newspapers that were "public nuisances," specifically scandal sheets that made scurrilous attacks on the police and minority racial groups. But in its interpretation of the First Amendment, the Supreme Court found this law, as it has most other attempts at censorship, illegal. In another ruling, the Supreme Court struck down a state law that would have imposed a tax *only* on newspapers and other publications. The justices said that taxes imposed on other businesses may also be imposed on newspapers and other publications. But taxes that single out the press can be a potential tool for censorship that abridges freedom of the press.

The famous Pentagon Papers incident in 1971 is another case in point. A multivolume Department of Defense study, entitled *History of U.S. Decisionmaking Process on Viet Nam Policy,* was classified as top secret but was leaked to the press. Both the *New York Times* and the *Washington Post* decided to publish stories and excerpts based on the material in the 47 volumes. The Justice Department obtained a temporary court injunction to prevent publication of the material. Because of its significance, the case quickly went to the Supreme Court. In a 6–3 landmark decision, the Court ruled in favor of the newspapers and freedom of the press.

Although the Court's decision clarified the First Amendment, it did not really broaden the protection of freedom. The newspapers hoped that the Court would rule that the First Amendment guaranteed an *absolute* freedom. In the Pentagon Papers case, however, the Court held that the government had not provided sufficient evidence to justify prior restraint of the publications. This left the door open for courts in the future to decide how much justification the government must provide in order to censor a publication. But the six concurring opinions of the Supreme Court justices gave ample support to the general theory of freedom from prior restraint by the government.

For years, motion pictures have not had this protection. In 1915, the Supreme Court, in the case *Mutual Film Corporation* v. *Industrial Commission of Ohio,* upheld the right of individual states to censor motion pictures on the grounds that they are "a business, pure and simple." They are a "spectacle or show and not such vehicles of thought as to bring them within the press of the country." However, in 1952, a Supreme Court decision changed this ruling somewhat and laid the groundwork for increasing freedom for motion pictures. In the case *Burstyn* v. *Wilson,* which involved the film *The Miracle,* the Supreme Court stated:

> We conclude that expression by means of motion pictures is included within the free speech and free press guarantee of the First and Fourteenth Amendments. To the extent that language in the opinion in the Ohio case is out of harmony with the views here set forth, we no longer adhere to it.

Decisions since then have continually weakened efforts to censor movies. Not a single state now has a movie-censorship board. Of the last four

Figure 17.6 The front page of the *Washington Post* on the day after the Supreme Court's decision in the Pentagon Papers case.

states to have such a board, New York, Kansas, and Virginia phased theirs out in the 1970s, and Maryland's was abolished in 1981. Only two cities—Chicago and Dallas—still require motion pictures to be submitted to a board for examination prior to public showing.

It should be noted that when we speak of movie censorship, we are referring primarily to censorship of obscenity, and obscenity is not protected by the First Amendment. For example, Section 223 of the Federal Communications Act makes it illegal for anyone who uses the telephone to make comments or statements that are "obscene, lewd, lascivious, filthy, or indecent." Freedom of speech does not provide protection for obscene use of the telephone. The penalty for violation is a fine of up to $500 and imprisonment for up to six months. In 1983, the FCC used this statute to investigate the growing "Dial-a-Porn" business, but that business has not yet been outlawed.

Censorship of obscenity, however, does not give government the right to revoke broadcast licenses. In 1982, a small town in Utah passed an ordinance prohibiting the transmission of both pornographic and indecent material over cable TV. A federal judge struck down the ordinance, calling it "overbroad" because it would have threatened revocation of the cable company's license for broadcasting such films. However, in 1983, a Cincinnati cable firm was indicted on obscenity charges for having broadcast the Playboy channel programs, including the movies *Maraschino Cherry* and *The Opening of Misty Beethoven*. To some extent, the movie review boards have viewed themselves as consumer-protection agencies, not merely as censors of obscenity. The Dallas Motion Picture Classification Board, for example, gives films a public rating to warn the moviegoer in advance; ratings are for explicit sex (S), excessive violence (V), drugs (D), rough language (L), nudity (N), and perversion (P).

All other forms of government censorship, which exist in some countries and have sometimes been tried in the United States, have been declared unconstitutional.

Restrictions on Importation, Distribution, and Sale of Pornography

It is legal to regulate some aspects of mass communication without causing prior restraint or suppression. The government has generally held that the morals of the community should be protected by restricting the importation, distribution, and sale of certain types of pornographic communication that could be objectionable to the average person. These restrictions apply primarily to obscene publications, but also to gambling and lottery information and, in some cases, treasonous propaganda.

The Customs Bureau of the Treasury Department has the right to impound obscene material or gambling and lottery information and thus keep it from being imported into the United States. But a Supreme Court decision in the late 1950s declared unconstitutional the role of Customs in

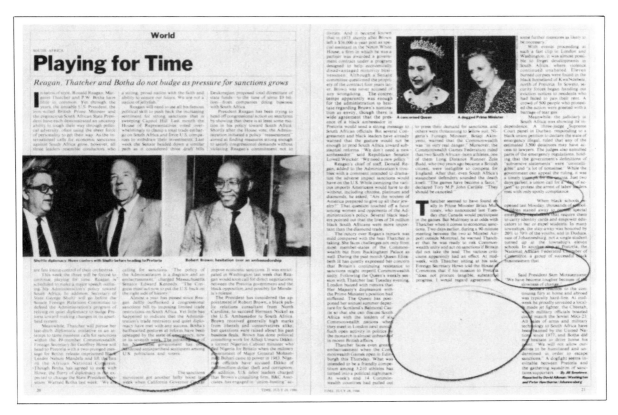

Figure 17.7 Censorship in South Africa. *Time*'s international edition is widely circulated in Africa, but the magazine was ordered to remove certain pictures and text before this 1986 issue could be sold in South Africa.

restricting the importation of propaganda materials. In 1938, Congress passed the Foreign Agents Registration Act, which says that any person who represents a foreign government must register with the Justice Department, and any foreign publication that contains propaganda to influence the American public must be labeled as propaganda. In 1983, the Justice Department attempted to restrict three Canadian films by forcing them to be preceded by a message stating that the films were political propaganda and expressed views not supported by the United States. The films were *If You Love This Planet*, an antinuclear film that was nominated for an Academy Award, and two films exposing the problems of acid rain, said to come from America: *Acid Rain: Requiem or Recovery* and *Acid from Heaven*.

The U.S. Postal Service exercises the right to restrict the distribution of obscene publications or lottery advertisements through the public mails. It can stop the mailing of such material and issue an order to refrain from further mailings. However, the Postal Service has greatly reduced its fulfill-ment of this responsibility in the past decade. It requires senders of ob-scene materials merely to put them in a plain wrapper and label them accordingly. This supposedly protects those who do not want to be ex-posed to pornography. The Postal Service also requires senders of pornog-raphy to remove from their mailing lists the names of all those who request such action.

The Supreme Court has upheld the right of local courts and legisla-tures to forbid the sale of obscene material. A person who violates a local ordinance against the sale of such material is subject to arrest and punish-ment, as called for in the ordinance. It was such a local authority that brought *Hustler* publisher Larry Flynt to court for having distributed por-nography.

In the 1980s, a number of state and local authorities have been passing increasingly restrictive laws concerning the sale of pornographic material, sometimes inspired by pressure groups. However, these laws have been frequently challenged as violations of First Amendment rights, and the Supreme Court has been active in further defining the constitutional limits of the law. For example, at the urging of women's groups, Indianapolis passed an ordinance banning the sale of pornography, on the grounds that it discriminates against women by portraying them as sex objects. The ordinance allowed any woman who said she had been harmed because of the sale of pornographic material to seek damages from businesses that sold or exhibited it. In 1986, the Court ruled that such an ordinance carries the law beyond the limits of constitutional guarantees.

In another case, in 1985, Virginia passed a law barring newsstands from displaying such sexually explicit magazines as *Playboy*, *Penthouse*, and *Hustler*. In 1986, the Supreme Court ruled that such a law is too sweeping. Laws can prevent businesses from selling pornography to minors, said the Court, but laws that force sellers to hide such material unreasonably inter-fere with adults' ability to exercise free choice in the purchase of material. But the Court has upheld the constitutionality of laws that force sellers to keep pornography "behind the counter" or away from shelves on which food products are displayed.

It is important to note that in all cases of such restrictions by the Customs Bureau, the Postal Service, and local authorities, none has the right to censor or prevent publication. It should also be noted that social mores are changing rapidly, and certainly in the 1980s, many forms of obscenity might not be considered as harmful as in previous decades. In the 1980s, the Customs Bureau was concerned primarily with confiscating pornography featuring children. Forms of obscenity that earlier might have been seized were by the mid-1980s considered too benign to cause concern.

Criminal Libel and Sedition

Government has assumed the right to protect society and the public from libel and to protect itself from seditious acts. Criminal libel is interpreted as a false and malicious attack on society that would cause a breach of the peace or disrupt by force the established public order. Criminal libel might also apply to libelous statements made against groups or against dead persons who cannot defend themselves in a civil action; thus the state becomes the prosecutor, and the libel becomes a crime. Cases of criminal libel have been extremely rare.

The government also has a right to protect itself from acts of treason, and the public communication of information that might endanger the security of the nation increasingly has been considered seditious or treasonous. Among the first laws passed by the new American Congress were the Alien Acts of 1798 and the Sedition Act of 1798. The Sedition Act made it a crime for a newspaper to criticize the government, on the theory that such criticism could harm the new government. This philosophy prevails in many newly independent countries today. But Thomas Jefferson and many others felt that the Alien and Sedition Acts were a clear violation of constitutional rights, and when Jefferson became president, the law expired.

When governments can label communication as a threat, freedom of speech and of the press is in danger. Between the demise of the Alien and Sedition Acts and the outbreak of World War I, the American government was reluctant to pass laws that would limit freedoms in order to protect national security. However, as the United States has become a national power with much to protect, as wars have become world wars, and as threats to national security have increased, the American people have allowed the government to make exceptions to freedom of speech and of the press during wartime. During World War I, Congress passed the Espionage Act, which made it a crime to publish information that could have been used by the enemy against America. The law lapsed when the war ended. A similar act was enacted during World War II, and it too lapsed at war's end. However, with the dawn of the Cold War and the nuclear age, Congress felt that national security was again vulnerable, and in 1950, it passed a law that makes it a crime to disclose communications intelligence or to publish classified information concerning the communications-intelligence activities of the United States.

Since such a law raises sensitive First Amendment issues, no news organization has ever been prosecuted under that law, as of 1986. In 1985, however, the government successfully prosecuted its first case against an individual who had disclosed classified information to the media. In this case, a government employee was found guilty of having sold three classified U.S. spy-satellite photos to a British defense magazine. As government has grown more cautious about its secrets, it has turned again to the 1950 law, which is still on the books. In 1986, the late William J. Casey, former director of the CIA, informed the *Washington Post,* the *New York Times,* and NBC News that they could be convicted of the felony of espionage under the 1950 law if they published or broadcast information that was being leaked to the press as a result of several spy trials. It was the first time that a government official had made such an overt, official threat against the press and indicates the growing problems in this area of government restriction of the press.

Libel of Government and Public Officials

Governments in totalitarian countries can suppress the critical press with criminal prosecution for seditious libel, but this is not possible in America. The trial of John Peter Zenger in New York in 1735 first established the unqualified right of the press to criticize the government, even if the facts are false and the criticism is malicious. Various attempts have been made by government to protect itself from such criticism—for example, the Alien and Sedition Acts of 1798. But the courts have steadily upheld the impunity of the press as goad and critic of government.

One of the most far-reaching Supreme Court decisions was *The New York Times Co. v. Sullivan* ruling in 1964. This ruling gives the press almost as much right to libel public officials as it has the right to criticize government. The case came about as the result of an advertisement appearing in the *Times* in 1960; the ad, it was claimed, libeled, among others, one L. B. Sullivan, then commissioner of public affairs for Montgomery, Alabama. The Court ruled that the press has a right to publish defamatory falsehoods about public officials if the statements are made in good faith, concern the official's public rather than private life, and are not made in reckless disregard of the truth. However, in 1981, the Supreme Court refined and limited this ruling when it decided that government consultants are *not* considered to be "public figures," and thus, unlike individuals considered to be public figures, consultants can bring suits for libel against the mass media. In this way, laws concerning libel and government regulation of mass communication are constantly being interpreted and clarified.

Protection of the Judicial System

Government also exercises the right to protect the administration of justice against the interference of the mass media. If a journalist, for instance, in the course of professional work, disobeys a court order, disturbs a courtroom, attempts to influence court decisions or participants, or (in some states) refuses to testify as to sources of news, that journalist can be cited for contempt of court. Court officials have used this power to subpoena reporters' notes, tapes, photographs, and film in an effort to use this material in court cases. However, 26 states have laws that provide some protection of the journalist's right not to reveal confidential sources of information.

In a 5–4 decision in 1972, the Supreme Court ruled that journalists have no *absolute* privilege to protect their sources of information if they are subpoenaed to testify in court proceedings, unless there is a state law giving them such protection. Medical doctors do not have to reveal the nature of their relationships with their patients, nor lawyers with clients, nor ministers with parishioners, nor teachers with students, but the Court held that such a privilege does not necessarily apply to the relationship between a journalist and a news source under the First Amendment. The ruling was made on the basis of three cases. Paul Pappas of WTEV-TV in New Bedford, Massachusetts, had refused to tell a grand jury what he had seen in a Black Panthers headquarters. Earl Caldwell, a *New York Times* reporter, also had refused to testify about a Black Panther case. And Paul M. Branzburg, a reporter for the *Louisville* (Kentucky) *Courier Journal,* had refused to tell a state grand jury the names of individuals he had written about in a drug story.

Since that ruling, an increasing number of journalists have gone to jail for contempt of court after they refused to divulge information in court

Figure 17.8 *New York Times* reporter Myron Farber was sent to jail for 40 days for contempt of court. His reporting had convinced a New Jersey prosecutor to reopen a murder case, and Farber was subpoenaed to testify about his knowledge of the case. His refusal to name sources cited in his articles brought him the contempt citation. (Photo: UPI/Bettmann Newsphotos, courtesy of the *Columbia Journalism Review.*)

CAPITOL GAMES   By James Stevenson

(Courtesy of the *Los Angeles Times.*)

proceedings. For example, Peter Bridge, a former reporter for the *Newark (New Jersey) News,* was sentenced to an indefinite jail term for having refused to answer a grand jury's questions that went beyond his story about an alleged bribe attempt. He was ultimately released. In Fresno, California, four journalists from the *Fresno Bee*—the managing editor, the newspaper's ombudsman, and two court reporters—went to jail in 1976 for an indefinite term for having refused to tell a judge the source of secret grand-jury testimony used in a news story. They, too, ultimately were released. In 1981, the Supreme Court was still of the opinion that reporters should have no special protection from the courts. It let stand an order that a *Philadelphia Inquirer* reporter be jailed for having refused to answer questions about her source for a story about the Abscam under-cover operation.

Congress also can cite journalists for contempt, as it did in the 1976 case of Daniel Schorr, the CBS reporter who refused to tell the House of Representatives how he had obtained a copy of a congressional commit-tee's report on intelligence activities. Congress ultimately decided not to punish Schorr.

Restrictions on Court Coverage

The judicial branch of government can also restrict news media in their coverage of court news by closing the courtroom to reporters. For example, in 1975, a Nebraska judge ordered restrictions on news coverage of a mass-murder trial, on the grounds that the trial was too sensational. But "secret trials" have always been anathema in free societies, and in 1976, the Su-preme Court, in a unanimous decision, ruled that the Nebraska gag order, as it was called, was an unconstitutional restraint of freedom of the press. The Court did not rule out the possibility that such orders could be issued to protect the right of a defendant to a fair trial, but such orders should be issued only when there is a clear threat to the fairness of the trial.

In 1983, a U.S. District Court judge issued gag orders barring CBS's "60 Minutes" from broadcasting a story about a New Orleans criminal case, saying that it would prejudice the case. But a U.S. Court of Appeals in New Orleans postponed the trial so the effects of the publicity would not affect the jury, and the Supreme Court refused to change the ruling. Such battles between the courts and the press will, no doubt, continue.

The problem of free press versus a fair trial, the First Amendment versus the Sixth Amendment, has posed difficulties for both the news media and the courts. Journalists and lawyers have increasingly clashed over the issues of prejudicial publicity, on the one hand, and censorship of the news, on the other. Some restrictions have been eased, however.

In 1956, Colorado was the first state to relax its rules about cameras in the courtroom. By the mid-1980s, 37 states were in various stages of opening their courts to photographers, tape recorders, and video cameras. Twenty-one states have permanent laws opening their courts to cameras. Sixteen states have experimental programs. Congress has also changed its ban on television coverage. The Senate opened its session to televised coverage on an experimental basis for the first time in 1986. A closed-circuit television system had already become a permanent fixture in the House of Representatives. Cameras have been placed at various locations around the House and Senate, providing "gavel-to-gavel" coverage of floor proceedings. Live or taped broadcasts can be used by television correspondents and networks. Some cable systems carry the floor proceedings in their entirety.

Protection of Property

The government also regulates communication by protecting the property rights of communicators. The present copyright law was revised in 1976 for the first time since its passage as a federal statute in 1909. The copyright law protects the property rights of authors, composers, artists, and photographers and establishes a system of penalties and a method of redress for violations of those rights. Among other restrictions, the 1976 revision also limits the amount of photocopying that can be done on copyrighted works and extends the life of a copyright. It is important to note that facts and ideas cannot be copyrighted, only the order and selection of words, phrases, clauses, and sentences and the arrangement of paragraphs.

The government has sometimes invoked the right of protection of property as a means of restricting media access to a news event. In a few cases, the media have been cited for trespass in covering events such as fires. The news media contend that they should not have to obtain the permission of a property owner to enter the scene of a news event, but court rulings on such cases have not yet established clear precedents.

The government also protects property rights through the application of antitrust laws to the mass media. For example, newspaper mergers that eliminated actual or potential competition in a newspaper-market area were formerly considered to be a violation of the antitrust laws. But because so many newspapers have succumbed to financial pressures, antitrust law pertaining to newspaper mergers has been recast somewhat: the Newspaper Preservation Act of 1970 gives newspapers special antitrust privileges.

Copyright laws were the center of attention in two major legal battles fought by the mass media in the early 1980s. The first was the debate over whether manufacturers of home video-recording equipment must pay copyright royalties to producers of TV programs because video-recorder owners tape movies and shows that are aired on television. Sony Corporation argued that owners of video recorders have a First Amendment right to copy publicly aired programming and replay the tapes as often as they like for their own, private use. Universal City Studios and Walt Disney Productions countered that there is no such right allowing wholesale, cost-free taping of copyrighted films. They contended that the practice illegally deprives them of fair compensation for use of their movies. If viewers cannot record the programs, they have to watch television, and the producers receive royalties each time a program is aired. The Court ruled that the public has a limited right to record video programs off the air for personal use, but not for resale.

The second battle was over who owns syndicated television films. FCC rules have prohibited the three major national networks from directly owning most programming and syndication rights, since they are the prime distributors of the films. The networks sought the ownership rights, while the film and independent television studios in Hollywood claimed that they should own the rights to TV films and syndicated programs. The Court held that the producer is the owner of the copyright.

Regulation of Broadcasting

Unlike the other mass media, radio and television stations are licensed by the government, but the government cannot censor or suppress any broadcast once the broadcaster has a license. The government began its regulation of broadcasting in the 1920s when major broadcasters requested help to maintain order in the scramble for limited frequencies and channels. The Supreme Court later upheld the notion that broadcasters use public property—the airwaves—and government has an obligation to administer property that is not private. In 1927, the Federal Radio Commission was established; in 1934, it became the Federal Communications Commission (FCC), which was charged with regulating radio, telephone and telegraph, and, later, television. By the mid-1980s, reduction in the FCC's regulating powers was being pushed on a broad front.

Like the courts, the FCC interprets rather than makes the law. Congress enacts the law. A broadcast station must be licensed by the FCC, and the license must be renewed. Stations used to be required to renew their licenses every three years. Now, radio stations are given a seven-year license and television stations, a five-year license. At the time of renewal, the station and its programming were formerly reviewed, and if the commission ruled that the station had not acted in the public interest, the license could be rescinded. These reviews are now greatly reduced under deregulation. The FCC can still levy fines of up to $10,000 for specific violations of its rules and regulations. But these regulatory powers do not give the FCC the right to censor.

It is rare for licenses not to be renewed because of single violations; the station's overall performance is evaluated. Few licenses have been revoked, since the burden of proof falls on the FCC, and the definition of "public interest" is vague. Nevertheless, the government does have more power to regulate a broadcaster than to regulate a publisher.

The FCC also has controlled the extent of broadcast ownership, so that it could prevent monopolies. Formerly, no one could own more than one AM, one FM, and one TV station in any one listening area, and no one could own more than a total of seven of each of these stations in the entire country. In television, no more than five of these outlets could be very-high-frequency (VHF, channels 2 to 13) stations. Under deregulation, a person or corporation can now own 12 AM, 12 FM, and 12 TV stations, and in 1990, ownership of radio will become unlimited. The FCC has also sought to prevent monopolies in local media by not giving licenses to applicants who already own a daily newspaper in the same market.

The FCC has also regulated some broadcast program content, especially in the areas of politics and public affairs. Section 315 of the FCC code required the broadcaster to furnish equal time and equal opportunity to all political candidates for a given office. Excepted were news programs, which have been carefully qualified to allow debates between candidates of principal political parties when covered as a bona-fide news event. In 1983, the FCC voted to abolish this requirement.

Another FCC regulation, the so-called Fairness Doctrine, charges broadcasters with the duty of seeking out and broadcasting contrasting viewpoints on controversial issues of public importance. However, the Fairness Doctrine is different from the equal-time provision of Section 315; the Fairness Doctrine requires broadcasters only to present contrasting views, not to give them equal time on the air. The constitutionality of the Fairness Doctrine was upheld by the Supreme Court in 1969 in the case *Red Lion Broadcasting Co.* v. *FCC.* The Court ruled that the public's right to hear all points of view is more important than the broadcaster's right to express only one point of view. The Fairness Doctrine has continued, despite deregulation.

The FCC has had specific regulations for cable television. Until the mid-1960s, the FCC paid little attention to cable TV, regarding it as a passing phenomenon. But in 1972, the commission adopted a set of rules specifically for this expanding area of television. The rules established which broadcast stations the cable systems could transmit and which ones they could not; they required the systems to have a minimum 20-channel capacity; they made provisions for a public-access channel; and they stipulated that cable systems build in the capacity for two-way circuitry, allowing for feedback from a subscriber to the system. But the FCC has relaxed many of these rules in an effort to allow cable systems to grow; for example, it has eased the rule on the stations that the system can carry and the rule on local origination and access.

In fact, most regulations on broadcasting were lessened considerably in the 1980s. Broadcasters had spent years lobbying on Capitol Hill for deregulation of their industry, and the Reagan administration stimulated and speeded the process.

By the mid-1980s, radio was the most deregulated broadcasting medium. Stations were no longer obligated to devote a certain percentage of their programming to nonentertainment or public-service programs. They were no longer required to ascertain the interests of their communities, maintain program logs, or produce a limited number of programs on issues relevant to their communities. Perhaps most important, stations were no longer required to limit commercials to 18 minutes per hour; they could run as many commercials as they wanted. Finally, the amount of paperwork required to apply for a license renewal was drastically reduced.

Deregulation of television has not come as swiftly, but by the mid-1980s, Congress and the FCC had agreed to eliminate the restrictions on TV stations and networks that had prevented them from owning cable systems. The FCC voted to reduce the requirement that TV stations broadcast a minimum amount of public-affairs and new programming and to ease the requirement that stations regularly assess community needs for guidance in programming. The commission had also proposed an end to the 16-minute limit on commercials during each hour of TV broadcasting.

Controversy over the Fairness Doctrine has continued in the 1980s. Much discussion was held on making the license period indefinite. But licensing, some control of ownership, and some degree of regulation probably will always apply to the broadcast media in our society.

Regulation of Advertising

The Federal Trade Commission Act of 1941 established the Federal Trade Commission (FTC), which was meant to regulate unfair competition in business, but checking dishonest advertising has become an important aspect of its work. It is also paying particular attention to dishonest advertising aimed at children, especially in television commercials.

A recent case illustrates the FTC's actions in regulating advertising. In 1985, the R. J. Reynolds Tobacco Company placed a "public-issue message" advertisement in selected mass media stating that a medical study had shown there was no proof that smoking increases health risks. "This controversy over smoking and health remains an open one," the ad concluded. But the FTC issued a complaint against Reynolds, accusing the company of deliberately misrepresenting both the purpose and the results of a 10-year study by the National Institutes of Health, which had concluded that smoking is hazardous to one's health. The FTC charged that the Reynolds ad was fraudulent. But Reynolds contended that it had a First Amendment right to express its views.

It should be noted that the FTC is concerned only with fraudulence in advertising. It does not view its role as protector of the public's morals or taste, as reflected in advertising. It seeks only to protect the public from being cheated by dishonest advertising.

Other government agencies have more specific tasks in the regulation of advertising. The Food and Drug Administration controls labeling in the important area of food and drugs. The FCC does not regulate advertising on radio and television, but it does note whether a station is complying with the profession's own codes (the code of the National Association of Broadcasters, which seeks to limit advertising for hard liquor, for example). An act of Congress denied broadcasters the right to advertise cigarettes, although broadcasters can advertise pipe tobacco, cigars, and snuff. The Postal Service controls fraudulent advertising sent throught the mails. And the Securities and Exchange Commission can regulate advertising about stocks and bonds.

In all these cases, there is still no censorship or suppression on the part of the government. It can ask for voluntary compliance, and, if the advertiser refuses, it can issue a cease-and-desist order. Violation of such an order can bring about a $5,000 fine, six months in jail, or both. The FTC can also publicize deceitful advertising and thus warn the public.

In sum, the government can and does regulate and restrict mass media in certain areas, and in these areas, the Supreme Court has determined that there is no conflict with the intent of the First Amendment to the Constitution. These regulations are aimed at protecting society from damage by the mass media and protecting the rights of some media from damage by competing media, individuals, or the state itself.

THE CONTENT SOURCE AS REGULATOR

The source of information can also be a regulator, providing a form of control at the very beginning of the communication process. Although communication has grown massive and complicated, the forms of regulation that are used by the content source can be assigned to fairly distinct categories.

Strategic Releasing

The source regulates communication by strategically timing and packaging the message in a letter, publication, or (if the content source has enough money) radio, television, or motion-picture production. Or the source

Figure 17.9 President Reagan can regulate the flow of news out of the White House, to a certain extent, by deciding what information to release and to whom to release it. Here he meets with five reporters in the Oval Office. (Photo: Pete Souza, The White House.)

might choose to release the message to the media through a news release, a press conference, or an exclusive interview.

Strategic Withholding

The source can also regulate the communication flow by blocking the media from getting a certain message or parts of a message. The government can do this by classifying documents or claiming executive privilege. The Freedom of Information Act of 1967 set forth the rationale for what can be legally withheld by the federal government and what cannot, and it established the judicial procedures to make the government prove in court why information should be withheld. Many states have statutes that define the categories of public records to which the media can and cannot have access.

When President Reagan was shot in an assassination attempt in 1981, for example, the White House press office withheld certain details of his injury soon after the shooting. The press office told journalists that the president was only slightly injured, that he was joking and laughing at the hospital, and that he would be back at work soon. Later, the officials admitted that they had withheld information about the gravity of the president's wounds to avoid overreaction.

When American troops invaded the tiny Caribbean island of Grenada in 1983, news about the invasion was withheld from the press for a number of hours. And even after the news had been released, reporters were at first not allowed to go to Grenada for firsthand coverage. Later, a "pool" was established; only a few reporters were allowed to go to Grenada and then share their reports with a large number of grumbling and angry reporters waiting on a nearby island.

Another form of withholding has been to deny news media access to meetings. But in 1976, Congress passed the Government in Sunshine Act, which requires about 50 federal agencies, boards, and commissions with 2 or more heads or directors to open their meetings and their records to the public. There are 10 exceptions under which meetings may be closed, but in these cases, transcripts must be kept to allow scrutiny in case of legal action. Some states have passed sunshine laws to open meetings at state and local government levels as well.

The Reagan administration made strenuous efforts in the early and mid-1980s to reduce the effectiveness of the Freedom of Information Act and to increase the penalties for government employees who leaked information to the press. The Intelligence Identities Protection Act of 1982 makes it a crime to expose the identities of American intelligence agents. The Defense Department in 1982 also broadened its practice of giving employees lie-detector tests, in an effort to prevent leaking of information, and the Reagan administration urged Congress to pass a law making all government employees subject to lie-detector tests for the rest of their lives, in order to protect information. But the Senate delayed voting on the issue.

Strategic Staging

The source can also regulate the flow of communication by deliberately staging a situation or an event in such a way that a certain kind of message gets into the media. For example, a senator who wishes to express his point of view about a particular issue holds a hearing and calls a group of witnesses, from whom he can elicit the type of testimony that will get news headlines. The president, not wanting to see this point of view emphasized in the media, announces that he is traveling to Europe at the same time that the senator is holding his hearing. The president takes many reporters with him, attracting daily coverage in the newspapers and newscasts and overshadowing the hearing called by the senator. Meanwhile, a citizen's group holds a rally on the steps of the Capitol to get media (and public) attention for its position on the problem. These concurrent events will affect what news and how much of it will be covered by the press.

The terrorists who hijacked a TWA plane in the Middle East in 1985 certainly used that staged event to capture the attention of the American

Figure 17.10 The president can regulate the flow of news by staging events, such as press conferences and public speeches. Because of his prominence, he is guaranteed front-page and prime-time coverage. (Photo: Bill Fitz-Patrick, The White House.)

people. Indeed, many people believed that the media—as well as the airplane passengers—were being held hostage by the situation. It was news that could not be ignored. Thus the people who controlled the event also controlled the media.

THE ADVERTISER AS REGULATOR

Advertisers obviously play a role in the regulation of mass media, but theirs can be a subtle, unspecific control. David Potter, a historian who has studied advertising as a force in molding the American character, wrote in his book *People of Plenty*:

> . . . in the mass media we have little evidence of censorship in the sense of deliberate, planned suppression imposed by moral edict (by advertisers) but much evidence of censorship in the sense of operative suppres-

sion of a great range of subjects. . . . The dynamics of the market . . . would seem to indicate that freedom of expression has less to fear from the control which large advertisers exercise than from the control which these advertisers permit the mass market to exercise.[2]

Individual instances can be cited in which advertisers used their economic power to "regulate" the media. For example, advertisers in a Wisconsin town withdrew their advertising from the local newspaper to protest the use of its production shop to print an underground newspaper. Their action could have put the newspaper out of business, but the newspaper stood its ground and ultimately won the battle. The news offices of most mass media are separate from the advertising offices, and news officials rarely want to accept the dictates of the advertising offices.

Another example is an episode in the life of the "Desilu Playhouse," this one from late 1958. In one drama, a military officer was depicted warning the people of Hawaii of an imminent attack by the Japanese prior to the bombing of Pearl Harbor. The army authorities were shown declaring the officer as incompetent and removing him from headquarters. But "Desilu Playhouse" was sponsored by Westinghouse, a firm with a multitude of government and military contracts. It would not do, cried Westinghouse, to depict the military as being blind to the hero's warnings. The CBS network censors cut the show under pressure from the advertiser.

Theoretically, the more independent the medium can be from advertising, the less power of regulation the advertiser will have. Radio and television, which receive 100 percent of their revenue from advertising, run the risk of great pressures from sponsors. Newspapers and magazines, which, for the most part, receive 33 to 50 percent of their revenue directly from subscribers, have less direct obligation to paid advertisers. Books, the recording industry, and motion pictures, which receive 100 percent of their revenue directly from their audiences, can afford to ignore Madison Avenue altogether.

THE CONSUMER AS REGULATOR

In a system of free mass communication, the consumer is perhaps the most important regulator of the media. In two areas, consumers can resort to court procedures to help protect themselves from the media as well as keep the media within acceptable boundaries. These areas are civil libel and the right of privacy.

Civil Libel

Libel is false defamation of a person's character through printed or broadcast means. Slander is false defamation through spoken words. Defama-

---

[2] David Potter, *People of Plenty* (Chicago: University of Chicago Press, 1954), 184.

tion is communication that exposes a person to hatred, ridicule, or contempt; lowers him in the esteem of his fellows; causes him to be shunned; or injures him in his business or calling. The concept of defamation as a punishable act has a long history; the ancient Egyptians cut out the tongues of those who were found guilty of having lied maliciously about their neighbors.

Those who feel that damage has been done to them by communication can bring a civil suit against those responsible and seek payment for damages. The legal action is not much different from a lawsuit in which a person seeks to be paid for the actual damage to a car fender in an automobile accident. In a libel suit, tradition holds that a person's reputation is a priceless commodity (unlike an automobile) and that little just compensation can be paid for actual damages. Thus the plaintiff can ask for punitive damages, an amount of compensation so great that it will punish the libeler. Some punitive damages for libel have run into the millions of dollars, especially when the libel was shown to have been published or broadcast with malicious intent.

The publisher or broadcaster of a defamatory statement can defend the publication or broadcast under certain conditions that might absolve the defamer completely or lessen the damages he or she may be ordered to pay. Truth is now accepted as an absolute defense for the publication of a defamation, and a defamer who can prove the truth of a statement can be completely absolved. Certain statements are privileged; that is, the communicator has a right to repeat those statements without fear of libel suits. Such privileged statements are those recorded in legislative, judicial, and other official public proceedings. Also, statements made as a matter of fair comment or criticism about public matters are defensible—even if defamatory.

Perhaps the most famous libel suit of the early 1980s was that brought by television star Carol Burnett against the *National Enquirer*. The *Enquirer* had published a story indicating that Burnett had been drunk and disorderly in a Washington restaurant. She proved the description to be false and libelous, and a California court awarded her $1.6 million in damages, which was subsequently lowered to $750,000 by an appeals court.

Two other widely publicized libel suits in the mid-1980s were lost by the individuals who had brought the suits against the mass media. In the early 1980s, CBS produced a documentary about the Vietnam War that charged General William Westmoreland with having covered up information about the extent of Vietcong victories. Westmoreland sued CBS for millions, contending that the program defamed him as a professional soldier. When CBS presented its facts in court, Westmoreland withdrew his suit. In another famous case, *Time* produced a cover story on the war in Lebanon; in the story, it accused Israeli Defense Minister Ariel Sharon of having encouraged acts of atrocities against Palestinians in refugee camps. *Time* admitted that it had accepted the report of a correspondent without double-checking it because of the pressures of deadline, but it contended that it had not maliciously defamed the Israeli general. The court ordered *Time* to pay $1 for its offense.

The Right of Privacy

Individuals have the right to be private, even from mass media. Unlike libel, however, this is a relatively new concept of communication regulation. Citizens have the right to recover damages from the media for having intruded on their solitude, published private matters that violate ordinary decencies, used their names publicly in a false manner, or used their names or likenesses for commercial purposes. Individuals can bring a civil action in court to seek compensation for damages done to them from such invasion of privacy.

An individual sometimes can lose the right of privacy. For example, a person who is involved in a newsworthy act or a person who becomes newsworthy by virtue of public actions loses the right to privacy in those matters. Or someone who gives consent to an invasion of privacy—for example, by signing a waiver on entering a studio to become a member of a television audience—cannot recover any damages through loss of privacy.

Some states have passed laws that have added to the privacy of individuals, but these laws may, in fact, lead to abuses in secrecy. In 1975, for example, Oregon passed a law preventing the police from disclosing the names and addresses of people arrested, detained, indicted, charged, sentenced, serving time, and released, in an effort to protect those individuals who might have been falsely arrested or charged or sentenced. But the law allowed the police and courts to carry out secret arrests and jailings and secret trials, in the name of protecting the few. Certainly, no greater abuse can be perpetrated in a free and open society than police action without the scrutiny of the public through the watchdog eyes of the press. In such cases, it would seen, the right to know would be more important to a free society than the right to privacy.

Control through Consumption

No doubt, the greatest area of consumer regulation is in the marketplace. Those publications that sell stay in business, and those that cannot obtain or maintain an audience go bankrupt. Broadcast programs that do not attract large audiences go off the air. Because the media are in business to make a profit, they are usually sensitive to their customers and pay careful attention to the moods and habits of their readers, listeners, and viewers. Of course, what the audience wants may not always be the best or most constructive content for the social good. Violence and sex seem to be more popular than news analysis and interpretation of public issues. Thus control by the marketplace has to be balanced against other considerations to achieve social well-being.

THE PRESSURE GROUP AS REGULATOR

Although mass media are sensitive to individual responses, as media grow, the individual voice gets weaker. Increasingly, people have joined together in groups and associations to make their voices heard and their opinions felt. These groups have been able to pressure mass media, thus serving as regulators of mass communication. Nearly every religious, ethnic, occupational, and political group has an association that can speak for the members of the group, such as exerting pressure on television to stop portraying Italians as criminals, on newspapers to publish stories about gun laws, on radio to present antismoking commercials, on magazines to stop obscenity.

One such pressure group, Action for Children's Television (ACT), petitioned the FCC for a rule barring advertisements on children's shows. The efforts were a major force behind all three networks' appointments of executives to supervise children's programming. Such pressure is also often applied to the media through government regulatory agencies. For example, enforcement of the FCC's Fairness Doctrine is most often triggered by complaints from pressure groups whose members disagree with an opinion that has been broadcast.

The National Council of Churches has taken an active role in pressuring the broadcast media about sex and violence in programs. In 1985, in an effort to have an impact on the regulation of television, the religious group widely publicized a report that concluded the following:

1. Laboratory and field studies show a link between "viewing violence on television and subsequent aggressive behavior."
2. Violent sexual material stimulates aggression toward women and children and sexual violence.
3. Music video—combining erotic relationships, teen idols, and violence in a "repetitive context"—has a "serious negative effect" on young people.
4. Frequent TV viewers develop a "greater sense of insecurity and apprehension" about the world—a "mean world" syndrome heightening fears and feelings of vulnerability that foster violence.[3]

It remains to be seen what impact the National Council of Churches will have on television programming.

Another pressure group that became active in the mid-1980s was the Parents Music Resource Center, started by a group of prominent Washington, D.C., women who objected to "dirty" lyrics in popular recordings. The women's interest in the issue was sparked particularly by Prince, one of

---

[3] Associated Press, "Condemning FCC, Church Council Says TV 'Pollution' Imperils Quality of Life," *Washington Post*, 21 September 1985, A16.

Figure 17.11 Record album jacket showing sexual explicitness.

the sultriest stars of the mid-1980s. The women's group was also offended by lyrics in songs by Sheena Easton and Frankie Goes to Hollywood and by Madonna gyrating about in a music-video version of her album "Like a Virgin." The group won the support of the NAB to urge record companies to provide radio stations with advance copies of record lyrics so that the stations could judge the records' suitability for broadcast. They also pressed for laws requiring that song lyrics and the label "Explicit Lyrics—Parental Advisory" be printed on album covers. But record companies resisted, saying that the requirement would be costly, burdensome, and possibly a violation of music-publishing rights.

Books have also suffered from the pressures of public groups that have sought to ban books from libraries and schools. Between 1982 and 1985, there were 22 public book burnings in 17 states. A citizens' review committee in Midland, Michigan, recommended banning Shakespeare's *Merchant of Venice* from the public schools on the grounds that it is anti-Semitic. In Waukegan, Illinois, a city alderman proposed banning from public schools books that give an unflattering portrayal of blacks, including such classics as *Gone with the Wind, Uncle Tom's Cabin, To Kill a Mockingbird,* and *The Adventures of Huckleberry Finn.*

One group that is increasingly applying pressure on all media is women. A number of women's groups have lobbied in various forums for more balanced coverage and an end to employment discrimination by the mass media. For example, a number of women complained about the first edition of this textbook, saying that it contained too many sexist references, such as the constant use of the term *newsman*. As a result, the authors were encouraged (not forced) by their editor to change or modify such references in later editions. We were happy to comply with the request, for the first edition did reflect outdated usage, and, more important, the changes have improved the book.

In 1976, the National Commission on the Observance of International Women's Year produced a set of guidelines for mass media coverage of and employment of women. Many of these guidelines have been adopted by mass media communicators and gatekeepers, for the mass media could certainly not continue to be mass if they continued to offend so large a segment of their audience.

SUMMARY

The mass media are regulated by internal and external forces, but because of constitutional guarantees of freedom of speech and of the press, the media in the United States are subject to less government regulation than is true in most other countries of the world.

Internal gatekeepers—media editors, producers, directors, managers, publishers, and lawyers—provide preliminary regulation of media content before it is communicated publicly.

The government, in its interpretation of the meaning of the Constitution, has usually been prevented from exercising prior restraint, or censorship, of messages before they are publicly communicated. The one exception has been the motion picture, which the Supreme Court has ruled can be censored, but the federal government has never exercised this option, and few state or local authorities now do.

Although the government cannot censor, it can restrict the mass media in a variety of ways. It can restrict the importation, distribution, and sale of pornography. It can bring legal action for criminal libel and, in certain instances, for communication that is seditious or treasonous. It can restrict the media to some extent to protect the judicial system and the fairness of trials. It can protect communicators' rights to their property. It can regulate broadcasting, although that regulation has decreased in the 1980s. And it can regulate fraudulent advertising, but it cannot regulate taste or moral values expressed in advertising.

The source of information can regulate media by controlling the way information is released, withheld, or staged. The advertiser can exercise some regulatory power over the media when the sponsor is more powerful than the medium.

The consumer can control the media's impact on individuals by using the courts to protect against defamation and invasion of privacy. But most important, the consumer can regulate the mass media by deciding which medium to buy in the marketplace. And increasingly, consumers are joining into pressure groups in order to exercise greater power over media conduct and content.

BIBLIOGRAPHY

Ashley, Paul P. *Say It Safely: Legal Limits in Publishing, Radio, and Television.* 5th ed. Seattle: University of Washington Press, 1976.

Ashmore, Harry S. *Fear in the Air: Broadcasting and the First Amendment: The Anatomy of a Constitutional Crisis.* New York: Norton, 1973.

Barron, Jerome A. *Freedom of the Press for Whom? The Right of Access to Mass Media.* Bloomington: Indiana University Press, 1973.

Berner, Richard Olin. *Constraints on the Regulatory Process: A Case Study of Regulation of Cable Television.* Cambridge, Mass.: Ballinger, 1976.

Cantor, Muriel G. *Prime-Time Television: Content and Control.* Beverly Hills, Calif.: Sage, 1980.

Chamberlin, Bill F., and Charlene J. Brown. *The First Amendment Reconsidered: New Perspectives on the Meaning of Freedom of Speech and Press.* New York: Longman, 1982.

Clark, David G., and Earl R. Hutchison. *Mass Media and the Law: Freedom and Restraint.* New York: Wiley, 1970.

Cole, Barry, and Mal Oettinger. *Reluctant Regulators: The FCC and the Broadcast Audience.* Reading, Mass.: Addison-Wesley, 1978.

François, William E. *Mass Media Law and Regulation.* Columbus, Ohio: Grid, 1975.

Glassman Don. *Writers' & Artists' Rights.* Washington, D.C.: Writers Press, 1978.

Heller, Melvin S. *Sexuality, Television and Broadcast Standards.* New York: American Broadcasting Companies, 1984.

Kittross, John M., and Kenneth Harwood. *Free & Fair: Courtroom Access and the Fairness Doctrine.* Philadelphia: Association for Professional Broadcasting Education, 1970.

Krasnow, Erwin G., and Lawrence D. Longley. *The Politics of Broadcast Regulation.* New York: St. Martin's Press, 1973.

Lawhorne, Clifton O. *Defamation and Public Officials: The Evolving Law of Libel.* Carbondale: Southern Illinois University Press, 1971.

Levin, Harvey J. *Fact and Fancy in Television Regulation.* New York: Russell Sage Foundation, 1980.

Lofton, John. *The Press as Guardian of the First Amendment.* Columbia: University of South Carolina Press, 1980.

Media Law Reporter. The Bureau of National Affairs, 231 25th Street, N.W., Washington, D.C. 20037.

Nelson, Harold L., and Dwight L. Teeter, Jr. *Law of Mass Communications: Freedom and Control of Print and Broadcast Media.* 3d ed. Mineola, N.Y.: Foundation Press, 1978.

News Media and the Law. Reporters Committee for Freedom of the Press, 1125 15th Street, N.W., Room 403, Washington, D.C.   20005.

Phelps, Robert H., and E. Douglas Hamilton. *Libel: A Guide to Rights, Risks, Responsibilities*. London: Collier Books, 1966.

Pool, Ithiel de Sola. *On Free Speech in an Electronic Age: Technologies of Freedom*. Cambridge, Mass.: The Belknap Press of Harvard University Press, 1983.

Rowan, Ford. *Broadcast Fairness: Doctrine, Practice, Prospects*. New York: Longman, 1984.

Schmidt, Benno C., Jr. *Freedom of the Press vs. Public Access*. New York: Praeger, 1976.

Simon, Morton J. *Public Relations Law*. New York: Meredith, 1969.

Simons, Howard, and Joseph A. Califano, Jr. *The Media and the Law*. New York: Praeger, 1976.

18

Audiences and Their Filters

Millions of Americans drive to and from work every day. Most of those caught up in rush hour drive their radios as well as their cars. Many of them could not tell you a single commercial they heard during the mad scramble of "drive-time."

It is the nature of the mass communication experience for most audience members to understand and retain only a limited portion of the media day. The better the media environment, the more likely the audience will better filter and understand the experience.

In effect, the audience, their filters, and the environment interact to make the communication process work or fail.

THE CONCEPT OF AUDIENCE

Distinctions have to be drawn between the terms *public* and *audience* and between the conditions that differentiate mass communication audiences from interpersonal communication receivers.

Public refers to a total pool of available people, whereas *audience* refers to the individuals who actually use the content produced by a media unit. For the mass communicator, the public is an abstraction; the audience is a reality because audience members actually consume what the media produce. An individual has only to exist to be a part of the public, but a person must take action to become a part of an audience. The individual must read or listen or watch. The members of the audience are active participants in mass communication. Audiences interact with the media, and the results are complex and powerful.

In Chapter 15, we saw how the sender becomes a conglomerate communicator when the mass media become involved in the communication process. The receiver also changes from one person—who, in interpersonal communication, remains a discrete, discernible, and recognizable individual in close physical and/or emotional contact with the sender—to part of the total audience for mass communication. Individuals are examined as parts of aggregates called readership, listenership, or viewership. Readers, listeners, and viewers make up mass communication audiences. Note the use of the plural here. It is not a singular audience because there are many audiences, over time, for any given unit of media content. Mass communication audiences exhibit five basic characteristics.

1. *The audience tends to be composed of individuals who are apt to have shared experiences and are affected by similar interpersonal social relationships.* These individuals choose the media products they use by conscious selection or habitual choice. Some people react to audiences as unthinking masses, following the line of thought developed by Gustave LeBon in *The Crowd,* according to which the masses (the mass audience) follow a leader (a TV program or magazine) in zombie-like obedience. The "crowd mentality" and "mass audience" are not well-thought-out concepts. The audience member remains an individual throughout the mass communication process.

2. *The audience tends to be large.* Charles Wright says, "We consider as 'large' any audience exposed during a short period of time and of such a size that the communicator could not interact with its members on a face-to-face basis."[1] There is no numerical cut-off point intended in the definition of large. Audience size is relative. A "large" audience for a hardback textbook might be a "small" audience for a prime-time network series like "Miami Vice."

3. *The audience tends to be heterogeneous rather than homogeneous.* Individuals within a given audience represent a wide variety of social categories. Some basic media units increasingly seek specialized audiences, but even these groups tend to be more heterogeneous than homogeneous. In actuality, audiences for some basic media units are relatively narrow in scope. For example, the target audience for "Video Soul" is young black Americans in predominantly urban markets. *Working Woman* magazine has a relatively limited audience, based on sex, age, and employment. The younger, college-educated professional is more likely to read *Working Woman*

---

[1] Charles Wright, *Mass Communication: A Sociological Perspective,* 2d ed. (New York: Random House, 1975), p. 6.

than is her older, grade-school-educated grandmother. The audience for *Mass Media V* is very specialized, but its readers are still part of a mass communication audience. To coin a phrase, audiences exhibit a "selective heterogeneity." Certainly, most mass media are available to a heterogeneous public, even if they are not actually used by a heterogeneous audience.

4. *The audience tends to be relatively anonymous.* Communicators normally do not know the specific individuals with whom they are communicating, although they may be aware of general audience characteristics. For example, Madonna does not personally know the individuals who are listening to her latest record.

5. *The audience tends to be physically separated from the communicator.* The movie *Top Gun* was seen by audience members months after it had been shot and miles from the studio where it had been produced. Audiences are separated from the conglomerate communicator in both time and space.

Audiences are also identified with a variety of subclassifications. We talk about available audiences in television (those who have their sets on) versus the actual audience (those who are tuned to a specific show). Print-readership studies focus on primary readers (those who buy the publications) versus pass-along readers (those who read the publications bought by others). Advertisers are interested in target audiences, those individuals who match prospective buyer characteristics or are "heavy users" of a specific brand or product class.

In *Theories of Mass Communication*, sociologists Melvin DeFleur and Sandra Ball-Rokeach analyze three perspectives of how audiences interact with the mass media and the messages that the media carry: the Individual-Differences Perspective, the Social-Categories Perspective, and the Social-Relationships Perspective.[2] In effect, DeFleur and Ball-Rokeach are looking at the effects of mass media—audience interaction, or how the audience acts on the content of the media.

The Individual Differences Perspective

The Individual Differences Perspective describes audiences in terms of behaviorism, according to which learning takes place on a stimulus–response basis. According to this view, there is no uniform mass audience; the mass media affect each audience member differently in terms of that individual's psychological make-up derived from past experiences.

In the Individual Differences Perspective, illustrated in Figure 18.1, the individual audience members (A_1, A_2, A_3) act on the media content by selectively attending to and perceiving the same messages using different,

---

[2] Melvin L. DeFleur and Sandra Ball-Rokeach, *Theories of Mass Communication*, 3d ed. (New York: Longman, 1975), pp. 202–225.

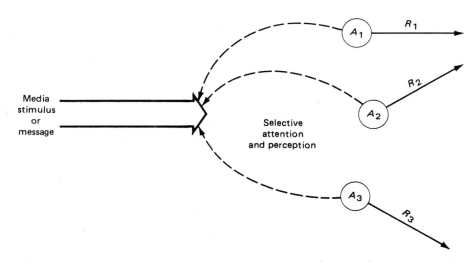

Figure 18.1 A visualization of the Individual Difference Perspective illustrates the behavioral nature of this concept. When an audience member is exposed to a media experience, he or she responds differently from others, based on his or her unique make-up.

individual filters. Therefore, each individual responds differently (A_1 produces R_1; A_2 reacts with R_2; and A_3 responds with R_3). This perspective suggests that each of us responds independently to the same message.

The Social Categories Perspective

The Social Categories Perspective takes the position that there are social aggregates in American society based on the common characteristics of sex, age, education, income, occupation, and so forth. Since these social aggregates have had shared experiences, audience members have similar social norms, values, and attitudes. According to this view, there are broad audience groups (for example, working mothers, males aged 18 to 49, southern white females with two children) that react similarly to specific message inputs.

In the Social Categories Perspective, illustrated in Figure 18.2, the members of the audience (A_1, A_2, A_3) are culturally linked and have a frame of reference in common; therefore, their responses to the same message are similiar, given that other conditions remain the same.

The Individual Differences and Social Categories perspectives, in combination, produce the "who says what to whom with what effect" approach in the following manner:

> While these two perspectives on mass communication remain useful and contemporary, there have been further additions to the set of variables intervening between media stimuli and audience response. One addi-

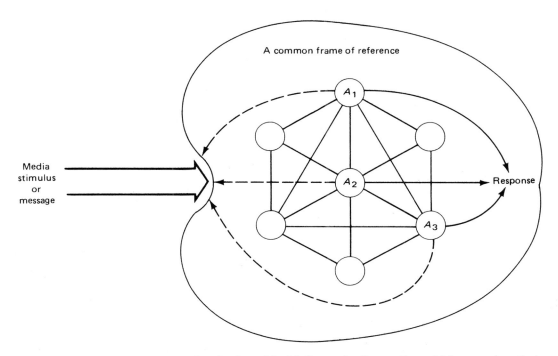

Figure 18.2 A visualization of Social Categories Perspective, which recognizes that audience members not only are individuals, but also belong to social aggregates. Because of their group membership, they may respond in ways similar to the response patterns of other members of their group.

tional elaboration of the S–R formula represents a somewhat belated recognition of the importance of patterns of interaction between audience members.[3]

The Social Relationships Perspective

The Social Relationships Perspective, which is based on the research of Paul Lazarsfeld, Bernard Berelson, Elihu Katz, and others, suggests that informal relationships significantly affect audiences. The impact of a given mass communication is altered tremendously by persons who have strong social relationships with the audience member. As a result, the individual is affected as much by other audience members' attitudes as by the mass communication itself.

In the Social Relationships Perspective, illustrated in Figure 18.3, the audience members (A_1, A_2, A_3) and an opinion leader (OL) receive a message. According to this view, it is not the media stimulus that has the

---

[3] Ibid., p. 206.

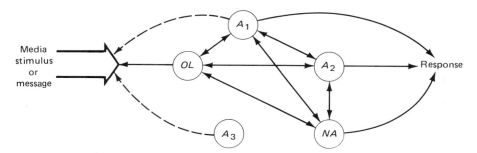

Figure 18.3 A visualization of the Social Relationships Perspective suggests that interpersonal interaction occurs before, during, and after the mass communication event and that these interactions are significant in terms of individuals' responses to media content. The model also suggest that there are opinion leaders (OL), influential individuals who may be relatively important in audience members' thinking as they make up their minds on a given issue.

significant impact; the informal interaction with others and a significant other (opinion leader) creates a common response. Audience member A_3 has no observable reaction, but an individual (NA) who did not receive the media message but did interact with audience members now reacts as they do. The interaction, rather than the message in isolation, has the significant impact.

If we combine aspects of all three perspectives, we come up with the following description of a possible audience "theory": no one mass audience of the media system exists; rather, a variety of audiences exists for each media event. All of us are members of a large number of audiences, but each audience member reacts individually. His or her individual reaction may be similar, however, to that of other audience members who have shared experiences. Our interaction with other audience members, nonmembers, and opinion leaders also has an impact on how we respond and may lead to a common reaction. As a result of being a member of an audience, an individual is changed by the total media experience, not just by the content of that experience.

THE CONCEPT OF FILTRATION

Filtration is the process of removing impurities, of separating particles from liquids or gases, or of eliminating certain light and sound wavelengths. When the filtering is over, one is left with less, yet one hopes it is more.

In mass communication, messages must struggle one against the other because there are so many of them. The average American is involved in thousands of communication exhanges a day. Communication overload is a reality, and our filters help us eliminate the useless, the annoying, and the unwanted. To some extent, filtration is our communication life jacket.

The filtering process depends on "frames of reference" within each individual member of the audience. Filters are the complex mechanisms that we use to "decode" messages. Your filters are a part of you; they are learned, and they can be relearned. They can be improved, and their improvement will make you a better audience member. Filters are, in effect, frames of reference.

The Conditions of Filtration

Four basic sets of conditions have an impact on our ability to filter messages: (1) informational or linguistic filters or conditions; (2) psychological filters or conditions; (3) cultural filters or conditions; and (4) physical filters or conditions. These filters or conditions are the ways in which we learn or are trained to receive or ignore messages in our daily communication activities.

Informational and Linguistic Filters. Do you have the basic "linguistic sets" necessary to decode a message? Can you understand the nuances of the language, whether verbal or part of the communicator's body language?

Each of us has learned a variety of languages and the responses to those codes. When you do not know the signs and symbols, you are at a serious disadvantage. Egyptian hieroglyphs slept for centuries until the work of Jean François Champollion unlocked the secret of the Rosetta stone. Champollion discovered that the Egyption symbols are syllabic and alphabetic rather than pictographic. The mysteries and the glories of ancient Egypt became readable once the message was filterable.

Without accurate informational filters, no positive communication can occur. If you cannot decode the message, you cannot communicate. The specialized codes of science and technology baffle us not because we are not intelligent, but because we do not possess the necessary language skill. That is why in mass communication, the primary directive of the conglomerate communicator is to code the content not in a private language, but in a symbolic form that the audience can filter accurately and easily.

As the world grows more complex, the problems of cross-occupational communication, in one sense at least, grow greater rather than smaller. As people become more specialized in the functions they perform, their filters become more specialized. They acquire a specialized vocabulary and language for their tasks. Engineers do not speak the language of doctors. The people who live in a neighborhood may have less in common with one another than they have with professional colleagues whom they meet only occasionally. We have to make new maps of the world informationally.

Specialized media have developed to accommodate the growing specialization of people. Almost every day, a new publication is born in Amer-

ica to serve a distinct audience, whether it is a group of prosthetics specialists or an association of terrazzo and mosaic experts. These new media
vehicles for new audiences develop new languages, which require specialized informational filters.

The front page of *Variety* may drive the point home (Figure 18.4). The
"show-biz" jargon is made up of nontraditional symbols. But as one reads
along and becomes familiar with the style, one's informational filters
"clock on." The theatrical nature of the words becomes not only comprehensible, but also more meaningful than standard English. You do not
even need a Rosetta stone. That's show biz!

And that is how our linguistic and informational filters work. We see
the world through "Rosetta-colored" frames of reference.

Psychological Filters. Each of us has a personality based on individual
experiences. We are more than one-dimensional; we are multifaceted. Our
personal receptivity to a specific communication is based on psychological
sets. These psychological sets are complex, and under various conditions,
psychological filters can reflect a variety of responses to the same content.

Our psychological sets, in effect, are what make us intellectually and
emotionally selective regarding the communication process. The psychological sets define other people, situations, and events. As receivers of
messages, we know that certain situations, individuals, interactions, symbols, words, and so on have more impact than others.

We structure our perception of the world in terms that are meaningful
to us, according to our frames of reference, or filters. This process has
been described as selective exposure, selective perception, and selective
retention. Wilbur Schramm defines three problems that communicators
must expect to face when they try to communicate meaning. First, receivers will interpret the message in terms of their own experiences and the
ways in which they have learned to respond to them. For example, a jungle
tribesman who has never seen an airplane will tend to interpret the first
airplane he sees as a bird. Second, receivers will interpret messages in such
a way as to resist any change in strong personality structures. For instance,
a woman who is strongly committed to the Democratic party will tend to
ignore the campaign information of the Republicans. Third, receivers will
tend to group characteristics on the basis of their experiences in order to
make whole patterns. As is the case when we look at abstract art, we "fill
in" the meaning. We add to what the artist provides based on our individual experiences with other works of art. Our enjoyment of a painting or
sculpture depends on our personal understanding or taste in art. We psychologically filter the work to give it personal meaning.

Rape is a powerful word psychologically because it connotes one person brutalizing another. Ask a group of men if they have been raped.
There are sometimes responses such as "not lately," which often gets a big
laugh. Then ask those same men if they have seen *Deliverance,* a film in

Figure 18.4 Specialized informational or linguistic filters are required to decode the "show-biz" jargon of *Variety*. (Copyright 1986 by Variety, Inc. All rights reserved.)

495

Figure 18.5 The film *Deliverance* is extremely powerful because of its impact on its audiences' cultural filters. This well-made and intelligent film brings an intense, emotional meaning to the word *rape* and to the concept of rape, especially for men in the audience.

which a man is raped by another man. Now the situation changes, and the laughter dies. Most men understand the terror of the concept, and the psychological impact is sobering. The filter changed with the situation, rather than with the symbol or source.

So the litany of power words depends on the source and the situation as well as on the symbol because our psychological filters are discerning.

Cultural Filters. Our filters—the senses—are colored, distorted, and polarized by our culture. Edward T. Hall, a cultural anthropologist, has written effectively about the role of culture in human communications efforts. In his book *The Silent Language,* he shows how culture affects the way a person sends and receives messages. We are fully aware, he writes, of "the broad extent to which culture controls our lives. Culture is not an exotic notion studied by a select group of anthropologists in the South Seas. It is a mold in which we are all cast, and it controls our daily lives in many unsuspected ways."[4]

Ten kinds of human activity are "primary message systems": interaction, association, subsistence, sexuality, territoriality, temporality, learning, play, defense, and exploitation (or use of materials). These systems vary from individual to individual and from culture to culture. They constitute a vocabulary and a language of their own, a silent language of which most of us are not aware.

Consider temporality, for example. To the average American of European origin, time exists as a continuum; there is a past, a present, and a future. Such a person is able to compartmentalize time, to recognize distinctions in time, and to do one thing at a time. The American-European culture is basically linear, and that is perhaps one cultural reason for this perceptual phenomenon. But to the Navajo, time has no limits. Some American Indian cultures, without written languages, were nonlinear. For the Navajo, time has no beginning, middle, or end. Time starts when the Navajo is ready, not at a given point. The future has little reality because it does not exist in the Navajo's time; nor does the past. The Cherokee, on the other hand, developed a written language with a dictionary and a very different, perhaps more complex, culture.

Territoriality is also a cultural message system. The average American of European origin has a strong sense of space and knows where things belong and to whom they belong. Individuals with this cultural background establish their rights to territory. For example, students take certain seats in a classroom; these chairs become *their* seats, and the students may well return to the same seats throughout the semester, as if they had established rights to them. But to the Hopi, space does not belong to anyone; they are apt to settle down wherever it suits them, regardless of whose territory they are invading.

Obviously, the Navajo and the Hopi have different message systems regarding time and space from those exhibited by Americans of European origin. This cannot help but affect their message intake and output on any subject that involves temporality or territoriality. We can make an almost endless list of cultural traits and subcultural habits of mind that influence our patterns of communication and our ability to make the act of communication a sharing of an understanding.

Cultures are social systems composed of people who have attitudes, mores, beliefs, and opinions in common. In a pluralistic society such as ours, the subgroups to which we belong are often stronger in molding our cultural communication filters than is the parent society. The enduring subcultural attitudes, mores, beliefs, and opinions, however, are undergoing homogenization carried out by the mass media.

---

[4] Edward T. Hall, *The Silent Language* (Garden City, N.Y.: Doubleday, 1959).

Figure 18.6 The film *Apocalypse Now* generates tremendous power by not stereotyping the Vietnamese. Indeed, all the major characters play against type in this film. The stereotypical heroes and heroic acts in many war films are totally absent from this document of the Vietnam War, which is based on Joseph Conrad's novel *Heart of Darkness.* (Photo: Courtesy of Zoetrope Studios. All rights reserved.)

Stereotyping was discussed at length by Walter Lippmann in a pioneering work, *Public Opinion,* originally published in 1922. He borrowed the term *stereotyping* from the printing industry. It refers to the plates, molded from type, that are used to reproduce printed copies, each of which is the same as the original. Lippmann used the term to characterize the human tendency to reduce perceptions to convenient categories, cataloging people, ideas, and actions according to frames of reference for the purpose of easy recognition.

"The pictures inside peoples' heads," Lippmann wrote, "do not automatically correspond with the world outside." Yet the pictures in our heads are our public opinions, and when those pictures "are acted upon by groups of people, or by individuals acting in the name of groups, they are Public Opinion with capital letters."[5] The Public Opinion is the "national

---

[5] Walter Lippman, *Public Opinion* (New York: Free Press, 1922; reprint, 1965).

will," which is supposed to inform the public about the truth of the world outside. But communicators themselves cannot keep from shaping the news in terms of the pictures in their heads and the stereotypes of their audiences.

We can see one example of stereotyping in our attitudes toward people of other nations. Two social psychologists, William Buchanan and Hadley Cantril, studied the images that one national group had of another and found a definite tendency to ascribe certain characteristics to certain people. For example, Americans think of Russians as cruel, hard-working, domineering, backward, conceited, and brave. Americans think of themselves as peace-loving, generous, intelligent, progressive, hard-working, and brave. The British think of Americans as intelligent, hard-working, brave, peace-loving, and self-controlled. Buchanan and Cantril found that people who live in countries that are on friendly terms tend to use less derogatory adjectives in describing one another's characteristics and that people invariably describe their own national characteristics in flattering terms.

Physical Filters. No two people experience the world exactly alike. Our perception is limited or expanded by the way we have conditioned our eyes, ears, fingers, mouth, and nose. Our responses to the world are dependent on the fidelity of our seeing, hearing, touching, tasting, and smelling and the training of these senses.

Why does one person take better photographs than another? She has learned to see better compositions.

Why does a blind person hear things that a sighted person cannot? He has trained himself, consciously and unconsciously, to listen more carefully.

Why does a weaver choose the fibers she does? Her sense of touch is developed through practice of her craft.

Why does one person enjoy cooked cabbage or raw oysters or retsina wine or steak tartare or—believe it or not—even chicken, while another gags at the mention of them? The one who enjoys has cultivated a taste for these delights.

Why does a smoker not realize that her house, car, clothes, hair, and breath reek of cigarette smoke? She has reoriented her olfactory mechanism to disregard or enjoy these smells. The nonsmoker has not.

Our physical sensors are the receivers we use to gather in the communication around us. They are our communication response mechanism. Our sensory perception is heightened, diminished, accepted, or rejected by two sets of physical characteristics: internal physical conditions and external physical conditions.

Internal physical conditions refer to the well-being or health of the individual audience member. A person who is physically ill filters messages in a different way from that in which he or she does when in good health. A migraine headache, a bleeding ulcer, or an abcessed tooth can radically alter message filtering. The pain of a smashed thumb affects the sense of touch so intensely that sight and sound are impaired. In some cases, physical discomfort may heighten the communication experience; for example, a person with an upset stomach may be more than usually receptive to a Pepto-Bismol commercial. In the extreme, the absence or impairment of one sense significantly heightens the effectiveness of another. Blind individuals tend to develop acute hearing. Blindness filters motion-picture messages negatively but may increase positively the filtering of phonographic music.

External physical conditions refer to the environment or surroundings in which members of an audience receive messages. If the room in which you are reading this book is too hot, too cold, too dark, or too noisy, the environment will affect your senses and the way you filter the content of this page. Most motion-picture theaters are constructed in such a way that the result is the most satisfactory environment possible for viewing films. Every sense is catered to in order to improve the way movies are filtered. Compare watching a film in a theater with watching a movie on television. The room is lighted. People wander in and out. The phone rings. Commercials interrupt. Your senses are bombarded by an array of competing stimuli. No wonder seeing a movie in a theater is a better experience than seeing the same movie at home. We filter these two experiences in entirely different physical environments. Every medium is affected in significantly different ways by the way people feel and the physical surroundings in which they use the medium.

These two physical conditions also relate to two major problems that mass media communicators must face: information overload and clutter.

Information overload is a fact of life. There is just too much communication in our lives. The amount of mass communication would overwhelm us if we let it, and so audience members at times just shut the mass media off with the switches on the sets and the filters in their heads. Because there is so much to digest in print, we are a society of speed-readers. We physically filter all but the necessary words.

Look at the three triangles in Figure 18.7. There is an error in each triangle. Find the error.

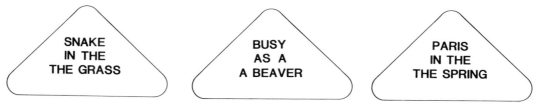

Figure 18.7 *Read aloud the phrases in the three triangles to determine the error in each. If you have trouble finding the mistake, read each phrase backward and point to each word as you proceed.*

If you have not found the error, look again. Each triangle repeats a word (Snake in the *the* grass. Busy as a *a* beaver. Paris in the *the* spring). Because each phrase is so familiar and because we speed-read, we misread. There is too much to read; we cope by deleting what we think is unnecessary. Information overload leads to filtering out some of the wheat with the chaff.

Unfortunately, time has not expanded to meet the demands of increased mass communication, and so we physically react with more intense philtering. Philtering? You mean filtering. No, "philtering" stops you for a microsecond and makes you concentrate. The communicator is trying to combat your filters with philters.

Clutter is a broadcasting term that refers to too many bits and pieces of information in a time slot. For example, in the average 2-minute commercial break, there are four 30-second ads. Because of clutter, advertisers must ensure that their spots stand out amid the clutter. The adult viewer often "shuts down" during the commercial breaks or gets something to drink or talks to other viewers or goes to the bathroom. It is the opposite with many toddlers. They play during the show and run in to watch the commercials. Why? Television ads are intense visual experiences because of increased volume, more arresting visuals, and rapid, dynamic editing of both sound and picture.

WHY AUDIENCES NEED FILTERS

Marshall McLuhan described the audience situation in terms of the concept of *implosion*. In this description, the audience is central to mass communication and is under constant bombardment from the media. Instead of talking about a communication explosion, we may have to refer to a communication implosion.

McLuhan argued that the medium itself, not the content of that medium, "massages" the audience.

> Societies have always been shaped more by the nature of the media by which men communicate than by the content of the communication. The alphabet, for instance, is a technology that is absorbed by the very young child in a completely unconscious manner, by osmosis so to speak. Words and the meaning of words predispose the child to think and act automatically in certain ways. The alphabet and print technology fostered and encouraged a fragmenting process, a process of specialism and of detachment. Electric technology fosters and encourages unification and involvement. It is impossible to understand social and cultural changes without a knowledge of the workings of media.[6]

The individual American resides in a mass media vortex and is pummeled on all sides by the experience. Mass communication implodes on the

---

[6] Marshall McLuhan, *The Medium Is the Message* (New York: Bantam Books, 1967), pp. 26–72.

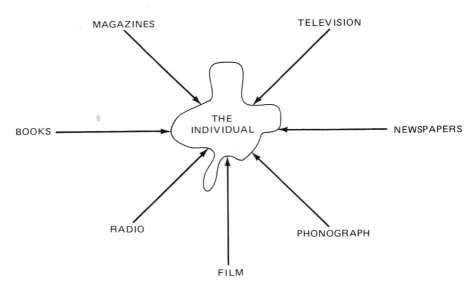

Figure 18.8 *Marshall McLuhan developed the concept of implosion to sensitize readers to the idea that the mass media are so pervasive that they literally massage individual members of an audience and their cultural outlook.*

individual. The media are so pervasive that they are almost impossible for audiences to escape. In addition, each individual is a member of a great number of audiences and receives thousands of mass messages daily. People have developed barriers that resist most mass communication and filter in those messages that might be helpful for a particular need.

There are informational, physical, psychological, and cultural limits to our ability to perceive and understand. As the mass media provide more and more information and as entertainment and implosion increase, an audience's filtering systems become ever-increasingly taxed, so much so that an individual can or may stop receiving anything at all for a period of time. We daydream, we drift, we lose concentration, we "bail out." The mass media can be overwhelming and our filters allow us to make decisions about what we will receive and retain when we read, listen to, and view the mass media.

Audience Environments

Audiences filter mass media content in a variety of specialized environments. And the media re-create or modify environments when they are introduced into them. Television has changed the living room forever. In a like manner, the physical conditions in which media are used affect the audience response.

Reading Environments. Print media are highly mobile; they can be used almost anywhere if the user is literate and there is enough light to read by.

Interestingly, some print-use environments establish physical constraints on the user. The library, presumably a place where people go to concentrate, usually demands quiet. Reading a textbook or studying for a test usually requires *low*-level sound. Freedom of movement is not restricted, however. It is amazing how irritating noise can be in a library but how unobtrusive it becomes on the subway ride to work. The rider conditions himself or herself to the reading of magazines, newspapers, and books in this noisy environment.

All of us learn to use media in a variety of environments. When these environmental conditions are altered, the audience member may become upset. Today's older generation learned to study quietly, and parents cannot fathom their children's use of rock music for background purposes while doing homework. The amount of retention required affects the reading situation. Reading for pleasure and reading for school are different acts and demand different levels of concentration because each requires us to learn different amounts and kinds of information.

The reading of a magazine, newspaper, or book can take place in many environments. Studying, however, tends to be most successful if done in environments that have little distraction. Nevertheless, the tremendous mobility of most printed matter allows readers to function anywhere they can establish satisfactory physical and psychological environments.

Listening and Viewing Environments. Radio has great mobility if the audience member owns a portable radio or has a car radio. In addition to having the physical device, the radio user must have an electrical source, be it dry-cell batteries, the car battery, or the standard alternating current. The automobile environment requires primary concentration on driving. For this reason, one hopes that the radio gets less attention than the road. Despite this, the driver is a captive audience unless he or she turns off the radio or leaves the car. The portable radio has no single physical setting for its use; portable use is inhibited where radio volume would disturb others, but the Sony Walkman has solved this problem.

The TV set tends to be located in a specific place, generally the living room or family room, which is often modified for the viewing experience. If a house has more than two sets, the extra sets generally go into bedrooms. There are portable TV sets, but the TV receiver tends to be less portable than radio or print media. The TV room is often the focus of family activity, and normal distractions and interruptions are accepted as part of the viewing experience. They are not only permissible, but also encouraged.

The environment for listening to records or tapes depends greatly on whether the phonograph or tape deck in use is the portable that belongs to the youngsters or the family stereo. The portable usually gets around more, and because it has little sound quality, it has to be played louder. The stereo is often housed in a visible area—immovable and supreme. The portable and the 45-rpm record can be adapted to new environments by means of increased volume. The album and the stereo modify the environment in which they are kept. Perhaps the best phonograph environment is provided by headsets, which eliminate other aural stimuli.

The motion-picture-viewing environment is the least portable and the most institutionalized of all the media environments. Watching a movie at home, on television, or in the classroom is completely unlike the experience of watching it in a movie theater. The movie house is created to increase the involvement of the audience with the film experience: the screen is huge; the theater is dark; the seats are designed for comfort; interruptions are minimal; the sound is usually good. Without question, motion pictures are shown in the best of all possible controlled media environments.

SUMMARY

Audiences use their filters to understand the contents presented by the mass media.

A distinction is made between the *public* (those available) and the *audience* (those attending the mass medium in question). The audiences of the mass communication media can be described as (1) composed of individuals who may have shared characteristics, (2) large, (3) heterogenous rather than homogenous, (4) relatively anonymous, and (5) physically separated from the communicator.

Audiences are also evaluated by the advertisers who buy them, in terms of being available or actual (in broadcasting) and primary or pass-along (in print).

Three theories developed by DeFleur and Ball-Rokeach attempt to describe how audiences respond to media stimuli. The Individual Differences theory describes audience members as reacting independently to each media event. The Social Categories theory suggests that individuals aggregate and respond similarly based on commonly shared characteristics such as age, sex, education, and income. The Social Relationships theory suggests that informal relationships and interpersonal communications before, during, and after media exposure impact on the effects of the experiences.

Audiences use all their senses to perceive messages and filter those messages with four filters: (1) *informational and linguistic* filters—do we understand the code/language used? (2) *psychological* filters—How do we selectively expose ourselves to respond to and retain media messages, and how are these behaviors related to our psychological/emotional makeup? (3) *Cultural* filters—How does our upbringing/background associations affect the reception and understanding of mass communication? (4) *Physical* filters—How does our comfort and well being (internal) and the environments (external) in which we receive messages impact on our responses.

In effect, a wide variety of individuals and audiences use many filters (frames of reference) to their advantage in the process of mass communication.

BIBLIOGRAPHY

Beville, Hugh M., Jr. *Audience Ratings: Radio, Television, and Cable*. Hillsdale, N.J.: Erlbaum, 1985.

Bower, Robert T. *The Changing Television Audience in America*. New York: Columbia University Press, 1985.

DeFleur, Melvin L., and Sandra Ball-Rokeach. *Theories of Mass Communication*. 4th ed. New York: Longman, 1982.

Dominick, Joseph R., and James Fletcher. *Broadcasting Research Methods*. Boston: Allyn and Bacon, 1985.

Fowles, Jib. *Television Viewers vs. Media Snobs: What TV Does for People*. New York: Stein and Day, 1982.

Frank, Ronald E., and Marshall G. Greenberg. *The Public's Use of Television: Who Watches and Why*. Beverly Hills, Calif.: Sage, 1980.

Marc, David. *Demographic Vistas: Television in American Culture*. Philadelphia: University of Pennsylvania Press, 1984.

Murray, John P. *Television and Youth: Twenty-Five Years of Research and Controversy*. Boystown, Neb.: Boystown Center, 1980.

Percy, Larry, and Arch G. Woodside, eds. *Advertising and Consumer Psychology*. Lexington, Mass.: Lexington Books, 1983.

19

Feedback, Noise, and Amplification

In the 1985/1986 television season, the NBC program "Remington Steele" ranked number 48 out of the year's 82 shows, averaging a 14.4 rating (percentage of TV homes that watched "Remington Steele") and a 25 share (percentage of TV homes watching television that were tuned to "Remington Steele"). On the basis of this feedback, NBC canceled the program. This is the normal pattern of mass communication feedback—representative, delayed information being sent back to the communicator in quantitative form by audience research companies such as Nielsen and Arbitron.

But as a result of a rare instance of direct, personal, qualitative (at least partially), and nonrepresentative feedback, NBC reversed its decision and renewed "Remington Steele" for the 1986/1987 season. The impetus for reviving the show, NBC said, came from over 8,700 calls and letters from loyal fans. Even after the show was renewed, letters at the rate of 150 to 200 a day kept arriving in support of the program.

In network television, Nielsen ratings are usually the only feedback used to make programming decisions. The same is true across other mass media, although the exact form of feedback is different—circulation figures for newspapers and magazines, sales of tickets for motion pictures, or sales of books and records or tapes for the publishing and recording industries. These forms of media feedback have a major impact on the process of mass communication.

Figure 19.1 In a rare instance of direct viewer feedback (letters and telephone calls), "Remington Steele," starring Pierce Brosnan and Stephanie Zimbalist, was taken off the canceled list and put back into NBC's program schedule.

THE CHARACTERISTICS OF FEEDBACK

Communication, by definition, is a two-way process, a cooperative and collaborative venture. It is a joint effort, a mutual experience, an exchange between two parties—a sender and a receiver. The communication experience is not complete until an audience is able to respond to the message of the communicator. That response is called *feedback*.

In interpersonal communication, the receiver usually responds naturally, directly, and immediately to the message and sender. We may flutter our eyelids or raise an eyebrow, ask for explanation or repetition, or even argue a point. In this way, a message is shaped and reshaped by the participants until the meaning becomes clear. The sender and the receiver interact and constantly exchange roles.

On the surface, many responses to mass communication seem to resemble those in interpersonal communication. An audience member may frown, yawn, cough, swear, throw down a magazine, kick a television set, or talk back. None of these responses is observable to the mass communicator, however, and all are ineffective responses unless they lead to further

Figure 19.2 Interpersonal feedback enhances and enlivens this communication experience. (Photo: Brendan Beirne.)

action—writing a letter, making a phone call, canceling a subscription, or turning off the television set.

Because of the distance in time and space between communicator and audience in the mass communication process, feedback in mass communication assumes different characteristics from feedback in interpersonal communication. Instead of being individual, direct, immediate, one-time, and personal, mass communication feedback is representative, indirect, delayed, cumulative, quantitative, institutionalized, and costly.

Despite what seem to be complicating obstacles—obstacles not worth the effort in overcoming—feedback for mass communicators is extremely important. All of us want our communication to be efficient; that is, we want to achieve the goals of our communication with as little effort as possible. Mass communicators are similarly concerned. Communicating by mass media involves enormous expense that has to be justified to executives and stockholders. The communicator must bring a return on the investment, must demonstrate that his or her communication is efficient; and feedback is necessary to provide the proof. Each of the three national TV networks pays $3.5 million for Nielsen basic data. Newspapers and magazines have had their circulation figures verified since 1914 by the Audit Bureau of Circulation (ABC). The cost of this service, about $5 million a year, is born by the newspapers and magazines through service fees to the ABC. Just these two forms of feedback cost over $15 million a year. Add to this figure feedback costs for such information as Arbitron (ARB) diaries, Starch reports, and Simmons Market Research Bureau studies, and you have some indication of how important feedback is to the mass media. Therefore, feedback in mass communication is not simply desirable; it is required. Because it is required, the mass media have gone to elaborate lengths to ensure that it is received on a regular basis. Let us look in more detail at the characteristics of mass communication feedback.

Representative

The audiences of mass media are so large that it is impossible to measure feedback from each member of every audience. Instead, a representative sample of the audience is selected for measurement, and the response of this sample is projected scientifically to the whole. A letter to the editor or a change of channels may be noted by the mass communicator, but these responses usually have little significance unless they can be shown to be statistically representative of the feelings and actions of a large portion of that medium's total audience. In measuring the feedback of mass media audiences, the specific responses of every individual are replaced by the responses of a representative sample of the total population.

Sampling is perhaps the least understood and most controversial aspect of mass communication survey research. In determining the size of the sample, the idea is to use as few units as possible and still maintain reasonable accuracy. What makes for "reasonable accuracy" varies, but the standard rule of thumb in media-audience research is that samples of fewer than 100 units are often unreliable and samples of more than 1,000 are seldom needed. Nielsen, for example, uses a national sample of about 1,700 households to determine national TV ratings. It may be difficult to accept that 1,700 homes can represent all the TV homes in the United States, but sampling technique is a proven method that has stood the test of time.

Nielsen, like most research companies, takes great care to create a national sample that is representative of the whole population. It uses a sample drawn from U.S. census maps by a method known as *multistage area probability sampling*. Basically, the method guarantees that the number of sample members from each geographical area is proportionate to the total population of the area. For its individual-market ratings, Nielsen uses special, current telephone directories.

As developments in media technology expand, especially in television, questions are being raised about traditional sampling methods. Special attention has been focused on the Nielsen national TV ratings because of their effect on the TV industry. The Nielsen sampling process involves a small, randomly dispersed sample with no weighting made to correct for sample imbalances. The process works when the viewer has the option of

Figure 19.3 An unusual example of television-viewer feedback occurred in 1984 when a young woman prepared to throw a brick at the screen when Howard Cosell appeared on ''Monday Night Football.'' (Photo: AP/World Wide Photo.)

choosing among 5 or so programs, but it is overly taxed when the viewer has the option of viewing any of 30, 40, or even 100 channel opportunities. With the advancement of cable and satellite technology, which promises to bring 100 channels and more into the cable-TV household, a much closer look must be given to the sampling process that affects Nielsen's audience measurements.

In the past, when TV viewing was confined to broadcast, most of it network, a distortion in Nielsen's sample was not critical, for all viewing was restricted to the same programming regardless of household characteristics. Today's TV usage can include either network or nonnetwork broadcasting, cable, or, most important, videocassette recording and/or playback. The need to differentiate accurately among these opportunities grows in importance as costs continue to escalate.

As VCR penetration jumped from 11 percent in 1984 to over 35 percent in 1986, the effect of time shifting, fast forwarding past commercials (known as "zapping"), or not playing the recorded program has become of deep concern to the network broadcaster. In the past, Nielsen credited all VCR taping as viewing, but advertisers recognized that this is not the case and have succeeded in persuading Nielsen to inaugurate a supplementary ratings report that will eliminate credit for taping. Any inconsistencies in the composition of the Nielsen sample may well distort audience selection and levels. Sensitive to such criticism, Nielsen uses audimeters, mechanical devices attached to sample-home television sets, to measure the program and channel viewing of the household and diaries, filled out by the sample viewers, to supply demographic information. The method has built-in limitations and potential for error, however, especially if the diaries are not filled out promptly.

With the recent proliferation of viewing choices, the television industry recognized the need for a method of recording audiences that would be more precise than audimeters and diaries. Nielsen responded in 1985 by testing its "people meter."

The people meter is an electronic box fixed to a family's television set. On the box are a number of buttons; each family member is assigned a specific button. The individual is required to press the appropriate button each time he or she views, stops viewing, or leaves the room. The people meter's main advantage over the diary method is its ability, if operated properly, to calculate the minute-by-minute viewing of each member of a household, recorded by the members themselves.

Nielsen's test of these meters showed that the technology is both workable and more accurate than the diary method. So in the autumn of 1985, Nielsen announced that it would replace its diary sample with a national people-meter sample for the 1986–1987 broadcast year. This announcement caused no ripples at the time it was made.

The situation was relatively calm as Nielsen began installing people meters and reporting data—first from 400 homes in January 1986 and then from 600 in February 1986, targeting toward a full sample of 1,000 people-meter homes by June 1986.

Researchers at the networks and advertising agencies began to compare the people-meter data with the diary data still being supplied. Not surprisingly, the effects of "diary-bias" now showed up in black and white. While total television usage was about the same in both samples, such key demographic audiences as women aged 18 to 49 and women aged

25 to 54 were 5 to 10 percent lower for network programs in the people-meter sample than in the diary sample during prime time. In daytime, audiences of women aged 25 to 54 for network programs, as measured by the people meter, were about 5 percent below those recorded in the diary.

With the reported ratings in prime time and daytime suddenly shrinking, and the up-front marketplace fast approaching, reconsideration of Nielsen's decision to abandon the diary method by the end of the broadcast year suddenly acquired critical importance for the networks. Financially, two concerns arose. In a "competitive" marketplace, they feared that larger network advertisers would use the new, lower people-meter audience estimates to drive much harder bargains with them, relative to prices paid on diary numbers. The comparison of cost efficiencies based on people meters in 1986 and 1987 with efficiencies based on diaries in 1985 and 1986, the networks felt, was apples versus oranges. Advertisers, of course, countered with the claim that apparently they have been overpaying for their "oranges" by 5 to 10 percent for the past several years.

The second financial worry for the networks was the question of guarantees. Large network advertisers typically receive guarantees on the demographic delivery of the packages they buy. The networks claimed that there is not enough of a track record with people meters to permit them to offer such guarantees.

Faced with strong pressure from the networks and a split among advertisers, Nielsen announced that it would continue the diary system until the 1987–1988 broadcast season.

The people-meter issue not only points out the tremendous importance of media feedback, but also highlights the representative nature of media feedback and the significance of accurate representation to the media communicator—in this case, the major TV networks.

Indirect

Rarely does a performer on television or a reporter for a newspaper receive any direct response from audience members. Rather, the feedback comes through a third party: a rating organization or a polling company. Even when a performer or reporter receives a telephone call from a listener or a letter from a reader, the response seldom offers much opportunity for direct interaction or substantially changes specific media content, unless the response is felt to be representative of the opinion of a large part of the audience. Because mass communication feedback is filtered through a third party, such as a rating organization, there is less variety in form and type of feedback. As we discuss later, one form—quantitative feedback—dominates. In effect, a rating organization such as Arbitron or Simmons acts as a gatekeeper in reverse, altering, modifying, or even preventing feedback from reaching the communicator.

Delayed

Mass media feedback is delayed from the moment of original transmission. There are overnight TV ratings, but most network ratings are published weekly. Local-TV reports are published three to eight times a year, depending on the size of the market. Letters to the editor must go through the mail and face even further delay because of periodical publishing deadlines. The following letter to the editor, which contains feedback that significantly alters the original communication, appeared in *Business Week* six weeks after the original article.

> The statement in "Magic Chef's new recipe calls for upscale appliances" (Product Development, June 20) that Magic Chef replaced "heavy, expensive, die-cast aluminum doors with plastic doors" on its microwave oven line to cut more than 20 lb. from the weight and pare the price tag by at least $200 is both untrue and unfair.
>
> The large weight savings looks questionable, but the cost saving is unbelievably high.
>
> LARRY BUCHTMANN
Sunnymead, California

> *The article should have stated that changes in design and production in addition to the door contributed to the weight saving and that the price reduction stemmed in part from a more competitive pricing strategy by Magic Chef.*

Surveys and polls take time to conduct and evaluate. The reaction of the communicator to feedback from the audience is also delayed by the particular technological and industrial characteristics of a medium. For example, once a motion picture is "in the can," it can be modified in only minor ways after an audience's reaction to preview screenings. Michael Cimino's film *Heaven's Gate* was scheduled to be released in late 1980. Preview screenings resulted in such universally negative feedback that the $33 million film was not released. Here was the ultimate consequence of delayed mass communication feedback: the potential loss of a huge amount of money because the content was completed, at great cost, before significant audience reaction was received. The film was eventually released in 1984 and flopped at the box office.

In some instances, feedback from preview audiences can be used to modify content in positive ways. James Bridges used a preview of his film *Mike's Murder,* which he described as "disastrous," to make major changes. The preview forced Bridges to think twice about a particular sequence in which the title character is killed. He decided to eliminate the sequence altogether and simply suggest the murder. While toning down the volume, Bridges also decided to alter the film's musical score to include more dramatic and traditional music by John Barry.

In the daily newspaper, modifications and corrections are played down and put on the back pages because they are not timely and newsworthy. Before the first episode of a new network-TV series appears in the fall, 13 episodes of that series have usually been completed. Therefore, because of the financial investment and contractual commitments involved, poor ratings (negative feedback) rarely spell the immediate termination of a new TV program; this usually occurs at the end of the first, or fall, quarter (the 13-week period from September to December).

Feedback to this book occurs primarily through published reviews and letters to the authors. Because the authors and publisher believe that more feedback is required, you will find a form at the back of the book to fill out and return. Response even to this improved feedback is delayed until the next edition is published, usually at least three years. The effect of delay, for this book or for other forms of mass communication, is the necessity of continuing inefficient communication beyond a natural stopping point. So despite the mass communicator's great concern over efficiency, by the very nature of the feedback process, a great deal of inefficiency is built into the original message.

Cumulative

In mass communication, the immediate and individual response is infrequent and therefore not too important. Rather, emphasis is placed on cumulative and collective responses over a substantial period of time. Since the response is usually delayed, there is little chance for immediate reaction, and so the communicator accumulates data over time from a variety of sources. The communicator stores the data, and this information influences future decisions, especially concerning what the public wants in the way of media content. The spin-off concept in TV programming is evidence of this. "The Mary Tyler Moore Show," for example, was very successful for several years. This success was attributed to the various characters in the series, including Mary's two female friends, Rhoda and Phyllis, and her boss, Lou Grant. Based on this cumulative feedback, series were created around each of these characters. The cumulative success of "Rich Man, Poor Man" stimulated the use of the anthology drama on prime-time television. Motion pictures such as *Indiana Jones and the Temple of Doom* (1984), *The Karate Kid: Part II* (1986), and *Rocky IV* (1985) are the result of cumulative feedback from the original motion picture. The enormous success of *People* magazine spawned a large number of similar efforts (*Us, We, Self*). These print spin-offs were the result of favorable cumulative feedback received by *People* in the form of subscriptions and newsstand sales. For radio ratings, the quarter-hour (the standard time unit of measurement) is so short that research organizations such as Arbitron compile cumulative audience figures known as cumes. For a radio station, cumes can represent many listeners over different quarter-hours or the same quarter-hour over a number of weeks. Cume persons are identified as the estimated number of different persons who listened at home and away to a station for a minimum of 5 minutes within a given daypart (specific time period such as 4 to 6 P.M.). Table 19.1 illustrates this feedback.

TABLE 19.1. AVERAGE QUARTER-HOUR AND CUME LISTENING ESTIMATES

Station call letters	Adults 25–29						Adults 25–54					
	Total area		Metro survey area				Total area		Metro survey area			
	Avg. pers (00)	Cume pers (00)	Avg. pers (00)	Cume pers (00)	Avg. pers rtg.	Ave pers shr.	Avg. pers (00)	Cume pers (00)	Avg. pers (00)	Cume pers (00)	Avg. pers rtg.	Avg. pers shr.
WABC	543	12608	476	10780	.9	4.7	595	14031	524	11975	.6	4.5
WADO	322	2467	322	2467	.6	3.2	398	2872	398	2872	.5	3.4
* WALK	1	64	1	64			3	140	3	140		
WALK FM	32	555	32	555	.1	.3	37	805	37	781	.1	.3
TOTAL	33	590	33	590	.1	.3	40	840	40	516	.1	.3
WBAB	39	480	39	480	.1	.4	39	480	39	480	.1	.3
WBLI	152	1775	151	1713	.3	1.5	157	1613	156	1751	.2	1.3
WBLS	648	7561	639	7448	1.2	6.4	672	7862	663	7749	1.0	5.7
WCBS	403	9270	342	7777	.6	3.4	517	11754	438	9891	.7	3.7
WCBS FM	668	10012	644	9535	1.2	6.4	685	10452	660	9927	1.0	5.6
WCTC	26	439	26	439		.3	33	597	33	597	.1	.3
WCTO	49	660	49	660	.1	.5	55	785	55	785	.1	.5
WEVD	36	583	36	583	.1	.4	40	899	40	599	.1	.3
* WHLI	52	614	52	614	.1	.5	78	1077	78	1077	.1	.7
WHM	353	6436	322	5885	.6	3.2	474	7593	439	6878	.7	3.7
WHUD	99	1118	53	634	.1	.5	143	1577	71	784	.1	.6
WINS	371	9342	368	9271	.7	3.7	472	11637	469	11566	.7	4.0
WJIT	242	2111	242	2111	.4	2.4	300	2263	300	2283	.5	2.6
WKHK	317	3852	286	3540	.5	2.8	346	4309	315	3955	.5	2.7
WKTU	779	9422	778	9360	1.4	7.7	786	9702	785	9540	1.2	6.7
* WLIB	79	1005	79	1005	.1	.8	87	1122	87	1122	.1	.7
WLIR	58	942	58	938	.1	.5	58	968	58	954	.1	.5
WMCA	161	2497	156	2384	.3	1.6	255	3533	250	3420	.4	2.1

Quantitative

For the most part, mass communication feedback is sought and measured in quantitative terms. Examples include box-office figures for motion pictures, ratings for TV programs, sales figures for records and books, and circulation figures for newspapers and magazines. Mass media critics provide qualitative judgments through book, photograph, movie, and TV reviews. But the mass communicator is more interested in knowing how many people responded rather than how one person (for example, a critic) responded, unless the critic's view can affect or represent the opinions of a number of people. In particular, the review of a book or movie, especially the review by a well-known critic, such as the *New York Times* film critic Vincent Canby or the *New Yorker*'s Pauline Kael, can seriously affect purchases or attendance. In television, the review of a particular program has little impact because it usually appears after the telecast. However, the cumulative effect of television criticism, especially that aimed at general issues or themes, can, if written by a major critic, influence the medium. A few critics claim that bad reviews can affect a program's success. However, this viewpoint is contradicted by the evidence. For instance, Bert Briller, of the Television Information Office, made an in-depth analysis of major reviews of new series for 1976, 1977, and 1979 and found "little correlation between what TV critics say about a new show and its chances of gaining a sizable audience."[1] Little or no consistent critical evaluation of newspapers, magazines, or radio is available to audiences. Numbers are what count in mass communication. As the Nielsen Company states in one of its promotional brochures, "These are quantitative measurements. The word rating is a misnomer because it implies a measurement of program quality—and this we never do. Never!"[2]

This fact creates some problems. When you consistently measure the success or efficiency of your message in terms of *how* many responses rather than *what kind* of response, you are severely limiting your ability to judge the quality of your message. A TV program may have a large audience at 9:00 P.M. on Tuesday, not because it is a good program, but because the competition is weak. Placed in another time slot or on another day, the same program may fail. In network television, for example, Saturday night is known as "the graveyard" because fewer people watch television on this night than on any other night.

The quality of quantitative feedback varies with the questions being asked. In terms of *how many people are exposed*, media research data are excellent within the limits of statistical error. As to *who the audience is*, the feedback is also superior within these statistical limits. In terms of *how*

---

[1] Richard Pack, "Can Critics Really Influence Television's Decision Makers?" *Television/Radio Age*, 19 August 1985, 106.

[2] Undated A. C. Nielsen Co. brochure, 5.

messages are perceived and *the effects of this perception,* reliable feedback is extremely limited, however.

Communication research firms are sensitive to criticism and are increasingly analyzing the why and who as well as the what of media audiences. Nielsen supplements its audimeter figures with diary responses, and more and more communicators are utilizing interviews and detailed questionnaires to go beyond a simple quantitative measure of response. Arbitron (ARB) specializes in radio ratings using the diary method. By such means, a radio-station manager can determine where the audience members live, how long they listen, when they listen, their age and sex, where they listen, and when they switch stations. Birch Radio's *Prism,* a semiannual ratings report, examines the listening preferences of 12 life-style groups that it profiles in what it terms "geo-demographic cluster groups."

Despite a strong quantitative bias, mass communication feedback is occasionally provided in qualitative measures. The most ambitious attempt to provide qualitative data on a large-scale basis has been the recent work of a company called Television Audience Assessment (TAA). Since 1982, TAA has conducted qualitative-ratings studies—primarily experimental— to assess the potential of the instrument and methodology. Based on findings from its studies, TAA developed two measures of viewer response to television programming: Program Impact and Program Appeal. Program Impact measures the emotional and intellectual stimulation a program provides its viewers, while Program Appeal measures the overall entertainment value of a program. The results of TAA studies indicate that programs with high Impact and Appeal are more likely to capture viewers' attention and increase their receptivity to commercials. Program Impact was especially meaningful.

Clearly, there are a number of applications of qualitative program ratings. Certainly, advertisers and agencies seeking greater advertising effectiveness will find qualitative ratings systems helpful. In today's highly competitive media environment, qualitative ratings provide the means for identifying who is actually watching, noticing, and reacting favorably to advertisers' messages. Examination of measures such as TAA's Impact and Appeal scores can help industry executives make better informed judgments about the values of different programs as environments for advertisements.

Institutionalized

Mass communication feedback is institutionalized. That is, large and complex organizations are required to provide meaningful feedback to mass communicators. Research organizations—such as the A. C. Nielsen Company, Arbitron (ARB), and Pulse, Inc.—provide quantitative feedback data

34   PROGRAM AUDIENCE ESTIMATES (Alphabetic)   2ND JAN. 1984 REPORT

WEEKDAY DAYTIME CONT'D

PROGRAM NAME (WK# DAY / START TIME / DUR / NET / PROG TYPE)	T/C THIS SEASON	STATIONS WK1	WK2	KEY	AVG AUD %	SHARE %	AVG AUD (0,000)	TOTAL PERSONS (2+)	LADY OF HOUSE	WORK-ING WOM	WOMEN TOTAL	18-34	18-49	25-54	35-64	55+	MEN TOTAL	18-34	18-49	25-54	35-64	55+	TEENS (12-17) TOTAL	FEM	CHILDREN (2-11) TOTAL	6-11
NEWSBREAK-3.57 M-F 3.57P 2 CBS N	75	188 / 94	187 / 94	A	7.3	19	612	1297	798	148	869	208	390	345	369	448	210	59^	93	77^	83^	111	119	102	99	62^
				B	6.5	19	545	1329	825	154	921	251	439	384	404	436	187	61	86	61	78	94	135	92	86	43
ONE LIFE TO LIVE M-F 2.00P 60 ABC DD	79	202 / 99	203 / 99	A	9.2	28	771	1227	759	232	854	429	582	456	322	214	244	109	168	120	106	55^	63^	57^	66^	13v
				B	8.3	27	696	1314	793	243	908	458	653	511	344	203	228	117	163	112	80	54	104	75	74	23
2.00 - 2.30				A	9.1	28	763	1227	756	237	852	432	586	462	325	204	256	116	178	136	114	53^	61^	56^	58^	8v
2.30 - 3.00				A	9.3	29	779	1211	758	225	853	427	578	451	318	218	225	99	155	103	96	52^	63^	55^	70^	14v
PEOPLE TO PEOPLE-M-F(S) 1 M-F 11.00A 30 ABC U		184	88	A	2.8	11	235	1383	804	123^	902	430^	574	433^	408^	213^	361^	72v	107v	60v	90v	254^	51v	21v	69v	47v
PRESS YOUR LUCK M-F 10.30A 30 CBS QP	80	161 / 83	161 / 83	A	6.0	23	503	1223	562	125	696	205	316	249	254	356	333	111^	178	152	129	143	43^	32^	151	66^
				B	4.6	20	385	1260	660	142	750	202	336	300	309	379	315	110	173	138	107	136	59	35	136	51
PRICE IS RIGHT 1 M-F 11.00A 30 CBS AP	77	204 / 99	202 / 99	A	8.8	32	737	1288	610	137	716	217	331	265	270	368	365	110	168	148	124	174	44^	26^	163	42^
				B	7.2	30	603	1306	668	116	756	224	351	306	288	373	366	113	170	142	125	179	54	32	130	44
PRICE IS RIGHT 2 M-F 11.30A 30 CBS AP	77	204 / 99	202 / 99	A	11.6	41	972	1254	640	138	740	213	335	281	293	380	337	95	153	136	130	165	37^	22^	140	35^
				B	9.5	38	796	1314	679	117	764	228	353	309	297	375	369	113	172	138	132	181	55	31	126	42
RYAN'S HOPE M-F 12.30P 30 ABC DD	80	177 / 94	177 / 94	A	5.7	18	478	1207	647	226	754	374	488	391	260	194	276	94^	185	163	142	70^	52^	38^	125	27v
				B	5.0	18	419	1269	743	220	846	436	596	461	288	198	229	100	153	112	86	68	85	58	109	24
SALE OF THE CENTURY M-F 10.30A 30 NBC QG	74	159 / 88	157 / 88	A	5.1	19	427	1527	774	100^	801	198	412	365	354	375	431	131^	194	201	150	222	70^	33v	225	65^
				B	4.6	19	385	1437	737	113	804	225	395	327	331	375	367	110	177	155	145	171	90	57	176	64

Figure 19.4 *This sample page from the National Nielsen Television Report illustrates the complexity and quantitative nature of institutionalized media feedback. (Courtesy the A. C. Nielsen Company.)*

for broadcasting in the form of ratings. Companies such as Simmons Market Research Bureau and Politz survey print-media audiences. Standard Rate and Data Service provides information on newspaper costs and circulation. Joseph Dominick speaks of this as "media-originated" feedback. In addition, market-research and public-opinion survey groups—such as Gallup, Harris, and Roper—go directly to the public to find out what messages have come through and what changes have resulted in levels of information, attitudes, and actions.

Most media institutions not only purchase the raw data, but also seek an analysis of the information by the research organization. In fact, little feedback is interpreted directly by the majority of mass communicators.

This third-party function regarding the indirect nature of mass communication feedback further complicates the issue. The organization that collects responses and then communicates them to the sender essentially performs a gatekeeping function, with all its potential concerns and problems. The broadcast industry has recognized the potential problems and established the Broadcast Ratings Council. The council functions as an accrediting agency and checks on such areas as sample design, field work, and type of reporting. In essence, mass communication feedback is mass communication in reverse, containing many of the same elements—complex communicators, specific codes and symbols, gatekeepers, regulators, filters, and so forth.

Costly

Mass communication feedback is expensive. Measuring a national audience over a long period of time and with precise sampling methods is costly. The institutions and organizations that provide this service are in business to make money. We have already noted the $3.5 million paid yearly by each TV network to Nielsen and the $5 million price tag for the Audit Bureau of Circulation. In addition, Arbitron prices its service according to a broadcast station's commercial rates. Fees range from $2,600 a year for small stations to $85,000 a year for large stations, with the average for all stations being approximately $17,000. Because of the costs involved, elaborate or qualitative feedback is not common in mass media. Sales figures, TV sets in use, average listeners per quarter-hour, and circulation statistics are relatively gross measures of feedback. Rarely do media communicators know the attitudes or ideas of audience members, even though this information may be important. Cost is a mass communication feedback characteristic that, in the final analysis, greatly limits feedback and prevents media communicators from knowing as much about their audiences as they want and need to be efficient and effective.

TECHNIQUES OF OBTAINING FEEDBACK

It should be obvious by now that feedback is essential in mass communication. Whether the originator of the message is an advertiser, a public-relations official, a politician, an entertainer, or a newspaper publisher, all have to ask questions concerning responses to their messages.

The answers to these questions are obtained through conducting research and using scientific methods developed by sociologists, psychologists, and survey researchers. As noted, correct sampling procedures are a critical aspect of such research. Although there are many ways to conduct mass communication research, five techniques are common to most research organizations.

Personal Interview

The personal interview is used in media research because it can provide lengthy, detailed responses that involve the personal interaction of respondent and interviewer. It offers the greatest flexibility in questioning methods. The drawbacks of this method are that it is time consuming, relatively expensive, and often depends on recall rather than the immediate responses of audience members. As a result of these and other drawbacks, personal door-to-door surveys have declined in recent years. In broadcasting, only Pulse uses personal interviews as the basis of its reports on local-radio ratings. However, the print media use interviewing for two major forms of feedback: Starch reports and Simmons Market Research Bureau reports.

Coincidental Telephone Survey

The coincidental telephone survey provides immediate feedback about what an individual is doing at the time of the call. It is fast, simple, and relatively inexpensive. Extremely lengthy and detailed answers are difficult to obtain, however, and because of the prevalent use of the telephone as a sales tool, many people who are called in such surveys are suspicious and refuse to cooperate. Therefore, coincidental telephone surveys normally require large samples. This method also automatically limits the sample to people with telephones, to those who have not moved recently, and to those at home or not using the phone when called. Despite these drawbacks, the telephone-coincidental method provides the most accurate information on TV-audience size.

Telephone recall is another method of collecting audience data, primarily about TV sets in use or programs viewed. It is less reliable than the telephone coincidental because it relies on respondents' memories, although recent advances in polling techniques have improved the results.

Diary

The diary method, whereby respondents keep a log of their own or their family's use of media, has the advantage of providing a record over a substantial period of time (usually a week). Detailed information regarding viewer habits and consumer behavior also can be obtained. Major disadvantages are respondents' failure to maintain the diary, thus depending on recall to fill in data, and to return the diary. The diary method is also more expensive than the telephone technique, although not as expensive as the personal interview. In addition, the TV diary has room for a limited number of channels, often not enough to accommodate viewers in heavily cabled cities. Diary keepers are supposed to compile a quarter-hour record of the programs that all family members and visitors have watched for five minutes or more during a week (Figure 19.5). The diaries have space to record the names, ages, and sex of family members. The incentive for cooperating is normally 50 cents, but can run to $2 for hard-to-reach categories of audience. Arbitron uses its diaries for local-market ratings only, while Nielsen uses diaries to supplement its meter ratings.

Mechanical Device

The mechanical device, such as the audimeter used by the A. C. Nielsen Company, records the minute-by-minute use of a TV set. However, the audimeter supplies information only about whether the set is on and the station to which it is tuned. No data are provided about who the viewers are or even how many viewers are watching (this will likely change soon with the spreading use of the people meter). Also, because of the expense of setting up a meter in a sample home, the sample, especially in the Nielsen surveys, is relatively permanent. Each meter remains in place for

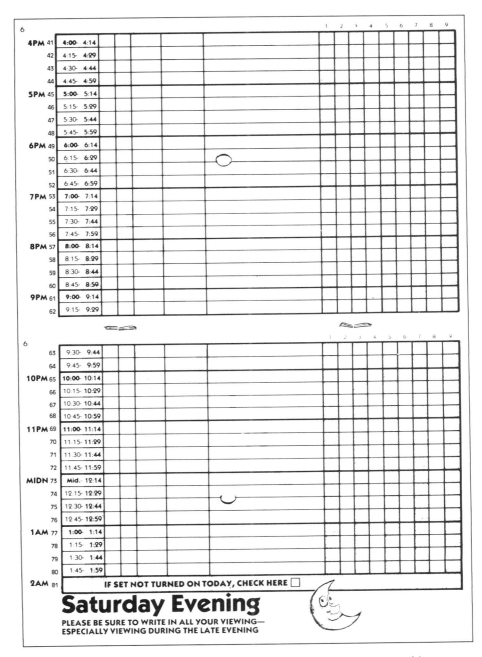

Figure 19.5 When completed, this page from an Arbitron diary can provide detailed feedback on TV viewing habits, including an individual viewer's use of television. (Courtesy the Arbitron Company.)

five years. Arbitron is also beginning to develop a metered rating system in major cities. People who allow Arbitron to install the meters are given free TV repairs, reimbursement for the electricity used, and a $10 thank-you check.

Preview

Another technique used by a number of mass communication organizations is the so-called preview theater. Randomly selected people are shown various TV programs (usually pilots) and/or advertisements in a theater and responds to the messages by pushing buttons or turning dials that signal positive or negative feelings. The American Research Institute of Los Angeles uses this technique. It is gaining in popularity because it provides data that show how people react at different stages of the message, not simply at the end. Of course, the motion-picture "sneak preview" has existed for almost 50 years. Today, it is used in increasingly sophisticated ways that involve detailed questionnaires that are filled out by audience members and follow-up interviews with selected viewers. Another technique used primarily by TV production companies is concept testing, in which sample viewers are asked to respond to a one- or two-paragraph description of a new series or show.

The ways in which these research methods have been used tend to fall into general patterns. The diary and the mechanical device are used almost exclusively in providing feedback for the broadcast media. The personal interview and the coincidental telephone survey are essential tools in public-opinion surveys. The coincidental telephone survey is also used as a fast method of obtaining broadcast-audience information, and the personal interview is used almost exclusively for print-media feedback.

FEEDBACK IN THE MEDIA

Motion Pictures and Sound Recordings

For commercial films and recordings, box-office receipts and sales provide the most important feedback in determining the kinds of feature-length movies and singles or albums that will be produced in the future. For both motion pictures and recordings, critics have some impact, but the communicator usually focuses on ticket and record or tape sales rather than on reviews. The data compiled by *Variety* and *Billboard*, shown in Figures 19.6 and 19.7, represent a major form of feedback for movie and record producers because they reveal the number of people buying a particular product during a limited time.

In addition to gross sales, the record charts reflect movement up and down the list, indicating a record's relative popularity from week to week and its performance against competitors. The *Billboard* "Hot 100" is actually

50 Top-Grossing Films

Based On Variety's Theater Sample

(WEEK ENDING FEBRUARY 11)

Compiled by Standard Data Corp., N.Y.

TITLE	DISTR	THIS WEEK SAMPLE $	RANK	LAST WEEK SAMPLE $	RANK	TOTALS					WEEKS ON CHART	SAMPLE TOTAL TO DATE $
						CITIES	FIRST RUN	SHOW CASE	TOTAL SCREENS	AVG. $ PER SCREEN		
PLATOON	ORI	3,441,228	1	3,785,540	1	20	1	219	220	15,641	8	16,074,481
OUTRAGEOUS FORTUNE	BV	2,355,225	2	2,713,362	2	19	1	227	228	10,347	2	4,870,849
BLACK WIDOW	FOX	1,589,113	3			17	3	157	160	9,931	1	1,589,113
LIGHT OF DAY	TST	1,376,059	4			17	2	196	198	6,949	1	1,376,059
RADIO DAYS	ORI	1,356,718	5	1,405,835	3	16	5	88	93	14,588	2	2,705,107
FROM THE HIP	DEG	868,040	6			16	2	181	183	4,743	1	868,040
THE GOLDEN CHILD	PAR	577,222	7	850,038	7	20	2	155	157	3,676	9	20,483,613
THE BEDROOM WINDOW	DEG	565,482	8	905,544	5	17	4	163	167	3,386	4	3,684,262
STAR TREK IV-THE VOYAGE HOME	PAR	543,332	9	878,920	6	17	1	145	146	3,721	11	28,191,234
CRITICAL CONDITION	PAR	537,194	10	1,091,344	4	15	4	141	145	3,704	4	5,023,974
CROCODILE DUNDEE	PAR	524,146	11	627,623	10	15	1	127	128	4,094	20	29,749,372
DEAD OF WINTER	MGM	519,057	12			16	2	118	120	4,325	1	519,057
LITTLE SHOP OF HORRORS	WB	408,149	13	741,277	8	18	4	102	106	3,850	8	12,510,401
ALLAN QUATERMAIN & LOST CITY	CAN	305,262	14	677,350	9	18	7	136	143	2,134	2	979,296
THE MISSION	WB	249,715	15	347,241	13	18	6	82	88	2,837	15	3,980,748
CRIMES OF THE HEART	DEG	215,550	16	405,402	12	16	6	53	59	3,653	9	6,482,005
DEAD TIME STORIES	CMG	183,200	17	432,100	11	6	1	61	62	2,954	3	676,535
THE MORNING AFTER	FOX	117,412	18	301,259	15	9	3	31	34	3,453	7	7,089,535
THE KINDRED	FME	109,650	19	345,800	14	8	4	35	39	2,811	5	1,266,912
THERESE	CCL	61,300	20	46,500	31	5	4	2	6	10,216	8	277,653
HOOSIERS	ORI	60,000	21	87,000	22	1		12	12	5,000	9	533,340
ASSASSINATION	CAN	57,000	22	124,950	18	2		11	11	5,181	5	2,030,365
DECLINE OF AMERICAN EMPIRE	CPO	54,100	23	69,050	24	9	8	5	13	4,161	13	1,018,502
LADY & THE TRAMP	BV	53,000	24	113,955	19	5	1	19	20	2,650	27	10,617,582
BLUE VELVET	DEG	48,450	25	67,100	25	8	9		9	5,383	21	3,926,756
AN AMERICAN TAIL	U	48,100	26	38,397	34	5	1	51	52	925	12	8,084,647
THE MOSQUITO COAST	WB	46,300	27	163,693	17	7	2	25	27	1,714	11	4,837,539
SCORPION	CWN	45,000	28			1		42	42	1,071	2	73,500
ROOM WITH A VIEW	CIM	42,600	29	57,400	27	5	4	9	13	3,276	49	7,495,403
WANTED DEAD OR ALIVE	NW	41,682	30	183,643	16	6	4	6	10	4,168	4	1,786,166
BRIGHTON BEACH MEMOIRS	U	40,000	31	107,800	20	2		15	15	2,666	7	4,189,336
BETTY BLUE	ALV	39,700	32	50,900	28	7	7		7	5,671	14	787,731
MY SWEET LITTLE VILLAGE	CCL	31,900	33	17,200	48	5	5		5	6,380	5	118,180
ANIMATION CELEBRATION	EXE	29,100	34	71,661	23	4	3	2	5	5,820	2	252,531
MALIBU BIKINI SHOP	IFM	26,000	35			1		7	7	3,714	2	40,150
SCENE OF THE CRIME	KNO	25,000	36	32,826	35	1	1		1	25,000	3	89,083
SID AND NANCY	GWN	23,550	37	30,578	36	5	6		6	3,991	17	1,258,696
DEFENCE OF THE REALM	HMD	23,537	38	22,187	38	5	5		5	4,707	11	191,821
HEARTBREAK RIDGE	WB	21,600	39	39,200	33	5	3	10	13	1,661	10	8,674,452
EL AMOR BRUJO/LOVE MAGICIAN	ORC	20,900	40	20,500	40	4	4		4	5,225	7	190,057
NATIVE SON	CIM	19,600	41	49,700	29	6	6		6	3,266	7	636,359
ONE WOMAN OR TWO	ORC	18,000	42			1	1		1	18,000	1	18,000
MARLENE	ALV	17,500	43	15,500	49	2	2		2	8,750	14	329,881
MENAGE	CIM	16,500	44	11,500		2	2		2	8,250	17	632,765
THE COLOR OF MONEY	BV	16,185	45	5,000		2	1	7	8	2,023	15	13,557,447
THE COLOR PURPLE	WB	15,700	46	98,200	21	3	2	1	3	5,233	31	30,685,846
ROUND MIDNIGHT	WB	15,000	47	18,500	45	2	2		2	7,500	19	1,522,021
CRYSTAL HEART	NW	15,000	48			6	4	9	13	1,153	1	15,000
CHILDREN OF A LESSER GOD	PAR	14,598	49	17,283	47	4	4		4	3,649	18	9,111,707
PEGGY SUE GOT MARRIED	TST	13,900	50	20,000	41	3	3		3	4,633	18	12,478,233
ALL OTHERS		210,257		489,822		44	21	65		3,234		11,100,671,467
GRAND TOTAL		$17,057,213		$17,580,854		197	2671	2868		5,947		11,374,452,809

Figure 19.6 This chart from *Variety* provides weekly feedback on feature motion pictures in the form of gross box-office receipts. (Copyright © 1987, Variety Inc. Reprinted by permission.)

Billboard. TOP POP ALBUMS™

Compiled from a national sample of retail store, one-stop, and rack sales reports.

THIS WEEK	LAST WEEK	2 WKS. AGO	WKS. ON CHART	ARTIST — LABEL & NUMBER/DISTRIBUTING LABEL (SUG. LIST PRICE)*	TITLE
1	1	1	24	★★ NO. 1 ★★ BON JOVI ▲⁵ MERCURY 830264-1/POLYGRAM — 7 weeks at No. One	SLIPPERY WHEN WET
2	2	4	13	BEASTIE BOYS ▲ DEF JAM BFC 40238/COLUMBIA (CD)	LICENSED TO ILL
3	4	3	32	CINDERELLA ▲ MERCURY 830076-1/POLYGRAM (CD)	NIGHT SONGS
4	5	5	36	BRUCE HORNSBY & THE RANGE ▲ RCA AFL1-5904 (8.98) (CD)	THE WAY IT IS
5	3	2	56	BANGLES ▲² COLUMBIA BFC 40039 (CD)	DIFFERENT LIGHT
6	7	9	51	JANET JACKSON ▲³ A&M SP-5106 (9.98) (CD)	CONTROL
7	9	12	35	GENESIS ▲² ATLANTIC 81641 (9.98) (CD)	INVISIBLE TOUCH
8	11	17	17	GEORGIA SATELLITES ▲ ELEKTRA 60496 (8.98) (CD)	GEORGIA SATELLITES
9	6	6	19	BOSTON ▲³ MCA 6188 (9.98) (CD)	THIRD STAGE
10	8	7	24	HUEY LEWIS & THE NEWS ▲ CHRYSALIS OV 41534 (CD)	FORE!
11	12	10	32	MADONNA ▲⁴ SIRE 25442/WARNER BROS. (9.98) (CD)	TRUE BLUE
12	10	11	26	LIONEL RICHIE ▲³ MOTOWN 6158ML (9.98) (CD)	DANCING ON THE CEILING
13	15	16	24	PAUL SIMON ▲ WARNER BROS. 25447 (9.98) (CD)	GRACELAND
14	17	18	19	LUTHER VANDROSS ▲ EPIC FE 40415 (CD)	GIVE ME THE REASON
15	14	13	10	DURAN DURAN ▲ CAPITOL PJ-12540 (9.98) (CD)	NOTORIOUS
16	20	22	12	BILLY VERA & THE BEATERS ● RHINO RNLP 70858/CAPITOL (8.98) (CD)	BY REQUEST
17	19	19	22	CAMEO ▲ ATLANTA ARTISTS 830 265-1/POLYGRAM (CD)	WORD UP
18	24	24	45	ANITA BAKER ▲ ELEKTRA 60444 (8.98) (CD)	RAPTURE
19	16	14	37	RUN-D.M.C. ▲² PROFILE 1217 (8.98) (CD)	RAISING HELL
20	18	15	21	CYNDI LAUPER ▲ PORTRAIT OR 40313/EPIC (CD)	TRUE COLORS
21	29	29	10	ROBERT CRAY MERCURY/HIGHTONE 830 568-1/POLYGRAM (CD)	STRONG PERSUADER
22	25	38	12	EUROPE EPIC BFE 40241 (CD)	THE FINAL COUNTDOWN
23	22	23	17	GREGORY ABBOTT ● COLUMBIA BFC 40437 (CD)	SHAKE YOU DOWN
24	13	8	13	BRUCE SPRINGSTEEN ▲³ COLUMBIA C5X 40558 (CD)	BRUCE SPRINGSTEEN & THE E STREET BAND 1975-1985
25	26	33	13	SAMANTHA FOX JIVE 1012-1-J/RCA (8.98) (CD)	TOUCH ME
26	28	28	37	PETER GABRIEL ▲ GEFFEN GHS 24088/WARNER BROS. (8.98) (CD)	SO
27	23	20	28	BILLY JOEL ▲ COLUMBIA OC 40402 (CD)	THE BRIDGE
28	30	25	15	FREDDIE JACKSON ▲ CAPITOL ST 12495 (8.98) (CD)	JUST LIKE THE FIRST TIME
29	21	21	16	BILLY IDOL ▲ CHRYSALIS OV 41514 (CD)	WHIPLASH SMILE
30	50	—	2	BRUCE WILLIS ● MOTOWN 6222ML (8.98) (CD)	THE RETURN OF BRUNO
31	34	34	12	STEVE WINWOOD ▲ ISLAND 25448/WARNER BROS. (8.98) (CD)	BACK IN THE HIGHLIFE
32	33	41	12	READY FOR THE WORLD ● MCA 5829 (9.98) (CD)	LONG TIME COMING
33	27	27	22	GLASS TIGER ● MANHATTAN ST-53032/EMI-AMERICA (8.98) (CD)	THIN RED LINE
34	39	57	4	DEEP PURPLE MERCURY 831 318 IMI/POLYGRAM (CD)	THE HOUSE OF BLUE LIGHT
35	36	30	26	EDDIE MONEY ● COLUMBIA FC 40096 (CD)	CAN'T HOLD BACK
36	31	26	14	THE POLICE ● A&M SP 3902 (9.98) (CD)	EVERY BREATH YOU TAKE-THE SINGLES
37	35	35	42	JOURNEY ▲ COLUMBIA OC 39936 (CD)	RAISED ON RADIO
38	45	42	15	THE PRETENDERS ● SIRE 25488/WARNER BROS. (9.98) (CD)	GET CLOSE
39	44	50	19	CHICAGO ● WARNER BROS. 25509 (9.98) (CD)	18
40	46	6	8	ERIC CLAPTON WARNER BROS. 25476 (9.98) (CD)	AUGUST
41	59	78	3	CLUB NOUVEAU WARNER BROS. 25531 (8.98)	LIFE, LOVE AND PAIN
42	37	37	13	ROBBIE NEVIL ● MANHATTAN ST 53006/EMI-AMERICA (8.98) (CD)	ROBBIE NEVIL
43	38	31	12	KOOL & THE GANG ▲ MERCURY 830 398 1/POLYGRAM (CD)	FOREVER
44	47	58	42	THE JETS ● MCA 5667 (8.98) (CD)	THE JETS
45	48	55	28	DAVID & DAVID A&M SP 65134 (6.98) (CD)	BOOMTOWN
46	40	36	20	IRON MAIDEN ● CAPITOL SJ 12524 (9.98) (CD)	SOMEWHERE IN TIME
47	51	51	100	WHITNEY HOUSTON ▲⁷ ARISTA ALB-8212 (8.98) (CD)	WHITNEY HOUSTON
48	58	69	6	SOUNDTRACK GEFFEN GHS 24125/WARNER BROS. (9.98) (CD)	LITTLE SHOP OF HORRORS
49	41	40	15	ARETHA FRANKLIN ● ARISTA AL-8442 (9.98) (CD)	ARETHA
50	43	43	10	NEW EDITION ● MCA 5912 (8.98) (CD)	UNDER THE BLUE MOON
51	32	32	14	STRYPER ● ENIGMA PJAS 73237/CAPITOL (9.98) (CD)	TO HELL WITH THE DEVIL
52	52	52	24	THE SMITHEREENS ENIGMA ST 73208/CAPITOL (8.98) (CD)	ESPECIALLY FOR YOU
53	42	39	15	KANSAS MCA 5838 (8.98) (CD)	POWER
54	54	54	33	PETER CETERA ● WARNER BROS. 25474 (8.98) (CD)	SOLITUDE/SOLITAIRE
55	57	71	4	SOUNDTRACK MCA 39096 (9.98)	AN AMERICAN TAIL
56	50	45	22	TINA TURNER ▲ CAPITOL PJ 12530 (9.98) (CD)	BREAK EVERY RULE
57	56	53	10	STEVIE RAY VAUGHAN & DOUBLE TROUBLE EPIC E2-40511 (CD)	LIVE
58	55	47	38	SOUNDTRACK ▲⁴ COLUMBIA SC 40323 (CD)	TOP GUN
59	49	44	21	TALKING HEADS ● SIRE 25512/WARNER BROS. (9.98) (CD)	"TRUE STORIES"
60	74	84	9	WORLD PARTY ENSIGN BFV 41552/CHRYSALIS (CD)	PRIVATE REVOLUTION
61	53	49	16	SURVIVOR SCOTTI BROS./CBS ASSOCIATED FZ-40457/EPIC (CD)	WHEN SECONDS COUNT
62	64	75	9	DEAD OR ALIVE EPIC FE 40572 (CD)	MAD, BAD AND DANGEROUS TO KNOW
63	69	64	18	RATT ▲ ATLANTIC 81683 (9.98) (CD)	DANCIN' UNDERCOVER
64	65	62	17	WANG CHUNG GEFFEN GHS 24115/WARNER BROS. (8.98) (CD)	MOSAIC
65	112	—	2	LOS LOBOS SLASH 25523/WARNER BROS. (8.98) (CD)	BY THE LIGHT OF THE MOON
66	67	67	66	ROBERT PALMER ▲ ISLAND 90471/ATLANTIC (8.98) (CD)	RIPTIDE
67	61	59	23	SOUNDTRACK ▲ ATLANTIC 81677 (9.98) (CD)	STAND BY ME
68	79	80	15	JEFF LORBER WARNER BROS. 25492 (8.98) (CD)	PRIVATE PASSION
69	63	63	19	COREY HART ● EMI-AMERICA PW 17217 (8.98) (CD)	FIELDS OF FIRE
70	80	135	3	THE ALAN PARSONS PROJECT ARISTA AL-8448 (9.98) (CD)	GAUDI
71	72	60	21	TIMBUK 3 I.R.S. 5739/MCA (8.98) (CD)	GREETINGS FROM TIMBUK 3
72	71	65	15	STEVE MILLER CAPITOL PJ 12445 (9.98) (CD)	LIVING IN THE 20TH CENTURY
73	70	72	21	VINNIE VINCENT INVASION CHRYSALIS BFV 41529 (CD)	VINNIE VINCENT INVASION
74	76	68	25	KENNY G. ▲ ARISTA AL 8-8427 (8.98) (CD)	DUOTONES
75	75	77	16	KBC BAND ARISTA AL 8440 (8.98) (CD)	KBC BAND
76	73	61	20	LONE JUSTICE GEFFEN GHS 24122 (9.98) (CD)	SHELTER
77	120	—	2	SHIRLEY MURDOCK ELEKTRA 60443 (8.98) (CD)	SHIRLEY MURDOCK
78	101	113	30	POISON ENIGMA ST 12523/CAPITOL (8.98) (CD)	LOOK WHAT THE CAT DRAGGED IN
79	87	126	4	TESLA GEFFEN GHS 24120/WARNER BROS. (8.98) (CD)	MECHANICAL RESONANCE
80	68	46	66	MIAMI SOUND MACHINE ▲ EPIC BFE 40131 (CD)	PRIMITIVE LOVE
81	81	83	10	THE KINKS MCA 5822 (8.98) (CD)	THINK VISUAL
82	84	91	17	LOVE & ROCKETS BIG TIME 6011-1-B/RCA (8.98) (CD)	EXPRESS
83	85	73	18	'TIL TUESDAY EPIC FE 40314 (CD)	WELCOME HOME
84	62	56	41	BILLY OCEAN ▲² JIVE JL8-8409/ARISTA (8.98) (CD)	LOVE ZONE
85	106	180	3	CROWDED HOUSE CAPITOL ST-12485 (8.98)	CROWDED HOUSE
86	73	61	20	THE HUMAN LEAGUE A&M/VIRGIN SO 5129/A&M (8.98) (CD)	CRASH
87	82	76	10	KATE BUSH EMI-AMERICA ST 17242 (8.98) (CD)	THE WHOLE STORY
88	92	85	24	TOTO COLUMBIA FC 40273 (CD)	FAHRENHEIT
89	89	87	18	MEGADETH CAPITOL ST 12526 (8.98)	PEACE SELLS...BUT WHO'S BUYING?
90	98	98	19	IGGY POP A&M SP 5145 (8.98) (CD)	BLAH, BLAH, BLAH
91	96	94	14	JASON & THE SCORCHERS EMI-AMERICA ST 17219 (8.98) (CD)	STILL STANDING
92	66	66	23	AMY GRANT A&M SP 3900 (9.98) (CD)	THE COLLECTION
93	83	74	17	HOWARD JONES ELEKTRA 60499 (8.98) (CD)	ONE TO ONE
94	88	79	46	VAN HALEN ▲³ WARNER BROS. 25394 (8.98) (CD)	5150
95	90	96	16	CHICO DEBARGE MOTOWN 6214 ML (8.98) (CD)	CHICO DEBARGE
96	99	103	16	BERLIN GEFFEN GHS 24121/WARNER BROS. (8.98)	COUNT THREE AND PRAY
97	86	86	16	BENJAMIN ORR ELEKTRA 60460 (8.98) (CD)	THE LACE
98	77	72	17	THE TONIGHT SHOW BAND/DOC SEVERINSEN AMHERST AMH7 3311 (8.98) (CD)	THE TONIGHT SHOW BAND
99	128	—	2	JENNIFER WARNES CYPRESS 661 111-1/POLYGRAM (CD)	FAMOUS BLUE RAINCOAT
100	93	100	72	BON JOVI ● MERCURY 824 509-1/POLYGRAM (CD)	7800 DEGREES FAHRENHEIT
101	103	93	16	METAL CHURCH ELEKTRA 60493 (8.98) (CD)	THE DARK
102	124	—	2	DAVID SANBORN WARNER BROS. 25479 (9.98) (CD)	A CHANGE OF HEART
103	107	112	10	THE COMMUNARDS MCA 5794 (8.98) (CD)	THE COMMUNARDS
104	102	99	27	GEORGE THOROGOOD AND THE DESTROYERS ● EMI-AMERICA ST 17214 (8.98) (CD)	LIVE
105	95	89	13	THE POINTER SISTERS RCA 5609-1-R (9.98) (CD)	HOT TOGETHER
106	100	110	54	BON JOVI ● MERCURY 814 982-1/POLYGRAM (CD)	BON JOVI
107	110	101	43	BOB SEGER & THE SILVER BULLET BAND ▲ CAPITOL PT 12398 (8.98) (CD)	LIKE A ROCK
108	111	111	11	DEBBIE HARRY GEFFEN GHS 24123/WARNER BROS. (8.98)	ROCKBIRD
109	109	109	9	GEORGE HOWARD MCA 5855 (8.98) (CD)	A NICE PLACE TO BE

○ Albums with the greatest sales gains this week. (CD) Compact disk available. ● Recording Industry Assn. Of America (RIAA) certification for sales of 500,000 units. ▲ RIAA certification for sales of 1 million units, with each additional million indicated by a numeral following the symbol. *CBS Records and PolyGram Records do not issue a suggested list price for their product.

Figure 19.7 Similar to the *Variety* chart, the *Billboard* "Top Pop Albums" provides the recording industry with weekly "standings," based on airplay on radio stations and sales to individual consumers. (Copyright © 1987, Billboard Publications, Inc. Compiled by the Billboard Research Department and reprinted with permission.)

based on feedback from two sources: record and tape sales from the top markets and radio play lists from major-market radio stations.

Although this feedback cannot alter the content of a completed film or recording, it can affect the booking and distribution of a film or record and, more important, greatly influence the future production of films and recordings with similar themes. One has only to look at the top grossing films of the late 1970s and early 1980s to see the pattern of spin-off, reproduction, duplication, and sequel at work. As the cost of producing and marketing a feature-length motion picture soars, few individuals or corporations are willing or able to risk huge sums of money on untried or unproven themes. As a result, sequels to successful movies like *Star Wars*, *Rocky*, and *Superman* are commonplace. The reissue of successful films has also become a prominent feature of the past several years. Such movies as *E.T.* and *Close Encounters of the Third Kind* often bring as much revenue in reissue as in their original run.

Most music-oriented radio stations have long obtained some recording feedback by monitoring best-selling albums and singles at local record stores. With prices up and sales down, however, stations can no longer rely on record sales alone to indicate music popularity. Also, statistics on record sales do not always pinpoint favorite songs or match listening patterns. Recently, more sophisticated research programs have been introduced, designed to profile the average listener and provide insight into his or her characteristics. The new wave of research is concerned with the "passive" listener, who does not call the radio station's request line or buy many records but who listens to radio on a regular basis.

A new form of research known as *call-out* involves playing short musical excerpts over the telephone followed by a series of questions to the respondent. This method is virtually limitless in potential. Although many stations have adopted call-out strictly for tracking the appeal of individual songs and artists, other programmers have used it to explore their listeners' life styles—to find out where they eat, what they eat, how much they earn, how many concerts they attend, what kinds of cars they drive, what they think of a particular announcer, when they want news, and so on.

Other forms of research include *auditorium testing*, in which a large group is asked to rate music or other program-related elements. Personal interviews are also frequently employed wherever possible—for example, at shopping malls.

One other form of feedback important to motion pictures and sound recordings is professional recognition, symbolized by awards. The Oscars and Grammys are important forms of feedback to film and recording artists. These awards can and often do serve as recognition of a specific film or recording, or they reward exceptional careers. The most important effect of this feedback, however, is monetary. An award often brings increased sales for a film or record and gives the performers additional leverage with future employers.

In 1983, for example, the group Toto collected several Grammys. As a result, its album *Toto IV* returned to the top-10 list and stayed there for another 12 weeks. The 1984 Grammy success of Michael Jackson and *Thriller* boosted sales from 25 million to over 30 million. In motion pictures, an already established hit benefits less from an Oscar win, since the audience has already turned out for it. *Terms of Endearment*, 1984's big Oscar winner, attracted the infrequent moviegoer and a repeat audience, but its total box-office gross did not increase dramatically after its Oscar success. But *Annie Hall* earned an extra $10 million after it had won the Oscar for best picture in 1977, and *Ghandhi*'s Oscar for best picture added over $16 million to the $38 million it had already taken in at the box offices.

The Broadcast Media

As we have discussed, for radio and television, critics' feedback has little impact, and awards in the form of Emmys are often used by actors and others to criticize TV business decisions.

Feedback in the form of sales of radio or TV sets as well as subscriptions to cable-television systems also has little direct effect on programming practices of stations or networks, because it provides no information about specific content—it merely implies that the medium is popular.

In radio and television, five forms of feedback are dominant: (1) cumulative audience (cume), (2) homes using television (HUT), (3) rating, (4) share, and (5) cost per thousand (CPM). HUTs are television-only feedback; cumes, as described earlier, are radio feedback.

Cume. For more than two decades, Arbitron has been the dominant organization providing radio stations with feedback. The company claims over 2,700 radio clients and a staff of 3,000 interviewers, who collect listening information from 2 million households across the country. All markets are measured at least once a year during the spring; however, larger markets are measured up to four times a year.

Radio feedback has become increasingly sophisticated in recent years. Age and sex represent only a small portion of the information available to agencies and advertisers. Information based on income, marital status, family size, presence of children, occupation, employment status, home ownership, education, race, and geo-demography are available. Recently, Arbitron introduced new ratings books that provide even more audience data than before. Each market report contains nine major sections: (1) audience trends, (2) discrete demographics, (3) audience composition, (4) demographic buyer, (5) hour-by-hour average cumes, (6) listening locations, (7) loyal and exclusive cume audience, (8) overnight listening, and (9) ethnic composition. Research companies such as Simmons also define specific demographic groups and then repackage the information into "clusters"—socioeconomic profiles of prospective product users.

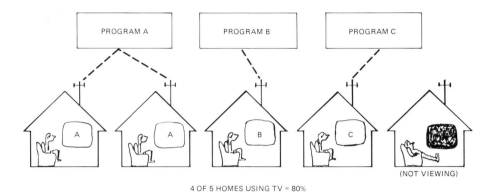

4 OF 5 HOMES USING TV = 80%

Figure 19.8 *The television feedback measurement HUT (homes using TV).*

HUT. As Figure 19.8 illustrates, HUT measures the number of homes that are using television at a given time and is the most basic form of television feedback.

Ratings. Ratings are a further refinement of broadcast feedback and are expressed as the percentage of individuals or homes exposed to a particular program (Figure 19.9).

The ratings most of us are familiar with are the national ratings compiled by the A. C. Nielsen Company. Actually, Nielsen compiles four ratings, the most important of which involve network-TV programs. The national TV ratings obtained by Nielsen are a percentage of the estimated number of American households watching certain TV programs at a particular time. A program rating of 20 means that 20 percent of all American homes equipped with TV sets are watching a particular program. In the mid-1980s, there were 85 million TV homes. Thus a rating of 20 means that 17 million homes are tuned to that program.

To calculate a rating, two numbers are needed: (1) the total number of homes with television; and (2) the number of TV homes watching a certain program. To obtain the rating for a particular program, you divide the number of homes watching a certain program by the total number of homes *with* television. It should be emphasized that these ratings usually represent households, not individuals, and that they are based on only homes with TV sets.

The most specialized ratings are based on product usage, a practice initiated in the mid-1960s by the Brand Rating Index (BRI). Viewers of TV programs are reported as percentages (ratings) of users of a product class. For example, a BRI rating of 20 indicates that 20 percent of the viewers are heavy users of a product class (gasoline, prepared cereal, beer). The rationale for this system is that the advertiser on TV is more interested in feed-

Homes with television   = 80,000,000

Homes tuned to Program A = 30,000,000

$$\text{Rating for Program A} = \frac{30{,}000{,}000}{80{,}000{,}000} = 37.5\%$$

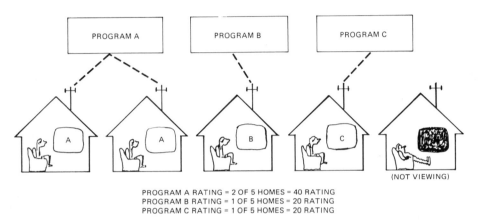

PROGRAM A RATING = 2 OF 5 HOMES = 40 RATING
PROGRAM B RATING = 1 OF 5 HOMES = 20 RATING
PROGRAM C RATING = 1 OF 5 HOMES = 20 RATING

Figure 19.9 Television ratings as the percentage of *homes with television* exposed to particular programs.

back that indicates product use than in feedback that indicates audience characteristics and demographics. This feedback is obtained through personal interviews to get product information and diaries to get viewer information.

Ratings to obtain radio and TV feedback for local markets are also prepared by Statistical Research, Inc.; Pulse, Inc.; and Arbitron (ARB). The organizations use different methods of obtaining feedback. Statistical Research, Inc., uses the telephone-coincidental method for network-radio research. Pulse, Inc., uses the personal-interview-aided recall method for local-radio ratings. ARB uses the diary method for local radio and is also the major competitor of Nielsen in providing local-TV feedback.

Local-TV ratings for more than 200 markets are reported nationally from one to seven times a year, depending on market size and demand; the most common time frame is four times a year. In addition, Arbitron and Nielsen provide continuous daily and weekly reports in four (ARB) and six (Nielsen) major cities. Arbitron also provides ratings to over 250 radio markets, usually twice a year.

Share. A share is an equally important measurement of the broadcast audience. A share is a measure of homes watching a TV program based on

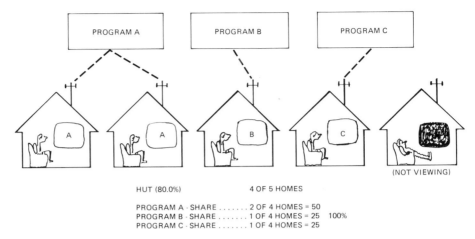

HUT (80.0%)   4 OF 5 HOMES

PROGRAM A - SHARE . . . . 2 OF 4 HOMES = 50
PROGRAM B - SHARE . . . . 1 OF 4 HOMES = 25   100%
PROGRAM C - SHARE . . . . 1 OF 4 HOMES = 25

Figure 19.10 Television-viewing shares as the percentage of *homes using television* tuned to particular programs.

homes using television (HUT) at that time (Figure 19.10), whereas a rating measures homes watching a program based on all homes with a television set. The percentage of a TV audience accounted for by a share provides a more accurate measure of how a particular program did in competition with other programs broadcast at the same time. To obtain the share for a particular program, you divide the number of homes tuned to a particular program by the total number of homes using television.

Table 19.2 shows feedback in the form of ratings and shares for the syndicated program "To Tell the Truth" according to a specific kind of audience. The program was viewed, for example, in Providence by 32 percent of all TV households in the station's market area. The 43 percent share figure indicates the percentage of households watching television at that time who were tuned to "To Tell the Truth." The information is further broken down by estimating figures (in thousands) for people aged 18 to 49 and 18 to 34, and for two groups of housewives. This kind of information is obtained by using diaries, because it deals with *viewers* rather than *sets*. In using this feedback, mass communicators place as much importance on the share as on the rating because a share indicates how many households watching TV tuned into a program, thus providing a more significant measure of popularity.

CPM. Ultimately, cumes, HUTs, ratings, and shares lead to the most critical form of feedback for media: cost per thousand (CPM). This is the most widely used comparative tool for evaluating the efficiency of a particular medium. A CPM represents the advertiser's cost in reaching 1,000 of its target population using a specific medium or combination of media. A

TABLE 19.2. Selected Market Analysis of "To Tell the Truth"

Market		Station	ADI		METRO		Homes	Total	18–49	18–34	Housewives	
			Rating	Share	Rating	Share					Total	Under 50
Providence	(WED)	WJAR	32	43	38	51	215	218	61	34	183	51
Chattanooga	(THURS)	WDEF	25	36	29	48	60	51	20	11	47	20
Spokane	(MON)	KXLY	24	39			64	52	20	14	46	17
Memphis (6:30 CST)	(WED)	WREC	29	41	29	42	159	161	68	37	137	55
Albany	(FRI)	WTEN	23	36	27	42	97	93	43	25	79	37
Columbus, O.	(FRI)	WTVN			20	39	98	87	39		77	
Phoenix (6:30 CST)	(MON)	KOOL	23	43	24	45	93	85	24		80	
Indianapolis	(WED)	WISH	22	33	25	38	162	155			138	
St. Louis (6:30 CST)	(THURS)	KTVI	20	33	18	31	184	163	58		145	49
Fresno	(THURS)	KMJ	22	37	25	42	54	50	24		46	21
Roanoke	(MON)	WSLS	28	39	35	49	91	90	44	21	77	36

Source: Arbitron Television Syndicate Program Analysis.

TABLE 19.3. WE USE CPM TO EVALUATE ALTERNATIVES

	Cost: 30	Delivery (000)		CPM	
		Homes	Women	Homes	Women
Program A	$30,000	8,000	5,000	$3.75	$6.00
Program B	$40,000	12,000	10,000	$3.33	$4.00
	Cost Page 4-Color	Delivery (000)		CPM	
		Total Women	Women 25–54	Total Women	Women 25–54
Women's Day	$57,270	19,706	11,919	$2.91	$4.80
Good Housekeeping	$45,235	17,498	9,865	$2.59	$4.59

CPM is calculated as follows:

$$\frac{\text{cost}}{\text{audience}/1000} = \text{CPM}$$

As Table 19.3 indicates, CPM is used to evaluate alternatives.

The main criticism leveled at the various forms of radio and television feedback just discussed is the emphasis placed on them by networks, stations, and advertisers. A low rating, share, or cume bumps a program off the air because a program with a rating or share of 10 costs its sponsor twice as much for each home reached as does a program with a 20 rating. A television program stays on the air or is canceled almost exclusively according to how much it costs the sponsor of the program to reach 1,000 people (CPM).

As long as there is a commercial system of broadcasting in the United States, ratings, shares, cumes, and CPM will play an important role in the medium. Broadcasters and advertisers must know what they are getting for their money in television and radio as in any other advertising medium.

The Print Media

Feedback for books, newspapers, and magazines comes from critics, award committees, and sales. All three provide a good indication of a book's success. For newspapers and magazines, the most important feedback comes from subscription and sales figures. Most newspapers and magazines subscribe to the Audit Bureau of Circulation (ABC), which verifies their circulation figures. Begun in 1914 as a check against deceptive "circulation-boosting" practices, the ABC currently audits approximately 75 percent of all print media in the United States and Canada. The system requires the cooperation of the print media to submit twice yearly circulation figures to the ABC, which audits these figures on an annual basis. The critical importance of verified figures is, of course, economic. The ABC figures help determine advertising rates (which are based on the number of readers) and assist the advertiser in creating an appropriate and cost-effective media plan. This information indicates only the newspaper's and magazine's paid circulation. Additional feedback on both media is provided by readership studies conducted by companies such as Simmons and Starch. Simmons provides extremely detailed feedback for the magazine industry similar to the ARB radio diaries. Starch measures advertising readership through detailed interviews and then categorizes readers into four groups: (1) *nonreader*, a person who does not remember seeing the ad, (2) *noted reader*, a person who remembers having previously seen the ad, (3) *associated reader*, a person who not only notes the ad but also sees or reads some part of it that indicates the advertiser, and (4) *read-most reader*, a person who reads more than half the written material in the ad. The range of readers provides the advertising industry with information on individual ad effectiveness, including specific layout and copy features.

Telephone calls and letters from readers have not had a significant impact on the print media. These forms of feedback have always been popular with readers, however, and there is a growing sensitivity to readers' opinions, as reflected in letters to the editor. The *New York Times*, for example, receives over 40,000 letters to the editor a year. Readers' cancellation of subscriptions and boycott of the shops and products of advertisers are additional means of feedback, but are rarely effective unless done by a large number of individuals.

THE IMPACT OF FEEDBACK

Given the reliance on institutionalized and largely quantitative feedback, it is no wonder that the average viewer or reader feels that he or she does not have an impact on specific television programs, magazines, or motion pictures. Still, individual or group feedback can have an effect if it is directed at the right target. This often takes the form of going beyond the local communicator to other agencies or groups, which, in turn, can exert pressure on the particular medium.

Many dissatisfied audience members of radio and TV stations write to the Federal Communications Commission rather than to the specific station. The FCC—under public pressure—then provides the station with indirect feedback that might be more effective than that of the local audience. For example, WLBT-TV in Jackson, Mississippi, lost its license in 1969 because of indirect feedback on that station's policy in regard to racial issues. Action by the FCC can also serve as feedback for other stations, indicating that certain actions are frowned on.

Television is not the only medium in which this kind of feedback is effective. The establishment by the Motion Picture Producers Association of a production code and a self-regulating agency was a result, in part, of public feedback to Congress, which then transmitted this public opinion to the film industry. In addition, public reaction to increased violence and nudity in film has been communicated to local newspapers and national magazines, which, in turn, transmit it to the film industry. In the early 1980s, religious groups used economic threat and boycott to pressure advertisers to drop their sponsorship of programs that contained what they thought was too much violence and sex.

Public feedback over references to drugs in rock-music lyrics led the FCC to send a notice in 1971 to radio stations, reminding them that they were responsible for putting this material on the air. The stations, in turn, pressured the recording industry to change the music or to send the stations printed lyrics of all new releases so that they could be evaluated in the light of the FCC policy statement.

There is some indication that the public feels its direct, negative feedback goes unheeded when sent directly to the media. Letters alone usually cannot keep a TV series on the air or change the content of movies or the lyrics of rock music. This is, in part, correct—a few letters are ineffective. Nevertheless, as we indicated with "Remington Steele," a barrage of letters or telephone calls or a boycott by regular users of a medium can have some effect. Reform feedback in mass communication must consist of extensive, long-term pressure on the appropriate source in order to be successful in accomplishing major change.

Equally important to consistent long-term feedback is the organized group that responds to a specific issue. In the past, group pressure has been one of the more effective means of supplying a media communicator with important feedback. In the early 1970s, the TV series "Maude" was the subject of organized-group feedback when several church organizations opposed the showing of a two-episode program dealing with abortion. The groups were concerned that the programs did not condemn abortion, and as a result of their pressure, over 30 CBS network-affiliated stations refused to clear the episode. Similar actions by the National Rifle Association in 1975 resulted in a CBS documentary, "The Guns of Autumn," being shown with only minimal sponsor support because advertisers refused to run spots in fear of the powerful NRA's threat of boycott of their products. Another example is the Reverend Jerry Falwell's threatened boycott of sponsors of ABC's controversial drama "The Day After."

Feedback in mass communication can be effective. However, what the viewing, listening, or reading audience must recognize is that like the original media message, feedback must travel through a complex process of communication in order to be heard or read. The simple act of turning off a television or radio set or of not reading an article or advertisement is not enough. To be effective, the individuals' acts must be amplified through significant numbers and/or specific pressure.

NOISE

All along the route of a message from communicator to audience and back, there are many possibilities for distraction, and this element of the communication process should not be minimized. This breakdown in mass communication is called *interference, static,* or *noise.* In person-to-person communication, the listener may look away from the speaker or may interrupt the flow of conversation, or other people may be talking at the same time. In mass communication, the possibilities of noise are greatly multiplied. Noise can result from weak signals, clutter, environmental distractions, and information overload.

It is important to distinguish between interference, or noise, and filters. Both have the ability to distort the sender's message. The key difference is the ability of senders to control noise, at least partially, and their inability to control filters. In other words, a sender can work to eliminate noise by reducing static, increasing power, or sending fewer messages. Nevertheless, distortion can still occur because of audience filters. The sender has little or no control over filters.

Weak Signals

Weak signals—such as poor sound levels in radio; distorted pictures on television; or poor quality of paper and printing in newspapers, magazines, and books—can result in a message reaching an audience in distorted form or not at all. This type of technical noise is the most easily controlled, since the sender often has direct influence on the source of the noise. VHF television stations are received more clearly in a larger geographical region than are UHF stations. The noise of a weak UHF signal, therefore, can have major economic consequences. Similarly, FM radio signals are essentially free from the static interference that exists on AM stations. This has a major impact on the economic and aesthetic success of FM radio.

Clutter

Clutter—such as the variety of sounds and images in broadcasting, the jumble of stories splashed on the newspaper page, or the profusion of books and magazines lined up on the newsstand rack—can cause intense competition for the attention of an audience. The audience members' minds essentially turn off and receive no messages or receive so many different and conflicting messages that none make any impression. This is especially prevalent in commercial radio, where a 5-minute segment can contain as many as seven or eight message units.

An example of clutter in books may be found in some textbooks. If you examine used books at your college bookstore, you probably see that they are not "clean." One or more former readers have underlined, written in the margins, and, in general, created visual and cognitive noise for you as a

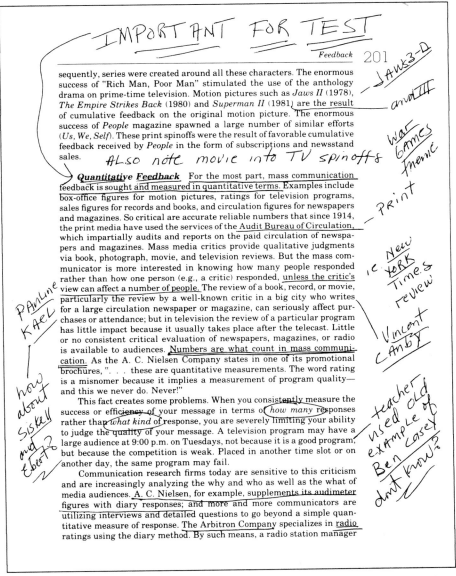

Figure 19.11 Copious notes and underlining on this page from a used edition of *Mass Media* result in noise for the reader and may interfere with the message sent by the authors.

reader. Figure 19.11 illustrates how this clutter can create visual and cognitive confusion by emphasizing parts of the page and thus calling the reader's attention to those parts instead of allowing him or her to read the material "cleanly."

Environmental Distractions

Environmental distractions are a frequent source of noise in mass communication. The home television set often competes with the dishwasher, the telephone, the radio, and even other television sets. As radio became more of an "out-of-home" medium, the noise potential increased significantly. The popularity of the Walkman radio is a clear illustration of the listener's attempt to eliminate enviromental noise. The motion picture is designed to be exhibited in a more-or-less noise-free environment, but out-of-focus projection, poor sound, and a talkative audience can interfere with the message.

Information Overload

Information overload also can interfere with the message. The audiences of mass media receive so much continuous information that the barrage often distracts from the meaning of the message. The difference between clutter and information overload is that information overload results primarily from the barrage of messages. People are surrounded by mass media messages, and given the number of messages bombarding the audience, it is remarkable that any come through.

AMPLIFICATION

Those messages that acutally get through the maze of mass communication do so because they are amplified. Somewhere along the line, a message gets amplified and so stands out from the other facts and ideas clamoring for our attention. Amplification may be the result of front-page headlines, frequent reproduction of a message in many media over a period of time, or the approval of a third party. The very fact that one message gets into the media, while others do not, serves to emphasize that message and deemphasize others. Gatekeepers play a critical role in this process, as the analysis in Chapter 17 demonstrated.

Strong signals can amplify the message. Bold, black type in a front-page headline can make one item stand out more than another. Powerful radio transmission, color television, Technicolor and stereophonic wide-screen movies, slick paper, and artful typography can add to the effectiveness of a message.

Repetition of the message over a period of time can also amplify it. The name of a person who is mentioned in the headlines day after day becomes a household word and acquires status and prestige; people listen to that person more carefully than they would if they had never heard the name. Products, ideas, and events, too, can be amplified if they are repeated in the mass media.

Endoresment may be one of the most important elements amplifying a message. An attractive woman is often used to endorse an idea. A baseball

Figure 19.12 Pinchas Zuckerman's personal endorsement of Smirnoff vodka is a means of amplifying this advertisement and making it stand out from other advertisements. (Copyright © 1983 by Ste. Pierre Smirnoff Fils. Reprinted by permission.

hero, movie star, or popular politician can also amplify a message by verifying it for the sender, or approving it. John Houseman is paid very well for his effectiveness in selling a financial service, as is Karl Malden for selling traveler's checks.

SUMMARY

Communication, by definition, is a two-way process, a cooperative and collaborative venture. In order for communication to succeed, it is important that feedback take place. In interpersonal communication, feedback is usually a natural response, direct and immediate. In mass communication, however, feedback characteristics are different from those in interpersonal communication. Instead of being individual, direct, immediate, one-time, and personal, mass communication feedback is representative, indirect, delayed, cumulative, quantitative, institutionalized, and costly.

Mass communication feedback is *representative* because audiences of mass media are so large that it is impossible to measure feedback from each member. Instead, a representative sample of the audience is selected for measurement, and the response of this sample is projected scientifically to the whole.

Mass communication feedback is also *indirect*. It comes through a third party: a rating organization or a polling company. Even when a performer or reporter receives a telephone call from a listener or a letter from a reader, the response seldom offers much opportunity for direct interaction.

Mass communication feedback is *delayed* from the moment of original transmission. There are overnight television ratings, but most network ratings are published weekly. Letters to the editor must go through the mail and face even further delay because of periodical publishing deadlines.

Mass communication feedback is *cumulative*. The immediate and individual response is infrequent and, therefore, not important. Rather, emphasis is placed on the cumulative and collective responses to a program or a periodical over a substantial period of time.

Mass communication feedback is measured, for the most part, in *quantitative* terms, including box-office figures for motion pictures, ratings for television programs, sales figures for records and books, and circulation figures for newspapers and magazines.

Mass communication feedback is *institutionalized*. Large and complex organizations, such as the A. C. Nielsen Company, Arbitron, and Pulse, Inc., are required to provide meaningful feedback to mass communicators.

Finally, mass communication feedback is *costly*. Each television network pays $3.5 million yearly to Nielsen for television ratings, and the Audit Bureau of Circulation provides periodical and newspaper circulation figures at a cost of $5 million per year.

There are many different techniques for obtaining feedback in mass communication, but five are most predominant: (1) the personal interview, (2) the coincidental telephone survey, (3) the diary, (4) the mechanical device, and (5) the preview.

Despite some similarities in their methods of obtaining feedback, the different media also use different forms of feedback. The motion picture and sound recording industries depend primarily on sales and box-office receipts to analyze the degree of success of a particular picture or record, even though they do receive some feedback from critics' reviews.

In broadcasting, feedback from critics has had little impact. In radio and television, five forms of feedback are dominant: (1) cumulative audience (CUME), (2) homes using television (HUT), (3) rating, (4) share, and (5) cost per thousand (CPM). Cumes are especially important for radio feedback, whereas HUTs, ratings, and shares are critical for television feedback.

Mass communication feedback has a major impact on media programming. Negative feedback results in radio and television stations canceling programs, newspapers and magazines ceasing production, and motion picture corporations going bankrupt.

In addition to feedback, two other important elements in the mass communication process are noise and amplification. The breakdown in mass communication is called *interference, static,* or *noise.* Noise in mass communication is the result of four major factors: (1) weak signals, such as poor sound levels in radio, distorted pictures on television, or poor quality of paper and printing in newspapers, magazines, and books; (2) clutter, such as the variety of sounds and images in broadcasting or the jumble of stories splashed on a newspaper page; (3) environmental distractions, such as people talking in a motion picture theater, the shaking of a commuter train, which disturbs a newspaper reader, or household sounds that compete with television; (4) information overload, in which audiences of mass media receive so much continuous information that it distracts from the meaning of the message.

Amplification is important because those messages that actually get through the maze of mass communication do so because they are amplified. There are three ways in which media messages become amplified: (1) strong signals, such as bold, black type in a front-page headline or a powerful radio transmission; (2) repetition of a message over a period of time; and (3) endorsement, in which a message is amplified by a well-known person.

Ultimately, feedback is necessary, because mass communication, like all forms of communication, must be a two-way process in order to succeed. Even though mass communication is not direct and immediate, it is relatively effective and efficient in determining the ways messages are perceived by audiences.

BIBLIOGRAPHY

Berger, Arthur Asa. *Media Analysis Techniques.* Beverly Hills, Calif.: Sage, 1982.
Beville, Hugh M., Jr. *Audience Measurement in Transition.* New York: Television/ Radio Age, 1983.

————— . *Audience Ratings: Radio, Television and Cable.* Hillsdale, N.J.: Erlbaum, 1985.

Bollier, D. *How to Appraise and Improve Your Daily Newspaper: A Manual for Readers.* Washington, D.C.: Disability Rights Center, 1978.

Christensen, Mark, and Cameron Stauth. *The Sweeps: Behind the Scenes in Network TV.* New York: Morrow, 1984.

Dominick, Joseph R., and James E. Fletcher. *Broadcasting Research Methods.* Boston: Allyn and Bacon, 1985.

Hiber, Jhan. *Hibernetics: A Guide to Radio Ratings and Research.* Los Angeles: R & R Books, 1984.

Himmelstein, Harold. *On the Small Screen: New Directions in Television and Video Criticism.* New York: Praeger, 1981.

PART IV

What Are the Key Mass Communication Issues?

20

International Systems

Lella Vigo is a schoolteacher. Aldo Vigo is an engineer. They have three children: Matteo, Cristiana, and Andrea. They have two cars and two television sets, a black-and-white set in the kitchen and a color set in the living room. As a family, they watch television for about 24 hours a week. After supper, Aldo watches the news, usually on the black-and-white in the kitchen because his children are watching cartoons. They especially like "The Smurfs." Lella watches "Dallas" and especially enjoyed the mini-series "The Thorn Birds." A typical American family. Not quite. The Vigos live in Milan, Italy.

The Vigos consider themselves selective viewers. "I can't understand how some parents can use the television as a baby-sitter," says Lella Vigo.

"We enjoy the television and watch it when there is something worthwhile on. We rarely decide ahead of time what to watch during the week or plan our evenings around it."

The Vigos are in the middle bracket among Italian television audiences—the 37 percent who watch between 23 and 32 hours of television weekly. Another 37 percent watch from 12 to 22 hours a week; 25 percent watch between 33 and 56.

Average daily viewing is 3.6 hours, or slightly less than the Vigos watch. Italians' TV viewing appears to be much like Americans' viewing.

And, in some ways, the same is true of Italian programming. In Milan, for example, midday, a relatively new viewing time, now contains an American-style game show.

But it is not merely a new show here or there that is fueling the growth of midday viewing. Italian life styles are changing too. Increasingly, Italian men are eating near their workplaces rather then rushing home to a noonday meal with their families. That leaves Mom at home alone, in front of the TV set.

Lella Vigo, however, works outside the home. And, "no," she replies quickly, she does not watch TV during the afternoon after she comes home. Often, no one in the Vigo household watches daytime TV. Andrea has after-school activities, while Christiana and Matteo play outside in the garden. Some days, the children attend religious instruction. When they do get around to watching TV, the younger Vigo children generally tune in cartoons. But not 11-year-old Andrea. "They bore me," he explains. "There are a lot of shows about animal life and plants, and we recently watched a program about human kidney operations," says Andrea. Andrea also confesses to a preference for American imports, such as "CHiPs" or "T. J. Hooker," which his brother and sister watch, too.

When Aldo Vigo comes home, dinner is put on the table, and both TV sets are turned off. After dinner, TV watching resumes, this time including the family patriarch. "I regularly watch the evening news," says Aldo. The news he watches is an 8:00 P.M. broadcast by the state network. (Commercial stations are not allowed to broadcast news.) The program typically captures a 60 percent share of the viewing audience. Like many Italians, Aldo is an armchair politician, annoyed with news programming because it is, well, so "political." "I watched the debates during the elections last year, and I didn't find them well done at all," he complains. "There is little balance and even less controversy. The politicians are evasive, and the journalists let them get away with it."

Aldo Vigo has another complaint: those infernal game shows. "Ridiculous," he says, rolling his eyes skyward. "They ask the most inane questions and award huge prizes. I don't approve of what it teaches the children—that such nonsense is rewarded like that."

Generally, though, the Vigos feel that television has a great deal to offer and can be educational. They get 12 channels, and there is always a broad enough selection in programming, Aldo says. They do not subscribe to any viewers' guides, so they consult the daily newspaper to see if there is anything they want to watch. They refuse to become slaves to series, especially Aldo, who avoids shows such as "Dallas." "I won't watch it, I absolutely refuse to watch it," Aldo says of the popular American import. "It just can't be real. How can Americans relate to something like that?" Many Italians obviously find something to relate to. "Dallas" is one of Italy's most popular shows, commanding a 20 percent share of the audience weekly. Lella, who watches "Dallas," says, "I don't see anything wrong with watching these kinds of programs. If it's a half-hour of living vicariously or dreaming, so what?"[1]

---

[1] Claire Wilson, "Peeking at an Italian Family's Viewing Habits," *Electronic Media* 3 January 1985, 118–119.

The Vigos use mass media, and by doing so, they interact with the world. Although the mass media experience is international, each nation has evolved its own mass communication system, based on its unique conditions and factors. The way people use mass media is based, in part, on the kind of media systems they have. And the kind of media system is based, in part, on the way people use mass media. The system is the result of this interaction and relationship. The study of how these systems work is called *metacommunication*. Although this text is concerned primarily with the American system of mass media, it is important to look at the media systems of other countries and try to understand why they differ from both the American and one another. By doing so, we will be better able to understand why they are used differently. And by comparing the American system with others, we will come to a fuller understanding of our own use of mass media.

POLITICAL PHILOSOPHIES AND MASS MEDIA SYSTEMS

There are many ways to analyze and attempt to understand a nation's mass communication system. Political philosophies are an important frame of reference for such analysis, and so let us look at the major political theories of mass communication.

In a sense, all political philosophies are either libertarian or authoritarian. A libertarian political philosophy basically holds that the individual is most important in society; the state, government, and media exist to serve the needs of the individual. If they are not serving these needs, the individual can change them.

An authoritarian political philosophy basically holds that some higher order has authority over the individual. That higher order may be the church, the state, a political leader, a teacher, or a parent. In an authoritarian society, the individual exists to serve the needs of the higher order.

Historically, authoritarian societies have existed longer and have been more prevalent than libertarian ones. Although the United States came into being as a libertarian society, many American social institutions, such as the family and the educational system, are still largely authoritarian. Libertarian societies have been prominent only in ancient democratic Greece, in Western Europe and North America since the seventeenth century, and in Japan since the end of World War II.

In an authoritarian system, the press and the other media are controlled by the government and exist to serve the needs of the state or authority in power. In a libertarian society, mass media exist to serve the needs of the individual and are free to provide whatever individuals want from them. But these descriptions are two extremes at either end of a political continuum. No society is as simple as either–or. Nations can be analyzed for degrees of freedom and/or control of mass media.

One method used to describe, analyze, and compare different media systems and their political philosophies was outlined in the mid-1950s by Frederick Siebert, Theodore Peterson, and Wilbur Schramm in their book *Four Theories of the Press.* They reasoned that throughout the world, all media systems can be broken down into four basic types: (1) the authoritarian system; (2) the Soviet Communist system, a derivative of the authoritarian; (3) the libertarian system; and (4) the social-responsibility system, a derivative of the libertarian.

The Authoritarian System

The authoritarian system is as old as humankind. Throughout history, governments have controlled public expression. As soon as the printing press was developed in fifteenth-century Europe, those in power realized that it had to be controlled. This media philosophy is based on the political assumption that absolute power should rest in the hands of a monarch, a dictator, the ruling church, or the aristocracy.

Under the authoritarian system, the mass media may be privately owned (although the broadcast media are often owned by the state), but they are directly controlled by the government through laws and licenses. Direct criticism of the government by the media is usually forbidden because the media is supposed to support the state. Media owners can have their property taken away, and they and their editors and writers can be put in jail, if their products detract from or compete with the power of political authority.

Much of the non-Communist world—including many countries in Latin America, Africa, the Middle East, and Asia—still operates under this system. The fascist regimes in Germany and Italy were modern European examples. Adolf Hitler expressed the basic idea of the authoritarian system when he said:

> Our law concerning the press is such that divergencies of opinion between members of the government are no longer an occasion for public exhibitions, which are not the newspapers' business. We've eliminated that conception of political freedom which holds that everybody has the right to say whatever comes into his head.[2]

The Soviet Communist System

The Soviet Communist system is an extension of the authoritarian system. It developed from the application of Marxist-Leninist-Stalinist philosophy to mass communication in the twentieth century. Its basic assumption is that the individual needs to be changed so that he or she will share with and support society as a whole. The purpose of mass communication is to support the Communist party in its efforts to revolutionize society, to

---

[2] "Hitler's Secret Conversations," in *The Great Quotations,* comp. George Seides (New York: Lyle Stuart, 1966), 321.

make each person work for the good of the whole rather than for his or her selfish interests.

Under the Soviet Communist system, the mass media are owned by the state, and the media communicators are loyal party members because they must interpret all communication from the party's point of view. Owning and operating a private printing press under this kind of system is as serious a crime as printing counterfeit money is in the United States. Nicolai Lenin expressed this philosophy in a speech he gave in Moscow in 1920:

> Why should freedom of speech and freedom of the press be allowed? Why should a government which is doing what it believes to be right allow itself to be criticized? It would not allow opposition by lethal weapons. Ideas are much more fatal things than guns. Why should any man be allowed to buy a printing press and disseminate pernicious opinion calculated to embarrass the government?[3]

The Soviet Communist system prevails not only in the Soviet Union, but also in all other Communist countries. When the Communist revolution succeeded in Cuba, for example, the first act of the new regime was to take over all institutions of communication and education, including news-

"...WITH LESS THAN ONE PERCENT OF THE VOTE IN, WE ARE PROJECTING COMRADE CHERNENKO THE WINNER... BACK TO YOU, BORIS!...."

(Drawing by Gary Brookins, courtesy the *Richmond Times-Dispatch*.)

---

[3] Quoted in H. L. Mencken, comp., *A News Dictionary of Quotations on Historical Principles from Ancient and Modern Sources* (New York: Knopf, 1966), 966.

paper, magazine, and book publishing companies and radio and television stations. The mass media and the schools were reorganized so that they would be owned by the state and run by members of Fidel Castro's Marxist party.

The Libertarian System

The libertarian system struggled into existence in seventeenth- and eighteenth-century Europe as a revolutionary act against the repressive authoritarianism of the established monarchies. Philosophers John Locke and John Milton gave libertarianism its most eloquent rationale. They argued that the state exists to serve the needs of the people, not the people to serve the needs of the state. Governments that are not responsive to their citizens can be overthrown. Individuals have the right to seek and know the truth and to express their ideas and opinions.

Under the libertarian system, government should not be involved in mass communication. To ensure complete freedom of expression, the media should be privately owned. Indeed, the mass media under a libertarian system should function as watchdogs of government, to make sure that government is serving the needs of the people. The only restraints on media should be laws designed to protect the rights of individuals, such as libel laws to protect people's reputations and privacy laws to protect them from the media's invasion of their privacy.

The Founding Fathers, especially Thomas Jefferson and Benjamin Franklin—were imbued with the philosophy of the Enlightenment, libertarianism, and democracy. They wrote the libertarian theory of the press into the First Amendment to the Constitution, which guarantees freedom of speech and of the press. James Madison, signer of the Declaration of Independence, framer of the Constitution, and fourth president of the United States, expressed the essential argument for libertarianism in this manner:

> Nothing could be more irrational than to give the people power and to withhold from them information without which power is abused. A people who mean to be their own governors must arm themselves with power which knowledge gives. A popular government without popular information or the means of acquiring it is but a prologue to a farce or a tragedy, or perhaps both. . . . To the press alone, checkered as it is with abuses, the world is indebted for all the triumphs which have been obtained by reason and humanity over error and oppression.[4]

Social-Responsibility System

The social-responsibility system of mass media came into existence in some democratic societies in the mid-twentieth century. The realities of mass society have caused many thoughtful people to conclude that absolute

---

[4] Quoted in *Speaking of a Free Press* (New York: ANPA Foundation, 1970), 15.

freedom for the individual may no longer be possible; too many people live close to one another and are dependent on one another for survival. After World War II, the nongovernmental Commission on Freedom of the Press was established in the United States to discuss the relationship between the press and society in a Cold War world. Under the leadership of a Harvard philosophy professor, W. E. Hocking, the commission issued a two-volume report that concluded that freedom of the press should be preserved but that it can be maintained only if the mass media accept their responsibility to society as a whole.

Many argue that a free press acts irresponsibly when it serves only its own interest in making money. Publishers and broadcasters reap great profits by sensationalizing the news. A lurid picture or headline sells many more thousands of copies of a newspaper than a sedate one sells. If two magazines—say, *Time* and *Newsweek*—are placed side by side on a newsstand and if one features a cover picture of the president of the United States and the other shows a bikini-clad beauty, the magazine with the young woman on the cover usually far outsells the other. Indeed, the annual issue of *Sports Illustrated* devoted to new styles in women's bathing suits is bought by more people at newsstands than is any other issue. Appealing to what some consider to be the lowest common denominator and prurient interests also pays off for radio, television, and movies. "Happy-talk" television newscasts, which are designed to attract a large number of viewers and, hence, advertising dollars, have been the subject of great scorn and concern in recent years.

Is such mass communication in the best interests of society? One could argue that question, depending on one's moral or ethical values. But suppose that a publisher decides to publish a magazine article explaining how to build a hydrogen bomb in a basement. Would that be in the best interests of society? In a libertarian system, the freedom of people to do whatever they want often prevails, and in 1979, the government withdrew its case against a Wisconsin magazine, the *Progressive,* allowing it the legal right to publish an article on how to build a hydrogen bomb. Under the social-responsibility theory, such an article would probably not be allowed to be published. The mass media are still privately owned and operated under the social-responsibility theory, but they operate with the sanction of society. If they do not serve the interests of society or if they threaten the security of society, they can be taken over by the government to ensure public welfare and safety.

The social-responsibility theory exists in the United States to some extent in the broadcast media, but not in the print media. Radio and TV stations in the United States are privately owned, but they are licensed by the government. The Supreme Court in the early 1930s ruled that this was constitutional because broadcasters use public property, the airwaves, to communicate. Therefore, the public has a right, through its government, to exercise some control over broadcasting. And if the government, through the Federal Communications Commission, finds that a broadcaster is not serving the public interest, the broadcaster's license can be revoked or not renewed, or a fine can be levied. As Chapter 17 indicates, however, deregulation of broadcasting is increasing, and radio and TV stations may soon resemble newspapers and magazines in their freedom from government regulation.

Although the social-responsibility theory exists in the United States to some degree, it exists to an even larger degree in most of the democracies of Western Europe. In some European countries that consider themselves libertarian and democratic, journalists are licensed and are bound to abide by certain journalistic regulations, or they can lose their license. In Britain, the Offical Secrets Act gives the government power over any mass communication that might endanger the security of the nation. Thus the article on building a hydrogen bomb would no doubt have been banned in Britain.

OTHER MASS MEDIA MODELS

The four theories of the press serve as a starting point for the analysis of media systems. However, many countries fail to fit neatly into any of the four groups. For example, Spain and Portugal seem to be shifting away from their traditional authoritarian systems of control. In terms of the individual media, print media in the English-speaking democracies tend to reflect the libertarian theory, whereas broadcast media in most of these countries reflect the social-responsibility philosophy. Censorship of the press, be it under Hitler, Stalin, or Castro, is not significantly different whether it is called authoritarian or Communist. In fact, considerable repressive control of the media is exercised in some democracies during periods of civil strife or war. In other words, too many national media systems deviate from the four basic types to rely exclusively on the "four theories" approach to media systems analysis. Other ways to analyze mass media systems include the open–closed model and the ownership-control model.

Open–Closed Model

As Figure 20.1 indicates, a media system can be categorized according to the extent to which both the receiver system and the message system are open or closed. The open mass communication system allows as much audience and message freedom as possible. This system is similar to the libertarian and social-responsibility theories of the press. The private system, which incorporates such communications as telephone calls and mail, is the opposite of the open system. The controlled mass communication system exists when the audience is free to receive messages, but the mes-

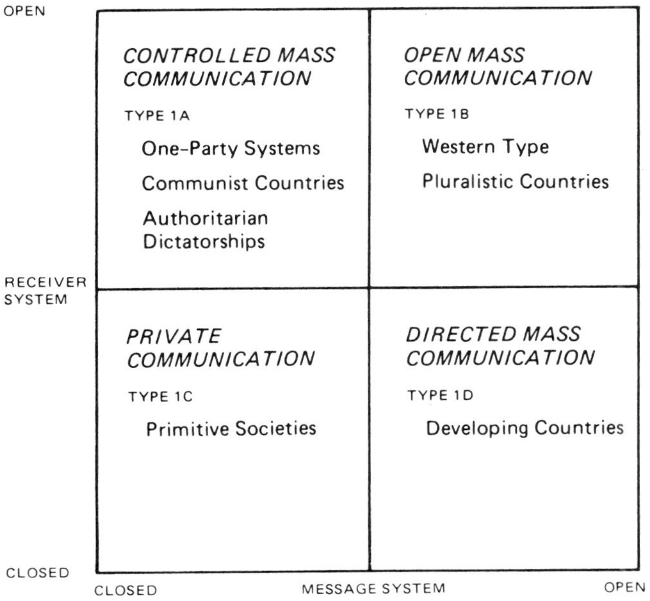

Figure 20.1 This model of comparative media systems, developed by L. John Martin and Anju Chaudhary, categorizes systems by the manner in which messages and audiences are open (free) or closed (controlled).

sages are censored. This system most closely approximates the authoritarian and Communist theories. In the directed mass communication system, the audience is cut off from many messages. Examples of a directed system exist in Asian and Southeast Asian countries where multilingualism prevents portions of the population from receiving the message.

Ownership-Control Model

The ownership-control model posits four media systems based on variables of public versus private ownership and decentralized versus centralized control. In Figure 20.2, Type 2A, the decentralized public model, is best exemplified in Western and northern European countries such as France and Denmark, where broadcasting companies are publicly owned, but the control system is decentralized so that no one central authority can control the messages. Type 2B, the centralized public model, is a typical socialist or Communist model, in which the media are owned by society and centrally controlled by the dominant political party. Type 2C, the decentralized private model, is typical of the media in the United States and most newspapers in Western Europe. Finally, Type 2D, the centralized private model, is found in many Latin American countries where the media are privately owned and controlled by the countries' rulers.

Although both these models are useful, they, like the four-theories system, have limitations because they *prescribe* rather than *describe* various media systems.

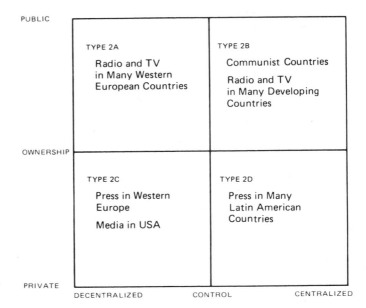

Figure 20.2 Martin and
Chaudhary also categorize media
systems by patterns of ownership
and control.

THE MEDIA-SYSTEMS PARADIGM

In an attempt to develop a more descriptive model that captures the dynamic *interactive* relationships of media and society, we present a media-systems paradigm. Rather than attempt to "fit" a certain nation into a particular political philosophy or system of media ownership, we use the media-systems paradigm to describe the many interactions that make up and create a nation's mass communication system.

The relationship between media and societies is reciprocal. A country creates a national media system, and this media system, in turn, modifies that society. Since every nation differs from every other nation, and media systems vary from nation to nation, the interaction between a given country and its media is unique. For example, the deaths of Mao Zedong and Zhou Enlai were political events of great significance in the People's Republic of China. The society and media interacted so that the nation, the people, and the media system were all changed. With the Cultural Revolution no longer the guiding philosophy, the media began to "open up" and reflect more cultural diversity.

For our purposes, then, it seems advisable to analyze each national media system as a distinct entity. The media-systems paradigm is designed to reflect the interplay between media and societies, as well as to help describe similarities and dissimilarities in national media systems. The media-systems paradigm is based on the theory that in every country, special

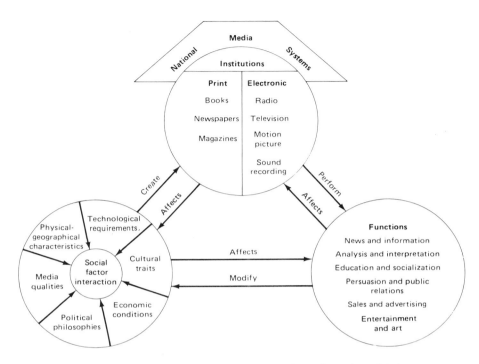

Figure 20.3 The media-systems paradigm is an action-oriented model that visualizes the theory that in every country, certain factors interact in unique ways to create a media system that performs a variety of functions that helps shape the country's society.

factors or social forces interact in unique ways (1) to create a national media system that (2) performs a variety of functions that (3) eventually participate in reshaping that society. The paradigm is action oriented (dynamic versus static) to emphasize the changing nature and interaction of media and societies.

As shown in Figure 20.3, six social factors or forces interact in the development of a media system: (1) physical and geographical characteristics, (2) technological requirements, (3) cultural traits, (4) economic conditions, (5) political philosophies, and (6) media qualities. The interaction of these factors, rather than their independent action, is crucial in the media system's evolution. Other factors also affect a country's media system, but the six mentioned here are the most critical.

Every national media system has a variety of individual media institutions. Seven major media merit special consideration: (1) books, (2) newspapers, (3) magazines, (4) radio, (5) television, (6) motion pictures, and (7) recordings.

These media institutions and others are used to perform six basic functions: (1) news and information, (2) analysis and interpretation, (3) education and socialization, (4) persuasion and public relations, (5) sales and advertising, and (6) entertainment and art. As the media perform these functions, they change the societies that created them. The extent and kinds of effects the media have on society are debatable, but it is commonly agreed that the media participate in modifying every society of the world.

Factors that Influence the Development of Media Systems

As we examine each of the six forces that affect media development, it is important to reemphasize that each of these factors seldom operates independently. It is the interaction of all six that stimulates significant differences in media systems. All six are influential to varying degrees in different situations. In fact, it is impractical to designate one factor as the only variable influencing any one aspect of a given media system.

Physical and Geographical Characteristics. A country's climate, geography, and other physical characteristics affect the development of its media system, just as they alter population patterns and economic development. For example, many nations have developed frequency-modulation (FM) rather than amplitude-modulation (AM) radio because the technical characteristics of the FM signal are better suited to mountainous regions. Because film stock tends to deteriorate more rapidly in the tropics than in temperate zones, nations located in tropical areas must take this fact into consideration when setting up facilities for film production, distribution, and exhibition. In most regions of the United States, winters are less hospitable than summers for outdoor activity. For this reason, audiences available for TV viewing in warmer months are decidedly smaller than in colder months. Climate, audience size, and TV economics interact to stimulate the use of reruns or low-cost replacements during the summer quarter of the television year.

Other factors affect media in other countries. In Tanzania, for example, few trees are available for wood pulp. Because all paper stock must be imported, there are very few newspapers and magazines. In most societies, newspapers and magazines are an urban phenomenon. As a result, a country like the Netherlands, which has a predominantly urban geographical make-up, has many daily newspapers and magazines. The enormous size of the Soviet Union has promoted several layers of regional media and has fostered the use of longwave and shortwave transmission of radio signals. Newspapers in the Soviet Union, as in most other large countries, are published on a regional basis. Indeed, whether to have a national newspaper is primarily determined by a nation's size. Israel's principal papers, for example, are sold nationwide, as are most newspapers in Scandinavian countries and in Great Britain. In the United States, only the *Christian Science Monitor,* the *Wall Street Journal,* and *USA Today* can be regarded as national newspapers.

In countries that span vast areas, such as Russia and China, or those composed of scattered land masses, such as the Philippines and other nations in the South Pacific, radio, because of its long-distance signal ability (AM), is a particularly strong medium of communication.

The proximity of a country to other countries also has an impact on the development of its media system. This is perhaps nowhere more evident than in Canada. Originally, radio broadcasting in Canada developed along the same lines as it did in the United States. Privately owned commercial stations were licensed to use certain frequencies, with few, if any, restrictions. Within a short time, however, Canadian broadcasting became an extension of the American system; most programming was directly "imported," and Canadian radio stations were formally affiliated with American networks. In order to provide motivation for Canadian programming and to develop an east–west network, the Canadian Parliament passed the Broadcasting Act of 1932, which established the Canadian Radio Broadcasting Commission (CRBC), whose main task was to set up a national service. The Canadian Broadcasting Commission (CBC) soon replaced the CRBC and today regulates all electronic communication in Canada. One regulation establishes a quota for Canadian content that all stations must meet. Content quotas are intended to help maintain a Canadian cultural identity in the face of influence from the United States.

The CBC also attempts to protect the broadcast system's economic well-being from intrusion northward across the border. Television stations are protected at the moment from competition from American border stations in two ways. First, advertisers cannot claim business-tax deductions for ads in non-Canadian-owned media (including print and radio). Second, if a show is aired on a Canadian station at the same time that an American station is broadcasting a show, cable operators are required to substitute the Canadian signal, so that no matter which button the viewer punches, only the Canadian station ads will be seen.

Nevertheless, American stations nationally have a 24 percent share of the Canadian viewing market. That figure is higher in border areas, going as high as an 81 percent share in the Windsor, Ontario, area—only a bridge span away from Detroit.

In Nicaragua, television has no monopoly on how the local population perceives the world. About one-half of the population watches local television at least 1 hour a day. But in the border areas, Costa Rican, Honduran, and Salvadoran television can also be received. AM-radio broadcasts from Mexico, Cuba, and United States are heard throughout the country. And the Spanish-language shortwave broadcasts of the Voice of America and the BBC attract an immense audience.

The porousness of Nicaragua's frontiers, as far as the electronic media are concerned, may be one reason the Sandinistas make no attempt to restrict programming severely.

As satellite systems continue to develop, many countries, especially those in Western Europe, are realizing that they essentially have no geographical border. In January 1985, enough television programming to fill five channels around the clock—3,560 hours—was transmitted internationally by satellite. Rupert Murdoch's Sky Channel cable network is looming as a significant programming, economic, and cultural force. It is creating significant changes in European television, primarily in forcing a second service of commercial and/or private television in Norway, Sweden, and Denmark.

Technological Requirements. In order for a mass communication system to evolve, four technological competencies are needed. First, a society must have a basic scientific capability, since both pure and applied research are necessary to develop media. Early research in electricity, for example, was not aimed at creating television, but the results of that research were essential to its application. This ability to apply research findings to improve mass communication is a critical technological prerequisite for media development.

Second, a nation needs raw materials to develop mass media or the economic resources to obtain them. In order to have books, magazines, and newspapers, paper, ink, and the machinery to print pages are essential. Paper requires suitable trees, rice, rags, or other source of fibrous material that can be turned into pulp. As we observed in the case of Tanzania, a shortage of trees precludes the development of many newspapers in the system. Ink requires acids, tints, resins, oils, drying agents, and other chemical components. Machines to produce print media need lead for type, aluminum for offset plates, various steels for presses, rubber for belts and rollers, and lubrication oils to keep the presses rolling. Electronic media make similar demands on a nation's natural resources.

Third, a country must have the industrial capability to mass-produce media products or the money to buy these finished goods. A nation must have vast quantities of transistors, cameras, typesetting machines, film stocks, printing presses, TV sets, inks, vacuum tubes, and other components if its media are to function optimally.

Fourth, trained personnel are needed to make these complex systems function. A medium cannot function satisfactorily without a technical staff to operate the equipment, a production staff to create content, and a managerial staff to handle the day-to-day operations of the system. This process requires an ongoing program to recruit and train personnel.

Lack of technical competence can often inhibit the development of mass communication systems. In Pakistan, for example, the national language is Urdu, and until recently, newspapers published in this language depended on copy that was handwritten by calligraphers. An Urdu paper of 10 pages requires at least 50 calligraphers, and as a result, the work force necessary to produce these papers is enormous. An Urdu keyboard developed in the late 1960s eliminated the need for transcribing by hand, but Pakistani newspapers have been slow to use it. Their readers like the calligraphers' script because it is decorative and easy to read.

In Southeast Asia, radio and TV operations have been greatly limited by a lack of trained production personnel. Because of the personnel shortage (and the high cost of producing programs), many developing countries in Asia and the Pacific import programs whose content is often unrelated to local cultures and values. In addition, the lack of electricity in these countries, in parts of China, and in the developing nations of Africa and South America has led to a radio-dominated electronic media environment because transistors and batteries allow radio to operate effectively where television cannot. As transistorized and battery-operated television becomes more of a reality, it will gain a stronger foothold in these countries' media systems.

Cultural Traits. Every society has unique ways of doing things, of evaluating what is important, and of modifying behavior. There are social laws, taboos, norms, mores, values, and attitudes. All these are important in the development of media systems.

In Czechoslovakia, for example, each of the two national groups, the Czechs and the Slovaks, has its own distinct language. Films are made in each of the two national languages to reflect the differences in these two cultures. In Switzerland, the government recognizes four national languages. Broadcasts are provided in German, French, Italian, and Romansch.

Danish cultural values have allowed pornographic material to appear in some media. Films, books, and magazines banned as obscene in most countries have been openly available in Denmark. In the United States, there is considerable disagreement on the sexual content of the mass media. Recent Supreme Court decisions have not always followed a consistent pattern, and the various media voices have not been unanimous in their thinking. The civil-rights and women's movements have changed American cultural attitudes tremendously; the mass media as well as business and industry are hiring minorities and women for senior positions throughout their organizations. Their abilities as journalists aside, Connie Chung, Ed Bradley, Diane Sawyer, Jane Pauley, and Bryant Gumbel can be cited as a reflection of this cultural change.

A number of cultural or social factors deeply influence media development; they include urbanization, population, sexual taboos, religion, race relations, labor organizations, youth culture, and education. Every mass society is a mixture of stability and change—the resulting conflict deeply involves and affects the development of media systems.

One of Japan's biggest television stars is a character called Ultraman, star of a show by the same name. Mark Siegel, a professor at the University of Wyoming, has analyzed the appeal and popularity of "Ultraman" and concludes that the program is more than a simple martial-arts fantasy. It represents a "reassuring ritual, deeply rooted in the nation's history, hopes, and fears."[5] According to Siegel, the key to "Ultraman" lies in the Japanese society's mixed feelings about things foreign.

For almost 2,000 years, the Japanese have been the greatest cultural borrowers in the world. At the same time, they remain a unique and tradition-oriented society, adapting outside influences to fit their culture and discarding what does not seem beneficial.

But in the past century and a half, the Japanese have been shocked into an awareness of their extreme vulnerability to outside forces. In 1853, after Japan had spent two centuries of almost complete isolation under the Tokugawa shoguns, Commodore Matthew Perry brought the United States Navy to Tokyo Bay. Forced to open its ports and accept a series of colonialist tariffs, Japan began to thrive by adapting Western industrialization to its own culture.

At the same time, the densely populated country, lacking natural resources, came to rely heavily on trade. Thus when the West's Great Depression arrived in the 1930s, Japan believed that was virtually forced into World War II in a hunt for new markets and resources.

"Ultraman" borrows from this history a number of elements that have particular resonance for the Japanese. Earth faces inevitable attack by the evil monstrosities that populate various alien worlds. To defend the planet, the benevolent Ultra family comes from a distant nebula and builds a major base in Japan, manned by 300 scientists and monster-fighters as well as by a number of elite assistants to Ultraman.

The hero himself gives up his own off-duty life to assume the identity of Iota, a Japanese family man whom he accidentally killed. When crisis comes, Iota changes into the giant in the rubberized jumpsuit to do battle with monsters who can be defeated only by someone possessing similar size and power. Just as the Japanese responded to the oddly dressed barbarians brought in by Commodore Perry, Ultraman adopts the invader's size and technology.

His fighting style is partly traditional Japanese and partly technological hocus-pocus. He does not fear the monsters' strength. The Japanese admire strength, and almost always seek to turn it to their advantage through a kind of cultural jujitsu.

Society is presented as healthy and stable in "Ultraman" and in nearly every one of its dozens of spin-offs. The threat comes from inhuman forces or forces seen to be of outside origin, such as modern technology. When Ultraman defeats the monster of the week, society is not advanced, improved, or moved in some new direction—it is returned to its original

---

[5] Marc Siegel, "Japan: The Ritual Roots of 'Ultraman' " *Channels*, July/August 1985, 85.

state. Despite enormous progress and change over the past 150 years, the Japanese tend to see their society as continuing in the proud tradition of two millennia and to see the alien intruders as bizarre and powerful, offering opportunity but threatening disruption and cultural devastation.

The literacy rate is a critical characteristic that determines to a great extent the growth and diffusion of print media. In Tanzania, the literacy rate has only recently reached 60 percent, and so print media are almost nonexistent. In the Netherlands, there is almost a 100 percent literacy rate, and so print media are very strong. In the Mediterranean nations of Spain, Portugal, Italy, Greece and Turkey, where there is poverty as well as illiteracy, especially in the rural areas, broadcast media are more important than print media. Even in Italy, the number of newspapers per 1,000 people is less than one-fifth that of Sweden and Britain, and most Italian newspapers are sold in the industrialized northern third of the country.

Another important factor in many countries is cultural and linguistic diversity. In Africa and the Arab states, especially, the number of discrete languages and dialects can range from 800 to 2,000. Additionally, many of these languages and dialects have no written form or literature. The oral tradition, which dominates in Africa and the Middle East, results in a poorly developed print-media system. Electronic media are also affected by the number of languages. In Cameroon, for example, with a population of slightly more than 8 million people, 100 languages are spoken. Gabon, with only 650,000 people, has 10 discrete languages. Radio broadcasting in the Soviet Union is done in 67 languages, and because of the linguistic diversity, radio has developed on regional and local levels rather than as a national system. Multilingualism is also a factor in the development of media systems in Asia and the South Pacific. In New Guinea, for example, broadcasts are made in 33 languages. Daily newspapers exist only in major urban centers in these countries, and the few regional papers are published haphazardly. Economics also is an interrelating factor, since it is less expensive to speak many languages than to print them.

Another cultural factor is a country's particular value system. In Sweden, for example, a concern for violence has led to film censorship, especially of films imported from the United States. But censorship of sexual content in film as well as in other media is nonexistent. In many ways, this attitude is the opposite of the attitude prevailing in the United States; we are more concerned about restricting sexual content than violence. Some people claim that in America, two historical features—the Puritan tradition and the westward expansion—resulted in this strange standard. Puritanism produced sexual constraints, and violence was an accepted part of the move West; our media content reflects our history.

In Canada, the power of the "marketplace" in determining and even regulating broadcast content is much weaker than it is in the United States. John Meisel, former chairman of the Canadian Radio-Television and Telecommunications Commission, wrote in *Channels* magazine that whatever the merits of the arguments about broadcast regulation, Canada and the United States will unlikely arrive at similar resolutions because they have different cultural traits and characteristics.

For one thing, says Meisel, Canadians do not seem to have developed the Americans' finely honed suspicion of government. Why did the forces of law and order—personified in the Royal Canadian Mounted Police—play such a prominent role in the settlement of the Canadian West, while the settlement of the American frontier was much more freewheeling? Why does Canada's constitution speak of "peace, order, and good government," while America's reveres "life, liberty, and the pursuit of happiness"? Why do Canadian responses to surveys consistently reveal higher levels of trust and confidence in government? A variety of explanations have been suggested: Canada's lack of a revolutionary past; the dispersion of the small Canadian population over vast distances; a sensitivity to society as community.

According to Meisel, Canadian attitudes bespeak more than an absence of distrust. Canadians have used the state as an instrument for common purposes much more often than have Americans. Heavy government involvement in the building of railways was, in large part, prompted by the need of a vast, sparsely settled country for an effective transportation system. Similarly, broadcasting and telecommunications are considered vitally important in forging and maintaining links among the country's various regions and groups.

Economic Conditions. The physical devices, content, and personnel that made mass communication systems possible cost vast sums of money. A country's or an individual's attitude toward a given medium can be assessed, in part, by the economic commitment made to that medium. The fact that Americans were willing to pay $500 for a television set in 1950 (in today's dollars, this would be over $2,000) indicated the strength of the public's commitment to this new medium. A nation's economic philosophy, structure, and conditions determine in great measure the ways and the extent to which media are funded. Capitalistic countries are more likely to allow the media to be profit-oriented, while Communist nations are less likely to have advertising in their media.

The economic conditions of a state also determine how the audience gains access to media. Are television sets purchased by individual viewers, or does the state provide receivers for group use? If a family buys a receiver, its members tend to exercise somewhat more control over how, when, and where their viewing takes place than do members of a communal audience. This makes communal viewing decidedly different from family or individual viewing.

In the United States, campus newspapers distributed free of charge have wider circulation than do those that students must purchase. Nevertheless, the student press that supports itself is less likely to bend to administrative pressure when sensitive issues arise.

A complex, sophisticated media system cannot thrive in an economically impoverished nation. A poor country with starving people can support only those media that help alleviate immediate problems. In most modern states, media survive and prosper because mass communication is a valuable asset to the states' economic process.

In Tanzania, for example, the average person's income is $136 a year; thus the country has a poorly developed media system. The media contain no advertising, not because of the state's political philosophy, but simply because the people do not earn enough money to buy the goods that would be advertised. In many Third World countries, newspapers are a form of mass communication among the urban elite. An advertiser support base is possible only in urban centers with a middle-class to upper-middle-class audience. In some cases, however, television has developed in spite of economic conditions. Television is regarded by many Third World governments as a symbol of prestige and power. Therefore, despite few TV sets and poor production facilities, TV systems are developed in order to enhance the government's prestige in the eyes of its neighbors and the world.

Political Philosophies. A country's political structure and the attitudes of its inhabitants influence the development of media systems more than any other factor, with the occasional exception of cultural and social traits. The amount and kind of control over mass communication are determined by the nature and structure of the government. Political forces establish the laws under which media institutions must operate. Media regulations may be repressive or permissive, depending on the political atmosphere of a particular society.

In the People's Republic of China, the media system is a political arm of the state used to implement party policy. For example, all Chinese television programming is linked in one way or another to social-policy goals. TV is first regarded primarily as a means for leadership to communicate with the people. Thus it is difficult to distinguish between entertainment and education offerings.

On Chinese television, there is little emphasis on personality; there are few, if any, "up-close-and-personal" programs. Many of the scheduled offerings, such as "Middle School Chemistry Experiments," suggest group audiences—in factories or schools or villages—and the use of television as a mass social reformer and educator.

Changes in China's geopolitical posture are also evident, however. The prominence of foreign-language instruction and the open rebroadcasting of foreign news speaks to China's commitment to join the world community.

An interesting development in China was the release in Peking of Sylvester Stallone's movie *First Blood*. The 1982 action film about a Vietnam veteran who loses control in Alaska was one of four foreign films released in China in the fall of 1985. But because China rarely allows American films to be shown there, the approval of this anti-Establishment movie by the Chinese authorities is a mystery.

One theory is economics. They probably did not pay more than $10,000 for it. But still, the movie applauds rebellion against authority, which the Chinese government will not accept.

For whatever reason, *First Blood* was a hit. At theaters around Peking, Chinese fans lined up three deep before breakfast to buy advance tickets. One possible reason that the film was so popular is that the Chinese are starved for entertainment. The other three foreign movies—from India, Romania, and the Netherlands—released that fall also attracted crowds.

During times of severe political stress, such as war, governments tend to exercise greater political control over media systems than in normal times. Both Iraq and Iran censor all media content, foreign as well as domestic, because they are currently at war with each other. During the Vietnam War, newspapers in South Vietnam that disagreed with the political policies of the Thieu government were shut down in the name of national security. After the war, that policy continued, but the papers that were permitted to publish changed. Newspapers that were not a part of the "reunification" effort ceased operation when the North Vietnamese and Vietcong assumed power.

The events of Watergate led to a major political struggle, which had an impact on the mass media of this country. Significant pressures from a variety of political sources affected the news media during the eclipse of the Nixon administration. The "fairness" tradition of the press remained a political force throughout this dark period in American political history.

In many African countries, direct censorship is the result of the political heritage of colonialism. This tradition has significantly influenced the new governments' attitudes toward mass media. In Tanzania, the government operates the broadcasting system and has "absolute discretion and rights" over content. The government also censors films and stage plays. The president of the country is the editor in chief of both newspapers. The government of South Africa, in its increasingly desperate attempt to maintain apartheid, regularly exercises press censorship by declaring "states of national emergency" and expelling foreign journalists.

As John C. Merrill notes in his book *Global Journalism*, government pressures on the world's press fall into four basic categories: (1) legal pressures, (2) economic and political pressures, (3) secrecy, and (4) direct censorship. Merrill states that legal pressures consist of constitutional provisions, security laws, press laws, and penal laws. The critical point of reference for most political systems' interface with the media is the nation's constitution. It defines the freedom and the limits of the media system. The

Russian constitution speaks of freedom of the press, but sets limits on that freedom and, in practice, controls the media system. The government administers both press and broadcasting through state committees that operate under the Council of Ministers, which is ultimately responsible to and controlled by the Communist party. Even newspaper and magazine circulation and book sales are controlled by the party.

In most socialist countries, the media are financed by the government through use taxes or other forms of tax revenue, but the content is basically not controlled. In Norway, for example, both motion-picture theaters and television are run by the state, but no significant censorship results.

The degree and kinds of political controls vary in each country, depending on that nation's political philosophies and goals. This aspect may well be the most potent single factor influencing media development because political power can be physical as well as philosophical.

Media Qualities. Technical features, media-use patterns, and overall institutional characteristics affect the development of media systems. For example, the development of commercial television in the United States radically changed radio and motion-picture institutions. Radio stations and motion-picture companies had to reevaluate and change their roles. This form of media interaction is constantly reshaping the total media system of the United States and every other nation.

Some media are inherently more expensive to operate than others. Television is a more costly medium than radio; high-quality magazines have a higher per-copy production cost than newspapers; it costs less to produce a phonograph record than a motion picture. The unique qualities of each of these media contribute to the per-unit cost, and this cost affects the way the medium is used and its place in the overall system.

As we have seen, print media can be highly effective only in literate societies; electronic media require no more than a speaking knowledge of a given language. Print media are more portable, however, and do not require expensive playback equipment. Radio is more portable than television, which contributes greatly to the use of radio in countries with large rural populations.

The use of satellites to broadcast television shows throughout Western European countries has made it all but impossible to carry on a strictly national broadcasting policy. In Belgium and Holland, for example, TV audiences can now choose from among 10 foreign services. As we noted, with the increase in satellite transmission, the concept of a national media system is being altered significantly.

Physical and geographical conditions, technological competencies, cultural traits, economic conditions, political philosophies, and media qualities interact to create unique media systems. Media are then used by the society to perform tasks that are essential to the society, including disseminating news, analyzing, educating, persuading, advertising, and entertaining.

The roles that the media perform in a nation cannot help but modify that nation, and as the parent society changes, the social forces and the uses made of media also change. This interaction of media systems and societies is critical to the development and well-being of the modern industrial state.

THE THIRD WORLD
AND A NEW INFORMATION ORDER

By and large, the mass media of the main spheres of political power, the capitalistic West and the Communist East, dominate world mass communication. But a large and increasingly vocal segment of the world does not want to be dominated by either. This is the so-called Third World, which is made up primarily of countries in Latin America, Africa, the Middle East, and Asia.

The countries of the Third World have been growing increasingly restive about the domination of media from East and West. As American media, especially, have grown massive and popular, much of the Third World has come to regard the American media invasion as exploitative and imperialistic. Mass media have become one of the biggest exports of the United States. Particularly in the Third World, where quality mass media are not readily available, those who want information and entertainment often turn to *Time, Reader's Digest,* and American movies, TV programs, and recorded music (especially rock music).

Much of the world's news is reported by American journalists through the news services of the Associated Press and United Press International. These are, of course, not the only news agencies in the world, but they have the largest staffs, the most equipment, and the most customers. Again, particularly in Third World nations, which do not have well-developed news agencies, people have to depend on agencies in the East and West for news and information, even about their own regions.

These problems were raised in the United Nations by Third World countries. In 1976, UNESCO proposed the adoption of a Soviet Union declaration stipulating the use of state-controlled news for certain purposes. Western governments responded with deep concern; as a result, the International Commission for the Study of Communication Problems was established under the leadership of Sean MacBride. The MacBride Commission delivered its report at a conference in 1980 to mixed reviews, and UNESCO Director General M'Bow refused to present it for formal adoption. The essence of the commission's report was a call for a "new world information order" that supposedly would help protect the communication integrity of every nation in the world. However, the more extreme elements of the "information order" clashed with traditional tenets of American freedom of the press. Ultimately, UNESCO adopted a resolution calling for the free flow of information, the need to protect freedom of information, and the repudiation of censorship and licensing.

One result of this 1980 conference was the establishment of the International Program for the Development of Communications (IPDC), which began a variety of programs designed to help address the world information imbalance. Meanwhile, the United States and Great Britain, weary of the politicization of UNESCO, withdrew from the organization in 1984, leaving it to an uncertain future because of loss of funding.

The concerns and questions about the free and balanced flow of information continue and are not easily resolved. However, awareness exists, and IPDC and other organizations continue to press for better understanding.

SUMMARY

The mass media experience is international. Each nation has evolved its own mass communication system based on unique conditions and factors. The study of how these systems work is called *metacommunications*. Although this text is concerned primarily with the American system of mass media, it is important to look at the media systems of other countries and try to understand why they are different from both the American system and one another.

There are many ways to analyze a nation's mass communication system. One of the most important is the impact of political philosophies on mass communication. Although a variety of political philosophies exist, four major theories of political/media systems have emerged. These are summarized in the book *Four Theories of the Press* and include: (1) the authoritarian system, in which government controls public expression; (2) the Soviet Communist system, in which the purpose of mass communication is to support the Communist party in its efforts to revolutionize society; (3) the libertarian system, which holds that the state exists to serve the needs of the people and that there should be complete freedom of expression; and (4) the social-responsibility system, which asserts that freedom of the press can be maintained only if the mass media accept their responsibility to society as a whole.

In addition to these four theories of the press, a media system can be categorized according to the extent to which both the receiver system and the message system are open or closed. The open mass communication system allows as much audience and message freedom as possible. This system is similar to the libertarian and social-responsibility theories of the press. The closed mass communication system exists when the audience is free to receive messages, but the messages are censored. This system most closely approximates the authoritarian and Communist theories of the press.

Both the open and closed models, like the four-theories system, have limitations because they *prescribe* rather than *describe* various media systems. In an attempt to develop a more descriptive model that captures the dynamic interactive relationships of media and society, we have developed a media-systems paradigm. The paradigm attempts to describe the relationship between the media and society. The paradigm is based on the theory that in every country, special factors or social forces interact in unique ways to create a national media system that performs a variety of functions that eventually participate in reshaping that society.

We have identified six social factors or forces that interact in the development of a media system: (1) physical and geographical characteristics, (2) technological requirements, (3) cultural traits, (4) economic conditions, (5) political philosophies, and (6) media qualities. The interaction of these factors, rather than their independent action, is crucial in the media system's evolution.

All these characteristics and qualities interact to create a unique media system. Media are then used by the society to preform essential tasks, including disseminating news, analyzing, educating, persuading, advertising, and entertaining.

By and large, the mass media of the capitalistic West and the Communist East dominate world mass communication. But a large and increasingly vocal segment of the world does not want to be dominated by either. This is the so-called Third World, which is made up primarily of countries of Latin America, Africa, the Middle East, and Asia. With much of the world's news dominated by American journalists, Third World countries have formally proposed the adoption of new principles that call for a Third World Information Order. There are a number of questions regarding this new information order, many of them political. However, the issues generated by this discussion and controversy are important for any study of international mass communication.

BIBLIOGRAPHY

Altbach, P. G., and E. M. Rathgeber. *Publishing in the Third World: Trend Report and Bibliography.* New York: Praeger, 1980.

Brown, Timothy G. *International Communications Glossary.* Washington, D.C.: Media Institute, 1984.

Burke, Richard C. *Comparative Broadcasting Systems.* Chicago: SRA, 1984.

Gerbner, George, and Marsha Siefert. *Global Frenzy: International Telecommunications in Transition.* Washington D.C.: Television Digest, 1984.

———— . *World Communications: A Handbook.* New York: Longman, 1984.

Hamelink, Cees J. *Cultural Autonomy in Global Communications: Planning National Information Policy.* New York: Longman, 1983.

Head, Sydney W. *World Broadcasting Systems: A Comparative Analysis.* Belmont, Calif.: Wadsworth, 1985.

Howkins, John. *International TV & Video Guide: 1986.* New York: New York Zoetrope, 1985.

———. *Mass Communication in China.* New York: Longman, 1982.

MacBride, Sean. *Many Voices, One World: Towards a New, More Just and More Efficient World Information and Communication Order.* Paris: UNESCO, 1980.

McLean, Mick, ed. *The Information Explosion: The New Electronic Media in Japan and Europe.* Westport, Conn.: Greenwood Press, 1985.

Martin, L. John, and Anju Grover Chaudhary. *Comparative Mass Media Systems.* New York: Longman, 1983.

Mattelart, Armand, and Hector Schmucler. *Communication and Information Technologies: Freedom of Choice for Latin America.* Norwood, N.J.: Ablex, 1985.

Merrill, John C. *Global Journalism.* New York: Longman, 1983.

Powell, Jon. *International Broadcasting by Satellite: Issues of Regulation, Barriers to Communication.* Westport, Conn.: Greenwood Press (Quorum Books), 1985.

Rogers, Everett M., and Francis Balle, eds. *The Media Revolution in America and Western Europe.* Norwood, N.J.: Ablex, 1985.

Smith, A. *The Newspaper: An International History.* London: Thames and Hudson, 1979.

Wendell, George, ed. *Mass Communications in Western Europe: An Annotated Bibliography.* Manchester, Eng.: European Institute for the Media, 1985.

21

Economics

America's capitalistic economic system is based on free enterprise and private ownership, which encourage competition, revenue generation, and profit taking. Our mass media actively participate in the process. The media have a significant impact on the United States economy, which, in turn, influences how and to what extent the mass media share in the rewards of the marketplace. But how does that work? For most students, economic issues are the most puzzling and least interesting—until it comes time to look for a job.

The headlines proclaiming the salaries of media talent (news actors as well as entertainment actors) does not reflect the reality of the job market in terms of job availability, employment patterns, or job security—let alone salary levels. Mass medialand is a tough, stressful, competitive, and modest-paying environment, and there is a lot less glamour once you get inside. It is a *work*place. It is a workplace in which careers rapidly become jobs.

The economic reality is just as rough-and-tumble for media businesses as it is for employees. Because of costs, entry into and survival within the media marketplace is rough sledding. Even Cable News Network and *U.S.A. Today*, which have substantial financial backing and large audiences, have had a rough time gaining advertisers and are not yet profitable.

Remember that the content that the movies, broadcasting, music industry, and print media produce must pay the bills through direct sales, ticket purchases, subscriptions, and advertising. Economically, *good* movies, books, records, TV shows, and magazines are those that attract paying consumers. Art is not an economic ethic, unless it pays for itself. Those who create content know that their arena is one of status, influence, power, and profit.

MEDIA ECONOMICS AND THE AMERICAN DREAM

The 1980s have been a "boom time" for the businesses of mass communication. And the mass media have influenced the American economic viewpoint that there will always be more of everything for everyone. The news, as well as the entertainment media, glorify economic growth, consumerism, and financial hedonism in the form of the "Yuppie ethic." What do "Lifestyles of the Rich and Famous," *Money* magazine, "Wall $treet Week" (on PBS), the movie *Trading Places,* the *Wall Street Journal,* and the depiction of the economic benefits of dealing drugs (even if the bad guys are punished in the last 30 seconds) on "Miami Vice" tell us about the real values in the world today?

The mass media are the tools of capitalism, in terms of both trumpeting the rewards of those who make it in the world of free enterprise and validating that American economic dream.

The media not only tell us to dream big, but also participate actively. They invest huge sums of money and gamble that they will make a profit. But how does the system work for all of us?

THE BASICS OF MEDIA ECONOMIC THEORY

Economic thought in the marketplace of mass communication is rooted in and best explained as the interaction of consumers, audiences, advertisers, and the purchases of goods and services influenced by supply and demand.

Levels of Consumer Decision Making

Individual decisions to spend money and time on the media are significant because those decisions determine whether a medium will succeed or fail. The consumer has three basic levels of purchasing power in regard to media consumption.

1. The consumer can choose between media and nonmedia goods and services. A family can spend its money on a new living-room sofa, a week's vacation, or a media product.
2. The consumer can choose among various media. The family that decides to spend its money on a media product must determine whether it wants $2,000 worth of books, a stereo system, or a video beam projector.

3. Once the decision is made to purchase a stereo system, the family must then choose among competing brands. Many consumers turn to foreign manufacturers, and many American companies now build their products overseas with components from many nations. In the area of electronic hardware, the zero-defect work ethic of the Japanese has helped Japanese companies gain a tremendous share of the American market and has silenced jokes of an earlier era about products made in Japan.

Dual Consumers in the Media Marketplace

An individual or a corporation that buys the goods and services of the newspaper, TV, recording, magazine, radio, motion-picture, or book industry becomes a media consumer. Media consumers use their time and money to purchase mass communication goods and services. Media consumers can be placed in two distinct categories: audiences and advertisers.

The Audience as Consumer. The audience buys media products so that it can receive and consume media content. Television, radio, and recording audiences use their financial resources to buy the equipment necessary to listen to and view the content. Audiences buy books, newspapers, and magazines in order to read the content.

Short-term and long-term consumption patterns are also realities of the media marketplace; the faster a given item is consumed, the sooner it must be replaced. Media audiences are willing to invest money and time in short-term consumption of media goods and services. Paperback books and magazines are bought and discarded almost as easily as the daily newspaper. Close to 40 percent of a TV network's prime-time programming is changed yearly. This rapid turnover is one of the major factors making media businesses viable economic enterprises. The willingness of audiences to spend money and time on short-term media goods and services is one indication of the value they place on them.

The Advertiser as Consumer. Traditionally, advertisers have been said to be buyers of time in the electronic media and of space in the print media. This labeling process is technically accurate but somewhat misleading as to what is actually being bought. The purchase of a 30-second commercial spot on NBC's "Cosby Show" or of a full-page advertisement in the *Chicago Tribune* is a meaningless act—and a poor business decision—unless audiences watch "The Cosby Show" or read the *Chicago Tribune*. In reality, advertisers buy audiences, not space and time. The estimated audiences for commercial broadcasting stations and for most newspapers and magazines are more valuable in the end than the original product—the minutes and pages of content. Although advertisers talk about buying 60-second spots on radio or full pages in magazines, their major concern is the audiences that consume these seconds and pages. Advertisers buy people because people consume the products advertised in the media.

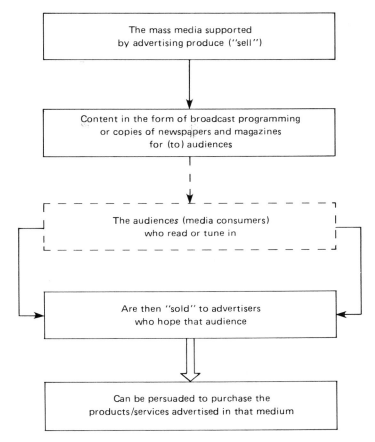

Figure 21.1 This model visualizes the dual-consumer concept, according to which the mass media produce content for audiences, which, in turn, are sold to advertisers, who persuade these readers, listeners, and viewers to buy the products and services advertised.

The Basic Conditions of the Marketplace

The economic conditions of the mass media are based on the same major principles as the rest of America's enterprises in our essentially capitalistic system.

Media Goods and Services. In popular economic language, there are two kinds of goods: *free goods,* which are supplied by nature; and *economic goods,* those goods to which human effort has added utility. Mass communication industries use free goods to produce economic goods. Trees, a free good, are used to produce newsprint, an economic good. Industrial diamonds are used to make phonograph needles. Within the category of economic goods, there are two classes: *producer goods and services,* which are used in the production of other goods and services; and *consumer goods and services,* which are used directly by the buyer without significant modification. Using the previous examples and extending them, we can say that free goods (trees and diamonds) are used to make producer goods (newsprint and phonograph needles), which, in turn, are used to make consumer goods (newspapers and record players).

The distinction between media goods and media services, at its simplest level, is that media goods are physical things (TV sets, transistor radios, copies of books and magazines), and media services are the content or activities that supplement or supply goods (the stories in magazines and books, the programs on radio and television).

Media Supply and Demand. The law of supply and demand is always at work in the media marketplace. *Consumer demand* is the desire to use and the ability to pay for goods and services. *Producer supply* refers to the quantity of goods available for purchase at a particular time and at an attractive price. When the consumer demand for VCRs exceeds the producer supply, the price tends to increase. When the supply of VCRs exceeds the demand, the price tends to drop. Media people, like any other businesspeople, seek to supply the demand at the most economically rewarding level for themselves (and sometimes even for consumers). Newspapers, magazines, and TV series that consistently misread the media marketplace are headed for economic disaster and oblivion.

THE MODELS OF MEDIA SUPPORT

There are essentially four kinds of media support systems: (1) media supported by audiences, (2) media supported by advertisers, (3) media supported by advertisers and audiences, and (4) media supported by public and private subsidy.

Audience-Supported Media

Record companies, the film industry (with the exception of films made expressly for television), pay cable-TV services, and book publishers derive practically all their revenue from audiences. The audiences bear the full brunt of the cost of producing these goods and services. The audience is not resold to advertisers. Ads can be and occasionally are inserted between chapters of books or cuts on LP records or scenes in motion pictures (as they are when shown on television), but the traditions of our media system have established that the audience pays the entire cost of these three media.

Advertiser-Supported Media

Radio and TV stations and some cable services produce programs that they provide "free of charge" to audiences. Stations and networks earn their money by selling these audiences to advertisers, which must recoup their ad costs when they sell their products to the public.

Audience- and Advertiser-Supported Media

Most general-circulation newspapers and magazines derive revenue from both audiences and advertisers. Audiences buy media content directly through subscriptions or newsstand purchases, but advertisers also pay for these audiences. Although the exact amount varies from publication to publication, audiences usually provide only 30 percent of the total revenue earned by general-circulation newspapers and magazines.

Private- and Corporate-Subsidized Media

Some media are supported by state and federal agencies, foundations, nonprofit organizations, or private corporations. These media obtain little or no consumer support. Public television and radio, student newspapers, corporate house organs, and subsidized government publishing are supported in this manner. The public pays part of the bill indirectly through local, state, and federal taxes; tuition; or support of these corporations involved with the media. Recently, public-radio and -TV stations have had to turn more and more to listener and viewer support and use auctions as well as other fund-raising activities. The Reagan administration has openly encouraged radical rethinking of the traditional support of public broadcasting. There is considerable consternation among local commercial

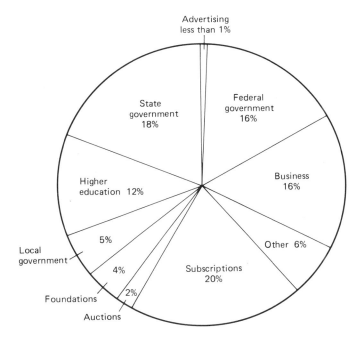

Figure 21.2 Public broadcasting is testing the advertising waters with enhanced underwriting, but it is a minuscule portion of most stations' budgets. The primary source of funding—39 percent—comes from governments, but if state-college support is included, that contribution rises to 51 percent. Subscriptions and auctions combine for 22 percent; business contributes 16 percent; foundations provide 4 percent; and the remaining 7 percent comes from other sources. Governments are trying to reduce their support, and in hard times, business also cut back contributions, as have the oil companies. During the next decade, public stations may see major changes in funding sources. (Source: Corporation for Public Broadcasting.)

broadcasters and video production houses over two new policies of public-TV stations:

1. *Enhanced Underwriting.* Many PBS stations are actively soliciting paid, 30-second "information announcements," which are defined by the FCC as having *no* inducement to buy a product or service; *no* call to action or encouragement of a consumer to buy a product or service; and *no* quotation of prices. In effect, public stations are selling institutional advertising, and if ad sales substantially increase, commercial stations' grumblings may grow louder.
2. *Production Services.* PBS outlets are also renting studios and equipment and editing facilities at very competitive prices. Some, such as WPBT-TV in Miami, have spun off production companies like Comtel, which compete with small production facilities that have to live off the economy.

These two actions were necessitated by changes in federal and state funding policies and by public broadcasting audiences' growing disenchantment with interruptions of program schedules to beg for dollars.

THE ECONOMICS OF ADVERTISING

Four mass media groups—newspapers, magazines, radio, and television—depend on advertising revenue for all or most of their support. Therefore, an understanding of the economics of advertising is necessary if we are to understand why ad media are the way they are.

Economic Value in Advertising

The value of a magazine, newspaper, radio, or TV advertisement depends on both the size of and the characteristics of the audience. To an advertiser, the most important audiences are composed of those individuals who are most likely to buy the product being advertised. These target audiences are critical to the ad media because they have real economic value based on the following dimensions:

1. If Mobil does not have many service stations in a given state, it is not worthwhile to advertise its gasoline products in that state. The *geographical location* of the potential consumer is critical to the advertiser. It would obviously be foolish for a snowmobile manufacturer to buy time on a New Orleans TV station.
2. Frequent airline travelers live primarily in metropolitan areas, and so United Airlines advertises mainly in large urban newspapers. *Population density* is an important dimension of the target audience.

3. The Kellogg Company sells most of its presweetened cereals to children. Saturday morning is a good time to advertise its products on television. *Age* is the relevant dimension here. For years, "The Lawrence Welk Show" was sponsored by Geritol.

4. Women buy Revlon cosmetics, so advertising lipstick in *Esquire* would be foolhardy. *Sex* is a dimension of the target audience.

5. Purchases of convenience foods are affected by *family size, income,* and *employment patterns.* Large families eat more and spend a larger portion of the family income for food. Women who work outside the home use more convenience foods than do women who remain at home.

Research methods are also beginning to report media usage based on product category. For example, in Atlanta, how many coffee drinkers read *Family Circle* or watch Cable News Network (CNN)? This kind of information has a significant impact on traditional advertising patterns. MTV now attracts a substantial number of subteens, teens, and young adults, especially white males 18 to 24 years old. Advertisers seeking this target audience determine MTV's economic value compared with that of other available media before buying time on this cable service. Advertisers must know their target audience and a specific media vehicle's ability to deliver that potential consumer.

Advertising Efficiency of the Media Buy

Advertisers seek to reach the largest number of consumers at the lowest possible price. Advertisers tend to use media vehicles that provide the best advertising efficiency.

$$\text{advertising efficiency} = \frac{\text{advertising cost}}{\text{audience size}}$$

We assign relative value to each medium's audience by dividing the cost of an ad by the size of the audience to determine specific cost efficiency, which is expressed as cost per thousand (CPM). In other words, how much does it cost to reach 1,000 households or viewers?

$$\text{cost per thousand (CPM)} = \frac{\text{advertising cost}}{\text{audience (in units of 1,000)}}$$

In effect, advertisers have to compare cost efficiencies. They work with CPM readers, listeners, and viewers as one means of assigning easily understandable and easily comparable economic weight to each buy.

Under normal conditions, newspapers with large circulations have higher advertising rates than do papers with fewer readers; when a newspaper's audience increases, its rates go up. For example, a large daily newspaper charges a one-time advertiser about $15,000 to use a full-page ad to reach its approximately 800,000 daily readers. On Sunday, the paper charges $18,750 for the same size ad because Sunday circulation exceeds 1 million. When the cost efficiencies of the two editions of the paper are compared, the CPM circulation is the same because the higher cost is offset by the increase in circulation of the Sunday edition.

Cost Efficiency

Daily

$$\frac{\$15,000 \text{ cost of ad}}{800,000 \text{ circulation}} = \$18.75 \text{ CPM}$$

Sunday

$$\frac{\$18,750 \text{ cost of ad}}{1,000,000 \text{ circulation}} = \$18.75 \text{ CPM}$$

In terms of advertiser cost, both editions have the same efficiency ($18.75), based on paid circulation estimates made by the Audit Bureau of Circulation.

Audience Characteristics and Cost Efficiency

Advertisers must know more about audiences than how many people use a particular media product; they need to know what kinds of people use a given newspaper, magazine, radio, or TV station. In television, for example, total audience size is usually less important than the characteristics or composition of a program's audience. If we compare two network programs, this point may become clearer. For example, an advertiser of a diet beer, if such a product exists, has to choose between buying a 30-second spot during a situation comedy for $100,000 or another during a football game for $150,000. The sitcom reaches 15 million viewers, while the football game reaches only 10 million viewers.

CPM Total Audience

Situation comedy

$$\frac{\$100,000 \text{ cost of spot ad}}{15,000,000 \text{ audience}} = \$6.67 \text{ CPM}$$

Football game

$$\frac{\$150,000 \text{ cost of spot ad}}{10,000,000 \text{ audience}} = \$15 \text{ CPM}$$

Comparing CPMs, the sitcom ($6.67) seems to be a better buy than the football game ($15) because it has a larger total audience. But the advertiser's target audience is men aged 18 to 49, and so the situation changes markedly. The sitcom has only 5 million male viewers (18–49), while the football game has 8 million male viewers (18–49).

CPM Men (18–49)

Situation comedy

$$\frac{\$100,000}{5,000,000 \text{ men (18–49)}} = \$20 \text{ CPM}$$

Football game

$$\frac{\$150,000}{8,000,000 \text{ men (18–49)}} = \$18.75 \text{ CPM}$$

At this point, the football game ($18.75 CPM) becomes a more efficient buy than the sitcom ($20 CPM). Football, then, is a better buy for this advertiser because it reaches more of the target audience at a lower unit cost.

The diet beer's audience would be in terms of "heavy-user" data that disregard traditional demographic variables and rely totally on product consumption. The situation comedy has only 1.5 million people in this new target audience, while the football game has 5 million.

CPM Heavy Users

Situation comedy

$$\frac{\$100,000}{1,500,00 \text{ heavy users}} = \$66.67 \text{ CPM}$$

Football game

$$\frac{\$150,000}{5,000,000 \text{ heavy users}} = \$30 \text{ CPM}$$

At this point, the football game ($30 CPM) becomes more than twice as efficient as the situation comedy ($66.67 CPM). This is true even though the situation-comedy spot costs $50,000 less than the football-game spot and the situation comedy has a substantially larger (5 million) number of total viewers.

Every advertiser tries to spend as many dollars on the product's target audience as possible. That is the essence of using cost efficiency to the economic advantage of the advertiser.

Current Cost Efficiencies

Obviously, CPM audience data vary among media and among competitors within a medium, but some averages are available. Television CPMs run from $2 for "daytime" to $8 for prime time. Radio CPMs vary by market, but $2 to $6 are usual costs. Cable household CPMs are harder to predict because of less consistent audience research data; a $5 to $10 range probably covers the major services. The cable services CNN, MTV, and ESPN, which run commercials of up to 2 minutes, are very attractive for adver-

Figure 21.3 This advertisement from the newspaper edition of *Standard Rates and Data* attempts to emphasize the ability of the *New York Times* to reach up-scale residents in five areas in and around "the City." The *Times* ad emphasizes education and income, which are hallmarks of the "Yuppie" target audience.

tisers that can use a longer format to "tell their story" to the potential consumer. There is evidence that the demographics of cable audiences are good in terms of providing "up-scale" audiences.

Print CPMs for newspapers run about $10 for a full-page ad in the major markets. Interestingly, smaller newspapers are less efficient, and CPMs go up as markets decrease in size. The cost efficiencies of a newspaper's Sunday edition traditionally are about 10 percent lower than those of the same paper's weekday editions. Magazine CPMs are higher than those of newspapers, but that is because magazines tend to reach very specialized target audiences.

Figure 21.4 Audiences and advertising costs have a symbiotic relationship. The target audience for *GQ* is the up-scale, well-educated, fashion-conscious, young, urban, white male. If this is also an advertiser's target audience, the $16,750 cost of a full-page, four-color ad should be very cost efficient.

Advertiser Production Costs

Besides paying for the costs incurred by the media, advertisers must produce ads to fill their space and time buys. The cost of producing advertisements has skyrocketed in the past 10 years. Print ads for major advertisers run as high as $50,000 per layout. Photographing models, retouching photographs, designing paper, setting type, and making gravure negatives and screen prints—these are complicated and time-consuming activities done by well-paid technicians using expensive, sophisticated equipment. Radio ad campaigns by recognized talent can run from $25,000 to $50,000 per 60-second spot. The average cost of a 30-second TV spot is $100,000, which is equal to the per-minute cost of a $10 million feature film.

Figure 21.5 Because of the high costs of both advertising space and advertising production, advertisers and their agencies are very demanding. They want their advertisements to reach the right audience and be visually arresting. That is why premium prices are paid for photography, layout, and design. This beautifully printed high-fashion ad appeared in *Ebony* and was targeted to weight-conscious consumers.

THE STRUCTURE OF THE MEDIA INDUSTRY

The mass communication industries have traditionally been described as having three layers: production, distribution, and exhibition.

1. *Production* is the creative development of content.
2. *Distribution* is the moving of product from the producer to the retail outlet.
3. *Exhibition* is the provision of content to the audience by the local retailer.

It is at the distribution level, the delivery of content, that the revolution in mass communication is occurring. News and entertainment "product" (actually a media service) are much the same from year to year, although "soft" news has grown.

News, for example, is at the edge of a significant change in how audiences will gain access to information. The time for videotex and teletext displays of information on a TV screen or personal computer is near; newspapers, especially the (Chicago) Tribune Company and the Knight-Ridder organization, are very active in this new technology. The newspaper will not disappear, but it will probably be reshaped along the lines of local versions of *USA Today*, which is essentially a headline service. The 24-hour TV news service pioneered by Ted Turner's Cable News Network (CNN) is another radical shift in news distribution. The "superstations" (WTBS, WOR, WGN) are legally local "broadcast" operations that distribute their programs nationally via satellite, using local cable operators and thus short-circuiting traditional broadcast network and station linkages.

Perhaps the most significant change in distribution has occurred in the motion-picture industry. In the past 10 years, major companies have dominated film distribution: Buena Vista (Disney), Columbia, MGM/United Artists, Orion and Tri-Star, Paramount, Twentieth Century-Fox, Universal, and Warner Brothers. They have financed 60 to 70 independent productions. They literally have controlled the industry in production and distribution.

To ensure product, superstation WTBS-TV in Atlanta bought MGM/UA for $6.5 billion in 1986, after Ted Turner had failed in his bid to gain control of CBS. This purchase by Turner guarantees that this distributor's film library (3,700 feature-length films) will provide programming for years to come for his exhibition outlet, WTBS. In a few years, savings on programming costs will almost pay the entire purchase price. Turner will also syndicate the films to other TV stations and sell videos for the home market. Turner became embroiled in controversy when he colorized the black and white films in that collection in order to increase ratings for the TV broadcasts and videocassette sales. Film artists protested the "defamation" of their work. It was a struggle of economics and audience taste versus artistic integrity.

Time, Inc., needs roughly 200 films each year for the Home Box Office (HBO)/Cinemax 24-hour pay-cable schedule via RCA's *Satcom 1* satellite. Obviously, the movie studios control the product HBO needs, and they raised pay-cable rental fees of successful theatrical movies to levels that are nearly equal to the total production costs of the films. Home Box Office countered by buying American pay-cable rights from independent producers for roughly 25 percent of production costs before the producers cut distribution deals for theatrical release with one of the major distribution companies. This was the case with hits like *Tootsie* and misses like *Nobody's Perfect*. But, hit or miss, it filled the HBO schedule adequately because HBO does not live by daily viewings, as do movie theaters. The subscriber's monthly flat fee covers all investments.

In effect, the traditional economic associations are breaking down. Media giants are diversifying and are buying into one another's "turf." The shape of things to come for all media is up for grabs, especially in the area of distribution.

THE HIGH COST OF FAILURE

Although the huge dollar amounts used to measure media advertising, sales, rentals, profits, and incomes seem exorbitant, it is important to keep in mind that every medium and every business unit within that medium has to meet extremely high labor and material costs.

The revenue derived from consumers and nonconsumers alike goes to pay media's bills. Media industries incur huge start-up costs. They also incur large operating expenses as they continue to pay for the production costs involved in making media content, the distribution costs incurred in delivering goods and services to the consumer, and the exhibition costs involved in making media products easily available to audiences.

Initial Costs

Some media businesses can start up with relatively little capital investment, whereas others require enormous initial costs. A phonograph record can be produced for whatever a local band can scrape together to rent a studio, cut the necessary tracks, and produce a "demo." Urban monthly magazines can be started with relatively little capital outlay. Books can be produced inexpensively using typed masters, rubber plates, offset printing, and glued binding.

Nevertheless, low initial costs are not the rule in media economics. A textbook such as *Mass Media V* requires a commitment of over $250,000 on the part of the publisher in terms of total investment in editorial, manufacturing, and promotion costs, as well as the advance payment to the authors. Even a bargain-basement film like *Invasion, U.S.A.* costs $3 million to $5 million to make. *Aliens, Back to the Future, The Untouchables,* and *Inner-Space* cost tens of millions. To start a newspaper in a major metropolitan area would require an investment of $10 million to $15 million. Moderately successful TV stations sell for millions of dollars. The impact of these large start-up costs is felt and reflected in the high advertising rates, admission prices, and subscription rates charged by most media.

Operating Expenses

Most media enterprises involve long-term commitments in the form of operating expenses: supplies, labor overhead, interest, modernization, and expansion. Newspapers alone spend more than $150 million annually to improve their operations. Radio operations purchase music rights, news, and sports information for programming because they are relatively inexpensive ways to serve their specialized audiences. To cut production costs, newspapers use newsprint rather than high-quality book paper.

Production Costs

Newspapers must pay a staff of reporters (or hire free lance writers), artists, editors, and syndicated services to generate content. Magazines must pay staff costs as well as "job out" articles to nonstaff writers, who are paid well for their work. Radio stations must pay music royalties and local talent costs, as well as cover the costs of news and sports programming.

The most publicized costs are those in television. Network prime-time productions run from about $750,000 to $1.5 million per hour-long episode; made-for-TV movies average $2 million to $3 million per 2-hour film; and miniseries like "Shogun," "The Thorn Birds," "The Winds of War," and "Chiefs" cost upward of $1.5 million an hour. The three networks spend approximately $6 billion a year on 1,500 hours of programming.

The networks pay only a portion of the production cost of each episode—usually 50 percent to 80 percent, depending on the series. They pay for two showings of each episode. The producer of the series must make her profit in syndication. The profits can be phenomenal on series that last more than five years on a network. "M*A*S*H" sold for $250,000 per episode in its first syndication run in the 1970s and $900,000 for each of the same syndicated episodes in the 1980s. "Magnum, P.I." now sells for $1,750,000 per episode in syndication, and estimates are that "The Cosby Show" will go for about $3 million per episode in syndication. The production cost of "The Cosby Show" is $550,000 per episode, and NBC pays all but $100,000 of that; so Viacom, the syndicator, should make $2.9 million on its investment of $100,000 an episode when "The Cosby Show" is syndicated.

Because of rampant off-network syndication costs, first-run dramatic series have become cost effective. "The New Gidget," "9 to 5," "Charles in Charge," "Silver Spoons," "One Big Family," "Throb," and "What a Country!" are producing at least 25 new episodes for syndication to local stations. These new shows will cost substantially less per showing than reruns now cost.

The syndication market is still dominated by shows that first appeared on ABC, CBS, and NBC but are owned by syndicators. Of the syndication market, 70 to 80 percent is still cornered by programs that were broadcast first on the networks.

Shows like "Entertainment Tonight," "Solid Gold," and game shows do well because their production costs are lower (approximately $100,000 per hour on the average). The Federal Communications Commission under the Reagan administration is trying to amend the rule that prevents networks from competing in the syndication market. Some programs can be aired live, but because most programs are videotaped or filmed, TV economics has been a primary reason for the death of live programming.

High production costs have forced the industry to use reruns, which means that programs must be recorded. Most prime-time TV series produce about 20 episodes each season, so it is possible for each show to be run two or three times each year. In theory, this practice cuts production costs for a season by at least 60 percent.

For prime time, nearly all variety series are videotaped and dramatic series are filmed. In the 1970s, situation comedies such as "All in the Family," under impetus from Norman Lear, turned from film to electronic production techniques. Without international markets and the ability to use reruns as syndicated series, few, if any, network prime-time shows would be economically successful. "Star Trek," for example, achieved greater success as a syndicated series than it did on the network, and this success even spawned a new "Star Trek" series.

Television production costs fall into two basic categories.

1. Above-the-line costs cover all items related to creative elements of production, including writing, directing, acting, and producing a program.
2. Below-the-line costs relate to physical or technical elements of a program, including the production staff, scenery, costumes, location costs, equipment rental, editing, processing, and overhead.

For videotaped variety shows, above-the-line elements account for 50 to 65 percent of the total production cost because of high talent costs. For filmed dramas, below-the-line items account for 50 to 65 percent of the total production cost because of high labor, scenery, location, and equipment costs.

Distribution Costs

The cost of producing a movie, a book, or a cable-TV show remains the same whether 10,000 or 10 million see it or read it. All media try to spread the cost over the largest possible audience in order to make their product profitable. It must be distributed.

Charges for network television time are based on available audience, that percentage of American TV homes with their sets turned on, rather than on the actual audience tuned to a specific program within a specific time slot. The available audience (and, therefore, network distribution costs) is affected by five variables: (1) the number of homes equipped with TV sets; (2) the coverage of the stations affiliated with the network; (3) the scope of the available interconnection system; (4) the season of the year; and (5) the daypart, or time segment—daytime, prime time, and so on.

Books, magazines, newspapers, records, radio shows, and cable services all have to be delivered. That costly, essential job falls to distributors and exhibitors—the wholesalers and retailers of the mass media. For example, magazine publishers depend on 750 wholesalers and more than

100,000 retail outlets to help sell their wares. The recording industry uses record clubs, distributors, retailers, and rack jobbers to get their records into the hands of the public.

THE BOTTOM LINE: ECONOMIC ISSUES AND TRENDS

The mass media are growth industries, but like every sector of the economy, they have experienced ups and downs in the past decade. As a rule of thumb, business is off and prices are up.

The Broadcast Media

Radio and television growth continues in both new stations being constructed and established stations being sold. This activity is, in part, the result of the FCC's decision that companies may now own 12 TV and 12 radio stations as long as neither group covers more than 25 percent of the country's population. Station sales are in excess of $3 billion a year at present. Various broadcast groups are gobbling up one another to improve their position in terms of the 12-station limit. When the dust settles, there will be fewer, bigger, more powerful, and heavily indebted companies controlling the future of broadcasting. Some analysts worry that too much was paid in these buyouts and the bubble could burst unless overall economic growth improves. Station income, however, has helped both network owned-and-operateds (O&O's) and affiliates attain strong financial positions. In terms of local stations for both affiliates and independents, news remains the profit center, and ratings battles at both the local and the national news desk is intense. The news department is a critical economic force in the finances of most stations.

The most dramatic changes have occurred in network economics, where Capital Cities Communications took over ABC for $3.4 billion. After a number of bidders failed to gain control of CBS, Loew's Corporation, led by Laurence Tisch, bought a major chunk of that network to prevent further hostile takeovers. And the granddaddy of the networks, NBC, was bought, along with its parent company, RCA, by General Electric for $6.3 billion. The network itself had also bought back a large share of stock and incurred a heavy debt in doing so.

These changes are bound to bring shake-ups at the networks, because all three parent organizations invested in their new networks for economic reasons. These three corporations are very profit-oriented. Changes in programming and network personnel's life styles will be rethought economically.

In addition, the Australian-born newspaper magnate Rupert Murdock hopes to start a fourth commercial television network built around the six stations he bought from Metromedia ($1.5 billion) and his investment in

Twentieth Century-Fox. It is estimated that it takes 200 stations to make a network viable at today's production cost levels and that potential for a fourth network does exist. The TV-network picture is further clouded by the fact that the three networks' share of the audience dropped from 90 percent in the late 1970s to only 75 percent in the mid-1980s. Under the FCC's financial-interest rule, the networks are allowed to produce and thus own the syndication rights to only three to five hours of their prime-time schedule. General Electric is committed to trying to change that FCC rule to improve the economic picture for NBC by allowing it to produce more of its prime-time schedule.

Radio's position is growing strong as newspaper and television advertising rates continue to increase. Demand for radio time is growing. However, radio stations' share of the pie will continue to fragment because of the new 689 FM stations being allocated by the FCC, and the competition will increase in an already crowded market. There is some concern that network radio may be in a precarious position because of the recent takeovers of the networks by companies interested in the bottom line. However it is too early to predict the economic outlook for radio networks.

Revenue earned from cable subscribers has reached $10 billion a year, with the average basic cable rate at about $10 a month, or $120 a year. Profit for most systems should increase substantially in the next few years as they pay off their indebtedness. There are now over 30 satellite cable services supported by advertising and by the fee of a few cents to 50 cents per subscriber paid by the cable operator to the programmer. Time-Life's HBO/ Cinemax combination accounts for 18 million subscribers and has become a major producer of movies because of its large audience. Satellite-dish sales are off because of scrambled signals. Cable advertising revenue reached $1 billion in 1986, partly because 50 percent of the homes in the United States are now cable subscribers, with an average of 12 channels in the basic service. And 55 percent of cable subscribers also pay another $11 a month for premium services, such as HBO, the Disney Channel, or Showtime.

The growth of pay cable TV, however, has slowed appreciably. Pay cable is the first service disconnected by subscribers when they buy a VCR and rent videotapes, which allows greater selectivity and costs less ($1 to $2 a movie).

The Home Shopping Network (HSN) is the hottest news in cable programming in the mid-1980s. It is the first profitable, interactive cable operation in broadcasting history. Its success is made possible by computer technology, telephones, and the buying of surplus goods at discount prices. HSN is a shop-at-home, low-margin retailer that operates 24 hours a day, 7 days a week, and depends on impulse buying of discounted items by viewers. HSN-2, which sells slightly up-scale items, went on the air in 1986, and both HSN and HSN-2 pay the local cable operator 5 percent of what is sold in that market, regardless of whether the consumer is a cable subscriber. It is a cable garage sale. Interest in pay-per-view showing is also picking up steam because of technological advances that make it easy to order programs and bill subscribers. However, this remains in the test-market phase and is not yet economically viable.

Motion Pictures and Recordings

The key growth factor in the economics of feature-length films has to be the development of a truly affordable VCR. Revenue from sales of videotapes of feature films now equals box-office revenue, which doubles film income and expands the audience by adding stay-at-homes to the traditional body of moviegoers. The prerecorded cassette has been and will continue to be a bonanza for Hollywood. Forty percent of homes have a VCR, and that number will reach 65 to 70 percent by 1990. In 1986, revenue from studios' rentals of films ran about $1.7 billion (of the annual $3.8 billion box-office receipts), and the studios receive another $2.3 from sales of cassettes at wholesale prices. Rather than being a threat to the motion-picture industry, the cassettes are expanding the audience by lowering costs so families can see films at home. This phenomenon may even help marginal films at the box office become profitable. The comedy hit *Beverly Hills Cop* sold 1.4 million copies and made $25 million for Paramount at the $29.95 retail price. Profit can run as high as $50 a cassette at current levels and can help defray production costs. Two-thirds of the $5 billion annual revenue from video rentals based on the "first-sale" concept remains with the retail outlets that rent them. Most movies on tape are priced in the $59.95 to $89.95 range and will remain so until video stores begin to share the profits from film rentals. The National Video Stores chain is testing a shared-rental scheme in 10 of its 650 stores that may become the model for the future.

The potential box-office and video-rental market has influenced to some extent the movement of B-movie companies into up-scale production rivalry with major producers. Cannon films is the flagship in a group that includes Avco-Embassy, Filmways, and American International. New low-end companies, such as New World Pictures (from the legendary Roger Corman), see a sure market for $1 million to $3 million projects because TV sales and the cassette market can supplement fall-off at the box office.

For the distributors of big-budget films, $15 million to $25 million production budgets are problematic. Even George Lucas's two big projects of 1986—*Labyrinth* (with a David Bowie sound track and Jim Henson Muppets) and *Howard the Duck*—were theatrical disasters. Tape sales will help. It is now *Top Gun, Rambo: First Blood, Part II, Police Academy III, Karate Kid II, Ferris Bueller's Day Off, Down and Out in Beverly Hills,* and *Back to School*—which have reasonable budgets and good box-office draw—that make profits. Tape sales of these films will be frosting on the cake.

A strong link continues between film and recording via pop-music sound tracks, for which rights can cost up to $1 million but average in the $300,000 to $400,000 range and can help sell the film on MTV, as happened with *White Nights, Running Scared,* and *Top Gun.*

Figure 21.6 *E.T. The Extra-Terrestrial*, Steven Spielberg's wonderful fantasy and testament to friendship, remains the box-office champion of all time, having earned about $228 million in American and Canadian box-office receipts. Never released to cable, television, syndication, or videotape, its future financial value is a wonder to behold.

In the record business, the compact disc (CD) is making economic waves. About 50 million discs were sold in 1986. One in five sales of albums is in the CD format, despite the fact only 2 percent of American homes have CD players. CDs are unquestionably the premier growth opportunity in the music business. Sales are so brisk that production cannot meet record stores' demand, which means that high prices ($15.00) will continue for the short run. Obviously, the sale of CD players is responsible for this new demand. This recording format provides higher quality sound and greater durability of the recording itself. The player is essentially a monopoly of Japanese firms that are now selling machines in the $100-plus range. It is estimated that CD sales could reach 300 million units a year in the early 1990s. Although total revenue from record sales was about $4.4 million in the mid-1980s, sales of CDs, even at reduced prices, could double the music industry's income by the late 1990s.

The Print Media

Newspapers are in a very strong position economically because of the trends of independent newspapers being acquired by newspaper chains and small chains being absorbed by larger chains at high prices. Group ownership dominates the business. In the mid-1980s, 156 chains controlled 71 percent of the newspapers (1,186 papers) and 78 percent of total circulation (49.3 million homes) in the United States. The continued growth of these large, strongly capitalized, and well-managed chains is assured, and newspapers will be a good investment into the next century.

Growth in circulation is less than 1 percent a year, and more than one-third of that growth is due to the pioneering but unprofitable national newspaper, the Gannett chain's *USA Today*. Increased newspaper revenue comes from higher per-copy prices, higher run-of-press (ROP) advertising rates, increases in classified ad volume, and substantial growth (about 15 percent per year) in preprinted advertising inserts and cents-off coupon campaigns, which account for over $4 billion of the annual $26 billion spent on newspaper advertising. Newspapers are now actively competing with direct mail, which has had to absorb or pass along the 13 percent increase in third-class postage rates. This successful campaign to compete with direct mail takes two forms: (1) the inclusion of inserts in less than a full run, which helps reach selected target audiences; and (2) the continued acquisition and start-up of penny-savers, or shoppers, delivered free to every home in a market, including those households that do not subscribe to the local newspaper. The 3,000 U.S. shoppers have a circulation of over 34 million homes. These free papers provide total-market as well as select-market coverage on demand through an alternative distribution system. The shopper gives 100 percent market coverage, whereas the paid newspaper reaches an average of only 60 percent of the households in a market zone. Either way, the newspaper company profits, because it owns both the newspaper and the shopper.

The trends toward fewer dailies, more Sunday editions, and morning editions continue. Rising costs have also led to such a situation as two local papers, with separate news staffs, sharing production plants and advertising sales departments. This has helped profit margins stay at the 15 to 20 percent level for the past decade, in spite of increases in newsprint costs. More than half of the newsprint used in the United States comes from Canadian suppliers. Reasonable union contracts and new computer-assisted technology have allowed papers to cut costs by reducing staff size.

The number of pages of advertising in magazines is increasing by 1 percent a year and ad revenue by 8 to 10 percent a year; therefore, the major economic gains for magazines in the mid-1980s are due to increased advertising rates, which have driven CPM readers for a one-page, four-color ad to $15.00. This is still viable because of the selectivity of magazine audiences. Per-copy and subscription prices are expected to continue to increase above their mid-1980 levels of $2.05 a copy and $22.35 an annual subscription rate. This will offset what is essentially slow growth in total copies sold. The increase in number of subscribers is offset by the drop in single-copy sales. About three of every four magazines are purchased by subscription, with total sales in excess of 320 million copies a year.

Because magazines clearly target specialized audiences and TV ad costs are very high ($1.1 million a minute in Super Bowls, and $400,000 for a 30-second spot on "The Cosby Show" in 1986), advertisers with clearly defined markets and strained budgets are using magazines effectively. Magazines are easy to carry and read, are relatively inexpensive to produce with high-quality graphics, are more timely because of technology that cuts production time, and cover a tremendous range of subjects. Paper prices are down, which has balanced increased postal rates. Magazine costs are broken down as production and distribution, 36.6 percent; circulation, 24.9 percent; advertising, 9.5 percent; editorial, 8.7 percent; administration, 5.9 percent; and miscellaneous, 3.3 percent.

Over 200 book publishers begin business each year, swelling the ranks to 1,700 publishing houses at the present time. Although the major houses still dominate the industry, many small publishers can corner a particular segment of a selected market. Computer technology in book production is rapidly opening the publishing industry to low-cost entry. The book business is not concentrated; it is labor intensive; and printing is jobbed out. Because of fixed costs, books with small runs have a high per-copy cost. Hardcover books sell for more than $31.50 a copy; trade paperbacks can cost more than $13.50; and mass-market paperbacks go for over $3.50. Total book sales are now in the $12 billion-plus range annually.

The more than 1,400 distributors and jobbers and 21,600 bookstores in the United States and Canada sell 2 billion copies of the 53,000 titles published each year.

Because of costs, publishers are reexamining their return policies, which have caused discomfort for distributors and retail outlets. Publisher, distributor, and bookstores are faced with the reality that only 20 percent of the books published earn a profit. A few titles must support the rest, and because of information obsolescence, nonfiction books must be revised every few years, especially texts and professional books. And for leading textbooks, the major competitor has become used copies of the same book. College bookstores indicate that they lose money on the sale of new books, while they clear 10 percent on used copies. At the beginning of each term, there is a shortage of used books and a surplus of new books. The sale of new texts increased only approximately 4 percent in recent years, while the sale of used texts increased over 50 percent. This is causing the prices of new books to be artificially inflated and the profits of used-book distributors to soar. Instead of buying new books, college students are renting used copies at very high costs from jobbers and campus outlets. In most cases, a student loses half the purchase price when she sells a used book back to the bookstore. Eventually, the student bears the economic burden, and the used-book distributors make substantial profits. If a book dealer buys a $30 list-price book back from a student for $15 and sells it for $20, he makes $5, and the student has "rented" the book for $15. In all later transactions (buying back at $10 and selling at $20), the outlet earns $100 "renting" the used book 10 times in five or six years. This process is forcing the prices of new textbooks into a sharp upward spiral, because publishers must pay their costs and make a profit on a dwindling number of sales for each revised or new text published.

Without the library market, many titles would never be published because 9 of every 10 books sell fewer than 20,000 copies. More than half of these 20,000 books are purchased by 29,000 libraries that buy 1 of every 10 books sold—usually higher priced, hard-cover, limited-sales editions.

As a result of all of these factors, merger-mania has also struck the book industry. Publishers are merging with one another, and outsiders are buying in. As an example, Gulf and Western bought Prentice-Hall for $705 million. It is a wild and woolly and profitable book world out there. Fortunes are being made in all areas of print publishing by starting specialized publications and then selling them off.

Advertising

Advertising in the United States is a $100 billion a year business, and revenue may well double by the year 2000 if current economic trends continue. At this date, three advertisers spend more than $1 billion a year—Proctor and Gamble ($1.6 billion), Phillip Morris Companies ($1.4 billion), and RJR/Nabisco ($1.1 billion)—and every one of the top-10 ad agencies in the United States had between $2 billion and $4 billion in worldwide billings in the mid-1980s.

Figures 21.7 and 21.8 provide a comparison among various mass media buys by *all* advertisers and the top-500 ad agencies. The agencies prefer to run campaigns in and on the four mass media and prefer the broadcast media and magazines over newspapers. This is because the top-500 agencies represent relatively few local advertisers. Newspapers earn nearly $9 of every $10 of their revenue from local rather than national sources.

Advertising is also caught up in the merger mania that bigger is better. Over 30 agency mergers have occurred recently, creating mega-agencies with hugh billing. This may not lead to better services for clients, but profitability should definitely improve. Some clients have revolted and left their large agencies, taking with them key agency creative personnel, who start a new ad shop specifically to serve the client.

THE EFFECTS OF MEDIA ECONOMICS

There is no question that costs and profits are of considerable importance in mass communication. Some critics voice concerns that not all the necessary changes have been for the best.

TOP AGENCIES' MEDIA BILLINGS AS PERCENT OF AD AGE 500

| | Top 25 Agencies | | | $ as % of top 500 U.S. billings | |
| | U.S. billings | | | | |
Media	1985	1984	% changing	1985	1984
Newspapers	$1,659.2	$1,529.0	8.5	48.1	50.9
Business papers	225.6	210.2	7.3	24.8	26.1
Medical journals	131.9	87.1	51.4	32.2	28.0
Magazines	3,257.5	2,836.9	14.8	56.2	58.2
Supplements	132.5	96.2	37.8	59.8	52.3
Farm publications	66.0	64.6	2.1	40.9	41.0
Radio	1,193.9	948.5	25.9	46.4	46.9
Network TV	7,485.6	7,025.2	6.6	79.3	82.1
Spot TV	4,397.5	3,701.5	18.8	57.0	58.7
Cable TV	270.3	181.8	48.7	65.2	68.5
Transit advertising	8.0	12.0	(32.9)	12.4	20.8
Outdoor	443.1	464.9	(4.7)	56.6	62.4
Direct response*	825.9	507.0	62.9	39.6	38.3
Point of sale	57.8	26.7	116.8	31.8	19.8
Other	738.0	511.7	44.2	59.0	53.7
Totals	20,892.7	18,203.2	14.8	58.9	61.3

NOTE: Dollar figures in millions

* Direct response includes Yellow Pages, direct mail, catalogs, direct response TV, direct response radio, direct response newspaper, direct response magazine, telemarketing, and free-standing inserts.

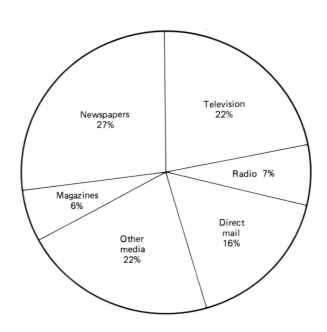

Top 100 Agencies			$ as % of top 500 U.S. billings		Top 500 Agencies		
U.S. billings					U.S. billings		
1985	1984	% changing	1985	1984	1985	1984	% changing
$2,243.7	$2,067.4	8.5	65.0	68.8	$3,451.8	$3,006.7	14.8
336.8	306.7	9.8	37.1	38.2	908.2	804.0	13.0
136.0	87.1	56.1	33.2	28.0	409.5	311.6	31.4
4,321.8	3,700.0	16.8	74.6	75.9	5,794.7	4,877.2	18.8
161.7	128.0	26.3	72.9	69.6	221.7	183.9	20.6
71.2	66.8	6.6	44.1	42.3	161.5	157.8	2.3
1,641.2	1,294.7	26.8	63.8	64.0	2,572.2	2,022.6	27.2
8,720.6	8,001.7	9.0	92.4	93.6	9,439.0	8,551.8	10.4
5,825.0	4,898.7	18.9	75.5	77.7	7,710.2	6,301.2	22.4
344.2	223.8	53.8	83.0	84.4	414.8	265.3	56.4
35.2	39.6	(11.1)	54.4	68.8	64.7	57.5	12.5
584.2	600.7	(2.8)	74.6	80.6	783.3	745.7	5.0
1,197.7	734.5	63.1	57.5	55.5	2,084.3	1,323.3	57.5
81.7	58.7	39.1	45.0	43.6	181.5	134.6	34.8
816.2	617.1	32.3	65.2	64.8	1,251.8	952.5	31.4
26,517.3	22,825.6	16.2	74.8	76.9	35,449.1	29,695.7	19.4

Figure 21.7 The four advertising mass media (newspapers, magazines, television, and radio) account for 62 percent of all advertising dollars; 56 percent of all ad dollars go to national media and 44 percent are spent locally. These market shares have changed relatively little in the past 10 years, which means that dollar volume growth is spread rather evenly across media; but the splits within media depend on the size of the market, the number of competitors, and the target audiences reached.

The three TV networks, because of debt, must now maximize their worth. That economic move may not always be in the best interests of the audience and the programming the public is offered. CBS News went through a series of personnel convulsions in 1986 that revolved around the reduction of staff and the increase in entertainment quotient in newscasts. Ratings, staff morale, and income had slipped. Many staff members were rubbed raw by the firing of lower salaried employees, while sports and news stars' incomes at all three networks exploded: Dan Rather of CBS earns $2.5 million; Tom Brokaw of NBC, $1.5 million; Ed Bradley of CBS, Bryant Gumbel of NBC, and Pat Summerall of CBS, $1 million; Peter Jennings of ABC and Ted Koppell of ABC, $800,000; and Marv Albert, $1.4 million. The networks created haves and have-nots, and some have-nots are being let go. Many are fired after years of good service. More of this may follow to maximize worth.

It is becoming increasingly difficult to buy media because of the large

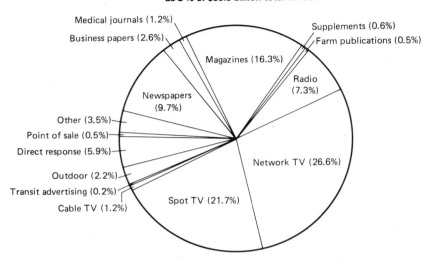

Top 500 agencies' U.S. media billings as a % of $35.5 billion total in 1985

Medical journals (1.2%)
Business papers (2.6%)
Supplements (0.6%)
Farm publications (0.5%)
Magazines (16.3%)
Radio (7.3%)
Newspapers (9.7%)
Other (3.5%)
Point of sale (0.5%)
Direct response (5.9%)
Network TV (26.6%)
Outdoor (2.2%)
Transit advertising (0.2%)
Cable TV (1.2%)
Spot TV (21.7%)

Figure 21.8 This detailed breakdown of billings and percentages of billings offers a number of insights into advertising economics. Network TV remains the number-one choice of the top 25, 100, and 500 agencies. Spot TV is second and, when combined with network and cable buys, accounts for 49.5 percent of all dollars spent by major agencies. Radio increased its revenue significantly and had the highest growth rate of the four major media. Magazines held steady and had growth rates with all three agency categories. Newspapers dipped to less than 1 of every 10 from the top 500 agencies, despite good growth in dollars. Although cable advertising accounts for only 1.2 percent of the total pie, its growth percentage was higher than that of any other category of the major mass media. The four major advertising mass media (newspapers, magazines, television, and radio) account for more than 80 percent of the top 500 agencies' billings. That is considerably higher than for all advertisers, as seen in Figure 21.7, for the mass media ad categories.

sums required to start and operate them. This is of special concern to minority groups. However, the Rupert Murdocks can be naturalized and still buy in. The best arena to break into is the specialized book and magazine computer-assisted publishing business. The "hackers" may have their economic day yet in the mass media.

Groups that are already involved in media operations are, in general, succeeding at a rapid rate. Successful companies seem to get bigger and more powerful. Because of the economics, media have become "big business," with chain and cross-media ownership. In the most lucrative TV markets, over 70 percent of the stations are licensed to group owners.

In the newspaper business, the control of content is narrowing. In a more tumultuous social climate, this could cause problems, some fear, by controlling access to the press or deciding centrally the general policies for local media outlets. The fear is there, but not the proof.

Figure 21.9 News is a profit center at the local level, but there are mixed economic reviews at the national level. Peter Jennings's high salary is offset somewhat by the knowledge that a shift upward by 1 share point in a monthly rating sweep will generate this amount of money before the next rating book is out. (Photo: Copyright © 1986 Capital Cities/ABC, Inc.)

Because of the enormous sums risked in the media marketplace, the media, in general, have become more competitive in trying to capture the largest, most valuable audience available, instead of attempting to meet the special needs of all segments of society. Even public broadcasters now struggle to reach a mass audience. The specialized audience is not being well served by TV networks or newspapers, but magazines, books, recordings, cable TV, and radio do offer selective content. The question remains: Can it continue to be done profitably?

Some media businesspeople seem to be sensitive to only the demands of the marketplace. Some media investors refuse to take anything other than mild positions on sensitive issues. Coverage of radical and reactionary positions is threatening and is generally ignored.

Today, most newspaper circulation comes from papers that are controlled by few multiple ownerships, and the top chains control more than half the newspapers as well as numerous broadcast stations. Fewer than 50 cities in the United States have more than one newspaper. This situation is directly attributable to the economics of mass communication and is less than satisfactory. The suburban press helps but does not reflect the voices of the disfranchised; rather, these papers are designed to serve the suburbanites who have moved out on the disfranchised.

Networks, syndicates, news services, and other corporate giants operate increasingly within media oligopolies. Only a limited number of powerful competitors exist in every media institution. In a free-enterprise and democratic society, competition and countervailing opinions are essential. The voices and the competition are decreasing. This is not the best of all possible trends in a free society—not economically and not politically.

SUMMARY

Media ownership has a significant impact on what Americans read, hear, and watch; and control of content in the news and entertainment media is in an ever-shrinking number of hands. The chains are getting bigger, and there are fewer and fewer independents. Conglomerates must be of special concern because of the power they hold and because they are increasingly involved in many media rather than one medium. The marketplace of ideas is shrinking as independent viewpoints are reduced through sales and mergers. As long as the media are booming and part of the American dream, they will succeed.

Consumers' decisions affect that success. Consumers can be audiences buying media goods and services or advertisers buying target audiences and thus generating ad revenue for four media (TV, radio, magazines, and newspapers). Books, movies, and music must be bought and paid for by the user, based on the laws of supply and demand.

The value, economically, of an ad is based on the medium's ability to reach the advertiser's target market at a reasonable price. Advertising is measured in terms of cost effectiveness, comparing the CPMs of competing media vehicles. The advertiser spends large sums to create ad campaigns that persuade audiences to buy once they are tuned in.

To serve consumers, the media, like other businesses, operate on three levels: producing, distributing, and exhibiting (retailing) their product.

All the media are buying out one another: consolidating newspaper chains, enlarging broadcast groups, developing cross-media interests, and merging into mega-advertising agencies.

Even the TV networks are being bought and sold. Everyone is paying premium prices for content and hoping that content draws the necessary readers, listeners, and viewers to be economically viable. The initial costs, operating expenses, and production, distribution, and exhibition costs are astronomical and continue to rise. As consumers, we eventually pay for the increases.

The bottom line is that all the media industries are healthy. Some are healthier than others. But that health has side effects. Competition is healthy; free enterprise needs it. Consolidation must be carefully watched to ensure that many voices will be heard.

BIBLIOGRAPHY

Aronoff, Craig E., ed. *Business and the Media*. Santa Monica, Calif.: Goodyear, 1979.

Bagdikian, Ben H. *The Media Monopoly*. Boston: Beacon Press, 1983.

Buono, Thomas J. *Investing on Television*. Washington, D.C.: Broadcast Investment Analysts, 1986.

Burns, George A. *Playing the Positioning Game: Aiming at the Core*. Studio City, Calif.: Burns Media Consultants, 1981.

The Cable TV Financial Datebook. Carmel, Calif.: Paul Kagan Associates, 1986.

Compaine, Benjamin J. et al. *Who Owns the Media? Concentration of Ownership in the Mass Communications Industry*. 2d ed. White Plains, N.Y.: Knowledge Industry Publications, 1982.

Economic Forecasts, Election Years, and the Media. Washington, D.C.: Media Institute, 1984.

Hamburg, Morton I. *Making Millions in Telecommunications: How to Invest Your Money, Mind and Expertise in this Exploding Industry*. New York: Rawson Associates, 1985.

Levin, Harvey J. *Fact and Fancy in Television Regulation: An Economic Study of Policy Alternatives*. New York: Russell Sage Foundation, 1980.

Miller, Roger Leroy, and Arline Alchian Hoel. *Media Economics Sourcebook*. St. Paul, Minn.: West, 1982.

Paiva, Bob. *The Program Director's Handbook*. Blue Ridge Summit, Pa.: Tab Books, 1983.

Radio Financial Report. Washington, D.C.: National Association of Broadcasters, 1985.

Webb, G. Kent. *The Economics of Cable Television*. Lexington, Mass.: Lexington Books, 1983.

22

Ethics

The press was everywhere. For every mourner in the congregation, there was at least one reporter, photographer or cameraman. They jammed the entrance to the . . . church. They were in the choir loft. They clomped up and down the stairs with their heavy equipment. Cameramen roamed the aisles. Often they would turn on their bright light, causing mourners to shield their eyes. So many cameramen stood up on the pews to get better footage that the next day the church's janitor had to be dispatched to remove the mud and grime from the benches.[1]

Not a pleasant scene and one that, unfortunately, is not uncommon. This particular description is of the television and press coverage of the memorial service for Christa McAuliffe, a crew member of the space shuttle *Challenger*. It represents one of the more recent and disturbing examples of press coverage of ordinary citizens in a crisis. Howard Ploskin wrote concerning this coverage of McAuliffe's memorial service:

While human suffering and grief are an essential part of the grist of daily journalism, the area between coverage and intrusion is a twilight zone that often strains the boundaries of taste, news judgment and human decency. And television, with its glaring lights, cumbersome equipment and inquiring reporters, tests these boundaries more than any other medium.[2]

---

[1] Howard Ploskin, *TV Guide* (June 28, 1986), p. 35.

[2] *Ibid.*, p. 36.

Figure 22.1 In *Absence of Malice*, Sally Field stars as an overzealous newspaper reporter who, in her eagerness to get a story, ignores basic ethical concerns. The film is a good, albeit dramatized, illustration of media ethics (or absence of them) at work. (Photo: Movie Star News. Courtesy Columbia Pictures.)

In 1981, the movie *Absence of Malice* dramatically focused the public's attention on yet another aspect of media ethics. In this film, the issue was the narrow distinction between accuracy and truth in reporting, as illustrated by the actions of a reporter played by Sally Field. In presenting the facts about how and why a person accused of a crime could not have been involved, she causes the death of one of the people in the story. Accuracy in this case was not necessarily the truth. All the facts of the story did not have to be reported in order for the "truth" of the story to be told.

Another example is reported in *Media Ethics* by Clifford G. Christians, Kim B. Rotzoll, and Mark Fackler. In 1976, the editors of the *Dallas Times Herald* chose to publish a story identifying a man as a Soviet spy, even after the individual had told the editors that such a disclosure would leave him no choice but suicide. The man killed himself on the day the story appeared.

As the authors indicate, the people at the paper made several critical choices: (1) to investigate and write the story; (2) to publish it as originally scheduled; and (3) to ignore a man's suicide threat. Their choices reflect an attitude that should cause concern for any student of mass communication. The first choice involved the public's *need* to know versus the public's *desire* to know. The choice to publish on schedule, despite the man's appeal, is little better than the wartime cry "damn the torpedoes, full speed ahead."

As the authors in *Media Ethics* point out, the story was clearly one that could keep. It was newsworthy, but the criterion of timeliness was not an inherent part of the story. The third choice—to ignore the man's suicide threat—involves not simple media ethics, but basic human ethics. Again, as the authors note, the failure of the editors to alert someone to the problem, to make any attempt to prevent the suicide, is "remarkable." The paper not only violated a journalistic principle, but, more important, a basic moral principle: we should not cause harm, and we should prevent harm when doing so does not subject us to a risk of comparable harm.[3]

On the night of March 4, 1983, in Jacksonville, Alabama, Cecil Andrews held a lighted match to his lighter fluid–dosed clothing. Two television reporters from WHMA-TV stared in disbelief as their camera recorded the scene. The flame moved up Andrews's leg and exploded just as one of the reporters approached him. Andrews rolled on the ground in flames and then ran across the town square. Quickly, a fireman doused the flames. All the while—82 seconds, to be exact—the television cameras were rolling.

Immediately the question was asked, "Why did the reporters not stop Andrews from setting himself on fire?" They said that they were just doing their job. The issue here was how deeply journalists should get involved in stories they are covering. Should journalists intervene in the events they are recording? What happens when the values of good reporting and basic human principles collide? The questions are not easy ones, and the answers are equally difficult.

Ethics in mass communication is a little like the weather: everyone likes to talk about it, but not very much is done about it. Today, however, both the public's and the profession's concern with media ethics and responsibility has gone beyond the talking stage. *Ethics* has become, along with *megatrends, information age,* and *one-minute managers,* one of the important buzzwords of this generation.

While there seems to be renewed interest in media ethics and responsibility, the issue itself is one of this country's most hallowed traditions. Freedom of the press and debate over the rights and responsibilities of the press are deeply ingrained in the historical, political, and cultural fabric of Western civilization. The libertarian philosophy of the press developed out of struggles against the repressive governments of the established monarchies in seventeenth- and eighteenth-century Europe. Under this philosophy, the press should act as a watchdog of government to make sure that government is serving the needs of the people. In order to do this, the press must be completely free. This absolutist position—freedom of the press—was incorporated into the First Amendment of the U.S. Constitution.

---

[3] Clifford G. Christians, Kim B. Rotzoll, and Mark Fackler, *Media Ethics: Cases and Moral Reasoning* (White Plains, N.Y.: Longman, 1983), pp. 114–117.

The libertarian system still prevails in several countries of Western Europe and North America. However, in many of these nations, including the United States, absolute freedom of speech and of the press has been tempered by the realities of mass society, including political conflict, global war, economic recession, and population expansion. In essence, the media proclaim the twin themes of Jeffersonian freedom of the press and twentieth-century social responsibility—the press must be free *and* responsible. Being free allows it to be responsible, and being responsible allows it to remain free.

SOCIAL RESPONSIBILITY AND THE MEDIA

It is precisely the issue of responsibility around which ethics in contemporary society and, for our analysis, media ethics revolve. In a media environment where freedom is considered paramount, where the First Amendment is carried like an armored shield, words such as *accountability* and *responsibility* are often not understood or even heard. Increasingly, however, they are watchwords for today's media. The regulation of media, especially the broadcast media, has decreased in recent years, and the need for ethical and moral responsibility in media has become especially important.

In 1984, at radio station KTTL-FM in Dodge City, Kansas, broadcasts by two self-styled preachers created a wave of controversy and criticism. With such remarks as "if the Jews even fool around with us . . . every rabbi in Los Angeles will die within 24 hours" and "blacks and browns are the enemy," the issues of First Amendment rights and broadcast regulation were brought into sharp relief. On the one side was Charles Ferris, a former FCC chairman, who stated: "You can't take the license away because of what they said. Some things are very distasteful or offensive but you have to be patient with the remedy. It's the price you pay to protect First Amendment rights."[4] On the other side were those who claimed that the preachers' statements were irresponsible calls for violence—the equivalent of a person shouting "Fire!" in a crowded theater—and were therefore unprotected by the First Amendment. On the surface, the issue involved the legal apparatus concerning a challenge to a radio license. But the deeper issue involved the sense of social responsibility (or lack of it) on the part of the owners of KTTL. The regulatory apparatus of the FCC is of little concern here. Whether a radio station is operating in the "public interest, convenience or necessity" is at the heart of the crisis.

Most ethical situations in the media have little to do with regulation, but have everything to do with responsibility, judgment, and, in many cases, common sense. The issues are not always clear. The conflict experi-

---

[4] Quoted in Merrill Brown, "KTTL's License to Malign," *Channels* 4 (March/April 1984): 15–16.

enced by a reporter between getting involved and just observing and reporting is one of the most troublesome. In referring to the 1983 Jacksonville, Alabama, story, one journalist said, "If a guy wanted to set himself
on fire and I tried to talk him out of it, I'd cover it. But I wouldn't hand him
the match."[5]

Fred Friendly, former president of CBS News, states emphatically,
"You don't show your tripod. You don't become part of the story. . . . By
being a good Samaritan we get in the way of our lenses."[6] But Tom Wicker,
political columnist for the *New York Times* who acted as a mediator for
prisoners in the 1971 Attica prison uprising, states, "I have always maintained that the journalist owes his duty to humanity. When there's a conflict between being a journalist and a human being, I'll always hope I'll be a
human being: It's a grave error for reporters to set themselves aside from
humanity."[7]

Objectivity and noninvolvement are cornerstones of the journalism
profession. There are, however, no hard rules to govern individual conduct in specific situations. There is only a sense of responsibility.

ETHICS AND TECHNOLOGY

As new technologies explode into reality, old rules concerning such fundamental issues as censorship, privacy, the right to know, and the right to a
fair trial are being questioned and are often challenged successfully. Interactive cable television, as developed by Warner-Amex in Columbus,
Ohio—the system known as Qube—revealed tremendous potential for
viewer feedback and participation in everything from choosing a certain
ending to a dramatic program to expressing opinions and even "voting" on
major issues affecting the community. The Qube technology cuts two
ways, however, and its potential for invading the privacy of homes
equipped with it is real and dangerous. The expansion of this wired model
to satellite distribution of content raises even more questions. Visions of
George Orwell's *1984* begin dancing in the heads of responsible media
professionals and educators.

Technology itself has no inherent value. The values, the ethical decisions, lie not in the machinery but in the choices made by the individuals
who use the machinery. In medicine, technology that allows victims of
kidney failure to live is, in itself, neither good nor evil. But the ethical
questions regarding who should receive such treatment and who should
pay for it involve choices and value decisions. Similarly, lightweight and
unobtrusive cameras are reshaping traditional attitudes toward televising

---

[5] Howard Ploskin, *TV Guide* (June 28, 1986), p. 36.

[6] *Ibid.*

[7] *Ibid.*, p. 37.

trials in courtrooms, not to mention proceedings in the United States Congress. The "gavel-to-gavel" TV coverage of a New Bedford, Massachusetts, trial of six men on gang-raping charges aroused great controversy. Controversial, too, is the televising of the execution of criminals. Ted Koppel, the ABC journalist, favors televising executions because, in his opinion, TV viewers have witnessed plenty of evil and can stomach a little more. This kind of thinking misses the point; it confuses and obscures the concept of social responsibility, of ethics, of a basic morality in such a decision.

In all these illustrations, the technical ability to *achieve* communication conflicts with both the social responsibility of and the legal right of the communicator to *publish* or *air* the content. These three elements—technology, regulation, and social responsibility—are at the heart of many ethical issues in mass media. As technology becomes more and more "user friendly" and regulations become more difficult to enforce and interpret (three of every four libel cases in which the jury found in favor of the defendant and "against" the press have, in recent years, been overturned on appeal), the critical issue in maintaining a basic sense of social responsibility in mass media becomes the professional and personal responsibility of the men and women who work in the system, from corporate-board chairpersons to editors to reporters and camera operators.

CODES OF CONDUCT

One way of looking at this issue in greater detail is to differentiate among institutional ethics, professional ethics, and personal ethics; that is, among formal codes of professional conduct and vaguely developed and often vaguely articulated institutional and personal value systems and morality.

Institutional Ethics

Before examining several of the formal codes more carefully, we should examine the gray area that lies between formal codes of conduct and individual morality. This is the informal ethical system that operates in most media institutions and is known as the "raised eyebrow" or "consensus of upper management." This *institutional* ethical system is most often associated with gatekeepers and involves both personal and professional values. For example, many major-city newspapers hire ombudsmen to investigate and recommend action on ethical issues involving news stories and reporting procedures. These individuals do not operate from a fixed code of conduct, but apply personal, professional, and institutional "codes" to specific situations. Charles Seib, a former *Washington Post* ombudsman, has urged that in training future journalists, more attention be given to basic matters such as personal integrity and the making of ethical judgments. The ombudsman often acts as the bridge among personal, professional, and institutional ethics and attempts to apply all three standards to specific issues.

The three major TV networks have departments of broadcast standards, whose gatekeeping function we discussed in Chapter 17. In the past, these standards were unwritten, with most tenets a matter of "common understanding." However, because of the increased interest in and awareness of programming standards, especially on television, these institutional standards are increasingly being formalized. CBS-TV recently published and made public its "Program Standards," excerpts of which follow.

General Standards
A CBS television program is a guest in the home. It is expected to entertain and enlighten but not to offend or advocate. CBS entertainment programs are intended to conform to generally accepted boundaries of public taste and decorum. . . .

Language
The language in a broadcast must be appropriate to a public medium and generally considered to be acceptable by a mass audience. Coarse or potentially offensive language is generally avoided. . . . Blasphemy and obscenity are not acceptable for broadcast.

Nudity and Sexuality
If consonant with prevailing societal standards, used for legitimate dramatic or historical purposes and not perceived as exploiting the body for prurient interests, certain degrees of undress are acceptable. The depiction of sexual intercourse is unacceptable for broadcast. . . .

Characterizations
Creative imperatives of the script will dictate the behavior and mannerisms of all characters. Character portrayals must be carefully crafted and sensitive to current ethnic, religious, sexual and other prominent social concerns and unacceptable stereotypes. Care is also to be exercised when depicting characters subject to physical or mental disabilities to ensure that such persons are not demeaned.

Accuracy and Misapprehension
. . . Programs or scenes containing elements whose technical accuracy is important to maintaining public confidence in the integrity of a profession or institution must strive to be accurate in all material regards. Consultation with qualified advisers is encouraged.

Presentations which could convey the misapprehension that a dramatized or prerecorded event is occurring "live" or in the form of spontaneous news coverage of a contemporary event are not permitted. Use of words such as "bulletin" or devices such as a "horizontal crawl" are unacceptable and reserved solely for the use of CBS News. . . .

Violence
As a component of human experience, the dramatic depiction of violence is permitted. Here, violence is defined as "the use of physical force against persons, or the articulated, explicit threat of physical force to compel particular behavior on the part of a person." Accidents and incidents of comic violence are not included in this definition. Any depiction of vio-

lence must be relevant to plot and/or character development. It should not be gratuitous, excessive or glamorized. Violence should not be used exploitatively to entice or shock an audience. . . . The use or portrayals of animals shall conform to accepted standards of humane treatment.

Substance Abuse

Character portrayals and scenes depicting the consumption of alcohol, drugs, cigarettes and similar substances must be thoughtfully considered, essential to plot and role development and not glamorized. When the line is crossed between normal, responsible consumption of a particular substance and abuse, the distinction must be clear and the adverse consequences of abuse specifically noted and explored.

Children and Television

Protagonists, ''heroes,'' should exemplify the most positive elements of social and personal codes of conduct such as honesty, fairness, compassion and respect for authority. Attitudinally, such characters should show respect for important societal institutions, concern for distinguishing right from wrong and commitments to such ideals as justice, ethics and humanity. Characters which represent unacceptable social and personal conduct need not be avoided but must clearly be portrayed as undesirable.

Violence should not be portrayed as a socially acceptable means of conflict resolution. It should not be glorified, made to seem fascinating, amusing or palatable. While villains may exhibit some violent behavior, this action should not be imitatable, horrific or extended in its presentation. Acts which carry the potential for violence should be clearly set in the realm of fantasy. Human beings should not be severely harmed or killed. . . . Characters should not be placed in circumstances that provoke excessive or prolonged anxiety, or suggest gratuitous psychological pain. Characters should not be placed in hopeless situations and those in peril should be presented with ways to overcome their predicaments. . . . Program content and commercial messages must be clearly distinct.

Unsubstantiated elements may be included only if they do not distort the material factual elements of the historical record. Omissions of historical information which materially distort the perception of historical events are not acceptable.

Editing or condensation in the portrayal of historical events should maintain accuracy or value of those events. Distortions of time, changes in the sequence of events or composite events which materially alter the historical record are to be avoided.

All characters, including composite characters, based on real persons must accurately reflect those persons in reality and their actual roles and behavior in any significant events in which they are portrayed. . . . Composite or fictional characters used in roles essential to development of the main plot(s) must be carefully reviewed to ensure that their fictional or representative nature does not undermine in any material way the overall accuracy of the historical events portrayed.

Care should be exercised in the employment of production techniques, such as casting, character and dialogue interpretation which have the potential to alter or distort the historical record. . . .

Dramas Based on Fact

. . . Dramas based on fact adapted for television from another published source, and so denominated, must faithfully represent, in all material regards, the plot and characterizes of the original work. . . . The original television drama based on fact, sometimes referred to as the docudrama, is a particularly challenging program form. Its material factual components should be accurate and cannot be changed merely to enhance dramatic value. Fictionalized elements consistent with the events being presented may amplify or enhance the story, so long as they do not materially alter or distort history. Any presentation of a significant controversy should be done in a fair and balanced way. . . .

Theatrical Films

Standards for programs created for television are applicable to films originally created for theatrical release and subsequently broadcast on the CBS Television Network. . . .

Game Shows

CBS has adopted and continuously refines rules and procedures to ensure that game shows are conducted honestly, fairly and as they appear to the public. These procedures guard against contestant access to information which could jeopardize the firmness and integrity of the game. . . . Disruptions that necessitate editing of the broadcast must be disclosed. All programs must conform to Sections 317, 507 and 508 of the Communications Act of 1934.

Promotional Materials

All promotional material must accurately and tastefully reflect the content of the program to which it refers. . . . On-air promotion will be scheduled to ensure that it is appropriate to the program in which it is placed.[8]

The reason CBS chose to publish its standards arose out of public controversy surrounding the CBS docudramas *The Atlanta Child Murders* and *Robert Kennedy and His Times.* The network discovered that the absence of written standards led some people to believe that they had no standards. According to Donald Wear, Vice President for Policy at CBS/Broadcast Group:

Now, when we air anything that is daring, provocative or controversial the public will know, as it should have before, that the programs have been carefully scrutinized according to standards for mass audience entertainment that, until now, have been just spoken and understood.

The written standards demonstrate in a tangible way that we are not cavalier about our public responsibilities.[9]

Both NBC and ABC program standards are in writing. Network standards are, therefore, not run on the whim or fancy of the person in charge. Rather, the ethical system is an agreed-on set of values that combines personal, professional, and institutional values. Within the past decade, about 66 percent of media institutions have either revised or written policy

---

[8] Diane Mermigas, *Electronic Media* (May 2, 1985), p. 3.

[9] *Ibid.*, p. 2.

guidelines or codes of conduct for their staffs. Almost 60 percent of the management personnel of news organizations who responded to a recent survey of media ethics said that their organizations have formal written policies.

Not all institutional ethics evolve from or into written form. In 1984, for example, the *New York Post* banned from its pages all advertising of pornographic films, burlesque houses, and topless bars. This decision was made by a "consensus at an upper management level" at the paper. This "consensus," in effect, is an institutional ethical system at work. The following article, from the *Ithaca* (New York) *Journal*, illustrates yet another attempt to develop and implement institutional ethics. Having no code or doctrine to regulate fairness comparable with the one that currently exists in broadcasting, newspapers have recently developed a wide variety of systems and procedures related to issues of ethics and social responsibility. In the article, the *Journal* states that its goal is primarily "to reinforce the perception that we are concerned about accuracy and fairness."

> Accuracy and fairness are two cornerstones of any successful newspaper.
>
> A newspaper can be dynamic and profitable, but if it fails to meet high standards of accuracy and fairness consistently, then it is failing its mission.
>
> Accuracy is more than spelling someone's name correctly. It's a reporter taking the time to double check the spelling of Cascadilla; it's an editor taking the time to make sure the mayor is 41 years old; it's the publisher taking the time to reinforce the notion that we are best when we are accurate.
>
> Fairness is more than giving both sides in a debate the chance to present a point of view: It's a reporter making sure that the presentation of all sides is not skewed by personal opinions; it's an editor making sure that diverse opinions are offered to the readers and that all angles have been given adequate consideration; it's a publisher making sure that all aspects of a community are given consideration and that biases toward businesses and minorities are shelved.
>
> With this in mind, the *Journal* is introducing a means of measuring our accuracy and fairness as we report the news.
>
> Lacking a better name, I'll call it an "accuracy check."
>
> I will be sending these one-page questionnaires to residents of the Eastern Finger Lakes whose names appear in the *Journal*.
>
> A coach in Watkins Glen might receive one after he is quoted in a basketball story; a Dryden funeral director might get one in connection with a funeral he handled; the subject of a feature article might find one in the mail.
>
> The reason for this "accuracy check" is twofold:
>
> —To reinforce the perception that we are concerned about accuracy and fairness.
>
> —To give reporters and editors an idea of what their readers think of the job being done every day on the second floor at 123 W. State Street.[10]

---

[10] Joe Junod, *Ithaca Journal*, July 14, 1983, p. 5.

Professional Ethics

In distinct contrast to the somewhat gray area of institutional ethics is the system of codes and, in some cases, regulations that forms the environment of *professional* ethics. Most of these codes relate to news, for the press has traditionally been the least controlled of any mass communication institution in the United States. Two of the most respected codes are those of the Society of Professional Journalists, Sigma Delta Chi (SPJ/SDC); and the Radio-Television News Directors Association (RTNDA). The SPJ/SDC code essentially preaches social responsibility. The code covers six areas:

1. *Responsibility* emphasizes both the public's right to know and the public-trust mission of mass media.

2. *Freedom of the press* stresses the right and responsibility of the media to question and challenge society's institutions, particularly government.

3. *Ethics* addresses personal "life-style" issues, such as moonlighting, as well as areas of news judgment, such as protecting the confidentiality of news sources.

4. The section on *accuracy* and *objectivity* looks at the concept of truth and attempts to draw the line between news and opinion.

5. *Fair play* discusses in a more technical way such issues as invasion of privacy, correcting errors, and the right to reply.

6. The *pledge* section simply indicates that compliance with the code is voluntary, signified by a pledge charging journalists to "ensure and prevent violations of these standards."

The RTNDA code addresses many of the same issues but applies them specifically to broadcast news. The RTNDA "Code of Broadcast News Ethics" contains 10 articles and covers such areas as right to privacy, confidentiality of sources, fair trial, and conflict of interest. Other codes, such as "A Statement of Principles" of the American Society of Newspaper Editors and the "Code of Professional Standards" of the Public Relations Society of America, emphasize many of the same basic issues.

One form of media content that has developed a relatively elaborate and systematic code of conduct is advertising. Self-regulation in advertising has existed for most of this century. In 1924, the American Association of Advertising Agencies asked its members to cooperate with its "Creative Code," which set forth some ground rules for ethical behavior (Figure 22.2). The code was a detailed instrument that articulated a philosophy of advertising and commented on specific practices. It was divided into areas dealing with a particular community, product, or medium. In 1971, this division changed, and with the creation of the National Advertising Review Board (NARB), the chief advertising organizations formed the most comprehensive self-regulation system ever established in advertising.

The NARB is concerned primarily with deceptive advertising and is one branch of the National Advertising Review Council. The National Advertising Division of the Better Business Bureaus employs a full-time professional staff that works to resolve advertising-practice complaints in a

CREATIVE CODE

American Association of Advertising Agencies

The members of the American Association of Advertising Agencies recognize:

1. That advertising bears a dual responsibility in the American economic system and way of life.

To the public it is a primary way of knowing about the goods and services which are the products of American free enterprise, goods and services which can be freely chosen to suit the desires and needs of the individual. The public is entitled to expect that advertising will be reliable in content and honest in presentation.

To the advertiser it is a primary way of persuading people to buy his goods or services, within the framework of a highly competitive economic system. He is entitled to regard advertising as a dynamic means of building his business and his profits.

2. That advertising enjoys a particularly intimate relationship to the American family. It enters the home as an integral part of television and radio programs, to speak to the individual and often to the entire family. It shares the pages of favorite newspapers and magazines. It presents itself to travelers and to readers of the daily mails. In all these forms, it bears a special responsibility to respect the tastes and self-interest of the public.

3. That advertising is directed to sizable groups or to the public at large, which is made up of many interests and many tastes. As is the case with all public enterprises, ranging from sports to education and even to religion, it is almost impossible to speak without finding someone in disagreement. Nonetheless, advertising people recognize their obligation to operate within the traditional American limitations: to serve the interests of the majority and to respect the rights of the minority.

Therefore we, the members of the American Association of Advertising Agencies, in addition to supporting and obeying the laws and legal regulations pertaining to advertising, undertake to extend and broaden the application of high ethical standards. Specifically, we will not knowingly produce advertising which contains:

a. False or misleading statements or exaggerations, visual or verbal.

b. Testimonials which do not reflect the real choice of a competent witness.

c. Price claims which are misleading.

d. Comparisons which unfairly disparage a competitive product or service.

e. Claims insufficiently supported, or which distort the true meaning or practicable application of statements made by professional or scientific authority.

f. Statements, suggestions or pictures offensive to public decency.

We recognize that there are areas which are subject to honestly different interpretations and judgment. Taste is subjective and may even vary from time to time as well as from individual to individual. Frequency of seeing or hearing advertising messages will necessarily vary greatly from person to person.

However, we agree not to recommend to an advertiser and to discourage the use of advertising which is in poor or questionable taste or which is deliberately irritating through content, presentation or excessive repetition.

Clear and willful violations of this Code shall be referred to the Board of Directors of the American Association of Advertising Agencies for appropriate action, including possible annulment of membership as provided in Article IV, Section 5, of the Constitution and By-Laws.

Conscientious adherence to the letter and the spirit of this Code will strengthen advertising and the free enterprise system of which it is part.   *Adopted April 26, 1962*

Endorsed by

Advertising Association of the West, Advertising Federation of America, Agricultural Publishers Association, Associated Business Publications, Association of Industrial Advertisers, Association of National Advertisers, Magazine Publishers Association, National Business Publications, Newspaper Advertising Executives Association, Radio Code Review Board (National Association of Broadcasters), Station Representatives Association, TV Code Review Board (NAB)

Figure 22.2 Codes, such as the "Creative Code" of the American Association of Advertising Agencies, represent the collective moral and ethical sensibilities of the members of a profession. (Courtesy the American Association of Advertising Agencies.)

private and personal way. If this procedure does not work, then the "case" is given to the NARB, which reviews the information and then communicates with the advertiser. If the advertiser still does not correct the deceptive material, the issue is referred to an appropriate government agency, such as the Federal Trade Commission, the Securities and Exchange Commission, or the United States Postal Service.

Easily the most comprehensive and systematic self-regulatory system is that used by the motion-picture industry. Developed out of a long-established "code," the current system is known primarily by the rating classifications G, PG, PG-13, R, and X, which are assigned to American motion pictures. The ratings are made by the Classification and Rating Administration (CARA), under the administration of the Motion Picture Association of America (MPAA), in accordance with a vaguely developed set of criteria that considers "among others as deemed appropriate the treatment of theme, language, violence, nudity and sex." In Chapter 17, we discussed MPAA in terms of its role as gatekeeper. It is also important, however, to understand CARA as the formal embodiment of certain moral values and ethical principles. These principles and values are not set in stone, however.

Perhaps the best example of the principles and values by which the system works is found in the appeals process, during which a particular CARA rating is defended or attacked. Here, the personal value systems of the seven people who sit on the CARA board are more clearly illuminated. What ultimately emanates from such a process is the absence of rules. As one CARA board member stated: "Rules make decision easy but they rob it of wisdom." The member went on to say, in defending a PG rating for a movie using an infamous four-letter word, "I wanted us not to have an easy time, but to be wise. I wanted our rating system to be wise, not rigid. . . . I urged upon you only *one* commanding rule: the rule of reason."[11] The point here is that the bedrock of any professional-ethics system, be it a code or council, is a sense of individual *and* collective wisdom and reason.

The authority of the NARB, CARA, and other codes to "regulate" conduct and content is almost negligible. With virtually every professional code, council, or statement of principles, the authority is almost exclusively moral. Codes cannot stop content, impose fines, boycott advertisers, or remove people from their jobs. What codes do is bring the judgment of one's professional peers to bear on a particular case or issue. Ultimately, the codes represent the collective moral and ethical sensibilities of members of a profession—be it journalism, advertising, or entertainment. The success of a code depends on individual and institutional *acceptance* of the moral and ethical principles on which the code is based and *compliance* with the specific credos formulated in the code. This agreement in principle makes self-regulation possible. The demise of "The Television Code" and

---

[11] Personal interview with G. E. Landen, former CARA board member, September 20, 1984.

"The Radio Code" of the National Association of Broadcasters occurred because fewer than one-third of broadcast stations subscribed to the code. The code was unenforceable, yes; but that is true of almost every media code. It was the absence of professional consensus, coupled with increasing deregulation of broadcasters, that made these codes inappropriate and meaningless. The following comment from *Time* illustrates the problem.

> If the news is covered as badly as much of the public thinks it is, why doesn't the press clean its own house? Where is its professional responsibility? The difficulty begins with that word professional. Medicine and law, being professions, can expel or censure wrongdoers, even though fraternal coziness makes such action rare. Journalism has no admission standards. A plumber or a hairdresser must pass a test to get a license, but no journalist does, on the grounds that licensing would be abhorrent to the idea of a free and robust press. . . .
>
> The inability of the press to get together to reform itself is more than arrogance and orneriness. The need for a diverse press makes for strange and incompatible bedfellows. The sleazy *Hustler* magazine may have a legal right to exist, but few in the press consider its publisher a colleague. Yet most members of the press feel that editorial independence, which tolerates the worst of journalism, is essential to producing the best.[12]

Personal Ethics

Ultimately, then, institutional ethics and professional ethics are grounded in personal ethics. This becomes the point at which all ethical systems finally arrive, and media ethical systems are no exception. The following column by the *Chicago Tribune* columnist Bob Greene graphically and dramatically illustrates this position.

> I may have blown this one. I don't think so, but I have enough doubts that I'm not sure. I think I'd like your opinion on it.
>
> In Chicago, there is a very prominent businessman who has gained great wealth largely on the strength of patronage by Jewish customers. The man is not Jewish.
>
> I received a copy of a personal letter the man wrote. He and his wife were engaged in a dispute with a dry-cleaning store; the couple charged that the store had ruined one of the woman's garments and had refused to pay for it. The owner of the dry-cleaning store was Jewish. In the letter, the gentile businessman—who depends on Jews for much of his income—called the dry-cleaning store owner a "kike."
>
> I telephoned the dry-cleaning store. The manager told me that he was not at fault. He said he had tried to reach a settlement with the businessman, and then the letter had arrived. So I called the businessman.
>
> "That's right, I called the man a kike," he told me. "He is a kike. There's a difference between a Jew and a kike."

---

[12] Robert McCloskey, "Journalism under Fire," *Time*, December 12, 1983, pp. 76–93.

When I asked him what the difference was, he said: "The low-class Jew is a kike. The immoral Jew is a kike. Everyone knows that.

"The man who runs that dry-cleaning store proved himself to be a kike by the way he did business with us, and he proved himself to be even more of a kike by showing that letter to you."

The man readily admitted to me that he did a high percentage of his business with Jewish customers. But he told me he was confident those customers would not resent his attitude.

"They won't be offended. Even a Jew knows that a low-class Jew is a kike. I have always referred to the immoral, low-class Jew as a kike."

He said to me:

"You're not Jewish, are you?"

I told him that indeed I was.

"Well, are you offended?" he said.

I said that "kike" was probably the ugliest name you could call a Jew; I couldn't imagine anyone, including any of his Jewish customers, who wouldn't be offended.

He seemed surprised. "Anyone who says I am anti-Semitic is an absolute liar," he said. "I do 90% of my business with Jews, and 90% of my friends are Jews." He said that he had always used the term "kike" and that he thought it was a perfectly acceptable way to refer to a "bad Jew."

I asked him what he called "bad Protestants."

"I never knew there was a name you called bad Protestants," he said.

That ended our conversation. He called back a little later. "I feel like Patton, at the end of that movie," he said. "Remember, he had slapped the soldier? And at the end of the movie he said, 'I wish I had kissed him instead of slapped him.' "

So I had a strong column, which I wrote. I intended to run it in my home paper, the *Chicago Tribune*. The peg was perfect: Here was a man who made his living off Jews, who readily admitted he used the word "kike." I moved the column, naming the man, and the page proofs came up. There it was, ready to be seen by all the people who read the *Tribune* every day.

And I killed it.

I requested that my editors yank it out of the paper. My column did not appear the next day.

My reason was this:

The man is a bigot. He has a foul mouth, an ugly temper and a nasty streak of prejudice.

However, the more I thought about it, the more I was unsure whether his bigotry ought to be exposed to the more than a million people who read the *Tribune*. If some guy on the street says something that ugly, you don't print it, because it's not news. If Chicago Mayor Jane Byrne says it (not that she would), you print it, because she's a public figure.

This guy fell somewhere in between. I knew what the reaction would be if the column appeared. His business would be damaged, and damaged badly. The whole public image of his company would change. For the rest of his life, he would be known not as a successful businessman, but as a Jew-hater. (I know he said he didn't hate Jews, but when you start writing letters calling people ''kikes'' and then try to defend it, you are pretty well branded.)

So why didn't I just run the column? Five years ago I might have just thrown it in there and watched the reaction. But now . . . the man seemed stupid and naive, but I wasn't sure that the punishment of the mass-distributed column was worth the crime of his ignorant remarks. There are a lot of bigots out there; by picking him out, I wasn't sure what I was accomplishing. Proving that such bigotry exists? I think we all know that.

I have given a lot of thought in recent months to the press as bully. We have grown so powerful; on the surface the column would have appeared to be exposing a wrong, but the *Chicago Tribune* is so much bigger than this one ugly-spirited businessman . . . should the full weight of the *Tribune* really be brought down on him because of his muddled attitude?

Many people I respected greatly, including a number of my editors, urged me to run the column. In a way, there was unintentional humor to the situation: Here was a columnist trying to kill a controversial column he had written, and his bosses trying to persuade him to go ahead and run it. The exact opposite of the way things are alleged to be. (As a matter of fact, a Jewish man who works in the *Tribune's* composing room saw the column in proofs and then saw the paper come out without the column. He called me to ask me why my bosses had killed the column, and seemed skeptical when I told him that they hadn't; I had.)

Anyway . . . I decided that the column would not run. But a week later, I'm still thinking about it. I honestly don't know if I did the correct thing or not—and that's the purpose of today's column. You and I have this regular interchange, through the paper. I'd be grateful to hear your opinion.[13]

In his article, Greene points out forcefully and clearly that his ethical system had made the difference. His personal sense of social responsibility had killed the story.

A more recent example occurred in relation to the popular *Blondie* comic strip. Creator Dean Young publicly, in print, apologized to a reader who had taken offense at Young's portrayal of adopted children. The letter from Young (Figure 22.3) appeared in the January 10, 1986, edition of the *Des Moines Register*. Media communicators, such as Bob Greene and Dean Young, face such decisions daily.

Each situation is unique, and yet in practical terms, the ethical issues faced by individual media communicators seem to fall into six major categories: (1) conflict of interest; (2) truth and accuracy; (3) sources of information; (4) payola, gifts, and business pressure; (5) privacy; and (6) social justice and responsibility.

Conflict of Interest. Conflict of interest is, simply put, an issue of divided loyalty. The conflict usually occurs as a result of multiple employment or

---

[13] Bob Greene, *Chicago Tribune*, May 17, 1982, p. 47.

DEAN YOUNG
235 EAST 45TH STREET
NEW YORK, N.Y. 10017

December 18, 1985

Ms. Colleen Last
538 Fifth Avenue South
Clinton, Iowa

Dear Ms. Last:

I was most distressed by your comments concerning my "BLONDIE" daily comic strip of October 28th regarding adopted children. I was even more distressed (devasted!) by the hundreds of letters I have received from around the world, verifying your accurate and astute opionion. You, of course, were quite correct in your assertions as to my insensitivity and ignorance on that particular Friday in October.

Each day I try to transcend the imaginary world of "BLONDIE" and bring only wholesome fun and laughter into an all-too-real world already over-burdened with pain, tragedy, and despair. In the fifty-five year history of the strip, this has always been our credo. Our main focus is to win smiles, not enemies!

But in this instance a mistake (on my part) was made. And I accept total responsibility for it and am quite deserving of the wrath perpetrated by it.

I assure you that the mistake was made without malice and in blind innocence, a poor excuse, admittedly -- but one which I will beg your forgiveness for. Please know that the realization of what I have done, hurts me...as much as anyone.

Hoping that you will accept my apologies and assurances that it will not happen again and that your continued readership will justify the truth in what I have said, I remain,

      With heartfelt apologies,

      DEAN YOUNG

DY:vm

CC Des Moines Register

Figure 22.3 Demonstrating that creators of comic strips are indeed sensitive to issues of media ethics, Dean Young wrote this public letter apologizing for his comic-strip treatment of and comment on adopted children.

personal friendships. If a broadcast journalist works part time for a local bank, and the bank is the subject of an investigation, conflict occurs. Can the journalist perform the task of properly investigating and reporting the story and still be employed by the bank? Even if the bank applies no pressure to "close down" the story, the reporter still faces a personal ethical dilemma. To whom does he or she owe loyalty? Even more serious is the misuse of information based on multiple employment.

In covering business news, the *Wall Street Journal* frequently publishes stories about the misuse of inside information in stock purchases. In the early 1980s, the paper revealed that it had found such a case in its own news room. It disclosed that one of its reporters had acknowledged leaking to investors upcoming items from the influential "Heard on the Street" column, which features stock tips. The reporter, one of the column's two principal writers, admitted the leaks to the Securities and Exchange Commission, which had been investigating evidence that a group of traders was earning illicit profits after having received the information in advance. The reporter subsequently was fired. The *Wall Street Journal* noted that in a policy designed to prevent such cases, new employees are expected to sign a three-and-one-half page conflict-of-interest statement.

Many journalists take the issue of conflict of interest so seriously that they will not broadcast or act as a spokesperson for a commercial product. Frank McGee, when he anchored NBC's "Today Show," was adamant in his refusal even to introduce commercials on the air. He felt that his role as a journalist placed him in a position of public trust and acceptance, and he would be trading on that reputation if he were to sell a product.

Personal friendships obviously can interfere with a journalist's role. The concept of an adversarial role for a free press is grounded in the absence of conflict of interest. It would have been difficult for Roger Mudd of NBC to have interviewed presidential candidates Edward Kennedy (1980) and Gary Hart (1984) in a tough, inquiring manner had he been a close personal friend of either man. Mudd, or any reporter, does not have to dislike an interviewee in order to be an effective adversary. Adversary does not imply enemy. Nevertheless, as adversaries, Mudd and other reporters represent the public. Their role is to fairly question a person on behalf of the public. This is the public-trust role by which all journalists should live.

Truth and Accuracy. *Truth* and *accuracy* are perhaps the two hottest words in a reporter's lexicon. Almost all ethical codes begin with the need of reporters to tell the facts of a story under all conditions. This may seem like a simple task; but facts and truth in today's society are often not without major ambiguities. Truth is not simply collecting all the facts or not lying. Outright deceit rarely occurs in newswriting; however, deception is always a temptation, especially in the news-gathering process. A typical situation involves reporters posing as employees of a particular organization or as consumers in order to get a story. Misrepresentation in this sense is usually viewed as harmless and, in many cases, necessary. Too often, however, misrepresentation is used as an easy way to obtain a story rather than take the more difficult path of informed consent.

Perhaps the most ambiguous aspect of the truth issue is equating truth with facts. A small daily newspaper, the *Ithaca* (New York) *Journal,* found itself in an ethical dilemma in reporting the death of a local man in a car accident. Commenting on the death, which was caused in part by the young man's state of insobriety, the *Journal* also reported that this young man had been involved in a DWI (driving while intoxicated) accident two years before and had caused the death of his passenger. Many people in the community were angry about the reporting; they felt that the newspaper was being insensitive to the man's family by "digging up" past history that, in their opinion, was not relevant to the story. The *Journal* defended its story by stating that the young man's previous accident was part of a pattern of behavior that shed light on his death. Here is clearly a case in which reporting the facts and telling the truth are not necessarily the same thing. There are no easy answers to the ethical dilemmas posed by questions of truth and accuracy. What is important is that reporters, editors, and publishers be aware of the need to make difficult decisions and moral judgments. Objectivity is not a shield to hide behind and does not excuse the journalist from exercising his or her value system.

Sources of Information. Unnamed sources, the disclosure of sources, or both, have in recent years been the subjects of intense and often sensationalized controversy. The dilemma is a classic one. When personal ethics conflict with the law, is it wrong to follow one's ethics? The distinction lies between what is legally permitted and what is ethically correct. In refusing to disclose a source, a reporter is clearly breaking the law. Nevertheless, by naming the source after having given one's word not to do so, a reporter is being unethical. As John Merrill and S. Jack Odell argue in their book *Philosophy and Journalism,* for the most part, the law of the land reflects the ethical code of that land. But it does not have to, and sometimes it does not.

As Merrill and Odell indicate, this fact can easily be grasped if one considers what so often happens after a revolution and the seizing of political power by those outside the Establishment. Either the revolutionaries change the existing laws, altering some and dropping others, in order to guarantee what they conceive to be the basic ethical rights of each person, or the laws are changed to fit the political objectives of those who seized power at the expense of certain individuals or groups. The former alternative is evidenced by the American and French revolutions; the latter alternative, by the Nazis in Germany.

Injustices can be rectified only as long as people are willing to break existing laws for the sake of ethical principles. The survival of the community depends on it. The upshot of these considerations is that a reporter's refusal to divulge sources, even when it means incarceration, can, in general, be justified and even applauded.[14]

Therefore, no set of exact rules can be formulated that will always tell the reporter what to do. One can only hope to educate and sensitize reporters to ethical issues and trust in their ability and willingness to address these issues intelligently, forcefully, and ethically.

Payola, Gifts, and Business Pressure. In distinct contrast to the much publicized and controversial issue of disclosure is the "back-of-the-house" problem of accepting gifts. As Tony Mauro of Gannett News Service has said:

"The problem is not new. Walk into any newsroom, find an employee with graying hair, buy him a couple of drinks and you will hear stories about the old days when reporters who boosted their friends were rewarded with a bottle of J&B . . . at Christmas. One crusty editor I know lives by this rule: "Never accept a gift you can't consume in 24 hours."[15]

Unfortunately, this attitude toward gifts makes the issue less controversial and problematic for many journalists. Most media communicators would agree that covert "under-the-table" practices, such as the payola scandal involving disc jockeys, require ethical surveillance and legal regulation. The more subtle practices—a restaurant critic accepting free meals, a travel editor accepting free trips, or a business editor sitting on a corporate board—are considered to be ethical gray areas. Yet if a reader expects objective information and independent opinion from a restaurant critic or travel editor, this expectation can easily be compromised by free meals or lodging. The American Society of Newspaper Editors is very clear in emphasizing that journalists must avoid impropriety and conflict of interest. The line between proper and improper conduct in this arena is a thin one.

Once again, as with most personal ethical issues faced by today's journalists, the bottom line is individual integrity. No set of rules or code of ethics can prevent reporters from accepting gifts or yielding to business pressure. It is up to the individual media communicator to set personal standards for behavior.

Privacy. Another ethical issue that often ends up in a journalistic "twilight zone" is the right to privacy. There have been great gains in the legal definition of privacy in recent years, particularly in four areas: (1) intrusion on seclusion or solitude; (2) publicity that puts an individual in a false light; (3) public disclosure of embarrassing private affairs; and (4) use of an individual's name or likeness for personal gain. An interesting twist on the

---

14 John C. Merrill and S. Jack Odell, *Philosophy and Journalism* (White Plains, N.Y.: Longman, 1983), p. 99.
15 Tony Mauro, "Shooting Ourselves in the Foot," *USA Today*, April 5, 1984, p. 10a.

last issue is the privacy rights of deceased persons. IBM was sued for having used the likeness of the late silent-film star Charlie Chaplin to sell its product. Other companies have used W. C. Fields and Laurel and Hardy clones to sell everything from windshield wipers to wine.

The critical theme in the privacy issue is the public's "right to know" versus the individual's right to privacy. For example, a Montana newspaper recently lost its bid to force the state's board of regents to open meetings during which state-college presidents are evaluated. The *Missoulian,* a daily newspaper in Missoula, where the University of Montana is located, claimed that the policy of barring the press and public from such sessions violates a state open-meeting law. But the Montana Supreme Court upheld a lower court's finding that the college presidents' right to privacy outweighs the public's interest in attending the sessions. The justices noted "that alternately opening and closing the evaluation as sensitive private matters came up was burdensome and impractical" and that "frank employee evaluations are an essential part" of sound university administration.

Despite the increasing number of court decisions, legal definitions of privacy, as with most ethical issues, are an inadequate foundation for journalistic behavior. Journalists themselves must exercise judgment, taste, and good sense. In a compelling example of such judgment, a WLS-TV anchor apologized on the air for having broadcast a scene in which a CBS News crew taped the actual moment when Marine Corps officials reported to a family that their son had been killed in the bombing of the Beirut Marine barracks. NBC refused to show similar footage that its crews had shot—anchor Tom Brokaw felt the taping was a blatant intrusion so they did not put in on. The story about the memorial service for Christa McAuliffe, which began this chapter, is another example.

Restraint is not natural to journalists. Indeed, they have been taught to be curious, persistent, and aggressive. However, persistent probing for facts and evidence is one thing; callous exploration and intrusion are another. The public has a right to know. However, this right must be balanced against the individual's right to privacy.

Social Justice and Responsibility. Ultimately, then, the ethical issues faced by contemporary journalists are difficult ones that are not easily resolved by subscribing to a code of ethics or adhering to some law. The critical ingredient becomes the individual journalist's sense of values, his or her own concept of social responsibility. It should be noted that these issues are confronted and analyzed by virtually all media people, not only national columnists or major-city-newspaper journalists, and they do not always deal with issues of national importance. The column by Joe Junod in the small (27,000) city *Ithaca Journal* (Figure 22.4) illustrates that ethical issues are an everyday fact of life for all media communicators.

When the comics aren't so funny

By JOE JUNOD
Journal Managing Editor

A popular part of most newspapers (excepting The Wall Street Journal and The New York Times) is its comics.

It's often said that comics are the most popular part of a newspaper, that they provide the best diversion from the day's events, which quite often are not funny.

Comic strips are plentiful. There are dozens of them available for purchase.

Not all comic strips, however, are always funny. There are times when a strip, such as Beetle Bailey, goes beyond what I consider the mark of good taste and fairness.

We keep an eye on the comic strips we run in The Journal, reading them for content and taste before they get into the paper.

Printed here is an example of one Beetle Bailey strip that I did not publish — until today, and now only as an example of what I would call a cheap shot to about half the population of this country.

This strip, and others, sometimes portray women are objects of lust or scorn. The strip Nancy also edges into this category on occasion, usually when Sluggo makes some comment about "women drivers," or somesuch.

  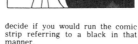 

By withholding certain comic strips, some people will accuse me of censorship, of being selective to suit my own tastes and biases.

I would argue that the job of being an editor is a process of being selective, choosing this picture over that one, writing a headline in one manner instead of another.

An editor has two jobs: Deciding what readers want to read and what they ought to read. I don't think they ought to read comic strips such as the one published here.

If you have a problem with this approach, try this: In place of the word woman, or the image woman, substitute the derogatory expression for a black person. Do that, and then decide if you would run the comic strip referring to a black in that manner.

I don't think that comic strips which treat women as sex objects, as stupid, or as objects of scorn are worth publishing. Since The Journal buys the rights to publication — most strips cost about $7 a week at this newspaper — I believe we also buy the rights to edit them.

Holding an individual up to ridicule is not a function of this newspaper.

In addition, I don't believe that such strips are beneficial as object lessons for children. If we are concerned that our children are not being exposed to a sufficient number of responsible adults, do we aggravate the situation by teaching them that half the population of America is dumb, or that they should be valued for the shape of their body? This newspaper endeavors to avoid passing such myths and stereotypes. Eyeballing the comic strips is one way we do this.

We are considering some changes in our comic strip selection. If you have an opinion about what strips should be dropped, or added, or about the process I described above, reach for the pen and paper, or the telephone.

Figure 22.4 This article by Joe Junod, former managing editor of the *Ithaca* (New York) *Journal*, illustrates that media ethics are ultimately personal ethics. In his article, Junod explains his personal concerns, which resulted in a professional decision. (Courtesy Joseph V. Junod, Managing Editor, *The Ithaca Journal*. "Beetle Bailey" cartoon Copyright © 1981, King Features Syndicate, Inc. World rights reserved.)

CENSORSHIP

Individual communicators are not the only ones involved in media ethics. The media also face generic issues that, although ultimately articulated on a personal level, are larger and more symptomatic of the system itself.

Perhaps no media issue is of greater concern and has as long and richly debated history as censorship. The word *censorship* itself almost immediately raises the collective temperature of the mass media. Here, too, long legal battles have been fought over the years. Similar to the conflict between the public's right to know and the individual's right to privacy, the censorship battle has centered on the right of freedom of the press versus the constraints and responsibility that such freedom requires. Chief Justice Oliver Wendell Holmes expressed it most simply when he said in 1918, that freedom of speech does not extend to allowing the cry of "Fire!"

in a crowded theater. The paradox was eloquently expressed 30 years later by William Hocking, a member of the Commission on Freedom of the Press:

> Are . . . thoughts all equally worthy of protection? Are there no ideas unfit for expression, insane, obscene, destructive? Are all hypotheses on the same level, each one, however vile or silly, to be taken with the same mock reverence because some academic jackass brings it forth? Is non-censorship so great a virtue that it can denounce all censorship as lacking in human liberality?[16]

Particularly troublesome is censorship in education. Perhaps because education has few powerful interest groups, perhaps because it is local, perhaps because, ironically, it receives so little media attention, the issues are at times clouded. Whatever the reason, nowhere in American society can censorship be more counterproductive than in education. Yet education remains particularly vulnerable to pressure groups when it is a question of the availability of literature and other learning materials.

In late summer 1986, a group of parents went to court in Greenville, Tennessee, in protest over some of the books that their children were being required to read in elementary school. Specifically, seven families from nearby Church Hill, Tennessee, claimed that "Goldilocks and the Three Bears," "The Three Little Pigs," "Jack and Jill," and a story about a little boy who cooks were undermining their religious beliefs. They wanted the public schools to buy their children alternative textbooks. They won their case, but it is being appealed.

Not your classic case of censorship, but it has enough of the trappings to make newspaper headlines across the country. The objections to the stories? Well, Goldilocks did not go to jail for breaking and entering; the Three Little Pigs dancing around a kettle suggests Satanism; and the boy who cooks promotes feminism. As one of the mothers said, "The man is the authority of the home with the wife in submission. These books are a direct attack on that."[17]

While it's difficult for some to take the issue seriously, the fight is wasting the valuable time of a federal court, and it is not the only instance of such arguments. It is clear that the religious fundamentalists attacking these readers will not rest unless the public schools teach their beliefs, their way.

They want religious creationism taught instead of, or alongside, the scientific process of evolution. They want books that exalt Christian values and exclude the values of other religions.

Tennessee is not the only state where religious fundamentalists are

---

[16] Quoted in Christians, Rotzoll, and Fackler, *Media Ethics*, p. 285.

[17] *USA Today*, July 23, 1986, p. 8a.

trying to attack schoolbooks. At least 123 incidents were reported during the 1985/1986 school year, an increase over the 97 of the year before.

In Alabama, a federal judge has been asked to declare that Mobile's schools teach "secular humanism" as a religion. In Florida, fundamentalists want schools to give students a handout challenging evolution and promoting creationism. And in Oregon, they failed to censor the same books now under attack in Tennessee.

School officials in some states, including Texas and California, are fighting back. They have rejected textbooks that were watered down to appease fundamentalist critics. That is a courageous step and is in the best interests of public education.

Librarians bear the brunt of these attacks because of their position in the community and in education as "supervisors of information." Teachers are vulnerable to "open, public retribution" for using certain materials in class. Interestingly, the lowest incidence of censorship is in the South and Southwest; the highest incidence is in New England and in Washington, D.C. More than half of all censorship attempts are successful.

As our culture becomes more combative, attempts at censorship are likely to increase. The tragedy of this fact lies in three areas:

1. The merits of the case aside, the kinds of materials available to students decrease. The users suffer.
2. The institution involved is painted into a corner; that is, it must lose support from *some* segments of the community.
3. The teacher, librarian, or media specialist involved is subjected to personal pressure and, at times, abuse. In some cases, the individual becomes "gun shy" and begins to make choices that are unnecessarily narrow.

In censorship attempts, books are attacked most often, and about one in four attacks concerns textbooks. Of the books attacked by would-be censors, *Catcher in the Rye,* by J. D. Salinger, is cited more often than any other work. *Catch-22,* by Joseph Heller, is another favorite target.

Two major areas of concern are (1) racial materials, with criticism arising from groups and individuals objecting to racism as well as radicalism; and (2) sexual references, which always draw fire from segments of the population, especially when the references occur in films, plays, and books.

Textbook censorship can occur at many levels. The pressure that surfaces in schools is normally addressed toward respected literary works by such writers as John Steinbeck, Ernest Hemingway, and Aldous Huxley. The public library that tends to offer a broad selection of popular works is another target; it is often pressured to remove works of lesser literary merit or works dealing with controversial issues.

Does a community, a society, have the right or responsibility to police media materials? There are no simple answers. To say "yes" in some cases (dealing with children?) and "no" in others (adults?) may be close to the facts of life in this society, but another question arises: When does a person become an adult?

A larger problem lies in the suppression of ideas. This should not be tolerated in a democratic society, but tragically, it is in some situations. Ultimately, in a democracy, too little censorship is undeniably better than too much.

The Media and the First Amendment

The interpretation of censorship in contemporary American society is, of course, centered in First Amendment law. A major distinction is made between print media and broadcast media in the application of this law. For print media, the First Amendment declares boldly that no government—federal, state, or local—can interfere with the right of publishers to print whatever information they care to put on paper. Of course, certain economic and labor regulations apply to print media, but in general, print media are free from repressive government controls. Broadcasting, on the contrary, is regulated by the federal government to the point of broadcasters being required to hold a license in order to communicate on radio or television. The basic licensing structure of broadcasting, established in 1927, has led to a wide variety of other controls, several of which directly affect the content of radio and television. These controls received their strongest judicial endorsement in the *Red Lion* decision of 1969, in which the Supreme Court ruled that the standard of the Fairness Doctrine, which requires broadcasters to balance their public-affairs programming and to provide air time to persons or points of view that the broadcaster might otherwise ignore, is constitutional.

In applying a different First Amendment standard to the broadcast media from the one that covers the print media, the Court stated: "Differences in the characteristics of news media justify differences in the First Amendment standards applied to them." The differences noted are grounded in the physical characteristics of broadcasting, primarily the scarcity of spectrum space (radio wave band), which prevents anyone who wants to from going on the air. But William Read points out a difficulty with this reasoning in his article "The First Amendment Meets the Information Society":

> At the heart of the distinction drawn by the U.S. Supreme Court between the press and broadcasting is the belief that "the broadcast media pose unique and special problems not present in the traditional free speech case." What the Court finds to be "special" is the technological nature of the medium. Because broadcast frequencies are finite (and thus for reasons of efficient use must be allocated), the Court concluded in *Red Lion* that "it is idle to posit an unabridgeable First Amendment right to broad-

cast comparable to the right of every individual to speak, write or publish.''

The upshot of all this is clear: The technological underpinnings of *Red Lion* are eroding as the technological distinctions among media blur. To cling to spectrum scarcity as a rationale for a divergent legal approach to broadcasting is no longer viable. Indeed it is risky. For as newspapers and magazines more and more come to rely on satellites and other regulated communications technologies the danger exists that they will be drawn into the regulatory web.

The conclusion to be drawn from the foregoing is simply this: The rationale for a divergent, two-track legal approach for mass media has eroded. Once seemingly clear distinctions between print and broadcasting are no longer clear; ''blur'' is fast becoming an appropriate word. The question then is whether, in an information society, both media should be placed under the print standard or under the broadcast standard? Or, perhaps, a standard yet to be developed?[18]

DEREGULATION AND THE BROADCAST MEDIA

Despite a long history of federal regulations, the broadcast media are finding it increasingly difficult to escape behind FCC rules and regulations and are faced with the full impact of a social-responsibility ethic that places them on a par with the print media. Whether the issues are the ''big-brother'' role of television, checkbook journalism, violence, or stereotyping, the bottom line again becomes a sense of media responsibility, media ethics, and media values.

The issue of checkbook journalism, in particular, has generated controversy not only within the print and broadcast media, but, more interestingly, between them. In 1984, CBS reportedly paid $500,000 for an interview with former President Richard Nixon. The payment raised the issue of checkbook journalism and what some journalists considered to be a bigger question: Was CBS News abdicating its editorial control—a former Nixon White House aide conducted the interview—and letting Nixon, in effect, produce his own program? The purchase was severely criticized by the *New York Times* and the *Los Angeles Times,* both of which, in turn, were accused of a ''double standard'' by Van Gordon Sauter, former president of CBS News. As Sauter stated in commenting on the newspapers' purchases of memoirs by Nixon and Jimmy Carter:

> There is nothing inherently wrong about the *New York Times* or *Los Angeles Times* publishing subjective judgments about the motivation or skills or shortcomings of CBS News, its executives or its journalists. But when will

---

[18] William Read, ''The First Amendment Meets the Information Society,'' in *Telecommunications,* ed. Jerry L. Salvaggio (White Plains, N.Y.: Longman, 1983), pp. 95–96.

those newspapers, or any other, render the same subjective judgments about, say, the *Washington Post,* or *USA Today,* or the *Daily News,* or the (Los Angeles) *Herald-Examiner*? Do not the editorial merits, or lack of them, of these communicators deserve the same scrutiny, the same subjective judgment, passed with such regularity on broadcast journalists?[19]

Whatever the specific issues—checkbook journalism, stereotyping, violence, deceptive advertising, conflict of interest—ethical conduct in broadcasting ultimately depends on the personal integrity of the individual communicator. As Muriel Reis, vice president of WNEW-TV in New York City, stated in a commentary on nonfiction programming:

> In reality programming, production techniques should be used for one purpose only—to clarify and enlighten, not to confuse, to obfuscate or deceive. If production techniques remove the program from the sphere of reality, then something is wrong.
>
> How does a broadcaster deal with these added responsibilities? And who should be responsible? Clearly, a general manager or a program director cannot be everywhere at all times. My recommendation is, from the general manager down, to develop an awareness of the responsibilities and of the problems that can arise. This awareness should be instilled among those directly responsible for production. Producers cannot be required to solve problems, but they should be able to recognize them. Management must also be aware that staffs change; there can be a well-educated staff one day and novices the next. Indoctrination into programming responsibilities must be an ongoing process.
>
> To insure the all-important integrity of reality programming, management must be ever-vigilant. Program directors should insure that their producers and staff understand the principles upon which their programming responsibilities are based. Setting forth lists of specific do's and don't's may appear to some to be the answer, but it can be a dangerous trap. Because it is impossible to anticipate all contingencies, relying on specific rules can provide false security. The key is for the principles and standards of honest and credible programming to be thoroughly understood at all levels. If reality programming is both accurate and honest, not only are legal problems avoided, but credibility insured. And unless there is credibility, no program will succeed.[20]

MEDIA FREEDOM

The theme running through this chapter is one of freedom. Freedom *of* media and freedom *for* media. Media must be free from inhibitory external controls in order to protect and correct society. However, as many in the media professions have noted, you can't hold on to a free press if it behaves irresponsibly.

Freedom of the press, like any other freedom, is a two-edged sword.

---

[19] *Broadcasting,* March 19, 1984, p. 48.

[20] Muriel Reis, *Broadcasting,* October 15, 1983, p. 15.

The press must be free to carry out its libertarian-based ethic of protecting the rights of the individual and acting as a check on government. However, it must also be held to a deep sense of responsibility. Journalists are aggressive partially because they perceive their essentially libertarian mission in David-versus-Goliath terms. However, like David, the press must be careful about how it uses its resources, whether against an ordinary individual or the president of the United States.

As David Brinkley, ABC News analyst, said in a recent conference on media ethics, "We are the only people I know who gather occasionally to discuss our ethics."[21] And this is as it should be. Ultimately, all the media have is their credibility—regardless of function—and without a basic sense of ethics, they lose credibility and, as a result, do not survive.

Making media ethics work is ultimately the responsibility of the individual media practitioner. Media systems are not ethical or unethical. Attacks on television or motion pictures do little to enlighten the debate. Mass communicators are not wholly discrete voices. They stand defined in relation to many others in the particular media context. It is the aggregate of these individuals and their day-to-day sense of responsibility that form a common ethic in mass communication.

SUMMARY

Although there is renewed interest in media ethics and responsibility today, the issue is one of this country's hallowed traditions. Most situations concerning ethics in the media have little to do with regulation but have everything to do with responsibility, judgment, and common sense.

New technologies are having a major impact on ethics. However, since technology itself has no inherent value, the values of the ethical decisions lie, not in the machinery, but in the choices of the individuals who use the machinery. One way to approach the issue of media responsibility and ethics is to differentiate among institutional ethics, professional ethics, and personal ethics.

Institutional ethics often take the form of informal codes of conduct, most often associated with gatekeepers. However, there are also formal codes of institutional conduct, such as the broadcast standards codes of the three major television networks. In addition, other media, such as newspapers, often have internal codes of conduct that help govern their professional conduct.

In contrast to the somewhat gray area of institutional ethics is the system of codes and regulations that forms the arena of professional ethics. Many of the codes relate to news, and two of the most respected are those of the Society of Professional Journalists and the Radio-Television News Directors Association. The advertising industry has developed a strong

---

[21] *Broadcasting*, June 23, 1986, p. 53.

self-regulation code of conduct, but the motion picture industry, with its rating and classification system, has developed what is perhaps the most comprehensive and systematic self-regulatory system of professional ethics.

Personal ethics are one of the most important areas of media responsibility and are ultimately at the heart of any ethical system. Each media situation is unique, but, in practical terms, the ethical issues faced by individual communicators fall into six categories: (1) conflict of interest; (2) truth and accuracy; (3) sources of information; (4) payola, gifts, and business pressure; (5) privacy; and (6) social justice and responsibility.

Perhaps the most major issue in media ethics is censorship. No media issue is of greater concern and has as long and richly debated a history. Particularly troublesome is censorship in education.

The interpretation of censorship in contemporary American society is centered in First Amendment law, in the application of which a major distinction is made between print media and broadcast media. For print media, the First Amendment states clearly that no government can interfere with the right of publishers to print whatever information they care to. Broadcasting, on the contrary, is regulated by the federal government to the point of broadcasters being required to hold a license in order to communicate on radio and television. Despite this long history of federal regulation, however, the broadcast media are increasingly being deregulated under the impact of recent Federal Communication Commission decisions.

Ultimately, the issue of media ethics and responsibility centers on freedom—freedom *of* media and freedom *for* media. Media must be free from external controls in order to protect and correct society; however, they must also be responsible to that society. Media ethics work because the individuals working in the media care about the system and their role in it. It is the individual communicator's day-to-day sense of responsibility that ultimately forms the basic ethical system of mass communication.

BIBLIOGRAPHY

Christians, Clifford G., Kim B. Rotzoll, and Mark Fackler. *Media Ethics: Cases and Moral Reasoning*. New York: Longman, 1983.

Goldstein, Tom *The News at Any Cost: How Journalists Compromise Their Ethics to Shape the News*. New York: Simon and Schuster, 1985.

Goodwin, H. Eugene. *Groping for Ethics in Journalism*. Ames: Iowa State University Press, 1983.

Hulteng, John L. *The Messenger's Motives: Ethical Problems of the News Media*. 2d ed. Englewood Cliffs, N.J.: Prentice-Hall, 1985.

Merrill, John C., and S. Jack Odell. *Philosophy and Journalism*. New York: Longman, 1983.

Phelan, John M. *Disenchantment: Meaning and Morality in the Media*. 2d ed. New York: Hastings House, 1980.

Rubin, Bernard, ed. *Questioning Media Ethics*. New York: Praeger, 1978.

Thayer, Lee, ed. *Ethics, Morality and the Media*. New York: Hastings House, 1980.

23

Effects: Mass Communication and the Individual

Given the problems in studying the effects of mass communication, why do we persist? Why continue the discussion? Why look for the answers to questions that we have not fully framed?

Because it is important! Because we need to know!

Admittedly, media science is in its infancy. But it is beginning to gather the wherewithall to emerge as an independent social science. And universities are beginning to graduate scholars who understand the mass media as well as research techniques.

What we think we know about the effects of mass communication has come from numerous field studies and laboratory experiments. Three basic methodologies have contributed to the current body of knowledge:

1. *Historical research* investigates past and current media events in order to make comparisons; recently, content analysis has broadened that endeavor.
2. *Survey research*, using representative, random, or stratified samples of audiences, has assessed media effectiveness in the diffused environment of the "real world" to determine who watches, listens to, and reads what the media produce.
3. *Experimental research*, done in the controlled environment of the laboratory, has contributed much toward determining specific short-term changes in behavior and attitudes as they relate to mass media content.

627

As should be expected, differences in design, methodology, and manipulation of the data have produced some disagreement among researchers and practitioners. They are not positive of the meaning of some of the results they have concerning the effectiveness of mass communication in our society. Also, they are more confident in some research areas than in others.

Mass communication research is currently facing up to a serious deficiency: most of what we have done is short-term rather than long-term. This is the case because longitudinal studies are (1) *costly,* and funding is inconsistent; (2) *topical,* and data have been collected to prove a point; (3) *time-consuming,* and researchers in the academic setting are pressed to produce results that can be published quickly; (4) *difficult to sustain* when human subjects are required for a study of sensitive issues, such as violence or erotica; (5) *subject to methodologies that change,* and some collected data cannot be compared with information gathered at an earlier date; and (6) *evaluated by very powerful pressure groups* that dispute answers that conflict with their position on the issue, affect their economic base, or both.

Mass communication inquiry uses a battery of mathematical and statistical models, techniques, and tests to collect, evaluate, and validate data. Researchers use partial and multiple correlations, parametric and nonparametric statistics, analysis of variance, and high-speed computers. In the laboratory, they manipulate the *independent* variable while the *dependent* variable is held constant and *extraneous* variables are controlled. A number of variables are tested on experimental groups large enough to determine if the probability level is significant when compared with results from a control group.

Some of you are confused by this litany, but it illustrates why the remaining discussion of reserach findings does not include these details. From this point onward, we attempt to distill what is known in ways that the beginner can comprehend.[1]

TRADITIONAL CONCERNS OF MASS COMMUNICATION RESEARCH

It is a fact that the mass media affect the course of human development. It is a fact that a causal relationship exists between exposure to the mass media and human behavior, even if it is not always possible to establish

---

[1] Although a huge amount of information thus is condensed and interpreted, which always generates honest disagreement, we feel that we have chosen the best course of action for the anticipated readership of this book. Some research is neglected and some may seem to be misinterpreted, but we are attempting to clarify complex issues in a very short space. We apologize if we have not given sufficient attention to concepts, results, and studies that you feel are essential and welcome feedback regarding how to make this important body of information more accurate and understandable to the beginning student of mass communication.

absolute cause-and-effect relationships for every individual in every situation. There are many variables in complex combinations in all media experiences. In 1948, Bernard Berelson framed his famous and cogent reply to questions about the effects of communication: "Some kinds of communication of some kinds of issues, brought to the attention of some kinds of people under some kinds of conditions, have some kinds of effect."[2] This statement remains valid. As to delineating these effects, Berelson, in conjunction with Morris Janowitz, commented:

> The effects of communication are many and diverse. They may be short-range or long-run. They may be manifest or latent. They may be strong or weak. They may derive from any number of aspects of the communication content. They may be considered as psychological or political or economic or sociological. They may operate upon opinions, values, information levels, skills, taste, or overt behavior.[3]

This statement, too, remains an accurate summary of the overall state of our knowledge. But we are learning more details about the "some kinds" of communication.

The effects of exposure to content in the mass media are seldom, if ever, simple, direct, or totally dependent on a specific experience. But media exposure is one of the important variables.

Research has focused primarily on three general areas:[4]

1. The effects of mass communication on cognition and comprehension.
2. The effects of mass communication on attitude and value change.
3. The effects of mass communication on behavior change, including both antisocial behavior (negative change) and prosocial behavior (positive change).

It has also focused on three specific topics:

1. The effects of violence in the mass media on American society.
2. The effects of erotica in the mass media on American society.
3. The effects of the mass media on children.

---

[2] Bernard Berelson, "Communications and Public Opinion," in *Mass Communication*, ed. Wilbur Schramm (Urbana: University of Illinois Press, 1949), p. 500.

[3] Bernard Berelson and Morris Janowitz, eds., *Reader in Public Opinion and Communication*, 2d ed. (New York: Free Press, 1966), p. 379.

[4] Walter Weiss, "The Effects of the Mass Media of Communication," in *Handbook of Social Psychology*, 2d ed., Gardner Lindzey and Eliot Aronson (Reading, Mass.: Addison-Wesley, 1968), vol. 2, pp. 77–195. This section is a modification of Weiss's comparison of research in Chapter 38 of the *Handbook of Social Psychology*. Weiss's summary is one of the best available and is a must for students interested in media effects. The *Handbook of Social Psychology* is an excellent source of historical data as well.

The issues of cognition, attitude, and behavior change are summarized first. The specific topics of violence, erotica, and children are then examined in relation to historical and current research.

Cognition and Comprehension

The communication process begins with gaining an audience's attention, then proceeds to generating awareness (cognition), and finally—optimally—results in comprehension. In mass communication, cognition is affected by the fact that the individual does not read all pages of a newspaper or listen to every minute of a newscast with equal attention. Audience members selectively expose themselves to media content; but by constant, repetitive exposure, the media can become highly effective on a wide variety of issues. A person's retention of information over a long time is least probable when he or she has no personal interest in the information.

Comprehension (as with all media effects) is, in large measure, the result of the interaction of media content with the direct, personal experiences of audience members. A person's ability to recall a media event also depends on repeated exposure to the stimulus and some reinforcement via interpersonal relationships. For example, if a person has a brother who is living in a Middle Eastern country that becomes a trouble spot, the very mention of that area will increase the person's awareness because he needs that information and is gratified by it.

Although Americans have one of the best overall information systems in the world, considerable misunderstanding occurs because people misinterpret, fail to hear, or refuse to accept the facts. Evidence also suggests that audience members' predispositions on a given issue create subtle, unconscious misconceptions in spite of repeated exposure to messages that contradict these notions. In other words, comprehension on a given issue can be distorted by personal beliefs.

Wilbur Schramm points out that "the mass media can widen horizons. . . . They can let a man see and hear where he has never been and know people he has never met."[5] Obviously, this is an important effect of mass media in developing societies in terms of the diffusion of innovations, but it is also relevant in any society caught up in rapid growth and change.

Attitude and Value Change

In media research on attitudes, there is general agreement that the mass media affect the values of a society and the attitudes of individuals. The extent, speed, and longevity of the effects remains in question.

Most research evidence supports the hypothesis that mass media can create opinions more easily than they can change opinions but that reinforcement of existing beliefs is the main effect of most mass communication

---

[5] Wilbur Schramm, *Mass Media and National Development* (Stanford, Calif.: Stanford University Press, 1964), p. 127.

experiences. One reason for this reinforcement is the tende
to protect themselves by means of selective exposure, select
and selective retention. We tend to expose ourselves only to messa
agree with our opinions; we tend to avoid communication that is unsympa-
thetic to our predispositions. When exposed to messages with which we
disagree, we tend to perceive only those elements that fit our preconcep-
tions. Finally, we tend to retain facts and ideas that agree with our opinions. Psychologist Leon Festinger studied this phenomenon and named it
cognitive dissonance.[6] Basically, the word *dissonance* replaces the word *incon-
sistency*, and *consonance* replaces *consistency*. Festinger's main hypothesis is
that the psychologically uncomfortable existence of dissonance motivates a
person to try to reduce it and achieve consonance. In addition to trying to
reduce dissonance, the person actively avoids situations and information
that would increase it. For example, a man who continues to smoke, even
though he knows that smoking is harmful, tries to reduce the dissonance.
He rationalizes that he enjoys smoking so much that it is worth the chances
of ill health; or he rationalizes that if he stopped smoking, he would put on
weight, which could be equally bad for his health.

Two sociologists, Paul F. Lazarsfeld and Robert K. Merton, have
pointed out the effects of mass communication on social values. The mass
media not only reinforce what we already believe, but also "enforce the
normal attitudes and behavior patterns of society. . . . Publicity closes the
gap between 'private attitudes' and 'public morality.' "[7] The mass media
expose deviations to public view, and this exposure usually forces some
degree of public action against what had been privately tolerated.

Considerable research has also verified the "bandwagon effect": people adopt opinions because they are, or seem to be, the opinions of a large
number of other people. This social conformity is most commonly demonstrated in advertising, which frequently uses such phrases as "9 out of 10,"
"more people use," or "millions recommend." Studies also show that
small, cohesive minority groups have an unusual amount of resistance to
the bandwagon effect but that most people, lacking the support of a
strong, active reference group, simply go along with the majority.

> The mass media bestow prestige and enhance the authority of individuals
> and groups by legitimizing their status. Recognition by the press or radio
> or magazines or newsreels testifies that one has arrived, that one is impor-
> tant enough to have been singled out from the large anonymous masses,
> that one's behavior and opinions are significant enough to require public
> notice.[8]

---

[6] Leon Festinger, *A Theory of Cognitive Dissonance* (Evanston, Ill.: Row, Peterson, 1957).

[7] Paul F. Lazarsfeld and Robert K. Merton, "Mass Communication, Popular Taste and Organized Action," in *Mass Communication*, ed. Wilbur Schramm (Urbana: University of Illinois
Press, 1960), p. 499.

[8] Ibid., p. 498.

Figure 23.1 A cover story in *Newsweek* relates the increasing problems faced by the *Playboy* empire because of the drop in circulation and the decreasing number of retail establishments that are willing to carry men's magazines in light of the increased pressures from conservative groups. The role of Hugh Hefner and his *Playboy* philosophy has been a topic of conversation throughout the so-called sexual revolution of the post–World War II era. The revolution is waning, however, and *Playboy* with it. (Copyright 1986, by Newsweek, Inc. All rights reserved. Reprinted by permission.)

This prestige enhancement is known as *status conferral,* and the news media confer it not only on persons in the news, but also on those who report the news. News "stars" are considered to be very powerful in terms of generating attitudes about events as well as providing information about them.

News may also be dysfunctional and cause an effect that was unintended. According to some sociologists and psychologists, news, which is invariably about deviations and abnormalities in society, may actually create anxieties among readers, listeners, and viewers. This anxiety could result in *privatization*—individuals who feel overwhelmed by the news react by turning inward to a private life over which they have more control. There is considerable support for the idea that heavy users of mass media develop negative attitudes about the world.

Behavior Change

Research has investigated both antisocial (negative) and prosocial (positive) changes in individual behavior to determine what the media's influences are on specific kinds of behavior. Among the behaviors studied are play patterns, voting behavior, and aggression.

As we allocate our discretionary or leisure time, the time allotted to the mass media is significant. Mass media dominate leisure-time activity in our society. Certain media usually generate much public interest if participation in them requires no skills (TV viewing, radio listening, and moviegoing). In effect, mass communication experiences are so attractive and rewarding that the individual consciously gives up or modifies other activities in order to partake of them.

The mass media are often employed to stimulate interest in specific activities, such as homemaking, sewing, or cooking. Most studies indicate that special-interest programs encourage passive rather than active behavior on the part of the viewer. But the media do not make a person more passive unless he or she has a very strong predisposition to be so anyway.

Studies have investigated various aspects of family-life patterns. In general, the media studies—specifically of television—indicate that television has not had a marked effect on family life styles. At a superficial level, members of a family spend slightly more time together (not necessarily interacting with one another) viewing television as a group until a second TV set is purchased. The specific fear that TV viewing negatively affects schoolwork seems to be unfounded. In fact, TV viewing may actually contribute to a faster start for some children. The bedtime of children also has not been changed markedly by television.

Considerable research has been devoted to the effects of mass communication on voting behavior. The mass media seem to be relatively ineffective in converting a voter from one party affiliation to another. Few voters seem to be influenced by specific political commercials for a candidate they dislike. The critical role of the media apparently is to reinforce political attitudes and maintain party-member support.

It takes considerable time for people to adopt specific behaviors, and depends on several factors, including the number of people involved in the decision; the economic and social risk necessary; the future ramifications of the action; the extent of departure from current practices; and the compatibility of the new behavior with the personality, values, and motives of the individual. The same factors influence making changes in purchasing behavior, wearing new styles of clothes, using "miracle cleaning agents," joining protest marches, participating in common-law marriages, adopting children of minority parentage, and other behavioral modifications. The interaction of media exposure and other personal experiences becomes the critical force in behavior change.

MAJOR STUDIES OF THE MASS MEDIA

Since the 1930s, numerous studies have been reported, but unfortunately not enough of them have been replicated. In addition, articles have appeared in the popular press that misrepresent or misinterpret study results and stress sensational or unsubstantiated findings.[9] However, several of the studies deserve a brief review.[10]

Early Studies of Motion Pictures, Radio, and Comic Books

The Payne Fund studies, conducted from 1929 to 1932, evaluated the influence of motion pictures on children. These 13 studies, published in 10 volumes, focused on audience composition and content analyses of themes. Results suggested that movies can affect information acquisition, modify cultural attitudes, stimulate emotions, and disturb sleep. Results even suggested that some films can produce negative "morals" and behaviors in some children. This report reinforced existing public concern and led to an industry self-censorship system that lasted until the 1960s.

The "Invasion from Mars" study was hastily done after the Orson Welles radio drama "War of the Worlds" was broadcast on October 30, 1938, and panicked an estimated 1 million listeners, who believed the drama to be real. The major findings were these:

1. The excellent quality of the production, designed around fictional news reports, contributed to the panic.
2. People who tuned in too late to hear disclaimers and who could not verify the broadcast's authenticity from another source were most likely to panic.
3. Individuals with "weak" personalities, lower education levels, and strong religious beliefs were most susceptible to panic.
4. Once frightened, people stopped listening altogether or refused to believe that all was well despite the fact that other stations were on the air.
5. Political tension in Europe and a depressed economy at home created cultural conditions that contributed to the overall panic.

In the aftermath of the broadcast, standards were mandated to prevent similar broadcasts. The power of radio was real.

---

[9] A number of articles and books have gained wide public acceptance without acceptable evidence or corroboration. This is the case with subliminal persuasion, which suggests that messages below the threshold of awareness can persuade audiences to purchase consumer goods. Another is the discovery of sex and death symbols in a limited number of print advertisements. These symbols can be discovered only after the closest scrutiny. "Pop scholarship" immediately assumed the existence of a plot that was somehow poisoning our minds. Such "scholarship" must stop. We have enough real problems in the area of mass communication research without creating straw men.

[10] Shearon Lowery and Melvin L. De Fleur, *Milestones in Mass Communication Research: Media Effects* (New York: Longman, 1983). The authors provide individual reviews of 11 major studies undertaken from the 1930s to the 1970s. This work is highly recommended as a comprehensive overview, even though it does not suggest that it is a complete study of many of the major works or that it selectively eliminates others.

Figure 23.2 Orson Welles's radio program "War of the Worlds" was broadcast on Halloween evening in 1938 and led to considerable panic among listeners. A study after the event by the Office of Radio Research at Princeton University, although hastily organized, found partial answers to the reason the program had been so effective in inducing mass hysteria. (Photo: AP/Wide World Photos.)

The "People's Choice" study analyzed voting predispositions in the 1940 presidential election. For the first time, the tools of the social scientist were used in a large-scale field study of communication. The study found that political propaganda persuades voters to remain loyal to their political beliefs rather than change parties. Variables such as religion, socioeconomic status, age, occupation, and urban versus rural residence were identified as important. The study also suggested that media content moves through a "two-step flow," in which opinion leaders influence less active information seekers, and these interpersonal social contacts are more important than exposure to the media.

The "Why We Fight" studies brought filmmakers and social scientists together at the beginning of World War II to create, produce, and test informational and motivational training films. Results showed that the effects of these films were caused by a variety of factors in addition to the films themselves. Yet the films proved (1) to be effective in imparting information, although the information was clearly forgotten over time; (2) to have had little effect on opinions regarding the war; and (3) to have had

Figure 23.3 Frank Capra's "Why We Fight" series was designed as propaganda aimed at troops and citizens alike to explain why America was fighting the Axis powers in World War II. Hollywood helped mightily in the efforts of the government to inform and persuade Americans of the rightness of the Allied cause. This series of films was studied intensely to determine the effect of these films on citizen soldiers.

no effect on recruits' motivation to serve their country. Results also demonstrated the value of giving one-sided presentations to less educated soldiers and two-sided arguments to better educated inductees.

Project Revere, conducted between 1951 and 1953, studied military propaganda but also was interested in airborne leaflet distribution to contact soldiers and noncombatants behind enemy lines. Results demonstrated that messages are *leveled* (shortened to fewer words), *sharpened* (emphasized selected ideas), and *assimilated* (understood) as they pass along interpersonal channels after the initial contact with the leaflets (medium).

The book *Interpersonal Communication Research* by Carl Hovland and Elihu Katz, working with Paul Lazarsfeld, had an impact on our understanding of mass communication effects in the 1940s and 1950s. The authors examined information and opinion exchange within social groups and shed light on the influence of source credibility, fear appeals, order of presentation, and explicit and implicit message variables. They also presented a more thorough analysis of the "two-step flow" theory. These studies found that there are many different opinion leaders, depending on the content of a communication. Most important, people interact over media content, and the interaction influences the effect perhaps more than the content.

The Wertham "Comic-Book" studies, published in 1954, analyzed the effects of selected sexually oriented or violent comic books on emotionally disturbed children.[11] Wertham's findings were based on his clinical work; he observed and solicited reports that such content contributed to the negative behavior of children with problems. The sensationalism of the media's coverage of Wertham's studies led to severe economic problems for comic-book publishers and the imposition of an industry "seal of approval" self-censorship. Interestingly, the hardiest survivors among comic books today are the types that Wertham condemned.

The studies discussed thus far found a variety of effects of mass communication and led to public consternation and strict self-regulation of motion pictures, radio, and comic books. This body of work strongly suggests that the media can have an impact on comprehension, attitudes, and behaviors and that different individuals react differently in the same situation. This conclusion negates the "magic-bullet theory," in which the exposure to one media experience is the sole cause of a specific response. It supports the belief that interpersonal interaction before, during, and after a media event is one, if not *the*, major determinant of the effect of that particular mass communication experience.

Early Studies of Television

Since the early 1950s, most research on the effects of mass communication has focused on television, especially the effect of television on children. A review of some of the significant work of the 1950s and 1960s reveals a variety of important information.

Television and the Child by Hilde Himmelweit, A. N. Oppenheim, and Pamela Vance was suggested by the British Broadcasting Corporation (BBC) and funded by the Nuffield Foundation to assess the impact of television on children in England.[12] Begun in 1954 and published in 1958, this field study matched children aged 10 through 14 in four cities in

---

[11] Frederic Wertham, *Seduction of the Innocent* (New York: Rinehart, 1954). Wertham's work is not documented by subject description and is difficult to apply beyond the two qualifications noted in the text: (1) violent and sexually oriented content; and (2) emotionally disturbed children. Yet press reports and personal appearances and writings by Wertham attempt to expand his work to include all comics and all children. His studies from 1948 to 1954 do not seem to justify this expansion.

[12] Hilde Himmelweit, A. N. Oppenheim, and Pamela Vance, *Television and the Child* (London: Oxford University Press, 1958). This book was the first major longitudinal study of TV's effects and makes a significant contribution to our understanding of the emergence of a new medium in a modern industrial society—in this case, Great Britain.

England. The study utilized questionnaires, observational techniques, mothers' diaries and viewing habits, interviews, personality measures, teachers' opinion studies, and school performance to gather information. It even compared children prior to television's coming to town and after its arrival. The 11 studies found the following:

1. Age, sex, emotional maturity, and personal need reflect taste and lead to program selection.
2. The more active, more intelligent, and more socially interested child needs television less.
3. Parental example is significant as to what and how much is viewed on television.
4. TV viewing influences children's ideas about jobs, success, and social surroundings.
5. TV dramas can frighten children, especially if they depict realistic violence and are viewed alone and in the dark.
6. Parental viewing with children reduces fright, but most children enjoy the excitement.
7. Knives are more fearful than guns; fisticuffs have little impact; and verbal aggression is often more frightening than physical acts of violence.
8. TV viewing takes time away from other leisure activities, but does not seem to have an impact on learning or school performance.
9. Viewing violence on television has little impact on the normal, active child, but does seem to affect the emotionally disturbed, heavy viewer.
10. Television affects children, but not to the degree that they are fundamentally changed.
11. Supervision of viewing and interaction with children by adults is the critical intervening variable in short-term and long-term effects of television on children.

The book *Television in the Lives of our Children* by Wilbur Schramm, Jack Lyle, and Edwin Parker included 11 studies funded by the National Television and Radio Center that were conducted from 1958 to 1960. They focused on the uses of gratifications, or the functions, that television served. The researchers found the following:

1. No harmful physical effects (eyestrain, loss of sleep) result from watching television.
2. Television helps children acquire information and stimulates their interest in subjects about which information is not otherwise available.

3. Children who are passive, under stress, possess inferior social skills, or are less intelligent make greater use of television.
4. As brighter, socially active children age, they watch television less.
5. Children watch television for thrills and play and seem to like being mildly frightened.
6. Adults and children alike seek out and use TV content to gratify certain needs.

The major conclusion of the studies was this:

> For some children, under some conditions, some television is harmful. For other children, under the same conditions, or for the same children under other conditions, it may be beneficial. For most children, under most conditions, most television is probably neither harmful nor particularly beneficial.[13]

The Effects of Mass Communication, a book by Joseph Klapper, has been neglected of late because of Klapper's association with the TV industry, as an employee of CBS, and his role as a defender of and apologist for industry positions on the effects of violence. Klapper's work is a summary of previous research and advocates the "phenomenistic" approach to television effects, that is, that television and other mass media must be viewed as only one of many factors rather than as the only factor in any consideration of the effects of the mass communication process on human behavior. Klapper suggested several general principles:

1. Children's reactions to television vary, based on use, gratification, and group association.
2. The content is not as powerful as we would like to believe, and mass communication normally is not an ordinary and sufficient cause, but a part of other "mediating factors and influences."
3. Regardless of other conditions, the mass media tend to reinforce rather than change.
4. When mass media do have an impact, it often is a result of other variables being inoperative or because the individual is actually desirous of change.
5. Media have measurable psychophysical impacts, but these are probably of short duration.
6. Media impact is influenced by the situation, the social climate, and the person's condition, as well as by the content.[14]

---

[13] Wilbur Schramm, Jack Lyle, and Edwin Parker, *Television in the Lives of Our Children* (Stanford, Calif.: Stanford University Press, 1961), p. 13. This was the first of many studies about the influence of television on children, and it remains a major contributor to our understanding of this process.

[14] Joseph T. Klapper, *The Effects of Mass Communication* (Glencoe, Ill.: Free Press, 1960), pp. 8–9.

The People Look at Television, funded by CBS and published in 1963, is a study of public attitudes toward the effects of television rather than a study of the effects themselves. It emphasizes that parents and other adult viewers felt that television had relatively little effect on them, but that they were concerned about the effects on children and about the amount of suggestive material on television.

Experimental and field studies done in the 1950s and 1960s demonstrated that violent TV content, regardless of the existence of other variables, led to aggressive behavior in children. The "Bobo" doll experiments done by Albert Bandura and his colleagues tested Bandura's social-learning theory and suggested that children learn personalities. These experiments were concerned with modeling, or imitative behavior, stimulated by TV violence, whether that violence was rewarded or punished. Bandura argued that TV violence has both a learning and a motivating effect. Bandura's much publicized article in *Look* magazine (1963) went beyond what his data demonstrated; many felt that it strayed back to the "magic-bullet" approach. Nevertheless, the research did demonstrate a relationship between TV violence and aggression in children in the laboratory setting.

The aggression-machine experiments of Leonard Berkowitz used a button-pushing situation in which helping or hurting could be simulated. The "hurting" consisted of pushing a button that supposedly administered an electric shock to another person. Both college students and children exhibited more aggression, as measured by the length of shocks they administered, after they were exposed to TV violence. Berkowitz suggested an instigation theory, according to which media violence somehow triggers aggressive behavior, especially when the violence appears to be justified.

The catharsis experiments conducted by S. Feshbach in 1955 posited the opposite result from that of Berkowitz. Feshbach concluded that TV violence reduces aggression by defusing the need and predisposition to act aggressively. When these experiments were replicated researchers who believe that TV violence stimulates violent behavior, they found nothing to corroborate cathartic effects. In the 1960s, Feshbach continued work in support of his theory and found TV violence to decrease aggression in aggressive boys but increase it in nonaggressive boys. This finding was also challenged by other researchers.

Comparing the major field studies and experiments presents a confusing, if not conflicting, picture of the effects of television. The experimenters demonstrate that TV violence does not make a difference in aggression, regardless of the other variables. The books by Himmelweit, Oppenheim, and Vance; Schramm, Lyle, and Parker; and Klapper argue that TV violence is one of many factors in the environmental mix and that other factors may be more powerful than the content of television when it comes to negative attitudes or antisocial behavior.

GOVERNMENT INVOLVEMENT
IN MEDIA RESEARCH

Throughout the 1950s and 1960s, politicians were uneasy about the impact and power of the mass media, especially television, and about that medium's effects on children. Senators Estes Kefauver (1954), Christopher Dodd (1961), and John Pastore (1968) held hearings on subjects related to the mass media and social ills. When cities exploded in riots in the 1960s, the violent and pornographic content that was widely available in the mass media was suspect as a contributing cause. Three large-scale governmental investigations sought answers to, and possibly scapegoats for, America's ills.

In June 1968, President Lyndon Baines Johnson created the National Commission on the Causes and Prevention of Violence in America to evaluate conditions that had led to the domestic turmoil: assassinations, antiwar protests, inner-city riots. A portion of the report submitted by the Media Task Force in December 1969 was a huge volume titled *Violence and the Media*. Among other findings, it included essays that linked violent media content to violent social behavior. The report suggested that portrayals of violence on television dominated the schedule (80 percent of programs) and refuted the networks' claim that violence had been reduced. The report implied that violent TV content was a contributor to turmoil in the streets. George Gerbner's violence index—a technique for counting the number of violent acts on a TV show—was the measurement used.[15] It was and remains a controversial instrument because of its all-inclusive definition of violence; it includes comic action and does not adequately adjust for the explicitness or degree of the violent act and its outcome. The report implied that television was culpable, and because television was and is a very visible target, lingering doubts remain.

Further political discussion and public disturbances led to *Television and Social Behavior: The Surgeon General's Report*, which was completed by the Surgeon General's Scientific Advisory Committee on Television and Social Behavior. The Surgeon General was directed by Congress, at the urging of Senator Pastore, to study TV violence as a public-health hazard. The committee's selection, research decisions, and summary report were all controversial. The political debacle that followed the report involved the blackballing of social scientists by the TV industry; the revelation of questionable funding practices; and the publication of the much-criticized, politically compromised summary volume (*Television and Growing Up: The Impact of Televised Violence*), which many of the researchers felt misrepre-

---

[15] George Gerbner, Larry Gross, Michael Morgan, and Nancy Signorielli, "The 'Mainstreaming' of America: Violence Profile Number 11, " *Journal of Communication* 30, no. 3 (Summer 1980).

Figure 23.4 *Violence on television and in films grew considerably more graphic in the late 1960s and early 1970s. The explicitness of the violence in both Stanley Kubrick's* Clockwork Orange *(1971) and Francis Ford Coppola's* Godfather *(1972) caused a considerable uproar, because both films were works of art and therefore very powerful. Gratuitous scenes of violence do not appear in these two movies, but the concern of pressure groups is that these films open the door for lesser works that do exploit graphic scenes of violence. (Photo: Movies Star News, Courtesy of Warner Brothers, Inc.)*

sented the findings of their 23 reports. In the studies, Gerbner continued to find high levels of violence in his content analyses; other researchers found that television can teach aggressive behavior; still other researchers decided that TV viewing decreases with age and developed a sociocultural description of those prone to excessively violent behavior; and content analyses described how the media portrayed an America with few blacks and Hispanics and depicted traditional stereotypes of women. In effect, the report seemed to repeat previous work and appeared to be an unwise expenditure of funds. It was widely quoted and roundly criticized. Senator Pastore, was so unhappy with the hedging and qualifications of the summation that he instituted another round of hearings to get to the bottom line—that television had a provable causal relationship with negative human behavior and needed to be changed.

In 1967, Congress established through Public Law 90–100 the Commission on Obscenity and Pornography, which, on September 30, 1970, submitted its report. The report contradicted many strongly held beliefs of politicians and citizens alike. The commission's majority report has gone the way of many other scientific-bureaucratic undertakings. The findings of the commission have been attacked, and the report's proposed legislation has been ignored.

The members of the Commission on Obscenity and Pornography were unable to reach unanimous agreement on the effects of obscene material.

The findings of the majority are these:

1. In the nonleglislative area, the major media involved in providing pornographic materials are paperback books, magazines, and films; however, with the advent of the new cassette videotape units, pornographic materials have become available more readily for use in the home.

2. In the legislative area, all local and state laws as well as federal statutes (Statutes 18 U.S.C. Sec. 1461, 1462, and 1465; 19 U.S.C. Sec. 1305; and 39 U.S.C. Sec. 3006) prohibiting the sale of pornographic materials to consenting adults should be repealed, because

    a. There is no empirical evidence that obscene materials cause antisocial attitudes or deviant behavior, although the material is sexually arousing.

    b. Increasingly, large numbers of persons (most frequently middle-aged, middle-income, and college-educated males) use pornography for entertainment and information, and these materials even appear to serve a positive function in healthy sexual relationships.

    c. Public-opinion studies indicate that the majority of Americans do not support legal restriction of adult uses of pornography and legal attempts to control the distribution of obscene material have failed.

    d. Obscenity laws are an infringement on Americans' constitutionally guaranteed right to freedom of speech.[16]

The commission also stated that although the empirical evidence suggests that pornography is in no way harmful to children, on ethical grounds, obscene material should not be made available without direct parental consent to persons under 18. The commission also argued that unsolicited mailings and public displays should be prohibited.

In other words, the majority of commissioners believed that there is no empirical evidence that pornography is harmful and that government at all levels should repeal obscenity laws for consenting adults. Three members of the commission objected to the findings on moral grounds (as did the Nixon administration) and questioned both the scientific studies and legal interpretations of the majority report of the Commission on Obscenity and Pornography.[17]

Erotica in the mass media is sexually oriented content that has as its purpose the physical and emotional arousal of the consumer. Books, magazines, and films are the traditional mass media for erotica, but sound recordings, cable television, and videocassettes are active in the distribution process. *Erotica* is a cultural term, whereas the word *pornography* has a legal, albeit a vague and arbitrary, definition at times.

---

[16] *The Report of the Commission on Obscenity and Pornography* (New York: Bantam Books, 1970), pp. 53–72.

[17] Ibid.

Pornography is any obscene material. Obscenity is based on these legal criteria:

1. The dominant theme, taken as a whole, must appeal to a prurient (morbid and unhealthy) interest in sex.
2. The material must be patently offensive and affront contemporary community standards.
3. The material must be without redeeming social value.

If a book or movie is shown to possess all three characteristics, it is legally obscene; in some communities, the distributor, exhibitor, and seller are liable for prosecution for making such material available to the public. A major change in dealing with pornography was the ruling by the Supreme Court in 1973 that "community standards" are local, not national. This means that something can be erotica in San Francisco but pornography in a small town in the Midwest. In 1987, the Court once again broadened the definition of *community* and implied a national standard.

Pornographic content falls within the definition of erotica, but not all erotica is obscene. The intensity of erotic stimuli varies from mild "cheesecake" photos to explicit "stag films." Research in the field is in its infancy because of social pressures and other difficulties in conducting it and because of problems in obtaining financial support. In general, mild erotica seems to generate a pleasurable emotional state in subjects, but there appears to be a link between erotica and aggressive behavior. There may also be a systematic transfer of sexual energy to negative kinds of behavior if other release is not possible. Arousal from erotica seems to have two major response patterns: if the material is perceived as entertaining, the subjects usually enjoy it; but if the subjects are bored, their response borders on disgust. Interestingly, the higher the arousal level, the more likely it is that the material will be judged pornographic. Studies also indicate that satiation occurs with repeated exposure, and the subject loses interest. Recent studies also seem to indicate that male and female responses are growing more alike and that exposure to erotica and the resultant arousal levels affect how subjects perceive attractiveness in others and the receptiveness of others to their own sexuality.

Limited research has been done relating erotica to anxiety, guilt, socially threatening situations, liberal or conservative views, and intellectual versus anti-intellectual variables. Without question, additional research is necessary before any final conclusions can be reached, but new findings suggest that arousal from sexual material may instigate more aggressive behavior than arousal from violent content. Relatively little experimental research takes place on this topic because of the difficulties in finding financial support and research subjects. William Masters and Virginia Johnson, among others, continue medical research on human sexuality that is tangentially related to this topic. One hopes that it may provide the necessary insights into this area of mass media content.

CURRENT RESEARCH ON THE MASS MEDIA

Before 1971, there were approximately 300 research titles relating to media effects. Over the next 10 years, another 2,500 works appeared. Thus about 90 percent of the research on media effects is recent.[18]

Most of that research revolves around three key words: *television* (medium); *violence* (content); and *children* (audience). Thus what is really the subject of the research is the effect of televised violence on children.

Television is studied because it is the most pervasive medium in human history. Children are studied because they are perceived as the most vulnerable audience segment and because they spend a significant amount of time watching television.[19] Violence is focused on because it is a central dramatic action in most TV programs and because there are very real concerns about its impact on youngsters.

Two other areas of interest to researchers are the effects of TV advertising on children and the effectiveness of television in imparting prosocial attitudes and behaviors to children.

Televised Violence and Children

Television is one of the most active participants in the socialization of the young. Television consumes more time in children's preschool lives than does any other waking activity. It is second only to school and, later, work as they grow up. There is evidence that heavy TV viewing by children can lead to unimaginative play and cause them to develop a negative view of the world. Children are relatively passive viewers of audiovisual thrills, and viewing is habituating.

Children's emotional responses tend to fall along a continuum from joy to excitement to surprise to fright to distress to fear. Youngsters seem to enjoy mild fright, and they seek out TV programs that produce this emotion.

There can no longer be any question that TV violence is arousing and that arousal can lead to aggressive behavior in normal children. The research overwhelmingly substantiates these premises. Under very special circumstances, aggression can become antisocial behavior. Audience research gives a relatively clear picture of the child who is an inordinately heavy viewer of television as one who is *habituated*.

---

[18] Robert M. Liebert, Joyce N. Sprafkin, and Emily S. Davidson, *The Early Window: Effects of Television on Children and Youth,* 2d ed. (New York: Pergamon Press, 1982). This work provides a comprehensive review of the research literature and expresses the major social concerns of political-action groups and social scientists. It is highly recommended for anyone interested in a secondary source on this topic. It is a major resource on prosocial behavior.

[19] U.S. Department of Health and Human Services, *Television and Human Behavior: Ten Years of Scientific Progress and Implications for the Future,* 2 vols. (Washington, D.C.: Government Printing Office, 1982). This project was funded by the National Institute of Mental Health and is a truly superior literature review and summary. The research volume contains a number of studies not otherwise available. It is highly recommended and serves as the major source for the section on TV violence and children.

Among children, there is also a correlation between heavy TV viewing and lower socioeconomic background, and children from disadvantaged homes rate violent behavior as more acceptable and more enjoyable to view on television than do youngsters from more economically advantaged backgrounds. In addition, children whose parents are heavy TV viewers invariably imitate that behavior.

We also know that children who are heavy viewers of television seek out violent programming and that as they grow older, they differ from light viewers of television in the following ways. Heavy TV viewers believe that there is more violence in the world they live in, are more accepting of violence in their society, and are more distrustful of others.

Socially deviant children who are prone to violent behavior enjoy violent TV content, and their exposure to TV violence stimulates antisocial behavior in the real world. Unquestionably, the viewing of TV violence by emotionally disturbed youngsters must be viewed as a *catalyst* for, if not a cause of, aggressive, antisocial actions. The correlation is stronger in boys than in girls.

Intervention of Adults. The research literature indicates that the single most important intervening variable in mitigating the negative effects of television is the parent (or older sister or brother or other adult), who acts as an opinion leader. Adults can take positive action regarding children's TV viewing by setting an example and avoiding habitual viewing patterns; by controlling the amount of time spent viewing; by supervising the kinds of programs viewed; and by viewing television with children and interacting with them before, during, and after the exposure.

A child does not have an inalienable right to view as much television as he or she wants. When attractive alternative activities are made available, children can break habitual viewing patterns. Parents who do not participate in the viewing decisions of children, especially "problem" children, are creating a potentially serious social problem.

Research, unfortunately, indicates that parents in most American families do not restrict either how much television their children watch or what TV shows their children view. And seldom, if ever, do parents discuss TV programs with their children. One reason why most parents do not worry about their children's TV viewing may be that parents do not know how much television their children watch. Yet, even as parents fail to supervise their children, more than one-half of American adults express the opinion that excessive TV viewing is responsible for the poor state of education in the United States.

Adults must be made aware of the TV-viewing problem and must be encouraged to exercise their responsibilities. The alternative is to impose censorship on TV content, and that solution may be even more dangerous to the health of future generations.

Figure 23.5 Expertly crafted films, such as *Kramer vs. Kramer* and *Ordinary People*, are emotionally arousing for adults. Can you imagine their effect on unsupervised youngsters? They deal with young people's deepest fears: verbal aggression and intimidation, being unlovable and rejected, and divorce. They may have more of an impact on the young than the stylized violence in *Raiders of the Lost Ark* or the silly sex in *Porky's*. Parental reassurance is important after a child has seen a problem film. If viewed with the family, complex films have significantly less impact, especially if they are then discussed. (Photos: *Kramer vs. Kramer*, Movie Star News, Courtesy of Columbia Pictures, Inc. *Ordinary People*, Copyright © 1980 by Paramount Pictures Corporation. All Rights Reserved. Courtesy of Paramount Pictures Corporation.)

Television Advertising and Children[20]

Political-action groups have had limited success in changing TV advertising directed at children. Action for Children's Television (ACT) prodded

---

[20] National Science Foundation, *Research on the Effects of Television Advertising on Children: A Review of the Literature and Recommendations for Future Research* (Washington, D.C.: Government Printing Office, 1977).

the National Science Foundation into sponsoring a review of research about the effects of advertising on youngsters. The findings, which appeared in 1977, reported the following:

1. Children do not understand that the primary intent of advertising is to sell.
2. Children do not understand disclaimers.
3. Commercials on television are effective in developing active consumerism in children.
4. As a result of seeing TV commercials, children attempt to persuade their parents to make certain purchases, which sometimes leads to conflict between parents and children.
5. Very strong evidence exists that TV advertising generates product awareness but that children become less accepting and finally skeptical of advertising claims by the time they reach their teens.
6. Very young children have difficulty perceiving the difference between advertising and program content.

This report and other actions by ACT contributed to the following changes in TV advertising directed at children:

1. Children's vitamin ads were discontinued.
2. Characters in shows no longer sell products.
3. Advertising time is limited on weekends.
4. Premiums in association with breakfast cereals were discontinued.

Television and Prosocial Learning

If TV content can lead to antisocial behavior, it has the potential to be used to educate and socialize children in positive ways. Studies show that TV programs help children's cognitive process at the three levels from *perceiving* to *comprehending* to *remembering*. Researchers have found that the process improves with age but that the very young do not understand much of what they view and tend to forget the little that they do understand. Specialized program content can lead to imaginative play and positive behaviors, such as altruism, friendliness, and self-control. And studies have shown that special "diets" of controlled TV programs can result in prosocial behaviors among behaviorally disturbed children.

The development of prosocial learning content is suspect because it is associated with cultural "mind control." Some people believe that the imposition of selected socially acceptable, middle-class values may actually be a handicap to the disadvantaged children they are designed to help.

A number of TV series have attempted prosocial learning; among them are "Sesame Street," "The Electric Company," and "Mister Rogers's Neighborhood." All appear on public television. The three commercial networks, especially CBS, have in the past actively developed Saturday-

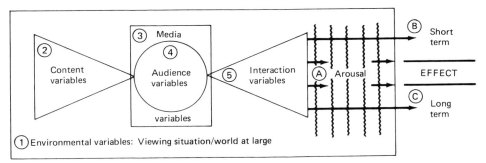

Figure 23.6 The Model of Media Effectiveness visualizes the interactive nature of the communication process. The eight elements of the model break into two groups: (1) the five variables that interact to produce (2) the three reactions, or effects of exposure, to mass communication. The modification of individual variables in any one of the sets affects the particular experience on specific individuals. The levels of arousal, short-term effects, and long-term impact depend on the nature of the environment, the type of content, the style of the medium, the personalities of the audience members, and the kinds of social interactions before, during, and after exposure.

morning programs—including "Fat Albert and the Cosby Kids," "The Harlem Globetrotters Popcorn Machine," "U.S. of Archie," "Shazam," and "Isis"—to impart positive social values. The CBS network also has conducted extensive research to determine the effectiveness of these shows. "After-school specials" at ABC use commercial techniques and rock music. The NBC network has generated fewer prosocial programs and less research.

The most researched TV series is the Children's Television Workshop's "Sesame Street." Some impressive results of the research indicate that children do learn as a result of watching the show. Nevertheless, children from disadvantaged families—the target audience of the series—are less likely to watch it than other children.

SUMMARY

The best way to understand the effects of mass communication is to summarize what we know into the Model of Media Effectiveness. This paradigm contains eight sets of elements. Five variables—environment, content, medium, audience, and interaction—lead to three types of reactions—arousal, short-term effects, and long-term impact.

Variables

There are five primary sets of variables in the Model of Media Effectiveness.

Environment. Environmental variables include the political, economic, and social conditions that exist at the time of exposure to a mass communication message. The radio broadcast "War of the Worlds" created panic partly because of the troubled economic situation and the dangerous international conditions in the 1930s. The environment itself also contributes to a medium's impact. The motion-picture theater, with its comfortable seats, large screen, and controlled environment, is relatively free of interruptions. But a dark house on a stormy night can be fearful for a child (or an adult) with or without TV violence.

Content. Content variables are manipulated by media artists. Most of the frightening films or TV programs we view use the following variables to arouse fear: explicit violence; a combination of erotic elements and violence; realism in the violent acts and settings; weapons of violence (knives are more threatening than guns or fist-fights); verbal aggression and threatening action, which have a strong impact on children; sympathetic villains, who are more difficult to understand than the traditional division between "good guys and bad guys"; identification of the audience with the characters, which makes violence directed at the characters more real (violence directed at youngsters and animals is the most fear-inducing for children); vulnerable characters; familiarity with continuing characters; and a relative powerlessness on the part of characters to control the situation.

Medium. Media variables refer to the style of the stimulus material using the inherent codes of a given medium. Loud music and flashy visual techniques—such as unusual camera angles, deep-shadow lighting, erratic camera movement, and rapid editing—contribute to arousal, regardless of content.

Audience. Audience variables are very significant because they involve the personality characteristics of individual audience members. Individuals who have had previous experiences with certain stimulus material react differently from those who are unfamiliar with it. Normal people respond differently from disturbed individuals. Any one person responds differently to even the same content based on his or her physical health or the degree of tension, anxiety, or stress he or she is experiencing.

Interaction. Interaction variables are dependent on the presence of others in the audience with whom we communicate before, during, and after the experience. Most of us have been "set up" by our friends to be frightened before a film begins. We have held one another's hands or tried to defuse tension by yelling or laughing. We have talked afterward to release our tension or have hidden around the corner and jumped out to startle others or have been startled by them. We know that children are less affected by violence when their parents also view the show and interact with them.

Reactions

The Model of Media Effectiveness also visualizes the reactions that the interacting variables produce as a result of the mass communication experience.

Arousal. Arousal is a straightforward, measurable response to a stimulus. Unquestionably, exposure to erotic content is biologically and sexually arousing for both men and women. In addition, exposure to fear-inducing and violent content stimulates human biochemistry and emotional reactions. That level of arousal is physiologically measurable. Anyone who has seen *Pyscho* or *The Shining* or *The Terminator* or *Rambo: First Blood, Part II* or *Aliens* can attest to sweaty palms and shortness of breath and increased heart rate and tension in the pit of the stomach. Films such as these definitely arouse and frighten audiences. And most users of erotic and fear-inducing content seek out that material for the stimulation it provides.

Short-Term Effects. Short-term changes in comprehension, attitudes and values, and behavior have been observed, and much of that research has been corroborated by subsequent studies that have replicated the original work. Audiences laugh at cruelty because much humor is based on inhumane actions—from pratfalls to tasteless ethnic jokes. We cover our eyes, grab hold of the person next to us, scream out warnings to the hero, and cheer the demise of the villain in the throes of physical agony. The audience loves the class clown, who "smarts off" during a tense moment so that we can release our built-up tensions. Children in this heightened state have been observed to act out mild antisocial behaviors in laboratory experiments where there is no prosocial adult intervention. There is also evidence that a causal relationship exists between exposure to violent content and negative aggressive reactions in disturbed or emotionally confused adults. There is a link between exposure to nonsexual violent content and aggressive sexual behavior.

Long-Term Impact. On this issue, there is *some* evidence that repeated exposure to *some* kinds of content, in *some* kinds of environments, on *some* kinds of audience members leads to *some* kinds of long-term changes in behavior and attitudes. In other words, we think we know that there are long-term effects on individuals, subcultures, and society as a whole from repeated exposure to media content, but hard evidence is not yet available. The long-term changes occur; we recognize them historically, but we have problems measuring them. The difficulty remains in isolating mass media involvement from the other cultural currents at work in our personal lives and in our society. We know that the mass media contributed to the changes wrought by the civil-rights, women's, and gay movements. Some of us have lived through the so-called sexual revolution, the changes in the young from socially committed to hedonistic, the protests during the Vietnam War, the cultural engineering that has tinkered with role models and the family, the political swings from conservative to liberal to conservative, and the rise of conservative religious groups that are mounting a media attack for a return to earlier values and traditions. We know that the mass media have been, are, and will be involved in these swings in human behavior and beliefs. We know that the media have been a catalyst, if not the most active change agent in that process. But we suspect that we do not know the full power of the mass media to influence our lives and the world in which we live.

BIBLIOGRAPHY

Brown, Ray, ed. *Children and Television*. Beverly Hills, Calif.: Sage, 1976.

Bryant, Jennings, and Dolf Zillman, eds. *Perspectives on Media Effects*. Hillsdale, N.J.: Erlbaum, 1985.

Liebert, Robert M., Joyce N. Sprafkin, and Emily S. Davidson. *The Early Window: Effects of Television on Children and Youth*. 2d ed. New York: Pergamon Press, 1982.

Lowery, Shearon, and Melvin L. DeFleur. *Milestones in Mass Communication Research: Media Effects*. New York: Longman, 1983.

Milasky, Ronald J. et al. *Television and Aggression: A Panel Study*. New York: Academic Press, 1982.

Palmer, Edward L., and Dorr Aimee. *Children and the Faces of Television: Teaching, Violence, and Selling*. New York: Academic Press, 1980.

Pornography and Prostitution in Canada: Report of the Special Committee on Pornography and Prostitution. 2 vols. Ottawa: Canadian Government Publishing Center, 1985.

Rosengren, Earl Erik et al., eds. *Media Gratifications Research: Current Perspectives*. Beverly Hills, Calif.: Sage, 1985.

Rowland, Willard D., Jr. *The Politics of TV Violence: Policy Uses of Communication Research*. Beverly Hills, Calif.: Sage, 1983.

U.S. Department of Health and Human Services. *Television and Human Behavior: Ten Years of Scientific Progress and Implications for the Future*. 2 vols. Washington, D.C.: Government Printing Office, 1982.

24

Impact:
Mass Media and Society

In a republic such as ours, the mass media play a vital role. They serve as the central nervous system of the United States—the critical information chain that vibrates without pause. Since a democracy cannot succeed without the support of the people, mass communication networks allow the public and their representatives to interact on a rapid, responsive, representative basis. The government and the governed inform and shape each other using mass communication.

MEDIA POWER AND OUR ABILITY
TO HARNESS IT

The mass media have tremendous power, but can it be harnessed? Can we control the process of mass communication? The answer must be—*absolutely!* For if we do not do it, someone else will. And we may not like that someone or what he or she does.

Take, for example, the enormously expensive operation that put an astronaut on the moon. Why were American taxpayers willing to put billions of dollars into that venture rather than, say, clean up the inner cities or build low-cost housing? Part of the answer may be that the space program benefited from compelling mass communication. The officials of NASA (National Aeronautics and Space Administration) realized early that in order to get sufficient congressional appropriations of funds to send astronauts to the moon, they would have to inform the American people of their intentions and persuade the public to support the space program.

Figure 24.1 The American public has walked in space, landed on the moon, and grieved at the loss of the *Challenger* crew. We have participated in those experiences "live" via the power of the mass media, especially television. We were with astronaut Bruce McCandless when he conducted experiments in space. It is *our* space program. (Photo: Courtesy National Aeronautics and Space Administration.)

NASA encouraged full media coverage of the space effort. Television, radio, and the other mass media were there when the first American rocketed into orbit; through the media, millions participated in the event. Mass communication stimulated public interest, allowing NASA to build its case with Congress, the president, and the people. By the time of the *Apollo* flights, which landed an astronaut on the moon, worldwide interest had been captured.

An estimated 528 million people around the world witnessed the moon landing, which was broadcast live on television. In nations where home TV sets were not yet common, great crowds gathered in public squares to watch the event on television. James Clayton, a *Washington Post* writer, referred to the *Apollo 11* flight as the most massive publicity effort in the history of the world. He meant that without the tremendous public exposure, NASA would not have been so successful.

In 1986, the disastrous *Challenger* accident and the investigation that followed received full media coverage. After a month or two, the tumult quieted down, and NASA went back to work. The news media covered the event; the country benefited; and the shuttle will fly again. That is how and why the American media work. It is the people's right to know and decide.

Presidents Gerald Ford and Jimmy Carter, both bright and good men, failed to kindle enough public support to be reelected. President Ford was unfairly characterized in the media as physically inept, and he lacked "media magic." Looking back on President Carter, the failure of his administration to solve the Iranian crisis—played out live and in color on television—was undoubtedly a major reason for his failure to win another term. President Carter's fall from power was not measured in loss of political clout, but in his disappearance from the front pages and television screens of America. The most powerful office in the world was media vacant for the last three months of the Carter administration. Ronald Reagan was already the focus of the news.

President Ronald Reagan is constantly under the media microscope because the presidency is central in a news environment that is insatiable. Whether one supports this president's policies or not, his media skills are second to none, not even John F. Kennedy, who was the darling of the news Establishment. President Reagan is a self-professed conservative ideologue, committed to doing what he set out to do. He has kept his promises to lower taxes, check domestic spending, reduce inflation, rebuild defense capability, and stand up to the Russians. He ran on these issues, and he has been true to his campaign pronouncements. Ronald Reagan communicates with courtesy, charm, witty self-deprecation, and goodwill. The press and the public have not always agreed with his policies, but it is hard to find fault with his style.

It is not only presidents who have the ability to harness media power. You must believe that ordinary citizens can, and do, have their say in America.

You can—you must—help harness media power for yourself, for those you love, for the things you believe in, and for the nation. Activists as well as audiences shape mass media and the media policies that affect America.

American public opinion is shaped by the ideas, information, and analysis provided by mass communication. The media play their roles very effectively and therefore are powerful instruments of stability and social progress. The mass media are neither saviors nor destroyers of our society, however. It is the people who gain access to and make skillful use of mass

Figure 24.2 They call him the "Great Communicator." And indeed he is. His mastery of communicating via the media with Americans is unmatched in history. He has personal style, grace and charm, and personal vision. Many disagree with that vision, but few fail to recognize his ability to express it. History will be his judge, but he may well turn out to be the first master of "the electric presidency." (Photo: AP/World Wide Photos.)

media who determine both positive and negative media contributions in this country.

HISTORICAL PERSPECTIVE

Harold A. Innis, a Canadian economic historian, was a pioneer in examining the effects of media on human activity. He was concerned primarily with the study of different currencies that various societies used, from bartering to beads and shells to coins to printed money. He came to the conclusion that the currency used by a society influences the nature of its commercial activity and its daily life style. He found that the printing of money had an important impact on the economics and politics of a society, and he thus posed the proposition that "Western civilization has been profoundly influenced by different media of communication."[1]

The Power of the Printed Word

The most influential communication development prior to the twentieth century occurred in 1450: Johannes Gutenberg's invention of movable type, which made mass-production printing possible. One of the first books to be printed was the Bible. Before the invention of the printing press, only the privileged few owned hand-copied Bibles. In fact, Bibles were so rare and precious that they were usually kept locked in the inner sanctums of churches and monasteries, and access to them was limited to those of high priestly rank. Those who had access to a Bible had great power to interpret the word of God for their own benefit.

The printing of the Bible changed the power of the Church and brought about a religious revolution. A Catholic priest, Martin Luther, who was born in Germany 30 years after the invention of the printing press, ultimately declared that his conscience was more important to him than was the pope in Rome, and thus he started the Reformation and the Protestant religion.

Luther felt that all people should be able to read the word of God for themselves and conduct themselves according to their own consciences, not according to the dictates of a priesthood. He translated the Bible from Latin into vernacular German (virtually inventing the German language in the process). When laymen could read the Scriptures, priests could be challenged in their role as mediators between the laity and God. Martin Luther understood the impact of the printed word, and he devoted much of his life to using it for his purposes. He was the most prolific serious writer in history; one edition of his works exceeds 100 volumes.

George Will, writing in 1983 on the five-hundredth anniversary of Luther's birth, called him "the first great life bound up with mass communication. . . . Luther showed how the tangible (a new technology, printing) can shape the intangible (the idea of an institutional church)."[2] Certainly, the Christian religion has never been the same since the invention of movable type.

Other revolutionary movements, in politics, economics, and science, occurred because of the printed word. The printed word made possible the rise of science by allowing facts and observations to be gathered and shared so that new and more valid conclusions could be drawn about the universe. Books could carry the message that the world was round, not flat. Less than 50 years after the invention of printing, Christopher Columbus set sail across the Atlantic and did not fall off the edge of the earth.

---

[1] Harold A. Innis, *Empire and Communications* (Toronto: University of Toronto Press, 1972), p. 14.

[2] George Will, "Luther's Quest," *Washington Post*, November 10, 1983, p. A21.

One can easily conjecture that without the printed word, the New World would not have been colonized by Europeans until a much later date.

The printed word also made possible the transfer of economic and commercial information necessary to the conduct of business. A new mercantile class, armed with information, arose to challenge the economic and political monopolies of the landed aristocracy. Out of the mercantile class came the middle class, which profoundly changed the economics and politics of Western civilization.

The printed word also brought about the political revolution that replaced monarchical and authoritarian governments with democracy and libertarianism. The printed word gave citizens access to information, and armed with the power of information, they could demand that governments serve their needs rather than the needs of the governors. These new revolutionary political ideas, culminating in the American and French revolutions, probably had their most succinct expression in the Declaration of Independence, which Thomas Jefferson penned to justify the withdrawal of the 13 colonies from the control of the British monarchy.

Indeed, without mass media, America as we know it would not exist. It was the printed word—broadside and pamphlet—that induced masses of Europeans to immigrate to the New World. Without the colonial weekly newspaper, the war against the British Crown would probably not have been fought or, if fought, would probably not have been successful.

From the founding of the country to the present day, mass media have played an important role in nearly all the important events of the nation. Antislavery publications, such as *Uncle Tom's Cabin*, did much to foment the Civil War, as did the newspaper editorials of Horace Greeley and James Gordon Bennett. William Randolph Hearst's sensational headlines help spark the Spanish-American War. Crusading newspaper and magazine reporters and editors at the turn of the century—the so-called muckrackers—stimulated much-needed political reform and social legislation to America.

Acoustic Space, the Alphabet, and Electric Circuitry

Marshall McLuhan, a scholar of English literature, startled and inspired the intellectual world of the mid-twentieth century with his ideas that media are more important than the messages they carry. The "medium is the message," he declared, and that single phrase reshaped much of our thinking about the impact of mass communication. McLuhan also suggested that human history can be divided into three great stages, each of which is caused by the dominant medium of the time.

In the first stage, the pre-alphabet, pre-written-language age, people lived in acoustic space. They knew only what they could hear and see in their immediate environment. Their world was small and tribal, governed by the group's emotions of the moment, a world of mystery and communal participation. Even today, in the few primitive societies that remain on

Earth, in which there is no written or mass communication, the inhabitants live in a culture of good and evil spirits rather than of laws, of feeling and emotion rather than of ideas and information.

The second great stage was marked by the development of alphabets, forcing people to think in logical terms. The advent of writing as the dominant mode of communication made people think in a linear, connected, and continuous fashion. One could think for oneself; become an individual separate from the tribe; and develop a rational universe, governed by laws based on logic, and a logical pattern of thought that could lead to science, invention, technology, an industrial society, the assembly line, and mass production.

The third great stage, according to McLuhan, came with the development of the electric media, starting with the telegraph in the nineteenth century. The electric media changed the linear way of thinking, making the aural and tactile senses important again in the perception of messages. High-speed information, sent over far distances by means of electronic waves, are changing our sense of time and space, reasoned McLuhan.

This third stage could be the most revolutionary. The electronic media may well be changing not only our perceptions, but also our thought patterns, our life styles, our values, and even our way of governing ourselves. With electronic media, for example, we can slow down or speed up our recording of reality and thus change our perceptions of physical phenomena. Using high-speed film, we can photograph a drop of water falling into a glass and observe the spire of water that rises as a result, with a small ball on the top. That scene will never be observable to the naked eye. The electronic media can give us "instant replay," allowing us to observe a football play, for example, from many different angles—in slow motion or fast motion.

Indeed, football is a good example of a sport that is uniquely suited to color television. And baseball is a sport that is uniquely suited to printed newspapers. Baseball is a linear sport; one thing happens at a time: the pitcher winds up and then throws the ball; the batter swings, hits the ball, runs to first base, and then to second, third, and home, all in a chronological sequence. Baseball is a perfect newspaper sport because it can be written about in a logical, linear manner, even with a "line score," which denotes the progress of the game in a sequential manner. Football, on the contrary, is more explosive than linear. Literally dozens of things happen at once. Each of the 22 men on the playing field has his own assignment on any given play. It would be impossible to do football complete justice by writing about it in the old-fashioned newspaper style. But television can use a variety of cameras to capture the explosion of action, with instant replay, from different angles, reverse angles, zooms, stills, and slow motion. Baseball may have been America's national sport during its newspaper days of the mid-nineteenth to the mid-twentieth century, but in the age of television, football seems much more appropriate as a national passion.

THE MASS MEDIA
AND SIGNIFICANT SOCIAL ACTIONS

As we discussed earlier, the mass media are very active in the economic, cultural, and political fabric of our society. And in this free society, we demand that mass communication help us have the opportunity to understand events and the consequences of those events so that we can form our own opinions and then take appropriate action for ourselves, our beliefs, and our institutions.

In the past 30 years many critical events and social changes that have shaped our future have occurred. In some of those events—civil rights, women's rights, sexual rights, politics, and war—the mass media played and continue to play a significant role as information providers, opinion shapers, persuaders, and instruments of socialization. America's view of itself and the world is shaped by news reports, advertising and entertainment, editorial comments, fair-minded documentaries, and the blatant propaganda of rock music. The media were there with the events—more often than some of us wanted.

The Mass Media and Social Justice

If you are white, compare your feelings about blacks with those of your parents and grandparents. If you are black, how does your self-concept differ from that of your parents and grandparents? The TV spectacle "Roots" opened the eyes of many white Americans and encouraged black Americans to take pride in their African heritage. The images of blacks in "Roots" was light-years away from the images of slaves in *Birth of a Nation* and *Gone with the Wind*. Film and other mass media reflect the times in which they are made as much as the historical period they cover. Media are both agents of change and reflections of what society wants to believe at a particular time. Political and economic groups that control the media can also control the images on the screen.

The past three decades have been a "30 years' war" for civil rights, and mass media have been major weapons. Events in the news and entertainment media have become the conscience of America. Covert discrimination may continue in our society; lynchings, segregated public facilities, and attacks on peaceful demonstrations are gone because the media exposed them. The news media continue to expose the resurgence of racial bigotry—such as the 1987 problems of integrating the all-white county of Forsyth County, Georgia, and, make tragically, the traffic death of a black man chased by a gang of white youths in Howard Beach, New York. Racism remains a critical social issue.

Television was a major news instrument used by black Americans to carry their grievances to the American body politic. Events—parades, speeches, boycotts, sit-ins, marches, freedom rides—were staged for the media and the white power structure.

A blossoming TV news industry was ready to bring dramatic events into 8 of every 10 American homes when a black woman, Rosa Parks, refused to surrender her seat on a Montgomery, Alabama, bus to a white man. The Montgomery bus boycott of 1954 and 1955 was one of the first successful mass challenges to public segregation. It also produced a black leader for the news media, especially for television. The Reverend Martin Luther King, Jr., was a master propagandist. His low-key, reasoned, Gandhi-inspired approach to nonviolent protest was perfect for the news. Television helped make Dr. King a symbol of change.

Because the media often deal in stereotypes and power symbols, King was essential as a symbol for black progress in a white society. Only his objection to this country's Vietnam policy (before it became popular to object) cast a negative shadow on his media standing as a symbol of the need for black progress.

Because civil-rights protests were covered by the media, the federal government as well as the people of America were moved to action in the 1960s. A protest is worthless unless the people and the power structure know what is happening. The freedom rides organized by the Congress of Racial Equality (CORE); the marches led by the Southern Christian Leadership Conference (SCLC); the manifestos, posturings, and programs of the Black Panthers; the urban riots in Harlem, Watts, Newark, and Detroit—mass media highlighted them and pressured politicians to act.

Murdered whites and blacks and, ultimately, the murdered Dr. Martin Luther King became martyrs under the glare of television. The violence of riots and the senseless stupidity of beatings and killings were given full media treatment. The civil-rights movement was a media movement; and because of news coverage, civil-rights legislation was passed. The media could focus society's attention on events and make visible the cancer of a racist society.

The entertainment industry (sound recording, motion pictures, and television) was also involved. The blatant racism of *The Wooing and Wedding of a Coon*, the "Sambo" and "Rastus" series, *The Nigger*, and *The Birth of a Nation* were supplanted in the 1920s and 1930s by black "fools" and "mammys." The tragedy of such great talents as Stepin Fetchit, Willie Best, and Mantan Moreland was not that they played buffoons but that these were the only roles available to them and the only blacks that movie audiences saw. With a few notable exceptions—*Hallelujah, Heart in Dixie, Green Pastures*, and *Cabin in the Sky*—the screen was lily white. Few white Americans knew that a black B-film industry was flourishing under the talents of Oscar Micheaux and other independents throughout the 1940s.

The watershed year for black images in white media was 1949, when four problem films were released: *Home of the Brave, Lost Boundaries, Pinky*, and *Intruder in the Dust*. This last film is notable as the first Hollywood portrayal of an independent black man. In the 1950s, one black star, Sidney Poitier, saved dozens of whites and emerged as a visible hero and im-

Figure 24.3 *King* was produced as a special by NBC and celebrated the contribution made by Martin Luther King, Jr., to America. Coretta Scott King was played by Cecily Tyson and King, by Paul Winfield.

proved white impressions of blacks. He is the only black actor to have won an Academy Award for best actor (in *Lilies of the Field*). By the mid-1960s, the "age of Poitier" had paved the way for a number of black talents, including Lou Gossett, who won an Academy Award for best supporting actor in *An Officer and a Gentleman.*

An economically viable black urban audience made it possible for "black exploitation" films to emerge. The superbad heroes of *Shaft, Superfly,* and *The Legend of Nigger Charlie* were important because black talent was providing black entertainment for black audiences. In the 1970s, both black and white directors produced a number of quality films—*Sounder, Lady Sings the Blues, Conrack, Claudine, Mahogany, The Wiz,* and *Blue Collar*— some of which centered on black living conditions in America.

A TV breakthrough came in 1965. After a virtual "whiteout" since the early 1950s, Bill Cosby starred in "I Spy." Cosby proved that black stars can attract high ratings, and he won two Emmy awards doing it. Many syndicated TV shows have featured black characters, and such shows as "Sanford and Son" and "The Jeffersons" pointed to the acceptance of a black style on television. "Julia," an often maligned series that starred Diahann Carroll, was important because it offered the example of a black professional woman making it in a white man's world. "The A Team," one of the

Figure 24.4 The hottest show on television at the present time is "The Cosby Show," and Bill Cosby's ads for a variety of products are testimony to his popularity among all Americans.

most successful TV shows, features a black character, Mr. T., who has become an international star. Also, Nell in "Gimme a Break" symbolized the emerging black identity on television.

In the late 1970s, "Roots" and "Roots II" validated early break-throughs. The public acceptance of "Roots" was evidenced by the highest ratings ever achieved by any program to that time. The combined minise-ries dealt with many issues that just a few years earlier would have been impossible to portray on television.

The key in both motion pictures and television was the presence of blacks in the shows and their acceptance by white audiences in a wide variety of roles. Blacks were no longer invisible. They lived and breathed and were heroes and villains. It was not a revolution, but it was a step forward; and the entertainment media were a part of the process of change.

Black ownership of broadcasting stations started to increase in the 1970s, and black radio has become a viable instrument in the advertising marketplace. In addition, special-interest magazines, such as *Ebony, Essence, Black Enterprise,* and *Players,* have continued to serve black readers. More job opportunities in all phases of the communication industry have also opened for blacks.

Figure 24.5 Today, Eddie Murphy is a star of the comedy circuit and of the music business and is one of the hottest properties in the motion-picture industry. His first three films—*48 Hours, Trading Places* (pictured here), and *Beverly Hills Cop*—have been box-office hits. *Beverly Hills Cop* is the largest selling videotape cassette in history. Murphy's brash, aggressive, street-smart characters are true delights to all his fans. (*Trading Places,* Copyright © 1983 by Paramount Pictures Corporation. All Rights Reserved. Courtesy of Paramount Pictures Corporation.)

Perhaps in no other medium does black artistic input dominate as it does in the recording industry. Traditionally, the entertainment entry point for blacks, records made by blacks now reach most white audiences. In the 1980s, Michael Jackson, a black singer, emerged as one of the most successful recording artists in history.

In all media, the fact that blacks appear as part of "the system" is a major change in the past 20 years. Tokenism still exists in mass media, but affirmative action is becoming a reality.

Without mass media, the progress made in civil rights may still have occurred, but not with the speed and impact that it did. Mass media have access to and influence on the power elites of this society. The media have challenged the old saw that you cannot legislate cultural change. Mass media have not done it on their own, but attitudes and behaviors on racial issues have changed because of what all of us read, heard, and saw in the media.

The Mass Media and Sexual Politics

Mass media are in the process of overhauling their presentation of women in America. It is fruitless to argue over whether mass media changed society's attitudes toward women or whether a changed society modified the media's portrayal of women. The best approach may be to accept the fact that a vital interaction took place. Most assuredly, a relationship exists between how men and women view themselves and each other and what media culture holds up as role models.

For the most part, the women's movement has made better use of the print media than it has of the electronic media. Women have had easier access to print, print costs are lower and offer a wide range of media vehicles, and more women are trained to write than are trained to use radio, television, and film. Books and magazines have been, by far, the most successful information and propaganda instruments of feminists.

Simone de Beauvoir's *Second Sex,* Betty Friedan's *Feminine Mystique,* Kate Millett's *Sexual Politics,* magazines such as *Ms.* and *Working Woman,* and myriad other media vehicles were involved in observing, redefining, and advocating new roles for women in society. Even such traditional magazines as *Cosmopolitan, Redbook,* and *Women's Day* have moved in new directions. Counterproposals to women's liberation ideas have also been mounted in the print media, most notably *The Total Woman,* which advocates a more conservative approach to male–female relationships.

The news media have assisted and resisted women's groups when staged events and other protests have occurred. By any measure, women's-rights events are covered more sparingly and less enthusiastically than were civil-rights stories in the 1960s. This is, in part, because the women's movement is *decentralized,* which makes it difficult for journalists to cover several groups that often seem to be at ideological odds; *localized,* made up of essentially independent local groups so that the news media cannot always identify important issues; not *hierarchical,* which does not give media a leader to focus on; *not ritualized,* so that mass media sometimes cover events that make "poor news," such as conferences, women's studies, and women's centers; and *internally opposed,* with some women's groups in public opposition to the goals of the movement—for example, passage of the Equal Rights Amendment.

The most significant progress in electronic journalism has been the increasing number and responsibilities of newswomen. The cumulative effect of daily TV appearances of Judy Woodruff, Connie Chung, and Jane Pauley on news shows and broadcasts has been important in consciousness raising, and affects the attitudes of men as well as women on a wide range of issues.

Some of the better TV series in the 1980s included "Kate and Allie" and the once-canceled "Cagney and Lacey," which a viewer letter-writing campaign succeeded in reinstating. The independent, intelligent women portrayed in these shows are a far cry from the earlier stereotypes of TV women in "I Love Lucy," "My Friend Irma," and "Father Knows Best." The new TV women can take care of themselves and, if they have to, can handle the bad guys in "Police Woman," the first successful adventure series with a woman (Angie Dickinson) in the title role. One of the biggest hits on television, now in syndication, "Charlie's Angels," stars rough-and-tumble beauties catered to by an affable male backup who is constantly in need of their help. This show's basis is sex, but it does present a new-for-television stereotype of women.

Even daytime soap operas and the TV commercials that sponsor them have changed their appeal for the stay-at-homes. The "soaps" are now peopled with career women involved in the business and professional worlds. Commercials project an image of women as attractive, childless, and wage earners, with male friends and husbands who are "liberated" as well as good-looking. Even if the TV characterizations of women have not come of age, signs of change exist.

In the motion-picture and sound-recording industries, the opportunity to express opinions corresponds with the ability to sell tickets and records. No woman at present can match the success of Barbra Streisand, an accomplished singer and actress who was also the executive producer of the rock remake of *A Star Is Born*. Her dominance in that film and her

Figure 24.6 Jane Fonda, Lily Tomlin, and Dolly Parton confront their sexist boss, played by Dabney Coleman, in *9 to 5*, truly a comedy for the working woman. The film was part of a series of films that attempted to integrate the themes of the women's movement into the story line. It certainly proved successful at the box office.

performance of "The Women in the Moon" is a political messag
ful as Helen Reddy's "I Am Woman." These songs may have
cultural impact than the amateur "librock" bands of the 196(
Streisand and Reddy reach audiences outside the women's movement. In
the early 1980s, Streisand expanded her roles, becoming actress, com-
poser, director, and producer of *Yentl*, a widely successful Hollywood film.

The very late 1970s and early 1980s saw the rebirth of "women's movies." The significant difference was that the women's roles included new
stereotypes and themes that are traditionally the province of male stars.
The films starring Jane Fonda, including *Klute, Julia, The Electric Cowboy, 9
to 5, Coming Home,* and *On Golden Pond,* display a broad range of heroines,
many of whom deviate from older Hollywood types. Many films—*Norma
Rae* (Sally Field), *Coal Miner's Daughter* (Sissy Spacek), *The Women's Room*
(Lee Remick), *Playing for Time* (Vanessa Redgrave), *The Turning Point* (Anne
Bancroft and Shirley MacLaine), *Terms of Endearment* (Shirley MacLaine and
Debra Winger), among others—offered fine women's parts.

The interpersonal-communication process has been central to the development of issues and platforms of the women's movement. For most
women, the key means of dissemination in mass media was print. Although the electronic media as a whole have been less supportive of wom-
en's crusade for equality than they were in the quest of black Americans for
civil rights, media images and media opportunities for women are growing
at a rapid rate.

The Mass Media and Human Rights

The sexual revolution that has taken place in our society in the past 30
years was begun, as was the women's movement, not by the mass electronic media, but by the more specialized print media. But in both cases,
and in the case of civil rights as well, the electronic media no doubt
changed Americans' perceptions of civil rights, women, and sex to make
possible the acceptance of the radical ideas espoused by the more specialized print media.

The sexual revolution really started with writers of books for very
narrow and specialized audiences. Their notions of sexual freedom finally
found their way into men's magazines that reached a national audience
with *Playboy,* which was started in the mid-1950s. The "*Playboy* philosophy" of sexual permissiveness and frank sexual pleasure had considerable
influence on other magazines and books, but it did not creep into such
mass media as newspapers, radio, television, or publicly shown motion
pictures until a decade or two later. Even in the late 1980s, the mass
media—prime-time television, metropolitan newspapers, national news
magazines—shy away from nudity and obscene language.

But these media have made a steady progression toward more sexual
explicitness. In 1972, ABC produced a prime-time drama called *That Certain
Summer,* which examined a homosexual relationship. Yet it was not until

Figure 24.7 Kathleen Turner is the newest in a long line of *female fatales*, and yet she brings a true modern strength to the characters she plays— the "hit woman" in *Prizzi's Honor* and, even more daringly, the upper-middle-class professional woman who prowls the streets as a hooker at night in *Crimes of Passion*, pictured here with Tony Perkins. *Vanity Fair* found her glamorous in a cover layout. Turner is the epitome of the I-can-have-it-all school of the modern woman.

1980 that a sitcom, "Love, Sidney," could deal with homosexuality with some ease. In 1974, *A Case of Rape* was the first major TV drama to investigate that crime from a woman's point of view. It was not until October 1983 that a network soap opera, "All My Children," used a continuing character who was clearly a lesbian. In 1983, NBC produced *Princess Daisy*, a tentative look at a brother–sister sexual relationship. And in 1984, ABC produced a two-hour drama, *Something about Amelia*, which was the first frank and honest treatment on national prime-time television of an incestuous father–daughter relationship.

The gay-rights movement has been largely confined to specialized print media. There are now newspapers and magazines that cater to gays. But most daily newspapers and national TV programs still treat homosexuality as an aberration in society, not as normal behavior. The film industry has produced some feature films with gay central characters—*Suddenly Last Summer, The Fox, The Boys in the Band, Reflections in a Golden Eye, Fortune and Men's Eyes, The Ritz, Outrageous,* and *My Beautiful Laundrette.* But in most TV shows, only a very infrequent episode alludes to "the problem." With the exception of *That Certain Summer*, television has not concerned itself with the gay issue in any significant drama. A sizable portion of the specialized erotic film industry, however, does exploit this sexual preference in films produced for urban markets.

One of the major motion picture hits of the 1970s was *La Cage Aux Folles*, a comedy about an aging gay couple. It was a major box-office success and attracted largely "straight" audiences. It was so popular that *La Cage Aux Folles II* continued the gay escapades at movie houses around the world. The point was not that gay characters were everywhere on the screen, but that when the issue of homosexuality was presented, it no longer created a sensation. It was just a part of the media scene.

Perhaps no other current media issue carries the emotional impact for audiences as does the issue of gay rights. With increasing numbers of activists, the gay-rights issue is bound to receive increasing coverage in the mass media. Unlike reistance to civil rights and the women's movement, which is subtle and diffuse, open resistance to gay rights is a reality.

Today, the mass media are moving to explore the AIDS epidemic as a heterosexual disease. AIDS is "out of the closet," and ads for condoms are gaining media acceptability as a preventer of disease as well as a contraceptive device. In 1987, the British television networks devoted hours of time to encourage the use of prophylactics as *the* effective agent against AIDS in a sexually permissive society. However, American mass media still have not persuaded most Americans that AIDS is anything other than a disease that affects gays, drug users, and an occasional unfortunate soul who contracts the disease via a blood transfusion. There is real concern in the medical community that this virulent disease has the potential to be the "black plague" of the last decade of the twentieth century. The entertainment media are just beginning to probe the dramatic possibilities

Figure 24.8 Films have become much more daring in recent years regarding sexual themes. *The Boys in the Band* moved with its cast from Broadway to film and sensitively portrayed some of the concerns of the gay community. *Personal Best* explored not only women's sports, but also lesbian relationships. And the most camp film in history, *The Rocky Horror Picture Show,* starred Tim Curry as "that sweet transvestite from transexual Transylvania." But television is taking the most daring steps, portraying everything from AIDS to incest, with excellent results. *Something about Amelia,* starring Ted Danson and Glenn Close, is a truly moving and troubling drama. (Photos: *The Boys in the Band,* copyright © 1970 Cinema Center Films, all rights reserved, The Museum of Modern Art/Film Stills Archive; *Personal Best,* copyright © 1981 by Warner Bros. Inc.; *The Rocky Horror Picture Show,* copyright © 1975, 20th Century-Fox Film Corporation, all rights reserved; *Something about Amelia,* the Leonard Goldberg Company.)

of the medical/sexual emergency. As the BBC said, "Safe sex is for everyone."

The Mass Media and Military Conflict

Electronic communication has certainly changed the nature of both war and politics since the mid-twentieth century. War has now become a media event, covered in color video from helicopters as though it were a movie in the making.

Before the age of radio and television, coverage of warfare by the news media was limited to the printed word, which could be more controlled and was less vivid about the realities of war. Before the Vietnam War, the U.S. government maintained wartime security measures over news dispatches that were sent from the front lines, and all news copy went through a government military review, a form of wartime censorship. Reports sent from the war front on this basis were usually carefully guarded and subdued, and as a result, news readers never received the full gruesome details of war.

The Vietnam War, however, was never officially declared as a war, so there were no official censorship procedures. In addition, TV networks had pressed very hard for uninhibited coverage of the war, and politicians needed television to convince the American public of the rightness of the war. As a consequence, the Vietnam War was the first to be reported, often live and in living color, without any government restraints on the coverage. For the first time, the American people could really see the gory details of war, and, ironically, the government could not hide the futility of its efforts.

Without doubt, TV coverage played a role in turning American opinion against the war, to such an extent that the government ultimately had to withdraw from the battle. Indeed, it may never again be possible to have a war such as the one in Vietnam as long as television is permitted to cover it freely and fully. So the nature of war will be changed as a result of television.

When Great Britain went to war with Argentina in 1982 over ownership of the Falkland Islands, Prime Minister Margaret Thatcher kept the British news media away from the war zone, and so the battle could not be covered live. The British government reasoned that it would be easier to win the war without the "prying" press providing coverage that might stir up negative public opinion. The negative public reaction was still widespread, however, despite what many Britons viewed as a form of press censorship.

On October 25, 1983, armed forces of the United States of America invaded Grenada to evacuate American medical students and oust a Marxist, Cuban-backed, and Russian-supplied government that had recently murdered its elected leader, Maurice Bishop. American troops were welcomed by both the students and the majority of Grenadians. The troops were "surrounded by friendlies" as they quickly defeated the Grenadian and Cuban forces, who were just as quickly repatriated to Cuba. The General Assembly of the United Nations overwhelmingly condemned America's armed intervention, even though some delegates quietly approved of it.

During the invasion, the American press corps was "out of action." The press was not informed by the Reagan administration as to the immi-

Figure 24.9 This banner headline is part of what many feel is yet to come in the "war against AIDS." The mosquito, if indeed a carrier, has no concern about infecting male or female, gay or straight. The media must become more active and prosocial in the battle against this disease, if we are to combat AIDS effectively. (© 1987 New York News Inc.)

Figure 24.10 Only one feature about the Vietnam War was made while it was being fought—*The Green Berets*, starring John Wayne. After the war, two films explored the conflict with great commercial and artistic success—Michael Cimino's Academy Award–winning *Deer Hunter* and Francis Ford Coppola's masterpiece *Apocalypse Now*. The most interesting trends are the strongly pro-America films such as *First Blood* and *Rambo: First Blood, Part II*, which deal with the returned Vietnam vet in the adventure-film format. (Photos: *The Green Berets*, Warner Bros. Television Distribution, a Warner Communications Company; *Deer Hunter*, © 1987 Universal City Studios, Inc.; *Apocalypse Now*, copyright © 1979 by United Artists Corporation, all rights reserved.)

nence of the invasion and was not allowed into Grenada during the two days of battle. When reporters attempted to enter Grenada by fishing boats, they were turned back by the U.S. Navy.

The press corps fumed. The public yawned, although some chuckled that President Reagan had tweaked the noses of "the fourth estate."

The congressional leadership of both parties fell into line by invoking the War Powers Act. A congressional study group flew to Grenada and determined that, indeed, the invasion had been justified "under the circumstances."

The rescued students thanked the president. The Grenadians thanked the president. American public opinion thanked the president by giving him the highest ratings of his tenure in office; 63 percent of those polled said they felt he was doing a good job.

The press corps fumed some more.

Who lost? Certainly not the president—and, in the long run, not the news media. We, the people, lost because a serious precedent had been set that abridges our freedom of communication.

Why were Americans not more concerned? Perhaps because we had won quickly and turned out to be the good guys for a change. And perhaps because we have become somewhat less than enamored of the egotistical exercise of power by some reporters, news stars, and ambush journalists, and by the news apparatus in general.

The British and the American governments succeeded in keeping the press out of those two engagements because they were short. If they had been long, drawn-out battles, the media and the public would no doubt have insisted on full coverage. The lessons that have been learned from all this, it seems, is that war can succeed if it amounts to quick skirmishes away from the limelight of media coverage. And wars of the future might be like that.

The electronic age has also spawned another kind of war—terrorism—in which the terrorist strikes in order to gain national or international publicity for political purposes. The taking of American hostages in Iran was an example of terrorist action motivated by the interest in achieving worldwide publicity for Iran's anger at the United States. Individual terrorist acts, aimed at getting electronic coverage, have become all too common in the electronic age. An American military officer is kidnapped in Italy, not for financial ransom, but for political publicity. A radical hijacks an airplane full of civilian passengers, not to get a free ride to his destination, but to get reporters to give some coverage to his point of view. An elderly gentleman fills a van of dynamite and drives it up to the Washington Monument, threatening to blow it up, not to satisfy some irrational or insane motive, but to warn the world of nuclear war.

THE MASS MEDIA, FREEDOM OF COMMUNICATION, AND THE CRITICAL CONSUMER

Can we agree that the media are powerful and have lasting impact on our society? Probably!

Do we, as a nation, agree to freedom of speech—freedom of mass communication? Probably not! Repeatedly in surveys, Americans do not recognize passages from the Bill of Rights and object to them as un-American.

The greatest danger we face is not someone conquering us and taking away our freedoms, but our giving them up unknowingly because we fail to realize we have them, do not understand their value, or believe someone else might abuse the privilege, especially the news fraternity.

Freedom of Communication

The purpose of freedom of speech, freedom of assembly, and freedom of the press is to guarantee the citizen's freedom of communication and create the potential for an informed electorate, one that is capable of making educated decisions, to emerge. "Free" speech, assembly, and press are not without costs. Maintaining these freedoms often involves struggle. A free press, for example, may step on the toes of members of powerful interest groups. A free press also has responsibilities and must coexist with the other rights Americans enjoy.

Our society is information dependent, but there are clouds on the horizon concerning a citizen's rights to inquire about what the government is doing and disclose that information to other citizens. Floyd Abrams, a noted attorney who specializes in constitutional law and represents media clients, summarized a series of disturbing events in 1983 in the *New York Times Magazine*.

A month ago today, the Reagan administration publicly released a contract that has no precedent in our nation's history. To be signed by all Government officials with access to high-level classified information, it will require these officials, for the rest of their lives, to submit for governmental review newspaper articles or books they write for the general reading public. . . .

The new requirement, warns the American Society of Newspaper Editors, is "peacetime censorship of a scope unparalleled in this country since the adoption of the Bill of Rights in 1791." . . .

In the two and a half years it has been in power, the Reagan administration has:

- Consistently sought to limit the scope of the Freedom of Information Act (F.O.I.A.).
- Barred the entry into the country of foreign speakers, including Hortensia Allende, widow of Chilean President Salvador Allende, because of concern about what they might say.
- Inhibited the flow of films into and even out of our borders; neither Canada's Academy Award-winning "If You Love This Planet" nor the acclaimed ABC documentary about toxic waste, "The Killing Ground," escaped Administration disapproval.
- Rewritten the classification system to assure that more rather than less information will be classified.
- Subjected governmental officials to an unprecedented system of lifetime censorship.
- Flooded universities with a torrent of threats relating to their right to publish and discuss unclassified information—usually of a scientific or technological nature—on campus.

So far, these efforts to control information have been noticed by those most directly affected, but by few others. The Administration's policies, says the American Civil Liberties Union, have been "quiet, almost stealthy, difficult to see and therefore hard to resist." There is also the feeling among many Americans that the actions of this Administration are less-than-threatening since they are fueled by the deeply felt conservative ideology of Ronald Reagan and not from the anger or meanness of spirit that, many feel, characterized the Nixon Presidency. Furthermore, wrote the Times's columnist Anthony Lewis, these actions "have had little attention from the press, perhaps because the press is not their principal target."[3]

The ability of citizens to discover the truth depends on the availability of countervailing opinions. The action that the current administration has taken concerning freedom of communication is restrictive at best, if not outright censorship. The administration's actions seriously impede our ability to make informed decisions. Our government must have more faith in "we, the people." What is most distressing in these events is the failure of the press to make us adequately aware of the consequences of these abridgements of our freedom of communication. Most Americans do not even realize they are occurring.

There is a natural tension between the press we support and the government we elect. That tension is positive for citizens. If the press and the government ever join forces, we may be in for a bad time.

The press corps has had a "bad press" of late. The TV show "60 Minutes," CBS, and Dan Rather went to court; although they won the case, they lost prestige. Cristine Craft won, then lost, then appealed a sex-discrimination suit against Metromedia. Reporters have been caught faking pot parties. A series carried in a respected newspaper, the *Washington Post*, was fabricated by a staff writer.

Astronomical salaries for press "stars" have been demanded, paid, and reported with glee. News has become a "profit center" in local TV stations; "happy talk," not the news itself, is the centerpiece of the show. Newspeople have badgered mothers weeping over the loss of their children. They have trampled and littered the lawns of citizens whom they deem newsworthy. They have ambushed citizens on their doorsteps to discuss allegations of guilt. Too many members of the press corps have exhibited unfettered ambition and arrogance. A politician who behaved in a similar manner would be exposed to the most excruciating news coverage.

And, finally, there was the disastrous, down-played civil war at CBS News in the summer of 1986. The primary issues were the profitability and entertainment quotient of the network's newscast, which had lost its previously undisputed grasp on number 1 in the ratings heap. There was a clash between the public's right to be well informed and the corporation's right

---

[3] Floyd Abrams, "The New Effort to Control Information," *New York Times Magazine*, September 25, 1983, pp. 22–23.

Figure 24.11 Although the press reviews of *Absence of Malice* claim that the story in the film, starring Paul Newman, could never happen, the American public, at least the moviegoing public, loved the film and were delighted that the press and the politicians got what was coming. Americans are less trusting of the news media than at anytime in our history. (Photo: Copyright © 1981, Columbia Pictures Industries, Inc., all rights reserved.)

to make a profit. The news department at CBS is under a cloud of exposé's being published, of giving in to a "happy-talk" format for "The CBS Morning News," and of being sullied by the William Westmoreland libel trial in 1985. Andy Rooney and Bill Moyers were in revolt. And wholesale firings, based on money rather than news judgments, have occurred. Corporate evaluations of the evening news have wondered why it was not more like "Entertainment Tonight." CBS News lost sight of the fact that its traditional viewers wanted to know—even if the news was *bad*. Freedom is demanding; it requires making hard choices—choices that cannot be made unless the public is informed.

It was a "Bad Day at Black Rock"—the euphemism for CBS's corporate headquarters. The rebellion in the news room ultimately led to the resignation of the CBS News president and the chairman of CBS, Inc. Whether these actions will put the news back in the newscast is yet to be seen. How can the public not doubt the news, when it suspects the overpaid oracles who present it.

And the public yawned and changed channels to "Wheel of Fortune!"

As in all areas of power brokering, the news corps needs to get its ethics and responsibilities in order. This country can ill afford more incidents like the one involving the press in Grenada—not because of the government's action, but because of the people's lack of reaction to it.

The Specter of Censorship

Censorship in time of war is accepted as essential to national survival. The censorship of unpopular views in time of peace endangers the survival of our democratic ideals, if not our very democracy. Censorship need not come from Washington. More frequently, the pressure to censor comes from political-action groups, and it is often directed at libraries and schools. Unfortunately, it is successful moré than 50 percent of the time.

Let us consider one recent example of an attempt at censorship. On November 20, 1983, ABC's movie *The Day After* blew the lid off the TV ratings; 48 million homes, or 62 percent of the viewing audience, were tuned in to the program. Yet this $7 million production had difficulty finding sponsors because it focused on the controversial subject of the aftermath of a nuclear war, and advertisers that sponsored the program were threatened with boycotts of their products. The threat came from the Reverend Jerry Falwell and the Moral Majority as part of their campaign against politically sensitive programs. Falwell's request for equal time was refused by ABC. The network did broadcast a discussion of the issues raised by the film and included nationally recognized authorities with differing viewpoints in the discussion.

Censorship of the program failed, although in some areas the action succeeded. The *Tallahassee Democrat* carried the following story from the Associated Press wire service prior to the airing of the program:

> *St. Petersburg.* Pinellas County School officials have barred a high-school social-studies teacher from showing a taped version of the controversial television movie, "The Day After," to a senior class next week.
>
> The movie was to have been video-taped and shown as part of a curriculum on war at Pinellas Park High School.
>
> But Scott Rose, the school superintendent, told teacher Jim Scott and others Thursday not to show the movie because it had not been pre-screened and approved under guidelines for teaching controversial issues.
>
> "When the Pentagon makes a make-more-bombs movie, we will be able to show it," Scott said.
>
> The National Education Association has advised that the film not be shown to children under 12, and that parents of children ages 13–16 view it with them.[4]

Pressures that TV networks can withstand with relative impunity are often too strong for a school system to fend off. *The Day After,* viewed at home by millions of children, usually with their parents, was unacceptable in the classroom even with parental approval and adult supervision in a course related to the show's subject.

Public television is not immune to public pressure, especially when it comes from Congress, because Congress gives the dollars that keeps the

---

[4] "School Officials Ban Film," *Tallahassee Democrat*, November 18, 1983.

Figure 24.12 *The Day After* is not a great work of art, but it had the potential to generate the kind of discussion that is important to a free society. Government representatives have a right to disagree with one another and an obligation to express dissenting points of view. Pressure groups should not have the power to intimidate a school system or censor expressions of unpopular viewpoints regarding issues of national concern. The real danger in this episode is that it could make other producers too timid to dramatize controversial subjects. (Photo: Dean Williams. Courtesy American Broadcasting Companies, Inc.)

Corporation for Public Broadcasting (CPB) in business. "The Lawmakers," a series of puff pieces on Congress's favorite topic—itself and its members—was funded and aired by PBS stations and failed to draw even small audiences and a little respect. Stations dropped it, and the CPB discontinued funding it. Then the show's staff lobbied Congress and Congress got to the CPB, and son of "Lawmakers"—"Capitol Journal"—was born. The president has not been shy to pressure public television and has done so on a number of occasions. President Nixon was concerned over the hiring

Figure 24.13 The TV networks refused to carry the television version of this W. R. Grace & Company ad about the national debt, called "The Deficit Trials," because they feared that, in accordance with the Fairness Doctrine, they might have to give up valuable ad time to opposing viewpoints.

of Sander Vanocur and Robert MacNeil. President Carter, with support from Mobil, tried to prevent *Death of a Princess* from airing. The Reagan administration totally eliminated funding for the CPB from its first budget and, after it was restored by Congress, cut it back at a later date. Public television must have an economic shield between it and political pressure if the public is to be served and the program fund is to be protected from stacked CPB boards, such as the one appointed by President Reagan, which refused to support attempts to exchange TV programs with the Soviet Union. The board is not supportive of controversial programming. That is a form of censorship.

The Fairness Doctrine, which requires broadcasters to devote time to controversial issues and have contrasting views expressed on those issues, is under siege. But under the Mark Fowler–led FCC's deregulation policies, the broadcasters' claim that fairness "chills" their freedom of speech on controversial issues is being given a hearing. Since when does airing a countervailing viewpoint retard free speech? The FCC has publicly announced against the doctrine of fairness, as has the so-called Freedom of Expression Foundation. In general, audience interest groups support the Fairness Doctrine, regardless of where they stand in the political spectrum, and both liberal and conservative broadcasters oppose it. It has served the nation well for over half a century; should we give it up?

The Potential Problems in Media Power

High costs and enormous profits have led to a concentration of media power and information control in the hands of a limited number of sources located in the Northeast. Critics have spoken of an "elite" that controls media content. They have expressed fears that these "media barons" exercise undue influence on the social, economic, and political structure of the United States.

The rise of media giants and corporate conglomerates is an understandable consequence of our economic system, but it is bothersome. It smacks of too much control in the hands of a few, a small minority that is also driven by the profit motive. The alternative seems to be government ownership and control of the media, and this is unacceptable in our society.

Two problems have to be faced:

1. There must be easier access to the media for all segments of society.
2. The media must serve all the functions required of them and not only those that are profitable.

Access and responsibility are the key issues in media today.

The state of the mass media may not be as dire as some people think, however. Cheaper means of publication and production are becoming available. Photo-offset lithography, cold-type composition, and inexpensive paper are bringing down the costs of publishing a newspaper. In many towns and cities in America, new publications, most of them weeklies, are getting established on low budgets through offset printing.

Even the electronic media are becoming less expensive. Hand-held cameras and videotape equipment are being manufactured at prices that many people can afford. This has brought about so-called people's television-neighborhood and inner-city groups that produce closed-circuit telecasting for local viewers.

And in spite of the economic warnings (explored in Chapter 21), mass media in the United States are more varied in their ownership and ideological commitment than are media in any other country in the world. One study, undertaken in the greater Washington, D.C., area, found more than 250 discrete information media to be available to the average citizen. These media included daily and weekly newspapers, regularly published local newsletters and magazines, AM and FM radio, and commercial and educational television. The average American can choose among a vast array of media.

Obviously, the media are important to us, or we would not spend the time and money on them that we do. The mass media are not without problems, however, and it is of increasing importance that both average citizen and mass communication respond to these problems with a sense of responsibility.

SUMMARY

The mass media are truly powerful institutions in American society. They are involved in every aspect of our economic, political, and cultural systems. They demand much from our leaders, and no president has been more successful than Ronald Reagan in harnessing media power to implement his vision of the future. American public opinion is shaped by what we read, watch, and listen to in the mass media.

Historically, we can trace the influence of the media. Certainly Johannes Gutenberg's printing press did more than make books; it remade how people thought about the world. Martin Luther reshaped Christian theology as the first media minister—a tradition that America's television clergy participate in fully.

The media are revolutionary instruments because they massage the very societies that give birth to them. The press parented in Great Britain came to the colonies and turned our ancestors into rebels and founders of a new nation. The peace movement, the civil-rights movement, and the women's and gay-rights movements were all revolutionary and used the mass media to reshape the world to make it a better nation for all to live in.

If we are to have social justice today and freedom for the future, you—the critical consumer—must participate fully in the mass communication process. You must manipulate the mass media, or they will manipulate you.

BIBLIOGRAPHY

Adler, Richard P., ed. *Understanding Television: Essays on Television as a Social and Cultural Force.* New York: Praeger, 1981.

Ball-Rokeach, Sandra J. *The Great American Values Test; Influencing Behavior and Belief Through Television.* New York: Free Press, 1984.

Barber, James David. *The Pulse of Politics: Electing Presidents in the Media Age.* New York: Norton, 1980.

Barcus, F. Earle. *Images of Life on Children's Television: Sex Roles, Minorities, and Families.* New York: Praeger, 1983.

Berry, Gordon L., and Claudia Mitchell-Kernan, eds. *Television and the Socialization of the Minority Child.* New York: Academic Press, 1982.

Comstock, George, *Television in America*. Beverly Hills, Calif.: Sage, 1980.

Fighting TV Stereotypes: An ACT Handbook. Newtonville, Mass.: Action for Children's Television, 1982.

Gallagher, Margaret. *Unequal Opportunities: The Case of Women and the Media*. Paris: UNESCO, 1981.

Greenberg, Bradley et al. *Mexican Americans and the Mass Media*. Norwood, N.J.: Albex, 1983.

Hill, George H. *Airwaves to the Soul: The Influence and Growth of Religious Broadcasting in America*. Saratoga, Calif.: R. and E. Publishers, 1983.

Horsfeld, Peter G. *Religious Television: The American Experience*. New York: Longman, 1984.

Katz, Elihu, and Tama Sezecsko, eds. *Mass Media and Social Change*. Beverly Hills, Calif.: Sage, 1981.

Lake, Sara. *Television's Impact on Children and Adolescents: A Special Interest Resource Guide in Education*. Phoenix: Oryx Press, 1981.

MacDonald, J. Fred. *Blacks and White TV: Afro-Americans in Television since 1948*. Chicago: Nelson-Hall, 1983.

Pell, Eve. *The Big Chill: How the Reagan Administration, Corporate America and Religious Conversations Are Subverting Free Speech and the Public Right to Know*. Boston: Beacon Press, 1984.

Rubin, Bernard, ed. *Small Voices and Great Trumpets: Minorities and the Media*. New York: Praeger, 1980.

Shaheen, Jack G. *The TV Arab*. Bowling Green, Ohio: Bowling Green University Press, 1986.

Tuchman, Gaye et al., eds. *Hearthland Home: Images of Women in the Mass Media*. New York: Oxford University Press, 1978.

Wilson, Clint C., and Felix Gutierrez. *Minorities and Mass Media: Diversity and the End of Mass Communication*. Beverly Hills, Calif.: Sage, 1985.

25

The Future of Mass Media

In the 1950s, when television was bursting onto the scene as a new mass medium, media philosopher Marshall McLuhan envisioned a new world brought about by electronic communication. He saw all humankind sitting at the hearth of television, watching the same pictures. Television, he said, would draw us all together and return us to an oral society in which, as in preliterate societies, spirit and feeling would replace the linear logic of the age of print, which had brought about the assembly line, mass production, and mass communication.

Indeed, in the 1950s, 1960s, and 1970s, television did bring us together in a way that mass communication had never done before. Almost everyone saw Milton Berle, Ed Sullivan, and Sid Caesar; Jackie Gleason in "The Honeymooners"; Lucille Ball in "I Love Lucy"; and Jack Parr on "The Tonight Show." The whole nation watched in shock as police dogs attacked civil-rights marchers; watched in grief as John F. Kennedy, Martin Luther King, Jr., and Robert Kennedy were buried; watched in horror as dissidents disrupted conventions and burned cities; watched in growing disillusionment as cameras in Vietnam brought war into our living rooms in living color; watched with renewed spirit and patriotism as an astronaut walked on the moon.

Mass communication, as we have seen, can bring about acculturation, melding distinct subcultures into a larger homogenous whole. In many ways, in the 1960s and 1970s, mass communication had that kind of effect on our society. Americans, all of whose ancestors came from different cultures, grew more alike in tastes, life styles, customs, and habits. We became consumers of McDonald's hamburgers and inhabitants of split-level houses. Critics said that the mass media were homogenizing America, reducing culture to its lowest common denominator. McLuhan went one step further, saying that the whole world would be acculturated by television and we would all live in one big global village.

By the mid-1980s, it was possible to note a number of areas in which the predictions of the philosophers and the woes of the critics were being realized. But the world was not as simple as most crystal-ball gazers of the 1960s and 1970s had thought. It is always difficult to predict the future. All kinds of unpredictable things happen. And that applies to what we are going to predict in this chapter. Mass communication has taken a slightly different turn from what we imagined it would 20 years ago. It may be quite different from what we think 20 years from now. But that should not keep us from looking into the future as best we can.

Few fields are more important to our future than mass media. And few fields have a future that seems so full of change. Fortunately, research on the future of mass media is growing. We are moving away from the notion that we can teach journalism and mass communication only on the basis of how it was done back in the good old days. Today we are looking ahead—to the future that will be inhabited by the students who are in school now.

In some ways, writing about the future of mass communication is like betting on a horse race. All sorts of possibilities and odds present themselves, and if we are not quick enough, the race is over before we have placed our bet. The media potentials outlined in this chapter may become a

"I just realized, Howard, that everything in this apartment is more sophisticated than we are."

(Drawing by Lorenz; © 1984 The New Yorker Magazine, Inc.)

reality before some people read this book. Also, making predictions in print is hazardous, as many sports writers can attest. Nevertheless, some fairly clear indications of the future of mass communication are apparent.

THE RISE OF PERSONALIZED MASS MEDIA

Perhaps the most important way in which media are changing and will continue to change in the immediate future is the growth of personalized mass media. New developments in mass media are usually dependent on innovations in technology. And most of the important innovations now seem to be leading us to "de-mass" the mass media, or at least to use mass media in a more personal way.

In general, human beings seem to prefer personal communication to mass communication. We would rather see and touch when we communicate. We want messages that are personal, that are directed to us as individuals, that come from communicators who understand our personal needs. Our spending on personal communication through the mail and over the telephone is increasing at a faster rate than is our spending on mass communication.

One reason for the increase in personalized communication is the growing need for special information. As our world becomes more complex, we must rely on more specialists, each of whom provides more information about a narrower field of expertise. The mass media usually provide only general information for a general audience, but as we become more specialized we need more specialized media. The new technologies are making it possible to produce personalized and specialized messages on a mass basis.

In *Goodbye Gutenberg*, a study of newspapers in the 1980s, Arthur Smith suggested that the changing production technology would make the newspaper a much more personal medium. He predicted that by 1990, newspaper publishers would find their readers looking to new systems for specialist and semispecialist offerings. One way or another, Smith wrote, the traditional mass audience for newspapers would break up. Selection, not "passive acceptance," would slice the market into smaller and smaller bits.

Alvin Toffler, author of *Future Shock* and *The Third Wave*, predicted that the 1980s would see the emergence of a new kind of consumer, a new kind of marketplace, and a new system of mass media to connect the two. He described a "de-massed" world in which ideas, media, and advertising were being changed from a mass orientation into segmental, regional, and local orientations. New technology, he predicted, would make small production runs profitable, while the greatly shortened distribution channels would make locally produced products price competitive and eventually cheaper than nationally distributed products, especially as energy costs climb.

Toffler predicted that this would bring about the end of the national advertising campaign. The United States has already moved part of the way from a national marketplace; it is a collection of regional economies that are becoming increasingly disparate. In fact, each is as large now as the national economy was 30 or 40 years ago. By the late 1980s, many of Smith's and Toffler's predictions were already becoming reality.

New Technologies of Change

Some of the important technical innovations that are changing the mass media into more personalized media should be described, even though some are no longer new. The following developments have changed and will continue to change the mass media in the forseeable future.

1. *Computers.* The computer is, without doubt, the most important tool in the information age. The rapid processing of information by computer enables mass communicators to make their messages more sophisticated, more efficient and inexpensive, and more personal.

Figure 25.1 The mass media have seized on the computer as an essential tool in the mass production and mass communication of messages. (Photo: AT&T Bell Laboratories.)

2. *Photo-offset lithography.* Photo-offset lithography is a relatively old technology; like the computer, it dates back to the early 1950s. It has changed print composition radically, and this will continue to bring changes to print media. Photo-offset lithography allows printing from a photosensitive plate. Now anything can be set in type easily and cheaply by taking a photograph instead of making an engraved metal plate.

3. *Paper and printing.* Changes in paper and printing are allowing more efficient and inexpensive printing. New printing presses are being developed that will simplify a process that has until now been based on complicated and outmoded nineteenth-century press design. Paper, too, is being improved and reduced in cost. The price of paper skyrocketed over the past decades as forests were felled to provide wood pulp for paper making. But a plant called kenaf has been discovered to have properties similar to wood pulp. One acre of kenaf can produce about 4 tons of pulp annually; softwood forests produce only about three-quarters of a ton per acre, and hardwoods produce even less. Because kenaf is an annual crop, additional pulp can be produced quickly to meet increasing annual demands. We are no longer locked into a 20-year cycle for growing trees, and the price of paper should decline.

4. *Earth-orbiting satellites.* Satellites have become indispensable to the technological revolution of the mass media. The development of rockets and the race to space have had a large payoff for the communication industries. Satellites are changing both the print and the broadcast media—allowing faster, more efficient message sending at reduced costs and increasing the choices available to audiences.

5. *Wired broadcasting.* Wired broadcasting is bringing about a major change in American mass media. Cable TV is slowly becoming commonplace in our country. Increasingly, we are talking of "*narrow*casting"—airing such a wide choice of programs that messages can be targeted to narrow, specialized audiences—rather than *broad*casting.

6. *Electronics.* Developments in electronics will continue to change the broadcast media, particularly the use of microprocessors and the miniaturization of equipment. These innovations have greatly reduced the size, weight, complexity, and cost of cameras, recorders, transmitters—indeed, of the whole range of electronic equipment needed to broadcast. One of the best examples is the development and rapid spread of the videocassette recorder.

7. *Laser fiber optics.* Laser fiber optics are bringing virtually unlimited communication capabilities to point-to-point transmission that will revolutionize any message-sending requiring a wire, including telephones, computer operations, and cable TV. A fiber-optics trans-

Figure 25.2 Satellites, hanging in stationary orbit 22,300 miles above the earth's surface, will have a major impact on all future mass communication—whether print or broadcast, whether for news or entertainment or business.

mission line is basically a fine, flexible glass fiber—approximately the diameter of a copper telephone line—that transmits light throughout its length by internal reflections. A bundle of these fibers can be placed within a cable smaller in diameter than a lead pencil. One fiber-optics cable of this size has the capability of transmitting every telephone conversation now taking place in the entire country.

8. *Very-high-speed integrated circuits.* VHSIC will dramatically change television in the twenty-first century. The technology, which packs literally billions of tiny circuits on a sapphire or gallium arsenide wafer, has already been perfected for defense uses but will gradually become available for commercial purposes in the late 1980s and the 1990s. VHSIC technology will make it possible to use our TV

sets to create our own TV dramas; we could put Humphrey Bogart into *Star Wars* or John Wayne into *Rambo,* using advanced computer-animation techniques. In the more immediate future, we will see a TV that will better serve the needs of the individual viewer, with freeze-frame, split-screen, optical dialogue for hearing-impaired viewers and with many other features made possible by digital signal-processing chips. Viewers could zoom in on a particular image frozen on the screen, store certain images in memory for individual future use, and "program out" images not wanted on the screen.

These are the kinds of technological innovations that are already making the media of the present and can make the media of the future more

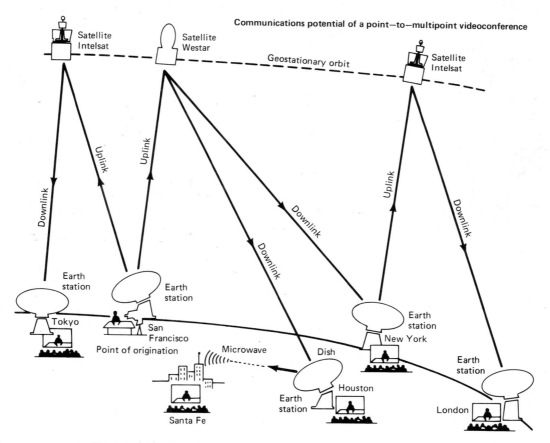

Figure 25.3 The new technology will increasingly make it possible for individuals to be interconnected on a global basis, as videoconferencing does. Organizations such as the Hilton Communications Network have already been formed to offer videoconferencing capabilities.

personalized, with implications that were not considered by Marshall McLuhan when he wrote about the global village.

NEWSPAPERS IN THE FUTURE

Newspapers have already been revolutionized by computers and electronics, and this trend will probably continue. As we have seen in earlier chapters, most newspapers now use computers to automate many of the functions of composition and printing and to store and retrieve material for editorial and advertising content. Newspapers will soon turn to computers and electronics to deliver the paper as well as process and publish the news.

Teletext is one system already perfected and being used. The British Broadcasting Corporation started the world's first and most extensive newspaper delivered by television in the early 1980s. Called CEEFAX, it was available 16 hours a day. It used a TV set and a decoder. By pressing a button on a recall pad, you could bring an index page to the screen. By keying in a three-digit number, you could get a headline page, the weather, highway conditions, or the latest sports scores. Whenever you wanted to read it, you could get whatever news of the day was stored in the system. And you could instruct your set to interrupt other shows with news bulletins flashing on the screen whenever they were sent along the system.

By the mid-1980s, a number of American newspaper companies had rushed into the teletext business, most set up to use personal computers and telephone modems at the receiving end. The Gannett Company, for example, formed Gannett New Media and offered to paying customers a variety of teletext services, such as banking, real-estate, insurance, and travel news and information. But teletext did not sell as well as anticipated, and by the late 1980s, many such experiments were either cut back or dropped.

Videotex is another system that may have more promise than teletext in the long run. It is interactive, a two-way system in which question-and-answer dialogue is possible. The store of data in this system is limited only

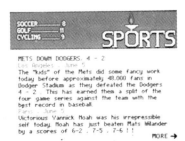

Figure 25.4 Teletext can provide information on a variety of subjects, selected by the user.

by the size of the data base at the other end of the telephone line, not by the amount of information that can be serially transmitted in a given period of time.

As time passes, the alternatives for newspaper communication will grow. And as home computers become a widespread commodity, persons in the home will be able to tap information from gigantic data bases. The important element here is that individuals will be able to create their own newspaper. They will be able to tailor information to their own choosing, selecting some material and eliminating others.

Of course, this means that there will be a greater need than ever for a larger data base. We will need more reporters to gather information and more editors to select and prepare the information for the data base. These new systems will not do away with the printed version of the newspaper. People will continue to demand the printed word. The newspaper will always have the advantage of being more portable than a TV set or a personal computer. We can read it wherever we choose—be it at the break-fast table, on the train, or at our desks. And it is separable: father can read the financial pages while mother is reading the editorials and the kids are reading the comics. That luxury will continue for many people.

National and international newspapers are now a technological possibility. The developments that allow media to be used more personally are also capable of creating more massive media. The best example is the Gannett Company's *USA Today*. By using earth-orbiting satellites, computerized composition, and high-speed printing, *USA Today* can be written and edited for a national audience and beamed by satellite simultaneously to dozens of printing plants around the United States so that it can be delivered first thing each morning to virtually every spot in America. Gan-

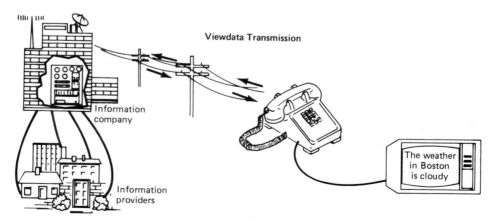

Figure 25.5 Videotex, as an interactive system, offers much potential for the future, although little was yet realized by the late 1980s.

Figure 25.6 Advances in satellite technology have moved a nationally distributed newspaper from a dream to a reality. *USA Today* converts the information on each page of the newspaper into a series of electronic signals that are beamed from the editorial headquarters in Arlington, Virginia, to print shops around the nation.

nett has already launched international editions of *USA Today* for Europe, Asia, and Africa.

MAGAZINES AND BOOKS IN THE FUTURE

Specialization and personalization are the keys to the future for these two media. Like newspapers, magazines and books have already turned increasingly to computers and electronic transmission to produce content and distribute it to targeted audiences.

Magazines have already become specialized, as we have seen. Using computers and demographics, publishers can target not only the individual magazine, but also advertising and editorial content within the magazine; this trend will continue into the late 1980s and 1990s. Twenty years ago, for example, one might have read *Time* or *Newsweek* for a variety of general news, such as sports, science, politics, and art. But as people grew more specialized in their professions—say, biology—these magazines could not provide specific enough science information, and so the readers subscribed to more specialized magazines—say, *Science*. As the readers became even more specialized, they added additional specialized magazines and journals to their subscription list. They subscribed not only to *Time* and *Science*, but also to *Biological Sciences*. Then they added the *Journal of Microbiology*; later, the *Quarterly on Lasers in Microbiology*; and, finally, the newsletter *Purple Lasers in Microbiology*.

Publishers are using the new technology with more efficient composition and printing processes to enable them to produce more book titles in smaller quantities for highly specialized audiences—and still make a profit. Some publishers allow authors to set their own books in type by writing the original on personal computers used to generate the composition for camera-ready copy needed to make plates for printing. This allows the publisher even greater economic leeway to produce limited editions.

BROADCASTING, MOTION PICTURES, AND RECORDINGS IN THE FUTURE

Radio, motion pictures, and recordings have already become highly specialized media, as we have seen in earlier chapters. Future developments in these media do not seem to be leading toward changing the media, but toward improving their quality. The medium that is changing the most is television. It rapidly became the most massive of all the mass media, and the changes on the horizon for TV seem to be moving it rapidly toward become a more personal and specialized medium. Only time will tell for sure.

THE POTENTIAL FOR POLARIZATION

As we have seen, the mass media can speed the process of acculturation, bringing us closer together and making us more like one another. Specialized media, on the contrary, pose the potential for polarization, separating and polarizing elements of society into narrow specializations, demographic groupings, and special interests.

In the past, for example, mass communication was often an experience shared by all the members of a family. Mom, Dad, and the children listened to the same radio programs; read the same magazines, newspapers, and books; and watched the same television programs and movies. By the mid-1980s, however, such shared media experiences were no longer the norm in the average American family. Mom might listen to only adult contemporary radio; Dad, to only country western; and the children, to only rock—and some of the children, to only acid rock, while others, to only black rock. Dad and Mom might watch only late-night adult TV; subteens, only late-afternoon serials and Saturday-morning cartoons; teenagers, only prime-time sitcoms. The men in the family might read only magazines espousing the *Playboy* philosophy; the women, only women's

"What do you mean 'we're polarized'? You're polarized!"

(Drawing by Opie; © 1980
The New Yorker Magazine,
Inc.)

lib magazines; and the children, only magazines for kids. Children and
young adults might be the only ones who watch movies; Mom and Dad
might not even go to the movies anymore, since they are not targeted for
older audiences.

These kinds of individual communication experiences might broaden
individual members of the family, giving more of the kind of information
and entertainment that he or she each needs and wants. That is the positive side. The negative is that communication may no longer be an experience shared by all. The family may have to find other means of coming
together if the members want to maintain some family unity. Yet since
each member of the family will have different facts and information, a
different perspective on those facts, and perhaps even specialized language to interpret those facts, unity will be harder to achieve. Dad might
well see only his version of men's lib; Mom, only hers; and the children
might want to be liberated as well.

Sociologists and psychologists have already noted the growing problem of a communication gap between parents and children, between men
and women, between young and old. If specialized media polarize audiences even further in the future, those gaps will grow.

If scientists, professionals, technicians, and specialists have time for
media only in their narrow specialties, how will they find out what is going
on in the rest of the world?

If whites use only those media targeted for white audiences, blacks
use only those media targeted for black audiences, and Hispanics use only

"We're lucky! Can you imagine the fights we'd have if we did communicate?"

(© 1972 Saturday Review magazine. Reprinted by permission.)

those media targeted for Hispanic audiences, how will these groups learn about one another, and what will keep them from growing even farther apart?

If Americans spend all their time reading, viewing, and listening to only local and special-interest media, how will we acquire a sense of the larger interests of society and the nation or the world as a whole? What will bring us all together? These will all be important questions for public policy about mass communication in the years ahead.

The new mass media could turn us into a different kind of global village than the one envisioned by Marshall McLuhan, in which we would all be sitting in front of the television set watching the same program. The new villages might not be global; we might all be sitting in front of the television tube, but we might all be watching different programs, unaware of and uninterested in the rest of the villages of the world, isolated in our own specialized languages and interests. The result could turn the world into a new version of the biblical city of Babel, whose inhabitants were doomed by God to speak many languages as punishment for having hoped to build a tower to heaven.

There are obvious advantages and disadvantages to increased specialization in communication. Part of America's strength in the past came from its rich cultural diversity. Homogenization by mass media, which destroys individualism and cultural diversity, can have serious negative effects. But polarization into isolated groups and narrow specializations that destroy social unity, community spirit, and national pride can be equally negative. The solution will come only by respecting individual differences while sharing commonalities, and that will take educated, thoughtful action and effective public communication policies.

As we become more specialized and polarized through media, we will also need to find new ways to share and communicate across cultures and languages and to respect the differences among people while still remaining a neighborhood, a corporation, a congregation, a university, or a nation.

THE ROLES OF CONSUMERS AND COMMUNICATORS

Communicators and the consumers of their messages will be the ones most responsible for the future of mass media. In a democratic society, it is usually the communicator and media gatekeepers, not government authorities, who make the final decisions about what becomes public communication. And those decisions are most largely influenced by the choices of the consumer in the marketplace. Consumers who make responsible and educated decisions about media will have the greatest impact on future directions of mass media, but responsible and educated communicators must be willing at times to rise above the demands of the marketplace. Perhaps education itself is the best key to the future, and education about mass media for both consumer and communicator is an essential first step.

The mass media of the future can offer far greater access to information than is available today. If we have more information, we should be able to make more personal choices about the alternatives in our lives and our life styles. The greater the array from which we can choose, the freer we will be as human beings. But we cannot lose sight of the fact that we are all part of the same world; we need to communicate with all the peoples of the world in order to survive.

If the mass media keep moving in these directions, we can be optimistic about the future. The mass media can become instruments that enable each individual human being to live a free, full, and rich personal life. That is the goal of a free and good society. That future depends on the people who will shape the mass media. The future depends on those who are reading this book. Serve it well.

BIBLIOGRAPHY

Cornish, Edward. *Communications Tomorrow: The Coming of the Information Society.* Bethesda, Md.: World Future Society, 1982.

Didsbury, Howard F., Jr. *Communications and the Future: Prospects, Promises, and Problems.* Bethesda, Md.: World Future Society, 1982.

Dizard, Wilson P., Jr. *The Coming Information Age: An Overview of Technology, Economics, and Politics.* New York: Longman, 1982.

The Futurist. World Future Society, 4916 St. Elmo Avenue, Bethesda, Md.   20814.

Grunig, James. *Decline of the Global Village: How Specialization Is Changing the Mass Media.* Bayside, N.Y.: General Hall, 1976.

Haigh, Robert W., George Gerbner, and Richard B. Byrne. *Communications in the Twenty-First Century.* New York: Wiley, 1981.

Hellman, Hal. *Communications in the World of the Future.* New York: Evans, 1969.

Maddox, Brenda. *Beyond Babel: New Directions Transforming Our Lives.* Boston: Beacon Press, 1972.

Naisbitt, John. *Megatrends: Ten New Directions Transforming Our Lives.* New York: Warner Books, 1982.

New Age. P. O. Box 853, Farmingdale, N.Y.   11735.

Robinson, Glen O. *Communications for Tomorrow: Policy Perspectives for the 1980s.* New York: Praeger, 1978.

Smith, Anthony. *Goodbye Gutenberg: The Newspaper Revolution in the 1980s.* Oxford: Oxford University Press, 1980.

Toffler, Alvin. *The Third Wave.* New York: Morrow, 1980.

Glossary

This is the first time we have included a glossary in *Mass Media*. Frankly, there are many reasons for glossaries:

1. To fill up space.
2. To bow to the publisher's demands.
3. To clarify or define technical terms and industry jargon.
4. To provide instructors with ready-made exam items.
5. To provide a measure of reader self-assessment.
6. To define major mass communication terms.
7. To help the reader locate terms and discussion about them.
8. To provide an alternative table of contents.

Our reasons for compiling a glossary for *Mass Media V* are, candidly, all of the above, with primary emphasis on the last three reasons. Unlike most glossaries, the terms are indexed to their first and/or most thorough discussion or definition in the book. In this way, we believe that you will *use* the glossary rather than simply memorize it for the midterm and final exams.

For the most part, we have omitted technical and engineering terms, production language, and industry jargon or slang. For example, in this glossary, you will not find *cuffo*, which means "work or participation done without pay or on speculation"; *cue cards*, "large pieces of cardboard held near the camera bearing songs, commercials, jokes, or other words to be spoken"; or *asphaltum*, "nondrying substance used as a base or a protective coating for images or lithographic plates." We have also not included, with some exceptions, generic terms that have a common meaning or understanding. For example, *column*, which means the "more or less regular output of a columnist"; or *departments*, "categories of editorial matter in a magazine, such as features, classifieds, letters to the editor."

Our glossary is also not a chronology, and we have therefore included very few events or time-related items.

Ultimately, glossaries are individual and idiosyncratic. They are the natural by-product of the text they accompany. As such, this glossary does not pretend to be all inclusive, but only faithful to *Mass Media V*, which, in turn, is faithful to the major ideas and discipline of mass communication.

Because mass communication is constantly growing and changing, a glossary must grow and change also. A glossary is a living thing, and you can contribute to this life by letting us know of terms and concepts that you feel should be in this glossary. Please send us *your* terms and definitions, and we will include them, as appropriate and possible, in our next edition.

MASS MEDIA V GLOSSARY
c/o Longman, Inc.
95 Church Street
White Plains, New York 10601

AAAA. American Association of Advertising Agencies. A national trade organization that is influential in developing self-regulation in advertising, specifically in developing standards of ethical practice.   p. 608

ABC. American Broadcasting Company. Founded in 1944, it is one of the three national television networks and is also a radio network.   p. 209

above-the-line costs. Costs that accrue to the artistic or creative side of a performing-arts production—for example, talent, writers, directors, producers, and script—before rehearsal or filming begins.   p. 584

A. C. Nielson. A company that specializes in broadcast ratings using an audimeter and diaries. It supplies ratings for network-television programming, among other services.   p. 510

Acta Diurna. The earliest form of newspaper. In 59 B.C., the Romans posted these public news sheets.   p. 41

Action for Children's Television (ACT). A consumer group that is dedicated to pressuring television, especially the networks, to produce better children's programming and to reduce and, eventually, eliminate what it considers to be harmful advertising aimed at children.   p. 482

ADI. A broadcast-ratings term meaning "Area of Dominant Influence." Television stations use this concept, developed by Arbitron, to define their markets for advertisers. A station's ADI is made up of the counties that cluster around its signal.   p. 528

advertising. Messages designed to inform and persuade consumers to buy a particular product or service.   p. 325

affiliate. A broadcast station that airs programs produced by or belonging to a national or regional network.   p. 209

alternative press. A form of newspaper, often called the *underground press* in its early (1960s) days. It is characterized as much by its form and style as by its content. Printed by inexpensive offset methods, these papers are often sold in the streets and often deal with radical politics and sexual topics.   p. 55

amplification. The process of boosting a message so that it stands out from other messages and commands audience attention. Amplification is achieved primarily by strong signals, repetition of message, and endorsement.   p. 536

AM radio. A form of radio transmission in which sound waves modulate the amplitude (length) of the carrier wave.   p. 161

Arbitron. A major broadcasting-ratings service that is especially important in local-market radio; it was formerly called the American Research Bureau.   p. 526

ASCAP. American Society of Composers, Authors, and Publishers. A music-licensing organization that collects fees from media that use the music of its members for profit.   p. 246

Associated Press (AP). A member-owned cooperative wire news service.   p. 272

audience. Receivers of media content who are active participants in mass communication, as distinguished from the *public*, which is the total pool of available people and a passive entity.   p. 487

audimeter. An electronic research device used by Nielsen to record television listening and viewing times and stations. It is used to determine national television-program ratings.   p. 520

Audit Bureau of Circulation (ABC). An organization that validates the circulation statements of member newspapers and periodicals.   p. 531

***auteur* theory.** A theory drawn from French film criticism and popularized in the United States by film critic Andrew Sarris that posits the director as artistically preeminent in the creation of a motion picture. Each director, according to the theory, has a recognizable touch or characteristic style.   p. 415

authoritarian theory. The oldest theory of the press, which asserts the government's control over the press, using such techniques as licensing, censorship, and imprisonment.   p. 546

barter. A term used in broadcasting to mean an agreement between stations and advertisers to use products or services by the advertiser in lieu of full or partial payment for air time. "Barter time" is often arranged through the services of a barter broker.   p. 343

below-the-line costs. Technical and production costs, including those for equipment, props, rentals, insurance, music, or special effects.   p. 584

blacklisting. An insidious method of preventing suspected Communists from working in radio, television, and motion pictures in the 1950s during the so-called Red Scare period.   p. 120

black press. Begun in 1827, the black press continues to serve the needs of many black Americans. About 200 black newspapers are published in the United States, with a circulation of 4 million.   p. 59

block booking. The practice of requiring a theater owner to take several films produced by a studio in order to get one or two good ones.   p. 140

BMI. Broadcast Music, Inc. A music-licensing organization that collects fees from media that use the music of its members for profit.   p. 246

cable television (CATV). Community antenna television. A service subscribed to by the viewer and transmitted to the viewing location by cable from a central receiving point.   p. 197

call letters. A broadcasting station's identifying letters—for example, WICB—assigned by the FCC. The letter *W* is usually the first letter in call signs of stations east of the Mississippi; the letter *K* begins most call signs of stations west of the Mississippi.   p. 163

Canons of Journalism. A code of ethical behavior adopted by the American Society of Newspaper Editors in 1933; it is strictly voluntary, with no means of punishment or enforcement.   p. 608

Canon 35. A voluntary guideline for the American Bar Association that prohibits cameras and audio-recording equipment from courtrooms during trials.   p. 470

CBS. Columbia Broadcasting System. Founded in 1927, it is one of the three national television networks and is also a radio network.   p. 209

CD. Compact disc. Developed in the mid-1980s, the CD—a digital sound recording—provides high-quality sound and will not scratch or wear out because of the laser stylus, which does not touch the disc.   p. 237

censorship. The systematic deletion of a message or parts of a message in order to prevent it from being received by the audience.   p. 619

channel. A band of frequencies in the UHF or VHF spectrum assigned by the FCC to a given television station or stations within which they must confine their broadcast signals.   p. 212

checkbook journalism. A controversial method of news gathering, by which news sources are paid for telling their stories to the press.   p. 623

cinematographe. The first motion-picture projector, invented in 1895 by the Lumière brothers in France.   p. 109

clear channel. A radio frequency usually reserved for a single, high-powered station to operate at night. Clear-channel stations broadcast on 50,000 watts.   p. 162

closed-circuit television. The transmission of television signals over a communications line or system (rather than broadcasting) for reception by only certain receivers. It is often used for major sports events and for industrial and educational applications.   p. 205

code. A media's symbol system; its language. In motion pictures, visual symbols, such as camera angle and focal length, carry much of the message; in newspapers, print symbols, such as typeface, create meaning.   p. 426

codex. An early (fourth century A.D.) form of book in which sheets of parchment were cut and tied together on the left side between boards. p. 23

comic. A particular form of magazine and newspaper content that can be a cartoon, comic strip, or comic book. A comic usually develops a narrative, uses continuing characters, and incorporates dialogue or description. p. 95

common carrier. A communications form that offers its services to the public and is regulated by the FCC. Ownership of the medium is divorced from control of the messages carried. Telephone is a common carrier; broadcast television is not. p. 472

communicator. The sender or initiator of a message. In mass communication, the communicator is rarely one individual acting alone. The media communicator is a complex network of people, each of whom has different functions and responsibilities. p. 403

conflict of interest. An ethical issue of divided loyalty, which often occurs in mass communication. It frequently takes place when a reporter has a personal relationship with a subject being written about. p. 613

conglomerate. A large corporation or holding company that owns a variety of businesses. In mass communication, a conglomerate may own media companies as well as industries totally unrelated to the media. p. 407

content analysis. A research procedure with many variations that is used for the purpose of understanding and summarizing the major qualitative and/or quantitative features of mass communication content. p. 627

cooperative advertising (CO-OP). Local advertising run in conjunction with a national sponsor, which usually provides the advertising materials and shares costs and mentions with the local advertiser. p. 343

copyright. Legal protection granted to the owner(s) of literary, musical, dramatic, pantomine, choreographic, pictorial, graphic and sculptural works; motion pictures; and other audiovisual works and sound recordings. The fundamental rights given by the law include reproduction, preparation of derivative works, distribution of copies, public performance of work, and right to publicly display the work. p. 471

Corporation for Public Broadcasting (CPB). The network office of the Public Broadcasting Service (PBS). p. 203

corrective advertising. Advertising required by the FTC to correct prior advertising that made false or misleading claims. p. 346

cost efficiency. Often referred to as cost per thousand (CPM) to place an advertisement before its actual or potential audience. p. 529

counter programming. In broadcasting, the airing or scheduling of a program designed to appeal to a different segment of the audience from that of competing stations, the same audience as that of the competition, or an entirely new or different audience from that of the competition. p. 209

cumulative audience. The total number of individuals reached by successive issues or broadcasts. Also called *cume,* it is especially important in radio ratings.   p. 526

DBS. Direct broadcast satellite transmission, in which a television signal is delivered directly to a home receiving dish by satellite.   p. 195

delayed-reward news. News that provides context and background for the receiver and does not affect the consumer until later—for example, public-affairs, education, and economic news.   p. 263

demographics. Usually computer-assisted ability to analyze audiences, subscribers, or consumers in terms of where they live, affluence, age, sex, and such, in order to target advertising or public-relations campaigns.   p. 517

deregulation. The process of reducing or eliminating government regulation in business and industry. It has become especially important in broadcasting in the 1980s.   p. 623

designated market area (DMA). Nielsen's term for a map or list of counties, usually adjacent, in which the larger share of the market is held by stations operating in these countries.   p. 510

diary. A rating system in which audiences keep written records of their TV and radio usage. It is used by Arbitron for radio ratings and by Nielsen for TV ratings.   p. 520

direct mail. A method of advertising and/or public relations that uses the postal system to send a message to potential readers who have something in common (target audience).   p. 338

disclosure of sources. An ethical issue involving the right of news reporters to maintain confidentiality of sources versus the right of the public to know the source of information.   p. 616

divorcement ruling. A major Supreme Court decision in 1950 that broke up the vertical monopoly of the major motion-picture studios by requiring them to "divorce" exhibition, production, and distribution.   p. 120

downlink/uplink. Jargon for a satellite earth station for receiving (downlink) or sending (uplink) satellite signals. They are also used as verbs.   p. 196

drive time. A radio term referring to the time when most people commute to and from work, normally from 7:00 to 9:00 A.M. and 4:30 to 6:30 P.M. Radio has its largest audience at these times, especially in urban areas. p. 168

electronic media. Broadcasting media—radio and television—derived from their method of transmission. The term *electronics* describes the area of technology dealing with currents of free electrons, as opposed to transmission through currents in wires only, which is generally termed *electric.* p. 12

electronic news gathering (ENG). The use of compact videotaping systems (minicams) to record news events and stories in the same manner as traditionally done with film cameras. p. 276

equal time. A provision by the FCC stating that stations selling or giving time to one candidate for public office are required to sell or give equal time to all legally qualified candidates for the same office. News programs are excluded from this provision. p. 473

ethnic press. Newspapers designed for a particular ethnic group, such as German-Americans or Spanish-Americans. They often are printed in the group's language and are confined to urban centers containing a significant percentage of a particular group. p. 58

Fairness Doctrine. The obligation imposed by the FCC on broadcasters to cover controversial issues. It stipulates that broadcasters must seek out and present contrasting points of view on controversial issues. p. 473

Federal Communications Commission (FCC). A U.S. government agency established in 1934 that regulates broadcasting, including licensing broadcast stations. It regulates all forms of broadcasting, including citizens'-band, marine, and police radio. p. 472

Federal Trade Commission (FTC). A U.S. government agency that regulates unfair and misleading advertising as well as other unfair competitive business practices. p. 346

feedback. Audience reactions that come back to the sender. Feedback is essentially communication in reverse and is ultimately designed to influence the sender and his or her future communication. p. 507

filter. A frame of reference through which audiences receive messages. Four types of filters—informational, physical, psychological, cultural—affect an individual's perception and reception of media content. p. 492

First Amendment. The constitutional guarantee of press, speech, and religious freedom. It reads: "Congress shall make no law respecting an establishment of religion, or prohibiting the free exercise thereof; or abridging the freedom of speech, or of the press; or the right of the people peaceably to assemble, and to petition the government for a redress of grievances." p. 622

FM radio. A form of radio transmission in which sound waves modulate the frequency of the carrier wave. FM frequencies have higher fidelity (88–108 megahertz) and are subject to less interference than AM frequencies. p. 162

format radio. Often called formula radio, radio formats are carefully constructed combinations of music, talk, and advertisements designed to appeal to a specific group of listeners. p. 165

freedom of information (FOI). Specifically, the Freedom of Information Act of 1966, which gives the media and members of the public access to federal government agency files.   p. 675

freeze. A four-year period between 1948 and 1952 when the FCC "froze" all further television station licensing in order to allow the medium to solve some technical and economic problems.   p. 181

gatekeeper. An individual or individuals who can determine and affect the information or entertainment received by an audience. A gatekeeper can block information, add to it, or alter it.   p. 453

global village. A term popularized by the communications scholar Marshall McLuhan. It refers to the "shrinking" of the world society because of the ability to communicate via mass media.   p. 15

homes using television (HUT). The percentage of homes viewing TV during a given time period.   p. 529

iconoscope. The first electronic television camera tube, invented by Vladimir Zworykin in 1928.   p. 178

immediate-reward news. News that provides instant satisfaction for the receiver—for example, sports, fire, and crime news. It is also characterized by its transitoriness.   p. 263

implosion. The opposite of explosion. A media-audience concept that describes the audience at the center being bombarded by media messages that converge on the individual.   p. 502

information society. A term popularized by John Naisbitt in his book *Megatrends,* which refers to a society in which information occupations are dominent and the greatest portion of the gross national product comes from information goods and services.   p. 686

institutional advertising. Advertising whose primary objective is not to promote a specific product or service, but to gain public good will or prestige for the advertiser or sponsor.   p. 341

institutional ethics. Media ethics that are informal and often associated with gatekeepers within media institutions.   p. 603

interactive. Referring to those technologies that permit users' participation, such as two-way cable, videotext, and certain optical videodiscs.   p. 371

invasion of privacy. Published or broadcast information that violates an individual's right to be let alone or damages one's peace of mind.   p. 617

inverted-pyramid structure. A method of news presentation that presents the most important facts, together with the necessary explanatory material, in the first paragraph (summary lead) of a news story and then moves into the detailed portion of the story (body) in descending order of importance.   p. 273

investigative news reporting. A style of reporting that goes beneath surface situations to probe the real cause or purpose, often to expose wrongdoing. It stresses careful assembling of facts in developing the story. p. 273

kinetograph. The first motion-picture camera, invented by Thomas Edison and his assistant William Dickson in 1888. p. 108

libel. A defamatory communication that is published or broadcast. Before libel is created in a communication, three conditions must exist: publication (published or broadcast); identification of the person, persons, or entity; and defamation (attack on a "good" name). p. 467

libertarian theory. The theory of the press that asserts that since the public is essentially rational, the government need never interfere in the free and unfettered competition of the various elements of the media. p. 547

linotype. A machine invented in 1884 by Ottmar Mergenthaler that molds and sets type from hot metal. It replaced hand setting of type and had a major impact on newspaper and book publishing. p. 49

low-power television (LPTV). A recent (early 1980s) form of television station licensed to broadcast at low power over a limited geographical area (10–15 miles in radius). p. 200

LP record. Long-playing record. First developed in 1948, the record is made and played at $33\frac{1}{3}$ rpm, providing up to 25 minutes of music per side. p. 255

mass communication. The process whereby mass-produced messages are transmitted to large, anonymous, and heterogeneous audiences. p. 3

mass media. The institutions of public communication that have as their physical channel of transmission a mass medium—television, radio, motion pictures, newspapers, books, magazines, and recordings. p. 12

MBS. Mutual Broadcasting System. Started in 1934, it is a national radio network that provides its affiliates with a variety of news, information, and sports programs. p. 153

media acculturation. The process by which mass communication creates cultural consensus and understanding among individual componets of society and brings people together on some common issues. p. 653

media-support system. The means by which a particular mass medium finances production, distribution, and exhibition of content. There are basically four types of support: audience; advertiser; audience and advertiser; and public and/or private subsidy. p. 572

media-systems paradigm. An action-oriented model that visualizes the theory that in every country, social factors interact in unique ways to create a national media system to perform a variety of functions that participate in reshaping that society. p. 552

Motion Picture Association of America (MPAA). A primary gatekeeper of the motion-picture industry. Its 1968 rating code classifies movies into G, PG, PG-13, R, and X categories.   p. 610

muckraking. Exposing political and social wrongdoing; synonymous with *investigative news reporting.* Although the term dates back to the seventeenth century, it was popularized mainly by Theodore Roosevelt.   p. 49

multistep flow theory. A process that suggests that the effects of mass media alone do not alter opinion or belief; rather, the media's message flows through and is filtered by a network of opinion leaders.   p. 492

National Public Radio (NPR). A network of approximately 200 noncommercial radio stations funded in part by the federal government through the Corporation for Public Broadcasting (CPB).   p. 164

NBC. National Broadcasting Company. Founded in 1926, it is one of the three national television networks and is also a radio network.   p. 209

network. Two or more radio or television stations connected by wire, microwave, or satellite to broadcast the same programs, usually—although not necessarily—simultaneously.   p. 209

new journalism. A style of journalism that emerged in the 1960s in which writers expressed their feelings and values and used techniques usually found in fiction.   p. 264

newsletter. A specialized form of print media. Written in letter form, it contains a wide variety of specialized and specific information for particular target audiences. It normally carries no advertising.   p. 98

new world information order. A philosophy emanating from several studies done in the late 1970s that postulates the communication integrity of every nation of the world. It is essentially a reaction by many Third World countries against what they term American and Western "media imperialism."   p. 564

noise. In mass media theory, anything that interferes with clear communications—from technical problems of reception to clutter in presentation to information overload.   p. 534

objectivity. A dominant theme of the journalism profession, to report events in a factual way, uninfluenced by attitudes or values of reporters, editors, or publishers.   p. 263

owned-and-operated (O&O). Broadcast outlets owned and operated by the networks. By FCC rules, each network is allowed only seven O&Os, no more than five of which can be VHF stations.   p. 210

participation. A program-sponsorship pattern in which the commercial messages of several advertisers are rotated through segments of the program. Station-lineup or program-content controls are not normally obtained by participating sponsors.   p. 343

pass-along reader. Person who reads a publication that he or she did not buy. Readers within households subscribing to the publication are included in the definition of *primary readers.* A periodical's total audience consists of both primary and pass-along readers. p. 532

payola. Reward in cash, goods, or services for the performance of undeserved favors; doing for pay what should be done without charge. The term originated in the 1950s to describe the practice of paying to have records played on radio. p. 617

pay TV. A system in which a viewer pays a per-program fee or a monthly fee to view specific programs or programming not available on regular television channels. HBO is a pay-TV channel for cable subscribers. p. 199

PBS. Public Broadcasting Service. Established in 1970 as the corporate voice of "educational and public" broadcasting in the United States, PBS manages programming, production, distribution, and station interconnection. p. 203

penny press. The first mass newspaper medium. Originating in the 1830s, the papers sold for a penny and offered news for less-educated, ordinary citizens. p. 46

persistence of vision. A phenomenon in which the eye retains an image for a short time after the object has been removed from view. Motion pictures are possible because of this phenomenon. p. 106

pornography. Any obscene material, as legally defined by dominant theme must appeal to a prurient interest in sex; material must be patently offensive and affront community standards; material is without socially redeeming value. p. 642

prime time. The time when television stations have their largest audiences; generally 7:30 to 11:00 P.M. on the East and West coasts and 6:30 to 10:00 P.M. elsewhere in the United States. p. 209

privacy. An ethical issue involving the right of an individual to privacy versus the public's right to know. p. 617

product advertising. Advertising that seeks to generate sales of a specific commodity. p. 341

professional ethics. Media ethics characterized by a system of codes and, in some cases, regulations that specifically "spell out" ethical practices and/or conditions. p. 608

PRSA. Public Relations Society of America. A professional trade association established to elevate and professionalize the practice of public relations. p. 310

public. The total pool of available people, as distinguished from an *audience,* which is defined by the individuals who actually use the media content. p. 487

public relations (PR). A management function that obtains, assesses, and evaluates public attitudes toward an organization, advertiser, or individual. Following this ongoing process, the policies and activities are identified with the public interest, and a program of action is executed to develop public understanding, good will, support, and acceptance. p. 303

quiz scandals. The relevation made in 1959 that many of television's popular quiz shows were "rigged," in that contestants were given answers before going on the show. The scandals signaled the end of television's first euphoric stage of growth. p. 187

rate card. A list or card giving important information concerning the medium's policies on its advertising, including space or time rate, plus data on mechanical requirements, closing dates, commissions, rate protection, spot length, color, rate inclusions, and so on. p. 337

ratings. Estimates of the number of people or households, usually expressed in percentages or percentage, who view or listen to a program or broadcasting station from a sample of homes or people with (*but not using*) television or radio. p. 527

recording. A generic term referring to a variety of sound-reproduction systems, including records, reel-to-reel tapes, cassettes, and videotape-music productions. p. 217

regulators. An individual or organization that exists *outside* the media institutions and is capable of altering, modifying, or stopping media content from reaching an audience—for example, the FCC and the Supreme Court. p. 453

sample. A portion of the total population involved in a survey, of whom questions are asked. To be valid, a sample should be representative of the total population involved. p. 510

share. An audience-measurement term usually referring to a percentage of homes *using* television that are tuned to a particular program. p. 528

Sixth Order and Report. Issued by the FCC in 1952, it ended a four-year "freeze" on television-station licensing and provided a master plan for television's development in the United States. p. 183

soap opera. A major form of daytime network television programming that features continuing stories and characters in a strip (five-day-a-week) format. The form was popular on network radio for almost 30 years. p. 193

social-responsibility theory. The theory of the press first presented in 1947 by the Commission on Freedom of the Press. It developed from the basic assumptions of the libertarian theory, but emphasized the need of occasional government encouragement of media idealism and performance. p. 548

Soviet Communist theory. The theory of the press that sees no tension between government and press because they are the same. p. 546

strategic releasing. A process by which a content source regulates communication by strategically timing and packaging the message for maximum effect. p. 475

strategic withholding. A process by which a content source regulates communication by blocking the media from receiving a message or parts of a message. p. 476

stringer. An unsalaried reporter or photographer, not regularly assigned to a news organization, who acts as a local contact on an irregular basis and who initiates story ideas and does photographing and/or reporting. Stringers work on retainers, word rates, negotiated article rates, or a combination of these methods of payment. p. 272

superstation. A local TV station whose signal is available by satellite relay to cable systems across the country. WTBS-TV in Atlanta is the original. p. 195

syndicate. A corporation that owns a group of newspapers or magazines or a group of radio or television stations. Syndicates also refer to organizations that sell comic strips and special columns to newspapers and magazines. p. 409

syndication. The sale of television or radio programs and series or newspaper features directly to individual stations or papers. Commercial television networks, for example, place successful series into syndication following their network runs. p. 411

tabloid. A newspaper of small page size, usually 5 columns wide and 16 to 18 inches deep, about half the size of a regular newspaper. It often is characterized by a great deal of photography, topical reporting, and emphasis on sensational headlines. p. 53

target audience. In advertising, the audience most likely to buy a particular product. In more general terms, a specific audience most likely to view, listen to, or read a particular media content. p. 345

teletext. A system for sending printed information to home television screens using scanning lines that are not needed for receiving TV programs. p. 201

textbook. A book prepared specifically for classroom use. It usually provides exposition of one subject area and serves as the content core of a given class. p. 35

trade book. A book produced for the mass market and usually sold through bookstores. p. 33

ultrahigh-frequency television (UHF). Television channels 14 through 83. p. 212

United Press International (UPI). A news wire agency that sells its services to subscribing news organizations.

very-high-frequency television (VHF). Television channels 2 to 13 on the lower end of the broadcasting band.   p. 212

VHS. Video Home System. The more popular of the two videocassette formats, it uses ½-inch tape; the other form is Beta.   p. 201

videodisc. A disc containing (potentially great amounts of) visual and aural information. It can be used to play back content, like a recording, and can be connected to a computer and function in an interactive mode. Television programs, motion pictures, or other visual materials can be played.   p. 201

video display terminal (VDT). An electronic typewriter and television screen connected to a computer. It is used by journalists and other writers to create and edit material.   p. 70

videotext. An information system that allows the receiver to control interactive cable or telephone lines. It can be used for information storage and retrieval, in-home banking, and shopping.   p. 200

wire service. An organization that gathers news stories, prepares them in a convenient form, and sends them (by wire or satellite) to newspapers and broadcasting stations around the country that pay for the service— for example, AP and UPI.   p. 272

yellow journalism. A derogatory term for sensation-mongering, irresponsible journalism. Reputedly short for "Yellow Kid journalism," it alludes to the cartoon *The Yellow Kid*, in the nineteenth-century *New York World*, a newspaper especially noted for its sensationalism.   p. 49

Index

Note: References to illustrations are in italic. An italic *n* following a page number indicates that the subject will be found in a footnote.